The Blair Reader

Fourth Edition

EDITED BY

Laurie G. Kirszner
University of the Sciences in Philadelphia

Stephen R. Mandell
Drexel University

Upper Saddle River, New Jersey 07458

Library of Congress Cataloging-in-Publication Data

The Blair reader / edited by Laurie G. Kirszner, Stephen R. Mandell, —4th ed.
    p.   cm.
    Includes index.
    ISBN 0–13–091066–X
    1. College readers. 2. English language—Rhetoric—Problems, exercises, etc. 3. Report writing—Problems, exercises, etc.
I. Kirszner, Laurie G II. Mandell, Stephen R.

PE1417 .B54 2001
808'.0427—dc21   2001031164
E   CIP

Editor in Chief: Leah Jewell
Acquisitions Editor: Corey Good
Editorial Assistant: Jennifer Collins
VP, Director of Production and Manufacturing: Barbara Kittle
Senior Managing Editor: Mary Rottino
Production Editor: Randy Pettit
Prepress and Manufacturing Manager: Nick Sklitsis
Prepress and Manufacturing Buyer: Mary Ann Gloriande
Director of Marketing: Beth Gillett Mejia
Marketing Manager: Rachel Falk
Marketing Assistant: Chrissie Moody
Cover Design Director: Jayne Conte
Cover Design: Bruce Kensellaar
Cover Art: "Tree", Diane Fenster
For permission to use copyrighted material, grateful
acknowledgment is made to the copyright holders listed
on pages 785–792, which is considered an extension of this
copyright page.

This book was set in 10/12 Palatino by Lithokraft II
and printed and bound by Courier-Westford.
The cover was printed by Phoenix Color Corp.

 © 2002, 1999, 1996, 1992 by Pearson Education, Inc.
Upper Saddle River, New Jersey 07458

Printed in the United States of America
10   9   8   7   6   5   4   3

ISBN 0-13-091066-X

Prentice-Hall International (UK) Limited, *London*
Prentice-Hall of Australia Pty. Limited, *Sydney*
Prentice-Hall Canada Inc., *Toronto*
Prentice-Hall Hispanoamerica, S.A., *Mexico*
Prentice-Hall of India Private Limited, *New Delhi*
Prentice-Hall of Japan, Inc., *Tokyo*
Pearson Education Asia Pte. Ltd., *Singapore*
Editora Prentice-Hall do Brasil, Ltda., *Rio de Janeiro*

Contents

Rhetorical Contents   viii

Topical Clusters   xiv

Preface   xxiii

INTRODUCTION: BECOMING A CRITICAL READER   1

CHAPTER 1   FAMILY AND MEMORY   10

Robert Hayden, "Those Winter Sundays"   11
Gary Soto, "One Last Time"   12
E. B. White, "Once More to the Lake"   20
Maxine Hong Kingston, "No Name Woman"   25
N. Scott Momaday, "The Way to Rainy Mountain"   36
Alice Walker, "Beauty: When the Other Dancer Is the Self"   42
Raymond Carver, "My Father's Life"   49

Focus: How Has Divorce Redefined the Family?   57

Alice Hoffman, "The Perfect Family"   57
Barbara Kingsolver, "Stone Soup"   60
Judith Wallerstein, "The Unexpected Legacy of Divorce"   67
Jane Smiley,
    "There They Go, Bad-Mouthing Divorce Again"   76

CHAPTER 2   ISSUES IN EDUCATION   82

John Holt, "School Is Bad for Children"   83
Plato, "Myth of the Cave"   89
Mark Twain, "Reading the River"   96
Walt Whitman,
    "When I Heard the Learn'd Astronomer" (poetry)   98
Lynda Barry, "The Sanctuary of School"   99
Maya Angelou, "Graduation"   102
Jonathan Kozol, "Savage Inequalities"   112
Brent Staples,
    "Why Colleges Shower Their Students With A's"   125
William Zinsser, "College Pressures"   127
William A. Henry III, "In Defense of Elitism"   134

Focus: What Is the Real Purpose of Education?   140

Leslie S. P. Brown,
   "Who Cares About the Renaissance?"   140
Aaron M. Shatzman, "When Learning Hurts"   142
Mark Edmundson,
   "On the Uses of a Liberal Education: Lite Entertainment for
   Bored College Students"   145

CHAPTER 3   THE POLITICS OF LANGUAGE   166

Frederick Douglass, "Learning to Read and Write"   167
Malcolm X, "A Homemade Education"   173
Barbara Lawrence, "Four-Letter Words Can Hurt You"   181
Amy Tan, "Mother Tongue"   184
Jonathan Kozol, "The Human Cost of an Illiterate Society"   189
S. I. Hayakawa, "Reports, Inferences, Judgments"   197
Alleen Pace Nilsen,
   "Sexism in English: Embodiment and Language"   203
Aldous Huxley, "Propaganda Under a Dictatorship"   214
George Orwell, "Politics and the English Language"   220

Focus: Should English Be the Law?   232

Richard Rodriguez, "Aria"   232
Robert D. King, "Should English Be the Law?"   238
Jorge Amselle, "¡Inglés, Sí!"   249

CHAPTER 4   MEDIA AND SOCIETY   256

Marie Winn, "Television: The Plug-In Drug"   257
Charles McGrath,
   "Giving Saturday Morning Some Slack"   266
Joe Saltzman,
   "Celebrity Journalism, the Public, and Princess Diana"   271
Gloria Steinem, "Sex, Lies, and Advertising"   274
Kevin J. H. Dettmar, "Grasping the Dark Images of Rock"   290
Kate Tuttle, "Television and African Americans"   297
Pico Iyer, "The Global Village Finally Arrives"   303
Wendy Kaminer, "Testifying: Television"   307

Focus: Does Media Violence Hurt?   318

John Grisham, "Unnatural Killers"   318
Richard Rhodes,
   "Hollow Claims About Fantasy Violence   326
John Leo, " When Life Imitates Video"   329

CHAPTER 5   GENDER AND SOCIETY   336

Marge Piercy, "Barbie Doll"   338
Sharon Olds, "Rite of Passage"   339
Virginia Woolf, "Professions for Women"   340
Scott Russell Sanders, "The Men We Carry in Our Minds"   345
Judy Brady, "Why I Want a Wife"   348
Arlie Hochschild, "The Second Shift"   351
Stephanie Gutmann, "Sex and the Soldier"   357
Deborah Tannen, "Marked Women"   366

Focus: Who Has It Harder, Women of Men?   372

Barbara Dafoe Whitehead, "The Girls of Gen X"   372
Christina Hoff Sommers, "The War Against Boys"   380
Susan Faludi, "The Future of Men"   385

CHAPTER 6   THE AMERICAN DREAM   391

Chief Seattle, "We May Be Brothers"   392
Alexis de Toqueville, "Why the Americans Are So Restless
   in the Midst of Their Prosperity"   395
Richard Wright, "The Library Card"   398
Bharati Mukherjee, "American Dreamer"   406
Judith Ortiz Cofer, "The Myth of the Latin Woman:
   I Just Met a Girl Named Maria"   412
Brent Staples, "Just Walk On By"   417
Lars Eighner, "On Dumpster Diving"   421
Zora Neale Hurston, "How It Feels to Be Colored Me"   432
Charles R. Lawrence III and Mari Matsuda, "The Telltale Heart:
   Apology, Reparation, and Redress"   436

Focus: What Is the American Dream?   449

Thomas Jefferson, "The Declaration of Independence"   449
Emma Lazarus, " The New Colossus"   452
John F. Kennedy, Inaugural Address   453
Martin Luther King, Jr., " I Have A Dream"   457

CHAPTER 7   THE WIRED REVOLUTION   464

Asley Dunn, "Two Views of Technology's Promise"   465
Nicholas Negroponte, "An Age of Optimism"   469
Lewis Thomas, "Computers"   473
Gregory J. E. Rawlins, "Pregnant With Possibility"   475
Ted Gup, "The End of Serendipity"   478
Peshe Kuriloff, "If John Dewey Were Alive Today,
   He'd Be a Webhead"   482

Philip Elmer-Dewitt, "Bards of the Internet: If E-Mail Represents the Renaissance of Prose, Why Is So Much of It Awful?" 495
Neil Postman, "Informing Ourselves to Death" 486

Focus: Is There Equality in Cyberspace? 499

Henry Louis Gates Jr., "One Internet, Two Nations" 499
Paula Span, "Women and Computers":
   Is There Equity in Cyberspace?" 502
Matthew Symonds, "Government and the Internet:
   Haves and Have-Nots" 514

CHAPTER 8 MEDICINE AND HUMAN VALUES 521

Barbara Tuchman, "The Black Death" 522
Richard Selzer, "Imelda" 532
Suzanne Gordon, "What Nurses Stand For" 543
Margaret Sanger, "The Turbid Ebb and Flow of Misery" 553
Jane Goodall, "A Plea for the Chimps" 559
Anna Mae Halgrim Seaver, "My World Now" 566
Dylan Thomas,
   "Do Not Go Gentle into That Good Night" (poetry) 569
Elizabeth Kübler-Ross, "On the Fear of Death" 570
Robert L. Borosage,
   "Misplaced Priorities: A Focus on Guns 577

Focus: Whose Life Is It Anyway? 581

Lawrence J. Schneiderman, "The Ethics of Euthanasia" 581
Jack Kevorkian, "A Case of Assisted Suicide" 587
Stephen L. Carter, "Rush to Lethal Judgment" 592

CHAPTER 9 NATURE AND THE ENVIRONMENT 600

Chief Seattle, "Letter to President Pierce, 1855" 601
Al Gore, "The Wasteland" 603
E. H. Forster, "My Wood" 611
Rachel Carson, "The Obligation to Endure" 614
William Rathje and Cullen Murphy,
   "Recycling: No Panacea" 620
Jerediah Purdy, "Shades of Green" 625
Sally Thane Christensen, "Is a Tree Worth a Life?" 630
T. Coraghessan Boyle, "Top of the Food Chain" (fiction) 632

Focus: Who Owns the Land? 637

Brenda Peterson, "Growing Up Game" 637
Anna Quindlen, "Our Animal Rites" 640
Barbara Ehrenreich, "The Myth of Man as Hunter" 643
William Stafford, "Traveling Through the Dark" 645

CHAPTER 10   MAKING CHOICES   651

Robert Frost, "The Road Not Taken" (poetry)   651
Linda Pastan, "Ethics" (poetry)   652
Annie Dillard, "The Deer at Providencia"   654
George Orwell, "Shooting an Elephant"   658
Henry David Thoreau, "Civil Disobedience"   664
Martin Luther King, Jr., "Letter from Birmingham Jail"   682
Garret Hardin,
   "Lifeboat Ethics: The Case Against 'Aid' That Harms"   697
Claire McCarthy, "Dog Lab"   707
Edward I. Koch, "Death and Justice:
   How Capital Punishment Affirms Life"   714
Russell Feingold,
   "The Need for a Moratorium on Executions"   719
Stanley Milgram, "The Perils of Obedience"   725
Carl Sagan, "The Rules of the Game"   738
Ursula Le Guin,
   "The Ones Who Walk Away from Omelas" (fiction)   747

Focus: Are All Ideas Created Equal?   **754**

Lawrence Krauss, "Equal Time for Nonsense"   754
Niles Eldridge, "Creationism Isn't Science"   757
Deborah Lipstadt, "Denying the Holocaust"   763
Franois Tremblay, "Revising Our Prejudices:
   The Holocaust and Freedom of Speech"   776

CREDITS   785

INDEX   793

Rhetorical Contents

Narrative

Gary Soto, "One Last Time"   12
E. B. White, "Once More to the Lake"   20
Maxine Hong Kingston, "No Name Woman"   25
Alice Walker, "Beauty: When the Other Dancer Is the Self"   42
Raymond Carver, "My Father's Life"   49
Lynda Barry, "The Sanctuary of School"   99
Maya Angelou, "Graduation"   102
Frederick Douglass, "Learning to Read and Write"   167
Amy Tan, "Mother Tongue"   184
Richard Rodriguez, "Aria"   232
John Grisham, "Unnatural Killers"   318
Sharon Olds, "Rite of Passage"   339
Richard Wright, "The Library Card"   398
Judith Ortiz Cofer, "The Myth of the Latin Woman"   412
Lars Eighner, "On Dumpster Diving"   421
Richard Selzer, "Imelda"   532
Margaret Sanger, "The Turbid Ebb and Flow of Misery"   553
Jack Kevorkian, "A Case of Assisted Suicide"   587
T. Coraghessan Boyle, "Top of the Food Chain"   632
William Stafford, "Traveling Through the Dark"   645
George Orwell, "Shooting an Elephant"   658
Claire McCarthy, "Dog Lab"   707
Ursula Le Guin,
    "The Ones Who Walk Away from Omelas"   747

Description

E. B. White, "Once More to the Lake"   20
N. Scott Momaday, "The Way to Rainy Mountain"   36
John Holt, "School Is Bad for Children"   83
Plato, "Myth of the Cave"   89
Mark Twain, "Reading the River"   96
Richard Rodriguez, "Aria"   232
Marge Piercy, "Barbie Doll"   338
Emma Lazarus, "The New Colossus"   452
Richard Selzer, "Imelda"   532
Anna Mae Halgrim Seaver, "My World Now"   566

Robert Frost, "The Road Not Taken"   651
George Orwell, "Shooting an Elephant"   658
Ursula Le Guin,
    "The Ones Who Walk Away from Omelas"   747

Process

Malcolm X, "A Homemade Education"   173
Marge Piercy, "Barbie Doll"   338
Lars Eighner, "On Dumpster Diving"   421
Margaret Sanger, "The Turbid Ebb and Flow of Misery"   553
Elisabeth Kübler-Ross, "On the Fear of Death"   570
Chief Seattle, "Letter to President Pierce, 1855"   601
Al Gore, "The Wasteland"   603
T. Coreghessan Boyle, "Top of the Food Chain"   632
Claire McCarthy, "Dog Lab"   707
Ursula Le Guinn,
    "The Ones Who Walk Away from Omelas"   747

Example

Judith Wallerstein, et al.,
    "The Unexpected Legacy of Divorce"   67
Jonathan Kozol, "The Human Cost of an Illiterate Society"   189
Alleen Pace Nilsen, "Sexism in English: A 1990s Update"   203
George Orwell, "Politics and the English Language"   220
Marie Winn, "Television: The Plug-In Drug"   257
Gloria Steinem, "Sex, Lies, and Advertising"   274
Kevin J. H. Dettmar, "Grasping the Dark Images of Rock"   290
Kate Tuttle, "Television and African Americans"   297
Pico Iyer, "The Global Village Finally Arrives"   303
Wendy Kaminer, "Testifying: Television"   307
Susan Faludi, "The Future of Men"   385
Judith Ortiz Cofer, "The Myth of the Latin Woman"   412
Brent Staples, "Just Walk on By"   125
Thomas Jefferson, "The Declaration of Independence"   449
Martin Luther King, Jr., "I Have a Dream"   457
Philip Elmer-Dewitt, "Bards of the Internet"   495
Suzanne Gordon, "What Nurses Stand For"   543
Jane Goodall, "A Plea for the Chimps"   559
Al Gore, "The Wasteland"   603
Brenda Peterson, "Growing Up Game"   637
Anna Quindlen, "Our Animal Rites"   640
Linda Pastan, "Ethics"   652

Russell Feingold,
"The Need for a Moratorium on Executions"   719
Deborah Lipstadt, "Denying the Holocaust"   763

Cause and Effect

E. B. White, "Once More to the Lake"   20
Alice Walker, "Beauty: When the Other Dancer Is the Self"   42
Judith Wallerstein, et al.,
"The Unexpected Legacy of Divorce"   67
Jane Smiley,
"There They Go, Bad-Mouthing Divorce Again"   76
Brent Staples,
"Why Colleges Shower Their Students with A's"   125
Mark Edmundson, "On the Uses of a Liberal Education"   145
Jonathan Kozol, "The Human Cost of an Illiterate Society"   189
George Orwell, "Politics and the English Language"   220
Aldous Huxley, "Propaganda Under a Dictatorship"   214
Marie Winn, "The Plug-In Drug"   257
Joe Saltzman,
"Celebrity Journalism, the Public, and Princess Diana"   271
Pico Iyer, "The Global Village Finally Arrives"   303
Wendy Kaminer, "Testifying: Television"   307
John Grisham, "Unnatural Killers"   318
Richard Rhodes,
"Hollow Claims About Fantasy Violence"   326
John Leo, "When Life Imitates Video"   329
Barbara Dafoe Whitehead, "The Girls of Gen X"   372
Susan Faludi, "The Future of Men"   385
Alexis de Tocqueville, "Why the Americans Are So Restless
in the Midst of Their Prosperity"   395
Richard Wright, "The Library Card"   398
Brent Staples, "Just Walk on By"   417
Ted Gup, "The End of Serendipity"   478
Peshe Kuriloff,
"If John Dewy Were Alive Today, He'd Be a Webhead"   482
Neal Postman, "Informing Ourselves to Death"   486
Barbara Tuchman, "The Black Death"   522
William Rathje and Cullen Murphy, "Recycling:
No Panacea"   620

Comparison and Contrast

Alice Hoffman, "The Perfect Family"   57
Jane Smiley,
"There They Go, Bad-Mouthing Divorce Again"   76
Plato, "Myth of the Cave"   89
Mark Twain, "Reading the River"   96

Walt Whitman, "When I Heard the Learn'd Astronomer"   98
Jonathan Kozol, "Savage Inequalities"   112
Alleen Pace Nilsen, "Sexism in English: A 1990s Update"   203
Charles McGrath, "Giving Saturday Morning Some Slack"   266
Virginia Woolf, "Professions for Women"   340
Scott Russell Sanders, "The Men We Carry in Our Minds"   345
Arlie Hochschild, "The Second Shift"   351
Deborah Tannen, "Marked Women"   396
Christina Hoff Sommers, "The War Against Boys"   380
Ashley Dunn, "Two Views of Technology's Promise"   465
Lewis Thomas, "Computers"   473
Henry Louis Gates, Jr., "One Internet, Two Nations"   499
Paula Span, "Women and Computers"   502
Matthew Symonds,
    "Government and the Internet: Haves and Have-nots"   514
Jane Goodall, "A Plea for the Chimps"   559
Robert L. Borosage,
    "Misplaced Priorities: A Focus on Guns"   577
Chief Seattle, "Letter to President Pierce, 1855"   601
Barbara Ehrenreich, "The Myth of Man as Hunter"   643
Robert Frost, "The Road Not Taken"   651
Niles Eldridge, "Creationism Isn't Science"   757
Francois Tremblay, "Revising Our Prejudices:
    The Holocaust and Freedom of Speech"   776

Classification and Division

William Zinsser, "College Pressures"   127
Aaron M. Shatzman, "When Learning Hurts"   142
Amy Tan, "Mother Tongue"   184
S. I. Hayakawa, "Reports, Inferences, Judgments"   197
Scott Russell Sanders, "The Men We Carry in Our Minds"   345
Judy Brady, "Why I Want a Wife"   348
Gregory J. E. Rawlins, "Pregnant with Possibility"   475
Philip Elmer-Dewitt, "Bards of the Internet"   495
Al Gore, "The Wasteland"   603
E. M. Forster, "My Wood"   611
Jerediah Purdy, "Shades of Green"   625

Definition

Alice Walker, "Beauty: When the Other Dancer Is the Self"   42
Barbara Kingsolver, "Stone Soup"   60
Leslie S. P. Brown, "Who Cares About the Renaissance"   140
Aaron M. Shatzman, "When Learning Hurts"   142
Barbara Lawrence, "Four-Letter Words Can Hurt You"   181
S. I. Hayakawa, "Reports, Inferences, Judgments"   197

Aldous Huxley, "Propaganda Under a Dictatorship"   214
Kevin J. H. Dettmar, "Grasping the Dark Images of Rock"   290
Virginia Woolf, "Professions for Women"   340
Judy Brady, "Why I Want a Wife"   348
Deborah Tannen, "Marked Women"   366
Bharati Mukherjee, "American Dreamer"   406
Anna Mae Halgrim Seaver, "My World Now"   566
Suzanne Gordon, "What Nurses Stand For"   626
Barbara Ehrenreich, "The Myth of Man as Hunter"   643
Deborah Lipstadt, "Denying the Holocaust"   763

Argument and Persuasion

John Holt, "School Is Bad for Children"   83
Lynda Barry, "The Sanctuary of School"   99
Jonathan Kozol, "Savage Inequalities"   112
Frederick Douglass, "Learning to Read and Write"   167
Barbara Lawrance, "Four-Letter Words Can Hurt You"   181
Amy Tan, "Mother Tongue"   184
Jonathan Kozol, "The Human Cost of an Illiterate Society"   189
Alleen Pace Nilsen, "Sexism in English: A 1990s Update"   203
Robert D. King, "Should English Be the Law"   238
Jorge Amsell, "¡Inglés, Sí!"   249
Marie Winn, "Television: The Plug-In Drug"   257
Joe Saltzman,
    "Celebrity Journalism, the Public, and Princess Diana"   271
John Grisham, "Unnatural Killers"   318
Richard Rhodes,
    "Hollow Claims About Fantasy Violence"   326
John Leo, "When Life Imitates Video"   329
Judy Brady, "Why I Want a Wife"   348
Brent Staples, "Just Walk on By"   417
Charles R. Lawrence III and Mari Matsuda, "The Telltale
    Heart"   436
Thomas Jefferson, The Declaration of Independence   449
Martin Luther King, Jr., "I Have a Dream"   457
Nicholas Negroponte, "An Age of Optimism"   469
Neal Postman, "Informing Ourselves to Death"   486
Dylan Thomas,
    "Do Not Go Gentle into That Good Night"   569
Elisabeth Kübler-Ross, "On the Fear of Death"   570
Robert L. Borosage,
    "Misplaced Priorities: A Focus on Guns"   577
Lawrence J. Schneiderman, "The Ethics of Euthanasia"   581
Jack Kevorkian, "A Case of Assisted Suicide"   587
Stephen L. Carter, "Rush to Lethal Judgment"   592
Rachel Carson, "The Obligation to Endure"   614

Sally Thane Christensen, "Is a Tree Worth a Life?" 630
William Stafford, "Traveling Through the Dark" 645
Annie Dillard, "The Deer at Providencia" 654
George Orwell, "Shooting an Elephant" 658
Henry David Thoreau, "Civil Disobedience" 664
Martin Luther King, Jr., "Letter from Birmingham Jail" 682
Edward Koch, "Death and Justice" 714
Russell Feingold,
    "The Need for a Moratorium on Executions" 719
Stanley Milgram, "The Perils of Obedience" 725
Lawrence Krauss, "Equal Time for Nonsense" 754
Niles Eldridge, "Creationism Isn't Science" 757
Deborah Lipstadt, "Denying the Holocaust" 763
Francois Tremblay, "Revising Our Prejudices:
    The Holocaust and Freedom of Speech" 776

Topical Clusters

The Arts and Popular Entertainment

Charles McGrath,
   "Giving Saturday Morning Some Slack"   266
Kevin J. H. Dettmar, "Grasping the Dark Images of Rock"   290
Kate Tuttle, "Television and African Americans"   297
John Grisham, "Unnatural Killers"   318
Richard Rhodes,
   "Hollow Claims About Fantasy Violence"   326
John Leo, "When Life Imitates Video"   329

Reading and Writing

Frederick Douglass, "Learning to Read and Write"   167
Malcolm X, "A Homemade Education"   173
Jonathan Kozol, "The Human Cost of an Illiterate Society"   189
S. I. Hayakawa, "Reports, Inferences, Judgments"   197
George Orwell, "Politics and the English Language"   220
Ted Gup, "The End of Serendipity"   478
Philip Elmer-Dewitt, "Bards of the Internet"   495

The College Years

Brent Staples,
   "Why Colleges Shower Their Students with A's"   125
William Zinsser, "College Pressures"   127
Leslie S. P. Brown, "Who Cares About the Renaissance?"   140
Aaron M. Shatzman, "When Learning Hurts"   142
Mark Edmundson, "On the Uses of a Liberal Education"   145
Barbara Dafoe Whitehead, "The Girls of Gen X"   372
Peshe Kuriloff,
   "If John Dewey Were Alive Today, He's Be a Webhead"   482
Claire McCarthy, "Dog Lab"   707

Innocence and Experience

E.B. White, "Once More to the Lake"   20
Alice Hoffman, "The Perfect Family"   57
John Holt, "School Is Bad for Children"   83
Plato, "Myth of the Cave"   89
Mark Twain, "Reading the River"   96

Walt Whitman, "When I Heard the Learn'd Astronomer" 98
Lynda Barry, "The Sanctuary of School" 99
Richard Rodriguez, "Aria" 232
E. M. Forster, "My Wood" 611
Claire McCarthy, "Dog Lab" 707
Ursula Le Guin,
    "The Ones Who Walk Away from Omelas" 747

Belief and Doubt

Plato, "Myth of the Cave" 89
Martin Luther King, Jr., "I Have a Dream" 457
Linda Pastan, "Ethics" 652
Lawrence Krauss, "Equal Time for Nonsense" 754
Niles Eldridge, "Creationism Isn't Science" 757
Deborah Lipstadt, "Denying the Holocaust" 763

Conformity and Rebellion

John Holt, "School Is Bad for Children" 83
Barbara Lawrence, "Four-Letter Words Can Hurt You" 181
Aldous Huxley, "Propaganda Under a Dictatorship" 214
Maya Angelou, "Graduation" 102
Gloria Steinem, "Sex, Lies, and Advertising" 274
Thomas Jefferson, The Declaration of Independence 449
Bharati Mukherjee, "American Dreamer" 406
Dylan Thomas,
    "Do Not Go Gentle into That Good Night" 569
George Orwell, "Shooting an Elephant" 658

Self-Image

Alice Walker, "Beauty: When the Other Dancer Is the Self" 42
Frederick Douglass, "Learning to Read and Write" 167
Richard Rodriguez, "Aria" 232
Wendy Kaminer, "Testifying: Television" 307
Marge Piercy, "Barbie Doll" 338
Virginia Woolf, "Professions for Women" 340
Deborah Tannen, "Marked Women" 366
Barbara Dafoe Whitehead, "The Girls of Gen X" 372
Christina Hoff Sommers, "The War Against Boys" 380
Susan Faludi, "The Future of Men" 385
Judith Ortiz Cofer, "The Myth of the Latin Woman" 412

Fear and Courage

Maxine Hong Kingston, "No Name Woman" 25
Richard Rodriguez, "Aria" 232

Virginia Woolf, "Professions for Women"   340
Brent Staples, "Just Walk on By"   417
Claire McCarthy, "Dog Lab"   707
Ursula Le Guin,
    "The Ones Who Walk Away from Omelas"   747

Property, Territoriality, and Space

Sharon Olds, "Rite of Passage"   339
Brent Staples, "Just Walk on By"   417
Lars Eighner, "On Dumpster Diving"   421
E. M. Forster, "My Wood"   611
Garrett Hardin, "Lifeboat Ethics: The Case Against 'Aid' That
    Harms"   697

What's in a Name?

Maxine Hong Kingston, "No Name Woman"   25
Barbara Lawrence, "Four-Letter Word Can Hurt You"   181
Alleen Pace Nilsen, "Sexism in English"   203
Judy Brady, "Why I Want a Wife"   348
Judith Ortiz Cofer, "The Myth of the Latin Woman"   412

Exiles

Maxine Hong Kingston, "No Name Woman"   25
Jonathan Kozol, "The Human Cost of an Illiterate Society"   189
Lars Eighner, "On Dumpster Diving"   421
Charles R. Lawrence III and Mary Matsuda, "The Telltale Heart"
    436
Emma Lazarus, "The New Colossus"   452
Gregory J. E. Rawlins, "Pregnant with Possibility"   475
Henry Louis Gates, "One Internet, Two Nations"   499
Matthew Symonds,
    "Government and the Internet: Haves and Have-Nots"   514
Margaret Sanger, "The Turbid Ebb and Flow of Misery"   553
Anna Mae Halgrim Seaver, "My World Now"   566
Ursula Le Guin,
    "The Ones Who Walk Away from Omelas"   747

Teenage Wasteland

Kevin J. H. Dettmar, "Grasping the Dark Images of Rock"   290
John Grisham, "Unnatural Killers"   318
John Leo, "When Life Imitates Video"   329
Barbara Dafoe Whitehead, "The Girls of Gen X"   372
Christina Hoff Sommers, "The War Against Boys"   380

The Generation Gap

Judith Wallerstein, et al.,
"The Unexpected Legacy of Divorce"   67
Jane Smiley,
"There They Go, Bad-Mouthing Divorce Again"   76
Mark Edmundson, "The Uses of a Liberal Education"   145
Barbara Lawrence, "Four-Letter Words Can Hurt You"   181
Charles McGrath, "Giving Saturday Morning Some Slack"   266
Kevin J. H. Dettmar, "Grasping the Dark Images of Rock"   290
Barbara Dafoe Whitehead, "The Girls of Gen X"   372
Bharati Mukherjee, "American Dreamer"   406
Peshe Kuriloff,
"If John Dewey Were Alive Today, He's Be a Webhead"   482

Fathers and Sons

Robert Hayden, "Those Winter Sundays"   11
E. B. White, "Once More to the Lake"   20
Raymond Carver, "My Father's Life"   49
Richard Rodriguez, "Aria"   232
Scott Russell Sanders, "The Men We Carry in Our Minds"   345

Mothers and Sons

Gary Soto, "One Last Time"   12
Richard Rodriguez, "Aria"   232
Sharon Olds, "Rite of Passage"   339

Fathers and Daughters

Alice Walker, "Beauty: When the Other Dancer Is the Self"   42
Brenda Peterson, "Growing Up Game"   637

Mothers and Daughters

Maxine Hong Kingston, "No Name Woman"   25
Alice Hoffman, "The Perfect Family"   57
Amy Tan, "Mother Tongue"   184

Family Matters

Alice Hoffman, "The Perfect Family"   57
Barbara Kingsolver, "Stone Soup"   60
Judith Wallerstein, et al.,
"The Unexpected Legacy of Divorce"   67
Jane Smiley,
"There They Go, Bad-Mounting Divorce Again"   76

Lynda Barry, "The Sanctuary of School" 99
Marie Winn, "Television: The Plug-In Drug" 257
Arlie Hochschild, "The Second Shift" 351

Women in a Man's World

Alleen Pace Nilsen,
    "Sexism in English: Embodiment and Language" 203
Gloria Steinem, "Sex, Lies, and Advertising" 274
Virginia Woolf, "Professions for Women" 340
Arlie Hochschild, "The Second Shift" 351
Stephanie Gutmann, "Sex and the Soldier" 357
Deborah Tannen, "Marked Women" 366
Paul Span, "Women and Computers" 502

Law and Justice

Aldous Huxley, "Propaganda Under a Dictatorship" 214
Robert D. King, "Should English Be the Law?" 232
John Grisham, "Unnatural Killers" 318
Charles R. Lawrence and Mari Matsuda,
    "The Telltale Heart" 436
Martin Luther King, Jr., "I Have a Dream" 457
Stephen L. Carter, "Rush to Lethal Judgment" 592
Henry David Thoreau, "Civil Disobedience" 664
Martin Luther King, Jr., "Letter from Birmingham Jail" 682
Edward Koch, "Death and Justice" 714
Russell Feingold,
    "The Need for a Moratorium on Executions" 719
Ursula Le Guin,
    "The Ones Who Walk Away from Omelas" 747

Nationalism and Patriotism

Pico Iyer, "The Global Village Finally Arrives" 303
Bharati Mukherjee, "American Dreamer" 406
Aldous Huxley, "Propaganda Under a Dictatorship" 214
Thomas Jefferson, The Declaration of Independence 449
John F. Kennedy, Inaugural Address 453
Martin Luther King, Jr., "I Have a Dream" 457

Unwisdom in Government

Plato, "Myth of the Cave" 89
Robert L. Borosage,
    "Misplaced Priorities: A Focus on Guns" 577
Stephen L. Carter, "Rush to Lethal Judgment" 592
T. Coraghessan Boyle, "Top of the Food Chain" 632
George Orwell, "Shooting an Elephant" 658

Henry David Thoreau, "Civil Disobedience" 664
Martin Luther King, Jr., "Letter from Birmingham Jail" 682
Russell Feingold,
    "The Need for a Moratorium on Executions" 719
Ursula Le Guin,
    "The Ones Who Walk Away from Omelas" 747
Deborah Lipstadt, "Denying the Holocaust" 763

The Civil Rights Movement

Maya Angelou, "Graduation" 102
Kate Tuttle, "Television and African Americans" 297
Richard Wright, "The Library Card" 398
Martin Luther King, Jr., "I Have a Dream" 457
Charles R. Lawrence and Mari Matsuda,
    "The Telltale Heart" 436
Henry Louis Gates, "One Internet, Two Nations" 499
Martin Luther King, Jr., "Letter from Birmingham Jail" 682

Native Americans: Past and Present

N. Scott Momaday, "The Way to Rainy Mountain" 36
Chief Seattle, "We May Be Brothers" 392
Chief Seattle, "Letter to President Pierce, 1855" 601

Social and Economic Class

Gary Soto, "One Last Time" 12
Jonothan Kozol, "Savage Inequalities" 112
William A. Henry, III, "In Defense of Elitism" 134
Jonothan Kozol,
    "The Human Costs of an Illiterate Society" 189
Richard Rodriguez, "Aria" 232
Scott Russell Sanders, "The Men We Carry in Our Minds" 345
Alexis de Toqueville, "Why the Americans are so Restless
    in the Midst of Their Prosperity" 395
Lars Eighner, "On Dumpster Diving" 421
Gregory J. E. Rawlins, "Pregnant with Possibility" 475
Henry Louis Gates, "One Internet, Two Nations" 499
Matthew Symonds, "Government and the Internet:
    Haves and Have-Nots" 514
Margaret Sanger, "The Turbid Ebb and Flow of Misery" 553
Garrett Hardin,
    "Lifeboat Ethics: The Case Against 'Aid' That Harms" 697

Working

Gary Soto, "One Last Time" 12
Leslie S. P. Brown, "Who Cares About the Renaissance" 140

Gloria Steinem, "Sex, Lies, and Advertising"   274
Virginia Woolf, "Professions for Women"   340
Scott Russell Sanders, "The Men We Carry in Our Minds"   345
Arlie Hochschild, "The Second Shift"   351
Stephanie Gutmann, "Sex and the Soldier"   357
Susan Faludi, "The Future of Men"   385
Alexis de Toqueville, "Why the Americans are so Restless
   in the Midst of Their Prosperity"   395
Richard Selzer, "Imelda"   532
Suzanne Gordon, "What Nurses Stand For"   543

The Language of Prejudice

Maya Angelou, "Graduation"   102
Barbara Lawrence, "Four-Letter Words Can Hurt You"   181
Amy Tan, "Mother Tongue"   184
S. I. Hayakawa, "Reports, Inferences, Judgements"   197
Alleen Pace Nilsen, "Sexism in English"   203
Aldous Huxley, "Propaganda Under a Dictatorship"   214
Deborah Lipstadt, "Denying the Holocaust"   763
Francois Tremblay, "Revising Our Prejudices:
   The Holocaust and Freedom of Speech"   776

Mother Tongues

Amy Tan, "Mother Tongue"   184
Richard Rodriguez, "Aria"   232
Robert D. King, "Should English Be the Law?"   232
Jorge Amselle, "¡Inglés, Sí!"   249

Stereotypes

Alice Hoffman, "The Perfect Family"   57
Maya Angelou, "Graduation"   102
Leslie S. P. Brown, "Who Cares About the Renaissance"   140
Gloria Steinem, "Sex, Lies, and Advertising"   274
Kate Tuttle, "Television and African Americans"   297
Marge Piercy, "Barbie Doll"   338
Scott Russell Sanders, "The Men We Carry in Our Minds"   345
Judith Ortiz Cofer, "The Myth of the Latin Woman"   412
George Orwell, "Shooting an Elephant"   658

Developing Nations

Pico Iyer, "The Global Village Finally Arrives"   303
Richard Selzer, "Imelda"   532
Robert L. Borosage,
   "Misplaced Priorities: A Focus on Guns"   577

T. Coraghessan Boyle, "Top of the Food Chain"   632
George Orwell, "Shooting an Elephant"   658

Free Speech and Censorship

Aldous Huxley, "Propaganda Under a Dictatorship"   214
John Grisham, "Unnatural Killers"   318
Deborah Lipstadt, "Denying the Holocaust"   763
Francois Tremblay, "Revising Our Prejudices:
    The Holocaust and Freedom of Speech"   776

City Life

Jonathan Kozol, "Savage Inequalities"   112
Brent Staples, "Just Walk On By"   417
Lars Eighner, "On Dumpster Diving"   421
Margaret Sanger, "The Turbid Ebb and Flow of Misery"   553

Violence

John Grisham, "Unnatural Killers"   318
Richard Rhodes,
    "Hollow Claims About Fantasy Violence"   326
John Leo, "When Life Imitates Video"   329
Sharon Olds, "Rite of Passage"   339
Susan Faludi, "The Future of Men"   385
Brent Staples, "Just Walk On By"   417
Barbara Ehrenreich, "The Myth of Man as Hunter"   643
Stanley Milgram, "The Perils of Obedience"   725

Saving the Planet

Al Gore, "The Wasteland"   603
Rachel Carson, "The Obligation to Endure"   614
William Rathje and Cullen Murphy, "Recycling:
    No Panacea"   620
Jerediah Purdy, "Shades of Green"   625
Sally Thane Christensen, "Is a Tree Worth a Life?"   630
T. Coraghessan Boyle, "Top of the Food Chain"   632

Humans and Animals

Jane Goodall, "A Plea for the Chimps"   559
Brenda Peterson, "Growing Up Game"   637
Anna Quindlen, "Our Animal Rites"   640
William Stafford, "Traveling Through the Dark"   645
Annie Dillard, "The Deer at Providencia"   654
George Orwell, "Shooting an Elephant"   658
Claire McCarthy, "Dog Lab"   707

The Limitations of Science

Walt Whitman, "When I Heard the Lean'd Astronomer"   98
Ashley Dunn, "Two Views of Technology's Progress"   465
Nicholas Negroponte, "An Age of Optimism"   469
Lewis Thomas, "Computers"   473
Neal Postman, "Informing Ourselves to Death"   486
Richard Selzer, "Imelda"   532
T. Coraghessan Boyle, "Top of the Food Chain"   632
Niles Eldridge, "Creationism Isn't Science"   757

Life and Death

Barbara Tuchman, "The Black Death"   522
Anna Mae Halgrim Seaver, "My World Now"   566
Elisabeth Kübler-Ross, "On the Fear of Death"   570
Lawrence Schneiderman, "The Ethics of Euthanasia"   581
Jack Kevorkian, "A Case of Assisted Suicide"   587
Stephen L. Carter, "Rush to Lethal Judgment"   592
Sally Thane Christensen, "Is a Tree Worth a Life?"   630
Linda Pastan, "Ethics"   652
Edward Koch, "Death and Justice"   714
Russell Feingold,
    "The Need for a Moratorium on Executions"   719

Apocalypse

Barbara Tuchman, "The Black Death"   522
Robert L. Borosage,
    "Misplaced Priorities: A Focus on Guns"   577
Al Gore, "The Wasteland"   603
T. Coraghessan Boyle, "Top of the Food Chain"   632

Preface

After more than twenty-five years of teaching composition, we have come to believe that reading and writing are interrelated tasks. If students are going to write effectively, they must also read actively and critically. In addition, we believe that writing is both a private and a public act. As a private act, it enables students to explore their feelings and reactions and to discover their ideas about a variety of subjects. As a public act, writing enables students to see how their own ideas fit into a larger discourse community, where ideas gain meaning and value. In short, we believe that students are most enriched and engaged if they view the reading and writing they do as a way of participating in ongoing public discussions about subjects that matter to them. We created *The Blair Reader* to encourage students to make their own contributions to the public discussion and to help them realize that their ideas take shape only in response to the ideas of others.

Another reason we decided to create *The Blair Reader* was that we could not find a reader that satisfied our needs as teachers. We-like you— expect compelling reading selections that involve both instructors and students in a spirited exchange. We also expect selections that are enriched by the diversity of ideas that characterize our society. In addition, we expect questions that ask students to respond critically to what they have read. In short, we expect a book that stimulates discussion and that encourages students to discover new ideas and to see familiar ideas in new ways. These expectations guided us as we developed *The Blair Reader* and as we worked on this fourth edition.

What's New in the Fourth Edition?

Our main goal in the fourth edition was to sharpen the focus of each chapter, thereby expanding the student's insight into the issue being discussed. Taking into consideration the comments of the many teachers who generously shared their reactions to the third edition with us, we narrowed the themes of several chapters. We also added a new unit, Chapter 7, "The Wired Revolution, to examine the cultural and ethical implications of the Internet.

New to the fourth edition are two features that are designed to increase the flexibility and usefulness of the book. The first is aimed at strengthening students' visual literacy. At the end of each chapter is an image that relates to the **Focus** question. Following each image are two **Responding to the Image** questions that ask students to respond critically to what they see. For example, a photograph at the end of Chapter 10,

Additional Resources for Instructors and Students

Instructor's Manual

Because we wanted *The Blair Reader* to be a rich and comprehensive resource for instructors, we developed an Instructor's Resource Manual to accompany the text. This manual, designed to serve as a useful and accessible classroom companion, incorporates teaching techniques drawn from our years inn the classroom as well as reactions of our own students to the selections. The manual contains teaching strategies, collaborative activities, multimedia resources, suggested answers for "Responding to Reading" questions, and many other useful resources.

Companion Website: www.prenhall.com/kirszner

The Companion Website provides additional chapter exercises, links, and activities that reinforce and build upon the material presented in the text.

Website features include:

- Additional essay and short answer questions for *every* reading

- Web links that provide additional contextual information

- Visual analysis questions for each chapter

- Web destinations for each essay topic

- Message board and chat room

- Syllabus Manager™

The New American Webster Handy College Dictionary
(0-13-032870-7)

FREE when packaged with the text.

English on the Internet: Evaluating Online Resources
(0-13-019484-0)

FREE when packaged with the text.

NEW! The Writer's Guide Series

FREE when packaged with the text.
The Writer's Guide to Document and Web Design (0-13-018929-4)

The Writer's Guide to Writing Across the Curriculum and Oral Presentations (0-13-018931-6)

The Writer's Guide to Writing About Literature (0-13-018932-4)

www.turnitin.com

This online service makes it easy for teachers to find out if students are copying their assignments from the Internet, and it is now free to professors using the fourth edition of *The Blair Reader* In addition to helping educators easily identify instances of Web-based student plagiarism, Turnitin.com also offers a digital archiving system and an online peer review service. Professors set up a "drop box" at the Tumitin.com website where their students submit papers. Turnitin.com then cross-references each submission with millions of possible online sources. Within 24 hours, teachers receive a customized, color-coded "Originality Report," complete with live links to suspect Internet locations, for each submitted paper. Visit www.prenhall.com/english for more information.

We encourage you to use the Instructor's Manual to complement your own proven strategies. We also encourage you to let us know your reactions to the Manual and your suggestions for making it better. We are especially interested in hearing about classroom strategies that you use successfully and reading selections that have consistently appealed to your students. In future editions of the Instructor's Resource Manual, we would like to include these suggestions along with the names of the individuals who submitted them. Just write us in care of Prentice Hall, One Lake Street, Upper Saddle River, NJ 07458.

Acknowledgments

The Blair Reader is the result of a fruitful collaboration between the two of us, between us and our students, between us and Prentice Hall, and between us and you —our colleagues who told us what you wanted in a reader.

At Prentice Hall, we want to thank our editor, Corey Good. We appreciate the organizational skills of Production Editor Randy Pettit, and we thank him for his patience and professionalism as he guided the book through production. We also thank our exceptional copyeditor, Margaret Ritchie.

As always, Mark Gallaher's editorial instincts were exactly right; as always, his contributions are much appreciated. (And, as always, he deserves his own paragraph.)

In preparing *The Blair Reader,* Fourth Edition, we benefited at every stage from the assistance and suggestions of colleagues from across the country: Jack Lynch, Rutgers University; Brenda Borron, Irvine Valley

College; Norman Lanquist, Eastern Arizona College; Andrew Tomko, Bergen Community College; Rober Dornsife, Creighton University; Mary E. Hallet, Boston College; and Rosemary Day, Albuquerque, T-VI Community College.

On the home front, we once again "round up the usual suspects" to thank—Mark, Adam, and Rebecca Kirszner and Demi, David, and Sarah Mandell. And, of course, we thank each other: it really has been a "beautiful friendship."

—*Laurie G. Kirszner,*
Stephen R. Mandell

INTRODUCTION:
BECOMING A
CRITICAL READER

In his autobiographical essay "The Library Card" (p. 398), Richard Wright describes his early exposure to the world of books. He says, "The plots and stories in the novels did not interest me so much as the point of view revealed. I gave myself over to each novel without reserve, without trying to criticize it; it was enough for me to see and feel something different. Reading was like a drug."

It is a rare person today for whom reading can hold this magic or inspire this awe. Most of us take the access to books for granted. As a student, you've probably learned to be pragmatic about your reading. In fact, "reading" most likely has come to mean reading assigned pages in a textbook. Whether the book's subject is modern American history, principles of corporate management, or quantum mechanics, you probably tend to read largely for information, expecting a book's ideas to be accessible and free of ambiguity and the book to be clearly written and logically organized.

In addition to reading textbooks, however, you also read essays and journal articles, fiction and poetry. These present special challenges because you read them not just for information but also to discover your own ideas about what the writer is saying—what the work means to you, how you react to it, why you react as you do, and how your reactions differ from the responses of other readers. And because the writers express opinions and convey impressions as well as facts, your role as a reader must be more active than it is when you read a textbook. Here, reading becomes not only a search for information, but also a search for meaning.

Reading and Meaning

Like many readers, you may assume that the meaning of a text is hidden somewhere between the lines and that you only have to ask the right questions or unearth the appropriate clues to discover exactly what the writer is getting at. But reading is not a game of hide-and-seek in which you must find ideas that have been hidden by the writer. As current reading theory demonstrates, meaning is created by the interaction of a reader with a text.

1

One way to explain this interactive process is to draw an analogy between a text—a work being read—and a word. A word is not the natural equivalent of the thing it signifies. The word *dog*, for example, does not evoke the image of a furry, four-legged animal in all parts of the world. To speakers of Spanish, the word *perro* elicits the same mental picture *dog* does in English-speaking countries. Not only does the word *dog* have meaning only in a specific cultural context, but even within that context it evokes different images in different people. Some people may picture a collie, others a poodle, and still others a particular pet.

Like a word, a text can have different meanings in different cultures—or even in different historical time periods. Each reader brings to the text associations that come from the cultural community in which he or she lives. These associations are determined by experience and education as well as by ethnic group, class, religion, gender, and many other factors. Each of these factors contributes to how a person views the world. Each reader also brings to the text expectations, desires, and prejudices that influence how he or she reacts to and interprets it. Thus it is entirely possible for two readers to have very different, but equally valid, interpretations of the same text. (This does *not* mean, of course, that a text can mean whatever any individual reader wishes it to mean. To be valid, an interpretation must be supported by what actually appears in the text.)

To get an idea of the range of possible interpretations that can be suggested by a single text, consider some of the responses different readers might have to E. B. White's classic essay "Once More to the Lake" (p. 20).

In "Once More to the Lake," White tells a story about his visit with his son to a lake in Maine in the 1940s. White compares this visit with those he made as a boy with his own father. Throughout the essay, White describes the changes that have occurred since he was first there. Memories from the past flood his consciousness and cause him to remember things that he did when he was a boy. At one point, after he and his son have been feeding worms to fish, he remembers doing the same thing with his father and has trouble separating the past from the present. As a result, White realizes that he will soon be just a memory in his son's mind—just as his father is a memory in his.

White had specific goals in mind when he wrote this essay. His title, "Once More to the Lake," indicates that he intended to compare his childhood and adult visits to the lake. The organization of ideas in the essay, the use of flashbacks, and the choice of particular transitional phrases reinforce this structure. In addition, descriptive details—such as the image of the tarred road that replaced the dirt road—remind readers, as well as White himself, that the years have made the lake site different from what it once was. The essay ends with the father suddenly feeling the "chill of death."

Despite White's specific intentions, each person reading "Once More to the Lake" will respond to it somewhat differently. Young male readers might identify with the boy. If they have ever spent a vacation at a lake, they might have experienced the "peace and goodness and jollity" of the whole summer scene. Female readers might also want to share these experiences, but they might feel excluded because only males are described in the essay. Readers who have never been on a fishing trip might not feel the same nostalgia for the woods that White feels. To them, living in the woods away from the comforts of home might seem an unthinkably uncomfortable ordeal. Older readers might identify with White, the adult, sympathizing with his efforts to recapture the past and seeing his son as naively innocent of the hardships of life.

Thus, although each person who reads White's essay will read the same words, each will be likely to *interpret* it differently and to see different things as important. This is because much is left open to interpretation. All essays leave blanks or gaps—missing words, phrases, or images—that readers have to fill in. In "Once More to the Lake," for example, readers must imagine what happened in the years that separated White's last visit to the lake and the trip he took with his son.

These gaps in the text create *ambiguities*—words, phrases, descriptions, or ideas that need to be interpreted by the reader. For instance, when you read the words "One summer, along about 1904, my father rented a camp on a lake," how do you picture the camp? White's description of the setting contains a great deal of detail, but no matter how much information he supplies, he cannot paint a complete verbal picture of the lakeside camp. He must rely on the reader's ability to visualize the setting and to supply details from his or her own experience.

Readers also bring their *emotional associations* to a text. For example, how readers react to White's statement above depends, in part, on their feelings about their own fathers. If White's words bring to mind a parent who is loving, strong, and protective, they will most likely respond favorably; if the essay calls up memories of a parent who is distant, bad-tempered, or even abusive, they may respond negatively.

Because each reader views the text from a slightly different angle, each may also see a different *focus* as central to "Once More to the Lake." Some might see nature as the primary element in the essay and believe that White's purpose is to condemn the encroachment of human beings on the environment. Others might see the passage of time as the central focus. Still others might see the initiation theme as being the most important element of the essay: each boy is brought to the wilderness by his father, and each eventually passes from childhood innocence to adulthood and the knowledge of death.

Finally, each reader may *evaluate* the essay differently. Some readers might think "Once More to the Lake" is boring because it has little action and deals with a subject in which they have no interest. Others might believe the essay is a brilliant meditation that makes an impact through its vivid description and imaginative figurative language. Still others might see the essay as a mixed bag—admitting, for example, that

By" (p. 417)? Does the writer quote experts, as Deborah Tannen does in "Marked Women" (p. 366), or present anecdotal information, as William Zinsser does in "College Pressures" (p. 127)? Why does the writer choose a particular kind of support? Does he or she supply enough information to support the essay's points? Are the examples given relevant to the issues being discussed? Is the writer's reasoning valid, or do the arguments seem forced or unrealistic? Are any references in the work unfamiliar to you? If so, do they arouse your curiosity, or do they discourage you from reading further?

What beliefs, assumptions, or preconceived ideas do you have that color your responses to a work? Does the writer challenge any ideas that you accept as "natural" or "obvious"? For example, does Garrett Hardin's controversial stand in "Lifeboat Ethics: The Case against 'Aid' That Harms" (p. 697) shock you or violate your sense of fair play? Does the fact that you are against physician-assisted suicide prevent you from appreciating the perspective of Jack Kevorkian's essay "A Case of Assisted Suicide" (p. 587)?

Does your background or experience give you any special insights that enable you to understand or interpret the writer's ideas? Are the writer's experiences similar to or different from your own? Is the writer like or unlike you in terms of age, ethnic background, gender, and social class? How do the similarities and differences between you and the writer affect your reaction to the work? For example, you may be able to understand Amy Tan's "Mother Tongue" (p. 184) better than other students because you, too, speak one language at home and another in public. You may have a unique perspective on the problems Raymond Carver examines in "My Father's Life" (p. 49) because you, too, have an alcoholic parent. Or your volunteer work at a shelter may have helped you understand the plight of the homeless as described by Lars Eighner in "On Dumpster Diving" (p. 421). Any experiences you have can help you to understand a writer's ideas and shape your response to them.

Recording Your Reactions

It is a good idea to read a work at least twice: first to get a general sense of the writer's ideas and then to think critically about these ideas. As you read critically, you interact with the text and respond in ways that will help you to interpret it. This process of coming to understand the text will in turn prepare you to discuss the work with others and, if necessary, to write about it.

As you read and reread, record your responses; if you don't, you will forget some of your best ideas. Two activities can help you keep a record of the ideas that come to you as you read: **highlighting** (using a system of symbols and underlining to identify key ideas) and **annotating** (writing down your responses and interpretations).

When you react to what you read, don't be afraid to question or challenge the writer's ideas. As you read and make annotations, you may question or disagree with some of the writer's ideas. Jot your responses down in the margin; when you have time, you can think more about what you have written. These informal responses may be the beginning of a thought process that will lead you to an original insight.

Highlighting and annotating helped a student to understand the passage below, which is excerpted from Jane Goodall's essay "A Plea for the Chimps" (p. 559). As she prepared to write about Goodall's essay, the student identified the writer's key points; asked pertinent questions; made a connection with another essay, Claire McCarthy's "Dog Lab" (p. 707); and eventually reached her own conclusions. As she read, she underlined some of the passage's important words and ideas, using arrows to indicate relationships between them. She also circled the word *physiology,* to remind her to look up its meaning later on, and she wrote down questions and comments as they occurred to her.

The chimpanzee is more like us, genetically, than any other animal. It is because of similarities in physiology, in biochemistry, in the immune system, that medical science makes use of living bodies of chimpanzees in its search for cures and vaccines for a variety of human diseases.

There are also behavioral, psychological and emotional similarities between chimpanzees and humans, resemblances so striking that they raise a serious ethical question: are we justified in using an animal so close to us—an animal, moreover, that is highly endangered in its African forest home—as a human substitute in medical experimentation?

In the long run, we can hope that scientists will find ways of exploring human physiology and disease, and of testing cures and vaccines, that do not depend on the use of living animals of any sort. A number of steps in this direction have already been taken, prompted in large part by growing public awareness of the suffering that is being inflicted on millions of animals. More and more people are beginning to realize that nonhuman animals—even rats and guinea pigs—are not just unfeeling machines but are capable of enjoying their lives, and of feeling fear, pain and despair.

But until alternatives have been found, medical science will continue to use animals in the battle against human disease and suffering. And some of those animals will continue to be chimpanzees.

Marginal annotations: What us? · Is there an alternative? Other animals? Computer models? · Compare with "Dog Lab" · (Like humans) · Is this justified? Does Goodall think it is?

READING TO WRITE

Much of the reading you will do as a student will be done to prepare you for writing. Writing helps you focus your ideas about various issues; in addition, the process of writing can lead you in unexpected directions, thereby enabling you to discover new insights. With this in mind, we have included in *The Blair Reader* a number of features that will help you as you read and prepare to write about its selections.

The readings in *The Blair Reader* are arranged in ten thematic chapters, each offering a variety of different vantage points from which to view the theme. Each chapter in the book opens with a brief introduction, "Preparing to Read and Write." This feature provides a context for the chapter's theme and lists questions to guide your thinking as you read. These questions are designed to help you to see the reading selections from different angles and thus to sharpen your critical skills and begin to apply those skills effectively.

Following each reading are three questions to help you think about and respond—in discussion and perhaps in writing—to what you have read. These "Responding to Reading" questions focus on the reader's side of the interaction, encouraging you to think critically about the writer's ideas or to focus on a particular strategy a writer has used to achieve his or her purpose or, in some cases, to examine your own ideas or beliefs. (The images in the focus section are also followed by questions.)

Following the essays that develop each chapter's general theme is a "Focus" question that introduces three or four thought-provoking readings that take different positions on a single complex issue. For example, Chapter 4's Focus question, "Does Media Violence Hurt?" introduces John Grisham's "Unnatural Killers", Richard Rhodes's "Hollow Claims about Fantasy Violence," and John Leo's "When Life Imitates Video." A visual image on the focus topic follows this group of readings. (The essays are accompanied by "Responding to Reading" questions; "Responding to the Image" questions follow each picture.) The Focus section concludes with a "Widening the Focus" feature that identifies additional readings in other chapters in the book that shed light on the issue.

At the end of each chapter are ten writing suggestions that expand on the ideas developed by the "Preparing to Read and Write" and "Responding to Reading" questions. Writing suggestions ask you to discuss the chapter's theme, to relate the writer's ideas to your own experiences, or to analyze connections among different works in the chapter or among selections in different chapters. Following the writing suggestions is a Web Assignment that asks you to further explore the chapter's "Focus" issue by doing guided research on the Internet.

As you read and write about the selections in this book, remember that you are learning ways of thinking about yourself and about the world. By considering and reconsidering the ideas of others, by rejecting easy answers, by considering a problem from many different angles, and by appreciating the many factors that can influence your responses, you develop critical thinking skills that you will use throughout your life. In addition, by writing about the themes discussed in this book, you participate in an ongoing conversation within the community of scholars and writers who care deeply about the issues that shape our world.

1

FAMILY
AND MEMORY

PREPARING TO READ AND WRITE

Memory preserves past events and makes them accessible to us. In this chapter, writers search their memories, trying to understand, recapture, or re-create the past, to see across the barriers imposed by time. In some cases, memories appear in sharp focus; in others, they are blurred, confused, or even partially invented. Many writers focus on themselves; others focus on their parents or other family members, struggling to close generational gaps, to replay events, to see through the eyes of others —and thus to understand their families and themselves more fully.

In the Focus section of this chapter, "How Has Divorce Redefined the Family?" (p. 57), four writers zero in on a painful subject: the effects of divorce on families in general and on children in particular. Looking at divorce from a variety of perspectives, these writers consider how children's lives change (and how they stay the same) after a divorce, how divorcing adults come to terms with their decision to break up a family, and how adult children of divorce look back on their families' lives. More significantly, all four readings focus on the central questions of how *family* is defined and how divorce has changed that definition.

As you read and prepare to write about the selections in this chapter, you may consider the following questions:

- Does the writer focus on a single person, on a relationship between two people, or on family dynamics?

- Do you think the writer's perspective is *subjective* (shaped by his or her emotional responses or personal opinions) or *objective* (based mainly on observation and fact rather than on personal impressions)?

- Does the writer recount events from the perspective of an adult looking back at his or her childhood? If so, does the writer seem to have more insight now than when the events occurred? What has the writer learned—and how?

- Are the memories generally happy or unhappy ones?

- Are family members presented in a favorable, unfavorable, neutral, or ambivalent light?

- Does one family member seem to have a great influence over others in the family? If so, is this influence positive or negative?

- Does the writer feel close to or distant from family members? Does the writer identify with a particular family member?

- What social, political, economic, or cultural forces influence the way the family functions?

- Is the writer's purpose to observe, explore, discover, explain, rationalize, or to do something else?

- Do you identify with the writer or with another person described in the selection? What makes you identify with that person?

- Which selections seem most similar in their views of family? How are they similar?

- Which selections seem most different in their views of family? How are they different?

THOSE WINTER SUNDAYS

Robert Hayden

Robert Hayden (1913-1980) published his first book of poems, Heart-Shaped in the Dust, *in 1940. He taught at Fiske University and the University of Michigan and served as a consultant in poetry to the Library of Congress. His belief that racism is best understood through historical causes is evident in his poems about the slave rebellions. Some of his many works include* A Ballad of Remembrance *(1962),* Words in Mourning Time *(1970),* American Journal *(1978), and* Complete Poems *(1985). Hayden once said that "writing poetry is one way of coming to grips with both inner and external realities." "Those Winter Sundays" is from the 1975 collection* Angle of Ascent, New and Selected Poems.

Sundays too my father got up early
and put his clothes on in the blueblack cold,

I cut another bunch, then another, fighting the snap and whip of   4
vines. After ten minutes of groping for grapes, my first pan brimmed
with bunches. I poured them on the paper tray, which was bordered by
a wooden frame that kept the grapes from rolling off, and they spilled
like jewels from a pirate's chest. The tray was only half filled, so I hurried to jump under the vines and begin groping, cutting, and tugging at
the grapes again. I emptied the pan, raked the grapes with my hands to
make them look like they filled the tray, and jumped back under the
vine on my knees. I tried to cut faster because Mother, in the next row,
was slowly moving ahead. I peeked into her row and saw five trays
gleaming in the early morning. I cut, pulled hard, and stopped to gather
the grapes that missed the pan; already bored, I spat on a few to wash
them before tossing them like popcorn into my mouth.

So it went. Two pans equaled one tray—or six cents. By lunchtime I   5
had a trail of thirty-seven trays behind me while mother had sixty or
more. We met about halfway from our last trays, and I sat down with a
grunt, knees wet from kneeling on dropped grapes. I washed my hands
with the water from the jug, drying them on the inside of my shirt
sleeve before I opened the paper bag for the first sandwich, which I
gave to Mother. I dipped my hand in again to unwrap a sandwich without looking at it. I took a first bite and chewed it slowly for the tang of
mustard. Eating in silence I looked straight ahead at the vines, and only
when we were finished with cookies did we talk.

"Are you tired?" she asked.   6

"No, but I got a sliver from the frame," I told her. I showed her the   7
web of skin between my thumb and index finger. She wrinkled her forehead but said it was nothing.

"How many trays did you do?"   8

I looked straight ahead, not answering at first. I recounted in my   9
mind the whole morning of bend, cut, pour again and again, before
answering a feeble "thirty-seven." No elaboration, no detail. Without
looking at me she told me how she had done field work in Texas and
Michigan as a child. But I had a difficult time listening to her stories. I
played with my grape knife, stabbing it into the ground, but stopped
when Mother reminded me that I had better not lose it. I left the knife
sticking up like a small, leafless plant. She then talked about school, the
junior high I would be going to that fall, and then about Rick and Debra,
how sorry they would be that they hadn't come out to pick grapes
because they'd have no new clothes for the school year. She stopped
talking when she peeked at her watch, a bandless one she kept in her
pocket. She got up with an "*Ay, Dios,*" and told me that we'd work until
three, leaving me cutting figures in the sand with my knife and dread-
ing the return to work.

Finally I rose and walked slowly back to where I had left off, again   10
kneeling under the vine and fixing the pan under bunches of grapes. By

that time, 11:30, the sun was over my shoulder and made me squint and think of the pool at the Y.M.C.A. where I was a summer member. I saw myself diving face first into the water and loving it. I saw myself gleaming like something new, at the edge of the pool. I had to daydream and keep my mind busy because boredom was a terror almost as awful as the work itself. My mind went dumb with stupid things, and I had to keep it moving with dreams of baseball and would-be girlfriends. I even sang, however softly, to keep my mind moving, my hands moving.

I worked less hurriedly and with less vision. I no longer saw that 11 copper pot sitting squat on our stove or Mother waiting for it to whistle. The wardrobe that I imagined, crisp and bright in the closet, numbered only one pair of jeans and two shirts because, in half a day, six cents times thirty-seven trays was two dollars and twenty-two cents. It became clear to me. If I worked eight hours, I might make four dollars. I'd take this, even gladly, and walk downtown to look into store windows on the mall and long for the bright madras shirts from Walter Smith or Coffee's, but settling for two imitation ones from Penney's.

That first day I laid down seventy-three trays while Mother had a 12 hundred and twenty behind her. On the back of an old envelope, she wrote out our numbers and hours. We washed at the pump behind the farm house and walked slowly to our car for the drive back to town in the afternoon heat. That evening after dinner I sat in a lawn chair listening to music from a transistor radio while Rick and David King played catch. I joined them in a game of pickle, but there was little joy in trying to avoid their tags because I couldn't get the fields out of my mind: I saw myself dropping on my knees under a vine to tug at a branch that wouldn't come off. In bed, when I closed my eyes, I saw the fields, yellow with kicked up dust, and a crooked trail of trays rotting behind me.

The next day I woke tired and started picking tired. The grapes 13 rained into the pan, slowly filling like a belly, until I had my first tray and started my second. So it went all day, and the next, and all through the following week, so that by the end of thirteen days the foreman counted out, in tens mostly, my pay of fifty-three dollars. Mother earned one hundred and forty-eight dollars. She wrote this on her envelope, with a message I didn't bother to ask her about.

The next day I walked with my friend Scott to the downtown mall 14 where we drooled over the clothes behind fancy windows, bought popcorn, and sat at a tier of outdoor fountains to talk about girls. Finally we went into Penney's for more popcorn, which we ate walking around, before we returned home without buying anything. It wasn't until a few days before school that I let my fifty-three dollars slip quietly from my hands, buying a pair of pants, two shirts, and a maroon T-shirt, the kind that was in style. At home I tried them on while Rick looked on enviously; later, the day before school started, I tried them on again wondering not so much if they were worth it as who would see me first in those clothes.

Along with my brother and sister I picked grapes until I was fifteen, before giving up and saying that I'd rather wear old clothes than stoop like a Mexican. Mother thought I was being stuck-up, even stupid, because there would be no clothes for me in the fall. I told her I didn't care, but when Rick and Debra rose at five in the morning, I lay awake in bed feeling that perhaps I had made a mistake but unwilling to change my mind. That fall Mother bought me two pairs of socks, a packet of colored T-shirts, and underwear. The T-shirts would help, I thought, but who would see that I had new underwear and socks? I wore a new T-shirt on the first day of school, then an old shirt on Tuesday, then another T-shirt on Wednesday, and on Thursday an old Nehru shirt that was embarrassingly out of style. On Friday I changed into the corduroy pants my brother had handed down to me and slipped into my last new T-shirt. I worked like a magician, blinding my classmates, who were all clothes conscious and small-time social climbers, by arranging my wardrobe to make it seem larger than it really was. But by spring I had to do something—my blue jeans were almost silver and my shoes had lost their form, puddling like black ice around my feet. That spring of my sixteenth year, Rick and I decided to take a labor bus to chop cotton. In his old Volkswagen, which was more noise than power, we drove on a Saturday morning to West Fresno—or Chinatown as some call it—parked, walked slowly toward a bus, and stood gawking at the winos, toothy blacks, Okies, *Tejanos*[2] with gold teeth, whores, Mexican families, and labor contractors shouting "Cotton" or "Beets," the work of spring.

We boarded the "Cotton" bus without looking at the contractor who stood almost blocking the entrance because he didn't want winos. We boarded scared and then were more scared because two blacks in the rear were drunk and arguing loudly about what was better, a two-barrel or four-barrel Ford carburetor. We sat far from them, looking straight ahead, and only glanced briefly at the others who boarded, almost all of them broken and poorly dressed in loudly mismatched clothes. Finally when the contractor banged his palm against the side of the bus, the young man at the wheel, smiling and talking in Spanish, started the engine, idled it for a moment while he adjusted the mirrors, and started off in slow chugs. Except for the windshield there was no glass in the windows, so as soon as we were on the rural roads outside Fresno, the dust and sand began to be sucked into the bus, whipping about like irate wasps as the gravel ticked about us. We closed our eyes, clotted up our mouths that wanted to open with embarrassed laughter

---

[2] Texans. [Eds.]

because we couldn't believe we were on that bus with those people and the dust attacking us for no reason.

When we arrived at a field we followed the others to a pickup 17 where we each took a hoe and marched to stand before a row. Rick and I, self-conscious and unsure, looked around at the others who leaned on their hoes or squatted in front of the rows, almost all talking in Spanish, joking, lighting cigarettes—all waiting for the foreman's whistle to begin work. Mother had explained how to chop cotton by showing us with a broom in the backyard.

"Like this," she said, her broom swishing down weeds. "Leave one 18 plant and cut four—and cut them! Don't leave them standing or the foreman will get mad."

The foreman whistled and we started up the row stealing glances at 19 other workers to see if we were doing it right. But after awhile we worked like we knew what we were doing, neither of us hurrying or falling behind. But slowly the clot of men, women, and kids began to spread and loosen. Even Rick pulled away. I didn't hurry, though. I cut smoothly and cleanly as I walked at a slow pace, in a sort of funeral march. My eyes measured each space of cotton plants before I cut. If I missed the plants, I swished again. I worked intently, seldom looking up, so when I did I was amazed to see the sun, like a broken orange coin, in the east. It looked blurry, unbelievable, like something not of this world. I looked around in amazement, scanning the eastern horizon that was a taut line jutted with an occasional mountain. The horizon was beautiful, like a snapshot of the moon, in the early light of morning, in the quiet of no cars and few people.

The foreman trudged in boots in my direction, stepping awkwardly 20 over the plants, to inspect the work. No one around me looked up. We all worked steadily while we waited for him to leave. When he did leave, with a feeble complaint addressed to no one in particular, we looked up smiling under straw hats and bandanas.

By 11:00, our lunch time, my ankles were hurting from walking on 21 clods the size of hardballs. My arms ached and my face was dusted by a wind that was perpetual, always busy whipping about. But the work was not bad, I thought. It was better, so much better, than picking grapes, especially with the hourly wage of a dollar twenty-five instead of piece work. Rick and I walked sorely toward the bus where we washed and drank water. Instead of eating in the bus or in the shade of the bus, we kept to ourselves by walking down to the irrigation canal that ran the length of the field, to open our lunch of sandwiches and crackers. We laughed at the crackers, which seemed like a cruel joke from our Mother, because we were working under the sun and the last thing we wanted was a salty dessert. We ate them anyway and drank more water before we returned to the field, both of us limping in exaggeration. Working side by side, we talked and laughed at our predicament because our Mother had warned us year after year that if we didn't get on track in school we'd have to work in the fields and then we would see. We mimicked Mother's whining voice and smirked at her smoky view of the future in which we'd be trapped by marriage and screaming kids. We'd eat beans and then we'd see.

Rick pulled slowly away to the rhythm of his hoe falling faster and smoother. It was better that way, to work alone. I could hum made-up songs or songs from the radio and think to myself about school and friends. At the time I was doing badly in my classes, mainly because of a difficult stepfather, but also because I didn't care anymore. All through junior high and into my first year of high school there were those who said I would never do anything, be anyone. They said I'd work like a donkey and marry the first Mexican girl that came along. I was reminded so often, verbally and in the way I was treated at home, that I began to believe that chopping cotton might be a lifetime job for me. If not chopping cotton, then I might get lucky and find myself in a car wash or restaurant or junkyard. But it was clear; I'd work, and work hard.   22

I cleared my mind by humming and looking about. The sun was directly above with a few soft blades of clouds against a sky that seemed bluer and more beautiful than our sky in the city. Occasionally the breeze flurried and picked up dust so that I had to cover my eyes and screw up my face. The workers were hunched, brown as the clods under our feet, and spread across the field that ran without end—fields that were owned by corporations, not families.   23

I hoed trying to keep my mind busy with scenes from school and pretend girlfriends until finally my brain turned off and my thinking went fuzzy with boredom. I looked about, no longer mesmerized by the beauty of the landscape, no longer wondering if the winos in the fields could hold out for eight hours, no longer dreaming of the clothes I'd buy with my pay. My eyes followed my chopping as the plants, thin as their shadows, fell with each strike. I worked slowly with ankles and arms hurting, neck stiff, and eyes stinging from the dust and the sun that glanced off the field like a mirror.   24

By quitting time, 3:00, there was such an excruciating pain in my ankles that I walked as if I were wearing snowshoes. Rick laughed at me and I laughed too, embarrassed that most of the men were walking normally and I was among the first timers who had to get used to this work. "And what about you, wino," I came back at Rick. His eyes were meshed red and his long hippie hair was flecked with dust and gnats and bits of leaves. We placed our hoes in the back of a pickup and stood in line for our pay, which was twelve fifty. I was amazed at the pay, which was the most I had ever earned in one day, and thought that I'd come back the next day, Sunday. This was too good.   25

Instead of joining the others in the labor bus, we jumped in the back of a pickup when the driver said we'd get to town sooner and   26 were welcome to join him. We scrambled into the truck bed to be joined by a heavy-set and laughing *Tejano* whose head was shaped like an egg, particularly so because the bandana he wore ended in a point on the top of his head. He laughed almost demonically as the pickup roared up the dirt path, a gray cape of dust rising behind us. On the highway, with the wind in our faces, we squinted at the fields as if we were looking for someone. The *Tejano* had quit laughing but was smiling broadly, occasionally chortling tunes he never finished. I was scared of him, though Rick, two years older and five inches taller, wasn't. If the *Tejano* looked at him, Rick stared back for a second or two before he looked away to the fields.

I felt like a soldier coming home from war when we rattled into 27 Chinatown. People leaning against car hoods stared, their necks following us, owl-like; prostitutes chewed gum more ferociously and showed us their teeth; Chinese grocers stopped brooming their storefronts to raise their cadaverous faces at us. We stopped in front of the Chi Chi Club where Mexican music blared from the juke box and cue balls cracked like dull ice. The *Tejano*, who was dirty as we were, stepped awkwardly over the side rail, dusted himself off with his bandana, and sauntered into the club.

Rick and I jumped from the back, thanked the driver who said 28 *de nada* and popped his clutch, so that the pickup jerked and coughed blue smoke. We returned smiling to our car, happy with the money we had made and pleased that we had, in a small way, proved ourselves to be tough; that we worked as well as other men and earned the same pay.

We returned the next day and the next week until the season was 29 over and there was nothing to do. I told myself that I wouldn't pick grapes that summer, saying all through June and July that it was for Mexicans, not me. When August came around and I still had not found a summer job, I ate my words, sharpened my knife, and joined Mother, Rick, and Debra for one last time.

Responding to Reading

1. What does Soto learn from the events he describes? What more do you think he still has to learn?
2. In paragraph 1 Soto says he recognizes his relatives in the characters he sees in the film *Gandhi*. What does he mean? Do you recognize any of your own relatives in Soto's essay?
3. Why would Soto at age fifteen "rather wear old clothes than stoop like a Mexican" (15)? Does the adult Soto understand the reasons for this sentiment? What does this comment reveal about the society in which Soto grew up?

ONCE MORE TO THE LAKE

E. B. White

One of America's best-loved essayists, E. B. White (1899–1986) enjoyed an almost idyllic childhood in Mt. Vernon, New York, graduated from college in 1921, and embarked on a career writing for newspapers. Soon he was writing essays for the New Yorker *and* Harper's Magazine. *White wrote the children's classics* Charlotte's Web *(1952) and* Stuart Little *(1945); in 1959, he expanded Will Strunk's grammar book, which White had used as his student, into the now classic* The Elements of Style; *and he published essays in the collections* One Man's Meat *(1944) and* Essays of E. B. White *(1977). In his nostalgic "Once More to the Lake," White revisits the lake in Maine where he vacationed as a boy with his family and explores the themes of time and change.*

One summer, along about 1904, my father rented a camp on a lake in   1
Maine and took us all there for the month of August. We all got ringworm from some kittens and had to rub Pond's Extract on our arms and legs night and morning, and my father rolled over in a canoe with all his clothes on; but outside of that the vacation was a success and from then on none of us ever thought there was any place in the world like that lake in Maine. We returned summer after summer—always on August 1st for one month. I have since become a salt-water man, but sometimes in summer there are days when the restlessness of the tides and the fearful cold of the sea water and the incessant wind which blows across the afternoon and into the evening make me wish for the placidity of a lake in the woods. A few weeks ago this feeling got so strong I bought myself a couple of bass hooks and a spinner and returned to the lake where we used to go, for a week's fishing and to revisit old haunts.

I took along my son, who had never had any fresh water up his nose and who had seen lily pads only from train windows. On the journey   2
over to the lake I began to wonder what it would be like. I wondered how time would have marred this unique, this holy spot—the coves and streams, the hills that the sun set behind, the camps and the paths behind the camps. I was sure the tarred road would have found it out and I wondered in what other ways it would be desolated. It is strange how much you can remember about places like that once you allow your mind to return into the grooves which lead back. You remember one thing, and that suddenly reminds you of another thing. I guess I remembered clearest of all the early mornings, when the lake was cool and motionless, remembered how the bedroom smelled of the lumber it was made of and of the wet woods whose scent entered through the screen. The partitions in the camp were thin and did not extend clear to

the top of the rooms, and as I was always the first up I would dress softly so as not to wake the others, and sneak out into the sweet outdoors and start out in the canoe, keeping close along the shore in the long shadows of the pines. I remembered being very careful never to rub my paddle against the gunwale for fear of disturbing the stillness of the cathedral.

The lake had never been what you would call a wild lake. There 3 were cottages sprinkled around the shores, and it was in farming country although the shores of the lake were quite heavily wooded. Some of the cottages were owned by nearby farmers, and you would live at the shore and eat your meals at the farmhouse. That's what our family did. But although it wasn't wild, it was a fairly large and undisturbed lake and there were places in it which, to a child at least, seemed infinitely remote and primeval.

I was right about the tar: it led to within half a mile of the shore. But 4 when I got back there, with my boy, and we settled into a camp near a farmhouse and into the kind of summertime I had known, I could tell that it was going to be pretty much the same as it had been before—I knew it, lying in bed the first morning, smelling the bedroom, and hearing the boy sneak quietly out and go off along the shore in a boat. I began to sustain the illusion that he was I, and therefore, by simple transposition, that I was my father. This sensation persisted, kept cropping up all the time we were there. It was not an entirely new feeling, but in this setting it grew much stronger. I seemed to be living a dual existence. I would be in the middle of some simple act, I would be picking up a bait box or laying down a table fork, or I would be saying something, and suddenly it would be not I but my father who was saying the words or making the gesture. It gave me a creepy sensation.

We went fishing the first morning. I felt the same damp moss cov- 5 ering the worms in the bait can, and saw the dragonfly alight on the tip of my rod as it hovered a few inches from the surface of the water. It was the arrival of this fly that convinced me beyond any doubt that everything was as it always had been, that the years were a mirage and there had been no years. The small waves were the same, chucking the rowboat under the chin as we fished at anchor, and the boat was the same boat, the same color green and the ribs broken in the same places, and under the floor-boards the same freshwater leavings and débris—the dead helgramite,[1] the wisps of moss, the rusty discarded fishhook, the dried blood from yesterday's catch. We stared silently at the tips of our rods, at the dragonflies that came and went. I lowered the tip of mine into the water, tentatively, pensively dislodging the fly, which darted

---

[1] The nymph of the May-fly, used as bait. [Eds.]

two feet away, poised, darted two feet back, and came to rest again a little farther up the rod. There had been no years between the ducking of this dragonfly and the other one—the one that was part of memory. I looked at the boy, who was silently watching his fly, and it was my hands that held his rod, my eyes watching. I felt dizzy and didn't know which rod I was at the end of.

We caught two bass, hauling them in briskly as though they were 6 mackerel, pulling them over the side of the boat in a businesslike manner without any landing net, and stunning them with a blow on the back of the head. When we got back for a swim before lunch, the lake was exactly where we had left it, the same number of inches from the dock, and there was only the merest suggestion of a breeze. This seemed an utterly enchanted sea, this lake you could leave to its own devices for a few hours and come back to, and find that it had not stirred, this constant and trustworthy body of water. In the shallows, the dark, water-soaked sticks and twigs, smooth and old, were undulating in clusters on the bottom against the clean ribbed sand, and the track of the mussel was plain. A school of minnows swam by, each minnow with its small individual shadow, doubling the attendance, so clear and sharp in the sunlight. Some of the other campers were in swimming, along the shore, one of them with a cake of soap, and the water felt thin and clear and unsubstantial. Over the years there had been this person with the cake of soap, this cultist, and here he was. There had been no years.

Up to the farmhouse to dinner through the teeming, dusty field, 7 the road under our sneakers was only a two-track road. The middle track was missing, the one with the marks of the hooves and the splotches of dried, flaky manure. There had always been three tracks to choose from in choosing which track to walk in; now the choice was narrowed down to two. For a moment I missed terribly the middle alternative. But the way led past the tennis court, and something about the way it lay there in the sun reassured me; the tape had loosened along the backline, the alleys were green with plantains and other weeds, and the net (installed in June and removed in September) sagged in the dry noon, and the whole place steamed with midday heat and hunger and emptiness. There was a choice of pie for dessert, and one was blueberry and one was apple, and the waitresses were the same country girls, there having been no passage of time, only the illusion of it as in a dropped curtain—the waitresses were still fifteen; their hair had been washed, that was the only difference—they had been to the movies and seen the pretty girls with the clean hair.

Summertime, oh summertime, pattern of life indelible, the fade- 8 proof lake, the woods unshatterable, the pasture with the sweetfern and the juniper forever and ever, summer without end; this was the background, and the life along the shore was the design, the cottagers with their innocent and tranquil design, their tiny docks with the flagpole and the American flag floating against the white clouds in the blue sky, the little paths over the roots of the trees leading from camp to camp and the paths leading back to the outhouses and the can of lime for sprinkling, and at the souvenir counters at the store the miniature birch-bark canoes and the post cards that showed things looking a little better than they looked. This was the American family at play, escaping the city heat, wondering whether the newcomers in the camp at the head of the cove were "common" or "nice," wondering whether it was true that the people who drove up for Sunday dinner at the farmhouse were turned away because there wasn't enough chicken.

It seemed to me, as I kept remembering all this, that those times and those summers had been infinitely precious and worth saving. There had been jollity and peace and goodness. The arriving (at the beginning of August) had been so big a business in itself, at the railway station the farm wagon drawn up, the first smell of the pine-laden air, the first glimpse of the smiling farmer, and the great importance of the trunks and your father's enormous authority in such matters, and the feel of the wagon under you for the long ten-mile haul, and at the top of the last long hill catching the first view of the lake after eleven months of not seeing this cherished body of water. The shouts and cries of the other campers when they saw you, and the trunks to be unpacked, to give up their rich burden. (Arriving was less exciting nowadays, when you sneaked up in your car and parked it under a tree near the camp and took out the bags and in five minutes it was all over, no fuss, no loud wonderful fuss about trunks.) 9

Peace and goodness and jollity. The only thing that was wrong now, really, was the sound of the place, an unfamiliar nervous sound of the outboard motors. This was the note that jarred, the one thing that would sometimes break the illusion and set the years moving. In those other summertimes all motors were inboard; and when they were at a little distance, the noise they made was a sedative, an ingredient of summer sleep. They were one-cylinder and two-cylinder engines, and some were make-and-break and some were jump-spark,[2] but they all made a sleepy sound across the lake. The one-lungers throbbed and fluttered, and the twin-cylinder ones purred and purred, and that was a quiet sound too. But now the campers all had outboards. In the daytime, in the hot mornings, these motors made a petulant, irritable sound; at night, in the still evening when the afterglow lit the water, they whined about one's ears like mosquitoes. My boy loved our rented outboard, and his great desire was to achieve singlehanded mastery over it, and authority, and he soon learned the trick of choking it a little (but not too much), and the adjustment of the needle valve. Watching him I would remember the things you 10

---

[2] Methods of ignition timing. [Eds.]

could do with the old one-cylinder engine with the heavy flywheel, how you could have it eating out of your hand if you got really close to it spiritually. Motor boats in those days didn't have clutches, and you would make a landing by shutting off the motor at the proper time and coasting in with a dead rudder. But there was a way of reversing them, if you learned the trick, by cutting the switch and putting it on again exactly on the final dying revolution of the flywheel, so that it would kick back against compression and begin reversing. Approaching a dock in a strong following breeze, it was difficult to slow up sufficiently by the ordinary coasting method, and if a boy felt he had complete mastery over his motor, he was tempted to keep it running beyond its time and then reverse it a few feet from the dock. It took a cool nerve, because if you threw the switch a twentieth of a second too soon you would catch the flywheel when it still had speed enough to go up past center, and the boat would leap ahead, charging bull-fashion at the dock.

We had a good week at the camp. The bass were biting well and the 11
sun shone endlessly, day after day. We would be tired at night and lie down in the accumulated heat of the little bedrooms after the long hot day and the breeze would stir almost imperceptibly outside and the smell of the swamp drift in through the rusty screens. Sleep would come easily and in the morning the red squirrel would be on the roof, tapping out his gay routine. I kept remembering everything, lying in bed in the mornings—the small steamboat that had a long rounded stern like the lip of a Ubangi, and how quietly she ran on the moonlight sails, when the older boys played their mandolins and the girls sang and we ate doughnuts dipped in sugar, and how sweet the music was on the water in the shining night, and what it had felt like to think about girls then. After breakfast we would go up to the store and the things were in the same place—the minnows in a bottle, the plugs and spinners disarranged and pawed over by the youngsters from the boys' camp, the fig newtons and the Beeman's gum. Outside, the road was tarred and cars stood in front of the store. Inside, all was just as it had always been, except there was more Coca-Cola and not so much Moxie and root beer and birch beer and sarsaparilla. We would walk out with a bottle of pop apiece and sometimes the pop would backfire up our noses and hurt. We explored the streams, quietly, where the turtles slid off the sunny logs and dug their way into the soft bottom; and we lay on the town wharf and fed worms to the tame bass. Everywhere we went I had trouble making out which was I, the one walking at my side, the one walking in my pants.

One afternoon while we were there at that lake a thunderstorm 12
came up. It was like the revival of an old melodrama that I had seen long ago with childish awe. The second-act climax of the drama of the electrical disturbance over a lake in America had not changed in any important respect. This was the big scene, still the big scene. The whole

thing was so familiar, the first feeling of oppression and heat and a general air around camp of not wanting to go very far away. In midafternoon (it was all the same) a curious darkening of the sky, and a lull in everything that had made life tick; and then the way the boats suddenly swung the other way at their moorings with the coming of a breeze out of the new quarter, and the premonitory rumble. Then the kettle drum, then the snare, then the bass drum and cymbals, then crackling light against the dark, and the gods grinning and licking their chops in the hills. Afterward the calm, the rain steadily rustling in the calm lake, the return of light and hope and spirits, and the campers running out in joy and relief to go swimming in the rain, their bright cries perpetuating the deathless joke about how they were getting simply drenched, and the children screaming with delight at the new sensation of bathing in the rain, and the joke about getting drenched linking the generations in a strong indestructible chain. And the comedian who waded in carrying an umbrella.

When the others went swimming my son said he was going in too. He pulled his dripping trunks from the line where they had hung all 13 through the shower, and wrung them out. Languidly, and with no thought of going in, I watched him, his hard little body, skinny and bare, saw him wince slightly as he pulled up around his vitals the small, soggy, icy garment. As he buckled the swollen belt suddenly my groin felt the chill of death.

Responding to Reading

1. How is White's "holy spot" different when he visits it with his son from how it was when he visited it with his father?
2. Is this essay primarily about a time, a place, or a relationship? Explain.
3. Why does White feel "the chill of death" (13) as he watches his son? Do you identify more with White the father or White the child? Explain.

NO NAME WOMAN

Maxine Hong Kingston

Maxine Hong Kingston (1940–   ) a native of California, is a nonfiction writer who has taught English in high school and at the University of Hawaii. She also contributes to Ms., *the* New Yorker, American Heritage, *and other publications. Her most recent work is the novel* Tripmaster Monkey: His

Fake Book (1989). In her autobiography, The Woman Warrior: Memoirs of a Girlhood among Ghosts *(1976), and in* China Men *(1980), Kingston explores her Chinese ancestry. She said of* The Woman Warrior *in a 1983 interview, "One of the themes in* Warrior *was: what is it that's a story and what is it that's life? . . . Sometimes the boundaries are very clear, and sometimes they interlace and we live out stories." In the following selection from* The Woman Warrior, *Kingston tells the story of her aunt in China, who disgraced her family and suffered neglect and despair.*

"You must not tell anyone," my mother said, "what I am about to 1 tell you. In China your father had a sister who killed herself. She jumped into the family well. We say that your father has all brothers because it is as if she had never been born.

"In 1924 just a few days after our village celebrated seventeen 2 hurry-up weddings—to make sure that every young man who went 'out on the road' would responsibly come home—your father and his brothers and your grandfather and his brothers and your aunt's new husband sailed for America, the Gold Mountain. It was your grandfather's last trip. Those lucky enough to get contracts waved good-bye from the decks. They fed and guarded the stowaways and helped them off in Cuba, New York, Bali, Hawaii. 'We'll meet in California next year,' they said. All of them sent money home.

"I remember looking at your aunt one day when she and I were 3 dressing; I had not noticed before that she had such a protruding melon of a stomach. But I did not think, 'She's pregnant,' until she began to look like other pregnant women, her shirt pulling and the white tops of her black pants showing. She could not have been pregnant, you see, because her husband had been gone for years. No one said anything. We did not discuss it. In early summer she was ready to have the child, long after the time when it could have been possible.

"The village had also been counting. On the night the baby was to 4 be born the villagers raided our house. Some were crying. Like a great saw, teeth strung with lights, files of people walked zigzag across our land, tearing the rice. Their lanterns doubled in the disturbed black water, which drained away through the broken bunds. As the villagers closed in, we could see that some of them, probably men and women we knew well, wore white masks. The people with long hair hung it over their faces. Women with short hair made it stand up on end. Some had tied white bands around their foreheads, arms, and legs.

"At first they threw mud and rocks at the house. Then they threw 5 eggs and began slaughtering our stock. We could hear the animals scream their deaths—the roosters, the pigs, a last great roar from the ox. Familiar wild heads flared in our night windows; the villagers encircled us. Some of the faces stopped to peer at us, their eyes rushing like searchlights. The hands flattened against the panes, framed heads, and left red prints.

"The villagers broke in the front and the back doors at the same 6 time, even though we had not locked the doors against them. Their knives dripped with the blood of our animals. They smeared blood on the doors and walls. One woman swung a chicken, whose throat she had slit, splattering blood in red arcs about her. We stood together in the middle of our house, in the family hall with the pictures and tables of the ancestors around us, and looked straight ahead.

"At the time the house had only two wings. When the men came 7 back, we would build two more to enclose our courtyard and a third one to begin a second courtyard. The villagers pushed through both wings, even your grandparents' rooms, to find your aunt's, which was also mine until the men returned. From this room a new wing for one of the younger families would grow. They ripped up her clothes and shoes and broke her combs, grinding them underfoot. They tore her work from the loom. They scattered the cooking fire and rolled the new weaving in it. We could hear them in the kitchen breaking our bowls and banging the pots. They overturned the great waist-high earthenware jugs; duck eggs, pickled fruits, vegetables burst out and mixed in acrid torrents. The old woman from the next field swept a broom through the air and loosed the spirits-of-the-broom over our heads. 'Pig.' 'Ghost.' 'Pig,' they sobbed and scolded while they ruined our house.

"When they left, they took sugar and oranges to bless themselves. 8 They cut pieces from the dead animals. Some of them took bowls that were not broken and clothes that were not torn. Afterward we swept up the rice and sewed it back up into sacks. But the smells from the spilled preserves lasted. Your aunt gave birth in the pigsty that night. The next morning when I went for the water, I found her and the baby plugging up the family well.

"Don't let your father know that I told you. He denies her. Now that 9 you have started to menstruate, what happened to her could happen to you. Don't humiliate us. You wouldn't like to be forgotten as if you had never been born. The villagers are watchful."

Whenever she had to warn us about life, my mother told stories that 10 ran like this one, a story to grow up on. She tested our strength to establish realities. Those in the emigrant generations who could not reassert brute survival died young and far from home. Those of us in the first American generations have had to figure out how the invisible world the emigrants built around our childhoods fit in solid America.

The emigrants confused the gods by diverting their curses, mis- 11 leading them with crooked streets and false names. They must try to confuse their offspring as well, who, I suppose, threaten them in similar ways—always trying to get things straight, always trying to name the

desires delicate, wire and bone. She looked at a man because she liked the way the hair was tucked behind his ears, or she liked the question-mark line of a long torso curving at the shoulder and straight at the hip. For warm eyes or a soft voice or a slow walk—that's all—a few hairs, a line, a brightness, a sound, a pace, she gave up family. She offered us up for a charm that vanished with tiredness, a pigtail that didn't toss when the wind died. Why, the wrong lighting could erase the dearest thing about him.

It could very well have been, however, that my aunt did not take 22 subtle enjoyment of her friend, but, a wild woman, kept rollicking company. Imagining her free with sex doesn't fit, though. I don't know any women like that, or men either. Unless I see her life branching into mine, she gives me no ancestral help.

To sustain her being in love, she often worked at herself in the mir- 23 ror, guessing at the colors and shapes that would interest him, changing them frequently in order to hit on the right combination. She wanted him to look back.

On a farm near the sea, a woman who tended her appearance 24 reaped a reputation for eccentricity. All the married women blunt-cut their hair in flaps about their ears or pulled it back in tight buns. No nonsense. Neither style blew easily into heart-catching tangles. And at their weddings they displayed themselves in their long hair for the last time. "It brushed the backs of my knees," my mother tells me. "It was braided, and even so, it brushed the backs of my knees."

At the mirror my aunt combed individuality into her bob. A bun 25 could have been contrived to escape into black streamers blowing in the wind or in quiet wisps about her face, but only the older women in our picture album wear buns. She brushed her hair back from her forehead, tucking the flaps behind her ears. She looped a piece of thread, knotted into a circle between her index fingers and thumbs, and ran the double strand across her forehead. When she closed her fingers as if she were making a pair of shadow geese bite, the string twisted together catching the little hairs. Then she pulled the thread away from her skin, ripping the hairs out neatly, her eyes watering from the needles of pain. Opening her fingers, she cleaned the thread, then rolled it along her hairline and the tops of her eyebrows. My mother did the same to me and my sisters and herself. I used to believe that the expression "caught by the short hairs" meant a captive held with a depilatory string. It especially hurt at the temples, but my mother said we were lucky we didn't have to have our feet bound when we were seven. Sisters used to sit on their beds and cry together, she said, as their mothers or their slave removed the bandages for a few minutes each night and let the blood gush back into their veins. I hope that the man my aunt loved appreciated a smooth brow, that he wasn't just a tits-and-ass man.

Once my aunt found a freckle on her chin, at a spot that the almanac 26
said predestined her for unhappiness. She dug it out with a hot needle
and washed the wound with peroxide.

More attention to her looks than these pullings of hairs and pick- 27
ings at spots would have caused gossip among the villagers. They
owned work clothes and good clothes, and they wore good clothes for
feasting the new seasons. But since a woman combing her hair hexes
beginnings, my aunt rarely found an occasion to look her best. Women
looked like great sea snails—the corded wood, babies, and laundry they
carried were the whorls on their backs. The Chinese did not admire a
bent back; goddesses and warriors stood straight. Still there must have
been a marvelous freeing of beauty when a worker laid down her burden and stretched and arched.

Such commonplace loveliness, however, was not enough for my aunt. 28
She dreamed of a lover for the fifteen days of New Year's, the time for
families to exchange visits, money, and food. She plied her secret comb.
And sure enough she cursed the year, the family, the village, and herself.

Even as her hair lured her imminent lover, many other men looked 29
at her. Uncles, cousins, nephews, brothers would have looked, too, had
they been home between journeys. Perhaps they had already been
restraining their curiosity, and they left, fearful that their glances, like a
field of nesting birds, might be startled and caught. Poverty hurt, and
that was their first reason for leaving. But another, final reason for leaving the crowded house was the never-said.

She may have been unusually beloved, the precious only daughter, 30
spoiled and mirror gazing because of the affection the family lavished
on her. When her husband left, they welcomed the chance to take her
back from the in-laws; she could live like the little daughter for just a
while longer. There are stories that my grandfather was different from
other people, "crazy ever since the little Jap bayoneted him in the head."
He used to put his naked penis on the dinner table, laughing. And one
day he brought home a baby girl, wrapped up inside his brown western-
style greatcoat. He had traded one of his sons, probably my father, the
youngest, for her. My grandmother made him trade back. When he
finally got a daughter of his own, he doted on her. They must have all
loved her, except perhaps my father, the only brother who never went
back to China, having once been traded for a girl.

Brothers and sisters, newly men and women, had to efface their sex- 31
ual color and present plain miens.[2] Disturbing hair and eyes, a smile
like no other, threatened the ideal of five generations living under one
roof. To focus blurs, people shouted face to face and yelled from room
to room. The immigrants I know have loud voices, unmodulated to

---

[2] Appearances. [Eds.]

American tones even after years away from the village where they called their friendships out across the fields. I have not been able to stop my mother's screams in public libraries or over telephones. Walking erect (knees straight, toes pointed forward, not pigeon-toed, which is Chinese-feminine) and speaking in an inaudible voice, I have tried to turn myself American-feminine. Chinese communication was loud, public. Only sick people had to whisper. But at the dinner table, where the family members came nearest one another, no one could talk, not the outcasts nor any eaters. Every word that falls from the mouth is a coin lost. Silently they gave and accepted food with both hands. A preoccupied child who took his bowl with one hand got a sideways glare. A complete moment of total attention is due everyone alike. Children and lovers have no singularity here, but my aunt used a secret voice, a separate attentiveness.

She kept the man's name to herself throughout her labor and dying; she did not accuse him that he be punished with her. To save her inseminator's name she gave silent birth.

He may have been somebody in her own household, but intercourse with a man outside the family would have been no less abhorrent. All the village were kinsmen, and the titles shouted in loud country voices never let kinship be forgotten. Any man within visiting distance would have been neutralized as a lover—"brother," "younger brother," "older brother"—one hundred and fifteen relationship titles. Parents researched birth charts probably not so much to assure good fortune as to circumvent incest in a population that has but one hundred surnames. Everybody has eight million relatives. How useless then sexual mannerisms, how dangerous.

As if it came from an atavism[3] deeper than fear, I used to add "brother" silently to boys' names. It hexed the boys, who would or would not ask me to dance, and made them less scary and as familiar and deserving of benevolence as girls.

But, of course, I hexed myself also—no dates. I should have stood up, both arms waving, and shouted out across libraries, "Hey, you! Love me back." I had no idea, though, how to make attraction selective, how to control its direction and magnitude. If I made myself American-pretty so that the five or six Chinese boys in the class fell in love with me, everyone else—the Caucasian, Negro, and Japanese boys—would too. Sisterliness, dignified and honorable, made much more sense.

Attraction eludes control so stubbornly that whole societies designed to organize relationships among people cannot keep order, not even when they bind people to one another from childhood and

---

[3] The reappearance of a characteristic after a long absence. [Eds.]

raise them together. Among the very poor and the wealthy, brothers married their adopted sisters, like doves. Our family allowed some romance, paying adult brides' prices and providing dowries so that their sons and daughters could marry strangers. Marriage promises to turn strangers into friendly relatives—a nation of siblings.

In the village structure, spirits shimmered among the live creatures, 37 balanced and held in equilibrium by time and land. But one human being flaring up into violence could open up a black hole, a maelstrom that pulled in the sky. The frightened villagers, who depended on one another to maintain the real, went to my aunt to show her a personal, physical representation of the break she had made in the "roundness." Misallying couples snapped off the future, which was to be embodied in true offspring. The villagers punished her for acting as if she could have a private life, secret and apart from them.

If my aunt had betrayed the family at a time of large grain yields 38 and peace, when many boys were born, and wings were being built on many houses, perhaps she might have escaped such severe punishment. But the men—hungry, greedy, tired of planting in dry soil, cuckolded—had had to leave the village in order to send food-money home. There were ghost plagues, bandit plagues, wars with the Japanese, floods. My Chinese brother and sister had died of an unknown sickness. Adultery, perhaps only a mistake during good times, became a crime when the village needed food.

The round moon cakes and round doorways, the round tables of 39 graduated size that fit one roundness inside another, round windows and rice bowls—these talismans had lost their power to warn this family of the law: a family must be whole, faithfully keeping the descent line by having sons to feed the old and the dead, who in turn look after the family. The villagers came to show my aunt and her lover-in-hiding a broken house. The villagers were speeding up the circling of events because she was too shortsighted to see that her infidelity had already harmed the village, that waves of consequences would return unpredictably, sometimes in disguise, as now, to hurt her. This roundness had to be made coin-sized so that she would see its circumference: punish her at the birth of her baby. Awaken her to the inexorable. People who refused fatalism because they could invent small resources insisted on culpability. Deny accidents and wrest fault from the stars.

After the villagers left, their lanterns now scattering in various 40 directions toward home, the family broke their silence and cursed her. "Aiaa, we're going to die. Death is coming. Death is coming. Look what you've done. You've killed us. Ghost! Dead ghost! Ghost! You've never been born." She ran out into the fields, far enough from the house so that she could no longer hear their voices, and pressed herself against the earth, her own land no more. When she felt the birth coming, she thought that she had been hurt. Her body seized together. "They've hurt me too much," she thought. "This is gall, and it will kill me." With forehead and knees against the earth, her body convulsed and then relaxed. She turned on her back, lay on the ground. The black well of sky and stars went out and out and out forever; her body and her complexity seemed to disappear. She was one of the stars, a bright dot in blackness, without home, without a companion, in eternal cold and silence. And agoraphobia[4] rose in her, speeding higher and higher, bigger and bigger; she would not be able to contain it; there would be no end to fear.

Flayed, unprotected against space, she felt pain return, focusing her 41 body. This pain chilled her—a cold, steady kind of surface pain. Inside, spasmodically, the other pain, the pain of the child, heated her. For hours she lay on the ground, alternately body and space. Sometimes a vision of normal comfort obliterated reality: she saw the family in the evening gambling at the dinner table, the young people massaging their elders' backs. She saw them congratulating one another, high joy on the mornings the rice shoots came up. When these pictures burst, the stars drew yet further apart. Black space opened.

She got to her feet to fight better and remembered that old-fashioned 42 women gave birth in their pigsties to fool the jealous, pain-dealing gods, who do not snatch piglets. Before the next spasms could stop her, she ran to the pigsty, each step a rushing out into emptiness. She climbed over the fence and knelt in the dirt. It was good to have a fence enclosing her, a tribal person alone.

Laboring, this woman who had carried her child as a foreign growth 43 that sickened her every day, expelled it at last. She reached down to touch the hot, wet, moving mass, surely smaller than anything human, and could feel that it was human after all—fingers, toes, nails, nose. She pulled it up on to her belly, and it lay curled there, butt in the air, feet precisely tucked one under the other. She opened her loose shirt and buttoned the child inside. After resting, it squirmed and thrashed and she pushed it up to her breast. It turned its head this way and that until it found her nipple. There, it made little snuffling noises. She clenched her teeth at its preciousness, lovely as a young calf, a piglet, a little dog.

She may have gone to the pigsty as a last act of responsibility: she 44 would protect this child as she had protected its father. It would look after her soul, leaving supplies on her grave. But how would this tiny child without family find her grave when there would be no marker for her anywhere, neither in the earth nor the family hall? No one would give her a family hall name. She had taken the child with her into the wastes. At its birth the two of them had felt the same raw pain of separation, a wound that only the family pressing tight could close. A child

---

[4] Pathological fear of of being helpless or embarrassed in a pubic situation, characterized by avoidance of public places. [Eds.]

with no descent line would not soften her life but only trail after her, ghost-like, begging her to give it purpose. At dawn the villagers on their way to the fields would stand around the fence and look.

Full of milk, the little ghost slept. When it awoke, she hardened her   45
breasts against the milk that crying loosens. Toward morning she picked up the baby and walked to the well.

Carrying the baby to the well shows loving. Otherwise abandon it.   46
Turn its face into the mud. Mothers who love their children take them along. It was probably a girl; there is some hope of forgiveness for boys.

"Don't tell anyone you had an aunt. Your father does not want to   47
hear her name. She has never been born." I have believed that sex was unspeakable and words so strong and fathers so frail that "aunt" would do my father mysterious harm. I have thought that my family, having settled among immigrants who had also been their neighbors in the ancestral land, needed to clean their name, and a wrong word would incite the kinspeople even here. But there is more to this silence: they want me to participate in her punishment. And I have.

In the twenty years since I heard this story I have not asked for   48
details nor said my aunt's name; I do not know it. People who can comfort the dead can also chase after them to hurt them further—a reverse ancestor worship. The real punishment was not the raid swiftly inflicted by the villagers, but the family's deliberately forgetting her. Her betrayal so maddened them, they saw to it that she would suffer forever, even after death. Always hungry, always needing, she would have to beg food from other ghosts, snatch and steal it from those whose living descendants give them gifts. She would have to fight the ghosts massed at crossroads for the buns a few thoughtful citizens leave to decoy her away from village and home so that the ancestral spirits could feast unharassed. At peace, they could act like gods, not ghosts, their descent lines providing them with paper suits and dresses, spirit money, paper houses, paper automobiles, chicken, meat, and rice into eternity—essences delivered up in smoke and flames, steam and incense rising from each rice bowl. In an attempt to make the Chinese care for people outside the family, Chairman Mao[5] encourages us now to give our paper replicas to the spirits of outstanding soldiers and workers, no matter whose ancestors they may be. My aunt remains for-ever hungry. Goods are not distributed evenly among the dead.

My aunt haunts me—her ghost drawn to me because now, after fifty years of neglect, I alone devote pages of paper to her, though not origamied into houses and clothes. I do not think she always means me well. I am telling on her, and she was a spite suicide, drowning herself

---

[5] Mao Zedong (1893–1976), founder and leader of the communist People's Republic of China from 1949 until his death. [Eds.]

log. From one point of view, their migration was the fruit of an old prophecy, for indeed they emerged from a sunless world.

Although my grandmother lived out her long life in the shadow of 5 Rainy Mountain, the immense landscape of the continental interior lay like memory in her blood. She could tell of the Crows, whom she had never seen, and of the Black Hills, where she had never been. I wanted to see in reality what she had seen more perfectly in the mind's eye, and traveled fifteen hundred miles to begin my pilgrimage.

Yellowstone, it seemed to me, was the top of the world, a region of 6 deep lakes and dark timber, canyons and waterfalls. But, beautiful as it is, one might have the sense of confinement there. The skyline in all directions is close at hand, the high wall of the woods and deep cleavages of shade. There is a perfect freedom in the mountains, but it belongs to the eagle and the elk, the badger and the bear. The Kiowas reckoned their stature by the distance they could see, and they were bent and blind in the wilderness.

Descending eastward, the highland meadows are a stairway to the 7 plain. In July the inland slope of the Rockies is luxuriant with flax and buckwheat, stonecrop and larkspur. The earth unfolds and the limit of the land recedes. Clusters of trees, and animals grazing far in the distance, cause the vision to reach away and wonder to build upon the mind. The sun follows a longer course in the day, and the sky is immense beyond all comparison. The great billowing clouds that sail upon it are shadows that move upon the grain like water, dividing light. Farther down, in the land of the Crows and Blackfeet, the plain is yellow. Sweet clover takes hold of the hills and bends upon itself to cover and seal the soil. There the Kiowas paused on their way; they had come to the place where they must change their lives. The sun is at home on the plains. Precisely there does it have the certain character of a god. When the Kiowas came to the land of the Crows, they could see the dark lees of the hills at dawn across the Bighorn River, the profusion of light on the grain shelves, the oldest deity ranging after the solstices. Not yet would they veer southward to the caldron of the land that lay below; they must wean their blood from the northern winter and hold the mountains a while longer in their view. They bore Tai-me in procession to the east.

A dark mist lay over the Black Hills, and the land was like iron. At 8 the top of a ridge I caught sight of Devil's Tower upthrust against the gray sky as if in the birth of time the core of the earth had broken through its crust and the motion of the world was begun. There are things in nature that engender an awful quiet in the heart of man; Devil's Tower is one of them. Two centuries ago, because they could not do otherwise, the Kiowas made a legend at the base of the rock. My grandmother said:

Eight children were there at play, seven sisters and their brother. Suddenly the boy was struck dumb; he trembled and began to run upon his hands and feet. His fingers became claws, and his body was covered with fur. Directly there was a bear where the boy had been. The sisters were terrified; they ran, and the bear after them. They came to the stump of a great tree, and the tree spoke to them. It bade them climb upon it, and as they did so it began to rise into the air. The bear came to kill them, but they were just beyond its reach. It reared against the tree and scored the bark all around with its claws. The seven sisters were borne into the sky, and they became the stars of the Big Dipper.

From that moment, and so long as the legend lives, the Kiowas have kinsmen in the night sky. Whatever they were in the mountains, they could be no more. However tenuous their well-being, however much they had suffered and would suffer again, they had found a way out of the wilderness.

My grandmother had a reverence for the sun, a holy regard that 9 now is all but gone out of mankind. There was a wariness in her, and an ancient awe. She was a Christian in her later years, but she had come a long way about, and she never forgot her birthright. As a child she had been to the Sun Dances; she had taken part in those annual rites, and by them she had learned the restoration of her people in the presence of Tai-me. She was about seven when the last Kiowa Sun Dance was held in 1887 on the Washita River above Rainy Mountain Creek. The buffalo were gone. In order to consummate the ancient sacrifice— to impale the head of a buffalo bull upon the medicine tree—a delegation of old men journeyed into Texas, there to beg and barter for an animal from the Goodnight herd. She was ten when the Kiowas came together for the last time as a living Sun Dance culture. They could find no buffalo; they had to hang an old hide from the sacred tree. Before the dance could begin, a company of soldiers rode out from Fort Sill under orders to disperse the tribe. Forbidden without cause the essential act of their faith, having seen the wild herds slaughtered and left to rot upon the ground, the Kiowas backed away forever from the medicine tree. That was July 20, 1890, at the great bend of the Washita. My grandmother was there. Without bitterness, and for as long as she lived, she bore a vision of deicide.[1]

Now that I can have her only in memory, I see my grandmother in 10 the several postures that were peculiar to her: standing at the wood stove on a winter morning and turning meat in a great iron skillet; sitting at the south window, bent above her beadwork, and afterwards,

---

[1] The killing of a god. [Eds.]

when her vision failed, looking down for a long time into the fold of her hands; going out upon a cane, very slowly as she did when the weight of age came upon her; praying. I remember her most often at prayer. She made long, rambling prayers out of suffering and hope, having seen many things. I was never sure that I had the right to hear, so exclusive were they of all mere custom and company. The last time I saw her she prayed standing by the side of her bed at night, naked to the waist, the light of a kerosene lamp moving upon her dark skin. Her long, black hair, always drawn and braided in the day, lay upon her shoulders and against her breasts like a shawl. I do not speak Kiowa, and I never understood her prayers, but there was something inherently sad in the sound, some merest hesitation upon the syllables of sorrow. She began in a high and descending pitch, exhausting her breath to silence; then again and again—and always the same intensity of effort, of something that is, and is not, like urgency in the human voice. Transported so in the dancing light among the shadows of her room, she seemed beyond the reach of time. But that was illusion; I think I knew then that I should not see her again.

Houses are like sentinels in the plain, old keepers of the weather 11 watch. There, in a very little while, wood takes on the appearance of great age. All colors wear soon away in the wind and rain, and then the wood is burned gray and the grain appears and the nails turn red with rust. The windowpanes are black and opaque; you imagine there is nothing within, and indeed there are many ghosts, bones given up to the land. They stand here and there against the sky, and you approach them for a longer time than you expect. They belong in the distance; it is their domain.

Once there was a lot of sound in my grandmother's house, a lot of 12 coming and going, feasting and talk. The summers there were full of excitement and reunion. The Kiowas are a summer people; they abide the cold and keep to themselves, but when the season turns and the land becomes warm and vital they cannot hold still; an old love of going returns upon them. The aged visitors who came to my grandmother's house when I was a child were made of lean and leather, and they bore themselves upright. They wore great black hats and bright ample shirts that shook in the wind. They rubbed fat upon their hair and wound their braids with strips of colored cloth. Some of them painted their faces and carried the scars of old and cherished enmities. They were an old council of warlords, come to remind and be reminded of who they were. Their wives and daughters served them well. The women might indulge themselves; gossip was at once the mark and compensation of their servitude. They made loud and elaborate talk among themselves, full of jest and gesture, fright and false alarm. They went abroad in fringed and flowered shawls, bright beadwork and German silver. They were at home in the kitchen, and they prepared meals that were banquets.

There were frequent prayer meetings, and great nocturnal feasts. 13
When I was a child I played with my cousins outside, where the lamp-
light fell upon the ground and the singing of the old people rose up
around us and carried away into the darkness. There were a lot of good
things to eat, a lot of laughter and surprise. And afterwards, when the
quiet returned, I lay down with my grandmother and could hear the
frogs away by the river and feel the motion of the air.

Now there is funeral silence in the rooms, the endless wake of some 14
final word. The walls have closed in upon my grandmother's house.
When I returned to it in mourning, I saw for the first time in my life how
small it was. It was late at night, and there was a white moon, nearly
full. I sat for a long time on the stone steps by the kitchen door. From
there I could see out across the land; I could see the long row of trees by
the creek, the low light upon the rolling plains, and the stars of the Big
Dipper. Once I looked at the moon and caught sight of a strange thing.
A cricket had perched upon the handrail, only a few inches away from
me. My line of vision was such that the creature filled the moon like a
fossil. It had gone there, I thought, to live and die, for there, of all places,
was its small definition made whole and eternal. A warm wind rose up
and purled[2] like the longing within me.

The next morning I awoke at dawn and went out on the dirt road to 15
Rainy Mountain. It was already hot, and the grasshoppers began to fill
the air. Still, it was early in the morning, and the birds sang out of the
shadows. The long yellow grass on the mountain shone in the bright
light, and a scissortail hied above the land. There, where it ought to be,
at the end of a long and legendary way, was my grandmother's grave.
Here and there on the dark stones were ancestral names. Looking back
once, I saw the mountain and came away.

Responding to Reading

1. Momaday portrays his grandmother not only as an individual but also as a
   symbol. What larger idea do you think she stands for? Explain.
2. In paragraph 8, Momaday tells a story his grandmother told him. What
   does this story reveal about the Kiowa? What do you think it means to
   Momaday?
3. In what sense is the essay as much about Momaday himself as about his
   grandmother?

---

[2] Flowed; rippled. [Eds.]

this is what happened, I know my brothers will find ways to make me wish I had. But now I will say anything that gets me to my mother.

Confronted by our parents we stick to the lie agreed upon. They 11 place me on a bench on the porch and I close my left eye while they examine the right. There is a tree growing from underneath the porch that climbs past the railing to the roof. It is the last thing my right eye sees. I watch as its trunk, its branches, and then its leaves are blotted out by the rising blood.

I am in shock. First there is intense fever, which my father tries to 12 break using lily leaves bound around my head. Then there are chills: my mother tries to get me to eat soup. Eventually, I do not know how, my parents learn what has happened. A week after the "accident" they take me to see a doctor. "Why did you wait so long to come?" he asks, looking into my eye and shaking his head. "Eyes are sympathetic," he says. "If one is blind, the other will likely become blind too."

This comment of the doctor's terrifies me. But it is really how I look 13 that bothers me most. Where the BB pellet struck there is a glob of whitish scar tissue, a hideous cataract, on my eye. Now when I stare at people—a favorite pastime, up to now—they will stare back. Not at the "cute" little girl, but at her scar. For six years I do not stare at anyone, because I do not raise my head.

Years later, in the throes of a mid-life crisis, I ask my mother and sis- 14 ter whether I changed after the "accident." "No," they say, puzzled. "What do you mean?"

What do I mean?   15

I am eight, and, for the first time, doing poorly in school, where I 16 have been something of a whiz since I was four. We have just moved to the place where the "accident" occurred. We do not know any of the people around us because this is a different county. The only time I see the friends I knew is when we go back to our old church. The new school is the former state penitentiary. It is a large stone building, cold and drafty, crammed to overflowing with boisterous, ill-disciplined children. On the third floor there is a huge circular imprint of some partition that has been torn out.

"What used to be here?" I ask a sullen girl next to me on our way 17 past it to lunch.

"The electric chair," says she.   18

At night I have nightmares about the electric chair, and about all the 19 people reputedly "fried" in it. I am afraid of the school, where all the students seem to be budding criminals.

"What's the matter with your eye?" they ask, critically.   20

When I don't answer (I cannot decide whether it was an "accident"   21
or not), they shove me, insist on a fight.

My brother, the one who created the story about the wire, comes to   22
my rescue. But then brags so much about "protecting" me, I become sick.

After months of torture at the school, my parents decide to send me   23
back to our old community, to my old school. I live with my grandparents and the teacher they board. But there is no room for Phoebe, my
cat. By the time my grandparents decide there *is* room, and I ask for
my cat, she cannot be found. Miss Yarborough, the boarding teacher,
takes me under her wing, and begins to teach me to play the piano. But
soon she marries an African—a "prince," she says—and is whisked
away to his continent.

At my old school there is at least one teacher who loves me. She is   24
the teacher who "knew me before I was born" and bought my first
baby clothes. It is she who makes life bearable. It is her presence that
finally helps me turn on the one child at the school who continually
calls me "one-eyed bitch." One day I simply grab him by his coat and
beat him until I am satisfied. It is my teacher who tells me my mother
is ill.

My mother is lying in bed in the middle of the day, something I   25
have never seen. She is in too much pain to speak. She has an abscess in
her ear. I stand looking down on her, knowing that if she dies, I cannot
live. She is being treated with warm oils and hot bricks held against her
cheek. Finally a doctor comes. But I must go back to my grandparents'
house. The weeks pass but I am hardly aware of it. All I know is that my
mother might die, my father is not so jolly, my brothers still have their
guns, and I am the one sent away from home.

"You did not change," they say.   26

Did I imagine the anguish of never looking up?   27

I am twelve. When relatives come to visit I hide in my room. My   28
cousin Brenda, just my age, whose father works in the post office and
whose mother is a nurse, comes to find me. "Hello," she says. And then
she asks, looking at my recent school picture, which I did not want
taken, and on which the "glob," as I think of it, is clearly visible, "You
still can't see out of that eye?"

"No," I say, and flop back on the bed over my book.   29

That night, as I do almost every night, I abuse my eye. I rant   30
and rave at it, in front of the mirror. I plead with it to clear up before
morning. I tell it I hate and despise it. I do not pray for sight. I pray for
beauty.

"You did not change," they say.   31

I am fourteen and baby-sitting for my brother Bill, who lives in 32
Boston. He is my favorite brother and there is a strong bond between us.
Understanding my feelings of shame and ugliness he and his wife take
me to a local hospital, where the "glob" is removed by a doctor named
O. Henry. There is still a small bluish crater where the scar tissue was,
but the ugly white stuff is gone. Almost immediately I become a different person from the girl who does not raise her head. Or so I think. Now
that I've raised my head I win the boyfriend of my dreams. Now that I've
raised my head I have plenty of friends. Now that I've raised my head
classwork comes from my lips as faultlessly as Easter speeches did, and
I leave high school as valedictorian, most popular student, and *queen*,
hardly believing my luck. Ironically, the girl who was voted most beautiful in our class (and was) was later shot twice through the chest by a
male companion, using a "real" gun, while she was pregnant. But that's
another story in itself. Or is it?

"You did not change," they say. 33

It is now thirty years since the "accident." A beautiful journalist 34
comes to visit and to interview me. She is going to write a cover story
for her magazine that focuses on my latest book. "Decide how you want
to look on the cover," she says. "Glamorous, or whatever."

Never mind "glamorous," it is the "whatever" that I hear. Suddenly 35
all I can think of is whether I will get enough sleep the night before the
photography session: if I don't, my eye will be tired and wander, as
blind eyes will.

At night in bed with my lover I think up reasons why I should not 36
appear on the cover of a magazine. "My meanest critics will say I've
sold out," I say. "My family will now realize I write scandalous books."

"But what's the real reason you don't want to do this?" he asks. 37

"Because in all probability," I say in a rush, "my eye won't be 38
straight."

"It will be straight enough," he says. Then, "Besides, I thought 39
you'd made your peace with that."

And I suddenly remember that I have. 40

I remember: 41

I am talking to my brother Jimmy, asking if he remembers anything 42
unusual about the day I was shot. He does not know I consider that day
the last time my father, with his sweet home remedy of cool lily leaves,
chose me, and that I suffered and raged inside because of this. "Well,"
he says, "all I remember is standing by the side of the highway with
Daddy, trying to flag down a car. A white man stopped, but when
Daddy said he needed somebody to take his little girl to the doctor, he
drove off."

I remember: 43

I am in the desert for the first time. I fall totally in love with it. I am 44
so overwhelmed by its beauty, I confront for the first time, consciously,

the meaning of the doctor's words years ago: "Eyes are sympathetic. If one is blind, the other will likely become blind too." I realize I have dashed about the world madly, looking at this, looking at that, storing up images against the fading of the light. *But I might have missed seeing the desert!* The shock of that possibility—and gratitude for over twenty-five years of sight—sends me literally to my knees. Poem after poem comes—which is perhaps how poets pray.

On Sight

I am so thankful I have seen
The Desert
And the creatures in the desert
And the desert Itself.

The desert has its own moon   5
Which I have seen
With my own eye.
There is no flag on it.

Trees of the desert have arms
All of which are always up   10
That is because the moon is up
The sun is up
Also the sky
The stars
Clouds   15
None with flags.

If there were flags, I doubt
the trees would point.
Would you?

But mostly, I remember this: 45

I am twenty-seven, and my baby daughter is almost three. Since her   46
birth I have worried about her discovery that her mother's eyes are different from other people's. Will she be embarrassed? I think. What will she say? Every day she watches a television program called "Big Blue Marble." It begins with a picture of the earth as it appears from the moon. It is bluish, a little battered-looking, but full of light, with whitish clouds swirling around it. Every time I see it I weep with love, as if it is a picture of Grandma's house. One day when I am putting Rebecca down for her nap, she suddenly focuses on my eye. Something inside me cringes, gets ready to try to protect myself. All children are cruel about physical differences, I know from experience, and that they don't always mean to be is another matter. I assume Rebecca will be the same.

But no-o-o-o. She studies my face intently as we stand, her inside 47
and me outside her crib. She even holds my face maternally between
her dimpled little hands. Then, looking every bit as serious and lawyer-
like as her father, she says, as if it may just possibly have slipped my
attention: "Mommy, there's a *world* in your eye." (As in, "Don't be
alarmed, or do anything crazy.") And then, gently, but with great interest: "Mommy, where did you get that world in your eye?"

For the most part, the pain left then. (So what, if my brothers grew 48
up to buy even more powerful pellet guns for their sons and to carry
real guns themselves. So what, if a young "Morehouse man"[1] once
nearly fell off the steps of Trevor Arnett Library because he thought my
eyes were blue.) Crying and laughing I ran to the bathroom, while
Rebecca mumbled and sang herself off to sleep. Yes indeed, I realized,
looking into the mirror. There was a world in my eye. And I saw that it
was possible to love it: that in fact, for all it had taught me of shame and
anger and inner vision, I *did* love it. Even to see it drifting out of orbit in
boredom, or rolling up out of fatigue, not to mention floating back at
attention in excitement (bearing witness, a friend has called it), deeply
suitable to my personality, and even characteristic of me.

That night I dream I am dancing to Stevie Wonder's song "Always" 49
(the name of the song is really "As," but I hear it as "Always"). As I
dance, whirling and joyous, happier than I've ever been in my life,
another bright-faced dancer joins me. We dance and kiss each other and
hold each other through the night. The other dancer has obviously come
through all right, as I have done. She is beautiful, whole and free. And
she is also me.

Responding to Reading

1. Although she is remembering past events, Walker uses present tense ("It is
   a bright summer day in 1947") to tell her story. Why do you think she does
   this? Is the present tense more effective than the past tense ("It *was* a bright
   summer day in 1947") would be? Explain.
2. At several points in the essay, Walker repeats the words her relatives used
   to reassure her: "You did not change." Why does she repeat this phrase?
   Were her relatives correct?
3. What circumstances or individuals does Walker blame for the childhood
   problems she describes? Who do you think is responsible for her misery?
   Would you be as forgiving as Walker seems to be?

---

[1] A student at Morehouse College, a historically black college in Atlanta, Georgia. [Eds.]

MY FATHER'S LIFE
Raymond Carver

Raymond Carver (1939–1988) was a fiction and poetry writer who grew up in a working-class family in the Pacific Northwest. Influenced by his father's storytelling, he began writing stories himself as a boy. Collections of Carver's stories include Will You Please Be Quiet, Please? *(1976),* What We Talk about When We Talk about Love *(1981),* Cathedral *(1984), and* Short Cuts *(1993). Usually about desperate people struggling for daily survival, Carver's stories often have enigmatic endings. In "My Father's Life," which originally appeared in* Esquire *in 1984, Carver tells how his father first struggled financially during the Great Depression and later suffered from psychological depression.*

My dad's name was Clevie Raymond Carver. His family called him 1
Raymond and friends called him C. R. I was named Raymond Clevie
Carver Jr. I hated the "Junior" part. When I was little my dad called
me Frog, which was okay. But later, like everybody else in the family, he
began calling me Junior. He went on calling me this until I was thirteen
or fourteen and announced that I wouldn't answer to that name any
longer. So he began calling me Doc. From then until his death, on June
17, 1967, he called me Doc, or else Son.

When he died, my mother telephoned my wife with the news. I was 2
away from my family at the time, between lives, trying to enroll in the
School of Library Science at the University of Iowa. When my wife
answered the phone, my mother blurted out. "Raymond's dead!" For a
moment, my wife thought my mother was telling her that I was dead.
Then my mother made it clear *which* Raymond she was talking about
and my wife said, "Thank God. I thought you meant *my* Raymond."

My dad walked, hitched rides, and rode in empty boxcars when he 3
went from Arkansas to Washington State in 1934, looking for work. I
don't know whether he was pursuing a dream when he went out to
Washington. I doubt it. I don't think he dreamed much. I believe he was
simply looking for steady work at decent pay. Steady work was meaningful work. He picked apples for a time and then landed a construction
laborer's job on the Grand Coulee Dam.[1] After he'd put aside a little
money, he bought a car and drove back to Arkansas to help his folks, my
grandparents, pack up for the move west. He said later that they were
about to starve down there, and this wasn't meant as a figure of speech.
It was during that short while in Arkansas, in a town called Leola, that
my mother met my dad on the sidewalk as he came out of a tavern.

---

[1] On the Columbia River, northwest of Spokane, Washington. [Eds.]

the Vance Hotel and eat, I remember, at a place called the Dinner Bell Cafe. Once we went to Ivar's Acres of Clams and drank glasses of warm clam broth.

In 1956, the year I was to graduate from high school, my dad quit 18 his job at the mill in Yakima and took a job in Chester, a little sawmill town in northern California. The reasons given at the time for his taking the job had to do with a higher hourly wage and the vague promise that he might, in a few years' time, succeed to the job of head filer in this new mill. But I think, in the main, that my dad had grown restless and simply wanted to try his luck elsewhere. Things had gotten a little too predictable for him in Yakima. Also, the year before, there had been the deaths, within six months of each other, of both his parents.

But just a few days after graduation, when my mother and I were 19 packed to move to Chester, my dad penciled a letter to say he'd been sick for a while. He didn't want us to worry, he said, but he'd cut himself on a saw. Maybe he'd got a tiny sliver of steel in his blood. Anyway, something had happened and he'd had to miss work, he said. In the same mail was an unsigned postcard from somebody down there telling my mother that my dad was about to die and that he was drinking "raw whiskey."

When we arrived in Chester, my dad was living in a trailer that 20 belonged to the company. I didn't recognize him immediately. I guess for a moment I didn't want to recognize him. He was skinny and pale and looked bewildered. His pants wouldn't stay up. He didn't look like my dad. My mother began to cry. My dad put his arm around her and patted her shoulder vaguely, like he didn't know what this was all about, either. The three of us took up life together in the trailer, and we looked after him as best we could. But my dad was sick, and he couldn't get any better. I worked with him in the mill that summer and part of the fall. We'd get up in the mornings and eat eggs and toast while we listened to the radio, and then go out the door with our lunch pails. We'd pass through the gate together at eight in the morning, and I wouldn't see him again until quitting time. In November I went back to Yakima to be closer to my girlfriend, the girl I'd made up my mind I was going to marry.

He worked at the mill in Chester until the following February, when 21 he collapsed on the job and was taken to the hospital. My mother asked if I would come down there and help. I caught a bus from Yakima to Chester, intending to drive them back to Yakima. But now, in addition to being physically sick, my dad was in the midst of a nervous breakdown, though none of us knew to call it that at the time. During the entire trip back to Yakima, he didn't speak, not even when asked a direct question. ("How do you feel, Raymond?" "You okay, Dad?") He'd communicate if he communicated at all, by moving his head or by turning his palms up as if to say he didn't know or care. The only time he said anything on the trip, and for nearly a month afterward, was when I was speeding down a gravel road in Oregon and the car muffler came loose. "You were going too fast," he said.

Back in Yakima a doctor saw to it that my dad went to a psychia- 22
trist. My mother and dad had to go on relief,[2] as it was called, and the county paid for the psychiatrist. The psychiatrist asked my dad. "Who is the President?" He'd had a question put to him that he could answer. "Ike," my dad said. Nevertheless, they put him on the fifth floor of Valley Memorial Hospital and began giving him electroshock treatments. I was married by then and about to start my own family. My dad was still locked up when my wife went into this same hospital, just one floor down, to have our first baby. After she had delivered, I went upstairs to give my dad the news. They let me in through a steel door and showed me where I could find him. He was sitting on a couch with a blanket over his lap. *Hey,* I thought. *What in hell is happening to my dad?* I sat down next to him and told him he was a grandfather. He waited a minute and then he said, "I feel like a grandfather." That's all he said. He didn't smile or move. He was in a big room with a lot of other people. Then I hugged him, and he began to cry.

Somehow he got out of there. But now came the years when he 23
couldn't work and just sat around the house trying to figure what next and what he'd done wrong in his life that he'd wound up like this. My mother went from job to crummy job. Much later she referred to that time he was in the hospital, and those years just afterward, as "when Raymond was sick." The word *sick* was never the same for me again.

In 1964, through the help of a friend, he was lucky enough to be 24
hired on at a mill in Klamath, California. He moved down there by himself to see if he could hack it. He lived not far from the mill, in a one-room cabin not much different from the place he and my mother had started out living in when they went west. He scrawled letters to my mother, and if I called she'd read them aloud to me over the phone. In the letters, he said it was touch and go. Every day that he went to work, he felt like it was the most important day of his life. But every day, he told her, made the next day that much easier. He said for her to tell me he said hello. If he couldn't sleep at night, he said, he thought about me and the good times we used to have. Finally, after a couple of months, he regained some of his confidence. He could do the work and didn't think he had to worry that he'd let anybody down ever again. When he was sure, he sent for my mother.

He'd been off from work for six years and had lost everything in that 25
time—home, car, furniture, and appliances, including the big freezer that had been my mother's pride and joy. He'd lost his good name too—

---

[2] What would today be called "public assistance" or "welfare." [Eds.]

Raymond Carver was someone who couldn't pay his bills—and his self-respect was gone. He'd even lost his virility. My mother told my wife, "All during that time Raymond was sick we slept together in the same bed, but we didn't have relations. He wanted to a few times, but nothing happened. I didn't miss it, but I think he wanted to, you know."

During those years I was trying to raise my own family and earn a 26 living. But, one thing and another, we found ourselves having to move a lot. I couldn't keep track of what was going down in my dad's life. But I did have a chance one Christmas to tell him I wanted to be a writer. I might as well have told him I wanted to become a plastic surgeon. "What are you going to write about?" he wanted to know. Then, as if to help me out, he said, "Write about stuff you know about. Write about some of those fishing trips we took." I said I would, but I knew I wouldn't. "Send me what you write," he said. I said I'd do that, but then I didn't. I wasn't writing anything about fishing, and I didn't think he'd particularly care about, or even necessarily understand, what I was writing in those days. Besides, he wasn't a reader. Not the sort, anyway, I imagined I was writing for.

Then he died. I was a long way off, in Iowa City, with things still to 27 say to him. I didn't have the chance to tell him goodbye, or that I thought he was doing great at his new job. That I was proud of him for making a comeback.

My mother said he came in from work that night and ate a big sup- 28 per. Then he sat at the table by himself and finished what was left of a bottle of whiskey, a bottle she found hidden in the bottom of the garbage under some coffee grounds a day or so later. Then he got up and went to bed, where my mother joined him a little later. But in the night she had to get up and make a bed for herself on the couch. "He was snoring so loud I couldn't sleep," she said. The next morning when she looked in on him, he was on his back with his mouth open, his cheeks caved in. *Graylooking,* she said. She knew he was dead—she didn't need a doctor to tell her that. But she called one anyway, and then she called my wife.

Among the pictures my mother kept of my dad and herself during 29 those early days in Washington was a photograph of him standing in front of a car, holding a beer and a stringer of fish. In the photograph he is wearing his hat back on his forehead and has this awkward grin on his face. I asked her for it and she gave it to me, along with some others. I put it up on my wall, and each time we moved, I took the picture along and put it up on another wall. I looked at it carefully from time to time, trying to figure out some things about my dad, and maybe myself in the process. But I couldn't. My dad just kept moving further and further away from me and back into time. Finally, in the course of another move, I lost the photograph. It was then that I tried to recall it, and at the same time make an attempt to say something about my dad, and how I thought that in some important ways we might be alike. I wrote the poem when I was living in an apartment house in an urban area south of San Francisco, at a time when I found myself, like my dad, having trouble with alcohol. The poem was a way of trying to connect up with him.

Photograph of My Father in His Twenty-Second Year

October. Here in this dank, unfamiliar kitchen
I study my father's embarrassed young man's face.
Sheepish grin, he holds in one hand a string
of spiny yellow perch, in the other
a bottle of Carlsberg beer.   5

In jeans and flannel shirt, he leans
against the front fender of a 1934 Ford.
He would like to pose brave and hearty for his posterity,
wear his old hat cocked over his ear.
All his life my father wanted to be bold.   10

But the eyes give him away, and the hands
that limply offer the string of dead perch
and the bottle of beer. Father, I love you,
yet how can I say thank you, I who can't hold my
    liquor either
and don't even know the places to fish.   15

The poem is true in its particulars, except that my dad died in June   30
and not October, as the first word of the poem says. I wanted a word
with more than one syllable to it to make it linger a little. But more than
that, I wanted a month appropriate to what I felt at the time I wrote the
poem—a month of short days and failing light, smoke in the air, things
perishing. June was summer nights and days, graduations, my wedding anniversary, the birthday of one of my children. June wasn't a
month your father died in.

After the service at the funeral home, after we had moved outside,   31
a woman I didn't know came over to me and said, "He's happier where
he is now." I stared at this woman until she moved away. I still remember the little knob of a hat she was wearing. Then one of my dad's
cousins—I didn't know the man's name—reached out and took my
hand, "We all miss him," he said, and I knew he wasn't saying it just to
be polite.

I began to weep for the first time since receiving the news. I hadn't   32
been able to before. I hadn't had the time, for one thing. Now, suddenly,
I couldn't stop. I held my wife and wept while she said and did what she
could do to comfort me there in the middle of that summer afternoon.

I listened to people say consoling things to my mother, and I was ₃₃ glad that my dad's family had turned up, had come to where he was. I thought I'd remember everything that was said and done that day and maybe find a way to tell it sometime. But I didn't. I forgot it all, or nearly. What I do remember is that I heard our name used a lot that afternoon, my dad's name and mine. But I knew they were talking about my dad. *Raymond*, these people kept saying in their beautiful voices out of my childhood. *Raymond.*

Responding to Reading

1. Why does Carver include details about his father's work history? His drinking? His mental illness? The photograph? Do you think all these details are necessary? Explain.
2. What information is provided by the poem that follows paragraph 29 that is not provided by the essay itself? Could Carver have conveyed this information as effectively in prose?
3. What does Carver finally come to realize about his father, and about himself?

―――――――――――――― FOCUS ――――――――――――――

How Has Divorce Redefined the Family?

THE PERFECT FAMILY
Alice Hoffman

Alice Hoffman (1952–   ) was born in New York City and raised on Long Island, where she attended Adelphi University, receiving her B.A. in 1973. She later received an M.F.A. from Stanford University in California. A prolific novelist, Hoffman has written a number of best-sellers, including At Risk *(1988),* Seventh Heaven *(1990),* Turtle Moon *(1992),* Practical Magic *(1995), and most recently* The River King *(2000). Her work often focuses on families and the difficulties of communication, but her tales are generally optimistic, often incorporating elements of fantasy and magic. In the following essay published in the* New York Times Magazine *in 1992, Hoffman writes about her own childhood in the 1950s. Raised by a divorced working mother at a time when divorce was rare and most mothers stayed at home, Hoffman reflects on the stereotypical standards that define today's debate over family values.*

When I was growing up in the 50s, there was only one sort of 1 family, the one we watched on television every day. Right in front of us, in black and white, was everything we needed to know about family values: the neat patch of lawn, the apple tree, the mother who never once raised her voice, the three lovely children: a Princess, a Kitten, a Bud and, always, the father who knew best.[1]

People stayed married forever back then, and roses grew by the 2 front door. We had glass bottles filled with lightning bugs and brand-new swing sets in the backyard, and softball games at dusk. We had summer nights that lasted forever and well-balanced meals, three times a day, in our identical houses, on our identical streets. There was only one small bargain we had to make to exist in this world: we were never to ask questions, never to think about people who didn't have as much or who were different in any way. We ignored desperate marriages and piercing loneliness. And we were never, ever, to wonder what might be hidden from view, behind the unlocked doors, in the privacy of our neighbors' bedrooms and knotty-pine-paneled dens.

―――――

[1] *Father Knows Best* was a popular family comedy with a stay-at-home mother. [Eds.]

This was a bargain my own mother could not make. Having once ₃ believed that her life would sort itself out to be like the television shows we watched, only real and in color, she'd been left to care for her children on her own, at a time when divorce was so uncommon I did not meet another child of divorced parents until 10 years later when I went off to college.

Back then, it almost made sense when one of my best friends was ₄ not allowed to come to my house; her parents did not approve of divorce or my mother's life style. My mother, after all, had a job and boyfriend and, perhaps even more incriminating, she was the one who took the silver-colored trash cans out to the curb on Monday nights. She did so faithfully, on evenings when she had already balanced the checkbook and paid the bills and ministered to sore throats and made certain we'd had dinner; but all up and down the street everybody knew the truth: taking out the trash was clearly a job for fathers.

When I was 10, my mother began to work for the Department of ₅ Social Services, a world in which the simple rules of the suburbs did not apply. She counseled young unwed mothers, girls and women who were not allowed to make their own choices, most of whom had not been allowed to finish high school or stay in their own homes, none of whom had been allowed to decide not to continue their pregnancies. Later, my mother placed most of these babies in foster care, and still later, she moved to the protective-services department, investigating charges of abuse and neglect, often having to search a child's back and legs for bruises or welts.

She would have found some on my friend, left there by her right- ₆ eous father, the one who wouldn't allow her to visit our home but blackened her eye when, a few years later, he discovered that she was dating a boy he didn't approve of. But none of his neighbors had dared to report him. They would never have imagined that someone like my friend's father, whose trash cans were always tidily placed at the curb, whose lawn was always well cared for, might need watching.

To my mother, abuse was a clear-cut issue, if reported and found, ₇ but neglect was more of a judgment call. It was, in effect, passing judgment on the nature of love. If my father had not sent the child support checks on time, if my mother hadn't been white and college-educated, it could have easily been us in one of those apartments she visited, where the heat didn't work on the coldest days, and the dirt was so encrusted you could mop all day and still be called a poor housekeeper, and there was often nothing more for dinner than Frosted Flakes and milk, or, if it was toward the end of the month, the cereal might be served with tap water. Would that have meant my mother loved her children any less, that we were less of a family?

My mother never once judged who was a fit mother on the basis of ₈ a clean floor, or an unbalanced meal, or a boyfriend who sometimes spent the night. But back then, there were good citizens who were only too ready to set their standards for women and children, factoring out poverty or exhaustion or simply a different set of beliefs.

There are always those who are ready to deal out judgment with the 9 ready fist of the righteous. I know this because before the age of 10 I was one of the righteous, too. I believed that mothers were meant to stay home and fathers should carry out the trash on Monday nights. I believed that parents could create a domestic life that was the next best thing to heaven, if they just tried. That is what I'd been told, that in the best of all worlds we would live identical lives in identical houses.

It's a simple view of the world, too simple even for childhood. 10 Certainly, it's a vision that is much too limited for the lives we live now, when only one in 19 families is made up of a wage-earner father, a mother who doesn't work outside the home and two or more children. And even long ago, when I was growing up, we paid too high a price when we cut ourselves off from the rest of the world. We ourselves did not dare to be different. In the safety we created, we became trapped.

There are still places where softball games are played at dusk and 11 roses grow by the front door. There are families with sons named Bud, with kind and generous fathers, and mothers who put up strawberry preserves every June and always have time to sing lullabies. But do these families love their children any more than the single mother who works all day? Are their lullabies any sweeter? If I felt deprived as a child, it was only when our family was measured against some notion of what we were supposed to be. The truth of it was, we lacked for little.

And now that I have children of my own, and am exhausted at the 12 end of the day in which I've probably failed in a hundred different ways, I am amazed that women alone can manage. That they do, in spite of everything, is a simple fact. They rise from sleep in the middle of the night when their children call out to them. They rush for the cough syrup and cold washcloths and keep watch till dawn. These are real family values, the same ones we knew when we were children. As far as we were concerned our mother could cure a fever with a kiss. This may be the only thing we ever need to know about love. The rest, no one can judge.

Responding to Reading

1. What was so different about Hoffman's family? Would her family still be considered "different" in a suburb today? Do suburban families still live "identical lives in identical houses" (9)? Did they ever?

2. Consider the various combinations of individuals that can constitute a family today (one example is described in the opening paragraph of Barbara Kingsolver's "Stone Soup," p. 60). How is the current concept of *family* different from the 1950s definition? Despite these differences, do

you think most people's idea of the "perfect" or ideal family has changed significantly since the 1950s? How do you account for this?

3. Hoffman's mother worked for the Department of Social Services, "a world in which the simple rules of the suburbs did not apply" (5). What were the "simple rules of the suburbs"? Why didn't they apply? In what respects did the "perfect" suburban families resemble the families with whom Hoffman's mother worked? What do these similarities reveal about the 1950s suburban family?

STONE SOUP

Barbara Kingsolver

Born in Annapolis, Maryland, and raised in rural Kentucky, Barbara Kingsolver (1955–   ) received her B.A. from DePauw University and a master's degree in biology from the University of Arizona. She began her career as a technical writer and freelance journalist before turning to fiction and poetry in the 1980s. Among her works are the novels The Bean Trees *(1988),* The Poisonwood Bible *(1998), and* Prodigal Summer *(2000); a collection of poetry,* Another America *(1991); and* Homelands *(1989), a collection of short stories. She also wrote the nonfiction work* Holding the Line *(1989), about a 1983 mining strike spearheaded largely by Mexican-Americans in southern Arizona. "Stone Soup" is from her most recent work,* High Tide in Tucson *(1995), a collection of essays focusing on a variety of topics, including her own role as a single mother. In this essay, she discusses "nontraditional families," arguing that "[d]ivorce, remarriage, single parenthood, gay parents, and blended families" are not symptoms of some societal breakdown but simply "facts of our time."*

In the catalog of family values, where do we rank an occasion like 1 this? A curly-haired boy who wanted to run before he walked, age seven now, a soccer player scoring a winning goal. He turns to the bleachers with his fists in the air and a smile wide as a gap-toothed galaxy. His own cheering section of grown-ups and kids all leap to their feet and hug each other, delirious with love for this boy. He's Andy, my best friend's son. The cheering section includes his mother and her friends, his brother, his father and stepmother, a stepbrother and stepsister, and a grandparent. Lucky is the child with this many relatives on hand to hail a proud accomplishment. I'm there too, witnessing a family fortune. But in spite of myself, defensive words take shape in my head. I am thinking: I dare *anybody* to call this a broken home.

Families change, and remain the same. Why are our names for 2 home so slow to catch up to the truth of where we live?

When I was a child, I had two parents who loved me without cease. 3
One of them attended every excuse for attention I ever contrived, and
the other made it to the ones with higher production values, like piano
recitals and appendicitis. So I was a lucky child too. I played with a set
of paper dolls called "The Family of Dolls," four in number, who came
with the factory-assigned names of Dad, Mom, Sis, and Junior. I think
you know what they looked like, at least before I loved them to death
and their heads fell off.

Now I've replaced the dolls with a life. I knit my days around my 4
daughter's survival and happiness, and am proud to say her head is
still on. But we aren't the Family of Dolls. Maybe you're not, either. And
if not, even though you are statistically no oddity, it's probably been
suggested to you in a hundred ways that yours isn't exactly a real family, but an impostor family, a harbinger of cultural ruin, a slapdash substitute—something like counterfeit money. Here at the tail end of our
century, most of us are up to our ears in the noisy business of trying to
support and love a thing called family. But there's a current in the air
with ferocious moral force that finds its way even into political campaigns, claiming there is only one right way to do it, the Way It Has
Always Been.

In the face of a thriving, particolored world, this narrow view is so 5
pickled and absurd I'm astonished that it gets airplay. And I'm astonished that it still stings.

Every parent has endured the arrogance of a child-unfriendly 6
grump sitting in judgment, explaining what those kids of ours really
need (for example, "a good licking"). If we're polite, we move our crew
to another bench in the park. If we're forthright (as I am in my mind,
only, for the rest of the day), we fix them with a sweet imperious stare
and say, "Come back and let's talk about it after you've changed a thousand diapers."

But it's harder somehow to shrug off the Family-of-Dolls Family 7
Values crew when they judge (from their safe distance) that divorced
people, blended families, gay families, and single parents are failures.
That our children are at risk, and the whole arrangement is messy and
embarrassing. A marriage that ends is not called "finished," it's called
failed. The children of this family may have been born to a happy union,
but now they are called *the children of divorce*.

I had no idea how thoroughly these assumptions overlaid my cul- 8
ture until I went through divorce myself. I wrote to a friend: "This might
be worse than being widowed. Overnight I've suffered the same
losses—companionship, financial and practical support, my identity as
a wife and partner, the future I'd taken for granted. I am lonely, grieving, and hard-pressed to take care of my household alone. But instead
of bringing casseroles, people are acting like I had a fit and broke up the
family china."

Once upon a time I held these beliefs about divorce: that everyone 9
who does it could have chosen not to do it. That it's a lazy way out of
marital problems. That it selfishly puts personal happiness ahead of
family integrity. Now I tremble for my ignorance. It's easy, in fortunate
times, to forget about the ambush that could leave your head reeling:
serious mental or physical illness, death in the family, abandonment,
financial calamity, humiliation, violence, despair.

I started out like any child, intent on being the Family of Dolls. I set 10
upon young womanhood believing in most of the doctrines of my generation: I wore my skirts four inches above the knee. I had that Barbie
with her zebra-striped swimsuit and a figure unlike anything found in
nature. And I understood the Prince Charming Theory of Marriage, a
quest for Mr. Right that ends smack dab where you find him. I did not
completely understand that another whole story *begins* there, and no
fairy tale prepared me for the combination of bad luck and persistent
hope that would interrupt my dream and lead me to other arrangements. Like a cancer diagnosis, a dying marriage is a thing to fight, to
deny, and finally, when there's no choice left, to dig in and survive.
Casseroles would help. Likewise, I imagine it must be a painful reckoning in adolescence (or later on) to realize one's own true love will never
look like the soft-focus fragrance ads because Prince Charming (surprise!) is a princess. Or vice versa. Or has skin the color your parents
didn't want you messing with, except in the Crayola box.

It's awfully easy to hold in contempt the straw broken home, and 11
that mythical category of persons who toss away nuclear family for the
sheer fun of it. Even the legal terms we use have a suggestion of caprice.
I resent the phrase "irreconcilable differences," which suggests a stubborn refusal to accept a spouse's little quirks. This is specious. Every
happily married couple I know has loads of irreconcilable differences.
Negotiating where to set the thermostat is not the point. A nonfunc-
tioning marriage is a slow asphyxiation. It is waking up despised each
morning, listening to the pulse of your own loneliness before the radio
begins to blare its raucous gospel that you're nothing if you aren't
loved. It is sharing your airless house with the threat of suicide or other
kinds of violence, while the ghost that whispers, "Leave here and
destroy your children," has passed over every door and nailed it shut.
Disassembling a marriage in these circumstances is as much *fun* as
amputating your own gangrenous leg. You do it, if you can, to save a
life—or two, or more.

I know of no one who really went looking to hoe the harder row, 12
especially the daunting one of single parenthood. Yet it seems to be the
most American of customs to blame the burdened for their destiny.
We'd like so desperately to believe in freedom and justice for all, we
can hardly name that rogue bad luck, even when he's a close enough
snake to bite us. In the wake of my divorce, some friends (even a few

close ones) chose to vanish, rather than linger within striking distance
of misfortune.

But most stuck around, bless their hearts, and if I'm any the wiser 13
for my trials, it's from having learned the worth of steadfast friendship.
And also, what not to say. The least helpful question is: "Did you want
the divorce, or didn't you?" Did I want to keep that gangrenous leg, or
not? How to explain, in a culture that venerates choice: two terrifying
options are much worse than none at all. Give me any day the quick
hand of cruel fate that will leave me scarred but blameless. As it was, I
kept thinking of that wicked third-grade joke in which some boy comes
up behind you and grabs your ear, starts in with a prolonged tug, and
asks, "Do you want this ear any longer?"

Still, the friend who holds your hand and says the wrong thing is 14
made of dearer stuff than the one who stays away. And generally,
through all of it, you live. My favorite fictional character, Kate Vaiden
(in the novel by Reynolds Price), advises: "Strength just comes in one
brand—you stand up at sunrise and meet what they send you and keep
your hair combed."

Once you've weathered the straits, you get to cross the tricky junc- 15
ture from casualty to survivor. If you're on your feet at the end of a year
or two, and have begun putting together a happy new existence, those
friends who were kind enough to feel sorry for you when you needed it
must now accept you back to the ranks of the living. If you're truly
blessed, they will dance at your second wedding. Everybody else, for
heaven's sake, should stop throwing stones.

Arguing about whether nontraditional families deserve pity or tol- 16
erance is a little like the medieval debate about left-handedness as a
mark of the devil. Divorce, remarriage, single parenthood, gay parents,
and blended families simply are. They're facts of our time. Some of the
reasons listed by sociologists for these family reconstructions are: the idea
of marriage as a romantic partnership rather than a pragmatic one; a
shift in women's expectations, from servility to self-respect and independence; and longevity (prior to antibiotics no marriage was expected
to last many decades—in Colonial days the average couple lived to be
married less than twelve years). Add to all this, our growing sense of
entitlement to happiness and safety from abuse. Most would agree
these are all good things. Yet their result—a culture in which serial
monogamy and the consequent reshaping of families are the norm—
gets diagnosed as "failing."

For many of us, once we have put ourselves Humpty-Dumpty-wise 17
back together again, the main problem with our reorganized family is
that other people think we have a problem. My daughter tells me the
only time she's uncomfortable about being the child of divorced parents
is when her friends say they feel sorry for her. It's a bizarre sympathy,

given that half the kids in her school and nation are in the same boat, pursuing childish happiness with the same energy as their married-parent peers. When anyone asks how *she* feels about it, she spontaneously lists the benefits: our house is in the country and we have a dog, but she can go to her dad's neighborhood for the urban thrills of a pool and sidewalks for roller-skating. What's more, she has three sets of grandparents!

Why is it surprising that a child would revel in a widened family 18 and the right to feel at home in more than one house? Isn't it the opposite that should worry us—a child with no home at all, or too few resources to feel safe? The child at risk is the one whose parents are too immature themselves to guide wisely; too diminished by poverty to nurture; too far from opportunity to offer hope. The number of children in the U.S. living in poverty at this moment is almost unfathomably large: twenty percent. There are families among us that need help all right, and by no means are they new on the landscape. The rate at which teenage girls had babies in 1957 (ninety-six per thousand) was twice what it is now. That remarkable statistic is ignored by the religious right—probably because the teen birth rate was cut in half mainly by legalized abortion. In fact, the policy gatekeepers who coined the phrase "family values" have steadfastly ignored the desperation of too-small families, and since 1979 have steadily reduced the amount of financial support available to a single parent. But, this camp's most outspoken attacks seem aimed at the notion of families getting too complex, with add-ons and extras such as a gay parent's partner, or a remarried mother's new husband and his children.

To judge a family's value by its tidy symmetry is to purchase a book 19 for its cover. There's no moral authority there. The famous family comprised of Dad, Mom, Sis, and Junior living as an isolated economic unit is not built on historical bedrock. In *The Way We Never Were*, Stephanie Coontz writes, "Whenever people propose that we go back to the traditional family, I always suggest that they pick a ballpark date for the family they have in mind." Colonial families were tidily disciplined, but their members (meaning everyone but infants) labored incessantly and died young. Then the Victorian family adopted a new division of labor, in which women's role was domestic and children were allowed time for study and play, but this was an upper-class construct supported by myriad slaves. Coontz writes, "For every nineteenth-century middle-class family that protected its wife and child within the family circle, there was an Irish or German girl scrubbing floors . . . a Welsh boy mining coal to keep the homebaked goodies warm, a black girl doing the family laundry, a black mother and child picking cotton to be made into clothes for the family, and a Jewish or an Italian daughter in a sweatshop making ladies' dresses or artificial flowers for the family to purchase."

The abolition of slavery brought slightly more democratic arrange- 20 ments, in which extended families were harnessed together in cottage industries; at the turn of the century came a steep rise in child labor in mines and sweatshops. Twenty percent of American children lived in orphanages at the time; their parents were not necessarily dead, but couldn't afford to keep them.

During the Depression and up to the end of World War II, many 21 millions of U.S. households were more multigenerational than nuclear. Women my grandmother's age were likely to live with a fluid assortment of elderly relatives, in-laws, siblings, and children. In many cases they spent virtually every waking hour working in the company of other women—a companionable scenario in which it would be easier, I imagine, to tolerate an estranged or difficult spouse. I'm reluctant to idealize a life of so much hard work and so little spousal intimacy, but its advantage may have been resilience. A family so large and varied would not easily be brought down by a single blow: it could absorb a death, long illness, an abandonment here or there, and any number of irreconcilable differences.

The Family of Dolls came along midcentury as a great American 22 experiment. A booming economy required a mobile labor force and demanded that women surrender jobs to returning soldiers. Families came to be defined by a single breadwinner. They struck out for single-family homes at an earlier age than ever before, and in unprecedented numbers they raised children in suburban isolation. The nuclear family was launched to sink or swim.

More than a few sank. Social historians corroborate that the subur- 23 ban family of the postwar economic boom, which we have recently selected as our definition of "traditional," was no panacea. Twenty-five percent of Americans were poor in the mid-1950s, and as yet there were no food stamps. Sixty percent of the elderly lived on less than $1000 a year, and most had no medical insurance. In the sequestered suburbs, alcoholism and sexual abuse of children were far more widespread than anyone imagined.

Expectations soared, and the economy sagged. It's hard to depend 24 on one other adult for everything, come what may. In the last three decades, that amorphous, adaptable structure we call "family" has been reshaped once more by economic tides. Compared with fifties families, mothers are far more likely now to be employed. We are statistically more likely to divorce, and to live in blended families or other extra-nuclear arrangements. We are also more likely to plan and space our children, and to rate our marriages as "happy." We are less likely to suffer abuse without recourse, or to stare out at our lives through a glaze of prescription tranquilizers. Our aged parents are less likely to be destitute, and we're half as likely to have a teenage daughter turn up a mother herself. All in all, I would say that if "intact" in modern family-values jargon means living quietly desperate in the bell jar, then hip-hip-hooray for "broken." A neat family model constructed to service the Baby Boom economy seems to be returning gradually to a grand, lumpy shape that human families apparently have tended toward since they first took root in the Olduvai Gorge.[1] We're social animals, deeply fond of companionship, and children love best to run in packs. If there is a *normal* for humans, at all, I expect it looks like two or three Families of Dolls, connected variously by kinship and passion, shuffled like cards and strewn over several shoeboxes.

The sooner we can let go the fairy tale of families functioning per- 25 fectly in isolation, the better we might embrace the relief of community. Even the admirable parents who've stayed married through thick and thin are very likely, at present, to incorporate other adults into their families—household help and baby-sitters if they can afford them, or neighbors and grandparents if they can't. For single parents, this support is the rock-bottom definition of family. And most parents who have split apart, however painfully, still manage to maintain family continuity for their children, creating in many cases a boisterous phenomenon that Constance Ahrons in her book *The Good Divorce* calls the "binuclear family." Call it what you will—when ex-spouses beat swords into plowshares and jump up and down at a soccer game together, it makes for happy kids.

Cinderella, look, who needs her? All those evil stepsisters? That 26 story always seemed like too much cotton-picking fuss over clothes. A childhood tale that fascinated me more was the one called "Stone Soup," and the gist of it is this: Once upon a time, a pair of beleaguered soldiers straggled home to a village empty-handed, in a land ruined by war. They were famished, but the villagers had so little they shouted evil words and slammed their doors. So the soldiers dragged out a big kettle, filled it with water, and put it on a fire to boil. They rolled a clean round stone into the pot, while the villagers peered through their curtains in amazement.

"What kind of soup is that?" they hooted.   27

"Stone soup," the soldiers replied. "Everybody can have some 28 when it's done."

"Well, thanks," one matron grumbled, coming out with a shriveled 29 carrot. "But it'd be better if you threw this in."

And so on, of course, a vegetable at a time, until the whole suspi- 30 cious village managed to feed itself grandly.

Any family is a big empty pot, save for what gets thrown in. Each 31 stew turns out different. Generosity, a resolve to turn bad luck into good, and respect for variety—these things will nourish a nation of children. Name-calling and suspicion will not. My soup contains a rock or two of hard times, and maybe yours does too. I expect it's a heck of a bouillabaise.

---

[1] Many fossils of human ancestors have been discovered at the Olduvai Gorge in Tanzania. [Eds.]

Responding to Reading

1. In paragraph 1, Kingsolver describes a family group consisting of a child's "mother and her friends, his brother, his father and stepmother, a stepbrother and stepsister, and a grandparent." She continues, "I dare *anybody* to call this a broken home." Do you think most people *would* consider this a broken home? Would you?
2. What is the "Family of Dolls"? Is it the same family that Alice Hoffman (p. 57) watched on television in the 1950s? What is Kingsolver's attitude toward this kind of family? Do you think this attitude is justified, or do you think Kingsolver's status as a divorced parent colors her view?
3. Kingsolver cites examples of terms from the language of divorce that she finds inaccurate, biased, or misleading, for example, *broken home, irreconcilable differences, failed marriage,* and *children of divorce.* What view of the family do these terms suggest? Do you see such language as inaccurate or biased, or do you think it accurately reflects the status of the families it describes?

THE UNEXPECTED LEGACY OF DIVORCE

Judith Wallerstein

Born in New York City in 1922, Judith Wallerstein attended Hunter College and Columbia University and received her doctorate in psychology from Sweden's Lund University. She served on the faculty of the University of California, Berkeley, from 1966 to 1992 and in 1971 founded the California Study of Children of Divorce. She has devoted the last thirty years to this project and has kept in touch with many of the children she began working with at the outset. Since 1980, her Center for the Family in Transition has helped over 6,000 children and their divorcing parents. Her best-known books include Second Chances: Men, Women, and Children a Decade after Divorce *(1989, with Sandra Blakeslee) and* The Good Marriage *(1995, also with Blakeslee). The following is taken from the conclusion of her latest book,* The Unexpected Legacy of Divorce: A 25 Year Landmark Study *(2000, with Blakeslee and Julia M. Lewis).*

Having spent the last thirty years of my life traveling here and 1 abroad talking to professional, legal, and mental health groups plus working with thousands of parents and children in divorced families, it's clear that we've created a new kind of society never before seen in human culture. Silently and unconsciously, we have created a culture of divorce. It's hard to grasp what it means when we say that first marriages stand a 45 percent chance of breaking up and that second marriages have a 60 percent chance of ending in divorce. What are the consequences for all of us when 25 percent of people today between the ages of eighteen and forty-four have parents who divorced? What does it mean to a society when people wonder aloud if the family is about to disappear? What can we do when we learn that married couples with children represent a mere 26 percent of households in the 1990s and that the most common living arrangement nowadays is a household of unmarried people with no children? These numbers are terrifying. But like all massive social change, what's happening is affecting us in ways that we have yet to understand.

For people like me who work with divorcing families all the time, 2 these abstract numbers have real faces. . . . I can relate to the millions of children and adults who suffer with loneliness and to all the teenagers who say, "I don't want a life like either of my parents." I can empathize with the countless young men and women who despair of ever finding a lasting relationship and who, with a brave toss of the head, say, "Hey, if you don't get married then you can't get divorced." It's only later, or sometimes when they think I'm not listening, that they add softly, "but I don't want to grow old alone." I am especially worried about how our divorce culture has changed childhood itself. A million new children a year are added to our march of marital failure. As they explain so eloquently, they lose the carefree play of childhood as well as the comforting arms and lap of a loving parent who is always rushing off because life in the postdivorce family is so incredibly difficult to manage. We must take very seriously the complaint of children like Karen who declare, "The day my parents divorced is the day my childhood ended."

Many years ago the psychoanalyst Erik Erikson taught us that child- 3 hood and society are vitally connected. But we have not yet come to terms with the changes ushered in by our divorce culture. Childhood is different, adolescence is different, and adulthood is different. Without our noticing, we have created a new class of young children who take care of themselves, along with a whole generation of overburdened parents who have no time to enjoy the pleasures of parenting. So much has happened so fast, we cannot hold it all in our minds. It's simply overwhelming.

But we must not forget a very important other side to all these 4 changes. Because of our divorce culture, adults today have a greater sense of freedom. The importance of sex and play in adult life is widely accepted. We are not locked into our early mistakes and forced to stay in wretched, lifelong relationships. The change in women—their very identity and freer role in society—is part of our divorce culture. Indeed, two-thirds of divorces are initiated by women despite the high price they pay in economic and parenting burdens afterward. People want and expect a lot more out of marriage than did earlier generations. Although the divorce rate in second and third marriages is sky-high, many second marriages are much happier than the ones left behind. Children and adults are able to escape violence, abuse, and misery to create a better life. Clearly there is no road back.

The sobering truth is that we have created a new kind of society 5
that offers greater freedom and more opportunities for many adults,
but this welcome change carries a serious hidden cost. Many people,
adults and children alike, are in fact not better off. We have created new
kinds of families in which relationships are fragile and often unreliable.
Children today receive far less nurturance, protection, and parenting
than was their lot a few decades ago. Long-term marriages come apart
at still surprising rates. And many in the older generation who started
the divorce revolution find themselves estranged from their adult
children. Is this the price we must pay for needed change? Can't we do
better?

I'd like to say that we're at a crossroads but I'm afraid I can't be that 6
optimistic. We can choose a new route only if we agree on where we are
and where we want to be in the future. The outlook is cloudy. For every
person who wants to sound an alarm, there's another who says don't
worry. For everyone concerned about the economic and emotional
deprivations inherited by children of divorce there are those who argue
that those kids were "in trouble before" and that divorce is irrelevant,
no big deal. People want to feel good about their choices. Doubtless
many do. In actual fact, after most divorces, one member of the former
couple feels much better while the other feels no better or even worse.
Yet at any dinner party you will still hear the same myths: Divorce is a
temporary crisis. So many children have experienced their parents'
divorce that kids nowadays don't worry so much. It's easier. They
almost expect it. It's a rite of passage. If I feel better, so will my children.
And so on. As always, children are voiceless or unheard.

But family scholars who have not always seen eye to eye are con- 7
verging on a number of findings that fly in the face of our cherished
myths. We agree that the effects of divorce are long-term. We know that
the family is in trouble. We have a consensus that children raised in
divorced or remarried families are less well adjusted as adults than
those raised in intact families.

The life histories of this first generation to grow up in a divorce cul- 8
ture tells us truths we dare not ignore. Their message is poignant, clear,
and contrary to what so many want to believe. They have taught me the
following:

From the viewpoint of the children, and counter to what happens to 9
their parents, divorce is a cumulative experience. Its impact increases
over time and rises to a crescendo in adulthood. At each developmental
stage divorce is experienced anew in different ways. In adulthood it
affects personality, the ability to trust, expectations about relationships,
and ability to cope with change.

The first upheaval occurs at the breakup. Children are frightened 10
and angry, terrified of being abandoned by both parents, and they feel
responsible for the divorce. Most children are taken by surprise; few are

relieved. As adults, they remember with sorrow and anger how little support they got from their parents when it happened. They recall how they were expected to adjust overnight to a terrifying number of changes that confounded them. Even children who had seen or heard violence at home made no connection between that violence and the decision to divorce. The children concluded early on, silently and sadly, that family relationships are fragile and that the tie between a man and woman can break capriciously, without warning. They worried ever after that parent-child relationships are also unreliable and can break at any time. These early experiences colored their later expectations.

As the postdivorce family took shape, their world increasingly 11 resembled what they feared most. Home was a lonely place. The household was in disarray for years. Many children were forced to move, leaving behind familiar schools, close friends, and other supports. What they remember vividly as adults is the loss of the intact family and the safety net it provided, the difficulty of having two parents in two homes, and how going back and forth cut badly into playtime and friendships. Parents were busy with work, preoccupied with rebuilding their social lives. Both moms and dads had a lot less time to spend with their children and were less responsive to their children's needs or wishes. Little children especially felt that they had lost both parents and were unable to care for themselves. Children soon learned that the divorced family has porous walls that include new lovers, live-in partners, and stepparents. Not one of these relationships was easy for anyone. The mother's parenting was often cut into by the very heavy burdens of single parenthood and then by the demands of remarriage and stepchildren.

Relationships with fathers were heavily influenced by live-in lovers 12 or stepmothers in second and third marriages. Some second wives were interested in the children while others wanted no part of them. Some fathers were able to maintain their love and interest in their children but few had time for two or sometimes three families. In some families both parents gradually stabilized their lives within happy remarriages or well-functioning, emotionally gratifying single parenthood. But these people were never a majority in any of my work.

Meanwhile, children who were able to draw support from school, 13 sports teams, parents, stepparents, grandparents, teachers, or their own inner strengths, interests, and talents did better than those who could not muster such resources. By necessity, many of these so-called resilient children forfeited their own childhoods as they took responsibility for themselves; their troubled, overworked parents; and their siblings. Children who needed more than minimal parenting because they were little or had special vulnerabilities and problems with change were soon overwhelmed with sorrow and anger at their parents. Years later, when contemplating having their own children, most children in this study said hotly, "I never want a child of mine to experience a childhood like I had."

As the children told us, adolescence begins early in divorced 14 homes and, compared with that of youngsters raised in intact families, is more likely to include more early sexual experiences for girls and higher alcohol and drug use for girls and boys. Adolescence is more prolonged in divorced families and extends well into the years of early adulthood. Throughout these years children of divorce worry about following in their parents' footsteps and struggle with a sinking sense that they, too, will fail in their relationships.

But it's in adulthood that children of divorce suffer the most. The 15 impact of divorce hits them most cruelly as they go in search of love, sexual intimacy, and commitment. Their lack of inner images of a man and a woman in a stable relationship and their memories of their parents' failure to sustain the marriage badly hobbles their search, leading them to heartbreak and even despair. They cried, "No one taught me." They complain bitterly that they feel unprepared for adult relationships and that they have never seen a "man and woman on the same beam," that they have no good models on which to build their hopes. And indeed they have a very hard time formulating even simple ideas about the kind of person they're looking for. Many end up with unsuitable or very troubled partners in relationships that were doomed from the start.

The contrast between them and children from good intact homes, as 16 both go in search of love and commitment, is striking. . . . Adults in their twenties from reasonably good or even moderately unhappy intact families had a fine understanding of the demands and sacrifices required in a close relationship. They had memories of how their parents struggled and overcame differences, how they cooperated in a crisis. They developed a general idea about the kind of person they wanted to marry. Most important, they did not expect to fail. The two groups differed after marriage as well. Those from intact families found the example of their parent's enduring marriage very reassuring when they inevitably ran into marital problems. But in coping with the normal stresses in a marriage, adults from divorced families were at a grave disadvantage. Anxiety about relationships was at the bedrock of their personalities and endured even in very happy marriages. Their fears of disaster and sudden loss rose when they felt content. And their fear of abandonment, betrayal, and rejection mounted when they found themselves having to disagree with someone they loved. After all, marriage is a slippery slope and their parents fell off it. All had trouble dealing with differences or even moderate conflict in their close relationships. Typically their first response was panic, often followed by flight. They had a lot to undo and a lot to learn in a very short time.

Those who had two parents who rebuilt happy lives after divorce 17 and included children in their orbits had a much easier time as adults. Those who had committed single parents also benefited from that parent's attention and responsiveness. But the more frequent response in adulthood was continuing anger at parents, more often at fathers, whom the children regarded as having been selfish and faithless.

Others felt deep compassion and pity toward mothers or fathers who failed to rebuild their lives after divorce. The ties between daughters and their mothers were especially close but at a cost. Some young women found it very difficult to separate form their moms and to lead their own lives. With some notable exceptions, fathers in divorced families were less likely to enjoy close bonds with their adult children, especially their sons. This stood in marked contrast to fathers and sons from intact families, who tended to grow closer as the years went by. 18

Fortunately for many children of divorce, their fears of loss and betrayal can be conquered by the time they reach their late twenties and thirties. But what a struggle that takes, what courage and persistence. Those who succeed overcome their difficulties the hard way—by learning from their own failed relationships and gradually rejecting the models they were raised with to create what they want from a love relationship. Those lucky enough to have found a loving partner are able to interrupt their self-destructive course with a lasting love affair or marriage. 19

In other realms of adult life—financial and security, for instance— some children were able to overcome difficulties through unexpected help from fathers who had vanished long before. Still others benefit from the constancy of parents or grandparents. Many men and women raised in divorced families establish successful careers. Their workplace performance is largely unaffected by the divorce. But no matter what their success in the world, they retain some serious residues—fear of loss, fear of change, and fear that disaster will strike, especially when things are going well. They're still terrified by the mundane differences and inevitable conflicts found in every close relationship. 20

I'm heartened by the hard-won success of these adults. But at the same time, I can't forget those who've failed to straighten out their lives. I'm especially troubled by how many divorced or remained in wretched marriages. Of those who have children and who are now divorced, many, to my dismay, are not protecting their children in ways we might expect. They go on to repeat the same mistakes their own parents made, perpetuating problems that have plagued them all their lives. I'm also concerned about many who, by their mid- and late thirties, are neither married nor cohabiting and who are leading lonely lives. They're afraid of getting involved in a relationship they they think is doomed to fail. After a divorce or breakup, they're afraid to try again. And I'm struck by continuing anger at parents and flat-out statements by many of these young adults that they have no intention of helping their moms and especially their dads or stepparents in old age. This may change. But if it doesn't, we'll be facing another unanticipated consequence of our divorce culture. Who will take care of an older generation estranged form its children? 21

What We Can and Cannot Do

Our efforts to improve our divorce culture have been spotty and the   22
resources committed to the task are pitifully small. The courts have given
the lion's share of attention to the 10 to 15 percent of families that continue
to fight bitterly. Caught between upholding the rights of parents and protecting the interests of children, they have tilted heavily toward parents.
Such parents allegedly speak in the name of the child just as those who
fight bloody holy wars allegedly speak in the name of religion. Thus, as I
explained to the judge with whom I began this chapter, our court system
has unintentionally contributed to the suffering of children. At the same
time, most parents receive little guidance. Some courts offer educational
lectures to families at the time of the breakup, but the emphasis is on preventing further litigation. Such courses are typically evaluated according
to how much they reduce subsequent litigation and not on how they
might improve parenting. Curricula to educate teachers, school personnel, pediatricians, and other professionals about child and parenting
issues in divorce are rare. Few university or medical school programs in
psychiatry, psychology, social work, or law include courses on how to
understand or help children and parents after separation, divorce, and
remarriage. This lack of training persists despite the fact that a disproportionate number of children and adolescents from divorced homes are
admitted as patients for psychological treatment at clinics and family
agencies. In many social agencies, close to three-quarters of the children
in treatment are from divorced families. Some school districts have organized groups for children whose parents are divorcing. And some communities have established groups to help divorcing parents talk about
their children's problems. A few centers such as ours have developed programs to help families cope with high conflict and domestic violence. But
such efforts are not widespread. As a society, we have not set up services
to help people relieve the stresses of divorce. We continue to foster the
myth that divorce is a transient crisis and that as soon as adults restabi-
lize their lives, the children will recover fully. When will the truth sink in?

Let's suppose for a moment that we had a consensus in our society.   23
Suppose we could agree that we want to maintain the advantages of
divorce but that we need to protect our children and help parents mute
the long-term effects of divorce on future generations. Imagine we were
willing to roll up our sleeves and really commit the enormous resources
of our society toward supplementing the knowledge we have. Suppose
we gave as much time, energy, and resources to protecting children as
we give to protecting the environment. What might we try?

I would begin with an effort to strengthen marriage. Obviously,   24
restoring confidence in marriage won't work if we naively call for a
return to marriage as it used to be. To improve marriage, we need to fully
understand the nature of contemporary man-woman relationships. We
need to appreciate the difficulties modern couples confront in balancing

work and family, separateness and togetherness, conflict and cooperation. It's no accident that 80 percent of divorces occur in the first nine
years of marriage. These new families should be our target.

What threats to marriage can we change? First, there's a serious 25
imbalance between the demands of the workplace and the needs of family life. The corporate world rarely considers the impact of its policies on
parents and children. Some companies recognize that parents need time
to spend with their children but they don't understand that the workplace exerts a major influence on the quality and stability of marriage.
Heavy work schedules and job insecurity erode married life. Families
with young children especially postpone intimate talk, sex, and friendship. These are the ties that replenish a marriage. When the boss calls, we
go to the office. When the baby cries, we pick up the child. But when a
marriage is starving, we expect it to bumble along. Most Wester European
countries provide paid family leave. What about us? Why do we persist
in offering unpaid leave and pretend that it addresses the young family's
problem? One additional solution might be social security and tax benefits for a parent who wants to stay home and care for young children. That
alone would lighten the burden on many marriages. Other suggestions
for reducing the stresses on young families include more flex time, greater
opportunities for part-time work, assurances that people who take family
leave will not lose their place on the corporate ladder, tax advantages for
families, and many other ideas that have been on the table for years.
Public policy cannot create good marriages. But it can buffer some of the
stresses people face, especially in those early, vulnerable years when couples need time to establish intimacy, a satisfying sex life, and a friendship
that will hold them together through the inevitable challenges that lie
ahead. Ultimately, if we're really interested in improving marriage so that
people have time for each other and their children, we need to realign our
priorities away from the business world and toward family life.

We might also try to help the legions of young adults who complain 26
bitterly that they're unprepared for marriage. Having been raised in
divorced or very troubled homes, they have no idea how to choose a
partner or what to do to build the relationship. They regard their parents' divorce as a terrible failure and worry that they're doomed to follow in the same footsteps. Many adults stay in unhappy marriages just
to avoid divorce. We don't know if we can help them with educational
methods because we haven't tried. Our experience is too limited and our
experience models nonexistent. But when so many young people have
never seen a good marriage, we have a moral obligation to try to intervene preventively. Most programs that give marital advice are aimed at
engaged couples who belong to churches and synagogues. These are
very good beginnings that should be expanded. But many offer too little
and arrive too late to bring about changes in any individual's values or
knowledge. Nor is the excitement that precedes a wedding the best time

for reflection on how to choose a lifetime partner or what makes a marriage work. Academic courses on marriage mostly look at families from the lofty perch of the family scholar and not from the perspective of children of divorce who feel "no one ever taught me."

In my opinion, a better time to begin helping these youngsters is 27 during mid-adolescence, when attitudes toward oneself and relationships with the opposite sex are beginning to gel. Adolescence is the time when worries about sex, love, betrayal, and morality take center stage. Education for and about relationships should begin at that time, since if we do it right, we'll have their full attention. It could be based in the health centers that have been established in many schools throughout the country. Churches and synagogues and social agencies might provide another launching place. Ideally, adolescents in a well-functioning society should have the opportunity to think and talk about a wide range of relationships, issues, and conflicts confronting them. As an opening gambit, think about asking the deceptively simple question: "How do you choose a friend?" A group of teenagers considering this problem could be drawn to the important question of how to choose a lover and life partner—and even more important, how not to choose one. Specific topics such as differences between boys and girls, cultural subgroups, and how people resolve tensions would follow based on the teenagers' interests and their willingness to discuss real issues. Colleges could also offer continuing and advanced courses on an expanded range of subjects, including many problems that young men and women now struggle with alone.

We are on the threshold of learning what we can and cannot do for 28 these young people. Still one wonders, can an educational intervention replace the learning that occurs naturally over many years within the family? How do we create a corps of teachers who are qualified to lead meaningful courses on relationships? By this I mean courses that are true to life, honest, and respectful of students. I worry about the adult tendency to lecture or sermonize. In a society where the family has become a political issue, I'm concerned about attacks from the left and the right, about the many people who would attack such interventions the way they've attacked the Harry Potter books. Mostly I'm concerned about finding a constituency of adults who would rally behind an idea that has so many pitfalls. But I'm also convinced that doing nothing— leaving young people alone in their struggles—is more dangerous. We should not give up without a try.

Responding to Reading

1. In paragraph 1, the author states, "Silently and unconsciously, we have created a culture of divorce." She goes on in this paragraph to pose some

disturbing questions. How do you believe Barbara Kingsolver (p. 60) or Jane Smiley (p. 76) might respond to this statement and to the related questions?

2. In summing up the findings of a twenty-five-year study of the effects of divorce on children, the author enumerates many results, mostly negative, of the "divorce culture" she defines. What *positive* results does she identify? Can you think of others?

3. The author does not condemn divorce, but she does find it responsible for some very harmful long-term problems. She believes, for example, that because of divorce, "the family is in trouble" and that "children raised in divorced or remarried families are less well adjusted as adults than those raised in intact families" (7). What does the author believe ought to be done to "improve our divorce culture" (24)? Do you see her suggestions as realistic? Do you see them as necessary?

THERE THEY GO, BAD-MOUTHING DIVORCE AGAIN

Jane Smiley

Jane Smiley (1949–   ) was born in Los Angeles, California, and spent her childhood in St. Louis, Missouri. A graduate of Vassar College with M.A. and M.F.A. degrees from the University of Iowa, she has taught creative writing at Iowa State University. Smiley's widely acclaimed novels, which are noted for differing from one another in style and subject matter, include the Pulitzer Prize–winning A Thousand Acres *(1991), a modern-day retelling of Shakespeare's* King Lear; Moo *(1995), an academic satire;* The All-True Travels and Adventures of Lidie Newton *(1998), a historical fiction; and* Horse Heaven *(2000), set among horse breeders and trainers. Smiley also contributes articles and criticism to a variety of periodicals. The following essay appeared on the op-ed page of the* New York Times *in September 2000.*

Several years ago at a party, I asked a woman I had just met how   1
her Christmas had been. She said, "First good Christmas in 25 years."

"Why was that?"   2

"Oh, my father died."   3

"And that made it good?"   4

"Well, every year for 25 years, he would gather us all around the   5
Christmas tree and tell us how terrible his life was and how disappointed he was in everyone."

"How did your mother feel, though?"   6

"Oh, she was relieved. He'd been telling her for 60 years that she 7 wasn't pretty or smart enough for him. Now she's planning to do some of the things she's wanted to do all along."

I thought this was an excellent example of a thank-God-for-divorce 8 tale. Here's another one: When the grandfather of a friend of mine died many years ago, his last words to his wife of 50 years were, "I'm sorry I married you."

I admit that I am susceptible to such tales. I am the poster child for 9 the recent study by Judith Wallerstein et al. of the long-term effects of divorce on children—the child of parents who parted before I was a year old and divorced uncountable times (well, three).

Bad habits? Bad choices? Perhaps it is time to subject myself to 10 Wallersteinian analysis. But when I do my own little survey, and come up with the marital histories of my 32 closest friends and relatives, the picture grows more complex. All of the 32 are baby boomers or a bit older—oldest, 58, youngest, 40. Twenty-six are the offspring of long-term first marriages that ended in the death of one spouse or the other; six of them come from divorced families.

Of the 26 whose parents had long-term marriages, 17 have been 11 divorced at least once.

What does my mini-survey tell me? It tells me the same thing that 12 any cursory review of the last 50 years of married life in America tells us—most baby boomers were born into intact families. On the surface nearly all adhered to the ideal. Dad earned enough money so that Mom could stay home and take care of the 3.2 children and the house. Marital roles were divided by gender, and Mom was regularly advised by Ann Landers and Abigail Van Buren, not to mention everyone else, to cater to Dad's sense of privileged masculinity: Should she iron his shorts? If he didn't give her any money of her own, was it permissible to take it out of his pockets while he was sleeping? If, when she was doing the laundry, she found lipstick on his collar, should she mention it?

And most baby boomers, learning how to be married, as Ms. 13 Wallerstein suggests, by witnessing the examples of marriage that they grew up with, voted with their feet when the time came to endure or not in their own.

Twenty-six boomers from 26 intact marriages. Seventeen divorced. 14 That's about 65 percent.

The fact is, the goals of marriage have changed. In the first half of the 15 century people married to survive, reproduce, join properties, become a part of the mainstream community of adults. Individual happiness might have been foreseen and desired, but if as the marriage wore on happiness came to seem elusive, other goals dominated. Some marriages did work on both levels: several of my divorced peers had parents whose marriages I know to have been happy, compatible and peaceful.

Whatever the reasons for their parents' marital longevity, though, 16 the children in my group did not learn from their example how to choose their own partners wisely or how to stick with it, as Ms. Wallerstein would have expected. Some who were divorced chose to try again, and have found happiness. Others in second or third marriages have not. The person I know whose parents had the longest, happiest marriage recently wrote me: "We plug along." A thank-God-for-divorce tale, midlife version.

Americans born since mid-century marry for the same reason they 17 do anything else—to be happy. Yet literature of all periods tells us that marrying to be happy is at best an iffy proposition. Historians of domestic life have suggested that marriages in the premodern period were usually short—death did the work of divorce.

Marrying with the overriding goal of being happy for all your adult 18 life with a single other (since survival, reproduction, property joining and being part of a community of adults can be achieved now without marriage) is a new experiment. Divorce is its corollary. This is an experiment that our children will engage in, whatever models we give them.

Divorce is a right that took many generations to gain. It is no more 19 a guarantor of happiness than marriage, but also no less. The rate of divorce in our country tells us very little other than that our culture is in transition to new ways of organizing itself. Given the social and technological changes of the past century, this can hardly be surprising.

Personally, in spite of the testaments of the Wallersteinians, I'm glad 20 my parents divorced, and I have been since I first began to actually think about it. I can't speak for my children, but I do hope they try more than one way of being happy, rather than turning around at 84 and saying, "Free at last."

Responding to Reading

1. Responding to Wallerstein's study of divorce (p. 87), Smiley, who calls herself the "poster child" (9) for the study, conducts her own informal survey of friends and family. What does she conclude? What does she see as the significance of her conclusions?
2. In paragraph 15, Smiley states, "The goals of marriage have changed." Do you see this change as largely positive or negative? Do you think it is in any way responsible for creating what Wallerstein calls our "divorce culture"? Explain.
3. Unlike Wallerstein, Smiley bases her conclusions not on twenty-five years of research but on her own experiences with divorce and on the "mini-survey" she describes in paragraphs 10–12. Do you find the informal evidence she presents convincing?

———————— WIDENING THE FOCUS ————————

- Lynda Barry, "The Sanctuary of School" (p. 99)
- Marie Winn, "Television: The Plug-in Drug" (p. 257)
- Arlie Hochschild, "The Second Shift" (p. 351)

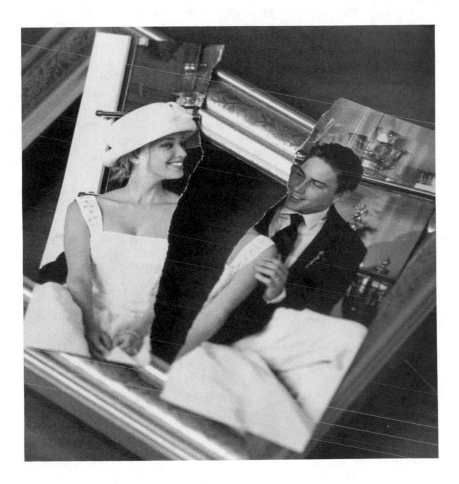

Responding to the Image

1. How do you interpret this image? Do you think that most people involved in a divorce want to obliterate memories of the past as the torn photograph suggests?
2. How do you think a child of divorce might respond to a torn photograph like this one of his or her own parents? What might divorced parents do to make the break easier on their children?

WRITING

Family and Memory

1. What exactly is a family? Is it a group of people bound together by love? By marriage? By blood? By shared memories? By economic dependency? By habit? Is a family what Alice Hoffman remembers from 1950s television: "the neat patch of lawn, the apple tree, the mother who never once raised her voice, the three lovely children" (1)? Is it Barbara Kingsolver's "stone soup"? Or is it something else? Define *family* as it is presented in several of the essays in this chapter.

2. Leo Tolstoy's classic Russian novel *Anna Karenina* opens with the sentence "Happy families are all alike; every unhappy family is unhappy in its own way." Write an essay in which you concur with or challenge this statement, supporting your position with references to several of the readings in this chapter.

3. In a sense, memories are like snapshots, a series of disconnected candid pictures, sometimes unflattering, often out of focus, eventually fading. Writers of autobiographical memoirs often explore this parallel; for example, Alice Walker sees her painful childhood as a series of snapshots, and Raymond Carver calls the poem that appears in his essay "Photograph of My Father in His Twenty-Second Year." Using information from your own family life as well as from your reading, discuss the relationship between memories and photographs. If you like, you may describe and discuss some of your own family photographs.

4. Several of the writers represented in this chapter—for example, Kingston, Momaday, and Carver—present fairly detailed biographical sketches of a family member. Using these essays as guides, write a detailed biographical sketch of a member of your family. If you can, prepare for this assignment by interviewing several family members.

5. Have you, like E. B. White, ever returned as an adult to a place that was important to you when you were a child? Write two brief descriptions, one from the point of view of your adult self and one from the point of view of your childhood self. In each description, consider both the physical appearance of the place and its significance to you. Then, expand your descriptions into an essay by writing introductory and concluding paragraphs comparing your two views.

6. How do your parents' notions of success and failure affect you? Do you think your parents tend to expect too much of you? Too little?

Explore these ideas in an essay, referring to one essay in this chapter and one in Chapter 6, "The American Dream."

7. Gary Soto comes to understand his parents better by seeing them in the role of workers. Discuss his changing attitude toward his parents' work, comparing his views with ideas expressed by Scott Russell Sanders in "The Men We Carry in Our Minds" in Chapter 5. (You may also discuss how your experience as a worker has helped you to understand or appreciate your own parents.)

8. Read the poem "Photograph of My Father in His Twenty-Second Year," which follows paragraph 29 of Raymond Carver's essay. Write an essay in which you compare and contrast this poem with Robert Hayden's "Those Winter Sundays" (p. 11).

9. What traits, habits, and values (positive or negative) have you inherited from your parents? What qualities do you think you will pass on to your children? Write a letter to your parents in which you explore these two questions, incorporating the ideas of several of the writers in this chapter.

10. After reading the four selections in the Focus section, write an essay in which you answer the question "How has divorce redefined the family?" In gathering support for your essay, you should consider information from the readings in the Focus section, but you may also wish to include information from your own personal experience or from the experience of friends or relatives.

11. **For Internet Research:** As the readings in the Focus section suggest, the increase in the number of divorces in the United States has led to considerable debate over the effects of divorce. Much of this debate, like so many others, is taking place on the Internet. The "Divorce Reform Page" at <http://patriot.net/~crouch/divorce.html> provides links to many resources both pro and con, as does the site <http://www.divorcereform.org>. The site <http://www.heart choice.com/divorceroom> offers advice as well as a forum for parents going through a divorce. Using these sites, the Focus readings, and other sources you may find, write an essay discussing whether or not you think it should be more difficult for parents to get a divorce today.

2

ISSUES
IN EDUCATION

It may seem odd to us today, when education is touted as a remedy for many of the social and economic problems of modern society, that a hundred years ago Mark Twain could imply that becoming educated meant paying a price: forfeiting youthful innocence and happiness. Yet that is precisely what he suggests in his essay "Reading the River," where he examines two different ways of viewing the world: one innocent and naive, the other experienced and educated; one accepting, the other questioning.

It is this view of education—as a process that radically changes a person from an unthinking, innocent child to a cognizant, questioning adult—that is largely missing from today's educational systems. In fact, more emphasis seems to be placed on increasing self-esteem and avoiding controversy than on challenging students to discover new ways of thinking and new contexts for viewing the world. As a result, classic books are censored or rewritten and ideas are presented as if they all have equal value. The result is an educational environment that has all the excitement of elevator music. Many people—educators included—seem to have forgotten that ideas *must* be unsettling if they are to make us think. What is education, after all, but a process that encourages us to think critically about the world and develop a healthy skepticism—to question, evaluate, and synthesize ideas and events?

The focus section in this chapter (p. 140) addresses the question, "What is the real purpose of education?" More specifically, the essays in this section consider whether a college education should prepare students for life or for a job. What, for example, is the place of a liberal arts curriculum in an increasingly practical educational environment? In such an environment, will literature and history courses ultimately be edged out by courses in management or computers?

As you read and prepare to write about the selections in this chapter, you may consider the following questions:

- How does the writer define education? Is this definition consistent with yours?

- What does the writer think the main goals of education should be? Do you agree?

- Which does the writer believe is more important, formal or informal education?

- On what aspect or aspects of education does the writer focus?

- Who does the writer believe bears primary responsibility for a student's education? The student? The school? The community? The government?

- Does the writer use personal experience to support his or her position? Or does he or she use facts and statistics or expert opinion as support? Do you find the writer's ideas convincing?

- What changes in the educational system does the writer recommend? Do you agree with the writer's recommendations?

- Are the writer's educational experiences similar to or different from yours? How do any similarities or differences affect your response to the essay?

- In what way is the essay you are reading similar to or different from other essays in this chapter?

SCHOOL IS BAD FOR CHILDREN

John Holt

Teacher and education theorist John Holt (1923–1985) believed that schooling undermines the curiosity and love of life that children have naturally. In his writings about education, Holt suggests that there should be more than one path for learning and that students should be allowed to pursue only what interests them. Some of his many books include How Children Fail *(1964),* How Children Learn *(1967),* Instead of Education *(1976), and* Learning All The Time *(1989). The following essay, first published in the* Saturday Evening Post *in 1969, makes a plea to free children from the classroom, a "dull and ugly place, where nobody ever says anything very truthful," and to "give them a chance to learn about the world at first hand."*

Almost every child, on the first day he sets foot in a school building, 1 is smarter, more curious, less afraid of what he doesn't know, better at finding and figuring things out, more confident, resourceful, persistent and independent than he will ever be again in his schooling—or, unless he is very unusual and very lucky, for the rest of his life. Already, by paying close attention to and interacting with the world and people around him, and without any school-type formal instruction, he has done a task far more difficult, complicated and abstract than anything he will be asked to do in school, or than any of his teachers has done for years. He has solved the mystery of language. He has discovered it— babies don't even know that language exists—and he has found out how it works and learned to use it. He has done it by exploring, by experimenting, by developing his own model of the grammar of language, by trying it out and seeing whether it works, by gradually changing it and refining it until it does work. And while he has been doing this, he has been learning other things as well, including many of the "concepts" that the schools think only they can teach him, and many that are more complicated than the ones they do try to teach him.

In he comes, this curious, patient, determined, energetic, skillful 2 learner. We sit him down at a desk, and what do we teach him? Many things. First, that learning is separate from living. "You come to school to learn," we tell him, as if the child hadn't been learning before, as if living were out there and learning were in here, and there were no connection between the two. Secondly, that he cannot be trusted to learn and is no good at it. Everything we teach about reading, a task far simpler than many that the child has already mastered, says to him, "If we don't make you read, you won't, and if you don't do it exactly the way we tell you, you can't." In short, he comes to feel that learning is a passive process, something that someone else does *to* you, instead of something you do for yourself.

In a great many other ways he learns that he is worthless, untrust- 3 worthy, fit only to take other people's orders, a blank sheet for other people to write on. Oh, we make a lot of nice noises in school about respect for the child and individual differences, and the like. But our acts, as opposed to our talk, say to the child, "Your experience, your concerns, your curiosities, your needs, what you know, what you want, what you wonder about, what you hope for, what you fear, what you like and dislike, what you are good at or not so good at—all this is of not the slightest importance, it counts for nothing. What counts here, and the only thing that counts, is what we know, what we think is important, what we want you to do, think and be." The child soon learns not to ask questions—the teacher isn't there to satisfy his curiosity. Having learned to hide his curiosity, he later learns to be ashamed of it. Given no chance to find out who he is—and to develop that person, whoever it is—he soon comes to accept the adults' evaluation of him.

He learns many other things. He learns that to be wrong, uncertain, 4 confused, is a crime. Right Answers are what the school wants, and he learns countless strategies for prying these answers out of the teacher, for conning her into thinking he knows what he doesn't know. He learns to dodge, bluff, fake, cheat. He learns to be lazy. Before he came to school, he would work for hours on end, on his own, with no thought of reward, at the business of making sense of the world and gaining competence in it. In school he learns, like every buck private, how to goldbrick, how not to work when the sergeant isn't looking, how to know when he is looking, how to make him think you are working even when he is looking. He learns that in real life you don't do anything unless you are bribed, bullied or conned into doing it, that nothing is worth doing for its own sake, or that if it is, you can't do it in school. He learns to be bored, to work with a small part of his mind, to escape from the reality around him into daydreams and fantasies—but not like the fantasies of his preschool years, in which he played a very active part.

The child comes to school curious about other people, particularly 5 other children, and the school teaches him to be indifferent. The most interesting thing in the classroom—often the only interesting thing in it—is the other children, but he has to act as if these other children, all about him, only a few feet away, are not really there. He cannot interact with them, talk with them, smile at them. In many schools he can't talk to other children in the halls between classes; in more than a few, and some of these in stylish suburbs, he can't even talk to them at lunch. Splendid training for a world in which, when you're not studying the other person to figure out how to do him in, you pay no attention to him.

In fact, he learns how to live without paying attention to anything 6 going on around him. You might say that school is a long lesson in how to turn yourself off, which may be one reason why so many young people, seeking the awareness of the world and responsiveness to it they had when they were little, think they can only find it in drugs. Aside from being boring, the school is almost always ugly, cold, inhuman— even the most stylish, glass-windowed, $20-a-square-foot schools.

And so, in this dull and ugly place, where nobody ever says any- 7 thing very truthful, where everybody is playing a kind of role, as in a charade, where the teachers are no more free to respond honestly to the students than the students are free to respond to the teachers or each other, where the air practically vibrates with suspicion and anxiety, the child learns to live in a daze, saving his energies for those small parts of his life that are too trivial for the adults to bother with, and thus remain his. It is a rare child who can come through his schooling with much left of his curiosity, his independence or his sense of his own dignity, competence and worth.

So much for criticism. What do we need to do? Many things. Some are easy—we can do them right away. Some are hard, and may take some time. Take a hard one first. We should abolish compulsory school attendance. At the very least we should modify it, perhaps by giving children every year a large number of authorized absences. Our compulsory school-attendance laws once served a humane and useful purpose. They protected children's right to some schooling, against those adults who would otherwise have denied it to them in order to exploit their labor, in farm, store, mine or factory. Today the laws help nobody, not the schools, not the teachers, not the children. To keep kids in school who would rather not be there costs the schools an enormous amount of time and trouble—to say nothing of what it costs to repair the damage that these angry and resentful prisoners do every time they get a chance. Every teacher knows that any kid in class who, for whatever reason, would rather not be there not only doesn't learn anything himself but makes it a great deal tougher for anyone else. As for protecting the children from exploitation, the chief and indeed only exploiters of children these days *are* the schools. Kids caught in the college rush more often than not work 70 hours or more a week, most of it on paper busywork. For kids who aren't going to college, school is just a useless time waster, preventing them from earning some money or doing some useful work, or even doing some true learning.

Objections. "If kids didn't have to go to school, they'd all be out in the streets." No, they wouldn't. In the first place, even if schools stayed just the way they are, children would spend at least some time there because that's where they'd be likely to find friends; it's a natural meeting place for children. In the second place, schools wouldn't stay the way they are, they'd get better, because we would have to start making them what they ought to be right now—places where children would *want* to be. In the third place, those children who did not want to go to school could find, particularly if we stirred up our brains and gave them a little help, other things to do—the things many children now do during their summers and holidays.

There's something easier we could do. We need to get kids out of the school buildings, give them a chance to learn about the world at first hand. It is a very recent idea, and a crazy one, that the way to teach our young people about the world they live in is to take them out of it and shut them up in brick boxes. Fortunately, educators are beginning to realize this. In Philadelphia and Portland, Oreg., to pick only two places I happen to have heard about, plans are being drawn up for public schools that won't have any school buildings at all, that will take the students out into the city and help them to use it and its people as a learning resource. In other words, students, perhaps in groups, perhaps independently, will go to libraries, museums, exhibits, court rooms, legislatures, radio and TV stations, meetings, businesses and laboratories to learn about their world and society at first hand. A small private school in Washington is already doing this. It makes sense. We need more of it.

As we help children get out into the world, to do their learning 11 there, we get more of the world into the schools. Aside from their parents, most children never have any close contact with any adults except people whose sole business is children. No wonder they have no idea what adult life or work is like. We need to bring a lot more people who are *not* full-time teachers into the schools and into contact with the children. In New York City, under the Teachers and Writers Collaborative, real writers, working writers—novelists, poets, playwrights—come into the schools, read their work, and talk to the children about the problems of their craft. The children eat it up. In another school I know of, a practicing attorney from a nearby city comes in every month or so and talks to several classes about the law. Not the law as it is in books but as he sees it and encounters it in his cases, his problems, his work. And the children love it. It is real, grown-up, true, not *My Weekly Reader,* not "social studies," not lies and baloney.

Something easier yet. Let children work together, help each other, 12 learn from each other and each other's mistakes. We now know, from the experience of many schools, both rich-suburban and poor-city, that children are often the best teachers of other children. What is more important, we know that when a fifth- or sixth-grader who has been having trouble with reading starts helping a first-grader, his own reading sharply improves. A number of schools are beginning to use what some call Paired Learning. This means that you let children form partnerships with other children, do their work, even including their tests, together, and share whatever marks or results this work gets—just like grownups in the real world. It seems to work.

Let the children learn to judge their own work. A child learning to 13 talk does not learn by being corrected all the time—if corrected too much, he will stop talking. *He* compares, a thousand times a day, the difference between language as he uses it and as those around him use it. Bit by bit, he makes the necessary changes to make his language like other people's. In the same way, kids learning to do all the other things they learn without adult teachers—to walk, run, climb, whistle, ride a bike, skate, play games, jump rope—compare their own performance with what more skilled people do, and slowly make the needed changes. But in school we never give a child a chance to detect his mistakes, let alone correct them. We do it all for him. We act as if we thought he would never notice a mistake unless it was pointed out to him, or correct it unless he was made to. Soon he becomes dependent on the expert. We should let him do it himself. Let him figure out, with the help of other children if he wants it, what this word says, what is the answer to that problem, whether this is a good way of saying or doing this or that. If right answers are involved, as in some math or science, give him the answer book, let him correct his own papers. Why should we teachers waste time on such donkey work? Our job should be to help the kid when he tells us that he can't find a way to get the right answer. Let's get rid of all this nonsense of grades, exams, marks. We don't know now, and we never will know, how to measure what another person knows or understands. We certainly can't find out by asking him questions. All we find out is what he doesn't know—which is what most tests are for, anyway. Throw it all out, and let the child learn what every educated person must someday learn, how to measure his own understanding, how to know what he knows or does not know.

We could also abolish the fixed, required curriculum. People remem- 14 ber only what is interesting and useful to them, what helps them make sense of the world, or helps them get along in it. All else they quickly forget, if they ever learn it at all. The idea of a "body of knowledge," to be picked up in school and used for the rest of one's life, is nonsense in a world as complicated and rapidly changing as ours. Anyway, the most important questions and problems of our time are not *in* the curriculum, not even in the hotshot universities, let alone the schools.

Children want, more than they want anything else, and even after 15 years of miseducation, to make sense of the world, themselves, and other human beings. Let them get at this job, with our help if they ask for it, in the way that makes most sense to them.

Responding to Reading

1. In what ways does Holt say that schools fail children?
2. According to Holt, what should schools do to correct their shortcomings? Are his suggestions realistic or unrealistic?
3. In paragraph 13, Holt says, "'Let's get rid of the all this nonsense of grades, exams, marks." Do you agree? What would be the advantages and disadvantages of this course of action?

THE MYTH OF THE CAVE
Plato

The ancient Greek philosopher Plato (428–347 B.C.E.) lived in Athens during a time of rich intellectual and artistic activity. The student of another famous philosopher, Socrates, he carried on his mentor's work after Socrates was put to death for heresy in 399. Most of his philosophic writings are cast in the form of dialogues between Socrates and various other characters, in which Socrates, through artful questioning, leads his listener to a new understanding of whatever topic they are discussing. "The Myth of the Cave," one of Plato's most famous and influential works, is part of The Republic, *a larger essay on the ideal aims of government. In it Socrates, as presented by Plato, muses on what humans can actually know—on the limits of perception and our understanding of what is true and good.*

And now, I said, let me show in a figure how far our nature is 1 enlightened or unenlightened—Behold! human beings living in an underground den, which has a mouth open toward the light and reaching all along the den; here they have been from their childhood, and have their legs and necks chained so that they cannot move, and can only see before them, being prevented by the chains from turning round their heads. Above and behind them a fire is blazing at a distance, and between the fire and the prisoners there is a raised way; and you will see, if you look, a low wall built along the way, like the screen which marionette players have in front of them, over which they show the puppets.

I see. 2

And do you see, I said, men passing along the wall carrying all 3 sorts of vessels, and statues and figures of animals made of wood and stone and various materials, which appear over the wall? Some of them are talking, others silent.

You have shown me a strange image, and they are strange prisoners. 4

Like ourselves, I replied; and they see only their own shadows, or 5 the shadows of one another, which the fire throws on the opposite wall of the cave?

True, he said; how could they see anything but the shadows if they 6 were never allowed to move their heads?

And of the objects which are being carried in like manner they 7 would only see the shadows?

Yes, he said. 8

And if they were able to converse with one another, would they not 9 suppose that they were naming what was actually before them?

Very true.   10

And suppose further that the prison had an echo which came from   11
the other side, would they not be sure when one of the passersby spoke
that the voice which they heard came from the passing shadow?

No question, he replied.   12

To them, I said, the truth would be literally nothing but the shad-   13
ows of the images.

That is certain.   14

And now look again, and see what will naturally follow if the   15
prisoners are released and disabused of their error. At first, when any
of them is liberated and compelled suddenly to stand up and turn his
neck round and walk and look toward the light, he will suffer sharp
pains; the glare will distress him, and he will be unable to see the realities of which in his former state he had seen the shadows; and then
conceive some one saying to him, that what he saw before was an illusion, but that now, when he is approaching nearer to being and his eye
is turned toward more real existence, he has a clearer vision—what
will be his reply? And you may further imagine that his instructor is
pointing to the objects as they pass and requiring him to name them—
will he not be perplexed? Will he not fancy that the shadows which he
formerly saw are truer than the objects which are now shown to him?

Far truer.   16

And if he is compelled to look straight at the light, will he not have   17
a pain in his eyes which will make him turn away to take refuge in the
objects of vision which he can see, and which he will conceive to be in
reality clearer than the things which are now being shown to him?

True, he said.   18

And suppose once more, that he is reluctantly dragged up a steep   19
and rugged ascent, and held fast until he is forced into the presence of
the sun himself, is he not likely to be pained and irritated? When he
approaches the light his eyes will be dazzled, and he will not be able to
see anything at all of what are now called realities.

Not all in a moment, he said.   20

He will require to grow accustomed to the sight of the upper   21
world. And first he will see the shadows best, next the reflections of
men and other objects in the water, and then the objects themselves;
then he will gaze upon the light of the moon and the stars and the
spangled heaven; and he will see the sky and the stars by night better
than the sun or the light of the sun by day?

Certainly.   22

Last of all he will be able to see the sun, and not mere reflections of   23
him in the water, but he will see him in his own proper place, and not
in another; and he will contemplate him as he is.

Certainly.   24

He will then proceed to argue that this is he who gives the season   25
and the years, and is the guardian of all that is in the visible world, and
in a certain way the cause of all things which he and his fellows have
been accustomed to behold?

Clearly, he said, he would first see the sun and then reason about   26
him.

And when he remembered his old habitation, and the wisdom of   27
the den and his fellow-prisoners, do you not suppose that he would
felicitate himself on the change, and pity them?

Certainly, he would.   28

And if they were in the habit of conferring honors among them selves   29
on those who were quickest to observe the passing shadows and to
remark which of them went before, and which followed after, and which
were together; and who were therefore best able to draw conclusions as
to the future, do you think that he would care for such honors and glories, or envy the possessors of them? Would he not say with Homer,

> Better to be the poor servant of a poor master,

and to endure anything, rather than think as they do and live after their
manner?

Yes, he said, I think that he would rather suffer anything than enter-   30
tain these false notions and live in this miserable manner.

Imagine once more, I said, such an one coming suddenly out of the   31
sun to be replaced in his old situation; would he not be certain to have
his eyes full of darkness?

To be sure, he said.   32

And if there were a contest, and he had to compete in measuring   33
the shadows with the prisoners who had never moved out of the den,
while his sight was still weak, and before his eyes had become steady
(and the time which would be needed to acquire this new habit of sight
might be very considerable), would he not be ridiculous? Men would
say of him that up he went and down he came without his eyes; and
that it was better not even to think of ascending; and if any one tried to
loose another and lead him up to the light, let them only catch the
offender, and they would put him to death.

No question, he said.   34

This entire allegory, I said, you may now append, dear Glaucon, to   35
the previous argument; the prison-house is the world of sight, the light
of the fire is the sun, and you will not misapprehend me if you interpret the journey upwards to be the ascent of the soul into the intellectual world according to my poor belief, which, at your desire, I have
expressed—whether rightly or wrongly God knows. But, whether true
or false, my opinion is that in the world of knowledge the idea of good

appears last of all, and is seen only with an effort; and, when seen, is also inferred to be the universal author of all things beautiful and right, parent of light and of the lord of light in this visible world, and the immediate source of reason and truth in the intellectual; and that this is the power upon which he who would act rationally either in public or private life must have his eye fixed.

I agree, he said, as far as I am able to understand you.   36

Moreover, I said, you must not wonder that those who attain to this   37 beatific vision are unwilling to descend to human affairs; for their souls are ever hastening into the upper world where they desire to dwell; which desire of theirs is very natural, if our allegory may be trusted.

Yes, very natural.   38

And is there anything surprising in one who passes from divine   39 contemplations to the evil state of man, misbehaving himself in a ridiculous manner; if, while his eyes are blinking and before he has become accustomed to the surrounding darkness, he is compelled to fight in courts of law, or in other places, about the images or the shadows of images of justice, and is endeavoring to meet the conceptions of those who have never yet seen absolute justice?

Anything but surprising, he replied.   40

Any one who has common sense will remember that the bewilder-   41 ments of the eyes are of two kinds, and arise from two causes, either from coming out of the light or from going into the light, which is true of the mind's eye, quite as much as of the bodily eye; and he who remembers this when he sees any one whose vision is perplexed and weak, will not be too ready to laugh; he will first ask whether that soul of man has come out of the brighter life, and is unable to see because unaccustomed to the dark, or having turned from darkness to the day is dazzled by excess of light. And he will count the one happy in his condition and state of being, and he will pity the other; or, if he have a mind to laugh at the soul which comes from below into the light, there will be more reason in this than in the laugh which greets him who returns from above out of the light into the den.

That, he said, is a very just distinction.   42

But then, if I am right, certain professors of education must be   43 wrong when they say that they can put a knowledge into the soul which was not there before, like sight into blind eyes.

They undoubtedly say this, he replied.   44

Whereas, our argument shows that the power and capacity or   45 learning exists in the soul already; and that just as the eye was unable to turn from darkness to light without the whole body, so too the instrument of knowledge can only by the movement of the whole soul be turned from the world of becoming into that of being, and learn by degrees to endure the sight of being, and of the brightest and best of being, or in other words, of the good.

Very true.   46

And must there not be some art which will effect conversion in the   47
easiest and quickest manner; not implanting the faculty of sight, for
that exists already, but has been turned in the wrong direction, and is
looking away from the truth?

Yes, he said, such an art may be presumed.   48

And whereas the other so-called virtues of the soul seem to be akin 49
to bodily qualities, for even when they are not originally innate they
can be implanted later by habit and exercise, the virtue of wisdom
more than anything else contains a divine element which always
remains, and by this conversion is rendered useful and profitable; or,
on the other hand, hurtful and useless. Did you never observe the narrow intelligence flashing from the keen eye of a clever rogue—how
eager he is, how clearly his paltry soul sees the way to his end; he is the
reverse of blind, but his keen eyesight is forced into the service of evil,
and he is mischievous in proportion to his cleverness?

Very true, he said.   50

But what if there had been a circumcision of such natures in the   51
days of their youth; and they had been severed from those sensual
pleasures, such as eating and drinking, which, like leaden weights,
were attached to them at their birth, and which drag them down and
turn the vision of their souls upon the things that are below—if, I say,
they had been released from these impediments and turned in the
opposite direction, the very same faculty in them would have seen the
truth as keenly as they see what their eyes are turned to now.

Very likely.   52

Yes, I said; and there is another thing which is likely, or rather a 53
necessary inference from what has preceded, that neither the uneducated and uninformed of the truth, nor yet those who never make an
end of their education, will be able ministers of State; not the former,
because they have no single aim of duty which is the rule of all their
actions, private as well as public; nor the latter, because they will not
act at all except upon compulsion, fancying that they are already
dwelling apart in the islands of the blest.

Very true, he replied.   54

Then, I said, the business of us who are the founders of the State   55
will be to compel the best minds to attain that knowledge which we
have already shown to be the greatest of all—they must continue to
ascend until they arrive at the good; but when they have ascended and
seen enough we must not allow them to do as they do now.

What do you mean?   56

I mean that they remain in the upper world: but this must not be   57
allowed; they must be made to descend again among the prisoners in
the den, and partake of their labors and honors, whether they are
worth having or not.

But is not this unjust? he said; ought we to give them a worse life, 58
when they might have a better?

You have again forgotten, my friend, I said, the intention of the leg- 59
islator, who did not aim at making any one class in the State happy
above the rest; the happiness was to be in the whole State, and he held
the citizens together by persuasion and necessity, making them benefactors of the State, and therefore benefactors of one another; to this
end he created them, not to please themselves, but to be his instruments in binding up the State.

True, he said, I had forgotten. 60

Observe, Glaucon, that there will be no injustice in compelling our 61
philosophers to have a care and providence of others; we shall explain
to them that in other States, men of their class are not obliged to share
in the toils of politics; and this is reasonable, for they grow up at their
own sweet will, and the government would rather not have them.
Being self-taught, they cannot be expected to show any gratitude for a
culture which they have never received. But we have brought you into
the world to be rulers of the hive, kings of yourselves and of the other
citizens; and have educated you far better and more perfectly than they
have been educated; and you are better able to share in the double
duty. Wherefore each of you, when his turn comes, must go down to
the general underground abode, and get the habit of seeing in the dark.
When you have acquired the habit, you will see ten thousand times
better than the inhabitants of the den, and you will know what the several images are, and what they represent, because you have seen the
beautiful and just and good in their truth. And thus our State which is
also yours will be a reality, and not a dream only, and will be administered in a spirit unlike that of other States, in which men fight with one
another about shadows only and are distracted in the struggle for
power, which in their eyes is a great good. Whereas the truth is that the
State in which the rulers are most reluctant to govern is always the best
and most quietly governed, and the State in which they are most eager,
the worst.

Quite true, he replied. 62

And will our pupils, when they hear this, refuse to take their turn 63
at the toils of State, when they are allowed to spend the greater part of
their time with one another in the heavenly light?

Impossible, he answered; for they are just men, and the commands 64
which we impose upon them are just; there can be no doubt that every
one of them will take office as a stern necessity, and not after the fashion of our present rulers of State.

Yes, my friend, I said; and there lies the point. You must contrive 65
for your future rulers another and a better life than that of a ruler, and
then you may have a well-ordered State; for only in the State which

offers this, will they rule who are truly rich, not in silver and gold, but in virtue and wisdom, which are the true blessings of life. Whereas if they go to the administration of public affairs, poor and hungering after their own private advantage, thinking that hence they are to snatch the chief good, order there can never be; for they will be fighting about office, and the civil and domestic broils which thus arise will be the ruin of the rulers themselves and of the whole State.

Most true, he replied.   66

And the only life which looks down upon the life of political ambi- 67
tion is that of true philosophy. Do you know of any other?

Indeed, I do not, he said.   68

And those who govern ought not to be lovers of the task? For, if 69
they are, there will be rival lovers, and they will fight.

No question.   70

Who then are those whom we shall compel to be guardians? Surely 71
they will be the men who are wisest about affairs of State, and by whom the State is best administered, and who at the same time have other honors and another and a better life than that of politics?

They are the men, and I will choose them, he replied.   72

And now shall we consider in what way such guardians will be 73
produced, and how they are to be brought from darkness to light—as some are said to have ascended from the world below to the gods?

By all means, he replied.   74

The process, I said, is not the turning over of an oyster-shell, but 75
the turning round of a soul passing from a day which is little better than night to the true day of being, that is, the ascent from below which we affirm to be true philosophy?

Quite so.   76

Responding to Reading

1. In what way does the allegory of the cave present Socrates' ideas about education?
2. Why, in paragraph 19, does the prisoner have to be dragged to the cave opening to look at the sun? What does this image imply about education? About the role of teachers?
3. What does Socrates mean when he says, "the State in which rulers are most reluctant to govern is always the best and most quietly governed, and the State in which they are most eager, the worst" (61). Does your experience with politics suggest that Socrates's observation is accurate or inaccurate?

READING THE RIVER

Mark Twain

Mark Twain (born Samuel Clemens, 1835–1910) remains today one of the most beloved of American writers. Raised in Hannibal, Missouri, he worked as a printer and later as a riverboat pilot on the Mississippi. During the Civil War, Twain went west, honing his writing talents at newspapers in Colorado and later in San Francisco. He published his first volume of humorous sketches and essays in 1867 and achieved fame and fortune with a variety of later works: accounts of his travels, such as Innocents Abroad *(1868) and* Roughing It *(1872); classic novels drawing on the rich material of his midwestern childhood, like* The Adventures of Tom Sawyer *(1876) and* The Adventures of Huckleberry Finn *(1884); the satiric* A Connecticut Yankee in King, Arthur's Court *(1889); and the story of his life as a riverboat pilot,* Life on the Mississippi *(1884). In the following excerpt from* Life on the Mississippi, *Twain reflects on the contrast between the experienced navigator's view of the river with that of an inexperienced passenger.*

Now when I had mastered the language of this water and had come to know every trifling feature that bordered the great river as familiarly as I knew the letters of the alphabet, I had made a valuable acquisition. But I had lost something, too. I had lost something which could never be restored to me while I lived. All the grace, the beauty, the poetry, had gone out of the majestic river! I still kept in mind a certain wonderful sunset which I witnessed when steamboating was new to me. A broad expanse of the river was turned to blood; in the middle distance the red hue brightened into gold, through which a solitary log came floating, black and conspicuous; in one place a long, slanting mark lay sparkling upon the water; in another the surface was broken by boiling, tumbling rings, that were as many-tinted as an opal; where the ruddy flush was faintest, was a smooth spot that was covered with graceful circles and radiating lines, ever so delicately traced; the shore on our left was densely wooded and the somber shadow that fell from this forest was broken in one place by a long, ruffled trail that shone like silver; and high above the forest wall a clean-stemmed dead tree waved a single leafy bough that glowed like a flame in the unobstructed splendor that was flowing from the sun. There were graceful curves, reflected images, woody heights, soft distances, and over the whole scene, far and near, the dissolving lights drifted steadily, enriching it every passing moment with new marvels of coloring.

I stood like one bewitched. I drank it in, in a speechless rapture. The world was new to me and I had never seen anything like this at home. But as I have said, a day came when I began to cease from noting the glories and the charms which the moon and the sun and the twilight wrought upon the river's face; another day came when I ceased altogether to note them. Then, if that sunset scene had been repeated, I should have looked upon it without rapture, and should have commented upon it inwardly after this fashion: "This sun means that we are going to have wind to-morrow; that floating log means that the river is rising, small thanks to it; that slanting mark on the water refers to a bluff reef which is going to kill somebody's steamboat one of these nights, if it keeps on stretching out like that; those tumbling 'boils' show a dissolving bar and a changing channel there; the lines and circles in the slick water over yonder are a warning that that troublesome place is shoaling up dangerously; that silver streak in the shadow of the forest is the 'break' from a new snag and he has located himself in the very best place he could have found to fish for steamboats; that tall dead tree, with a single living branch, is not going to last long, and then how is a body ever going to get through this blind place at night without the friendly old landmark?"

No, the romance and beauty were all gone from the river. All the value any feature of it had for me now was the amount of usefulness it could furnish toward compassing the safe piloting of a steamboat. Since those days, I have pitied doctors from my heart. What does the lovely flush in a beauty's cheek mean to a doctor but a "break" that ripples above some deadly disease?[1] Are not all her visible charms sown thick with what are to him the signs and symbols of hidden decay? Does he ever see her beauty at all, or doesn't he simply view her professionally and comment upon her unwholesome condition all to himself? And doesn't he sometimes wonder whether he has gained most or lost most by learning his trade?

[handwritten margin note: doc sees person as not sick just as healthy beauty is gone from river when becomes familiar]

Responding to Reading

1. In what way is the river like a book? What two ways of reading the river does Twain discuss? According to Twain, which way of reading is more valuable?

2. Twain uses his discussion of reading the river to express his ideas about education. According to Twain, what is gained by getting an education? What is lost? Does he think the gain is worth the price?

3. Twain ends his essay by saying that he has always pitied doctors. Why? In what way is being a doctor like being, a riverboat pilot?

---

[1] Red cheeks are one of the signs of tuberculosis. [Eds.]

WHEN I HEARD THE LEARN'D ASTRONOMER

Walt Whitman

Walt Whitman (1819–1892) was a bold, eccentric character who wrote radical poetry about sexuality, technology, and nature to unsettle "all the settled laws." He first published his best-known work, Leaves of Grass, *in 1855 with no author's name on the title page. Whitman was also a journalist who reported on the Civil War and an essayist who commented on American society and democracy. He wrote about and for working-class Americans, but his work appealed mostly to intellectuals. In the poem "When I Heard the Learn'd Astronomer," Whitman unites two of his favorite and seemingly incompatible themes: science and nature.*

When I heard the learn'd astronomer,
When the proofs, the figures were ranged in columns before
me,
When I was shown the charts and diagrams, to add, divide,
and measure them,
When I sitting heard the astronomer where he lectured with
much applause in the lecture-room,
How soon unaccountable I became tired and sick,   5
Till rising and gliding out I wander'd off by myself,
In the mystical moist night-air, and from time to time,
Look'd up in perfect silence at the stars.

Responding to Reading

1. What does the speaker in the poem dislike about the astronomer's lecture? Why does the speaker become "tired and sick" (5)?
2. Why does the speaker think that his view of the stars is preferable to that of the astronomer? Do you agree?
3. Whitman's poem can be divided into two four-line segments. What ideas about education are expressed in each segment?

THE SANCTUARY OF SCHOOL

Lynda Barry

Born in Richland Center, Wisconsin, Lynda Barry (1956–   ) grew up in Seattle, Washington, as part of an extended Filipino family (her mother was Filipino, her father an alcoholic Norwegian-Irishman). She majored in art at Evergreen State College—the first member of her family to go on to higher education—and began her career as a cartoonist shortly after graduation. Known as a chronicler of adolescent angst both in her syndicated comic strip Ernie Pook's Comeek *and in collections like* The Freddie Stories *(1997) and* Cruddy *(2000). Barry has also written a widely admired novel about adolescence,* The Good Times Are Killing Me *(1988), which was turned into a successful musical play. In "The Sanctuary of School," Barry remembers her Seattle grade school in a racially mixed neighborhood as a nurturing safe haven from her difficult family life.*

I was 7 years old the first time I snuck out of the house in the dark. 1 It was winter and my parents had been fighting all night. They were short on money and long on relatives who kept "temporarily" moving into our house because they had nowhere else to go.

My brother and I were used to giving up our bedroom. We slept on 2 the couch, something we actually liked because it put us that much closer to the light of our lives, our television.

At night when everyone was asleep, we lay on our pillows watch- 3 ing it with the sound off. We watched Steve Allen's mouth moving. We watched Johnny Carson's mouth moving. We watched movies filled with gangsters shooting machine guns into packed rooms, dying soldiers hurling a last grenade and beautiful women crying at windows. Then the sign-off finally came and we tried to sleep.

The morning I snuck out, I woke up filled with a panic about need- 4 ing to get to school. The sun wasn't quite up yet but my anxiety was so fierce that I just got dressed, walked quietly across the kitchen and let myself out the back door.

It was quiet outside. Stars were still out. Nothing moved and no one 5 was in the street. It was as if someone had turned the sound off on the world.

I walked the alley, breaking thin ice over the puddles with my 6 shoes. I didn't know why I was walking to school in the dark. I didn't think about it. All I knew was a feeling of panic, like the panic that strikes kids when they realize they are lost.

That feeling eased the moment I turned the corner and saw the dark 7 outline of my school at the top of the hill. My school was made up of about 15 nondescript portable classrooms set down on a fenced concrete lot in a rundown Seattle neighborhood, but it had the most beautiful view of the Cascade Mountains. You could see them from anywhere on the playfield and you could see them from the windows of my classroom—Room 2.

I walked over to the monkey bars and hooked my arms around the 8 cold metal. I stood for a long time just looking across Rainier Valley. The sky was beginning to whiten and I could hear a few birds.

In a perfect world my absence at home would not have gone unno- 9 ticed. I would have had two parents in a panic to locate me, instead of two parents in a panic to locate an answer to the hard question of survival during a deep financial and emotional crisis.

But in an overcrowded and unhappy home, it's incredibly easy for 10 any child to slip away. The high levels of frustration, depression and anger in my house made my brother and me invisible. We were children with the sound turned off. And for us, as for the steadily increasing number of neglected children in this country, the only place where we could count on being noticed was at school.

"Hey there, young lady. Did you forget to go home last night?" It 11 was Mr. Gunderson, our janitor, whom we all loved. He was nice and he was funny and he was old with white hair, thick glasses and an unbelievable number of keys. I could hear them jingling as he walked across the playfield. I felt incredibly happy to see him.

He let me push his wheeled garbage can between the different 12 portables as he unlocked each room. He let me turn on the lights and raise the window shades and I saw my school slowly come to life. I saw Mrs. Holman, our school secretary, walk into the office without her orange lipstick on yet. She waved.

I saw the fifth-grade teacher Mr. Cunningham, walking under the 13 breezeway eating a hard roll. He waved.

And I saw my teacher, Mrs. Claire LeSane, walking toward us in a 14 red coat and calling my name in a very happy and surprised way, and suddenly my throat got tight and my eyes stung and I ran toward her crying. It was something that surprised us both.

It's only thinking about it now, 28 years later, that I realize I was cry- 15 ing from relief. I was with my teacher, and in a while I was going to sit at my desk, with my crayons and pencils and books and classmates all around me, and for the next six hours I was going to enjoy a thoroughly secure, warm and stable world. It was a world I absolutely relied on. Without it, I don't know where I would have gone that morning.

Mrs. LeSane asked me what was wrong and when I said "Nothing," 16 she seemingly left it at that. But she asked me if I would carry her purse for her, an honor above all honors, and she asked if I wanted to come into Room 2 early and paint.

She believed in the natural healing power of painting and drawing 17 for troubled children. In the back of her room there was always a drawing table and an easel with plenty of supplies, and sometimes during the day she would come up to you for what seemed like no good reason and quietly ask if you wanted to go to the back table and "make some pictures for Mrs. LeSane." We all had a chance at it—to sit apart from the class for a while to paint, draw and silently work out impossible problems on 11 × 17 sheets of newsprint.

Drawing came to mean everything to me. At the back table in Room 18 2, I learned to build myself a life preserver that I could carry into my home.

We all know that a good education system saves lives, but the people of this country are still told that cutting the budget for public schools is necessary, that poor salaries for teachers are all we can manage and that art, music and all creative activities must be the first to go when times are lean.

Before- and after-school programs are cut and we are told that public schools are not made for baby-sitting children. If parents are neglectful temporarily or permanently, for whatever reason, it's certainly sad, but their unlucky children must fend for themselves. Or slip through the cracks. Or wander in a dark night alone.

We are told in a thousand ways that not only are public schools not 21 important, but that the children who attend them, the children who need them most, are not important either. We leave them to learn from the blind eye of a television, or to the mercy of "a thousand points of light"[1] that can be as far away as stars.

I was lucky. I had Mrs. LeSane. I had Mr. Gunderson. I had an abundance of art supplies. And I had a particular brand of neglect in my home that allowed me to slip away and get to them. But what about the rest of the kids who weren't as lucky? What happened to them?

By the time the bell rang that morning I had finished my drawing 23 and Mrs. LeSane pinned it up on the special bulletin board she reserved for drawings from the back table. It was the same picture I always drew—a sun in the corner of a blue sky over a nice house with flowers all around it.

Mrs. LeSane asked us to please stand, face the flag, place our right 24 hands over our hearts and say the Pledge of Allegiance. Children across the country do it faithfully. I wonder now when the country will face its children and say a pledge right back.

---

[1] Catchphrase for former president George Bush's plan to substitute volunteerism for government programs. [Eds.]

In the Store I was the person of the moment. The birthday girl. The center. Bailey[1] had graduated the year before, although to do so he had had to forfeit all pleasures to make up for his time lost in Baton Rouge.

My class was wearing butter-yellow piqué dresses, and Momma launched out on mine. She smocked the yoke into tiny crisscrossing puckers, then shirred the rest of the bodice. Her dark fingers ducked in and out of the lemony cloth as she embroidered raised daisies around the hem. Before she considered herself finished she had added a crocheted cuff on the puff sleeves, and a pointy crocheted collar.

I was going to be lovely. A walking model of all the various styles of fine hand sewing and it didn't worry me that I was only twelve years old and merely graduating from the eighth grade. Besides, many teachers in Arkansas Negro schools had only that diploma and were licensed to impart wisdom.

The days had become longer and more noticeable. The faded beige of former times had been replaced with strong and sure colors. I began to see my classmates' clothes, their skin tones, and the dust that waved off pussy willows. Clouds that lazed across the sky were objects of great concern to me. Their shiftier shapes might have held a message that in my new happiness and with a little bit of time I'd soon decipher. During that period I looked at the arch of heaven so religiously my neck kept a steady ache. I had taken to smiling more often, and my jaws hurt from the unaccustomed activity. Between the two physical sore spots, I suppose I could have been uncomfortable, but that was not the case. As a member of the winning team (the graduating class of 1940) I had outdistanced unpleasant sensations by miles. I was headed for the freedom of open fields.

Youth and social approval allied themselves with me and we trammeled memories of slights and insults. The wind of our swift passage remodeled my features. Lost tears were pounded to mud and then to dust. Years of withdrawal were brushed aside and left behind, as hanging ropes of parasitic moss.

My work alone had awarded me a top place and I was going to be one of the first called in the graduating ceremonies. On the classroom blackboard, as well as on the bulletin board in the auditorium, there were blue stars and white stars and red stars. No absences, no tardinesses, and my academic work was among the best of the year. I could say the preamble to the Constitution even faster than Bailey. We timed ourselves often: "WethepeopleoftheUnitedStatesinordertoformamoreperfectunion . . ." I had memorized the Presidents of the United States from Washington to Roosevelt in chronological as well as alphabetical order.

6

7

8

9

10

11

---

[1] Angelou's brother. The Store was run by Angelou's grandmother, whom she called Momma, and Momma's son, Uncle Willie. [Eds.]

My hair pleased me too. Gradually the black mass had lengthened 12 and thickened, so that it kept at last to its braided pattern, and I didn't have to yank my scalp off when I tried to comb it.

Louise and I had rehearsed the exercises until we tired out our- 13 selves. Henry Reed was class valedictorian. He was a small, very black boy with hooded eyes, a long, broad nose and an oddly shaped head. I had admired him for years because each term he and I vied for the best grades in our class. Most often he bested me, but instead of being disappointed I was pleased that we shared top places between us. Like many Southern Black children, he lived with his grandmother, who was as strict as Momma and as kind as she knew how to be. He was courteous, respectful and soft-spoken to elders, but on the playground he chose to play the roughest games. I admired him. Anyone, I reckoned, sufficiently afraid or sufficiently dull could be polite. But to be able to operate at a top level with both adults and children was admirable.

His valedictory speech was entitled "To Be or Not to Be." The rigid 14 tenth-grade teacher had helped him write it. He'd been working on the dramatic stresses for months.

The weeks until graduation were filled with heady activities. A 15 group of small children were to be presented in a play about buttercups and daisies and bunny rabbits. They could be heard throughout the building practicing their hops and their little songs that sounded like silver bells. The older girls (nongraduates, of course) were assigned the task of making refreshments for the night's festivities. A tangy scent of ginger, cinnamon, nutmeg and chocolate wafted around the home economics building as the budding cooks made samples for themselves and their teachers.

In every corner of the workshop, axes and saws split fresh timber as 16 the woodshop boys made sets and stage scenery. Only the graduates were left out of the general bustle. We were free to sit in the library at the back of the building or look in quite detachedly, naturally, on the measures being taken for our event.

Even the minister preached on graduation the Sunday before. His 17 subject was, "Let your light so shine that men will see your good works and praise your Father, Who is in Heaven." Although the sermon was purported to be addressed to us, he used the occasion to speak to backsliders, gamblers and general ne'er-do-wells. But since he had called our names at the beginning of the service we were mollified.

Among Negroes the tradition was to give presents to children going 18 only from one grade to another. How much more important this was when the person was graduating at the top of the class. Uncle Willie and Momma had sent away for a Mickey Mouse watch like Bailey's. Louise gave me four embroidered handkerchiefs. (I gave her crocheted doilies.) Mrs. Sneed, the minister's wife, made me an undershirt to wear for graduation, and nearly every customer gave me a nickel or maybe even a dime with the instruction "Keep on moving to higher ground," or some such encouragement.

Amazingly the great day finally dawned and I was out of bed 19 before I knew it. I threw open the back door to see it more clearly, but Momma said, "Sister, come away from that door and put your robe on."

I hoped the memory of that morning would never leave me. 20 Sunlight was itself young, and the day had none of the insistence maturity would bring it in a few hours. In my robe and barefoot in the backyard, under cover of going to see about my new beans, I gave myself up to the gentle warmth and thanked God that no matter what evil I had done in my life He had allowed me to live to see this day. Somewhere in my fatalism I had expected to die, accidentally, and never have the chance to walk up the stairs in the auditorium and gracefully receive my hard-earned diploma. Out of God's merciful bosom I had won reprieve.

Bailey came out in his robe and gave me a box wrapped in 21 Christmas paper. He said he had saved his money for months to pay for it. It felt like a box of chocolates, but I knew Bailey wouldn't save money to buy candy when we had all we could want under our noses.

He was as proud of the gift as I. It was a soft-leather-bound copy of a 22 collection of poems by Edgar Allan Poe, or, as Bailey and I called him, "Eap." I turned to "Annabel Lee" and we walked up and down the garden rows, the cool dirt between our toes, reciting the beautifully sad lines.

Momma made a Sunday breakfast although it was only Friday. 23 After we finished the blessing, I opened my eyes to find the watch on my plate. It was a dream of a day. Everything went smoothly and to my credit. I didn't have to be reminded or scolded for anything. Near evening I was too jittery to attend to chores, so Bailey volunteered to do all before his bath.

Days before, we had made a sign for the Store, and as we turned out 24 the lights Momma hung the cardboard over the doorknob. It read clearly: CLOSED. GRADUATION.

My dress fitted perfectly and everyone said that I looked like a sun- 25 beam in it. On the hill, going toward the school, Bailey walked behind with Uncle Willie, who muttered, "Go on, Ju." He wanted him to walk ahead with us because it embarrassed him to have to walk so slowly. Bailey said he'd let the ladies walk together, and the men would bring up the rear. We all laughed, nicely.

Little children dashed by out of the dark like fireflies. Their crepe- 26 paper dresses and butterfly wings were not made for running and we heard more than one rip, dryly, and the regretful "uh uh" that followed.

The school blazed without gaiety. The windows seemed cold and 27 unfriendly from the lower hill. A sense of ill-fated timing crept over me, and if Momma hadn't reached for my hand I would have drifted back to Bailey and Uncle Willie, and possibly beyond. She made a few slow jokes about my feet getting cold, and tugged me along to the now-strange building.

Around the front steps, assurance came back. There were my fellow 28 "greats," the graduating class. Hair brushed back, legs oiled, new dresses and pressed pleats, fresh pocket handkerchiefs and little handbags, all homesewn. Oh, we were up to snuff, all right. I joined my comrades and didn't even see my family go in to find seats in the crowded auditorium.

The school band struck up a march and all classes filed in as had 29 been rehearsed. We stood in front of our seats, as assigned, and on a signal from the choir director, we sat. No sooner had this been accomplished than the band started to play the national anthem. We rose again and sang the song, after which we recited the pledge of allegiance. We remained standing for a brief minute before the choir director and the principal signaled to us, rather desperately I thought, to take our seats. The command was so unusual that our carefully rehearsed and smooth-running machine was thrown off. For a full minute we fumbled for our chairs and bumped into each other awkwardly. Habits change or solidify under pressure, so in our state of nervous tension we had been ready to follow our usual assembly pattern: the American national anthem, then the pledge of allegiance, then the song every Black person I knew called the Negro National Anthem. All done in the same key, with the same passion and most often standing on the same foot.

Finding my seat at last, I was overcome with a presentiment of 30 worse things to come. Something unrehearsed, unplanned, was going to happen, and we were going to be made to look bad. I distinctly remember being explicit in the choice of pronoun. It was "we," the graduating class, the unit, that concerned me then.

The principal welcomed "parents and friends" and asked the 31 Baptist minister to lead us in prayer. His invocation was brief and punchy, and for a second I thought we were getting on the high road to right action. When the principal came back to the dais, however, his voice had changed. Sounds always affected me profoundly and the principal's voice was one of my favorites. During assembly it melted and lowed weakly into the audience. It had not been in my plan to listen to him, but my curiosity was piqued and I straightened up to give him my attention.

He was talking about Booker T. Washington, our "late great leader," 32 who said we can be as close as the fingers on the hand, etc. . . . Then he said a few vague things about friendship and the friendship of kindly people to those less fortunate than themselves. With that his voice nearly faded, thin, away. Like a river diminishing to a stream and then to a trickle. But he cleared his throat and said, "Our speaker tonight, who is also our friend, came from Texarkana to deliver the commencement address, but due to the irregularity of the train schedule, he's going to, as they say, 'speak and run.'" He said that we understood and wanted the man to know that we were most grateful for the time he was able to give us and then something about how we were willing always to adjust to another's program, and without more ado—"I give you Mr. Edward Donleavy."

Not one but two white men came through the door off-stage. The 33 shorter one walked to the speaker's platform, and the tall one moved to the center seat and sat down. But that was our principal's seat, and already occupied. The dislodged gentleman bounced around for a long breath or two before the Baptist minister gave him his chair, then with more dignity than the situation deserved, the minister walked off the stage.

Donleavy looked at the audience once (on reflection, I'm sure that 34 he wanted only to reassure himself that we were really there), adjusted his glasses and began to read from a sheaf of papers.

He was glad "to be here and to see the work going on just as it was 35 in the other schools."

At the first "Amen" from the audience I willed the offender to 36 immediate death by choking on the word. But Amens and Yes, sir's began to fall around the room like rain through a ragged umbrella.

He told us of the wonderful changes we children in Stamps had in 37 store. The Central School (naturally, the white school was Central) had already been granted improvements that would be in use in the fall. A well-known artist was coming from Little Rock to teach art to them. They were going to have the newest microscopes and chemistry equipment for their laboratory. Mr. Donleavy didn't leave us long in the dark over who made these improvements available to Central High. Nor were we to be ignored in the general betterment scheme he had in mind.

He said that he had pointed out to people at a very high level that 38 one of the first-line football tacklers at Arkansas Agricultural and Mechanical College had graduated from good old Lafayette County Training School. Here fewer Amen's were heard. Those few that did break through lay dully in the air with the heaviness of habit.

He went on to praise us. He went on to say how he had bragged 39 that "one of the best basketball players at Fisk² sank his first ball right here at Lafayette County Training School."

The white kids were going to have a chance to become Galileos and 40 Madame Curies and Edisons and Gauguins,³ and our boys (the girls weren't even in on it) would try to be Jesse Owenses and Joe Louises.⁴

---

² Highly regarded, predominantly black university in Nashville. [Eds.]

³ Inventors, scientists, and artists. [Eds.]

⁴ The black track star and Olympic gold medalist, and the longtime world heavyweight boxing champion, known as the "Brown Bomber." [Eds.]

Owens and the Brown Bomber were great heroes in our world, but   41
what school official in the white-goddom of Little Rock had the right to
decide that those two men must be our only heroes? Who decided that
for Henry Reed to become a scientist he had to work like George
Washington Carver, as a bootblack, to buy a lousy microscope? Bailey
was obviously always going to be too small to be an athlete, so which
concrete angel glued to what country seat had decided that if my
brother wanted to become a lawyer he had to first pay penance for his
skin by picking cotton and hoeing corn and studying correspondence
books at night for twenty years?

The man's dead words fell like bricks around the auditorium and   42
too many settled in my belly. Constrained by hard-learned manners I
couldn't look behind me, but to my left and right the proud graduating
class of 1940 had dropped their heads. Every girl in my row had found
something new to do with her handkerchief. Some folded the tiny
squares into love knots, some into triangles, but most were wadding
them, then pressing them flat on their yellow laps.

On the dais, the ancient tragedy was being replayed. Professor   43
Parsons sat, a sculptor's reject, rigid. His large, heavy body seemed
devoid of will or willingness, and his eyes said he was no longer with
us. The other teachers examined the flag (which was draped stage right)
or their notes, or the windows which opened on our now-famous playing diamond.

Graduation, the hush-hush magic time of frills and gifts and con-   44
gratulations and diplomas, was finished for me before my name was
called. The accomplishment was nothing. The meticulous maps, drawn
in three colors of ink, learning and spelling decasyllabic words, memo-
rizing the whole of *The Rape of Lucrece*[5]—it was for nothing. Donleavy
had exposed us.

We were maids and farmers, handymen and washerwomen, and   45
anything higher that we aspired to was farcical and presumptuous.

Then I wished that Gabriel Prosser and Nat Turner[6] had killed all   46
whitefolks in their beds and that Abraham Lincoln had been assassinated before the signing of the Emancipation Proclamation, and that
Harriet Tubman[7] had been killed by that blow on her head and
Christopher Columbus had drowned in the *Santa Maria*.

It was awful to be a Negro and have no control over my life. It was   47
brutal to be young and already trained to sit quietly and listen to
charges brought against my color with no chance of defense. We should
all be dead. I thought I should like to see us all dead, one on top of the

---

[5] *The Rape of Lucrece* is a long narrative poem by Shakespeare. [Eds.]

[6] Prosser and Turner both led slave rebellions. [Eds.]

[7] Harriet Tubman (1820–1913) was an African-American abolitionist who became one of the most
successful guides on the Underground Railroad. [Eds.]

other. A pyramid of flesh with the whitefolks on the bottom, as the broad base, then the Indians with their silly tomahawks and teepees and wigwams and treaties, the Negroes with their mops and recipes and cotton sacks and spirituals sticking out of their mouths. The Dutch children should all stumble in their wooden shoes and break their necks. The French should choke to death on the Louisiana Purchase (1803) while silkworms ate all the Chinese with their stupid pigtails. As a species, we were an abomination. All of us.

Donleavy was running for election, and assured our parents that if 48 he won we could count on having the only colored paved playing field in that part of Arkansas. Also—he never looked up to acknowledge the grunts of acceptance—also, we were bound to get some new equipment for the home economics building and the workshop.

He finished, and since there was no need to give any more than the 49 most perfunctory thank-you's, he nodded to the men on the stage, and the tall white man who was never introduced joined him at the door. They left with the attitude that now they were off to something really important. (The graduation ceremonies at Lafayette County Training School had been a mere preliminary.)

The ugliness they left was palpable. An uninvited guest who 50 wouldn't leave. The choir was summoned and sang a modern arrangement of "Onward, Christian Soldiers," with new words pertaining to graduates seeking their place in the world. But it didn't work. Elouise, the daughter of the Baptist minister, recited "Invictus,"[8] and I could have cried at the impertinence of "I am the master of my fate, I am the captain of my soul."

My name had lost its ring of familiarity and I had to be nudged to 51 go and receive my diploma. All my preparations had fled. I neither marched up to the stage like a conquering Amazon, not did I look in the audience for Bailey's nod of approval. Marguerite Johnson,[9] I heard the name again, my honors were read, there were noises in the audience of appreciation, and I took my place on the stage as rehearsed.

I thought about colors I hated: ecru, puce, lavender, beige and 52 black.

There was shuffling and rustling around me, then Henry Reed was 53 giving his valedictory address, "To Be or Not to Be." Hadn't he heard the whitefolks? We couldn't *be*, so the question was a waste of time. Henry's voice came out clear and strong. I feared to look at him. Hadn't he got the message? There was no "nobler in the mind" for Negroes

---

[8] An inspirational poem written in 1875 by William Ernest Henley (1849–1903). Its defiant and stoic sentiments made it extremely popular with nineteenth-century readers. [Eds.]

[9] Angelou's given name. [Eds.]

because the world didn't think we had minds, and they let us know it. "Outrageous fortune"? Now, that was a joke. When the ceremony was over I had to tell Henry Reed some things. That is, if I still cared. Not "rub," Henry, "erase." "Ah, there's the erase." Us.

Henry had been a good student in elocution. His voice rose on tides 54 of promise and fell on waves of warnings. The English teacher had helped him to create a sermon winging through Hamlet's soliloquy. To be a man, a doer, a builder, a leader, or to be a tool, an unfunny joke, a crusher of funky toadstools. I marveled that Henry could go through with the speech as if we had a choice.

I had been listening and silently rebutting each sentence with my 55 eyes closed; then there was a hush, which in an audience warns that something unplanned is happening. I looked up and saw Henry Reed, the conservative, the proper, the A student, turn his back to the audience and turn to us (the proud graduating class of 1940) and sing, nearly speaking,

> "Lift ev'ry voice and sing
> Till earth and heaven ring
> Ring with the harmonies of Liberty . . ."

It was the poem written by James Weldon Johnson. It was the music 56 composed by J. Rosamond Johnson. It was the Negro national anthem. Out of habit we were singing it.

Our mothers and fathers stood in the dark hall and joined the hymn 57 of encouragement. A kindergarten teacher led the small children onto the stage and the buttercups and daisies and bunny rabbits marked time and tried to follow:

> "Stony the road we trod
> Bitter the chastening rod
> Felt in the days when hope, unborn, had died.
> Yet with a steady beat
> Have not our weary feet   5
> Come to the place for which our fathers sighed?"

Each child I knew had learned that song with his ABC's and along 58 with "Jesus Loves Me This I Know." But I personally had never heard it before. Never heard the words, despite the thousands of times I had sung them. Never thought they had anything to do with me.

On the other hand, the words of Patrick Henry had made such an 59 impression on me that I had been able to stretch myself tall and trembling and say, "I know not what course others may take, but as for me, give me liberty or give me death."

And now I heard, really for the first time: 60

"We have come over a way that with tears
has been watered,
We have come, treading our path through
the blood of the slaughtered."

While echoes of the song shivered in the air, Henry Reed bowed his   61
head, said "Thank you," and returned to his place in the line. The tears
that slipped down many faces were not wiped away in shame.

We were on top again. As always, again. We survived. The depths   62
had been icy and dark, but now a bright sun spoke to our souls. I was
no longer simply a member of the proud graduating class of 1940; I
was a proud member of the wonderful, beautiful Negro race.

Oh, Black known and unknown poets, how often have your auc-   63
tioned pains sustained us? Who will compute the lonely nights made less
lonely by your songs, or the empty pots made less tragic by your tales?

If we were a people much given to revealing secrets, we might raise   64
monuments and sacrifice to the memories of our poets, but slavery
cured us of that weakness. It may be enough, however, to have it said
that we survive in exact relationship to the dedication of our poets
(include preachers, musicians and blues singers).

Responding to Reading

1. Angelou's graduation took place in 1940. What expectations did educators
   have for Angelou and her classmates? In what ways are these expectations
   different from the expectations of Angelou and her fellow students?
2. In what way does Mr. Donleavy's speech "educate" the graduates? How
   does Angelou's thinking change as she listens to him?
3. In paragraph 62, Angelou says, "We were on top again." In what way were
   she and the graduates "on top"? Do you think Angelou was being overly
   optimistic in light of what she had just experienced?

SAVAGE INEQUALITIES

Jonathan Kozol

Born in Boston into a "privileged and isolated" environment, Jonathan
Kozol (1936–   ) received his B.A. in literature from Harvard and drifted
into the civil rights movement in 1964. In 1967, he published Death at an
Early Age: The Destruction of the Hearts and Minds of Negro School

Children in the Boston Public Schools. *Based on his experiences as a fourth-grade teacher in an inner-city school, a position from which he was fired for "curriculum deviation," this controversial book led to a number of specific reforms. Since then, Kozol has divided his time between teaching and social activism, noting "It is a simple matter of humanity to use our limited resources in the places where they're the most needed." His books include* Illiterate America *(1985), an excerpt from which appears on page 189;* Rachel and Her Children *(1988), a study of homeless families; and* Savage Inequalities *(1991), an examination of the unequal resources available to suburban and inner-city public schools. His most recent book is* Ordinary Resurrections *(2000). In the following chapter from* Savage Inequalities, *Kozol looks at grade schools only a few miles apart in the Bronx, New York, where differences based on race and class could not be more apparent.*

"In a country where there is no distinction of class," Lord Acton 1 wrote of the United States 130 years ago, "a child is not born to the station of its parents, but with an indefinite claim to all the prizes that can be won by thought and labor. It is in conformity with the theory of equality . . . to give as near as possible to every youth an equal state in life." Americans, he said, "are unwilling that any should be deprived in childhood of the means of competition."

It is hard to read these words today without a sense of irony and 2 sadness. Denial of "the means of competition" is perhaps the single most consistent outcome of the education offered to poor children in the schools of our large cities; and nowhere is this pattern of denial more explicit or more absolute than in the public schools of New York City.

Average expenditures per pupil in the city of New York in 1987 3 were some $5,500. In the highest spending suburbs of New York (Great Neck or Manhasset, for example, on Long Island) funding levels rose above $11,000, with the highest districts in the state at $15,000. "Why . . . ," asks the city's Board of Education, "should our students receive less" than do "similar students" who live elsewhere? "The inequity is clear."

But the inequality to which these words refer goes even further than 4 the school board may be eager to reveal. "It is perhaps the supreme irony," says the nonprofit Community Service Society of New York, that "the same Board of Education which perceives so clearly the inequities" of funding between separate towns and cities "is perpetuating similar inequities" right in New York. And, in comment on the Board of Education's final statement—"the inequity is clear"—the CSS observes, "New York City's poorest . . . districts could adopt that eloquent statement with few changes."

New York City's public schools are subdivided into 32 school dis- 5 tricts. District 10 encompasses a large part of the Bronx but is, effectively, two separate districts. One of these districts, Riverdale, is in the northwest section of the Bronx. Home to many of the city's most sophisticated and well-educated families, its elementary schools have relatively few low-income students. The other section, to the south and east, is poor and heavily nonwhite.

The contrast between public schools in each of these two neighbor- 6 hoods is obvious to any visitor. At Public School 24 in Riverdale, the principal speaks enthusiastically of his teaching staff. At Public School 79, serving poorer children to the south, the principal says that he is forced to take the "tenth-best" teachers. "I thank God they're still breathing," he remarks of those from whom he must select his teachers.

Some years ago, District 10 received an allocation for computers. 7 The local board decided to give each elementary school an equal number of computers, even though the schools in Riverdale had smaller classes and far fewer students. When it was pointed out that schools in Riverdale, as a result, had twice the number of computers in proportion to their student populations as the schools in the poor neighborhoods, the chairman of the local board replied, "What is fair is what is determined . . . to be fair."

The superintendent of District 10, Fred Goldberg, tells the *New York* 8 *Times* that "every effort" is made "to distribute resources equitably." He speculates that some gap might exist because some of the poorer schools need to use funds earmarked for computers to buy basic supplies like pens and paper. Asked about the differences in teachers noted by the principals, he says there are no differences, then adds that next year he'll begin a program to improve the quality of teachers in the poorer schools. Questioned about differences in physical appearances between the richer and the poorer schools, he says, "I think it's demographics."[1]

Sometimes a school principal, whatever his background or his pol- 9 itics, looks into the faces of the children in his school and offers a disarming statement that cuts through official ambiguity. "These are the kids most in need," says Edward Flanery, the principal of one of the low-income schools, "and they get the worst teachers." For children of diverse needs in his overcrowded rooms, he says, "you need an outstanding teacher. And what do you get? You get the worst."

In order to find Public School 261 in District 10, a visitor is told to 10 look for a mortician's office. The funeral home, which faces Jerome Avenue in the North Bronx, is easy to identify by its green awning. The school is next door, in a former roller-skating rink. No sign identifies

---

[1] Marketing term tor the statistical characteristics—such as income and education—of particular population groups. [Eds.]

the building as a school. A metal awning frame without an awning supports a flagpole, but there is no flag.

In the street in front of the school there is an elevated public transit 11 line. Heavy traffic fills the street. The existence of the school is virtually concealed within this crowded city block.

In a vestibule between the outer and inner glass doors of the school 12 there is a sign with these words: "All children are capable of learning."

Beyond the inner doors a guard is seated. The lobby is long and 13 narrow. The ceiling is low. There are no windows. All the teachers that I see at first are middle-aged white women. The principal, who is also a white woman, tells me that the school's "capacity" is 900 but that there are 1,300 children here. The size of classes for fifth and sixth grade children in New York, she says, is "capped" at 32, but she says that class size in the school goes "up to 34." (I later see classes, however, as large as 37.) Classes for younger children, she goes on, are "capped at 25," but a school can go above this limit if it puts an extra adult in the room. Lack of space, she says, prevents the school from operating a pre-kindergarten program.

I ask the principal where her children go to school. They are 14 enrolled in private school, she says.

"Lunchtime is a challenge for us," she explains. "Limited space 15 obliges us to do it in three shifts, 450 children at a time."

Textbooks are scarce and children have to share their social studies 16 books. The principal says there is one full-time pupil counselor and another who is here two days a week: a ratio of 930 children to one counselor. The carpets are patched and sometimes taped together to conceal an open space. "I could use some new rugs," she observes.

To make up for the building's lack of windows and the crowded 17 feeling that results, the staff puts plants and fish tanks in the corridors. Some of the plants are flourishing. Two boys, released from class, are in a corridor beside a tank, their noses pressed against the glass. A school of pinkish fish inside the tank are darting back and forth. Farther down the corridor a small Hispanic girl is watering the plants.

Two first grade classes share a single room without a window, 18 divided only by a blackboard. Four kindergartens and a sixth grade class of Spanish-speaking children have been packed into a single room in which, again, there is no window. A second grade bilingual class of 37 children has its own room but again there is no window.

By eleven o'clock, the lunchroom is already packed with appetite 19 and life. The kids line up to get their meals, then eat them in ten minutes. After that, with no place they can go to play, they sit and wait until it's time to line up and go back to class.

On the second floor I visit four classes taking place within another 20 undivided space. The room has a low ceiling. File cabinets and movable blackboards give a small degree of isolation to each class. Again, there are no windows.

The library is a tiny, windowless and claustrophobic room. I count 21 approximately 700 books. Seeing no reference books, I ask a teacher if encyclopedias and other reference books are kept in classrooms.

"We don't have encyclopedias in classrooms," she replies. "That is 22 for the suburbs."

The school, I am told, has 26 computers for its 1,300 children. There 23 is one small gym and children get one period, and sometimes two, each week. Recess, however, is not possible because there is no playground. "Head Start,"[2] the principal says, "scarcely exists in District 10. We have no space."

The school, I am told, is 90 percent black and Hispanic; the other 10 24 percent are Asian, white or Middle Eastern.

In a sixth grade social studies class the walls are bare of words or 25 decorations. There seems to be no ventilation system, or, if one exists, it isn't working.

The class discusses the Nile River and the Fertile Crescent.   26

The teacher, in a droning voice: "How is it useful that these civi- 27 lizations developed close to rivers?"

A child, in a good loud voice: "What kind of question is that?"   28

In my notes I find these words: "An uncomfortable feeling—being 29 in a building with no windows. There are metal ducts across the room. Do they give air? I feel asphyxiated. . . ."

On the top floor of the school, a sixth grade of 30 children shares a 30 room with 29 bilingual second graders. Because of the high class size there is an assistant with each teacher. This means that 59 children and four grown-ups—63 in all—must share a room that, in a suburban school, would hold no more than 20 children and one teacher. There are, at least, some outside windows in this room—it is the only room with windows in the school—and the room has a high ceiling. It is a relief to see some daylight.

I return to see the kindergarten classes on the ground floor and feel 31 stifled once again by lack of air and the low ceiling. Nearly 120 children and adults are doing what they can to make the best of things: 80 children in four kindergarten classes, 30 children in the sixth grade class, and about eight grown-ups who are aides and teachers. The kindergarten children sitting on the worn rug, which is patched with tape, look up at me and turn their heads to follow me as I walk past them.

As I leave the school, a sixth grade teacher stops to talk. I ask her, 32 "Is there air conditioning in warmer weather?"

---

[2] Government program for disadvantaged preschoolers. [Eds.]

Teachers, while inside the building, are reluctant to give answers to 33
this kind of question. Outside, on the sidewalk, she is less constrained:
"I had an awful room last year. In the winter it was 56 degrees. In the
summer it was up to 90. It was sweltering."

I ask her, "Do the children ever comment on the building?" 34

"They don't say," she answers, "but they know." 35

I ask her if they see it as a racial message. 36

"All these children see TV," she says. "They know what suburban 37
schools are like. Then they look around them at their school. This was a
roller-rink, you know. . . . They don't comment on it but you see it in
their eyes. They understand."

On the following morning I visit P.S. 79, another elementary school 38
in the same district. "We work under difficult circumstances," says the
principal, James Carter, who is black. "The school was built to hold one
thousand students. We have 1,550. We are badly overcrowded. We need
smaller classes but, to do this, we would need more space. I can't add
five teachers. I would have no place to put them."

Some experts, I observe, believe that class size isn't a real issue. He 39
dismisses this abruptly. "It doesn't take a genius to discover that you
learn more in a smaller class. I have to bus some 60 kindergarten children elsewhere, since I have no space for them. When they return next
year, where do I put them?

"I can't set up a computer lab. I have no room. I had to put a class 40
into the library. I have no librarian. There are two gymnasiums upstairs
but they cannot be used for sports. We hold more classes there. It's
unfair to measure us against the suburbs. They have 17 to 20 children in
a class. Average class size in this school is 30.

"The school is 29 percent black, 70 percent Hispanic. Few of these 41
kids get Head Start. There is no space in the district. Of 200 kindergarten
children, 50 maybe get some kind of preschool."

I ask him how much difference preschool makes. 42

"Those who get it do appreciably better. I can't overestimate its 43
impact but, as I have said, we have no space."

The school tracks children by ability, he says. "There are five to 44
seven levels in each grade. The highest level is equivalent to 'gifted' but
it's not a full-scale gifted program. We don't have the funds. We have
no science room. The science teachers carry their equipment with
them."

We sit and talk within the nurse's room. The window is broken. 45
There are two holes in the ceiling. About a quarter of the ceiling has
been patched and covered with a plastic garbage bag.

"Ideal class size for these kids would be 15 to 20. Will these children 46
ever get what white kids in the suburbs take for granted? I don't think
so. If you ask me why, I'd have to speak of race and social class. I don't

say. When they are contemptuous of poor black people, their contempt is unadorned. When they're sympathetic and compassionate, their observations often go right to the heart of things. "Oh . . . they neglect these children," says the driver. "They leave them in the streets and slums to live and die." We stop at a light. Outside the window of the taxi, aimless men are standing in a semicircle while another man is working on his car. Old four-story buildings with their windows boarded, cracked or missing are on every side.

I ask the driver where he's from. He says Afghanistan. Turning in 73 his seat, he gestures at the street and shrugs. "If you don't, as an American, begin to give these kids the kind of education that you give the kids of Donald Trump, you're asking for disaster."

Two months later, on a day in May, I visit an elementary school in 74 Riverdale. The dogwoods and magnolias on the lawn in front of P.S. 24 are in full blossom on the day I visit. There is a well-tended park across the street, another larger park three blocks away. To the left of the school is a playground for small children, with an innovative jungle gym, a slide and several climbing toys. Behind the school there are two playing fields for older kids. The grass around the school is neatly trimmed.

The neighborhood around the school, by no means the richest part 75 of Riverdale, is nonetheless expensive and quite beautiful. Residences in the area—some of which are large, free-standing houses, others condominiums in solid red-brick buildings—sell for prices in the region of $400,000; but some of the larger Tudor houses on the winding and tree-shaded streets close to the school can cost up to $1 million. The excellence of P.S. 24, according to the principal, adds to the value of these homes. Advertisements in the *New York Times* will frequently inform prospective buyers that a house is "in the neighborhood of P.S. 24."

The school serves 825 children in the kindergarten through sixth 76 grade. This is approximately half the student population crowded into P.S. 79, where 1,550 children fill a space intended for 1,000, and a great deal smaller than the 1,300 children packed into the former skating rink; but the principal of P.S. 24, a capable and energetic man named David Rothstein, still regards it as excessive for an elementary school.

The school is integrated in the strict sense that the middle- and 77 upper-middle-class white children here do occupy a building that contains some Asian and Hispanic and black children; but there is little integration in the classrooms since the vast majority of the Hispanic and black children are assigned to "special" classes on the basis of evaluations that have classified them "EMR"—"educable mentally retarded"— or else, in the worst of cases, "TMR"—"trainable mentally retarded."

I ask the principal if any of his students qualify for free-lunch programs. "About 130 do," he says. "Perhaps another 35 receive their lunches at reduced price. Most of these kids are in the special classes. They do not come from this neighborhood."

The very few nonwhite children that one sees in mainstream classes tend to be Japanese or else of other Asian origins. Riverdale, I learn, has been the residence of choice for many years to members of the diplomatic corps.

The school therefore contains effectively two separate schools: one of about 130 children, most of whom are poor, Hispanic, black, assigned to one of the 12 special classes; the other of some 700 mainstream students, almost all of whom are white or Asian.

There is a third track also—this one for the students who are labeled "talented" or "gifted." This is termed a "pull-out" program since the children who are so identified remain in mainstream classrooms but are taken out for certain periods each week to be provided with intensive and, in my opinion, excellent instruction in some areas of reasoning and logic often known as "higher-order skills" in the contemporary jargon of the public schools. Children identified as "gifted" are admitted to this program in first grade and, in most cases, will remain there for six years. Even here, however, there are two tracks of the gifted. The regular gifted classes are provided with only one semester of this specialized instruction yearly. Those very few children, on the other hand, who are identified as showing the most promise are assigned, beginning in the third grade, to a program that receives a full-year regimen.

In one such class, containing ten intensely verbal and impressive fourth grade children, nine are white and one is Asian. The "special" class I enter first, by way of contrast, has twelve children of whom only one is white and none is Asian. These racial breakdowns prove to be predictive of the schoolwide pattern.

In a classroom for the gifted on the first floor of the school, I ask a child what the class is doing. "Logic and syllogisms," she replies. The room is fitted with a planetarium. The principal says that all the elementary schools in District 10 were given the same planetariums ten years ago but that certain schools, because of overcrowding, have been forced to give them up. At P.S. 261, according to my notes, there was a domelike space that had been built to hold a planetarium, but the planetarium had been removed to free up space for the small library collection. P.S. 24, in contrast, has a spacious library that holds almost 8,000 books. The windows are decorated with attractive, brightly colored curtains and look out on flowering trees. The principal says that it's inadequate, but it appears spectacular to me after the cubicle that holds a meager 700 books within the former skating rink.

The district can't afford librarians, the principal says, but P.S. 24, 84
unlike the poorer schools of District 10, can draw on educated parent
volunteers who staff the room in shifts three days a week. A parent
organization also raises independent funds to buy materials, including
books, and will soon be running a fund-raiser to enhance the library's
collection.

In a large and sunny first grade classroom that I enter next, I see 23 85
children, all of whom are white or Asian. In another first grade, there are
22 white children and two others who are Japanese. There is a computer
in each class. Every classroom also has a modern fitted sink.

In a second grade class of 22 children, there are two black children 86
and three Asian children. Again, there is a sink and a computer. A sixth
grade social studies class has only one black child. The children have
an in-class research area that holds some up-to-date resources. A set of
encyclopedias (World Book, 1985) is in a rack beside a window. The
children are doing a Spanish language lesson when I enter. Foreign languages begin in sixth grade at the school, but Spanish is offered also to
the kindergarten children. As in every room at P.S. 24, the window
shades are clean and new, the floor is neatly tiled in gray and green,
and there is not a single light bulb missing.

Walking next into a special class, I see twelve children. One is white. 87
Eleven are black. There are no Asian children. The room is half the size
of mainstream classrooms. "Because of overcrowding," says the principal, "we have had to split these rooms in half." There is no computer
and no sink.

I enter another special class. Of seven children, five are black, one is 88
Hispanic, one is white. A little black boy with a large head sits in the far
corner and is gazing at the ceiling.

"Placement of these kids," the principal explains, "can usually be 89
traced to neurological damage."

In my notes: "How could so many of these children be brain- 90
damaged?"

Next door to the special class is a woodworking shop. "This shop is 91
only for the special classes," says the principal. The children learn to
punch in time cards at the door, he says, in order to prepare them for
employment.

The fourth grade gifted class, in which I spend the last part of the 92
day, is humming with excitement. "I start with these children in the
first grade," says the teacher. "We pull them out of mainstream classes
on the basis of their test results and other factors such as the opinion
of their teachers. Out of this group, beginning in third grade, I pull out
the ones who show the most potential, and they enter classes such as
this one."

The curriculum they follow, she explains, "emphasizes critical think- 93
ing, reasoning and logic." The planetarium, for instance, is employed

not simply for the study of the universe as it exists. "Children also are designing their own galaxies," the teacher says.

A little girl sitting around a table with her classmates speaks with 94 perfect poise: "My name is Susan. We are in the fourth grade gifted program."

I ask them what they're doing and a child says, "My name is Laurie 95 and we're doing problem-solving."

A rather tall, good-natured boy who is half-standing at the table 96 tells me that his name is David. "One thing that we do," he says, "is logical thinking. Some problems, we find, have more than one good answer. We need to learn not simply to be logical in our own thinking but to show respect for someone else's logic even when an answer may be technically incorrect."

When I ask him to explain this, he goes on, "A person who gives an 97 answer that is not 'correct' may nonetheless have done some interesting thinking that we should examine. 'Wrong' answers may be more useful to examine than correct ones."

I ask the children if reasoning and logic are innate or if they're 98 things that you can learn.

"You know some things to start with when you enter school," Susan 99 says. "But we also learn some things that other children don't."

I ask her to explain this. 100

"We know certain things that other kids don't know because we're 101 *taught* them."

She has braces on her teeth. Her long brown hair falls almost to her 102 waist. Her loose white T- shirt has the word TRI-LOGIC on the front. She tells me that Tri-Logic is her father's firm.

Laurie elaborates on the same point: "Some things you know. Some 103 kinds of logic are inside of you to start with. There are other things that someone needs to teach you."

David expands on what the other two have said: "Everyone can 104 think and speak in logical ways unless they have a mental problem. What this program does is bring us to a higher form of logic."

The class is writing a new "Bill of Rights." The children already 105 know the U.S. Bill of Rights and they explain its first four items to me with precision. What they are examining today, they tell me, is the very *concept* of a "right." Then they will create their own compendium of rights according to their own analysis and definition. Along one wall of the classroom, opposite the planetarium, are seven Apple II computers on which children have developed rather subtle color animations that express the themes—of greed and domination, for example—that they also have described in writing.

"This is an upwardly mobile group," the teacher later says. "They 106 have exposure to whatever New York City has available. Their parents may take them to the theater, to museums. . . ."

Carlos: Here follows a tale of woe. I went home this weekend, had to help my Mom, & caught a fever so didn't have much time to study. My professor . . .

Carlos: Aargh! Trouble. Nothing original but everything's piling up at once. To be brief, my job interview . . .

Hey Carlos, good news! I've got mononucleosis.

Who are these wretched supplicants, scribbling notes so laden with   1
anxiety, seeking such miracles of postponement and balm? They are men and women who belong to Branford College, one of the twelve residential colleges at Yale University, and the messages are just a few of the hundreds that they left for their dean, Carlos Hortas—often slipped under his door at 4 A.M.—last year.

But students like the ones who wrote those notes can also be found   2
on campuses from coast to coast—especially in New England and at many other private colleges across the country that have high academic standards and highly motivated students. Nobody could doubt that the notes are real. In their urgency and their gallows humor they are authentic voices of a generation that is panicky to succeed.

My own connection with the message writers is that I am master   3
of Branford College. I live in its Gothic quadrangle and know the students well. (We have 485 of them.) I am privy to their hopes and fears—and also to their stereo music and their piercing cries in the dead of night ("Does anybody ca-a-are?"). If they went to Carlos to ask how to get through tomorrow, they come to me to ask how to get through the rest of their lives.

Mainly I try to remind them that the road ahead is a long one and   4
that it will have more unexpected turns than they think. There will be plenty of time to change jobs, change careers, change whole attitudes and approaches. They don't want to hear such liberating news. They want a map—right now—that they can follow unswervingly to career security, financial security, Social Security and, presumably, a prepaid grave.

What I wish for all students is some release from the clammy grip   5
of the future. I wish them a chance to savor each segment of their education as an experience in itself and not as a grim preparation for the next step. I wish them the right to experiment, to trip and fall, to learn that defeat is as instructive as victory and is not the end of the world.

My wish, of course, is naïve. One of the few rights that America   6
does not proclaim is the right to fail. Achievement is the national god, venerated in our media—the million-dollar athlete, the wealthy executive—and glorified in our praise of possessions. In the presence of such a potent state religion, the young are growing up old.

I see four kinds of pressure working on college students today: eco- 7
nomic pressure, parental pressure, peer pressure, and self-induced pressure. It is easy to look around for villains—to blame the colleges for
charging too much money, the professors for assigning too much work,
the parents for pushing their children too far, the students for driving
themselves too hard. But there are no villains; only victims.

"In the late 1960s," one dean told me, "the typical question that I got 8
from students was 'Why is there so much suffering in the world?' or
'How can I make a contribution?' Today it's 'Do you think it would look
better for getting into law school if I did a double major in history and
political science, or just majored in one of them?'" Many other deans
confirmed this pattern. One said: "They're trying to find an edge—the
intangible something that will look better on paper if two students are
about equal."

Note the emphasis on looking better. The transcript has become a 9
sacred document, the passport to security. How one appears on paper is
more important than how one appears in person. A is for Admirable and
B is for Borderline, even though, in Yale's official system of grading, A
means "excellent" and B means "very good." Today, looking very good
is no longer good enough, especially for students who hope to go on to
law school or medical school. They know that entrance into the better
schools will be an entrance into the better law firms and better medical
practices where they will make a lot of money. They also know that the
odds are harsh. Yale Law School, for instance, matriculates 170 students
from an applicant pool of 3,700; Harvard enrolls 550 from a pool of 7,000.

It's all very well for those of us who write letters of recommenda- 10
tion for our students to stress the qualities of humanity that will make
them good lawyers or doctors. And it's nice to think that admission officers are really reading our letters and looking for the extra dimension of
commitment or concern. Still, it would be hard for a student not to visualize these officers shuffling so many transcripts studded with As that
they regard a B as positively shameful.

The pressure is almost as heavy on students who just want to grad- 11
uate and get a job. Long gone are the days of the "gentleman's C," when
students journeyed through college with a certain relaxation, sampling
a wide variety of courses—music, art, philosophy, classics, anthropology, poetry, religion—that would send them out as liberally educated
men and women. If I were an employer I would rather employ graduates who have this range and curiosity than those who narrowly pursued safe subjects and high grades. I know countless students whose
inquiring minds exhilarate me. I like to hear the play of their ideas. I
don't know if they are getting As or Cs, and I don't care. I also like them
as people. The country needs them, and they will find satisfying jobs. I
tell them to relax. They can't.

Nor can I blame them. They live in a brutal economy. Tuition, room, 12
and board at most private colleges now comes to at least $7,000, not
counting books and fees. This might seem to suggest that the colleges
are getting rich. But they are equally battered by inflation. Tuition covers only 60 percent of what it costs to educate a student, and ordinarily
the remainder comes from what colleges receive in endowments,
grants, and gifts. Now the remainder keeps being swallowed by the
cruel costs—higher every year—of just opening the doors. Heating oil
is up. Insurance is up. Postage is up. Health-premium costs are up.
Everything is up. Deficits are up. We are witnessing in America the creation of a brotherhood of paupers—colleges, parents, and students,
joined by the common bond of debt.

Today it is not unusual for a student, even if he works part time at 13
college and full time during the summer, to accrue $5,000 in loans after
four years—loans that he must start to repay within one year after graduation. Exhorted at commencement to go forth into the world, he is
already behind as he goes forth. How could he not feel under pressure
throughout college to prepare for this day of reckoning? I have used
"he," incidentally, only for brevity. Women at Yale are under no less
pressure to justify their expensive education to themselves, their parents, and society. In fact, they are probably under more pressure. For
although they leave college superbly equipped to bring fresh leadership
to traditionally male jobs, society hasn't yet caught up with this fact.

Along with economic pressure goes parental pressure. Inevitably, 14
the two are deeply intertwined.

I see many students taking pre-medical courses with joyless tenacity. 15
They go off to their labs as if they were going to the dentist. It saddens
me because I know them in other corners of their life as cheerful people.

"Do you want to go to medical school?" I ask them.   16

"I guess so," they say, without conviction, or "Not really."   17

"Then why are you going?"   18

"Well, my parents want me to be a doctor. They're paying all this 19
money and . . ."

Poor students, poor parents. They are caught in one of the oldest 20
webs of love and duty and guilt. The parents mean well; they are trying
to steer their sons and daughters toward a secure future. But the sons
and daughters want to major in history or classics or philosophy—subjects with no "practical" value. Where's the payoff on the humanities?
It's not easy to persuade such loving parents that the humanities do
indeed pay off. The intellectual faculties developed by studying subjects
like history and classics—an ability to synthesize and relate, to weigh
cause and effect, to see events in perspective—are just the faculties that
make creative leaders in business or almost any general field. Still,
many fathers would rather put their money on courses that point

toward a specific profession—courses that are pre-law, pre-medical, pre-business, or, as I sometimes heard it put, "pre-rich."

But the pressure on students is severe. They are truly torn. One part 21 of them feels obligated to fulfill their parents' expectations; after all, their parents are older and presumably wiser. Another part tells them that the expectations that are right for their parents are not right for them.

I know a student who wants to be an artist. She is very obviously an 22 artist and will be a good one—she has already had several modest local exhibits. Meanwhile she is growing as a well-rounded person and taking humanistic subjects that will enrich the inner resources out of which her art will grow. But her father is strongly opposed. He thinks that an artist is a "dumb" thing to be. The student vacillates and tries to please everybody. She keeps up with her art somewhat furtively and takes some of the "dumb" courses her father wants her to take—at least they are dumb courses for her. She is a free spirit on a campus of tense students—no small achievement in itself—and she deserves to follow her muse.

Peer pressure and self-induced pressure are also intertwined, and 23 they begin almost at the beginning of freshman year.

"I had a freshman student I'll call Linda," one dean told me, "who 24 came in and said she was under terrible pressure because her roommate, Barbara, was much brighter and studied all the time. I couldn't tell her that Barbara had come in two hours earlier to say the same thing about Linda."

The story is almost funny—except that it's not. It's symptomatic of 25 all the pressures put together. When every student thinks every other student is working harder and doing better, the only solution is to study harder still. I see students going off to the library every night after dinner and coming back when it closes at midnight. I wish they would sometimes forget about their peers and go to a movie. I hear the clacking of typewriters in the hours before dawn. I see the tension in their eyes when exams are approaching and papers are due: *Will I get everything done?*

Probably they won't. They will get sick. They will get "blocked." 26 They will sleep. They will oversleep. They will bug out. *Hey Carlos, help!*

Part of the problem is that they do more than they are expected to 27 do. A professor will assign five-page papers. Several students will start writing ten-page papers to impress him. Then more students will write ten-page papers, and a few will raise the ante to fifteen. Pity the poor student who is still just doing the assignment.

"Once you have 20 or 30 percent of the student population deliber- 28 ately overexerting," one dean points out, "it's bad for everybody. When a teacher gets more and more effort from his class, the student who is doing normal work can be perceived as not doing well. The tactic works, psychologically."

Why can't the professor just cut back and not accept longer papers? 29
He can, and he probably will. But by then the term will be half over and
the damage done. Grade fever is highly contagious and not easily
reversed. Besides, the professor's main concern is with his course. He
knows his students only in relation to the course and doesn't know that
they are also overexerting in their other courses. Nor is it really his business. He didn't sign up for dealing with the student as a whole person
and with all the emotional baggage the student brought along from
home. That's what deans, masters, chaplains, and psychiatrists are for.

To some extent this is nothing new: a certain number of professors 30
have always been self-contained islands of scholarship and shyness,
more comfortable with books than with people. But the new pauperism
has widened the gap still further, for professors who actually like to
spend time with students don't have as much time to spend. They also
are overexerting. If they are young, they are busy trying to publish in
order not to perish, hanging by their finger nails onto a shrinking profession. If they are old and tenured, they are buried under the duties of
administering departments—as departmental chairmen or members of
committees—that have been thinned out by the budgetary axe.

Ultimately it will be the students' own business to break the circles 31
in which they are trapped. They are too young to be prisoners of their
parents' dreams and their classmates' fears. They must be jolted into
believing in themselves as unique men and women who have the
power to shape their own future.

"Violence is being done to the undergraduate experience," says 32
Carlos Hortas. "College should be open-ended: at the end it should
open many, many roads. Instead, students are choosing their goal in
advance, and their choices narrow as they go along. It's almost as if they
think that the country has been codified in the type of jobs that exist—
that they've got to fit into certain slots. Therefore, fit into the best-
paying slot.

"They ought to take chances. Not taking chances will lead to a life 33
of colorless mediocrity. They'll be comfortable. But something in the
spirit will be missing."

I have painted too drab a portrait of today's students, making them 34
seem a solemn lot. That is only half of their story; if they were so dreary
I wouldn't so thoroughly enjoy their company. The other half is that
they are easy to like. They are quick to laugh and to offer friendship.
They are not introverts. They are unusually kind and are more considerate of one another than any student generation I have known.

Nor are they so obsessed with their studies that they avoid sports 35
and extracurricular activities. On the contrary, they juggle their
crowded hours to play on a variety of teams, perform with musical and
dramatic groups, and write for campus publications. But this in turn is
one more cause of anxiety. There are too many choices. Academically,

they have 1,300 courses to select from; outside class they have to decide how much spare time they can spare and how to spend it.

This means that they engage in fewer extracurricular pursuits than 36 their predecessors did. If they want to row on the crew and play in the symphony they will eliminate one; in the '60s they would have done both. They also tend to choose activities that are self-limiting. Drama, for instance, is flourishing in all twelve of Yale's residential colleges as it never has before. Students hurl themselves into these productions— as actors, directors, carpenters, and technicians—with a dedication to create the best possible play, knowing that the day will come when the run will end and they can get back to their studies.

They also can't afford to be the willing slave of organizations like 37 the *Yale Daily News*. Last spring at the one-hundredth anniversary banquet of that paper—whose past chairmen include such once and future kings as Potter Stewart,[1] Kingman Brewster,[2] and William F. Buckley, Jr.[3]—much was made of the fact that the editorial staff used to be small and totally committed and that "Newsies" routinely worked fifty hours a week. In effect they belonged to a club; Newsies is how they defined themselves at Yale. Today's student will write one or two articles a week, when he can, and he defines himself as a student. I've never heard the word Newsie except at the banquet.

If I have described the modern undergraduate primarily as a driven 38 creature who is largely ignoring the blithe spirit inside who keeps trying to come out and play, it's because that's where the crunch is, not only at Yale but throughout American education. It's why I think we should all be worried about the values that are nurturing a generation so fearful of risk and so goal-obsessed at such an early age.

I tell students that there is no one "right" way to get ahead—that 39 each of them is a different person, starting from a different point and bound for a different destination. I tell them that change is a tonic and that all the slots are not codified nor the frontiers closed. One of my ways of telling them is to invite men and women who have achieved success outside the academic world to come and talk informally with my students during the year. They are heads of companies or ad agencies, editors of magazines, politicians, public officials, television magnates, labor leaders, business executives, Broadway producers, artists, writers, economists, photographers, scientists, historians—a mixed bag of achievers.

---

[1] Potter Stewart was an associate justice of the U. S. Supreme Court. [Eds.]

[2] Kingman Brewster is a former president of Yale. [Eds.]

[3] William F. Buckley, Jr., is a columnist and founder of the conservative journal *The National Review*. [Eds.]

―――――――――――――――――――――― FOCUS ――――――――――――――――――――――

What Is the Real Purpose of Education

WHO CARES ABOUT THE RENAISSANCE?
Leslie S. P. Brown

Leslie Brown was an Annenberg graduate fellow at the University of Pennsylvania, studying for a Ph.D. in Renaissance art history, when she contributed the following essay to Newsweek *magazine's "My Turn" column.*

Last September, with the aid of an unusually generous fellowship, I 1 enrolled in a doctoral program in Italian Renaissance art history. Although I had selected this particular career path as a college freshman and had never seriously considered any alternatives, I experienced severe doubts as I packed my bags and prepared to re-enter the academic life after a year away. For although my return to school elicited a few wistful wishes for happiness, and success, it primarily provoked a chorus of lugubrious warnings about the "lack of relevance" of my chosen field and the uncertainty of my professional and financial future.

I coped easily with the tired jokes about Ph.D.'s driving cabs from 2 the lawyers, doctors and M.B.A.'s of my acquaintance. But when a professor who had encouraged me to apply for graduate study sat me down and described in lurid detail his 20 years of frustration and comparative poverty as an academic, I began to be disturbed. And it was something of a shock to hear him say, as he leafed through the pages of his latest book, "I spent 10 years of my life on this thing, and what do I get? A thousand bucks and a pat on the back from a couple of colleagues. Sometimes I think it isn't worth it anymore."

Escapists: Not surprisingly, there aren't many of us left, we young 3 scholars of the past. Out of a total of 25 art-history majors at the college I attended, the vast majority went to law school. In these days of frantic attempts to gain admission to the best professional schools, the decision to pursue an advanced degree in literature, history, music or art is often viewed as a symptom of rapidly advancing lunacy—or, at least, as a sign of total disregard for the practical concerns of life. Media articles relentlessly describe the abysmal condition of the job market for Ph.D.'s in the humanities and the worry of department chairmen at universities where students are avoiding Chaucer and baroque music in favor of technical courses. Friends and family consider those of us who have chosen this course as aberrations. Some of us have been accused of being escapists, of refusing to face the constant changes of a technological society, of shutting ourselves up in ivory towers out of fear of competing with our pragmatic and computer-literate peers. In short, we hopeful scholars have had to accept the fact that we are considered anachronisms.

Why do we do it, then? Why have we, highly educated and raised, 4 for the most part, by ambitious and upwardly mobile parents, turned our backs on the 20th century in order to bury our noses in dusty books and write articles that only our colleagues will read?

Well, in part we do it for love. Despite the gibes and jeers of our 5 friends (and I might note that I have never once accused any of my lawyer friends of rampant materialism), we *are* realists. We are forced to be. We live in tiny, inexpensive apartments, take public transportation (or, more often, walk) and eat cheaply between long hours at the library. Many of us will be paying back huge educational loans for years and may never own a house or buy a new car. It is not a soft life, and sometimes we do complain. But usually we glory in it. We admire our contemporaries who are now making salaries that we only dream about, but we are secure in the knowledge that we have chosen to do what we love best. We have not relegated our joy in literature and art to the status of hobbies, and we can only hope that our passions will help us survive the lean years, the frustration and the occasional intellectual exhaustion.

Nor are we less competent or socially aware than our friends in 6 more practical professions. Several of my teachers and classmates have verbal and analytical abilities that would make them gifted lawyers or product managers; a small contingent is making fascinating discoveries about medieval architecture by performing astounding arithmetical gymnastics—with the aid of a computer. Many of us love science—several of my most enjoyable hours have been spent with a telescope in a freezing observatory—and we pay close attention to political developments. And many of us are enthusiastic sports fans. In other words, we are not social cripples or intellectual snobs with no interests beyond our own esoteric and rarefied disciplines. We have chosen to endure the raised eyebrows and the despair of our families because we hope that, with hard work and dedication, we will never have to mourn a lost love of Botticelli or Bach while working in jobs that fail to touch our souls or feed our human hunger for beauty.

Not long ago, a bright 16-year-old girl—a mathematics prodigy— 7 asked me who Michelangelo was. When I told her that he was one of the greatest artists who had ever lived, she asked me why she had never heard of him. Unfortunately, she is not alone. Universities today are wondering where they will find scholars of the humanities for new generations of students; perhaps it will be necessary to tell future freshmen that they cannot study literature, art, music or foreign languages because there is nobody to teach them.

field for me." For an uncertain student, eliminating something from the list of potential majors or careers is hardly a negative outcome.

Over the years, more than a few of the disconsolate visitors to my office have also come to discuss specific curricular or cocurricular incidents that have made life on campus hard to bear and that have undermined their inclination to remain. How does one respond to a student who complains that a faculty member forces a class to consider ideas or read books that are upsetting? What is a suitable reply to a report that a program or performance on campus was insensitive or offensive to some members of the community? The rich diversity that we seek in our academic communities helps fill our classrooms and residence halls with persons whose very difference makes it likely that ideas or programs presented by one group will trouble, if not hurt, others on campus.

Usually when I am confronted by a student raising these issues, I respond by saying that education often is painful because by definition it involves encountering that which is not already known. (This is among the best reasons, by the way, for making our campuses as diverse as possible.) Because the unfamiliar is often unsettling, threatening, even frightening, the process of learning may elicit a host of emotions, some of which are uncomfortable. If students, inside or outside the classroom, avoid difficult or challenging experiences because they want to be comfortable, they will miss what is potentially most valuable during their years on campus. Those who take the easy way, follow the familiar path, or fail to test themselves will miss the opportunity to become more than they were before they matriculated.

Sometimes when a student tells me that being on campus is painful, that a course is too difficult, that an idea is too upsetting, that a program is too offensive, I respond by talking about my friend Jesper. Were Jesper to follow the easy, painless path with massive pieces of mountain, were he to limit his activity merely to the exterior, then the forms inside never would be revealed. To release the treasures hidden in a twenty-ton block of marble, Jesper has to break through the surface, cut into the interior, saw, strike, and gouge. It is only after that brutal, even savage process has been completed (during which a beautiful form gradually emerges) that Jesper can refine the work by burnishing its surface. It seems to me that the hard treatment Jesper inflicts on those rough blocks of freshly quarried stone is analogous to what happens to some of our most successful students as they learn. Students who take the familiar route, who choose to follow the path of least resistance, who avoid the difficult course or stay away from the controversial lecture, who never feel tension or pain, who never test the ideas or challenge the beliefs they carried with them to college not only miss the very point of education but also diminish their potential. For those willing to push themselves, to dig deep rather than skim along the surface, the rewards (at least in retrospect) can be profound. But while the heavy excavation is in progress, they may feel a lot of pain.

On my wall hangs a small photo of an elegant, slender sculpture 8 that Jesper named after me. When advisees tell me they are uncertain or confused, or that learning hurts, I reach into a cabinet to retrieve a picture of the artist standing next to the block of freshly quarried marble from which "Aaron's Rod" may have emerged, note that students can be at once both sculptors and sculptures, and suggest that we get to work.

Responding to Reading

1. Why must learning hurt? According to Shatzman, what will happen to students who "take the easy way, follow the familiar path, or fail to test themselves" (6)?
2. What does Shatzman mean when he says, "The rich diversity that we seek in our academic communities . . . makes it likely that the ideas or programs presented by one group will trouble, if not hurt, others on campus" (5)? How do you think Shatzman would respond to a group of students who complain that a book on an instructor's reading list offends their sensibilities?
3. Shatzman begins and ends his essay with a discussion of the sculptor Jesper Neergaard. In what way is the process of creating a piece of sculpture like the process of getting an education?

ON THE USES OF A LIBERAL EDUCATION: LITE ENTERTAINMENT FOR BORED COLLEGE STUDENTS

Mark Edmundson

Mark Edmundson (1952–   ) grew up in Medford, Massachusetts. He received his B.A. from Bennington College and his Ph.D from Yale, and he currently teaches at the University of Virginia. He is also a contributing editor for Harper's *magazine. Edmundson has written on Freud and on literary theory, and his works include* Literature against Philosophy: A Defense of Poetry *(1995) and* Nightmare on Main Street: Angels, Sadomasochism, and the Culture of Gothic *(1997), a study of Gothic imagery in the 1990s. The following essay, which he says he wrote to "cause trouble of a useful sort," was published in* Harper's *in 1997. In it, Edmundson criticizes the "consumer culture" of higher education.*

Today is evaluation day in my Freud[1] class, and everything has   1
changed. The class meets twice a week, late in the afternoon, and the
clientele, about fifty undergraduates, tends to drag in and slump, looking disconsolate and a little lost, waiting for a jump start. To get the discussion moving, they usually require a joke, an anecdote, an
off-the-wall question—When you were a kid, were your Halloween
getups ego costumes, id costumes, or superego costumes? That sort of
thing. But today, as soon as I flourish the forms, a buzz rises in the room.
Today they write their assessments of the course, their assessments of
me, and they are without a doubt wide-awake. "What is your evaluation
of the instructor?" asks question number eight, entreating them to circle
a number between five (excellent) and one (poor, poor). Whatever inter-
pretive subtlety they've acquired during the term is now out the window. Edmundson: one to five, stand and shoot.

And they do. As I retreat through the door—I never stay around for   2
this phase of the ritual—I look over my shoulder and see them toiling
away like the devil's auditors. They're pitched into high writing gear,
even the ones who struggle to squeeze out their journal entries word by
word, stoked on a procedure they have by now supremely mastered.
They're playing the informed consumer, letting the provider know
where he's come through and where he's not quite up to snuff.

But why am I so distressed, bolting like a refugee out of my own   3
classroom, where I usually hold easy sway? Chances are the evaluations
will be much like what they've been in the past—they'll be just fine. It's
likely that I'll be commended for being "interesting" (and I am commended, many times over), that I'll be cited for my relaxed and tolerant
ways (that happens, too), that my sense of humor and capacity to connect the arcana of the subject matter with current culture will come in
for some praise (yup). I've been hassled this term, finishing a manuscript, and so haven't given their journals the attention I should have,
and for that I'm called—quite civilly, though—to account. Overall, I get
off pretty well.

Yet I have to admit that I do not much like the image of myself that   4
emerges from these forms, the image of knowledgeable, humorous
detachment and bland tolerance. I do not like the forms themselves,
with their number ratings, reminiscent of the sheets circulated after the
TV pilot has just played to its sample audience in Burbank. Most of all I
dislike the attitude of calm consumer expertise that pervades the
responses. I'm disturbed by the serene belief that my function—and,
more important, Freud's, or Shakespeare's, or Blake's[2] is to divert, entertain, and interest. Observes one respondent, not at all unrepresentative:

---

[1] Austrian psychiatrist Sigmund Freud (1856–1939); he posited that the human personality is
divided into the ego, the id, and the superego. [Eds.]
[2] English poet William Blake (1757–1827). [Eds.]

"Edmundson has done a fantastic job of presenting this difficult, important & controversial material in an enjoyable and approachable way."

Thanks but no thanks. I don't teach to amuse, to divert, or even, 5
for that matter, to be merely interesting. When someone says she
"enjoyed" the course—and that word crops up again and again in my
evaluations—somewhere at the edge of my immediate complacency I
feel encroaching self-dislike. That is not at all what I had in mind. The
off-the-wall questions and the sidebar jokes are meant as lead-ins to
stronger stuff—in the case of the Freud course, to a complexly tragic
view of life. But the affability and the one-liners often seem to be all
that land with the students; their journals and evaluations leave me little doubt.

I want some of them to say that they've been changed by the course. 6
I want them to measure themselves against what they've read. It's said
that some time ago a Columbia University instructor used to issue a
harsh two-part question. One: What book did you most dislike in the
course? Two: What intellectual or characterological flaws in you does
that dislike point to? The hand that framed that question was surely
heavy. But at least it compels one to see intellectual work as a confrontation between two people, student and author, where the stakes matter.
Those Columbia students were being asked to relate the quality of an
encounter, not rate the action as though it had unfolded on the big screen.

Why are my students describing the Oedipus complex and the 7
death drive[3] as being interesting and enjoyable to contemplate? And
why am I coming across as an urbane, mildly ironic, endlessly affable
guide to this intellectual territory, operating without intensity, generous,
funny, and loose?

Because that's what works. On evaluation day, I reap the rewards of 8
my partial compliance with the culture of my students and, too, with
the culture of the university as it now operates. It's a culture that's gotten little exploration. Current critics tend to think that liberal-arts education is in crisis because universities have been invaded by professors
with peculiar ideas: deconstruction, Lacanianism, feminism, queer theory. They believe that genius and tradition are out and that P.C., multiculturalism, and identity politics are in because of an invasion by tribes
of tenured radicals, the late millennial equivalents of the Visigoth
hordes that cracked Rome's walls.

But mulling over my evaluations and then trying to take a hard, 9
extended look at campus life both here at the University of Virginia and
around the country eventually led me to some different conclusions. To
me, liberal-arts education is as ineffective as it is now not chiefly
because there are a lot of strange theories in the air. (Used well, those
theories *can* be illuminating.) Rather, it's that university culture, like

---

[3] Important Freudian concepts. [Eds.]

American culture writ large, is, to put it crudely, ever more devoted to consumption and entertainment, to the using and using up of goods and images. For someone growing up in America now, there are few available alternatives to the cool consumer worldview. My students didn't ask for that view, much less create it, but they bring a consumer weltanschauung[4] to school, where it exerts a powerful, and largely unacknowledged, influence. If we want to understand current universities, with their multiple woes, we might try leaving the realms of expert debate and fine ideas and turning to the classrooms and campuses, where a new kind of weather is gathering.

From time to time I bump into a colleague in the corridor and we have what I've come to think of as a Joon Lee fest. Joon Lee is one of the best students I've taught. He's endlessly curious, has read a small library's worth, seen every movie, and knows all about showbiz and entertainment. For a class of mine he wrote an essay using Nietzsche's Apollo and Dionysus[5] to analyze the pop group The Supremes. A trite, cultural-studies bonbon? Not at all. He said striking things about conceptions of race in America and about how they shape our ideas of beauty. When I talk with one of his other teachers, we run on about the general splendors of his work and presence. But what inevitably follows a JL fest is a mournful reprise about the divide that separates him and a few other remarkable students from their contemporaries. It's not that some aren't nearly as bright—in terms of intellectual ability, my students are all that I could ask for. Instead, it's that Joon Lee has decided to follow his interests and let them make him into a singular and rather eccentric man; in his charming way, he doesn't mind being at odds with most anyone.

It's his capacity for enthusiasm that sets Joon apart from what I've come to think of as the reigning generational style. Whether the students are sorority/fraternity types, grunge aficionados, piercer/tattooers, black or white, rich or middle class (alas, I teach almost no students from truly poor backgrounds), they are, nearly across the board, very, very self-contained. On good days they display a light, appealing glow; on bad days, shuffling disgruntlement. But there's little fire, little passion to be found.

This point came home to me a few weeks ago when I was wandering across the university grounds. There, beneath a classically cast portico, were two students, male and female, having a rip-roaring argument. They were incensed, bellowing at each other, headstrong, confident, and wild. It struck me how rarely I see this kind of full-out

---

[4] German term referring to one's conception of the world. [Eds.]

[5] German philosopher Friedrich Nietzsche (1844–1900) used the opposing images of the Greek gods Apollo and Dionysus to classify artistic creators. [Eds.]

feeling in students anymore. Strong emotional display is forbidden. When conflicts arise, it's generally understood that one of the parties will say something sarcastically propitiating ("whatever" often does it) and slouch away.

How did my students reach this peculiar state in which all passion 13 seems to be spent? I think that many of them have imbibed their sense of self from consumer culture in general and from the tube in particular. They're the progeny of 100 cable channels and omnipresent Blockbuster outlets. TV, Marshall McLuhan famously said, is a cool medium. Those who play best on it are low key and nonassertive; they blend in. Enthusiasm, à la Joon Lee, quickly looks absurd. The form of character that's most appealing on TV is calmly self-interested though never greedy, attuned to the conventions, and ironic, ludicrous timing is preferred to sudden self-assertion. The TV medium is inhospitable to inspiration, improvisation, failures, slipups. All must run perfectly.

Naturally, a cool youth culture is a marketing bonanza for produc- 14 ers of the right products, who do all they can to enlarge that culture and keep it grinding. The Internet, TV, and magazines now teem with what I call persona ads, ads for Nikes and Reeboks and Jeeps and Blazers that don't so much endorse the capacities of the product per se as show you what sort of person you will be once you've acquired it. The Jeep ad that features hip, outdoorsy kids whipping a Frisbee from mountaintop to mountaintop isn't so much about what Jeeps can do as it is about the kind of people who own them. Buy a Jeep and be one with them. The ad is of little consequence in itself, but expand its message exponentially and you have the central thrust of current consumer culture—buy in order to be.

Most of my students seem desperate to blend in, to look right, not to 15 make a spectacle of themselves. (Do I have to tell you that those two students having the argument under the portico turned out to be acting in a role-playing game?) The specter of the uncool creates a subtle tyranny. It's apparently an easy standard to subscribe to, this Letterman-like, Tarantino-like cool, but once committed to it, you discover that matters are rather different. You're inhibited, except on ordained occasions, from showing emotion, stifled from trying to achieve anything original. You're made to feel that even the slightest departure from the reigning code will get you genially ostracized. This is a culture tensely committed to a laid-back norm.

Am I coming off like something of a crank here? Maybe. Oscar 16 Wilde,[6] who is almost never wrong, suggested that it is perilous to promiscuously contradict people who are much younger than yourself. Point taken. But one of the lessons that consumer hype tries to insinuate

---

[6] Oscar Wilde (1854–1900) was an Irish writer known for his intellectual wit and clever way of phrasing human truths. [Eds.]

gleaming aquatics building is a line by our founder, Thomas Jefferson, declaring that everyone ought to get about two hours' exercise a day. Clearly even the author of the Declaration of Independence endorses the turning of his university into a sports-and-fitness emporium.

But such improvements shouldn't be surprising. Universities need 25 to attract the best (that is, the smartest *and* the richest) students in order to survive in an ever more competitive market. Schools want kids whose parents can pay the full freight, not the ones who need scholarships or want to bargain down the tuition costs. If the marketing surveys say that the kids require sports centers, then, trustees willing, they shall have them. In fact, as I began looking around, I came to see that more and more of what's going on in the university is customer driven. The consumer pressures that beset me on evaluation day are only a part of an overall trend.

From the start, the contemporary university's relationship with 26 students has a solicitous, nearly servile tone. As soon as someone enters his junior year in high school, and especially if he's living in a prosperous zip code, the informational material—the advertising— comes flooding in. Pictures, testimonials, videocassettes, and CD ROMs (some bidden, some not) arrive at the door from colleges across the country, all trying to capture the student and his tuition cash. The freshman-to-be sees photos of well-appointed dorm rooms; of elaborate phys-ed facilities; of fine dining rooms; of expertly kept sports fields; of orchestras and drama troupes; of students working alone (no overbearing grown-ups in range), peering with high seriousness into computers and microscopes; or of students arrayed outdoors in attractive conversational garlands.

Occasionally—but only occasionally, for we usually photograph 27 rather badly; in appearance we tend at best to be styleless—there's a professor teaching a class. (The college catalogues I received, by my request only, in the late Sixties were austere affairs full of professors' credentials and course descriptions; it was clear on whose terms the enterprise was going to unfold.) A college financial officer recently put matters to me in concise, if slightly melodramatic, terms: "Colleges don't have admissions offices anymore, they have marketing departments." Is it surprising that someone who has been approached with photos and tapes, bells and whistles, might come in thinking that the Freud and Shakespeare she had signed up to study were also going to be agreeable treats?

How did we reach this point? In part the answer is a matter of demo- 28 graphics and (surprise) of money. Aided by the G.I. bill, the college-going population in America dramatically increased after the Second World War. Then came the baby boomers, and to accommodate them, schools continued to grow. Universities expand easily enough, but with tenure locking faculty in for lifetime jobs, and with the general reluctance of administrators to eliminate their own slots, it's not easy for a university to contract. So after the baby boomers had passed through—like a fat meal digested by a boa constrictor—the colleges turned to energetic promotional strategies to fill the empty chairs. And suddenly college became a buyer's market. What students and their parents wanted had to be taken more and more into account. That usually meant creating more comfortable, less challenging environments, places where almost no one failed, everything was enjoyable, and everyone was nice.

Just as universities must compete with one another for students, so 29 must the individual departments. At a time of rank economic anxiety, the English and history majors have to contend for students against the more success-insuring branches, such as the sciences and the commerce school. In 1968, more than 21 percent of all the bachelor's degrees conferred in America were in the humanities; by 1993, that number had fallen to about 13 percent. The humanities now must struggle to attract students, many of whose parents devoutly wish they would study something else.

One of the ways we've tried to stay attractive is by loosening up. 30 We grade much more softly than our colleagues in science. In English, we don't give many Ds, or Cs for that matter. (The rigors of Chem 101 create almost as many English majors per year as do the splendors of Shakespeare.) A professor at Stanford recently explained grade inflation in the humanities by observing that the undergraduates were getting smarter every year; the higher grades simply recorded how much better they were than their predecessors. Sure.

Along with softening the grades, many humanities departments 31 have relaxed major requirements. There are some good reasons for introducing more choice into curricula and requiring fewer standard courses. But the move, like many others in the university now, jibes with a tendency to serve—and not challenge—the students. Students can also float in and out of classes during the first two weeks of each term without making any commitment. The common name for this time span—shopping period—speaks volumes about the consumer mentality that's now in play. Usually, too, the kids can drop courses up until the last month with only an innocuous "W" on their transcripts. Does a course look too challenging? No problem. Take it pass-fail. A happy consumer is, by definition, one with multiple options, one who can always have what he wants. And since a course is something the students and their parents have bought and paid for, why can't they do with it pretty much as they please?

A sure result of the university's widening elective leeway is to give 32 students more power over their teachers. Those who don't like you can simply avoid you. If the clientele dislikes you en masse, you can be left without students, period. My first term teaching I walked into my introduction to poetry course and found it inhabited by one student, the gloriously named Bambi Lynn Dean. Bambi and I chatted amiably awhile, but for all that she and the pleasure of her name could offer, I was fast on the way to meltdown. It was all a mistake, luckily, a problem with the scheduling book. Everyone was waiting for me next door. But in a dozen years of teaching I haven't forgotten that feeling of being ignominiously marooned. For it happens to others, and not always because of scheduling glitches. I've seen older colleagues go through hot embarrassment at not having enough students sign up for their courses: they graded too hard, demanded too much, had beliefs too far out of keeping with the existing disposition. It takes only a few such instances to draw other members of the professoriat further into line.

And if what's called tenure reform—which generally just means the abolition of tenure—is broadly enacted, professors will be yet more vulnerable to the whims of their customer-students. Teach what pulls the kids in, or walk. What about entire departments that don't deliver? If the kids say no to Latin and Greek, is it time to dissolve classics? Such questions are being entertained more and more seriously by university administrators. 33

How does one prosper with the present clientele? Many of the most successful professors now are the ones who have "decentered" their classrooms. There's a new emphasis on group projects and on computer-generated exchanges among the students. What they seem to want most is to talk to one another. A classroom now is frequently an "environment," a place highly conducive to the exchange of existing ideas, the students' ideas. Listening to one another, students sometimes change their opinions. But what they generally can't do is acquire a new vocabulary, a new perspective, that will cast issues in a fresh light. 34

The Socratic method[9]—the animated, sometimes impolite give-and-take between student and teacher—seems too jagged for current sensibilities. Students frequently come to my office to tell me how intimidated they feel in class; the thought of being embarrassed in front of the group fills them with dread. I remember a student telling me how humiliating it was to be corrected by the teacher, by me. So I asked the logical question: "Should I let a major factual error go by so as to save discomfort?" The student—a good student, smart and earnest—said that was a tough question. He'd need to think about it. 35

Disturbing? Sure. But I wonder, are we really getting students ready for Socratic exchange with professors when we push them off into vast lecture rooms, two and three hundred to a class, sometimes face them with only grad students until their third year, and signal in our myriad professorial ways that we often have much better things to do than sit in our offices and talk with them? How bad will the student-faculty ratios have to become, how teeming the lecture courses, before we hear 36

---

[9] Based on the dialogues written by the ancient Greek philosopher Plato, the Socratic method involves rigorous questioning by both sides in a philosophical debate. [Eds.]

students righteously complaining, as they did thirty years ago, about the impersonality of their schools, about their decline into knowledge factories? "This is a firm," said Mario Savio at Berkeley during the Free Speech protests of the Sixties, "and if the Board of Regents are the board of directors, . . . then . . . the faculty are a bunch of employees and we're the raw material. But we're a bunch of raw material that don't mean . . . to be made into any product."

Teachers who really do confront students, who provide significant 37 challenges to what they believe, can be very successful, granted. But sometimes such professors generate more than a little trouble for themselves. A controversial teacher can send students hurrying to the deans and the counselors, claiming to have been offended. ("Offensive" is the preferred term of repugnance today, just as "enjoyable" is the summit of praise.) Colleges have brought in hordes of counselors and deans to make sure that everything is smooth, serene, unflustered, that everyone has a good time. To the counselor, to the dean, and to the university legal squad, that which is normal, healthy, and prudent is best.

An air of caution and deference is everywhere. When my students 38 come to talk with me in my office, they often exhibit a Franciscan humility.[10] "Do you have a moment?" "I know you're busy. I won't take up much of your time." Their presences tend to be very light; they almost never change the temperature of the room. The dress is nondescript: clothes are in earth tones; shoes are practical—cross-trainers, hiking boots, work shoes, Dr. Martens, with now and then a stylish pair of raised-sole boots on one of the young women. Many, male and female both, peep from beneath the bills of monogrammed baseball caps. Quite a few wear sports, or even corporate, logos, sometimes on one piece of clothing but occasionally (and disconcertingly) on more. The walk is slow, speech is careful, sweet, a bit weary, and without strong inflection. (After the first lively week of the term, most seem far in debt to sleep.) They are almost unfailingly polite. They don't want to offend me; I could hurt them, savage their grades.

Naturally, there are exceptions, kids I chat animatedly with, who 39 offer a joke, or go on about this or that new CD (almost never a book, no). But most of the traffic is genially sleepwalking. I have to admit that I'm a touch wary, too. I tend to hold back. An unguarded remark, a joke that's taken to be off-color, or simply an uncomprehended comment can lead to difficulties. I keep it literal. They scare me a little, these kind and melancholy students, who themselves seem rather frightened of their own lives.

Before they arrive, we ply the students with luscious ads, guaran- 40 teeing them a cross between summer camp and lotusland. When they

---

[10] That is, humility worthy of St. Francis, the thirteenth-century founder of the Franciscan order of priests, who was devoted to absolute poverty. [Eds.]

get here, flattery and nonstop entertainment are available, if that's what they want. And when they leave? How do we send our students out into the world? More and more, our administrators call the booking agents and line up one or another celebrity to usher the graduates into the millennium. This past spring, Kermit the Frog won himself an honorary degree at Southampton College on Long Island; Bruce Willis and Yogi Berra took credentials away at Montclair State; Arnold Schwarzenegger scored at the University of Wisconsin–Superior. At Wellesley, Oprah Winfrey gave the commencement address. (*Wellesley*—one of the most rigorous academic colleges in the nation.) At the University of Vermont, Whoopi Goldberg laid down the word. But why should a worthy administrator contract the likes of Susan Sontag, Christopher Hitchens, or Robert Hughes[11]—someone who might actually say something, something disturbing, something "offensive"—when he can get what the parents and kids apparently want and what the newspapers will softly commend—more lite entertainment, more TV?

Is it a surprise, then, that this generation of students—steeped in   41 consumer culture before going off to school, treated as potent customers by the university well before their date of arrival, then pandered to from day one until the morning of the final kiss-off from Kermit or one of his kin—are inclined to see the books they read as a string of entertainments to be placidly enjoyed or languidly cast down? Given the way universities are now administered (which is more and more to say, given the way that they are currently marketed), is it a shock that the kids don't come to school hot to learn, unable to bear their own ignorance? For some measure of self-dislike, or self-discontent—which is much different than simple depression—seems to me to be a prerequisite for getting an education that matters. My students, alas, usually lack the confidence to acknowledge what would be their most precious asset for learning: their ignorance.

Not long ago, I asked my Freud class a question that, however   42 hoary, never fails to solicit intriguing responses: Who are your heroes? Whom do you admire? After one remarkable answer, featuring T. S. Eliot[12] as hero, a series of generic replies rolled in, one gray wave after the next: my father, my best friend, a doctor who lives in our town, my high school history teacher. Virtually all the heroes were people my students had known personally, people who had done something local, specific, and practical, and had done it for them. They were good people, unselfish people, these heroes, but most of all they were people who had delivered the goods.

---

[11] Prominent contemporary intellectuals. [Eds.]

[12] American-British poet and critic T. S. Eliot (1888–1965) had a profound influence on twentieth-century literature. [Eds.]

My students' answers didn't exhibit any philosophical resistance to 43
the idea of greatness. It's not that they had been primed by their professors with complex arguments to combat genius. For the truth is that
these students don't need debunking theories. Long before college,
skepticism became their habitual mode. They are the progeny of Bart
Simpson and David Letterman, and the hyper-cool ethos of the box. It's
inane to say that theorizing professors have created them, as many conservative critics like to do. Rather, they have substantially created a university environment in which facile skepticism can thrive without being
substantially contested.

Skeptical approaches have *potential* value. If you have no all- 44
encompassing religious faith, no faith in historical destiny, the future of
the West, or anything comparably grand, you need to acquire your
vision of the world somewhere. If it's from literature, then the various
visions literature offers have to be inquired into skeptically. Surely it matters that women are denigrated in Milton and in Pope,[13] that some nov-
elistic voices assume an overbearing godlike authority, that the poor are,
in this or that writer, inevitably cast as clowns. You can't buy all of literature wholesale if it's going to help draw your patterns of belief.

But demystifying theories are now overused, applied mechanically. 45
It's all logocentrism, patriarchy, ideology. And in this the student environment—laid-back, skeptical, knowing—is, I believe, central. Full-out
debunking is what plays with this clientele. Some have been doing it
nearly as long as, if more crudely than, their deconstructionist teachers.
In the context of the contemporary university, and cool consumer culture, a useful intellectual skepticism has become exaggerated into a fun-
damentalist caricature of itself. The teachers have buckled to their
students' views.

At its best, multiculturalism can be attractive as well-deployed 46
theory. What could be more valuable than encountering the best work
of far-flung cultures and becoming a citizen of the world? But in the current consumer environment, where flattery plays so well, the urge to
encounter the other can devolve into the urge to find others who
embody and celebrate the right ethnic origins. So we put aside the
African novelist Chinua Achebe's abrasive, troubling *Things Fall Apart*
and gravitate toward hymns on Africa, cradle of all civilizations.

What about the phenomenon called political correctness? Raising 47
the standard of civility and tolerance in the university has been—who
can deny it?—a very good thing. Yet this admirable impulse has
expanded to the point where one is enjoined to speak well—and only
well—of women, blacks, gays, the disabled, in fact of virtually everyone. And we can owe this expansion in many ways to the student culture. Students now do not wish to be criticized, not in any form. (The

---

[13] British poets John Milton (1608–1674) and Alexander Pope (1688–1744). [Eds.]

culture of consumption never criticizes them, at least not *overtly*.) In the current university, the movement for urbane tolerance has devolved into an imperative against critical reaction, turning much of the intellectual life into a dreary Sargasso Sea. At a certain point, professors stopped being usefully sensitive and became more like careful retailers who have it as a cardinal point of doctrine never to piss the customers off.

To some professors, the solution lies in the movement called cultural 48 studies. What students need, they believe, is to form a critical perspective on pop culture. It's a fine idea, no doubt. Students should be able to run a critical commentary against the stream of consumer stimulations in which they're immersed. But cultural-studies programs rarely work, because no matter what you propose by way of analysis, things tend to bolt downhill toward an uncritical discussion of students' tastes, into what they like and don't like. If you want to do a Frankfurt School–style analysis of *Braveheart*, you can be pretty sure that by mid-class Adorno and Horkheimer[14] will be consigned to the junk heap of history and you'll be collectively weighing the charms of Mel Gibson. One sometimes wonders if cultural studies hasn't prospered because, under the guise of serious intellectual analysis, it gives the customers what they most want—easy pleasure, more TV. Cultural studies becomes nothing better than what its detractors claim it is—Madonna studies—when students kick loose from the critical perspective and groove to the product, and that, in my experience teaching film and pop culture, happens plenty.

On the issue of genius, as on multiculturalism and political correct- 49 ness, we professors of the humanities have, I think, also failed to press back against our students' consumer tastes. Here we tend to nurse a pair of—to put it charitably—disparate views. In one mode, we're inclined to a programmatic debunking criticism. We call the concept of genius into question. But in our professional lives per se, we aren't usually disposed against the idea of distinguished achievement. We argue animatedly about the caliber of potential colleagues. We support a star system, in which some professors are far better paid, teach less, and under better conditions than the rest. In our own profession we are creating a system that is the mirror image of the one we're dismantling in the curriculum. Ask a professor what she thinks of the work of Stephen Greenblatt, a leading critic of Shakespeare, and you'll hear it for an hour. Ask her what her views are on Shakespeare's genius and she's likely to begin questioning the term along with the whole "discourse of evaluation." This dual sensibility may be intellectually incoherent. But in its awareness of what plays with students, it's conducive to good classroom evaluations

---

[14] The Frankfurt School refers to a group of German philosophers who developed a Marxist-influenced method of "critical studies." Theodor Adorno (1903–1969) and Max Horkheimer (1895–1973) were among its influential members. [Eds.]

and, in its awareness of where and how the professional bread is buttered, to self-advancement as well.

My overall point is this: It's not that a leftwing professorial coup has taken over the university. It's that at American universities, left-liberal politics have collided with the ethos of consumerism. The consumer ethos is winning.

Then how do those who at least occasionally promote genius and high literary ideals look to current students? How do we appear, those of us who take teaching to be something of a performance art and who imagine that if you give yourself over completely to your subject you'll be rewarded with insight beyond what you individually command?

I'm reminded of an old piece of newsreel footage I saw once. The speaker (perhaps it was Lenin, maybe Trotsky[15]) was haranguing a large crowd. He was expostulating, arm waving, carrying on. Whether it was flawed technology or the man himself, I'm not sure, but the orator looked like an intricate mechanical device that had sprung into fast-forward. To my students, who mistrust enthusiasm in every form, that's me when I start riffing about Freud or Blake. But more and more, as my evaluations showed, I've been replacing enthusiasm and intellectual animation with stand-up routines, keeping it all at arm's length, praising under the cover of irony.

It's too bad that the idea of genius has been denigrated so far, because it actually offers a live alternative to the demoralizing culture of hip in which most of my students are mired. By embracing the works and lives of extraordinary people, you can adapt new ideals to revise those that came courtesy of your parents, your neighborhood, your clan—or the tube. The aim of a good liberal-arts education was once, to adapt an observation by the scholar Walter Jackson Bate, to see that "we need not be the passive victims of what we deterministically call 'circumstances' (social, cultural, or reductively psychological-personal), but that by linking ourselves through what Keats calls an 'immortal free-masonry' with the great we can become freer—freer to be ourselves, to be what we most want and value."

But genius isn't just a personal standard; genius can also have political effect. To me, one of the best things about democratic thinking is the conviction that genius can spring up anywhere. Walt Whitman[16] is born into the working class and thirty-six years later we have a poetic image of America that gives a passionate dimension to the legalistic brilliance of the Constitution. A democracy needs to constantly develop, and to do

---

[15] Vladimir Lenin (1870–1924) and Leon Trotsky (1879–1940) were leaders of the 1917 Russian Revolution; Lenin was the first leader of the USSR. [Eds.]

[16] American poet Walt Whitman (1819–1892), whose *Leaves of Grass* sang the praises of democracy and the universal spirit. See "When I Heard the Learn'd Astronomer," p. 98. [Eds.]

so it requires the most powerful visionary minds to interpret the present and to propose possible shapes for the future. By continuing to notice and praise genius, we create a culture in which the kind of poetic gamble that Whitman made—a gamble in which failure would have entailed rank humiliation, depression, maybe suicide—still takes place. By rebelling against established ways of seeing and saying things, genius helps us to apprehend how malleable the present is and how promising and fraught with danger is the future. If we teachers do not endorse genius and self-overcoming, can we be surprised when our students find their ideal images in TV's latest persona ads?

A world uninterested in genius is a despondent place, whose sad 55 denizens drift from coffee bar to Prozac dispensary, unfired by ideals, by the glowing image of the self that one might become. As Northrop Frye says in a beautiful and now dramatically unfashionable sentence "The artist who uses the same energy and genius that Homer and Isaiah[17] had will find that he not only lives in the same palace of art as Homer and Isaiah, but lives in it at the same time." We ought not to deny the existence of such a place simply because we, or those we care for, find the demands it makes intimidating, the rent too high.

What happens if we keep trudging along this bleak course? What 56 happens if our most intelligent students never learn to strive to overcome what they are? What if genius, and the imitation of genius, become silly, outmoded ideas? What you're likely to get are more and more one-dimensional men and women. These will be people who live for easy pleasures, for comfort and prosperity, who think of money first, then second, and third, who hug the status quo; people who believe in God as a sort of insurance policy (cover your bets); people who are never surprised. They will be people so pleased with themselves (when they're not in despair of the general pointlessness of their lives) that they cannot imagine humanity could do better. They'll think it their highest duty to clone themselves as frequently as possible. They'll claim to be happy, and they'll live a long time.

It is probably time now to offer a spate of inspiring solutions. Here 57 ought to come a list of reforms, with due notations about a core curriculum and various requirements. What the traditionalists who offer such solutions miss is that no matter what our current students are given to read, many of them will simply translate it into melodrama, with flat characters and predictable morals. (The unabated capitalist culture that conservative critics so often endorse has put students in a position to do little else.) One can't simply wave a curricular wand and reverse acculturation.

---

[17] The former is the ancient Greek poet to whom the great epics the Iliad and the Odyssey are attributed; the latter is the Hebrew writer to whom the biblical book of Isaiah is attributed. [Eds.]

Perhaps it would be a good idea to try firing the counselors and send- 58 ing half the deans back into their classrooms, dismantling the football team and making the stadium into a playground for local kids, emptying the fraternities, and boarding up the student-activities office. Such measures would convey the message that American colleges are not northern outposts of Club Med. A willingness on the part of the faculty to defy student convictions and affront them occasionally—to be usefully offensive—also might not be a bad thing. We professors talk a lot about subversion, which generally means subverting the views of people who never hear us talk or read our work. But to subvert the views of our students, our customers, that would be something else again.

Ultimately, though, it is up to individuals—and individual students 59 in particular—to make their own way against the current sludgy tide. There's still the library, still the museum, there's still the occasional teacher who lives to find things greater than herself to admire. There are still fellow students who have not been cowed. Universities are inefficient, cluttered, archaic places, with many unguarded corners where one can open a book or gaze out onto the larger world and construe it freely. Those who do as much, trusting themselves against the weight of current opinion, will have contributed something to bringing this sad dispensation to an end. As for myself, I'm canning my low-key one-liners; when the kids' TV-based tastes come to the fore, I'll aim and shoot. And when it's time to praise genius, I'll try to do it in the right style, full-out, with faith that finer artistic spirits (maybe not Homer and Isaiah quite, but close, close), still alive somewhere in the ether, will help me out when my invention flags, the students doze, or the dean mutters into the phone. I'm getting back to a more exuberant style; I'll be expostulating and arm waving straight into the millennium, yes I will.

Responding to Reading

1. According to Edmundson, his students have reached the "state in which all passion seems to be spent" (13). In what ways has America's consumer culture affected them? How have the media—particularly television and the Internet—shaped their sense of self?
2. "Over the past few years," says Edmundson, "the physical layout of my university has been changing" (24). In what ways has it been changing? How do these changes reflect (and reinforce) the consumer mentality that Edmundson sees in his students? How does Edmundson explain this phenomenon?
3. What does Edmundson think instructors and the university should do to correct the problems he sees? Do you think he is being fair when he says in his conclusion that ultimately it is up to individuals—especially individual students—to solve the problems he has pointed out?

——————————— WIDENING THE FOCUS ———————————

- Richard Rodriguez, "Aria" (p. 276)

- Peshe Kuriloff, "If John Dewey Were Alive Today, He'd Be a Webhead" (p. 482)

- Lawrence Krauss, "Equal Time for Nonsense" (p. 808)

"And this is Daniel, who is busy working toward his degree in money."

"English lit—how about you?"

Responding to the Images

1. What attitudes about education are suggested by these two cartoons? Do you agree with these viewpoints?
2. What might "Daniel" say to the two young men in the cornfield? What might they say to him?

WRITING

Issues in Education

1. Both Lynda Barry and Maya Angelou describe personal experiences related to their education. Write an essay in which you describe a positive or negative experience you have had with your education. Be specific, and make sure you include plenty of vivid descriptive details.

2. At the end of his essay, Jonathan Kozol describes a program for "talented" or "gifted" students. What would be the advantages and disadvantages of such a program in the kind of school he describes? Do you think children should be grouped according to their abilities?

3. What purpose do you think college should serve? Write an essay in which you explain your views, including specific references to essays in this chapter by Brown, Shatzman, and Edmundson, as well as examples from your own experience.

4. Both Maya Angelou in "Graduation" and Jonathan Kozol in "Savage Inequalities" look at ways in which in which race affects the educational experience. In what ways do your high school and college experiences support or contradict their views?

5. After reading Mark Edmundson's essay "On the Uses of a Liberal Education," develop a picture of the students whom Edmundson describes. Then, write a letter to Edmundson in which you discuss whether his characterization of students is accurate or inaccurate, pointing out where he hits and misses the mark.

6. Brent Staples says, "Grade inflation is in full gallop at every level, from struggling community institutions to the elites of the Ivy League" (2). Write an editorial for your school newspaper in which you agree or disagree with Staples's observation—at least as it applies to your school. Use your own experience as well as the ideas in Staples's essay to support your contentions.

7. Both Mark Twain in "Reading the River" and Walt Whitman in "When I Heard the Learn'd Astronomer" seem to value innocence. Aaron Shatzman, however, goes to great lengths to challenge his students' uninformed views. Write an essay in which you compare either Twain's or Whitman's ideas about education with Shatzman's. Be sure you use specific examples from each work to support your ideas.

8. "In Defense of Elitism," William A. Henry III argues that too many unqualified students go to college. To remedy this situation, he proposes limiting the number of high school students who are allowed

to attend college. Referring to "Savage Inequalities" by Jonathan Kozol, argue for or against Henry's proposal.

9. Write an essay in which you develop a definition of good teaching. As you write, consider the relationship of the teacher to the class, the standards teachers should use to evaluate students, and what students should gain from their educational experience. Make sure you refer to the ideas of John Holt and Mark Edmundson in your essay.

10. Write an essay in which you answer the Focus question, "What is the real purpose of education?" In your essay, refer to the ideas in Leslie S. P. Brown's "Who Cares about the Renaissance?" Aaron M. Shatzman's "When Learning Hurts," and Mark Edmundson's "On the Uses of a Liberal Education."

11. **For Internet Research:** Many colleges have posted sites discussing the value of a liberal arts education. At <http://www.hws.edu/new/pres/hersh/analysis.html> a college president analyzes a survey of opinion about the purpose of education. A site called "The Practical Value of the Liberal Arts" at <http://www. haverford.edu/publications/winter99/busarticle.htm> provides stories about liberal arts graduates of Haverford College. Lewis-Clark State College offers a student forum on the liberal arts at <http://www.lcsc.edu/forums/libartsbb.html>, and Colorado State has a site called "What Can I Do with a Degree in the Liberal Arts?" at <http://www.colo state.edu/Colleges/Libarts/careewha.htm>. A college newspaper's survey of students' lack of interest in academics can be found at <http://www.alligator.org/edit/issues/98-sprg/980113/>, and there is an interesting quiz titled "Should You Go to College?" at <http://www.parent-teen.com/collegeprep/collegequiz.html>. Using information from sources such as these as well as others you may find, write an article for your college newspaper on the role of the liberal arts in a college education.

3

THE POLITICS
OF LANGUAGE

PREPARING TO READ AND WRITE

During the years he spent in prison, political activist Malcolm X became increasingly frustrated by his inability to express himself in writing, so he began the tedious and often frustrating task of copying words from the dictionary—page by page. The eventual result was that for the first time, he could pick up a book and read it with understanding. "Anyone who has read a great deal," he says, "can imagine the new world that opened." In addition, by becoming a serious reader, Malcolm X was able to develop the ideas about race, politics, and economics that he would present so forcefully after he was released from prison.

In our society, language is constantly manipulated for political ends. This fact should come as no surprise if we consider the potential power of words. Often the power of a word comes not from its dictionary definitions, or *denotations,* but from its *connotations,* the associations that surround it. Often these connotations are subtle, giving language the power to confuse and even to harm. For example, whether a doctor who performs an abortion is "terminating a pregnancy" or "murdering a preborn child" is not just a matter of semantics. It is also a political issue, one that has provoked not only debate but violence. This potential for disagreement, and possibly danger, makes careful word choice very important.

The Focus section of this chapter (p. 232) addresses the question "Should English Be the Law?" On the one side, proponents of English-only laws in the United States say that unless something is done, the country will deteriorate into a polyglot society where language differences will divide one group from another. On the other side, proponents of multiculturalism, as well as bilingual education, say that the presence of other languages and cultures ultimately enriches our country and, for this reason, should be celebrated.

As you read and prepare to write about the essays in this chapter, you may consider the following questions:

- Does the selection deal primarily with written or spoken language?

- Does the writer place more emphasis on the denotations or the connotations of words?

- Does the writer make any distinctions between language applied to males and to females? Do you consider such distinctions valid?

- Does the writer discuss language in the context of a particular culture? Does he or she see language as a unifying or a divisive factor?

- In what ways would the writer like to change or reshape language? What do you see as the possible advantages or disadvantages of these changes?

- Does the writer believe that people are shaped by language or that language is shaped by people?

- Does the writer see language as having a particular social or political function? In what sense?

- Does the writer see language as empowering?

- Does the writer make assumptions about people's status on the basis of their use of language? Do these assumptions seem justified?

- Does the writer make a convincing case for the importance of language?

- Is the writer's focus primarily on language's ability to help or its power to harm?

- In what ways are your ideas about the power of words similar to or different from the writer's?

- How is the essay like and unlike other essays in this chapter?

LEARNING TO READ AND WRITE

Frederick Douglass

Frederick Douglass (1818–1895)—editor, author, lecturer, U.S. minister to Haiti—was born a slave in agricultural Maryland and later served a family in Baltimore. In the city, he had opportunities for personal improvement—and the luck to escape to the North in 1838. He settled in New

Bedford, Massachusetts, where he became active in the abolitionist move-ment. In 1845 Douglass wrote his most famous work, Narrative of the Life of Frederick Douglass. *Like other such narratives, extensions of the story-telling oratory and drama of former slaves in the abolitionist movement, it was distributed to a large and diverse audience. In the following excerpt from his* Narrative, *Douglass writes of outwitting his owners to become literate and find "the pathway from slavery to freedom."*

I lived in Master Hugh's family about seven years. During this time, 1
I succeeded in learning to read and write. In accomplishing this, I was compelled to resort to various stratagems. I had no regular teacher. My mistress, who had kindly commenced to instruct me, had, in compli-ance with the advice and direction of her husband, not only ceased to instruct, but had set her face against my being instructed by any one else. It is due, however, to my mistress to say of her, that she did not adopt this course of treatment immediately. She at first lacked the depravity indispensable to shutting me up in mental darkness. It was at least necessary for her to have some training in the exercise of irrespon-sible power, to make her equal to the task of treating me as though I were a brute.

My mistress was, as I have said, a kind and tender-hearted woman; 2
and in the simplicity of her soul she commenced, when I first went to live with her, to treat me as she supposed one human being ought to treat another. In entering upon the duties of a slaveholder, she did not seem to perceive that I sustained to her the relation of a mere chattel,[1] and that for her to treat me as a human being was not only wrong, but dangerously so. Slavery proved as injurious to her as it did to me. When I went there, she was a pious, warm, and tender-hearted woman. There was no sorrow or suffering for which she had not a tear. She had bread for the hungry, clothes for the naked, and comfort for every mourner that came within her reach. Slavery soon proved its ability to divest her of these heavenly qualities. Under its influence, the tender heart became stone, and the lamblike disposition gave way to one of tigerlike fierceness. The first step in her downward course was in her ceasing to instruct me. She now commenced to practice her husband's precepts. She finally became even more violent in her opposition than her husband himself. She was not satisfied with simply doing as well as he had commanded; she seemed anxious to do better. Nothing seemed to make her more angry than to see me with a newspaper. She seemed to think that here lay the danger. I have had her rush at me with a face made all up of fury, and snatch from me a newspaper, in a manner that fully revealed her apprehension. She was an apt woman;

---

[1] Property. [Eds.]

and a little experience soon demonstrated, to her satisfaction, that education and slavery were incompatible with each other.

From this time I was most narrowly watched. If I was in a separate 3 room any considerable length of time, I was sure to be suspected of having a book, and was at once called to give an account of myself. All this, however, was too late. The first step had been taken. Mistress, in teaching me the alphabet, had given me the *inch*, and no precaution could prevent me from taking the *ell*.

The plan which I adopted, and the one by which I was most 4 successful, was that of making friends of all the little white boys whom I met in the street. As many of these as I could, I converted into teachers. With their kindly aid, obtained at different times and in different places, I finally succeeded in learning to read. When I was sent on errands, I always took my book with me, and by going one part of my errand quickly, I found time to get a lesson before my return. I used also to carry bread with me, enough of which was always in the house, and to which I was always welcome; for I was much better off in this regard than many of the poor white children in our neighborhood. This bread I used to bestow upon the hungry little urchins, who, in return, would give me that more valuable bread of knowledge. I am strongly tempted to give the names of two or three of those little boys, as a testimonial of the gratitude and affection I bear them; but prudence forbids;—not that it would injure me, but it might embarrass them; for it is almost an unpardonable offense to teach slaves to read in this Christian country. It is enough to say of the dear little fellows, that they lived on Philpot Street, very near Durgin and Bailey's ship-yard. I used to talk this matter of slavery over with them. I would sometimes say to them, I wished I could be as free as they would be when they got to be men. "You will be free as soon as you are twenty-one, *but I am a slave for life!* Have not I as good a right to be free as you have?" These words used to trouble them; they would express for me the liveliest sympathy, and console me with the hope that something would occur by which I might be free.

I was now about twelve years old, and the thought of being *a slave* 5 *for life* began to bear heavily upon my heart. Just about this time, I got hold of a book entitled "The Columbian Orator."[2] Every opportunity I got, I used to read this book. Among much of other interesting matter, I found in it a dialogue between a master and his slave. The slave was represented as having run away from his master three times. The dialogue represented the conversation which took place between them, when the slave was retaken the third time. In this dialogue, the whole argument in behalf of slavery was brought forward by the master, all of which was disposed of by the slave. The slave was made to say some very smart as well as impressive things in reply to his master—things

---

[2] A popular textbook that taught the principles of effective public speaking. [Eds.]

write on the timber the name of that part of the ship for which it was intended. When a piece of timber was intended for the larboard side, it would be marked thus—"L." When a piece was for the starboard side, it would be marked thus—"S." A piece for the larboard side forward, would be marked thus—"L. F." When a piece was for starboard side forward, it would be marked thus—"S. F." For larboard aft, it would be marked thus—"L.A." For starboard aft, it would be marked thus—"S. A." I soon learned the names of these letters, and for what they were intended when placed upon a piece of timber in the shipyard. I immediately commenced copying them, and in a short time was able to make the four letters named. After that, when I met with any boy who I knew could write, I would tell him I could write as well as he. The next word would be, "I don't believe you. Let me see you try it." I would then make the letters which I had been so fortunate as to learn, and ask him to beat that. In this way I got a good many lessons in writing, which it is quite possible I should never have gotten in any other way. During this time, my copy-book was the board fence, brick wall, and pavement; my pen and ink was a lump of chalk. With these, I learned mainly how to write. I then commenced and continued copying the Italics in Webster's Spelling Book, until I could make them all without looking on the book. By this time, my little Master Thomas had gone to school, and learned how to write, and had written over a number of copy-books. These had been brought home, and shown to some of our near neighbors, and then laid aside. My mistress used to go to class meeting at the Wilk Street meetinghouse every Monday afternoon, and leave me to take care of the house. When left thus, I used to spend the time in writing in the spaces left in Master Thomas's copy-book, copying what he had written. I continued to do this until I could write a hand very similar to that of Master Thomas. Thus, after a long, tedious effort for years, I finally succeeded in learning how to write.

Responding to Reading

1. What does Douglass mean in paragraph 2 when he says that slavery proved as injurious to his mistress as it did to him? In spite of his owners' actions, what strategies did Douglass use to learn to read?
2. Douglass escaped from slavery in 1838 and became a leading figure in the antislavery movement. How did reading and writing help him develop his ideas about slavery? In what way did language empower him?
3. What comment do you think Douglass's essay makes on the conditions of African-Americans in the mid-nineteenth century? Does this essay have relevance today? Explain.

A HOMEMADE EDUCATION
Malcolm X

Writer, lecturer, and political activist Malcolm X (1925–1965) was born Malcolm Little in Omaha, Nebraska. His father, a Baptist minister, supported the back-to-Africa movement of the 1920s. Because of these activities the family was threatened by the Ku Klux Klan and forced to move several times. Eventually, his father was murdered, and his mother was committed to a mental institution. Malcolm X quit high school, preferring the street world of criminals and drug addicts. While he served time in prison from 1946 to 1952, he read books and studied the Black Muslim religion, finally becoming an articulate advocate of black separatism. Malcolm X later split with Elijah Muhammad, the Black Muslim leader, rejecting the notion that whites were evil and working for worldwide African-American unity and equality. For his defection, Malcolm X was assassinated. Some of his writings are The Autobiography of Malcolm X *(1965),* Malcolm X Talks to Young People *(1969), and* Malcolm X on Afro-American Unity *(1970). "A Homemade Education" is from Malcolm X's autobiography, which was written with Alex Haley.*

It was because of my letters that I happened to stumble upon starting 1 to acquire some kind of a homemade education.

I became increasingly frustrated at not being able to express what I 2 wanted to convey in letters that I wrote, especially those to Mr. Elijah Muhammad. In the street, I had been the most articulate hustler out there—I had commanded attention when I said something. But now, trying to write simple English, I not only wasn't articulate, I wasn't even functional. How would I sound writing in slang, the way I would *say* it, something such as, "Look, daddy, let me pull your coat about a cat, Elijah Muhammad—"

Many who today hear me somewhere in person, or on television, or 3 those who read something I've said, will think I went to school far beyond the eighth grade. This impression is due entirely to my prison studies.

It had really begun back in the Charlestown Prison, when Bimbi[1] 4 first made me feel envy of his stock of knowledge. Bimbi had always taken charge of any conversations he was in, and I had tried to emulate him. But every book I picked up had few sentences which didn't contain anywhere from one to nearly all of the words that might as well have been in Chinese. When I just skipped those words, of course, I really ended up with little idea of what the book said. So I had come to the Norfolk Prison Colony still going through only book-reading

---

[1] A fellow inmate. [Eds.]

motions. Pretty soon, I would have quit even these motions, unless I had received the motivation that I did.

I saw that the best thing I could do was get hold of a dictionary—to study, to learn some words. I was lucky enough to reason also that I should try to improve my penmanship. It was sad. I couldn't even write in a straight line. It was both ideas together that moved me to request a dictionary along with some tablets and pencils from the Norfolk Prison Colony school.

I spent two days just riffling uncertainly through the dictionary's pages. I'd never realized so many words existed! I didn't know *which* words I needed to learn. Finally, just to start some kind of action, I began copying.

In my slow, painstaking, ragged handwriting, I copied into my tablet everything printed on that first page, down to the punctuation marks.

I believe it took me a day. Then, aloud, I read back, to myself, every-thing I'd written on the tablet. Over and over, aloud, to myself, I read my own handwriting.

I woke up the next morning, thinking about those words— immensely proud to realize that not only had I written so much at one time, but I'd written words that I never knew were in the world. Moreover, with a little effort, I also could remember what many of these words meant. I reviewed the words whose meanings I didn't remember. Funny thing, from the dictionary first page right now, that "aardvark" springs to my mind. The dictionary had a picture of it, a long-tailed, long-eared, burrowing African mammal, which lives off termites caught by sticking out its tongue as an anteater does for ants.

I was so fascinated that I went on—I copied the dictionary's next page. And the same experience came when I studied that. With every succeeding page, I also learned of people and places and events from history. Actually the dictionary is like a miniature encyclopedia. Finally the dictionary's A section had filled a whole tablet—and I went on into the B's. That was the way I started copying what eventually became the entire dictionary. It went a lot faster after so much practice helped me to pick up handwriting speed. Between what I wrote in my tablet, and writing letters, during the rest of my time in prison I would guess I wrote a million words.

I suppose it was inevitable that as my word-base broadened, I could for the first time pick up a book and read and now begin to understand what the book was saying. Anyone who has read a great deal can imag-ine the new world that opened. Let me tell you something: from then until I left that prison, in every free moment I had, if I was not reading in the library, I was reading on my bunk. You couldn't have gotten me out of books with a wedge. Between Mr. Muhammad's teachings, my correspondence, my visitors—usually Ella and Reginald[2]—and my reading of books, months passed without my even thinking about being imprisoned. In fact, up to then, I never had been so truly free in my life.

The Norfolk Prison Colony's library was in the school building. A variety of classes was taught there by instructors who came from such 12 places as Harvard and Boston universities. The weekly debates between inmate teams were also held in the school building. You would be astonished to know how worked up convict debaters and audiences would get over subjects like "Should Babies Be Fed Milk?"

Available on the prison library's shelves were books on just about 13 every general subject. Much of the big private collection that Parkhurst[3] had willed to the prison was still in crates and boxes in the back of the library—thousands of old books. Some of them looked ancient: covers faded; old-time parchment-looking binding. Parkhurst, I've mentioned, seemed to have been principally interested in history and religion. He had the money and the special interest to have a lot of books that you wouldn't have in general circulation. Any college library would have been lucky to get that collection.

As you can imagine, especially in a prison where there was heavy 14 emphasis on rehabilitation, an inmate was smiled upon if he demonstrated an unusually intense interest in books. There was a sizable number of well-read inmates, especially the popular debaters. Some were said by many to be practically walking encyclopedias. They were almost celebrities. No university would ask any student to devour literature as I did when this new world opened to me, of being able to read and *understand*.

I read more in my room than in the library itself. An inmate who 15 was known to read a lot could check out more than the permitted maximum number of books. I preferred reading in the total isolation of my own room.

When I had progressed to really serious reading, every night at 16 about ten P.M. I would be outraged with the "lights out." It always seemed to catch me right in the middle of something engrossing.

Fortunately, right outside my door was a corridor light that cast a 17 glow into my room. The glow was enough to read by, once my eyes adjusted to it. So when "lights out" came, I would sit on the floor where I could continue reading in that glow.

At one-hour intervals the night guards paced past every room. Each 18 time I heard the approaching footsteps, I jumped into bed and feigned sleep. And as soon as the guard passed, I got back out of bed onto the floor area of that light-glow, where I would read for another fifty-eight minutes—until the guard approached again. That went on until three or

---

2 Ella was Malcolm's half sister, and Reginald was his brother. [Eds.]

3 A philanthropist. [Eds.]

four every morning. Three or four hours of sleep a night was enough for me. Often in the years in the streets I had slept less than that.

The teachings of Mr. Muhammad stressed how history had been 19 "whitened"—when white men had written history books, the black man simply had been left out. Mr. Muhammad couldn't have said anything that would have struck me much harder. I had never forgotten how when my class, me and all of those whites, had studied seventh-grade United States history back in Mason,[4] the history of the Negro had been covered in one paragraph, and the teacher had gotten a big laugh with his joke, "Negroes' feet are so big that when they walk, they leave a hole in the ground."

This is one reason why Mr. Muhammad's teachings spread so 20 swiftly all over the United States, among *all* Negroes, whether or not they became followers of Mr. Muhammad. The teachings ring true—to every Negro. You can hardly show me a black adult in America—or a white one, for that matter—who knows from the history books anything like the truth about the black man's role. In my own case, once I heard of the "glorious history of the black man," I took special pains to hunt in the library for books that would inform me on details about black history.

I can remember accurately the very first set of books that really 21 impressed me. I have since bought that set of books and I have it at home for my children to read as they grow up. It's called *Wonders of the World*. It's full of pictures of archeological finds, statues that depict, usually, non-European people.

I found books like Will Durant's *Story of Civilization*. I read H. G. 22 Wells' *Outline of History*. *Souls of Black Folk* by W. E. B. Du Bois gave me a glimpse into the black people's history before they came to this country. Carter G. Woodson's *Negro History* opened my eyes about black empires before the black slave was brought to the United States, and the early Negro struggles for freedom.

J. A. Rogers' three volumes of *Sex and Race* told about race-mixing 23 before Christ's time; about Aesop being a black man who told fables; about Egypt's Pharaohs; about the great Coptic Christian Empires; about Ethiopia, the earth's oldest continuous black civilization, as China is the oldest continuous civilization.

Mr. Muhammad's teaching about how the white man had been cre- 24 ated led me to *Findings in Genetics* by Gregor Mendel.[5] (The dictionary's G section was where I had learned what "genetics" meant.) I really studied this book by the Austrian monk. Reading it over and over, especially certain sections, helped me to understand that if you started with a black

---

[4] The junior high school that Malcolm X attended. [Eds.]

[5] Austrian monk (1822–1884) acknowledged as the father of modern genetics. [Eds.]

man, a white man could be produced; but starting with a white man, you never could produce a black man—because the white chromosome is recessive. And since no one disputes that there was but one Original Man, the conclusion is clear.

During the last year or so, in the *New York Times*, Arnold Toynbee[6] used the word "bleached" in describing the white man. (His words were: "White [i.e. bleached] human beings of North European origin. . . .") Toynbee also referred to the European geographic area as only a peninsula of Asia. He said there is no such thing as Europe. And if you look at the globe, you will see for yourself that America is only an extension of Asia. (But at the same time Toynbee is among those who have helped to bleach history. He has written that Africa was the only continent that produced no history. He won't write that again. Every day now, the truth is coming to light.)

I never will forget how shocked I was when I began reading about slavery's total horror. It made such an impact upon me that it later became one of my favorite subjects when I became a minister of Mr. Muhammad's. The world's most monstrous crime, the sin and the blood on the white man's hands, are almost impossible to believe. Books like the one by Frederick Olmstead[7] opened my eyes to the horrors suffered when the slave was landed in the United States. The European woman, Fannie Kimball, who had married a Southern white slaveowner, described how human beings were degraded. Of course I read *Uncle Tom's Cabin*. In fact, I believe that's the only novel I have ever read since I started serious reading.

Parkhurst's collection also contained some bound pamphlets of the Abolitionist Anti-Slavery Society of New England. I read descriptions of atrocities, saw those illustrations of black slave women tied up and flogged with whips; of black mothers watching their babies being dragged off, never to be seen by their mothers again; of dogs after slaves, and of the fugitive slave catchers, evil white men with whips and clubs and chains and guns. I read about the slave preacher Nat Turner, who put the fear of God into the white slavemaster. Nat Turner wasn't going around preaching pie-in-the-sky and "nonviolent" freedom for the black man. There in Virginia one night in 1831, Nat and seven other slaves started out at his master's home and through the night they went from one plantation "big house" to the next, killing, until by the next morning 57 white people were dead and Nat had about 70 slaves following him. White people, terrified for their lives, fled from their homes, locked themselves up in public buildings, hid in the woods, and some even left the state. A small army of soldiers took two months to

---

[6] English historian (1889–1975). [Eds.]

[7] American landscape architect and writer (1822–1903) who first achieved fame for his accounts of the South in the early 1850s. [Eds.]

When I discovered philosophy, I tried to touch all the landmarks of 40 philosophical development. Gradually, I read most of the old philosophers, Occidental and Oriental. The Oriental philosophers were the ones I came to prefer; finally, my impression was that most Occidental philosophy had largely been borrowed from the Oriental thinkers. Socrates, for instance, traveled in Egypt. Some sources even say that Socrates was initiated into some of the Egyptian mysteries. Obviously Socrates got some of his wisdom among the East's wise men.

I have often reflected upon the new vistas that reading opened to 41 me. I knew right there in prison that reading had changed forever the course of my life. As I see it today, the ability to read awoke inside me some long dormant craving to be mentally alive. I certainly wasn't seeking any degree, the way a college confers a status symbol upon its students. My homemade education gave me, with every additional book that I read, a little bit more sensitivity to the deafness, dumbness, and blindness that was afflicting the black race in America. Not long ago, an English writer telephoned me from London, asking questions. One was, "What's your alma mater?" I told him, "Books." You will never catch me with a free fifteen minutes in which I'm not studying something I feel might be able to help the black man.

Yesterday I spoke in London, and both ways on the plane across 42 the Atlantic I was studying a document about how the United Nations proposes to insure the human rights of the oppressed minorities of the world. The American black man is the world's most shameful case of minority oppression. What makes the black man think of himself as only an internal United States issue is just a catch-phrase, two words, "civil rights." How is the black man going to get "civil rights" before first he wins his *human* rights? If the American black man will start thinking about his *human* rights, and then start thinking of himself as part of one of the world's great peoples, he will see he has a case for the United Nations.

I can't think of a better case! Four hundred years of black blood and 43 sweat invested here in America, and the white man still has the black man begging for what every immigrant fresh off the ship can take for granted the minute he walks down the gangplank.

But I'm digressing. I told the Englishman that my alma mater was 44 books, a good library. Every time I catch a plane, I have with me a book that I want to read—and that's a lot of books these days. If I weren't out here every day battling the white man, I could spend the rest of my life reading, just satisfying my curiosity—because you can hardly mention anything I'm not curious about. I don't think anybody ever got more out of going to prison than I did. In fact, prison enabled me to study far more intensively than I would have if my life had gone differently and I had attended some college. I imagine that one of the biggest troubles with colleges is there are too many distractions, too much panty-raiding, fraternities, and boola-boola and all of that. Where else but in a prison could I have attacked my ignorance by being able to study intensely sometimes as much as fifteen hours a day?

Responding to Reading

1. What were Malcolm X's reasons for wanting to increase his skill in reading and writing? What else did his "homemade" education provide him?
2. Why didn't prison officials encourage Malcolm X to learn to read?
3. In what ways were Douglass's and Malcolm X's methods for learning to read similar? In what ways were they different? What message does Malcolm X's essay have for contemporary readers?

FOUR-LETTER WORDS CAN HURT YOU

Barbara Lawrence

Born in Hanover, New Hampshire, Barbara Lawrence holds a bachelor's degree from Connecticut College and a master's degree from New York University. She has worked as a magazine editor for Redbook *and* Harper's Bazaar, *among others, and she also served on the faculty of the State University of New York at Old Westbury. The following essay appeared in* The New York Times.

Why should any words be called obscene? Don't they all describe 1 natural human functions? Am I trying to tell them, my students demand, that the "strong, earthy, gut-honest"—or, if they are fans of Norman Mailer, the "rich, liberating, existential"—language they use to describe sexual activity isn't preferable to "phony-sounding, middle-class words like 'intercourse' and 'copulate'?" "Cop You Late!" they say with fancy and gagging grimaces. "Now, what is *that* supposed to mean?"

Well, what is it supposed to mean? And why indeed should one 2 group of words describing human functions and human organs be acceptable in ordinary conversation and another, describing presumably the same organs and functions, be tabooed—so much so, in fact, that some of these words still cannot appear in print in many parts of the English-speaking world?

The argument that these taboos exist only because of "sexual hang- 3 ups (middle-class, middle-age, feminist), or even that they are a result of class oppression (the contempt of the Norman conquerors for the language of their Anglo-Saxon serfs), ignores a much more likely explanation, it seems to me, and that is the sources and functions of the words themselves.

The best known of the tabooed sexual verbs, for example, comes 4 from the German *ficken,* meaning "to strike"; combined, according to Partridge's etymological dictionary *Origins,* with the Latin sexual verb *futuere;* associated in turn with the Latin *fustis,* "a staff or cudgel"; the Celtic *buc,* "a point, hence to pierce"; the Irish *bot,* "the male member"; the Latin *battuere,* "to beat"; the Gaelic *batair,* "a cudgeller"; the Early Irish *bualaim,* "I strike"; and so forth. It is one of what etymologists sometimes call "the sadistic group of words for the man's part in copulation."

The brutality of this word, then, and its equivalents ("screw," "bang," 5 etc.), is not an illusion of the middle class or a crotchet of Women's Liberation. In their origins and imagery these words carry undeniably painful, if not sadistic, implications, the object of which is almost always female. Consider, for example, what a "screw" actually does to the wood it penetrates; what a painful, even mutilating, activity this kind of analogy suggests. "Screw" is particularly interesting in this context, since the noun, according to Partridge comes from words meaning "groove," "nut," "ditch," "breeding sow" "scrofula" and "swelling," while the verb, besides its explicit imagery, has antecedent associations to "write on," "scratch," "scarify," and so forth—a revealing fusion of a mechanical or painful action with an obviously denigrated object.

Not all obscene words, of course, are as implicitly sadistic or 6 denigrating to women as these, but all that I know seem to serve a similar purpose: to reduce the human organism (especially the female organism) and human functions (especially sexual and procreative) to their least organic, most mechanical dimension; to substitute a trivializing deforming resemblance for the complex human reality of what is being described.

Tabooed male descriptives, when they are not openly denigrating to 7 women, often serve to divorce a male organ or function from any significant interaction with the female. Take the word "testes," for example, suggesting "witnesses" (from the Latin *testis*) to the sexual and procreative strengths of the male organ; and the obscene counterpart of this word, which suggests little more than a mechanical shape. Or compare almost any of the "rich," "liberating" sexual verbs, so fashionable today among male writers, with that much-derided Latin word "copulate" ("to bind or join together") or even that Anglo-Saxon phrase (which seems to have had no trouble surviving the Norman Conquest) "make love."

How arrogantly self-involved the tabooed words seem in compari- 8 son to either of the other terms, and how contemptuous of the female partner. Understandably so, of course, if she is only a "skirt," a "broad," a "chick," a "pussycat" or a "piece." If she is, in other words, no more than her skirt, or what her skirt conceals; no more than a breeder, or the broadest part of her; no more than a piece of a human being or a "piece of tail."

The most severely tabooed of all the female descriptives, inciden- 9 tally, are those like a "piece of tail," which suggest (either explicitly or through antecedents) that there is no significant difference between the female channel through which we are all conceived and born and the anal outlet common to both sexes—a distinction that pornographers have always enjoyed obscuring.

This effort to deny women their biological identity, their individual- 10 ity, their humanness, is such an important aspect of obscene language that one can only marvel at how seldom, in an era preoccupied with defini- tions of obscenity, this fact is brought to our attention. One problem, of course, is that many of the people in the best position to do this (critics, teachers, writers) are so reluctant today to admit that they are angered or shocked by obscenity. Bored, maybe, unimpressed, aesthetically, displeased, but—no matter how brutal or denigrating the material— never angered, never shocked.

And yet how eloquently angered, how piously shocked many 11 of these same people become if denigrating language is used about any minority group other than women; if the obscenities are racial or ethnic, that is, rather than sexual. Words like "coon," "kike," "spic," "wop," after all, deform identity, deny individuality and humanness in almost exactly the same way that sexual vulgarisms and obscenities do.

No one that I know, least of all my students, would fail to question 12 the values of a society whose literature and entertainment rested heavily on racial or ethnic pejoratives. Are the values of a society whose literature and entertainment rest as heavily as ours on sexual pejoratives any less questionable?

Responding to Reading

1. Lawrence begins her essay with a series of questions. Is this a good strategy? Does she answer all these questions in her essay?
2. Lawrence's title sums up the main point of her essay. Does she succeed in convincing you that "taboo sexual verbs" can, indeed, hurt you?
3. Do you agree with Lawrence when she says the use of obscene sexual references is as hurtful to women as the use of racial or ethnic epithets is to minorities? According to Lawrence, what should be done to remedy this situation?

MOTHER TONGUE

Amy Tan

Amy Tan (1952–   ) was born in Oakland, California, to parents who had emigrated from China only a few years earlier. (Her given name is actually An-mei, which means "blessing from America.") After receiving degrees from San Francisco State University (including a master's degree in linguistics), she became a business writer, composing speeches for corporate executives. A workaholic, Tan began writing stories as a means of personal therapy, and these eventually became the phenomenally successful The Joy Luck Club *(1987), a novel about Chinese-born mothers and their American-born daughters that was later made into a widely praised film. Tan's other books include two more novels,* The Kitchen God's Wife *(1991) and* The Hundred Secret Senses *(1995), and two illustrated children's books,* The Moon Lady *(1992) and* The Chinese Siamese Cat *(1994). In the following essay, which was originally delivered as a speech, Tan considers her relationship with her own mother, concentrating on the different "Englishes" they use to communicate with each other and with the world.*

I am not a scholar of English or literature. I cannot give you much 1 more than personal opinions on the English language and its variations in this country or others.

I am a writer. And by that definition, I am someone who has always 2 loved language. I am fascinated by language in daily life. I spend a great deal of my time thinking about the power of language—the way it can evoke an emotion, a visual image, a complex idea, or a simple truth. Language is the tool of my trade. And I use them all—all the Englishes I grew up with.

Recently, I was made keenly aware of the different Englishes I 3 do use. I was giving a talk to a large group of people, the same talk I had already given to half a dozen other groups. The nature of the talk was about my writing, my life, and my book, *The Joy Luck Club*. The talk was going along well enough, until I remembered one major difference that made the whole talk sound wrong. My mother was in the room. And it was perhaps the first time she had heard me give a lengthy speech, using the kind of English I have never used with her. I was saying things like, "The intersection of memory upon imagination" and "There is an aspect of my fiction that relates to thus-and-thus"—a speech filled with carefully wrought grammatical phrases, burdened, it suddenly seemed to me, with nominalized forms, past perfect tenses, conditional phrases, all the forms of standard English that I had learned in school and through books, the forms of English I did not use at home with my mother.

Just last week, I was walking down the street with my mother, and 4 I again found myself conscious of the English I was using, and the

English I do use with her. We were talking about the price of new and used furniture and I heard myself saying this: "Not waste money that way." My husband was with us as well, and he didn't notice any switch in my English. And then I realized why. It's because over the twenty years we've been together I've often used that same kind of English with him, and sometimes he even uses it with me. It has become our language of intimacy, a different sort of English that relates to family talk, the language I grew up with.

So you'll have some idea of what this family talk I heard sounds like, 5 I'll quote what my mother said during a recent conversation which I videotaped and then transcribed. During this conversation, my mother was talking about a political gangster in Shanghai who had the same last name as her family's, Du, and how the gangster in his early years wanted to be adopted by her family, which was rich by comparison. Later, the gangster became more powerful, far richer than my mother's family, and one day showed up at my mother's wedding to pay his respects. Here's what she said in part:

"Du Yusong having business like fruit stand. Like off the street kind. 6 He is Du like Du Zong—but not Tsung-ming Island people. The local people call putong, the river east side, he belong to that side local people. The man want to ask Du Zong father take him in like become own family. Du Zong father wasn't look down on him, but didn't take seriously, until that man big like become a mafia. Now important person, very hard to inviting him. Chinese way, came only to show respect, don't stay for dinner. Respect for making big celebration, he shows up. Mean gives lots of respect. Chinese custom. Chinese social life that way. If too important won't have to stay too long. He come to my wedding. I didn't see, I heard it. I gone to boy's side, they have YMCA dinner. Chinese age I was nineteen."

You should know that my mother's expressive command of English 7 belies how much she actually understands. She reads the Forbes report, listens to Wall Street Week, converses daily with her stockbroker, reads all of Shirley MacLaine's[1] books with ease—all kinds of things I can't begin to understand. Yet some of my friends tell me they understand 50 percent of what my mother says. Some say they understand 80 to 90 percent. Some say they understand none of it, as if she were speaking pure Chinese. But to me, my mother's English is perfectly clear, perfectly natural. It's my mother tongue. Her language, as I hear it, is vivid, direct, full of observation and imagery. That was the language that helped shape the way I saw things, expressed things, made sense of the world.

---

[1] Actress known for her autobiographical books, in which she traces her many past lives. [Eds.]

by the first pair, "*sunset* is to *nightfall*"—and I would see a burst of colors against a darkening sky, the moon rising, the lowering of a curtain of stars. And all the other pairs of words—red, bus, stoplight, boring—just threw up a mass of confusing images, making it impossible for me to sort out something as logical as saying: "A sunset precedes nightfall" is the same as "a chill precedes a fever." The only way I would have gotten that answer right would have been to imagine an associative situation, for example, my being disobedient and staying out past sunset, catching a chill at night, which turns into feverish pneumonia as punishment, which indeed did happen to me.

I have been thinking about all this lately, about my mother's English, 18 about achievement tests. Because lately I've been asked, as a writer, why there are not more Asian Americans represented in American literature. Why are there few Asian Americans enrolled in creative writing programs? Why do so many Chinese students go into engineering? Well, these are broad sociological questions I can't begin to answer. But I have noticed in surveys—in fact, just last week—that Asian students, as a whole, always do significantly better on math achievement tests than in English. And this makes me think that there are other Asian-American students whose English spoken in the home might also be described as "broken" or "limited." And perhaps they also have teachers who are steering them away from writing and into math and science, which is what happened to me.

Fortunately, I happen to be rebellious in nature and enjoy the chal- 19 lenge of disproving assumptions made about me. I became an English major my first year in college, after being enrolled as pre-med. I started writing nonfiction as a freelancer the week after I was told by my former boss that writing was my worst skill and I should hone my talents toward account management.

But it wasn't until 1985 that I finally began to write fiction. And 20 at first I wrote using what I thought to be wittily crafted sentences, sentences that would finally prove I had mastery over the English language. Here's an example from the first draft of a story that later made its way into *The Joy Luck Club*, but without this line: "That was my mental quandary in its nascent state." A terrible line, which I can barely pronounce.

Fortunately, for reasons I won't get into today, I later decided 21 I should envision a reader for the stories I would write. And the reader I decided upon was my mother, because these were stories about mothers. So with this reader in mind—and in fact she did read my early drafts— I began to write stories using all the Englishes I grew up with: the English I spoke to my mother, which for lack of a better term might be described as "simple"; the English she used with me, which for lack of a better term might be described as "broken"; my translation of her

Chinese, which could certainly be described as "watered down"; and what I imagined to be her translation of her Chinese if she could speak in perfect English, her internal language, and for that I sought to preserve the essence, but neither an English nor a Chinese structure. I wanted to capture what language ability tests can never reveal: her intent, her passion, her imagery, the rhythms of her speech and the nature of her thoughts.

Apart from what any critic had to say about my writing, I knew I had succeeded where it counted when my mother finished reading my book and gave me her verdict: "So easy to read."

Responding to Reading

1. Why does Tan begin her essay with the disclaimer "I am not a scholar of English or literature. I cannot give you much more than personal opinions" (1)? Does this opening add to her credibility or detract from it? Explain.

2. Tan implies that some languages are more expressive than others. Do you agree? Are there some ideas you can express in one language that are difficult or impossible to express in another? Give examples if you can.

3. Do you agree with Tan's statement in paragraph 15 that the kind of English spoken at home can have an effect on a student's performance on IQ tests and the SAT? Do you think the English you speak at home has had a positive or a negative effect on your command of English?

THE HUMAN COST
OF AN ILLITERATE SOCIETY

Jonathan Kozol

For over thirty years, Jonathan Kozol (see also p. 112) has written compassionately about many of the social problems confronting the United States, particularly those that affect the poor and the disadvantaged. In the following excerpt from his 1985 book Illiterate America, *Kozol exposes the problems facing the sixty million Americans who are unable to read well enough to function in society and argues that their plight has important implications for the literate among us as well.*

PRECAUTIONS. READ BEFORE USING.
Poison: Contains sodium hydroxide (caustic soda-lye).
Corrosive: Causes severe eye and skin damage, may cause blindness.
Harmful or fatal if swallowed.
If swallowed, give large quantities of milk or water.

Do not induce vomiting.
Important: Keep water out of can at all times to prevent contents from
violently erupting . . .

—warning on a can of Drano

Questions of literacy, in Socrates' belief, must at length be judged as   1
matters of morality. Socrates could not have had in mind the moral compromise peculiar to a nation like our own. Some of our Founding Fathers
did, however, have this question in their minds. One of the wisest of those
Founding Fathers (one who may not have been most compassionate but
surely was more prescient than some of his peers) recognized the special
dangers that illiteracy would pose to basic equity in the political
construction that he helped to shape.

"A people who mean to be their own governors," James Madison   2
wrote, "must arm themselves with the power knowledge gives. A popular government without popular information or the means of acquiring it,
is but a prologue to a farce or a tragedy, or perhaps both."

Tragedy looms larger than farce in the United States today. Illiterate   3
citizens seldom vote. Those who do are forced to cast a vote of questionable worth. They cannot make informed decisions based on serious
print information. Sometimes they can be alerted to their interests by
aggressive voter education. More frequently, they vote for a face, a
smile, or a style, not for a mind or character or body of beliefs.

The number of illiterate adults exceeds by 16 million the entire vote   4
cast for the winner in the 1980 presidential contest. If even one third of
all illiterates could vote, and read enough and do sufficient math to vote
in their self-interest, Ronald Reagan would not likely have been chosen
president. There is, of course, no way to know for sure. We do know this:
Democracy is a mendacious[1] term when used by those who are prepared
to countenance the forced exclusion of one third of our electorate. So long
as 60 million people are denied significant participation, the government
is neither of, nor for, nor by, the people. It is a government, at best, of those
two thirds whose wealth, skin color, or parental privilege allows them
opportunity to profit from the provocation and instruction of the written
word.

The undermining of democracy in the United States is one   5
"expense" that sensitive Americans can easily deplore because it represents a contradiction that endangers citizens of all political positions.
The human price is not so obvious at first.

Since I first immersed myself within this work I have often had the fol-   6
lowing dream: I find that I am in a railroad station or a large department

---

[1] Basely dishonest. [Eds.]

store within a city that is utterly unknown to me and where I cannot understand the printed words. None of the signs or symbols is familiar. Everything looks strange: like mirror writing of some kind. Gradually I understand that I am in the Soviet Union. All the letters on the walls around me are Cyrillic. I look for my pocket dictionary but I find that it has been mislaid. Where have I left it? Then I recall that I forgot to bring it with me when I packed my bags in Boston. I struggle to remember the name of my hotel. I try to ask somebody for directions. One person stops and looks at me in a peculiar way. I lose the nerve to ask. At last I reach into my wallet for an ID card. The card is missing. Have I lost it? Then I remember that my card was confiscated for some reason, many years before. Around this point, I wake up in a panic.

This panic is not so different from the misery that millions of adult 7 illiterates experience each day within the course of their routine existence in the U.S.A.

Illiterates cannot read the menu in a restaurant.   8

They cannot read the cost of items on the menu in the *window* of the 9 restaurant before they enter.

Illiterates cannot read the letters that their children bring home 10 from their teachers. They cannot study school department circulars that tell them of the courses that their children must be taking if they hope to pass the SAT exams. They cannot help with homework. They cannot write a letter to the teacher. They are afraid to visit in the classroom. They do not want to humiliate their child or themselves.

Illiterates cannot read instructions on a bottle of prescription 11 medicine. They cannot find out when a medicine is past the year of safe consumption; nor can they read of allergenic risks, warnings to diabetics, or the potential sedative effect of certain kinds of nonprescription pills. They cannot observe preventive health care admonitions. They cannot read about "the seven warning signs of cancer" or the indications of blood-sugar fluctuations or the risks of eating certain foods that aggravate the likelihood of cardiac arrest.

Illiterates live, in more than literal ways, an uninsured existence. 12 They cannot understand the written details on a health insurance form. They cannot read the waivers that they sign preceding surgical procedures. Several women I have known in Boston have entered a slum hospital with the intention of obtaining a tubal ligation and have emerged a few days later after having been subjected to a hysterectomy.[2] Unaware of their rights, incognizant of jargon, intimidated by the unfamiliar air of fear and atmosphere of ether that so many of us find oppressive in the confines even of the most attractive and expensive medical facilities, they have signed their names to documents they could not read and which

---

[2] A hysterectomy, the removal of the uterus, is a much more radical procedure than a tubal ligation, a method of sterilization that is a common form of birth control. [Eds.]

nobody, in the hectic situation that prevails so often in those overcrowded hospitals that serve the urban poor, had even bothered to explain.

Childbirth might seem to be the last inalienable right of any female 13 citizen within a civilized society. Illiterate mothers, as we shall see, already have been cheated of the power to protect their progeny against the likelihood of demolition in deficient public schools and, as a result, against the verbal servitude within which they themselves exist. Surgical denial of the right to bear that child in the first place represents an ultimate denial, an unspeakable metaphor, a final darkness that denies even the twilight gleamings of our own humanity. What greater violation of our biological, our biblical, our spiritual humanity could possibly exist than that which takes place nightly, perhaps hourly these days, within such over-burdened and benighted institutions as the Boston City Hospital? Illiteracy has many costs; few are so irreversible as this.

Even the roof above one's head, the gas or other fuel for heating that 14 protects the residents of northern city slums against the threat of illness in the winter months become uncertain guarantees. Illiterates cannot read the lease that they must sign to live in an apartment which, too often, they cannot afford. They cannot manage check accounts and therefore seldom pay for anything by mail. Hours and entire days of difficult travel (and the cost of bus or other public transit) must be added to the real cost of whatever they consume. Loss of interest on the check accounts they do not have, and could not manage if they did, must be regarded as another of the excess costs paid by the citizen who is excluded from the common instruments of commerce in a numerate society.

"I couldn't understand the bills," a woman in Washington, D.C., 15 reports, "and then I couldn't write the checks to pay them. We signed things we didn't know what they were."

Illiterates cannot read the notices that they receive from welfare 16 offices or from the IRS. They must depend on word-of-mouth instruction from the welfare worker—or from other persons whom they have good reason to mistrust. They do not know what rights they have, what deadlines and requirements they face, what options they might choose to exercise. They are half-citizens. Their rights exist in print but not in fact.

Illiterates cannot look up numbers in a telephone directory. Even if 17 they can find the names of friends, few possess the sorting skills to make use of the yellow pages; categories are bewildering and trade names are beyond decoding capabilities for millions of nonreaders. Even the emergency numbers listed on the first page of the phone book—"Ambulance," "Police," and "Fire"—are too frequently beyond the recognition of nonreaders.

Many illiterates cannot read the admonition on a pack of cigarettes. 18 Neither the Surgeon General's warning nor its reproduction on the package can alert them to the risks. Although most people learn by word of mouth that smoking is related to a number of grave physical disorders, they do not get the chance to read the detailed stories which can document this danger with the vividness that turns concern into determination to resist. They can see the handsome cowboy or the slim Virginia lady lighting up a filter cigarette; they cannot heed the words that tell them that this product is (not "may be") dangerous to their health. Sixty million men and women are condemned to be the unalerted, high-risk candidates for cancer.

Illiterates do not buy "no-name" products in the supermarkets. 19 They must depend on photographs or the familiar logos that are printed on the packages of brand-name groceries. The poorest people, therefore, are denied the benefits of the least costly products.

Illiterates depend almost entirely upon label recognition. Many 20 labels, however, are not easy to distinguish. Dozens of different kinds of Campbell's soup appear identical to the nonreader. The purchaser who cannot read and does not dare to ask for help, out of the fear of being stigmatized (a fear which is unfortunately realistic), frequently comes home with something which she never wanted and her family never tasted.

Illiterates cannot read instructions on a pack of frozen food. 21 Packages sometimes provide an illustration to explain the cooking preparations; but illustrations are of little help to someone who must "boil water, drop the food—*within* its plastic wrapper—in the boiling water, wait for it to simmer, instantly remove."

Even when labels are seemingly clear, they may be easily mistaken. 22 A woman in Detroit brought home a gallon of Crisco for her children's dinner. She thought that she had bought the chicken that was pictured on the label. She had enough Crisco now to last a year—but no more money to go back and buy the food for dinner.

Recipes provided on the packages of certain staples sometimes tempt 23 a semiliterate person to prepare a meal her children have not tasted. The longing to vary the uniform and often starchy content of low-budget meals provided to the family that relies on food stamps commonly leads to ruinous results. Scarce funds have been wasted and the food must be thrown out. The same applies to distribution of food-surplus produce in emergency conditions. Government inducements to poor people to "explore the ways" in which to make a tasty meal from tasteless noodles, surplus cheese, and powdered milk are useless to nonreaders. Intended as benevolent advice, such recommendations mock reality and foster deeper feelings of resentment and of inability to cope. (Those, on the other hand, who cautiously refrain from "innovative" recipes in preparation of their children's meals must suffer the opprobrium of "laziness," "lack of imagination. . . .")

Illiterates cannot travel freely. When they attempt to do so, they 24 encounter risks that few of us can dream of. They cannot read traffic signs and, while they often learn to recognize and to decipher symbols, they

"I come out of school. I was sixteen. They had their meetings. The 37
directors meet. They said that I was wasting their school paper. I was
wasting pencils . . ."

Another illiterate, looking back, believes she was not worthy of her 38
teacher's time. She believes that it was wrong of her to take up space
within her school. She believes that it was right to leave in order that
somebody more deserving could receive her place.

Children choke. Their mother chokes another way: on more than 39
chicken bones.

People eat what others order, know what others tell them, struggle 40
not to see themselves as they believe the world perceives them. A man
in California speaks about his own loss of identity, of self-location,
definition:

"I stood at the bottom of the ramp. My car had broke down on the 41
freeway. There was a phone. I asked for the police. They was nice. They
said to tell them where I was. I looked up at the signs. There was one
that I had seen before. I read it to them: ONE WAY STREET. They thought it
was a joke. I told them I couldn't read. There was other signs above the
ramp. They told me to try. I looked around for somebody to help. All the
cars was going by real fast. I couldn't make them understand that I was
lost. The cop was nice. He told me: 'Try once more.' I did my best. I
couldn't read. I only knew the sign above my head. The cop was trying
to be nice. He knew that I was trapped. 'I can't send out a car to you if
you can't tell me where you are.' I felt afraid. I nearly cried. I'm
forty-eight years old. I only said: 'I'm on a one-way street . . .'"

The legal problems and the courtroom complications that confront 42
illiterate adults have been discussed above. The anguish that may under-
lie such matters was brought home to me this year while I was working
on this book. I have spoken, in the introduction, of a sudden phone call
from one of my former students, now in prison for a criminal offense.
Stephen is not a boy today. He is twenty-eight years old. He called to ask
me to assist him in his trial, which comes up next fall. He will be on trial
for murder. He has just knifed and killed a man who first enticed him to
his home, then cheated him, and then insulted him—as "an illiterate
subhuman."

Stephen now faces twenty years to life. Stephen's mother was illit- 43
erate. His grandparents were illiterate as well. What parental curse did
not destroy was killed off finally by the schools. Silent violence is repaid
with interest. It will cost us $25,000 yearly to maintain this broken soul
in prison. But what is the price that has been paid by Stephen's
victim? What is the price that will be paid by Stephen?

Perhaps we might slow down a moment here and look at the realities 44
described above. This is the nation that we live in. This is a society that
most of us did not create but which our President and other leaders have

been willing to sustain by virtue of malign neglect. Do we possess the character and courage to address a problem which so many nations, poorer than our own, have found it natural to correct?

The answers to these questions represent a reasonable test of our 45 belief in the democracy to which we have been asked in public school to swear allegiance.

Responding to Reading

1. According to Kozol, how does illiteracy undermine democracy in the United States? Do you agree with him?
2. Do you think Kozol accurately describes the difficulties illiterates face in their daily lives, or does he seem to be exaggerating? If you think he is exaggerating, what motive might he have?
3. Kozol concludes his essay by asking whether we as a nation have "the character and the courage to address" illiteracy (44). He does not, however, offer any concrete suggestions for doing so. Can you offer any suggestions?

REPORTS, INFERENCES, JUDGMENTS

S. I. Hayakawa

Semanticist and psychologist S. I. Hayakawa (1906–1992) was born to Japanese immigrants in Vancouver, British Columbia, and attended the University of Manitoba, McGill University, and the University of Wisconsin, where he received his doctorate. For most of his teaching career, he was affiliated with San Francisco State College, serving as president there from 1968 to 1973, a time during which his conservative policies led to clashes with student militants. He was elected to the U.S. Senate in 1976, retiring in 1983 to spearhead the English Only movement. His classic linguistics text, Language in Thought and Action *(1938, revised 1978) remains one of the leading books in the field. The following is an excerpt from that text.*

For the purposes of the interchange of information, the basic sym- 1 bolic act is the report of what we have seen, heard or felt: "There is a ditch on each side of the road." "You can get those at Smith's Hardware Store for $2.75." "There aren't any fish on that side of the lake, but there are on this side." Then there are reports of reports: "The longest waterfall in the world is Victoria Falls in Rhodesia." "The Battle of Hastings took place in 1066." "The papers say that there was a smash-up on

Reports
-verifiable
- no
inferences
& judgments

Highway 41 near Evansville." Reports adhere to the following rules: first, they are *capable of verification;* second, they *exclude*, as far as possible, *inferences* and judgments. (These terms will be defined later.)

① **Verifiability** — *general agreement about event*

Reports are verifiable. We may not always be able to verify them our- 2
selves, since we cannot track down the evidence for every piece of history
we know, nor can we all go to Evansville to see the remains of the smash-
up before they are cleared away. But if we are roughly agreed upon the
names of things, upon what constitutes a "foot," or "yard," "bushel,"
"kilogram," "meter," and so on, and upon how to measure time, there is
relatively little danger of our misunderstanding each other. Even in a
world such as we have today, in which everybody seems to be quarreling
with everybody else, *we still to a surprising degree trust each other's reports.*
We ask directions of total strangers when we are traveling. We follow
directions on road signs without being suspicious of the people who put
them up. We read books of information about science, mathematics, auto-
motive engineering, travel, geography, the history of costume and other
such factual matters, and we usually assume that the author is doing his
best to tell us as truly as he can what he knows. And we are safe in so
assuming most of the time. With the interest given today to the discussion
of biased newspapers, propagandists, and the general untrustworthiness
of many of the communications we receive, we are likely to forget that we
still have an enormous amount of reliable information available and
that deliberate misinformation, except in warfare, is still more the exception than the rule. The desire for self-preservation that compelled men to
evolve means for the exchange of information also compels them to regard
the giving of false information as profoundly reprehensible.

At its highest development, the language of reports is the language 3
of science. By "highest development" we mean greatest general usefulness. Presbyterian and Catholic, workingman and capitalist, East
German and West German *agree* on the meanings of such symbols as
$2 + 2 = 4$, $100°$ C, HNO_3, 3:35 A.M., 1940 A.D., *1,000 kilowatts, Quercus agri-
folia,* and so on. But how, it may be asked, can there be agreement about
even this much among people who disagree about political philosophies, ethical ideas, religious beliefs, and the survival of my business
versus the survival of yours? The answer is that circumstances *compel
men to agree,* whether they wish to or not. If, for example, there were a
dozen different religious sects in the United States, each insisting on its
own way of naming the time of the day and the days of the year, the
mere necessity of having a dozen different calendars, a dozen different
kinds of watches, and a dozen sets of schedules for business hours,
trains, and television programs, to say nothing of the effort that would

② ?

be required for translating terms from one nomenclature to another, would make life as we know it impossible.[1]

The language of reports, then, including the more accurate reports 4 of science, is "map" language, and because it gives us reasonably accurate representations of the "territory," it enables us to get work done. Such language may often be dull reading: one does not usually read logarithmic tables or telephone directories for entertainment. But we could not get along without it. There are numberless occasions in the talking and writing we do in everyday life that *require that we state things in such a way that everybody will be able to understand and agree with our formulation.*

①

Inferences   Stmt about unknown from known info

. . . An inference, as we shall use the term, is a *statement about the* 5 *unknown made on the basis of the known.* We may *infer* from the material and cut of a woman's clothes her wealth or social position; we may *infer* from the character of the ruins the origin of the fire that destroyed the building; we may *infer* from a man's calloused hands the nature of his occupation; we may *infer* from a senator's vote on an armaments bill his attitude toward Russia; we may *infer* from the structure of the land the path of a prehistoric glacier; we may *infer* from a halo on an unexposed photographic plate its past proximity to radioactive materials; we may *infer* from the sound of an engine the condition of its connecting rods. Inferences may be carefully or carelessly made. They may be made on the basis of a broad background of previous experience with the subject matter or with no experience at all. For example, the inferences a good mechanic can make about the internal condition of a motor by listening to it are often startlingly accurate, while the inferences made by an amateur (if he tries to make any) may be entirely wrong. But the common characteristic of inferences is that they are statements about

---

[1] According to information supplied by the Association of American Railroads, "Before 1883 there were nearly 100 different time zones in the United States. It wasn't until November 18 of that year that . . . a system of standard time was adopted here and in Canada. Before then there was nothing but local or 'solar' time . . . The Pennsylvania Railroad in the East used Philadelphia time, which was five minutes slower than New York time and five minutes faster than Baltimore time. The Baltimore & Ohio used Baltimore time for trains running out of Baltimore, Columbus time for Ohio, Vincennes (Indiana) time for those going out of Cincinnati. . . . When it was noon in Chicago, it was 12:31 in Pittsburgh, 12:24 in Cleveland, 12:17 in Toledo, 12:13 in Cincinnati, 12:09 in Louisville, 12:07 in Indianapolis, 11:50 in St. Louis, 11:48 in Dubuque, 11:39 in St. Paul, and 11:27 in Omaha. There were 27 local time zones in Michigan alone.... A person traveling from Eastport, Maine, to San Francisco, if he wanted always to have the right railroad time and get off at the right place, had to twist the hands of his watch 20 times en route." Chicago *Daily News* (September 29, 1948).

matters which are not directly known, made on the basis of what has been observed.[2]

The avoidance of inferences . . . requires that we make no guesses as 6 to what is going on in other people's minds. When we say, "He was angry," we are not reporting; we are making an inference from such observable facts as the following: "He pounded his fist on the table; he swore; he threw the telephone directory at his stenographer." In this particular example, the inference appears to be safe; nevertheless, it is important to remember, especially for the purposes of training oneself, that it is an inference. Such expressions as "He thought a lot of himself," "He was scared of girls," "He has an inferiority complex," made on the basis of casual observation, and "What Russia really wants to do is to establish a communist world dictatorship," made on the basis of casual reading, are highly inferential. We should keep in mind their inferential character and . . . should substitute for them such statements as "He rarely spoke to subordinates in the plant," "I saw him at a party, and he never danced except when one of the girls asked him to," "He wouldn't apply for the scholarship, although I believe he could have won it easily," and "The Russian delegation to the United Nations has asked for A, B, and C. Last year they voted against M and N and voted for X and Y. On the basis of facts such as these, the newspaper I read makes the inference that what Russia really wants is to establish a communist world dictatorship. I agree."

Even when we exercise every caution to avoid inferences and to 7 report only what we see and experience, we all remain prone to error, since the making of inferences is a quick, almost automatic process. We may watch a car weaving as it goes down the road and say, "Look at that *drunken driver*," although what we see is only the *irregular motion of the car*. I once saw a man leave a dollar at a lunch counter and hurry out. Just as I was wondering why anyone should leave so generous a tip in so modest an establishment, the waitress came, picked up the dollar, put it in the cash register as she punched up ninety cents, and put a dime in her pocket. In other words, my description to myself of the event, "a dollar tip," turned out to be not a report but an inference.

All this is not to say that we should never make inferences. The 8 inability to make inferences is itself a sign of mental disorder. For example, the speech therapist Laura L. Lee writes, "The aphasic [brain-damaged] adult with whom I worked had great difficulty in making inferences about a picture I showed her. She could tell me what was happening at the moment in the picture, but could not tell me what

---

[2] The behaviorist school of psychology tries to avoid inferences about what is going on in other people's minds by describing only external behavior. A famous joke about behaviorism goes: Two behaviorists meet on the street. The first says, "You're fine. How am I?"

might have happened just before the picture or just afterwards."[3] Hence the question is not whether or not we make inferences; the question is whether or not we are aware of the inferences we make.

Report	Can be verified or disproved
Inference	A statement about the unknown made on the basis of the known
Judgement	An expression of the writer's approval or disapproval

Judgments *Approval / Disapproval of event or object being described*

. . . By judgments, we shall mean *all expressions of the writer's approval* 9 *or disapproval of the occurrences, persons, or objects he is describing.* For example, a report cannot say, "It was a wonderful car," but must say something like this: "It has been driven 50,000 miles and has never required any repairs." Again, statements such as "Jack lied to us" must be suppressed in favor of the more verifiable statement, "Jack told us he didn't have the keys to his car with him. However, when he pulled a handkerchief out of his pocket a few minutes later, a bunch of car keys fell out." Also a report may not say, "The senator was stubborn, defiant, and uncooperative," or "The senator courageously stood by his principles"; it must say instead, "The senator's vote was the only one against the bill."

Many people regard statements such as the following as statements 10 of "fact": "Jack *lied* to us," "Jerry is a *thief*," "Tommy is *clever*." As ordinarily employed, however, the word "lied" involves first an inference (that Jack knew otherwise and deliberately misstated the facts) and second a judgment (that the speaker disapproves of what he has inferred that Jack did). In the other two instances, we may substitute such expressions as, "Jerry was convicted of theft and served two years at Waupun," and "Tommy plays the violin, leads his class in school, and is captain of the debating team." After all, to say of a man that he is a "thief" is to say in effect, "He has stolen *and will steal again*—which is more of a prediction than a report. Even to say, "He has stolen," is to make an inference (and simultaneously to pass a judgment) on an act about which there may be a difference of opinion among those who have examined the evidence upon which the conviction was obtained. But to say that he was "convicted of theft" is to make a statement capable of being agreed upon through verification in court and prison records.

---

[3] "Brain Damage and the Process of Abstracting: A Problem in Language Learning," ETC.: *A Review of General Semantics,* XVI (1959), 154–62.

grown up with. Some of us became alcoholics, others got very good at bridge, while still others searched desperately for ways to contribute either to our families or to the Afghans.

When we returned in the fall of 1969 to the University of Michigan in   6
Ann Arbor, I was surprised to find that many other women were also questioning the expectations they had grown up with. Since I had been an English major when I was in college, I decided that for my part in the feminist movement I would study the English language and see what it could tell me about sexism. I started reading a desk dictionary and making note cards on every entry that seemed to tell something different about male and female. I soon had a dog-eared dictionary, along with a collection of note cards filling two shoe boxes.

The first thing I learned was that I couldn't study the language   7
without getting involved in social issues. Language and society are as intertwined as a chicken and an egg. The language a culture uses is telltale evidence of the values and beliefs of that culture. And because there is a lag in how fast a language changes—new words can easily be introduced, but it takes a long time for old words and usages to disappear—a careful look at English will reveal the attitudes that our ancestors held and that we as a culture are therefore predisposed to hold. My note cards revealed three main points. While friends have offered the opinion that I didn't need to read a dictionary to learn such obvious facts, the linguistic evidence lends credibility to the sociological observations.

Women Are Sexy: Men Are Successful

First, in American culture a woman is valued for the attractiveness   8
and sexiness of her body, while a man is valued for his physical strength and accomplishments. A woman is sexy. A man is successful.

A persuasive piece of evidence supporting this view are the   9
eponyms—words that have come from someone's name—found in English. I had a two-and-a-half-inch stack of cards taken from men's names but less than a half-inch stack from women's names, and most of those came from Greek mythology. In the words that came into American English since we separated from Britain, there are many eponyms based on the names of famous American men: Bartlett pear, boysenberry, Franklin stove, Ferris wheel, Gatling gun, mason jar, side-burns, sousaphone, Schick test, and Winchester rifle. The only common eponyms that I found taken from American women's names are Alice blue (after Alice Roosevelt Longworth), bloomers (after Amelia Jenks Bloomer), and Mae West jacket (after the buxom actress). Two out of the three feminine eponyms relate closely to a woman's physical anatomy, while the masculine eponyms (except for "sideburns" after General

Burnsides) have nothing to do with the namesake's body, but, instead, honor the man for an accomplishment of some kind.

In Greek mythology women played a bigger role than they did in   10 the biblical stories of the Judeo-Christian cultures, and so the names of goddesses are accepted parts of the language in such place names as Pomona, from the goddess of fruit, and Athens, from Athena, and in such common words as *cereal* from Ceres, *psychology* from Psyche, and *arachnoid* from Arachne. However, there is the same tendency to think of women in relation to sexuality as shown through the eponyms *aphrodisiac* from Aphrodite, the Greek name for the goddess of love and beauty, and *venereal disease* from Venus, the Roman name for Aphrodite.

Another interesting word from Greek mythology is *Amazon*.   11 According to Greek folk etymology, the *a-* means "without," as in *atypical* or *amoral*, while *-mazon* comes from *mazos*, meaning "breast," as still seen in *mastectomy*. In the Greek legend, Amazon women cut off their right breasts so they could better shoot their bows. Apparently, the storytellers had a feeling that for women to play the active, "masculine" role the Amazons adopted for themselves, they had to trade in part of their femininity.

This preoccupation with women's breasts is not limited to the   12 Greeks; it's what inspired the definition and the name for "mammals" (from Indo-European *mammae* for "breasts"). As a volunteer for the University of Wisconsin's *Dictionary of American Regional English (DARE)*, I read a western trapper's diary from the 1830s. I was to make notes of any unusual usages or language patterns. My most interesting finding was that the trapper referred to a range of mountains as "The Teats," a metaphor based on the similarity between the shapes of the mountains and women's breasts. Because today we use the French wording "The Grand Tetons," the metaphor isn't as obvious, but I wrote to mapmakers and found the following listings: Nipple Top and Little Nipple Top near Mount Marcy in the Adirondacks; Nipple Mountain in Archuleta County, Colorado; Nipple Peak in Coke County, Texas; Nipple Butte in Pennington, South Dakota; Squaw Peak in Placer County, California (and many other locations); Maiden's Peak and Squaw Tit (they're the same mountain) in the Cascade Range in Oregon; Mary's Nipple near Salt Lake City, Utah; and Jane Russell Peaks near Stark, New Hampshire.

Except for the movie star Jane Russell, the women being referred to   13 are anonymous—it's only a sexual part of their body that is mentioned. When topographical features are named after men, it's probably not going to be to draw attention to a sexual part of their bodies but instead to honor individuals for an accomplishment.

Going back to what I learned from my dictionary cards, I was   14 surprised to realize how many pairs of words we have in which the feminine word has acquired sexual connotations while the masculine word retains a serious businesslike aura. For example, a callboy is the person who calls actors when it is time for them to go on stage, but a callgirl is a prostitute. Compare sir and madam. *Sir* is a term of respect, while *madam* has acquired the specialized meaning of a brothel manager. Something similar has happened to master and mistress. Would you rather have a painting "by an old master" or "by an old mistress"?

It's because the word *woman* had sexual connotations, as in "She's his woman," that people began avoiding its use, hence such terminology as ladies' room, lady of the house, and girl's school or school for young ladies. Those of us who in the 1970s began asking that speakers use the term *woman* rather than *girl* or *lady* were rejecting the idea that *woman* is primarily a sexual term.   15

I found two-hundred pairs of words with masculine and feminine forms; for example, *heir/heiress, hero/heroine, steward/stewardess, usher/usherette.* In nearly all such pairs, the masculine word is considered the base, with some kind of a feminine suffix being added. The masculine form is the one from which compounds are made; for example, from king/queen comes kingdom but not queendom, from sportsman/sportslady comes sportsmanship but not sportsladyship. There is one—and only one—semantic area in which the masculine word is not the base or more powerful word. This is in the area dealing with sex, marriage, and motherhood. When someone refers to a virgin, a listener will probably think of a female unless the speaker specifies male or uses a masculine pronoun. The same is true for prostitute.   16

In relation to marriage, linguistic evidence shows that weddings are more important to women than to men. A woman cherishes the wedding and is considered a bride for a whole year, but a man is referred to as a groom only on the day of the wedding. The word *bride* appears in *bridal attendant, bridal gown, bridesmaid, bridal shower,* and even *bridegroom. Groom* comes from the Middle English *grom,* meaning "man," and in that sense is seldom used outside of the wedding. With most pairs of male/female words, people habitually put the masculine word first: *Mr. and Mrs., his and hers, boys and girls, men and women, kings and queens, brothers and sisters, guys and dolls, and host and hostess.* But it is the bride and groom who are talked about, not the groom and bride.   17

The importance of marriage to a woman is also shown by the fact that when a marriage ends in death, the woman gets the title of widow. A man gets the derived title of widower. This term is not used in other phrases or contexts, but widow is seen in widowhood, widow's peak, and widow's walk. A widow in a card game is an extra hand of cards, while in typesetting it is a leftover line of type.   18

Changing cultural ideas bring changes to language, and since I did my dictionary study three decades ago the word *singles* has largely replaced such gender-specific and value-laden terms as *bachelor, old*   19 *maid, spinster, divorcee, widow,* and *widower.* In 1970 I wrote that when people hear a man called "a professional," they usually think of him as a doctor or a lawyer, but when people hear a woman referred to as "a professional," they are likely to think of her as a prostitute. That's not as true today because so many women have become doctors and lawyers, it's no longer incongruous to think of women in those professional roles.

Another change that has taken place is in wedding announcements. 20 They used to be sent out from the bride's parents and did not even give the name of the groom's parents. Today, most couples choose to list either all or none of the parents' names. Also it is now much more likely that both the bride and groom's picture will be in the newspaper, while wenty years ago only the bride's picture was published on the "Women's" or the "Society" page. In the weddings I have recently attended, the official has pronounced the couple "husband and wife" instead of the traditional "man and wife," and the bride has been asked if she promises to "love, honor, and cherish," instead of to "love, honor, and obey."

Women Are Passive; Men Are Active

However, other wording in the wedding ceremony relates to a 21 second point that my cards showed, which is that women are expected to play a passive or weak role while men play an active or strong role. In the traditional ceremony, the official asks, "Who gives the bride away?" and the father answers, "I do." Some fathers answer, "Her mother and I do," but that doesn't solve the problem inherent in the question. The idea that a bride is something to be handed over from one man to another bothers people because it goes back to the days when a man's servants, his children, and his wife were all considered to be his property. They were known by his name because they belonged to him, and he was responsible for their actions and their debts.

The grammar used in talking or writing about weddings as well as 22 other sexual relationships shows the expectation of men playing the active role. Men *wed* women while women *become* brides of men. A man *possesses* a woman; he *deflowers* her; he *performs;* he *scores;* he *takes away* her virginity. Although a woman can *seduce* a man, she cannot offer him her virginity. When talking about virginity, the only way to make the woman the actor in the sentence is to say that "she lost her virginity," but people lose things by accident rather than by purposeful actions, and so she's only the grammatical, not the real-life, actor.

The reason that women brought the term Ms. into the language to re- 23 place Miss and Mrs. relates to this point. Many married women resent being identified in the "Mrs. Husband" form. The dictionary cards showed what appeared to be an attitude on the part of the editors that it was almost indecent to let a respectable woman's name march unaccompanied across the pages of a dictionary. Women were listed with male names whether or not the male contributed to the woman's reason for being in the dictionary or whether or not in his own right he was as famous as the woman. For example:

Charlotte Brontë = Mrs. Arthur B. Nicholls
Amelia Earhart = Mrs. George Palmer Putnam
Helen Hayes = Mrs. Charles MacArthur
Jenny Lind = Mme. Otto Goldschmit
Cornelia Otis Skinner = daughter of Otis
Harriet Beecher Stowe = sister of Henry Ward Beecher
Dame Edith Sitwell = sister of Osbert and Sacheverell*[2]

Only a small number of rebels and crusaders got into the dictionary without the benefit of a masculine escort: temperance leaders Frances Elizabeth Caroline Willard and Carry Nation, women's rights leaders Carrie Chapman Catt and Elizabeth Cady Stanton, birth control educator Margaret Sanger, religious leader Mary Baker Eddy, and slaves Harriet Tubman and Phillis Wheatley.

Etiquette books used to teach that if a woman had Mrs. in front of her 24
name, then the husband's name should follow because Mrs. is an abbreviated form of Mistress and a woman couldn't be a mistress of herself. As with many arguments about "correct" language usage, this isn't very logical because Miss is also an abbreviation of Mistress. Feminists hoped to simplify matters by introducing Ms. as an alternative to both Mrs. and Miss, but what happened is that Ms. largely replaced Miss to become a catch-all business title for women. Many married women still prefer the title Mrs., and some even resent being addressed with the term Ms. As one frustrated newspaper reporter complained, "Before I can write about a woman I have to know not only her marital status but also her political philosophy." The result of such complications may contribute to the demise of titles, which are already being ignored by many writers who find it more efficient to simply use names; for example, in a business letter: "Dear Joan Garcia," instead of "Dear Mrs. Joan Garcia," "Dear Ms. Garcia," or "Dear Mrs. Louis Garcia."

Titles given to royalty show how males can be disadvantaged by 25
the assumption that they always play the more powerful role. In British royalty, when a male holds a title, his wife is automatically given the

---

[2] Charlotte Brontë (1816–1855), author of *Jane Eyre*, Amelia Earhart (1898–1937), first woman to fly over the Atlantic; Helen Hayes (1900-1993), actress; Jenny Lind (1820-1887), Swedish soprano known as the "Swedish nightingale"; Cornelia Otis Skinner (1901–1979), actress and writer Harriet Beecher Stowe (1811–1896), author of *Uncle Tom's Cabin*; and Edith Sitwell (1877–1964), English poet and critic.

feminine equivalent. But the reverse is not true. For example, a count is a high political officer with a countess being his wife. The same pattern holds true for a duke and a duchess and a king and a queen. But when a female holds the royal title, the man she marries does not automatically acquire the matching title. For example, Queen Elizabeth's husband has the title of prince rather than king, but when Prince Charles married Diana, she became Princess Diana. If they had stayed married and he had ascended to the throne, then she would have become Queen Diana. The reasoning appears to be that since masculine words are stronger, they are reserved for true heirs and withheld from males coming into the royal family by marriage. If Prince Phillip were called "King Phillip," British subjects might forget who had inherited the right to rule.

The names that people give their children show the hopes and 26 dreams they have for them, and when we look at the differences between male and female names in a culture, we can see the cumulative expectations of that culture. In our culture girls often have names taken from small, aesthetically pleasing items; for example, Ruby, Jewel, and Pearl. Esther and Stella mean "star," and Ada means "ornament." One of the few women's names that refers to strength is Mildred, and it means "mild strength." Boys often have names with meanings of power and strength; for example, Neil means "champion"; Martin is from Mars, the God of war; Raymond means "wise protection"; Harold means "chief of the army"; Ira means "vigilant"; Rex means "king"; and Richard means "strong king."

We see similar differences in food metaphors. Food is a passive sub- 27 stance just sitting there waiting to be eaten. Many people have recognized this and so no longer feel comfortable describing women as "delectable morsels." However, when I was a teenager, it was considered a compliment to refer to a girl (we didn't call anyone a "woman" until she was middle-aged) as a cute tomato, a peach, a dish, a cookie, honey, sugar, or sweetie-pie. When being affectionate, women will occasionally call a man honey or sweetie, but in general, food metaphors are used much less often with men than with women. If a man is called "a fruit," his masculinity is being questioned. But it's perfectly acceptable to use a food metaphor if the food is heavier and more substantive than that used for women. For example, pin-up pictures of women have long been known as "cheesecake," but when Burt Reynolds posed for a nude centerfold the picture was immediately dubbed "beefcake," that is, a hunk of meat. That such sexual references to men have come into the language is another reflection of how society is beginning to lessen the differences between their attitudes toward men and women.

Something similar to the fruit metaphor happens with references to 28 plants. We insult a man by calling him a "pansy," but it wasn't considered particularly insulting to talk about a girl being a wallflower, a clinging vine, or a shrinking violet, or to give girls such names as Ivy, Rose, Lily, Iris, Daisy, Camelia, Heather, and Flora. A positive plant metaphor can be used with a man only if the plant is big and strong; for example, Andrew Jackson's nickname of Old Hickory. Also, the phrases *blooming idiots* and *budding geniuses* can be used with either sex, but notice how they are based on the most active thing a plant can do, which is to bloom or bud.

Animal metaphors also illustrate the different expectations for males 29 and females. Men are referred to as studs, bucks, and wolves, while women are referred to with such metaphors as kitten, bunny, beaver, bird, chick, and lamb. In the 1950s, we said that boys went "tom catting," but today it's just "catting around," and both boys and girls do it. When the term foxy, meaning that someone was sexy, first became popular it was used only for females, but now someone of either sex can be described as a fox. Some animal metaphors that are used predominantly with men have negative connotations based on the size and/or strength of the animals; for example, beast, bullheaded, jackass, rat, loanshark, and vulture. Negative metaphors used with women are based on smaller animals; for example, social butterfly, mousey, catty, and vixen. The feminine terms connote action, but not the same kind of large scale action as with the masculine terms.

Women Are Connected with Negative Connotations; Men with Positve Connotations

The final point that my note cards illustrated was how many posi- 30 tive connotations are associated with the concept of masculinity, while there are either trivial or negative connotations connected with the corresponding feminine concept. An example from the animal metaphors makes a good illustration. The word *shrew* taken from the name of a small but especially vicious animal was defined in my dictionary as "an ill-tempered scolding woman," but the word *shrewd* taken from the same root was defined as "marked by clever, discerning awareness" and was illustrated with the phrase "a shrewd businessman."

Early in life, children are conditioned to the superiority of the mas- 31 culine role. As child psychologists point out, little girls have much more freedom to experiment with sex roles than do little boys. If a little girl acts like a tomboy, most parents have mixed feelings, being at least partially proud. But if their little boy acts like a sissy (derived from *sister*), they call a psychologist. It's perfectly acceptable for a little girl to sleep in the crib that was purchased for her brother, to wear his hand-me-down jeans and shirts, and to ride the bicycle that he has outgrown. But few parents would put a boy baby in a white-and-gold crib decorated with frills and lace, and virtually no parents would have their little boy wear his sister's hand-me-down dresses, nor would they have their son ride a girl's pink bicycle with a flower-bedecked basket. The proper names given to girls and boys show this same attitude. Girls can have "boy" names—Cris, Craig, Jo, Kelly, Shawn, Teri, Toni, and Sam— but it doesn't work the other way around. A couple of generations ago, Beverly, Frances, Hazel, Marion, and Shirley were common boys' names. As parents gave these names to more and more girls, they fell into disuse for males, and some older men who have these names prefer to go by their initials or by such abbreviated forms as Haze or Shirl.

When a little girl is told to be a lady, she is being told to sit with her 32 knees together and to be quiet and dainty. But when a little boy is told to be a man, he is being told to be noble, strong, and virtuous—to have all the qualities that the speaker looks on as desirable. The concept of manliness has such positive connotations that it used to be a compliment to call someone a he-man, to say that he was doubly a man. Today many people are more ambivalent about this term and respond to it much as they do to the word *macho*. But calling someone a manly man or a virile man is nearly always meant as a compliment. Virile comes from the Indo-European *vir*, meaning "man," which is also the basis of *virtuous*. Consider the positive connotations of both virile and virtuous with the negative connotations of *hysterical*. The Greeks took this latter word from their name for uterus (as still seen in *hysterectomy*). They thought that women were the only ones who experienced uncontrolled emotional outbursts, and so the condition must have something to do with a part of the body that only women have. But how word meanings change is regularly shown at athletic events where thousands of *virtuous* women sit quietly beside their *hysterical* husbands.

Differences in the connotations between positive male and negative 33 female connotations can be seen in several pairs of words that differ denotatively only in the matter of sex. Bachelor as compared to spinster or old maid has such positive connotations that women try to adopt it by using the term *bachelor-girl* or *bachelorette*. Old maid is so negative that it's the basis for metaphors: pretentious and fussy old men are called "old maids," as are the leftover kernels of unpopped popcorn and the last card in a popular children's card game.

Patron and *matron* (Middle English for "father" and "mother") have 34 such different levels of prestige that women try to borrow the more positive masculine connotations with the word *patroness*, literally "female father." Such a peculiar term came about because of the high prestige attached to patron in such phrases as a *patron of the arts* or a *patron saint*. Matron is more apt to be used in talking about a woman in charge of a jail or a public restroom.

When men are doing jobs that women often do, we apparently try to 35 pay the men extra by giving them fancy titles. For example, a male cook is more likely to be called a "chef" while a male seamstress will get the title of "tailor." The armed forces have a special problem in that they recruit under such slogans as "The Marine Corps builds men!" and "Join the Army! Become a Man." Once the recruits are enlisted, they find themselves doing much of the work that has been traditionally thought of as "women's work." The solution to getting the work done and not insulting anyone's masculinity was to change the titles as shown below:

waitress = orderly
nurse = medic or corpsman
secretary=clerk-typist
assistant=adjutant
dishwasher = KP (kitchen police) or kitchen helper

Compare *brave* and *squaw*. Early settlers in America truly admired 36 Indian men and hence named them with a word that carried connotations of youth, vigor, and courage. But for Indian women they used an Algonquin slang term with negative sexual connotations that are almost opposite to those of brave. Wizard and witch contrast almost as much. The masculine *wizard* implies skill and wisdom combined with magic, while the feminine *witch* implies evil intentions combined with magic. When witch is used for men, as in witch-doctor, many mainstream speakers feel some carry-over of the negative connotations.

Part of the unattractiveness of both witch and squaw is that they have 37 been used so often to refer to old women, something with which our culture is particularly uncomfortable, just as the Afghans were. Imagine my surprise when I ran across the phrases *grandfatherly advice* and *old wives' tales* and realized that the underlying implication is the same as the Afghan proverb about old men being worth listening to while old women talk only foolishness.

Other terms that show how negatively we view old women as 38 compared to young women are *old nag* as compared to *filly*, *old crow* or *old bat* as compared to *bird*, and being *catty* as compared to being *kittenish*. There is no matching set of metaphors for men. The chicken metaphor tells the whole story of a woman's life. In her youth she is a chick. Then she marries and begins feathering her nest. Soon she begins feeling cooped up, so she goes to hen parties where she cackles with her friends. Then she has her brood, begins to henpeck her husband, and finally turns into an old biddy.

I embarked on my study of the dictionary not with the intention of 39 prescribing language change but simply to see what the language would tell me about sexism. Nevertheless, I have been both surprised and pleased as I've watched the changes that have occurred over the past three decades. I'm one of those linguists who believes that new language customs will cause a new generation of speakers to grow up with different expectations. This is why I'm happy about people's efforts to use inclusive languages, to say "he or she" or "they" when speaking about individuals whose names they do not know. I'm glad that leading publishers have developed guidelines to help writers use language that is fair to both sexes. I'm glad that most newspapers and magazines list women by their own names instead of only by their husbands' names. And I'm so glad that educated and thoughtful people no longer begin their business letters with "Dear Sir" or "Gentlemen," but instead use a memo form or begin with such salutations as "Dear Colleagues," "Dear Reader," or "Dear Committee Members." I'm also glad that such words as *poetess, authoress, conductress,* and *aviatrix* now sound quaint and old-fashioned and that *chairman* is giving way to *chair* or *head, mailman* to *mail carrier, clergyman* to *clergy,* and *stewardess* to *flight attendant.* I was also pleased when the National Oceanic and Atmospheric Administration bowed to feminist complaints and in the late 1970s began to alternate men's and women's names for hurricanes. However, I wasn't so pleased to discover that the change did not immediately erase sexist thoughts from everyone's mind, as shown by a headline about Hurricane David in a 1979 New York tabloid, "David Rapes Virgin Islands." More recently a similar metaphor appeared in a head-line in the *Arizona Republic* about Hurricane Charlie, "Charlie Quits Carolinas, Flirts with Virginia."

What these incidents show is that sexism is not something existing 40 independently in American English or in the particular dictionary that I happened to read. Rather, it exists in people's minds. Language is like an X-ray in providing visible evidence of invisible thoughts. The best thing about people being interested in and discussing sexist language is that as they make conscious decisions about what pronouns they will use, what jokes they will tell or laugh at, how they will write their names, or how they will begin their letters, they are forced to think about the underlying issue of sexism. This is good because as a problem that begins in people's assumptions and expectations, it's a problem that will be solved only when a great many people have given it a great deal of thought.

Responding to Reading

1. What point is Nilsen making about the culture in which she lives? Does your experience support her conclusions?
2. Does Nilsen use enough examples to support her claims? What others can you think of? In what way do her examples—and your own—illustrate the power of language to define the way people think?
3. Many of the connotations of the words Nilsen discusses are hundreds of years old and are also found in languages other than English. Given the widespread and long-standing linguistic bias against women, do you think attempts by Nilsen and others to change this situation succeed?

PROPAGANDA UNDER A DICTATORSHIP

Aldous Huxley

Aldous Huxley (1894–1963) was born in Surrey, England, and was educated at Eton and Balliol College, Oxford. Despite a serious eye disease, Huxley read with the aid of a magnifying glass and graduated from Oxford in 1915 with honors in English literature, after which he joined the staff of the Atheneum. *His brilliant social satires and wide-ranging essays on architecture, science, music, history, philosophy, and religion explore the relationship between humans and society.* Brave New World *(1932) is his best-known satire on how futuristic mass technology will achieve a sinister utopia of scientific breeding and conditioned happiness. Huxley's other works include* Eyeless in Gaza *(1936),* After Many a Summer *(1939),* Time Must Have a Stop *(1944), and* Ape and Essence *(1948). The* Doors Of Perception *(1954),* Heaven and Hell *(1956), and* Island *(1962) can be seen as attempts to search in new spiritual directions— through mysticism, mescaline, and parapyschology—as a reaction to the grim future he so devastatingly portrayed. In "Propaganda under a Dictatorship," from* Brave New World Revisited *(1958), Huxley reveals how the manipulation of language in the propaganda of Nazi Germany conditioned the thoughts and behavior of the masses.*

At his trial after the Second World War, Hitler's Minister for Arma- 1 ments, Albert Speer, delivered a long speech in which, with remarkable acuteness, he described the Nazi tyranny and analyzed its methods. "Hitler's dictatorship," he said, "differed in one fundamental point from all its predecessors in history. It was the first dictatorship in the present period of modern technical development, a dictatorship which made complete use of all technical means for the domination of its own country. Through technical devices like the radio and the loud-speaker, eighty million people were deprived of independent thought. It was thereby possible to subject them to the will of one man. . . . Earlier dictators needed highly qualified assistants even at the lowest level—men who could think and act independently. The totalitarian system in the period of modern technical development can dispense with such men; thanks to modern methods of communication, it is possible to mechanize the lower leadership. As a result of this there has arisen the new type of the uncritical recipient of orders."

In the Brave New World of my prophetic fable technology had 2 advanced far beyond the point it had reached in Hitler's day; consequently the recipients of orders were far less critical than their Nazi counterparts, far more obedient to the order-giving elite. Moreover, they had been genetically standardized and postnatally conditioned to perform their subordinate functions, and could therefore be depended upon to behave almost as predictably as machines. . . . This conditioning of "the lower leadership" is already going on under the Communist dictatorships. The Chinese and the Russians are not relying merely on the indirect effects of advancing technology; they are working directly on the psychophysical organisms of their lower leaders, subjecting minds and bodies to a system of ruthless and, from all accounts, highly effective conditioning. "Many a man," said Speer, "has been haunted by the nightmare that one day nations might be dominated by technical means. That nightmare was almost realized in Hitler's totalitarian system." Almost, but not quite. The Nazis did not have time—and perhaps did not have the intelligence and the necessary knowledge—to brainwash and condition their lower leadership. This, it may be, is one of the reasons why they failed.

Since Hitler's day the armory of technical devices at the disposal of 3 the would-be dictator has been considerably enlarged. As well as the radio, the loud-speaker, the moving picture camera and the rotary press, the contemporary propagandist can make use of television to broadcast the image as well as the voice of his client, and can record both image and voice on spools of magnetic tape. Thanks to technological progress, Big Brother can now be almost as omnipresent as God. Nor is it only on the technical front that the hand of the would-be dictator has been strengthened. Since Hitler's day a great deal of work has been carried out in those fields of applied psychology and neurology which are the special province of the propagandist, the indoctrinator and the brainwasher. In the past these specialists in the art of changing people's minds were empiricists. By a method of trial and error they had worked out a number of techniques and procedures, which they used very effectively without, however, knowing precisely why they were effective. Today the art of mind-control is in process of becoming a science. The practitioners of this science know what they are doing and why. They are guided in their work by theories and hypotheses solidly established on a massive foundation of experimental evidence. Thanks to the new insights and the new techniques made possible by these insights, the nightmare that was "all but realized in Hitler's totalitarian system" may soon be completely realizable.

But before we discuss these new insights and techniques let us take a 4 look at the nightmare that so nearly came true in Nazi Germany. What were the methods used by Hitler and Goebbels[1] for "depriving eighty million people of independent thought and subjecting them to the will of one man"? And what was the theory of human nature upon which those terrifyingly successful methods were based? These questions can be

---

[1] *Joseph Paul Goebbels (1897–1945):* the propaganda minister under Hitler, a master of the "big lie." [Eds.]

answered, for the most part, in Hitler's own words. And what remarkably clear and astute words they are! When he writes about such vast abstractions as Race and History and Providence, Hitler is strictly unreadable. But when he writes about the German masses and the methods he used for dominating and directing them, his style changes. Nonsense gives place to sense, bombast to a hard-boiled and cynical lucidity. In his philosophical lucubrations Hitler was either cloudily daydreaming or reproducing other people's half-baked notions. In his comments on crowds and propaganda he was writing of things he knew by firsthand experience. In the words of his ablest biographer, Mr. Alan Bullock, "Hitler was the greatest demagogue in history." Those who add "only a demagogue," fail to appreciate the nature of political power in an age of mass politics. As he himself said, "To be a leader means to be able to move the masses." Hitler's aim was first to move the masses and then, having pried them loose from their traditional loyalties and moralities, to impose upon them (with the hypnotized consent of the majority) a new authoritarian order of his own devising. "Hitler," wrote Hermann Rauschning in 1939, "has a deep respect for the Catholic church and the Jesuit order; not because of their Christian doctrine, but because of the 'machinery' they have elaborated and controlled, their hierarchical system, their extremely clever tactics, their knowledge of human nature and their wise use of human weaknesses in ruling over believers." Ecclesiasticism without Christianity, the discipline of a monastic rule, not for God's sake or in order to achieve personal salvation, but for the sake of the State and for the greater glory and power of the demagogue turned Leader—this was the goal toward which the systematic moving of the masses was to lead.

Let us see what Hitler thought of the masses he moved and how 5 he did the moving. The first principle from which he started was a value judgment: the masses are utterly contemptible. They are incapable of abstract thinking and uninterested in any fact outside the circle of their immediate experience. Their behavior is determined, not by knowledge and reason, but by feelings and unconscious drives. It is in these drives and feelings that "the roots of their positive as well as their negative attitudes are implanted." To be successful a propagandist must learn how to manipulate these instincts and emotions. "The driving force which has brought about the most tremendous revolutions on this earth has never been a body of scientific teaching which has gained power over the masses, but always a devotion which has inspired them, and often a kind of hysteria which has urged them into action. Whoever wishes to win over the masses must know the key that will open the door of their hearts." . . . In post-Freudian jargon, of their unconscious.

Hitler made his strongest appeal to those members of the lower 6 middle classes who had been ruined by the inflation of 1923, and then ruined all over again by the depression of 1929 and the following years. "The masses" of whom he speaks were these bewildered, frustrated and chronically anxious millions. To make them more masslike, more homogeneously subhuman, he assembled them, by the thousands and the tens of thousands, in vast halls and arenas, where individuals could lose their personal identity, even their elementary humanity, and be merged with the crowd. A man or woman makes direct contact with society in two ways: as a member of some familial, professional or religious group, or as a member of a crowd. Groups are capable of being as moral and intelligent as the individuals who form them; a crowd is chaotic, has no purpose of its own and is capable of anything except intelligent action and realistic thinking. Assembled in a crowd, people lose their powers of reasoning and their capacity for moral choice. Their suggestibility is increased to the point where they cease to have any judgment or will of their own. They become very excitable, they lose all sense of individual or collective responsibility, they are subject to sudden accesses of rage, enthusiasm and panic. In a word, a man in a crowd behaves as though he had swallowed a large dose of some powerful intoxicant. He is a victim of what I have called "herd-poisoning." Like alcohol, herd-poison is an active, extraverted drug. The crowd-intoxicated individual escapes from responsibility, intelligence and morality into a kind of frantic, animal mindlessness.

During his long career as an agitator, Hitler had studied the effects of 7 herd-poison and had learned how to exploit them for his own purposes. He had discovered that the orator can appeal to those "hidden forces" which motivate men's actions, much more effectively than can the writer. Reading is a private, not a collective activity. The writer speaks only to individuals, sitting by themselves in a state of normal sobriety. The orator speaks to masses of individuals, already well primed with herd-poison. They are at his mercy and, if he knows his business, he can do what he likes with them. As an orator, Hitler knew his business supremely well. He was able, in his own words, "to follow the lead of the great mass in such a way that from the living emotion to his hearers the apt word which he needed would be suggested to him and in its turn this would go straight to the heart of his hearers." Otto Strasser called him a "loud-speaker, proclaiming the most secret desires, the least admissible instincts, the sufferings and personal revolts of a whole nation." Twenty years before Madison Avenue embarked upon "Motivational Research," Hitler was systematically exploring and exploiting the secret fears and hopes, the cravings, anxieties and frustrations of the German masses. It is by manipulating "hidden forces" that the advertising experts induce us to buy their wares—a toothpaste, a brand of cigarettes, a political candidate. And it is by appealing to the same hidden forces—and to others too dangerous for Madison Avenue to meddle with—that Hitler induced the German masses to buy themselves a Fuehrer, an insane philosophy and the Second World War.

Unlike the masses, intellectuals have a taste for rationality and an 8 interest in facts. Their critical habit of mind makes them resistant to the kind of propaganda that works so well on the majority. Among the masses "instinct is supreme, and from instinct comes faith. . . . While the healthy common folk instinctively close their ranks to form a community of the people" (under a Leader, it goes without saying) "intellectuals run this way and that, like hens in a poultry yard. With them one cannot make history; they cannot be used as elements composing a community." Intellectuals are the kind of people who demand evidence and are shocked by logical inconsistencies and fallacies. They regard oversimplification as the original sin of the mind and have no use for the slogans, the unqualified assertions and sweeping generalizations which are the propagandist's stock in trade. "All effective propaganda," Hitler wrote, "must be confined to a few bare necessities and then must be expressed in a few stereotyped formulas." These stereotyped formulas must be constantly repeated, for "only constant repetition will finally succeed in imprinting an idea upon the memory of a crowd." Philosophy teaches us to feel uncertain about the things that seem to us self-evident. Propaganda, on the other hand, teaches us to accept as self-evident matters about which it would be reasonable to suspend our judgment or to feel doubt. The aim of the demagogue is to create social coherence under his own leadership. But, as Bertrand Russell has pointed out, "systems of dogma without empirical foundations, such as scholasticism, Marxism and fascism, have the advantage of producing a great deal of social coherence among their disciples." The demagogic propagandist must therefore be consistently dogmatic. All his statements are made without qualification. There are no grays in his picture of the world; everything is either diabolically black or celestially white. In Hitler's words, the propagandist should adopt "a systematically one-sided attitude towards every problem that has to be dealt with." He must never admit that he might be wrong or that people with a different point of view might be even partially right. Opponents should not be argued with; they should be attacked, shouted down, or, if they become too much of a nuisance, liquidated. The morally squeamish intellectual may be shocked by this kind of thing. But the masses are always convinced that "right is on the side of the active aggressor."

Such, then, was Hitler's opinion of humanity in the mass. It was a very low opinion. Was it also an incorrect opinion? The tree is known by its fruits, and a theory of human nature which inspired the kind of techniques that proved so horribly effective must contain at least an element of truth. Virtue and intelligence belong to human beings as individuals freely associating with other individuals in small groups. So do sin—and stupidity. But the subhuman mindlessness to which the demagogue makes his appeal, the moral imbecility on which he relies when he goads his victims into action, are characteristic not of men and women as individuals, but of men and women in masses. Mindlessness and moral idiocy are not characteristically human attributes; they are symptoms of herd-poisoning. In all the world's higher religions, salvation and enlightenment are for individuals. The kingdom of heaven is within the mind of a person, not within the collective mindlessness of a crowd. Christ promised to be present where two or three are gathered together. He did not say anything about being present where thousands are intoxicating one another with herd-poison. Under the Nazis enormous numbers of people were compelled to spend an enormous amount of time marching in serried ranks from point A to point B and back again to point A. "This keeping of the whole population on the march seemed to be a senseless waste of time and energy. Only much later," adds Hermann Rauschning, "was there revealed in it a subtle intention based on a well-judged adjustment of ends and means. Marching diverts men's thoughts. Marching kills thought. Marching makes an end of individuality. Marching is the indispensable magic stroke performed in order to accustom the people to a mechanical, quasi-ritualistic activity until it becomes second nature."

From his point of view and at the level where he had chosen to do 10 his dreadful work, Hitler was perfectly correct in his estimate of human nature. To those of us who look at men and women as individuals rather than as members of crowds, or of regimented collectives, he seems hideously wrong. In an age of accelerating over-population, of accelerating over-organization and even more efficient means of mass communication, how can we preserve the integrity and reassert the value of the human individual? This is a question that can still be asked and perhaps effectively answered. A generation from now it may be too late to find an answer and perhaps impossible, in the stifling collective climate of that future time, even to ask the question.

Responding to Reading

1. According to Huxley, why was Hitler's dictatorship different from its predecessors? What techniques did Hitler use to manipulate the German people? Why do you think he was so successful?

2. What was Hitler's opinion of the masses? Does Huxley agree with this evaluation?

3. In paragraph 3, Huxley says, "Since Hitler's day the armory of technical devices at the disposal of the would-be dictator has been considerably enlarged." What were some of these devices, and how did they make a dictator's job easier? Do you think the Internet makes it more likely or less likely that a dictator could control the masses?

POLITICS AND THE ENGLISH LANGUAGE

George Orwell

British Empire

Eric Blair (1903–1950) was an Englishman, born in Bengal, India, who took the pen name George Orwell. He attended school in England and then joined the Indian Imperial Police in Burma, where he came to question the British methods of colonialism. (See his essay "Shooting an Elephant," p. 658). An enemy of totalitarianism in any form and a spokesman for the oppressed, Orwell criticized totalitarian regimes in his bitterly satirical novels Animal Farm *(1945) and* 1984 *(1949). The following essay was written during the period between these two novels' publication, at the end of World War II, when jingoistic praise for "our democratic institutions" and blindly passionate defenses of Marxist ideology were the two common extremes of public political discourse. Orwell's plea for clear thinking and writing at a time when "political language . . . is designed to make lies sound truthful and murder respectable, and to give an appearance of solidity to pure wind" is as relevant today as when it was written.*

Most people who bother with the matter at all would admit that the English language is in a bad way, but it is generally assumed that we cannot by conscious action do anything about it. Our civilization is decadent and our language—so the argument runs—must inevitably share in the general collapse. It follows that any struggle against the abuse of language is a sentimental archaism, like preferring candles to electric light or hansom cabs to airplanes. Underneath this lies the half-conscious belief that language is a natural growth and not an instrument which we shape for our own purposes.

Now, it is clear that the decline of a language must ultimately have political and economic causes: it is not due simply to the bad influence of this or that individual writer. But an effect can become a cause, reinforcing the original cause and producing the same effect in an intensified form, and so on indefinitely. A man may take to drink because he feels himself to be a failure, and then fail all the more completely because he drinks. It is rather the same thing that is happening to the English language. It becomes ugly and inaccurate because our thoughts are foolish, but the slovenliness of our language makes it easier for us to have foolish thoughts. The point is that the process is reversible. Modern English, especially written English, is full of bad habits which spread by imitation and which can be avoided if one is willing to take the necessary trouble. If one gets rid of these habits one can think more clearly, and to think clearly is a necessary first step towards political regeneration: so that the fight against bad English is not frivolous and is not the exclusive concern of professional writers. I will come back to this presently, and I hope that by that time the meaning of what I have said here will have become clearer. Meanwhile, here are five specimens of the English language as it is now habitually written.

These five passages have not been picked out because they are ₃ especially bad—I could have quoted far worse if I had chosen—but because they illustrate various of the mental vices from which we now suffer. They are a little below the average, but are fairly representative samples. I number them so that I can refer back to them when necessary:

"(1) I am not, indeed, sure whether it is not true to say that the Milton who once seemed not unlike a seventeenth-century Shelley had not become, out of an experience ever more bitter in each year, more alien (*sic*) to the founder of that Jesuit sect which nothing could induce him to tolerate."

Professor Harold Laski (Essay in *Freedom of Expression*).

skipstones

"(2) Above all, we cannot play ducks and drakes with a native battery of idioms which prescribes such egregious collocations of vocables as the Basic *put up with* for *tolerate* or *put at a loss* for *bewilder*."

Armament

Professor Lancelot Hogben (*Interglossa*).

"(3) On the one side we have the free personality: by definition it is not neurotic, for it has neither conflict nor dream. Its desires, such as they are, are transparent, for they are just what institutional approval keeps in the forefront of consciousness; another institutional pattern would alter their number and intensity; there is little in them that is natural, irreducible, or culturally dangerous. But *on the other side*, the social bond itself is nothing but the mutual reflection of these self-secure integrities. Recall the definition of love. Is not this the very picture of a small academic? Where is there a place in this hall of mirrors for either personality or fraternity?"

Essay on psychology in *Politics* (New York).

Idioms =

"(4) All the 'best people' from the gentlemen's clubs, and all the frantic fascist captains, united in common hatred of Socialism and bestial horror of the rising tide of the mass revolutionary movement, have turned to acts of provocation, to foul incendiarism, to medieval legends of poisoned wells, to legalize their own destruction of proletarian organizations, and rouse the agitated petty-bourgeoisie to chauvinistic fervor on behalf of the fight against the revolutionary way out of the crisis."

Communist pamphlet.

ducks & drakes =

"(5) If a new spirit *is* to be infused into this old country, there is one thorny and contentious reform which must be tackled, and that is the humanization and galvanization of the B.B.C. Timidity here will bespeak cancer and atrophy of the soul. The heart of Britain may be sound and of strong beat, for instance, but the British lion's roar at present is like that of Bottom in Shakespeare's *Midsummer Night's Dream*—as gentle as any sucking dove. A virile new Britain cannot continue indefinitely to be traduced in the eyes, or rather ears, of the world by the effete languors of Langham Place, brazenly masquerading as 'standard English.' When the Voice of Britain is heard at nine o'clock, better far and infinitely less ludicrous to hear aitches honestly dropped than the present priggish, inflated, inhibited, school-ma'amish arch braying of blameless bashful mewing maidens!"

England Letter in *Tribune*.

Each of these passages has faults of its own, but, quite apart from avoidable ugliness, two qualities are common to all of them. The first is staleness of imagery: the other is lack of precision. The writer either has a meaning and cannot express it, or he inadvertently says something else, or he is almost indifferent as to whether his words mean anything or not. This mixture of vagueness and sheer incompetence is the most marked characteristic of modern English prose, and especially of any kind of political writing. As soon as certain topics are raised, the concrete melts into the abstract and no one seems able to think of turns of speech that are not hackneyed: prose consists less and less of *words* chosen for the sake of their meaning, and more and more of *phrases* tacked together like the sections of a prefabricated hen-house. I list below, with notes and examples, various of the tricks by means of which the work of prose-construction is habitually dodged:

Dying Metaphors

A newly invented metaphor assists thought by evoking a visual image, while on the other hand a metaphor which is technically "dead" (e.g. *iron resolution*) has in effect reverted to being an ordinary word and can generally be used without loss of vividness. But in between these two classes there is a huge dump of worn-out metaphors which have lost all evocative power and are merely used because they save people the trouble of inventing phrases for themselves. Examples are: *Ring the changes on, take up the cudgels for, toe the line, ride roughshod over, stand shoulder to shoulder with, play into the hands of, no axe to grind, grist to the mill, fishing in troubled waters, on the order of the day, Achilles' heel, swan song, hotbed.* Many of these are used without knowledge of their meaning (what is a "rift,"[1] for instance?), and incompatible metaphors

---

[1] Originally *rift* referred to a geological fault or fissure. Now it is commonly used to indicate a breach or estrangement. [Eds.]

are frequently mixed, a sure sign that the writer is not interested in what he is saying. Some metaphors now current have been twisted out of their original meaning without those who use them even being aware of the fact. For example, *toe the line* is sometimes written *tow the line*. Another example is the *hammer and the anvil*, now always used with the implication that the anvil gets the worst or it. In real life it is always the anvil that breaks the hammer, never the other way about: a writer who stopped to think what he was saying would be aware of this, and would avoid perverting the original phrase.

Operators or Verbal False Limbs

These save the trouble of picking out appropriate verbs and nouns, ₆ and at the same time pad each sentence with extra syllables which give it an appearance of symmetry. Characteristic phrases are: *render inoperative, militate against, make contact with, be subjected to, give rise to, give grounds for, have the effect of, play a leading part (role) in, make itself felt, take effect, exhibit a tendency to, serve the purpose of, etc., etc.* The keynote is the elimination of simple verbs. Instead of being a single word, such as *break, stop, spoil, mend, kill*, a verb becomes a *phrase*, made up of a noun or adjective tacked on to some general-purposes verb such as *prove, serve, form, play, render.* In addition, the passive voice is wherever possible used in preference to the active, and noun constructions are used instead of gerunds (*by examination of* instead of *by examining*). The range of verbs is further cut down by means of the *-ize* and *de-* formation, and the banal statements are given an appearance of profundity by means of the *not un-* formation. Simple conjunctions and prepositions are replaced by such phrases as *with respect to, having regard to, the fact that, by dint of, in view of, in the interests of, on the hypothesis that;* and the ends of sentences are saved from anticlimax by such resounding commonplaces as *greatly to be desired, cannot be left out of account, a development to be expected in the near future, deserving of serious consideration, brought to a satisfactory conclusion,* and so on and so forth.

Pretentious Diction

Words like *phenomenon, element, individual* (as noun), *objective,* ₇ *categorical, effective, virtual, basic, primary, promote, constitute, exhibit, exploit, utilize, eliminate, liquidate,* are used to dress up simple statements and give an air of scientific impartiality to biased judgments. Adjectives like *epoch-making, epic, historic, unforgettable, triumphant, age-old, inevitable, inexorable, veritable,* are used to dignify the sordid processes of international politics, while writing that aims at glorifying war usually takes on an archaic color, its characteristic words being: *realm, throne, chariot, mailed fist, trident, sword, shield, buckler, banner, jackboot, clarion.* Foreign words and expressions such as *cul de sac, ancien régime, deus ex machina, mutatis mutandis, status quo, gleichschaltung, weltanschauung,* are used to give an air of culture and elegance. Except for the useful abbreviations *i.e., e.g.,* and *etc.,* there is no real need for any of the hundreds of foreign phrases now current in English. Bad writers, and especially scientific, political and sociological writers, are nearly always haunted by the notion that Latin or Greek words are grander than Saxon ones, and unnecessary words like *expedite, ameliorate, predict, extraneous, deracinated, clandestine, subaqueous* and hundreds of others constantly gain ground from their Anglo-Saxon opposite numbers.[2] The jargon peculiar to Marxist writing (*hyena, hangman, cannibal, petty bourgeois, these gentry, lacquey, flunkey, mad dog, White Guard,* etc.) consists largely of words and phrases translated from Russian, German or French; but the normal way of coining a new word is to use a Latin or Greek root with the appropriate affix and, where necessary, the *-ize* formation. It is often easier to make up words of this kind (*deregionalize, impermissible, extra-marital, nonfragmentatory* and so forth) than to think up the English words that will cover one's meaning. The result, in general, is an increase in slovenliness and vagueness.

Meaningless Words

In certain kinds of writing, particularly in art criticism and literary 8 criticism, it is normal to come across long passages which are almost completely lacking in meaning.[3] Words like *romantic, plastic, values, human, dead, sentimental, natural, vitality,* as used in art criticism, are strictly meaningless in the sense that they not only do not point to any discoverable object, but are hardly ever expected to do so by the reader. When one critic writes, "The outstanding feature of Mr. X's work is its living quality," while another writes, "The immediately striking thing about Mr. X's work is its peculiar deadness," the reader accepts this as a simple difference of opinion. If words like *black* and *white* were involved, instead of the jargon words *dead* and *living,* he would see at once that language was being used in an improper way. Many political words are similarly abused. The word *Fascism* has now no meaning

---

[2] An interesting illustration of this is the way in which the English flower names which were in use till very recently are being ousted by Greek ones, *snapdragon* becoming *antirrhinum, forget-me-not* becoming *myosotis,* etc. It is hard to see any practical reason for this change in fashion: it is probably due to an instinctive turning-away from the more homely word and a vague feeling that the Greek word is scientific.

[3] Example: "Comfort's catholicity of perception and image, strangely Whitmanesque in range, almost the exact opposite in aesthetic compulsion, continues to evoke that trembling atmospheric accumulative hinting at a cruel, an inexorably serene timelessness. . . . Wrey Gardiner scores by aiming at simple bull's-eyes with precision. Only they are not so simple, and through this contended sadness—runs more than the surface bittersweet of resignation" (*Poetry Quarterly*).

except in so far as it signifies "something not desirable." The words *democracy, socialism, freedom, patriotic, realistic, justice,* have each of them several different meanings which cannot be reconciled with one another. In the case of a word like *democracy,* not only is there no agreed definition, but the attempt to make one is resisted from all sides. It is almost universally felt that when we call a country democratic we are praising it: consequently the defenders of every kind of regime claim that it is a democracy, and fear that they might have to stop using the word if it were tied down to any one meaning. Words of this kind are often used in a consciously dishonest way. That is, the person who uses them has his own private definition, but allows his hearer to think he means something quite different. Statements like *Marshal Pétain was a true patriot, The Soviet Press is the freest in the world, The Catholic Church is opposed to persecution,* are almost always made with intent to deceive. Other words used in variable meanings, in most cases more or less dishonestly, are: *class, totalitarian, science, progressive, reactionary, bourgeois, equality.*

Now that I have made this catalogue of swindles and perversions, 9 let me give another example of the kind of writing that they lead to. This time it must of its nature be an imaginary one. I am going to translate a passage of good English into modern English of the worst sort. Here is a well-known verse from *Ecclesiastes:*

> "I returned and saw under the sun, that the race is not to the swift, nor the battle to the strong, neither yet bread to the wise, nor yet riches to men of understanding, nor yet favor to men of skill; but time and chance happeneth to them all."

Here it is in modern English: 10

> "Objective consideration of contemporary phenomena compels the conclusion that success or failure in competitive activities exhibits no tendency to be commensurate with innate capacity, but that a considerable element of the unpredictable must invariably be taken into account."

This is a parody, but not a very gross one. Exhibit (3), above, for 11 instance, contains several patches of the same kind of English. It will be seen that I have not made a full translation. The beginning and ending of the sentence follow the original meaning fairly closely, but in the middle the concrete illustrations—race, battle, bread—dissolve into the vague phrase "success or failure in competitive activities." This had to be so, because no modern writer of the kind I am discussing—no one capable of using phrases like "objective consideration of contemporary phenomena"—would ever tabulate his thoughts in that precise and detailed way. The whole tendency of modern prose is away from concreteness. Now

shortest words that will cover one's meaning. What is above all needed is to let the meaning choose the word and not the other way about. In prose, the worst thing one can do with words is to surrender to them. When you think of a concrete object, you think wordlessly, and then, if you want to describe the thing you have been visualizing you probably hunt about till you find the exact words that seem to fit. When you think of something abstract you are more inclined to use words from the start, and unless you make a conscious effort to prevent it, the existing dialect will come rushing in and do the job for you, at the expense of blurring or even changing your meaning. Probably it is better to put off using words as long as possible and get one's meaning as clear as one can through pictures or sensations. Afterwards one can choose—not simply accept—the phrases that will best cover the meaning, and then switch round and decide what impression one's words are likely to make on another person. This last effort of the mind cuts out all stale or mixed images, all prefabricated phrases, needless repetitions, and humbug and vagueness generally. But one can often be in doubt about the effect of a word or a phrase, and one needs rules that one can rely on when instinct fails. I think the following rules will cover most cases:

(i) Never use a metaphor, simile or other figure of speech which you are used to seeing in print.
(ii) Never use a long word where a short one will do.
(iii) If it is possible to cut a word out, always cut it out.
(iv) Never use the passive where you can use the active.
(v) Never use a foreign phrase, a scientific word, or a jargon word if you can think of an everyday English equivalent.
(vi) Break any of these rules sooner than say anything outright barbarous.

These rules sound elementary, and so they are, but they demand a 20 deep change of attitude in anyone who has grown used to writing in the style now fashionable. One could keep all of them and still write bad English, but one could not write the kind of stuff that I quoted in those five specimens at the beginning of this article.

I have not here been considering the literary use of language, but 21 merely language as an instrument for expressing and not for concealing or preventing thought. Stuart Chase[5] and others have come near to claiming that all abstract words are meaningless, and have used this as a pretext for advocating a kind of political quietism. Since you don't know what Fascism is, how can you struggle against Fascism? One need not swallow such absurdities as this, but one ought to recognize that the present political chaos is connected with the decay of language, and that

---

[5] Author known for his advocacy of clear writing and clear thinking. [Eds.]

one can probably bring about some improvement by starting at the verbal end. If you simplify your English, you are freed from the worst follies of orthodoxy. You cannot speak any of the necessary dialects, and when you make a stupid remark its stupidity will be obvious, even to yourself. Political language—and with variations this is true of all political parties, from Conservatives to Anarchists—is designed to make lies sound truthful and murder respectable, and to give an appearance of solidity to pure wind. One cannot change this all in a moment, but one can at least change one's own habits, and from time to time one can even, if one jeers loudly enough, send some worn-out and useless phrase, some *jackboot, Achilles' heel, hotbed, melting pot, acid test, veritable inferno* or other lump of verbal refuse—into the dustbin where it belongs.

Responding to Reading

1. According to Orwell, what is the relationship between politics and the English language? Do you think he overstates his case?
2. What does Orwell mean in paragraph 14 when he says, "In our time, political speech and writing are largely the defense of the indefensible"? Do you believe his statement applies to current times as well? Look through some newspapers, and find several present-day examples of political language that support your conclusion.
3. Locate some examples of dying metaphors used in the popular press. Do you agree with Orwell that they undermine clear thought and expression? Why or why not?

———————————————— FOCUS ————————————————

Should English Be the Law?

ARIA[1]

Richard Rodriguez

Richard Rodriguez (1944–   ) was born in San Francisco, the son of Mexican immigrants. A graduate of Stanford University, he earned a Ph.D in Renaissance literature from the University of California at Berkeley. His first book, Hunger of Memory: The Education of Richard Rodriguez *(1982), focused on the experience of growing up in a Spanish-speaking home and adapting to an English-speaking community. His other books include* Mexico's Children *(1991) and* Days of Obligation: An Argument with My Mexican Father *(1992). Currently a Los Angeles-based journalist, Rodriguez is a frequent contributor to National Public Radio and a variety of magazines and journals. The following essay, from* Hunger of Memory, *is frequently anthologized as part of the debate over bilingual education.*

Supporters of bilingual education today imply that students like me   1
miss a great deal by not being taught in their family's language. What they seem not to recognize is that, as a socially disadvantaged child. I considered Spanish to be a private language. What I needed to learn in school was that I had the right—and the obligation—to speak the public language of *los gringos*.[2] The odd truth is that my first-grade classmates could have become bilingual, in the conventional sense of that word, more easily than I. Had they been taught (as upper-middle-class children are often taught early) a second language like Spanish or French, they could have regarded it simply as that: another public language. In my case such bilingualism could not have been so quickly achieved. What I did not believe was that I could speak a single public language.

Without question, it would have pleased me to hear my teachers   2
address me in Spanish when I entered the classroom. I would have felt much less afraid. I would have trusted them and responded with ease.

———————

[1] Solo vocal piece with instrumental accompaniment or melody. [Eds.]
[2] Foreigners, especially Americans. [Eds.]

But I would have delayed—for how long postponed?—having to learn the language of public society, I would have evaded—and for how long could I have afforded to delay?—learning the great lesson of school, that I had a public identity.

Fortunately, my teachers were unsentimental about their responsibil- 3 ity. What they understood was that I needed to speak a public language. So their voices would search me out, asking me questions. Each time I'd hear them, I'd look up in surprise to see a nun's face frowning at me. I'd mumble, not really meaning to answer. The nun would persist, "Richard, stand up. Don't look at the floor. Speak up. Speak to the entire class, not just to me!" But I couldn't believe that the English language was mine to use. (In part, I did not want to believe it.) I continued to mumble. I resisted the teacher's demands. (Did I somehow suspect that once I learned public language my pleasing family life would be changed?) Silent, waiting for the bell to sound, I remained dazed, diffident, afraid.

Because I wrongly imagined that English was intrinsically a public 4 language and Spanish an intrinsically private one, I easily noted the difference between classroom language and the language of home. At school, words were directed to a general audience of listeners. ("Boys and girls.") Words were meaningfully ordered. And the point was not self-expression alone but to make oneself understood by many others. The teacher quizzed: "Boys and girls, why do we use that word in this sentence? Could we think of a better word to use there? Would the sentence change its meaning if the words were differently arranged? And wasn't there a better way of saying much the same thing?" (I couldn't say. I wouldn't try to say.)

Three months. Five. Half a year passed. Unsmiling, ever watchful, 5 my teachers noted my silence. They began to connect my behavior with the difficult progress my older sister and brother were making. Until one Saturday morning three nuns arrived at the house to talk to our parents. Stiffly, they sat on the blue living room sofa. From the doorway of another room, spying the visitors, I noted the incongruity—the clash of two worlds, the faces and voices of school intruding upon the familiar setting of home. I overheard one voice gently wondering, "Do your children speak only Spanish at home, Mrs. Rodriguez?" While another voice added, "That Richard especially seems so timid and shy."

That Rich-heard!   6

With great tact the visitors continued, "Is it possible for you and 7 your husband to encourage your children to practice their English when they are home?" Of course, my parents complied. What would they not do for their children's well-being? And how could they have questioned the Church's authority which those women represented? In an instant, they agreed to give up the language (the sounds) that had revealed and accentuated our family's closeness. The moment after the visitors left, the change was observed, *"Ahora,* speak to us *en inglés,*[3] my father and mother united to tell us.

At first, it seemed a kind of game. After dinner each night, the fam- 8 ily gathered to practice "our" English. (It was still then *inglés,* a language foreign to us, so we felt drawn as strangers to it.) Laughing, we would try to define words we could not pronounce. We played with strange English sounds, often overanglicizing our pronunciations. And we filled the smiling gaps of our sentences with familiar Spanish sounds. But that was cheating, somebody shouted. Everyone laughed. In school, meanwhile, like my brother and sister, I was required to attend a daily tutoring session. I needed a full year of special attention. I also needed my teachers to keep my attention from straying in class by calling out, *Rich-heard*—their English voices slowly prying loose my ties to my other name, its three notes, *Ri-car-do.* Most of all I needed to hear my mother and father speak to me in a moment of seriousness in broken—suddenly heartbreaking—English. The scene was inevitable: One Saturday morning I entered the kitchen where my parents were talking in Spanish. I did not realize that they were talking in Spanish however until, at the moment they saw me, I heard their voices change to speak English. Those *gringo* sounds they uttered startled me. Pushed me away. In that moment of trivial misunderstanding and profound insight, I felt my throat twisted by unsounded grief. I turned away quickly and left the room. But I had no place to escape to with Spanish. (The spell was broken.) My brother and sisters were speaking English in another part of the house.

Again and again in the days following, increasingly angry, I was 9 obliged to hear my mother and father: "Speak to us *en inglés"* (*Speak.*) Only then did I determine to learn classroom English. Weeks after, it happened: One day in school I raised my hand to volunteer an answer. I spoke out in a loud voice. And I did not think it remarkable when the entire class understood. That day, I moved very far from the disadvantaged child I had been only days earlier. The belief, that calming assurance that I belonged in public, had at last taken hold.

Shortly after, I stopped hearing the high and loud sounds of *los grin-* 10 *gos.* A more and more confident speaker of English, I didn't trouble to listen to *how* strangers sounded, speaking to me. And there simply were too many English-speaking people in my day for me to hear American accents anymore. Conversations quickened. Listening to persons who sounded eccentrically pitched voices, I usually noted their sounds for an initial few seconds before I concentrated on *what* they were saying. Conversations became content-full. Transparent. Hearing someone's *tone* of voice—angry or questioning or sarcastic or happy or sad—I didn't

---

[3] "Now, speak to us in English." [Eds.]

distinguish it from the words it expressed. Sound and word were thus tightly wedded. At the end of a day, I was often bemused, always relieved, to realized how "silent," though crowded with words, my day in public had been. (This public silence measured and quickened the change in my life.)

At last, seven years old, I came to believe what had been technically   11 true since my birth; I was an American citizen.

But the special feeling of closeness at home was diminished by then.   12 Gone was the desperate, urgent, intense feeling of being at home, rare was the experience of feeling myself individualized by family intimates. We remained a loving family, but one greatly changed. No longer so close; no longer bound tight by the pleasing and troubling knowledge of our public separateness. Neither my older brother nor sister rushed home after school anymore. Nor did I. When I arrived home there would often be neighborhood kids in the house. Or the house would be empty of sounds.

Following the dramatic Americanization of their children, even my   13 parents grew more publicly confident. Especially my mother. She learned the names of all the people on our block. And she decided we needed to have a telephone installed in the house. My father continued to use the word *gringo*. But it was no longer charged with the old bitterness of distrust. (Stripped of any emotional content, the word simply became a name for those Americans not of Hispanic descent.) Hearing him, sometimes, I wasn't sure if he was pronouncing the Spanish word *gringo* or saying gringo in English.

Matching the silence I started hearing in public was a new quiet   14 at home. The family's quiet was partly due to the fact that, as we children learned more and more English, we shared fewer and fewer words with our parents. Sentences needed to be spoken slowly when a child addressed his mother or father. (Often the parent wouldn't understand.) The child would need to repeat himself. (Still the parent misunderstood.) The young voice, frustrated, would end up saying, "Never mind"—the subject was closed. Dinners would be noisy with the clinking of knives and forks against dishes. My mother would smile softly between her remarks; my father at the other end of the table would chew and chew at his food, while he stared over the heads of his children.

My *mother!* My *father!* After English became my primary language,   15 I no longer knew what words to use in addressing my parents. The old Spanish words (those tender accents of sound) I had used earlier— *mamá* and *papá*—I couldn't use anymore. They would have been too painful reminders of how much had changed in my life. On the other hand, the words I heard neighborhood kids call their parents seemed equally unsatisfactory. *Mother* and *Father; Ma, Papa, Pa, Dad, Pop* (how I hated the all American sound of that last word especially)—all these terms I felt were unsuitable, not really terms of address for my parents. As a result, I never used them at home. Whenever I'd speak to my parents, I would try to get their attention with eye contact alone. In public conversations, I'd refer to "my parents" or "my mother and father."

My mother and father, for their part, responded differently, as their children spoke to them less. She grew restless, seemed troubled and anxious at the scarcity of words exchanged in the house. It was she who would question me about my day when I came home from school. She smiled at small talk. She pried at the edges of my sentences to get me to say something more. (What?) She'd join conversations she overheard, but her intrusions often stopped her children's talking. By contrast, my father seemed reconciled to the new quiet. Though his English improved somewhat, he retired into silence. At dinner he spoke very little. One night his children and even his wife helplessly giggled at his garbled English pronunciation of the Catholic Grace before Meals. Thereafter he made his wife recite the prayer at the start of each meal, even on formal occasions, when there were guests in the house. Hers became the public voice of the family. On official business, it was she, not my father, one would usually hear on the phone or in stores, talking to strangers. His children grew so accustomed to his silence that, years later, they would speak routinely of his shyness. (My mother would often try to explain: Both his parents died when he was eight. He was raised by an uncle who treated him like little more than a menial servant. He was never encouraged to speak. He grew up alone. A man of few words.) But my father was not shy, I realized, when I'd watch him speaking Spanish with relatives. Using Spanish, he was quickly effusive. Especially when talking with other men, his voice would spark, flicker, flare alive with sounds. In Spanish, he expressed ideas and feelings he rarely revealed in English. With firm Spanish sounds, he conveyed confidence and authority English would never allow him.

The silence at home, however, was finally more than a literal silence. Fewer words passed between parent and child, but more profound was the silence that resulted from my inattention to sounds. At about the time I no longer bothered to listen with care to the sounds of English in public, I grew careless about listening to the sounds family members made when they spoke. Most of the time I heard someone speaking at home and didn't distinguish his sounds from the words people uttered in public. I didn't even pay much attention to my parents' accented and ungrammatical speech. At least not at home. Only when I was with them in public would I grow alert to their accents. Though, even then, their sounds caused me less and less concern. For I was increasingly confident of my own public identity.

I would have been happier about my public success had I not sometimes recalled what it had been like earlier, when my family had

conveyed its intimacy through a set of conveniently private sounds. 18
Sometimes in public, hearing a stranger, I'd hark back to my past.
A Mexican farmworker approached me downtown to ask directions to
somewhere, "¿Hijito. . . ?"[4] he said. And his voice summoned deep
longing. Another time, standing beside my mother in the visiting room
of a Carmelite convent, before the dense screen which rendered the
nuns shadowy figures, I heard several Spanish-speaking nuns—their
busy, singsong overlapping voices—assure us that yes, yes, we were
remembered, all our family was remembered in their prayers. (Their
voices echoed faraway family sounds.) Another day, a dark-faced old
woman—her hand light on my shoulder—steadied herself against me
as she boarded a bus. She murmured something I couldn't quite comprehend. Her Spanish voice came near, like the face of a never-before-
seen relative in the instant before I was kissed. Her voice, like so many
of the Spanish voices I'd hear in public, recalled the golden age of my
youth. Hearing Spanish then, I continued to be a careful, if sad, listener
to sounds. Hearing a Spanish-speaking family walking behind me, I
turned to look. I smiled for an instant, before my glance found the
Hispanic-looking faces of strangers in the crowd going by.

Today I hear bilingual educators say that children lose a degree of 19
"individuality" by becoming assimilated into public society. (Bilingual
schooling was popularized in the seventies, that decade when middle-
class ethnics began to resist the process of assimilation—the American
melting pot). But the bilingualists simplistically scorn the value and
necessity of assimilation. They do not seem to realize that there are *two*
ways a person is individualized. So they do not realize that while one suffers a diminished sense of *private* individuality by becoming assimilated
into public society, such assimilation makes possible the achievement of
public individuality.

The bilingualists insist that a student should be reminded of his 20
difference from others in mass society, his heritage. But they equate
mere separateness with individuality. The fact is that only in private—
with intimates—is separateness from the crowd a prerequisite for individuality. (An intimate draws me apart, tells me that I am unique,
unlike all others.) In public, by contrast, full individuality is achieved,
paradoxically, by those who are able to consider themselves members
of the crowd. Thus it happened for me: Only when I was able to think
of myself as an American, no longer an alien in *gringo* society, could I
seek the rights and opportunities necessary for full public individuality.
The social and political advantages I enjoy as a man result from the day
that I came to believe that my name, indeed, is *Rich-heard Road-ree-guess*.

---

[4] "Little boy. . . ?" [Eds.]

It is true that my public society today is often impersonal. (My public society is usually mass society). Yet despite the anonymity of the crowd and despite the fact that the individuality I achieve in public is often tenuous—because it depends on my being one in a crowd—I celebrate the day I acquired my new name. Those middle-class ethnics who scorn assimilation seem to me filled with decadent self-pity, obsessed by the burden of public life. Dangerously, they romanticize public separateness and they trivialize the dilemma of the socially disadvantaged.

My awkward childhood does not prove the necessity of bilingual 21 education. My story discloses instead an essential myth of childhood— inevitable pain. If I rehearse here the changes in my private life after my Americanization, it is finally to emphasize the public gain. The loss implies the gain: The house I returned to each afternoon was quiet. Intimate sounds no longer rushed to the door to greet me. There were other noises inside. The telephone rang. Neighborhood kids ran past the door of the bedroom where I was reading my school-books—covered with shopping-bag paper. Once I learned public language, it would never again be easy for me to hear intimate family voices. More and more of my day was spent hearing words. But that may only be a way of saying that the day I raised my hand in class and spoke loudly to an entire roomful of faces, my childhood started to end.

Responding to Reading

1. What distinction does Rodriguez make between public and private language? What point does this distinction help him make?
2. What does Rodriguez say he gains by speaking English? What does he say he loses? Do you agree with his assessment?
3. What is Rodriguez's main argument against those who support bilingual education? What evidence does he use to support his contention? How convincing is he?

SHOULD ENGLISH BE THE LAW?

Robert D. King

Robert D. King (1936–) was born in Hattiesburg, Mississippi. He received his B.S. and M.S. degrees in mathematics from the Georgia Institute of Technology and later earned an M.A. and a Ph.D in linguistics from the University of Wisconsin. He is currently a professor of linguistics at the University of Texas at Austin, where he also holds the Audre and Bernard Rappaport chair in Jewish Studies. His scholarly works include Historical Linguistics and Generative Grammar *(1969) and* Nehru and the Language Politics of India *(1997). The following essay for a general audience originally appeared in the* Atlantic Monthly *in 1997. In it, King surveys the "English Only" movement and uses the examples of Switzerland and India, countries whose linguistic diversity has never threatened national unity, to argue that we Americans should "relax and luxuriate in our linguistic richness and traditional tolerance of language differences."*

We have known race riots, draft riots, labor violence, secession, anti-war protests, and a whiskey rebellion, but one kind of trouble we've never had: a language riot. Language riot? It sounds like a joke. The very idea of language as a political force—as something that might threaten to split a country wide apart—is alien to our way of thinking and to our cultural traditions.

This may be changing. On August 1 of last year the U.S. House of Representatives approved a bill that would make English the official language of the United States. The vote was 259 to 169, with 223 Republicans and thirty-six Democrats voting in favor and eight Republicans, 160 Democrats, and one independent voting against. The debate was intense, acrid, and partisan. On March 25 of last year the Supreme Court agreed to review a case involving an Arizona law that would require public employees to conduct government business only in English. Arizona is one of several states that have passed "Official English" or "English Only" laws. The appeal to the Supreme Court followed a 6-to-5 ruling, in October of 1995, by a federal appeals court striking down the Arizona law. These events suggest how divisive a public issue language could become in America—even if it has until now scarcely been taken seriously.

Traditionally, the American way has been to make English the national language—but to do so quietly, locally, without fuss. The Constitution is silent on language: the Founding Fathers had no need to legislate that English be the official language of the country. It has always been taken for granted that English *is* the national language, and that one must learn English in order to make it in America.

To say that language has never been a major force in American history or politics, however, is not to say that politicians have always resisted linguistic jingoism. In 1753 Benjamin Franklin voiced his concern that German immigrants were not learning English: "Those [Germans] who come hither are generally the most ignorant Stupid Sort of their own Nation. . . . they will soon so outnumber us, that all the advantages we have will not, in My Opinion, be able to preserve our language, and even our government will become precarious."

Afraid people speak german if dont require people to learn English

Theodore Roosevelt articulated the unspoken American linguistic-melting-pot theory when he boomed, "We have room for but one language here, and that is the English language, for we intend to see that the crucible turns our people out as Americans, of American nationality, and not as dwellers in a polyglot boarding house." And: "We must have but one flag. We must also have but one language. That must be the language of the Declaration of Independence, of Washington's Farewell address, of Lincoln's Gettysburg speech and second inaugural."

One flag one lang.

Official English

TR's linguistic tub-thumping long typified the tradition of 5 American politics. That tradition began to change in the wake of the anything-goes attitudes and the celebration of cultural differences arising in the 1960s. A 1975 amendment to the Voting Rights Act of 1965 mandated the "bilingual ballot" under certain circumstances, notably when the voters of selected language groups reached five percent or more of a voting district. Bilingual education became a byword of educational thinking during the 1960s. By the 1970s linguists had demonstrated convincingly—at least to other academics—that black English (today called African-American vernacular English or Ebonics) was not "bad" English but a different kind of authentic English with its own rules. Predictably, there have been scattered demands that black English be included in bilingual-education programs.

It was against this background that the movement to make English 6 the official language of the country arose. In 1981 Senator S. I. Hayakawa, long a leading critic of bilingual education and bilingual ballots, introduced in the U.S. Senate a constitutional amendment that not only would have made English the official language, but would have prohibited federal and state laws and regulations requiring the use of other languages. His English Language Amendment died in the Ninety-seventh Congress.

In 1983 the organization called U.S. English was founded by 7 Hayakawa and John Tanton, a Michigan ophthalmologist. The primary purpose of the organization was to promote English as the official language of the United States. (The best background readings on America's "neolinguisticism" are the books *Hold Your Tongue,* by James Crawford, and *Language Loyalties,* edited by Crawford, both published in 1992.) Official English initiatives were passed by California in 1986, by Arkansas, Mississippi, North Carolina, North Dakota, and South Carolina in 1987, by Colorado, Florida, and Arizona in 1988, and by

Alabama in 1990. The majorities voting for these initiatives were generally not insubstantial: California's, for example, passed by 73 percent.

It was probably inevitable that the Official English (or English Only—the two names are used almost interchangeably) movement would acquire a conservative, almost reactionary undertone in the 1990s. Official English is politically very incorrect. But its cofounder John Tanton brought with him strong liberal credentials. He had been active in the Sierra Club and Planned Parenthood, and in the 1970s served as the national president of Zero Population Growth. Early advisers of U.S. English resist ideological pigeonholing: they included Walter Annenberg, Jacques Barzun, Bruno Bettelheim, Alistair Cooke, Denton Cooley, Walter Cronkite, Angier Biddle Duke, George Gilder, Sidney Hook, Norman Podhoretz, Arnold Schwarzenegger, and Karl Shapiro.[1] In 1987 U.S. English installed as its president Linda Chávez, a Hispanic who had been prominent in the Reagan Administration. A year later she resigned her position, citing "repugnant" and "anti-Hispanic" overtones in an internal memorandum written by Tanton. Tanton, too, resigned, and Walter Cronkite, describing the affair as "embarrassing," left the advisory board. One board member, Norman Cousins, defected in 1986, alluding to the "negative symbolic significance" of California's Official English initiative, Proposition 63. The current chairman of the board and CEO of U.S. English is Mauro E. Mujica, who claims that the organization has 650,000 members.

The popular wisdom is that conservatives are pro and liberals con. True, conservatives such as George Will and William F. Buckley Jr. have written columns supporting Official English. But would anyone characterize as conservatives the present and past U.S. English board members Alistair Cooke, Walter Cronkite, and Norman Cousins? One of the strongest opponents of bilingual education is the Mexican-American writer Richard Rodríguez, best known for his eloquent autobiography, *Hunger of Memory* (1982). There is a strain of American liberalism that defines itself in nostalgic devotion to the melting pot.

For several years relevant bills awaited consideration in the U.S. House of Representatives. The Emerson Bill (H.R. 123), passed by the House last August, specifies English as the official language of government, and requires that the government "preserve and enhance" the official status of English. Exceptions are made for the teaching of foreign languages; for actions necessary for public health, international relations, foreign trade, and the protection of the rights of criminal defendants; and for the use of "terms of art" from languages other than English. It would, for example, stop the Internal Revenue Service

---

[1] A diverse group of writers, academics, and media figures. [Eds.]

from sending out income-tax forms and instructions in languages other than English, but it would not ban the use of foreign languages in census materials or documents dealing with national security. *"E Pluribus Unum"* can still appear on American money. U.S. English supports the bill.

What are the chances that some version of Official English will become federal law? Any language bill will face tough odds in the Senate, because some western senators have opposed English Only measures in the past for various reasons, among them a desire by Republicans not to alienate the growing number of Hispanic Republicans, most of whom are uncomfortable with mandated monolingualism. Texas Governor George W. Bush, too, has forthrightly said that he would oppose any English Only proposals in his state. Several of the Republican candidates for President in 1996 (an interesting exception is Phil Gramm) endorsed versions of Official English, as has Newt Gingrich. While governor of Arkansas, Bill Clinton signed into law an English Only bill. As President, he has described his earlier action as a mistake. 11

Many issues intersect in the controversy over Official English: immigration (above all), the rights of minorities (Spanish-speaking minorities in particular), the pros and cons of bilingual education tolerance, how best to educate the children of immigrants, and the place of cultural diversity in school curricula and in American society in general. The question that lies at the root of most of the uneasiness is this: Is America threatened by the preservation of languages other than English? Will America, if it continues on its traditional path of benign linguistic neglect, go the way of Belgium, Canada, and Sri Lanka—three countries among many whose unity is gravely imperiled by language and ethnic conflicts? 12

Language and Nationality

Language and nationalism were not always so intimately intertwined. Never in the heyday of rule by sovereign was it a condition of employment that the King be able to speak the language of his subjects. George I spoke no English and spent much of his time away from England, attempting to use the power of his kingship to shore up his German possessions. In the Middle Ages nationalism was not even part of the picture: one owed loyalty to a lord, a prince, a ruler, a family, a tribe, a church, a piece of land, but not to a nation and least of all to a nation as a language unit. The capital city of the Austrian Hapsburg empire was Vienna, its ruler a monarch with effective control of peoples of the most varied and incompatible ethnicities, and languages, throughout Central and Eastern Europe. The official language, and the 13 lingua franca as well, was German. While it stood—and it stood for hundreds of years—the empire was an anachronistic relic of what for most of human history had been the normal relationship between country and language: none.

The marriage of language and nationalism goes back at least to 14 Romanticism and specifically to Rousseau,[2] who argued in his *Essay on the Origin of Languages* that language must develop before politics is possible and that language originally distinguished nations from one another. A little-remembered aim of the French Revolution—itself the legacy of Rousseau—was to impose a national language on France, where regional languages such as Provençal, Breton, and Basque were still strong competitors against standard French, the French of the Ile de France. As late as 1789, when the Revolution began, half the population of the south of France, which spoke Provençal, did not understand French. A century earlier the playwright Racine said that he had had to resort to Spanish and Italian to make himself understood in the southern French town of Uzès. After the Revolution nationhood itself became aligned with language.

In 1846 Jacob Grimm, one of the Brothers Grimm of fairy-tale fame 15 but better known in the linguistic establishment as a forerunner of modern comparative and historical linguists, said that "a nation is the totality of people who speak the same language." After midcentury, language was invoked more than any other single criterion to define nationality. Language as a political force helped to bring about the unification of Italy and of Germany and the secession of Norway from its union with Sweden in 1905. Arnold Toynbee observed—unhappily— soon after the First World War that "the growing consciousness of Nationality had attached itself neither to traditional frontiers nor to new geographical associations but almost exclusively to mother tongues."

The crowning triumph of the new desideratum was the Treaty 16 of Versailles, in 1919, when the allied victors of the First World War began redrawing the map of Central and Eastern Europe according to nationality as best they could. The magic word was "self-determination," and none of Woodrow Wilson's Fourteen Points[3] mentioned the word "language" at all. Self-determination was thought of as being related to "nationality," which today we would be more likely to call "ethnicity"; but language was simpler to identify than nationality or ethnicity. When it came to drawing the boundary lines of various countries—

---

[2] Jean-Jacques Rousseau (1712–1788), Swiss-French philosopher, novelist, and political theorist, who argued that humans in their natural state are good but are corrupted by society. [Eds.]

[3] President Woodrow Wilson formulated a fourteen-point European peace plan at the close of World War I; presented to Congress in 1918, it included a number of recommendations for redrawing the map of Europe. [Eds.]

Czechoslovakia, Yugoslavia, Romania, Hungary, Albania, Bulgaria, Poland—it was principally language that guided the draftsman's hand. (The main exceptions were Alsace-Lorraine, South Tyrol, and the German-speaking parts of Bohemia and Moravia.) Almost by default language became the defining characteristic of nationality.

And so it remains today. In much of the world, ethnic unity and 17 cultural identification are routinely defined by language. To be Arab is to speak Arabic. Bengali identity is based on language in spite of the division of Bengali-speakers between Hindu India and Muslim Bangladesh. When eastern Pakistan seceded from greater Pakistan in 1971, it named itself Bangladesh: *desa* means "country;" the *bangla* means not the Bengali people or the Bengali territory but the Bengali language.

Scratch most nationalist movements and you find a linguistic 18 grievance. The demands for independence of the Baltic states (Latvia, Lithuania, and Estonia) were intimately bound up with fears for the loss of their respective languages and cultures in a sea of Russianness. In Belgium the war between French and Flemish threatens an already weakly fused country. The present atmosphere of Belgium is dark and anxious, costive; the metaphor of divorce is a staple of private and public discourse. The lines of terrorism in Sri Lanka are drawn between Tamil Hindus and Sinhalese Buddhists—and also between the Tamil and Sinhalese languages. Worship of the French language fortifies the movement for an independent Quebec. Whether a united Canada will survive into the twenty-first century is a question too close to call. Much of the anxiety about language in the United States is probably fueled by the "Quebec problem": unlike Belgium, which is a small European country, or Sri Lanka, which is halfway around the world, Canada is our close neighbor.

Language is a convenient surrogate for nonlinguistic claims that are 19 often awkward to articulate, for they amount to a demand for more political and economic power. Militant Sikhs in India call for a state of their own: Khalistan ("Land of the Pure" in Punjabi). They frequently couch this as a demand for a linguistic state, which has a certain simplicity about it, a clarity of motive—justice, even, because states in India are normally linguistic states. But the Sikh demands blend religion, economics, language, and retribution for sins both punished and unpunished in a country where old sins cast long shadows.

Language is an explosive issue in the countries of the former Soviet 20 Union. The language conflict in Estonia has been especially bitter. Ethnic Russians make up almost a third of Estonia's population, and most of them do not speak or read Estonian, although Russians have lived in Estonia for more than a generation. Estonia has passed legislation requiring knowledge of the Estonian language as a condition of citizenship. Nationalist groups in independent Lithuania sought restrictions on the use of Polish—again, old sins, long shadows.

In 1995 protests erupted in Moldova, formerly the Moldavian 21 Soviet Socialist Republic, over language and the teaching of Moldovan history. Was Moldovan history a part of Romanian history or of Soviet history? Was Moldova's language Romanian? Moldovan—earlier called Moldavian—*is* Romanian, just as American English and British English are both English. But in the days of the Moldavian SSR, Moscow insisted that the two languages were different, and in a piece of linguistic nonsense required Moldavian to be written in the Cyrillic alphabet to strengthen the case that it was not Romanian.

The official language of Yugoslavia was Serbo-Croatian, which was 22 never so much a language as a political accommodation. The Serbian and Croatian languages are mutually intelligible. Serbian is written in the Cyrillic alphabet, is identified with the Eastern Orthodox branch of the Catholic Church, and borrows its high-culture words from the east—from Russian and Old Church Slavic. Croatian is written in the Roman alphabet, is identified with Roman Catholicism, and borrows its high-culture words from the west—from German, for example, and Latin. One of the first things the newly autonomous Republic of Serbia did, in 1991, was to pass a law decreeing Serbian in the Cyrillic alphabet the official language of the country. With Croatia divorced from Serbia, the Croatian and Serbian languages are diverging more and more. Serbo-Croatian has now passed into history, a language-museum relic from the brief period when Serbs and Croats called themselves Yugoslavs and pretended to like each other.

Slovakia, relieved now of the need to accommodate to Czech 23 cosmopolitan sensibilities, has passed a law making Slovak its official language. (Czech is to Slovak pretty much as Croatian is to Serbian.) Doctors in state hospitals must speak to patients in Slovak, even if another language would aid diagnosis and treatment. Some 600,000 Slovaks—more than 10 percent of the population—are ethnically Hungarian. Even staff meetings in Hungarian-language schools must be in Slovak. (The government dropped a stipulation that church weddings be conducted in Slovak after heavy opposition from the Roman Catholic Church.) Language inspectors are told to weed out "all sins perpetrated on the regular Slovak language." Tensions between Slovaks and Hungarians, who had been getting along, have begun to arise.

The twentieth century is ending as it began—with trouble in the 24 Balkans and with nationalist tensions flaring up in other parts of the globe. (Toward the end of his life Bismarck predicted that "some damn fool thing in the Balkans" would ignite the next war.) Language isn't always part of the problem. But it usually is.

Unique Otherness

Is there no hope for language tolerance? Some countries manage to 25 maintain their unity in the face of multilingualism. Examples are Finland, with a Swedish minority, and a number of African and Southeast Asian countries. Two others could not be more unlike as countries go: Switzerland and India.

German, French, Italian, and Romansh are the languages of 26 Switzerland. The first three can be and are used for official purposes; all four are designated "national" languages. Switzerland is politically almost hyperstable. It has language problems (Romansh is losing ground), but they are not major, and they are never allowed to threaten national unity.

Contrary to public perception, India gets along pretty well with a 27 host of different languages. The Indian constitution officially recognizes nineteen languages, English among them. Hindi is specified in the constitution as the national language of India, but that is a pious post-colonial fiction: outside the Hindi-speaking northern heartland of India, people don't want to learn it. English functions more nearly than Hindi as India's lingua franca.

From 1947, when India obtained its independence from the British, 28 until the 1960s blood ran in the streets and people died because of language. Hindi absolutists wanted to force Hindi on the entire country, which would have split India between north and south and opened up other fracture lines as well. For as long as possible Jawaharlal Nehru, independent India's first Prime Minister, resisted nationalist demands to redraw the capricious state boundaries of British India according to language. By the time he capitulated, the country had gained a precious decade to prove its viability as a union.

Why is it that India preserves its unity with not just two languages 29 to contend with, as Belgium, Canada, and Sri Lanka have, but nineteen? The answer is that India, like Switzerland, has a strong national identity. The two countries share something big and almost mystical that holds each together in a union transcending language. That something I call "unique otherness."

The Swiss have what the political scientist Karl Deutsch called 30 "learned habits, preferences, symbols, memories, and patterns of landholding": customs, cultural traditions, and political institutions that bind them closer to one another than to people of France, Germany, or Italy living just across the border and speaking the same language. There is Switzerland's traditional neutrality, its system of universal military training (the "citizen army"), its consensual allegiance to a strong Swiss franc—and fondue, yodeling, skiing, and mountains. Set against all this, the fact that Switzerland has four languages doesn't even approach the threshold of becoming a threat.

As for India, what Vincent Smith, in the *Oxford History of India,* calls 31 its "deep underlying fundamental unity" resides in institutions and beliefs such as caste, cow worship, sacred places, and much more. Consider *dharma, karma,* and *maya,* the three root convictions of Hinduism; India's historical epics; Gandhi; *ahimsa* (nonviolence); vegetarianism; a distinctive cuisine and way of eating; marriage customs; a shared past; and what the Indologist Ainslie Embree calls "Brahmanical ideology."[4] In other words, "We are Indian; we are different."

Belgium and Canada have never managed to forge a stable 32 national identity; Czechoslovakia and Yugoslavia never did either. Unique otherness immunizes countries against linguistic destabilization. Even Switzerland and especially India have problems; in any country with as many different languages as India has, language will never *not* be a problem. However, it is one thing to have a major illness with a bleak prognosis; it is another to have a condition that is irritating and occasionally painful but not life-threatening.

History teaches a plain lesson about language and governments: 33 there is almost nothing the government of a free country can do to change language usage and practice significantly, to force its citizens to use certain languages in preference to others, and to discourage people from speaking a language they wish to continue to speak (The rebirth of Hebrew in Palestine and Israel's successful mandate that Hebrew be spoken and written by Israelis is a unique event in the annals of language history.) Quebec has since the 1970s passed an array of laws giving French a virtual monopoly in the province. One consequence—unintended, one wishes to believe—of these laws is that last year kosher products imported for Passover were kept off the shelves, because the packages were not labeled in French. Wise governments keep their hands off language to the extent that it is politically possible to do so.

We like to believe that to pass a law is to change behavior; but 34 passing laws about language, in a free society, almost never changes attitudes or behavior. Gaelic (Irish) is living out a slow, inexorable decline in Ireland despite enormous government support of every possible kind since Ireland gained its independence from Britain. The Welsh language, in contrast, is alive today in Wales in spite of heavy discrimination during its history. Three out of four people in the northern and western counties of Gwynedd and Dyfed speak Welsh.

I said earlier that language is a convenient surrogate for other 35 national problems. Official English obviously has a lot to do with concern about immigration, perhaps especially Hispanic immigration. America may be threatened by immigration; I don't know. But America is not threatened by language.

---

[4] *Brahman* refers to a Hindu of the highest caste. [Eds.]

The usual arguments made by academics against Official English 36 are commonsensical. Who needs a law when, according to the 1990 census, 94 percent of American residents speak English anyway? (Mauro E. Mujica, the chairman of U.S. English, cites a higher figure: 97 percent.) Not many of today's immigrants will see their first language survive into the second generation. This is in fact the common lament of first-generation immigrants: their children are not learning their language and are losing the culture of their parents. Spanish is hardly a threat to English, in spite of isolated (and easily visible) cases such as Miami, New York City, and pockets of the Southwest and southern California. The everyday language of south Texas is Spanish, and yet south Texas is not about to secede from America.

But empirical, calm arguments don't engage the real issue: 37 language is a symbol, an icon. Nobody who favors a constitutional ban against flag burning will ever be persuaded by the argument that the flag is, after all, just a "piece of cloth." A draft card in the 1960s, was never merely a piece of paper. Neither is a marriage license.

Language, as one linguist has said, is "not primarily a means of 38 communication but a means of communion." Romanticism exalted language, made it mystical, sublime—a bond of national identity. At the same time, Romanticism created a monster: it made of language a means for destroying a country.

America has that unique otherness of which I spoke. In spite of all 39 our racial divisions and economic unfairness, we have the frontier tradition, respect for the individual, and opportunity; we have our love affair with the automobile; we have in our history a civil war that freed the slaves and was fought with valor; and we have sports, hot dogs, hamburgers, and milk shakes—things big and small, noble and petty, important and trifling. "We are Americans; we are different."

If I'm wrong, then the great American experiment will fail—not 40 because of language but because it no longer means anything to be an American; because we have forfeited that "willingness of the heart" that F. Scott Fitzgerald[5] wrote was America; because we are no longer joined by Lincoln's "mystic chords of memory."

We are not even close to the danger point. I suggest that we relax 41 and luxuriate in our linguistic richness and our traditional tolerance of language differences. Language does not threaten American unity. Benign neglect is a good policy for any country when it comes to language, and it's a good policy for America.

---

[5] Twentieth-century American writer. [Eds.]

Responding to Reading

1. According to King, what are the dangers of trying to maintain a bilingual society? What examples does he present to support his position? Does he offer enough examples?

2. What countries does King mention to support his argument that a multilingual society can maintain its unity? In what ways are these countries like the United States? In what ways are they different? Is King's argument convincing?

3. King says, "America may be threatened by immigration. . . . But America is not threatened by language" (35). Later, he says that "the great American experiment will fail—not because of language but because it no longer means anything to be an American" (40). How do you think Richard Rodriguez (p. 232) would respond to these statements?

¡INGLÉS, SÍ!

Jorge Amselle

Jorge Amselle (1969–) was born in Washington, D.C., to Nicaraguan immigrant parents. He spoke little English when he first started school, but he learned the language as part of his cultural assimilation. In 1992, he received a degree in economics from the University of Maryland and began to work for a variety of research organizations in the Washington area. Since 1994, he has been on the staff of the Center for Equal Opportunity, an organization that lobbies against affirmative action programs; he is currently its vice president for education. His writing has appeared in the Wall Street Journal, *the* Washington Times, *the* National Review, *and the* Weekly Standard, *among other periodicals. In the following essay, which appeared in the* National Review, *Amselle argues that most Hispanic parents are opposed to extensive bilingual education and want their children to learn English as quickly as possible.*

As the new school year gets under way, over one million Hispanic children are beginning their classroom experience in the United States in Spanish rather than English. For nearly thirty years professional Hispanic activists and bilingual-education proponents have been telling us that this is what Hispanic parents want, and that it is in the best interests of Hispanic children.

But every poll conducted of language-minority parents has shown that what they want for their children is English. The Center for Equal Opportunity recently commissioned a national survey of six hundred Hispanic parents—the first of its kind in more than eight years. This survey found that more than 80 per cent of Hispanic parents want their children taught in English and not in Spanish. And 63 per cent want their children to be taught English as quickly as possible—whereas bilingual-education theory calls for children to be taught academic content courses in their native language for five to seven years.

While the education establishment is resisting the deconstruction of 3 bilingual education, some progress is being made. In response to parents' protests, New York City is ending the automatic testing of children with Spanish names for placement in bilingual programs. The main problem with this approach was that students were being misidentified as needing bilingual education when their problem was that they had not been taught to read in any language. Hispanic children who scored below the 40th percentile in a standardized English exam, which by definition is 40 per cent of all the students taking the test, were automatically placed in Spanish-language programs, even if they did not speak Spanish.

In Los Angeles, over 100 Latino parents picketed their local school 4 for almost two weeks to protest the lack of English instruction. These parents had a legal right to request all-English instruction for their children, but their rights were nullified by the hurdles placed before them by school administrators.

The boycott ended only when the school promised to provide 5 classes in English. The school also promised to halt the practice of requiring parents to attend parent-teacher conferences before allowing children out of the bilingual program. Parent-teacher conferences are often used to bully, intimidate, and shame parents into leaving their children in bilingual programs they know don't work.

Indeed, bilingual education is working so poorly in California that 6 the State Board of Education is backing off from forcing school districts to use native-language instruction. The California Teachers Association has also joined the stampede away from bilingual education. Its newsletter states that the emphasis on using children's native language has "crippled the Spanish-speaking child's educational development."

Despite the mounting evidence, there are researchers and organiza- 7 tions, like Virginia Collier of George Mason University and the National Association for Bilingual Education (NABE), that continue to praise this failed educational technique. Professor Collier's study is often cited as proof that bilingual education works. However, her study has yet to be completed, let alone subjected to peer review.

In a monograph published by the New Jersey Teachers of English to 8 Speakers of Other Languages-Bilingual Education (NJTESOL-BE), Professor Collier shares some of her less publicized insights. "We must encourage language-minority parents to speak the first language at home, not to speak English. The worse advice [teachers] can give parents is to speak only English at home," she writes. She even suggests tha teaching children only in English is child abuse. She writes: "To deny a child the only means of communicating with his parents or to denigrate an adolescent for expressing her emotions through first language is tantamount to physical violence toward that student."

NABE readily admits that bilingual education is failing at least 9 some students, calling these cases "abhorrent aberration[s]." However, NABE ignores the fact that the few bilingual-education programs that work do so only because they are more English-intensive than what NABE advocates.

In fact, the vast majority of the research in favor of bilingual 10 education is desperately flawed. Professor Christine Rossell of Boston University has conducted an extensive review of over 300 bilingual-education studies. She found that only 60 measured reading ability in a methodologically acceptable way; of these, 78 per cent found bilingual education to be no better or actually worse than doing nothing. For math scores, 91 per cent of the 34 scientifically valid studies showed bilingual education to be no better than doing nothing.

In spite of this evidence, Latino parents who oppose bilingual 11 education often find themselves fighting a lonely battle. In fact, in both Los Angeles and New York City anti-bilingual-education parents' groups are being assisted by the religious organizations, not by traditional Hispanic advocacy groups. The reason is that traditional Hispanic organizations long ago sold out the interests of Latino parents to the bilingual education establishment. Now, whenever parents complain about a system that fails to teach their children English, their representatives not only ignore their pleas for help, but actually oppose them.

Some Members of Congress as well as many state legislators are 12 seeking far-reaching reforms of bilingual education. Unfortunately, because Congress ignored an opportunity to reform federal bilingual-education policy as part of the Official English legislation passed recently by the House, Hispanic children and parents will have to suffer through another year of bilingual education.

Responding to Reading

1. Amselle begins his essay by saying that there is a split between "what Hispanic parents want" and what "professional Hispanic activists and bilingual-education proponents" want (1). What evidence does he present to support this statement? Should he have offered more evidence? A different kind of evidence?

2. If, as Amselle contends, there is mounting evidence that bilingual education programs do not work, why does the federal government still require schools to use this method of teaching? Do you find his explanation plausible?
3. In "Should English Be the Law?" (p. 238), Robert D. King refutes a number of familiar arguments against bilingual education. Which of Amselle's points does King address? How convincing are these refutations?

─────── WIDENING THE FOCUS ───────

- John Holt, "School Is Bad for Children" (p. 83)

- Jonathan Kozol, "Savage Inequalities" (p. 112)

- Bharati Mukherjee, "American Dreamer" (p. 406)

Responding to the Image

1. How do you respond when you see information being provided in both English and Spanish, as in this image? Does the context make a difference?

2. This photograph was taken in a small Arkansas town that has experienced a significant influx of immigrants from Mexico to work in the poultry industry. Do you see a difference between offering adult education classes in Spanish and offering classes in Spanish to immigrant schoolchildren?

---------------------- WRITING ----------------------

The Politics of Language

1. Both Malcolm X and Frederick Douglass discuss how they undertook a program of self-education. Write an essay in which you discuss how their efforts were similar and different. Make certain you discuss what they learned about themselves and about their respective societies by learning to read and write.

2. In newspapers and magazines and on the Internet, look for examples of language that correspond to Hayakawa's definitions of reports, inferences, and judgments. Then, write an essay in which you present your examples and justify your conclusions.

3. Write an editorial for your local newspaper in which you argue for or against a constitutional amendment making English the official language of the United States. In your essay refer to Richard Rodriguez's "Aria," Robert D. King's "Should English Be the Law?" and Jorge Amselle's "¡Inglés, Sí!"

4. Over fifty years ago, both Huxley and Orwell wrote essays in which they discussed how governments use language to control people. Write an essay in which you discuss whether this situation is more or less likely to occur today. In your essay, make sure you refer specifically to "Propaganda under a Dictatorship" and "Politics and the English Language."

5. Both Amy Tan in "Mother Tongue" and Richard Rodriguez in "Aria" talk about how education can change one's use of language. Write an essay discussing the effect that education has had on your own spoken and written language. What do you think you have gained and lost as your language has changed?

6. Which of your daily activities would you be unable to carry out if, like the people Jonathan Kozol describes in "The Human Cost of an Illiterate Society," you could neither read nor write? Write an article for your local newspaper in which you report on a typical day. For example, begin by having breakfast and then walking, driving, or taking public transportation to class. Make sure you refer to specific tasks you could not do. In addition, explain some strategies you would use to hide the fact you couldn't read or write.

7. In paragraph 21 of his essay, Orwell says, "Political language . . . is designed to make lies sound truthful and murder respectable, and to give an appearance of solidity to pure wind." Write an essay in which you agree or disagree with this statement. Support your position with examples you find in newspapers and magazines, on TV, or on the Internet.

8. Write a letter to Barbara Lawrence in which you agree or disagree with her contention that sexual vulgarisms about women are as bad as racial or ethnic obscenities. In addition to Lawrence's essay, refer to Alleen Pace Nilsen's essay "Sexism in English: Embodiment and Language" as well as to your own experience.

9. In "Sexism in English: Embodiment and Language" Alleen Pace Nilsen says, "Language is like an x-ray in providing visible evidence of invisible thoughts" (40). Is this true of advertising? Find advertisements in several newspapers and magazines, and analyze their use of language, particularly their use of gender-specific words. Then, write an essay in which you agree or disagree with Pace's statement. If you wish, you may also refer to "Sex, Lies, and Advertising" by Gloria Steinem (p. 274).

10. Recently, there has been a great deal of debate about the benefits and drawbacks of a multilingual society. Supporters say that a multilingual society allows people to preserve their own cultures and thus fosters pride. Detractors say that a multilingual society reinforces differences and ultimately tears a country apart. What do you see as the benefits and drawbacks of a multilingual society? As a country, what would we gain if we encouraged multilingualism? What would we lose? Use any of the essays in this chapter to support your position.

11. Write an essay in which you answer the Focus question, "Should English Be the Law?" In your essay, refer to the ideas in Richard Rodriguez's "Aria," Robert D. King's "Should English Be the Law?" and Jorge Amselle's "¡Inglés, Sí!"

12. **For Internet research:** Links to sites in favor of accommodating non-English speakers can be found at <http://www.ourworld. compuserve.com/homepages/JWCRAWFORD/home.html>. Links to sites advocating that all Americans speak English can be found at <http://www.us-english.org/englishfirst.org/>. You may use these as supplemental research sources for the essay topic suggested in number 11 above.

4

MEDIA AND SOCIETY

PREPARING TO READ AND WRITE

The popular media—newspapers and magazines, radio, television, and film—have been around for a long time, but in recent years, they have come to have a particularly powerful and significant impact on our lives. Cable television has brought us literally hundreds of stations—along with sitcom reruns that endlessly recycle our childhood (and our parents' childhood). Satellites have brought immediacy: the Vietnam War was the first televised war, but we had to wait for the evening news to see it; during the Persian Gulf War, CNN brought us news as it happened. Talk radio has become so powerful that it may actually be shaping government policy. Other innovations have also appeared: film special effects that have the power to mystify or terrify, newspapers that seem to have more color and graphics than words, and, on television, tabloid journalism, home shopping, infomercials, and music videos. In addition, the Internet has made available a world of information—and with it, the ability to communicate easily with millions of people all over the planet.

The increasing power and scope of the media have helped to turn the world into what Canadian cultural critic Marshall McLuhan called a "global village," a world of nations that are more and more interconnected and interdependent. This is seen by many as a positive development. Ideally, as citizens of the global village, we should be able to understand one another as we increasingly come to share a common culture, with the same food, music, films, and television programs. But the power of the media has also brought problems. The tool that can unite, inform, instruct, entertain, and inspire can also misinform, stereotype, brainwash, and perhaps even incite violence.

As the Focus section of this chapter, "Does Media Violence Hurt?" (p. 318), suggests, some people believe that the violent images of films or TV shows may play a significant role in encouraging violent behavior. Whether or not we accept that there is a direct causal connection between media violence and the violence we see in our society, our awareness of the possible negative effects of the all-pervasive media has tempered our enthusiasm and made us embrace its virtues with caution.

As you read and prepare to write about the essays in this chapter, you may consider the following questions:

- Does the essay focus on one particular medium or on the media in general?

- Does the writer see the media as a positive, negative, or neutral force? Why?

- If the writer sees negative effects, where does he or she place blame? Do you agree?

- Does the writer make any recommendations for change? Do these recommendations seem reasonable?

- Is the writer focusing on the media's effect on society or on the media's effect on his or her own life?

- Does the writer discuss personal observations or experiences? If so, are they similar to or different from your own?

- When was the essay written? Has the situation the writer describes changed since then?

- Which writers' positions on the impact of the media (or on the media's shortcomings) are most alike? Most different? Most like your own?

TELEVISION: THE PLUG-IN DRUG

Marie Winn

Born in Czechoslovakia, Marie Winn (1936–) immigrated to the United States with her family in 1939. A graduate of Radcliffe College and Columbia University, she has written on a variety of subjects, but she is probably best known for her critiques of television's effects on children and families: The Plug-In Drug: Television, Children, and the Family *(1977, revised 1985);* Children without Childhood *(1983); and* Unplugging the Plug-In Drug *(1987). An avid urban naturalist, Winn has most recently published* Red-Tails in Love: A Wildlife Drama in Central Park *(1998). The following is a chapter from* The Plug-In Drug.

A quarter of a century after the introduction of television into 1 American society, a period that has seen the medium become so deeply ingrained in American life that in at least one state the television set has attained the rank of a legal necessity, safe from repossession in case of debt along with clothes, cooking utensils, and the like, television viewing has become an inevitable and ordinary part of daily life. Only in the early years of television did writers and commentators have sufficient perspective to separate the activity of watching television from the actual content it offers the viewer. In those early days writers frequently discussed the effects of television on family life. However, a curious myopia afflicted those early observers: almost without exception they regarded television as a favorable, beneficial, indeed, wondrous influence upon the family.

"Television is going to be a real asset in every home where there are 2 children," predicts a writer in 1949.

"Television will take over your way of living and change your children's habits, but this change can be a wonderful improvement," claims 3 another commentator.

"No surveys needed, of course, to establish that television has 4 brought the family together in one room," writes the *New York Times* television critic in 1949.

Each of the early articles about television is invariably accompanied 5 by a photograph or illustration showing a family cozily sitting together before the television set, Sis on Mom's lap, Buddy perched on the arm of Dad's chair, Dad with his arm around Mom's shoulder. Who could have guessed that twenty or so years later Mom would be watching a drama in the kitchen, the kids would be looking at cartoons in their room, while Dad would be taking in the ball game in the living room?

Of course television sets were enormously expensive in those early 6 days. The idea that by 1975 more than 60 percent of American families would own two or more sets was preposterous. The splintering of the multiple-set family was something the early writers could not foresee. Nor did anyone imagine the numbers of hours children would eventually devote to television, the common use of television by parents as a child pacifier, the changes television would effect upon child-rearing methods, the increasing domination of family schedules by children's viewing requirements—in short, the *power* of the new medium to dominate family life.

After the first years, as children's consumption of the new medium 7 increased, together with parental concern about the possible effects of so much television viewing, a steady refrain helped to soothe and reassure anxious parents. "Television always enters a pattern of influences that already exist: the home, the peer group, the school, the church and culture generally," write the authors of an early and influential study of television's effects on children. In other words, if the child's home life is all right, parents need not worry about the effects of all that television watching.

But television does not merely influence the child; it deeply influ- 8 ences that "pattern of influences" that is meant to ameliorate its effects. Home and family life has changed in important ways since the advent of television. The peer group has become television-oriented, and much of the time children spend together is occupied by television viewing. Culture generally has been transformed by television. Therefore it is improper to assign to television the subsidiary role its many apologists (too often members of the television industry) insist it plays. Television is not merely one of a number of important influences upon today's child. Through the changes it has made in family life, television emerges as *the* important influence in children's lives today.

Television's contribution to family life has been an equivocal one. For 9 while it has, indeed, kept the members of the family from dispersing, it has not served to bring them *together.* By its domination of the time families spend together, it destroys the special quality that distinguishes one family from another, a quality that depends to a great extent on what a family *does,* what special rituals, games, recurrent jokes, familiar songs, and shared activities it accumulates.

"Like the sorcerer of old," writes Urie Bronfenbrenner, "the televi- 10 sion set casts its magic spell, freezing speech and action, turning the living into silent statues so long as the enchantment lasts. The primary danger of the television screen lies not so much in the behavior it produces—although there is danger there—as in the behavior it prevents: the talks, the games, the family festivities and arguments through which much of the child's learning takes place and through which his character is formed. Turning on the television set can turn off the process that transforms children into people."

Yet parents have accepted a television-dominated family life so 11 completely that they cannot see how the medium is involved in whatever problems they might be having. A first-grade teacher reports:

"I have one child in the group who's an only child. I wanted to find 12 out more about her family life because this little girl was quite isolated from the group, didn't make friends, so I talked to her mother. Well, they don't have time to do anything in the evening, the mother said. The parents come home after picking up the child at the babysitter's. Then the mother fixes dinner while the child watches TV. Then they have dinner and the child goes to bed. I said to this mother. 'Well, couldn't she help you fix dinner? That would be a nice time for the two of you to talk,' and the mother said, 'Oh, but I'd hate to have her miss "Zoom."[1] It's such a good program!'"

---

[1] An educational program broadcast on PBS. [Eds.]

Even when families make efforts to control television, too often its 13
very presence counterbalances the positive features of family life. A
writer and mother of two boys aged 3 and 7 described her family's
television schedule in an article in the *New York Times*:

> We were in the midst of a full-scale War. Every day was a new bat-
> tle and every program was a major skirmish. We agreed it was a bad
> scene all around and were ready to enter diplomatic negotiations. . . .
> In principle we have agreed on 2 1/2 hours of TV a day, "Sesame
> Street," "Electric Company" (with dinner gobbled up in between) and
> two half-hour shows between 7 and 8:30 which enables the grown-ups
> to eat in peace and prevents the two boys from destroying one another.
> Their pre-bedtime choice is dreadful, because, as Josh recently admit-
> ted, "There's nothing much on I really like." So . . . it's "What's My
> Line" or "To Tell the Truth"[2] . . . Clearly there is a need for first-rate
> children's shows at this time. . . .

Consider the "family life" described here: Presumably the father 14
comes home from work during the "Sesame Street"–"Electric
Company" stint. The children are either watching television, gobbling
their dinner, or both. While the parents eat their dinner in peaceful privacy, the children watch another hour of television. Then there is only a
half-hour left before bedtime, just enough time for baths, getting pajamas on, brushing teeth, and so on. The children's evening is regimented
with an almost military precision. They watch their favorite programs,
and when there is "nothing much on I really like," they watch whatever
else is on—because *watching* is the important thing. Their mother does
not see anything amiss with watching programs just for the sake of
watching; she only wishes there were some first-rate children's shows
on at those times.

Without conjuring up memories of the Victorian era with family 15
games and long, leisurely meals, and large families, the question arises:
isn't there a better family life available than this dismal, mechanized
arrangement of children watching television for however long is
allowed them, evening after evening?

Of course, families today still do *special* things together at times: go 16
camping in the summer, go to the zoo on a nice Saturday, take various
trips and expeditions. But their *ordinary* daily life together is diminished—that sitting around at the dinner table, that spontaneous taking
up of an activity, those little games invented by children on the spur of
the moment when there is nothing else to do, the scribbling, the chatting, and even the quarreling, all the things that form the fabric of a family, that define a childhood. Instead, the children have their regular

---

[2] Long-running game shows. [Eds.]

schedule of television programs and bedtime, and the parents have their peaceful dinner together.

The author of the article in the *Times* notes that "keeping a family 17 sane means mediating between the needs of both children and adults." But surely the needs of adults are being better met than the needs of the children, who are effectively shunted away and rendered untroublesome, while their parents enjoy a life as undemanding as that of any childless couple. In reality, it is those very demands that young children make upon a family that lead to growth, and it is the way parents accede to those demands that builds the relationships upon which the future of the family depends. If the family does not accumulate its backlog of shared experiences, shared *everyday* experiences that occur and recur and change and develop, then it is not likely to survive as anything other than a caretaking institution.

Family Rituals

Ritual is defined by sociologists as "that part of family life that the 18 family likes about itself, is proud of and wants formally to continue." Another text notes that "the development of a ritual by a family is an index of the common interest of its members in the family as a group."

What has happened to family rituals, those regular, dependable, 19 recurrent happenings that gave members of a family a feeling of *belonging* to a home rather than living in it merely for the sake of convenience, those experiences that act as the adhesive of family unity far more than any material advantages?

Mealtime rituals, going-to-bed rituals, illness rituals, holiday ritu- 20 als, how many of these have survived the inroads of the television set?

A young woman who grew up near Chicago reminisces about 21 her childhood and gives an idea of the effects of television upon family rituals:

"As a child I had millions of relatives around—my parents both 22 come from relatively large families. My father had nine brothers and sisters. And so every holiday there was this great swoop-down of aunts, uncles, and millions of cousins. I just remember how wonderful it used to be. These thousands of cousins would come and everyone would play and ultimately, after dinner, all the women would be in the front of the house, drinking coffee and talking, all the men would be in the back of the house, drinking and smoking, and all the kids would be all over the place, playing hide and seek. Christmas time was particularly nice because everyone always brought all their toys and games. Our house had a couple of rooms with go-through closets, so there was always kids running in a great circle route. I remember it was just wonderful.

"And then all of a sudden one year I remember becoming suddenly 23 aware of how different everything had become. The kids were no longer playing Monopoly or Clue or the other games we used to play together. It was because we had a television set which had been turned on for a football game. All of that socializing that had gone on previously had ended. Now everyone was sitting in front of the television set, on a holiday, at a family party! I remember being stunned by how awful that was. Somehow the television had become more attractive."

As families have come to spend more and more of their time together 24 engaged in the single activity of television watching, those rituals and pastimes that once gave family life its special quality have become more and more uncommon. Not since prehistoric times when cave families hunted, gathered, ate, and slept, with little time remaining to accumulate a culture of any significance, have families been reduced to such a sameness.

Real People

It is not only the activities that a family might engage in together 25 that are diminished by the powerful presence of television in the home. The relationships of the family members to each other are also affected, in both obvious and subtle ways. The hours that the young child spends in a one-way relationship with television people, an involvement that allows for no communication or interaction, surely affect his relationships with real-life people.

Studies show the importance of eye-to-eye contact, for instance, in 26 real-life relationships, and indicate that the nature of a person's eye-contact patterns, whether he looks another squarely in the eye or looks to the side or shifts his gaze from side to side, may play a significant role in his success or failure in human relationships. But no eye contact is possible in the child-television relationship, although in certain children's programs people purport to speak directly to the child and the camera fosters this illusion by focusing directly upon the person being filmed. (Mr. Rogers is an example, telling the child "I like you, you're special," etc.) How might such a distortion of real-life relationships affect a child's development of trust, of openness, of an ability to relate well to other *real* people?

Bruno Bettelheim writes: 27

> Children who have been taught, or conditioned, to listen passively most of the day to the warm verbal communications coming from the TV screen, to the deep emotional appeal of the so-called TV personality, are often unable to respond to real persons because they arouse so much less feeling than the skilled actor. Worse, they lose the ability to learn from reality because life experiences are much more complicated than the ones they see on the screen. . . .

A teacher makes a similar observation about her personal viewing 28 experiences:

"I have trouble mobilizing myself and dealing with real people after 29 watching a few hours of television. It's just hard to make that transition from watching television to a real relationship. I suppose it's because there was no effort necessary while I was watching, and dealing with real people always requires a bit of effort. Imagine, then, how much harder it might be to do the same thing for a small child, particularly one who watches a lot of television every day."

But more obviously damaging to family relationships is the elimina- 30 tion of opportunities to talk, and perhaps more important, to argue, to air grievances, between parents and children and brothers and sisters. Families frequently use television to avoid confronting their problems, problems that will not go away if they are ignored but will only fester and become less easily resolvable as time goes on.

A mother reports: 31

"I find myself, with three children, wanting to turn on the TV set 32 when they're fighting. I really have to struggle not to do it because I feel that's telling them this is the solution to the quarrel—but it's so tempting that I often do it."

A family therapist discusses the use of television as an avoidance 33 mechanism:

"In a family I know the father comes home from work and turns on 34 the television set. The children come and watch with him and the wife serves them their meal in front of the set. He then goes and takes a shower, or works on the car or something. She then goes and has her own dinner in front of the television set. It's a symptom of a deeper-rooted problem, sure. But it would help them all to get rid of the set. It would be far easier to work on what the symptom really means without the television. The television simply encourages a double avoidance of each other. They'd find out more quickly what was going on if they weren't able to hide behind the TV. Things wouldn't necessarily be better, of course, but they wouldn't be anesthetized."

The decreased opportunities for simple conversation between 35 parents and children in the television-centered home may help explain an observation made by an emergency room nurse at a Boston hospital. She reports that parents just seem to sit there these days when they come in with a sick or seriously injured child, although talking to the child would distract and comfort him. "They don't seem to know *how* to talk to their own children at any length," the nurse observes. Similarly, a television critic writes in the *New York Times:* "I had just a day ago taken my son to the emergency ward of a hospital for stitches above his left eye, and the occasion seemed no more real to me than Maalot or 54th Street, south-central Los Angeles. There was distance and numbness and an inability to turn off the total institution. I didn't behave at all; I just watched. . . ."

A number of research studies substantiate the assumption that 36
television interferes with family activities and the formation of family
relationships. One survey shows that 78 percent of the respondents
indicated no conversation taking place during viewing except at
specified times such as commercials. The study notes: "The television
atmosphere in most households is one of quiet absorption on the part of
family members who are present. The nature of the family social life
during a program could be described as 'parallel' rather than interactive,
and the set does seem to dominate family life when it is on." Thirty-six
percent of the respondents in another study indicated that television
viewing was the only family activity participated in during the week.

In a summary of research findings on television's effect on family 37
interactions James Gabardino states: "The early findings suggest that
television had a disruptive effect upon interaction and thus presumably human development. . . . It is not unreasonable to ask: 'Is the fact
that the average American family during the 1950s came to include
two parents, two children and a television set somehow related to the
psychosocial characteristics of the young adults of the 1970s?'"

Undermining the Family

In its effect on family relationships, in its facilitation of parental 38
withdrawal from an active role in the socialization of their children, and
in its replacement of family rituals and special events, television has
played an important role in the disintegration of the American family.
But of course it has not been the only contributing factor, perhaps not
even the most important one. The steadily rising divorce rate, the
increase in the number of working mothers, the decline of the extended
family, the breakdown of neighborhoods and communities, the growing
isolation of the nuclear family—all have seriously affected the family.

As Urie Bronfenbrenner suggests, the sources of family breakdown 39
do not come from the family itself, but from the circumstances in which
the family finds itself and the way of life imposed upon it by those
circumstances. "When those circumstances and the way of life they
generate undermine relationships of trust and emotional security
between family members, when they make it difficult for parents to
care for, educate and enjoy their children, when there is no support or
recognition from the outside world for one's role as a parent and when
time spent with one's family means frustration of career, personal
fulfillment and peace of mind, then the development of the child is
adversely affected," he writes.

But while the roots of alienation go deep into the fabric of American 40
social history, television's presence in the home fertilizes them, encourages their wild and unchecked growth. Perhaps it is true that America's

commitment to the television experience masks a spiritual vacuum, an empty and barren way of life, a desert of materialism. But it is television's dominant role in the family that anesthetizes the family into accepting its unhappy state and prevents it from struggling to better its condition, to improve its relationships, and to regain some of the richness it once possessed.

Others have noted the role of mass media in perpetuating an unsat- 41 isfactory *status quo*. Leisure-time activity, writes Irving Howe, "must provide relief from work monotony without making the return to work too unbearable; it must provide amusement without insight and pleasure without disturbance—as distinct from art which gives pleasure through disturbance. Mass culture is thus oriented towards a central aspect of industrial society: the depersonalization of the individual." Similarly, Jacques Ellul rejects the idea that television is a legitimate means of educating the citizen: "Education . . . takes place only incidentally. The clouding of his consciousness is paramount. . . ."

And so the American family muddles on, dimly aware that some- 42 thing is amiss but distracted from an understanding of its plight by an endless stream of television images. As family ties grow weaker and vaguer, as children's lives become more separate from their parents', as parents' educational role in their children's lives is taken over by television and schools, family life becomes increasingly more unsatisfying for both parents and children. All that seems to be left is Love, an abstraction that family members *know* is necessary but find great difficulty giving each other because the traditional opportunities for expressing love within the family have been reduced or destroyed.

For contemporary parents, love toward each other has increasingly 43 come to mean successful sexual relations, as witnessed by the proliferation of sex manuals and sex therapists. The opportunities for manifesting other forms of love through mutual support, understanding, nurturing, even, to use an unpopular word, serving each other, are less and less available as mothers and fathers seek their independent destinies outside the family.

As for love of children, this love is increasingly expressed through 44 supplying material comforts, amusements, and educational opportunities. Parents show their love for their children by sending them to good schools and camps, by providing them with good food and good doctors, by buying them toys, books , games, and a television set of their very own. Parents will even go further and express their love by attending PTA meetings to improve their children's schools, or by joining groups that are acting to improve the quality of their children's television programs.

But this is love at a remove, and is rarely understood by children. 45 The more direct forms of parental love require time and patience, steady, dependable, ungrudgingly given time actually spent *with* a child, reading to him, comforting him, playing, joking, and working with him. But even if a parent were eager and willing to demonstrate that sort of direct love to his children today, the opportunities are diminished. What with school and Little League and piano lessons and, of course, the inevitable television programs, a day seems to offer just enough time for a good-night kiss.

Responding to Reading

1. Winn says, "Home and family has changed in important ways since the advent of television" (8). How, according to Winn, has family life changed? What kind of support does she offer for this conclusion? Is it enough?
2. Do you agree with Winn that television is an evil, addictive drug that has destroyed cherished family rituals, undermined family relationships, and "[anesthetized] the family into accepting its unhappy state and [prevented] it from struggling to better its condition, to improve its relationships, and to regain some of the richness it once possessed" (40)? How might Winn react to Charles McGrath's idea (p. 267) that watching TV can itself become a ritual? How might she react to his statement, "If . . . TV is a drug, then no opium den was ever sweeter" (3)?
3. Winn's essay was written nearly twenty-five years ago. In light of how much time has passed, could you argue that Winn's essay needs to be updated? If so, what kind of information should be added?

GIVING SATURDAY MORNING SOME SLACK

Charles McGrath

Charles McGrath was born in Boston, Massachusetts, in 1950. He graduated from Yale University and then studied abroad for two years on a Marshall scholarship, returning to Yale to complete his graduate work. A former editor at the New Yorker, *McGrath is currently editor of the* New York Times Book Review. *In addition, he contributes articles, essays, and reviews to a variety of other publications. The following essay, which appeared in the* New York Times Magazine, *offers a different perspective on children's television from that of Marie Winn in the previous essay.*

Remember Saturday morning? The expectancy, the blissfulness, the sense of utter freedom? The most sublime moment was the first—the instant when, unprodded by either alarm clock or parental summons, you emerged into consciousness and experienced an almost physical sense of release, a floating up from the mattress, as you realized that you didn't have to go to school. And the rest of the day—of the whole weekend—then seemed to spread out limitlessly from the edge of the bedcovers, a blank and beckoning horizon.

You could do absolutely anything you chose. You could turn over, tunnel under the pillow and go back to sleep. You could just lie there for a while, woolgathering and listening to Dad's snores rumble from down the hall. You could get up and play with your slot cars or your electric train. You could check on the gerbils, in hopes that they might be mating again. You could build a model plane, snuffling in deep, head-jolting whiffs of Testor's glue. You could even read—that was not unheard of back then.

But what you chose to do, of course, was watch TV. You sprang up and, still in your pj's, went to the kitchen and fixed yourself a bowl of Fruit Loops or Lucky Charms, which in violation of the first commandment of the household—no food in the living room!—you carried boldly over the forbidden threshold and set on top of the Magnavox. You turned on your favorite show and then curled up on the sofa or stretched out on the carpet in front, and with any luck you remained there, motionless, for hours. If, as the critics used to complain, TV is a drug, then no opium den was ever sweeter. On a good Saturday morning, one when Mom wasn't too cranky, you got to stay in your pajamas until noon.

In those days, of course, television was largely unregulated. No one, not even Mom, was paying much attention to what or how much we watched. In recent years, children's programming has been endlessly scrutinized, and thanks in large part to parental lobbying groups, it has come under more vigilant Federal controls. The newest set of regulations was supposed to go into effect this fall, requiring that stations devote at least three hours a week—most of them on Saturday, presumably—to educational programming for children under 16. So far, compliance has been spotty at best. Like those that preceded them, the new regulations are vague and unenforceable. No one can agree on what constitutes educational television, and the burden of policing falls not on the Government but on viewers, who are expected to keep tabs on their local stations. The stations claim, not unreasonably, that their hands are tied by the networks, which these days supply almost all the programming. The networks, meanwhile, have for the most part done little more than tinker with the existing shows and declare that they fit the bill. Disney's "101 Dalmatians," for example, turns out to teach friendship and responsibility, and "N.B.A. Inside Stuff," professional basketball's show for children, is said to impart "life lessons."

This is actually not as dumb as it sounds. *All* TV imparts life lessons 5 of a sort—if only lessons in how greedy or manipulative or boring television producers can be. And what we take away from the experience of watching television is more than what the programmers have put there. Watching television, even if you watch it alone, is also a social experience, and it's often a ritual. Part of the magic of the old Saturday-morning drill had almost nothing to do with content, or with anything that could be regulated. The magic was in the safeness and the sameness—the reassuring security—of the ritual itself.

What you watched, if you grew up in the 50's or early 60's, was not 6 the parade of otherworldly characters that nowadays lurches forth— robots and superheros mostly, so poorly animated that their dialogue and their expressionless mouths are forever out of sync and that Captain America, for example, walks as stiffly as if he had just had a hip replacement. In those days, what you watched, most likely, was a Saturday-morning program that originated at your local station. It featured an adult figure, either clownish or avuncular, depending on local custom, and perhaps a puppet or two or a dimwitted visitor, whose job it was to fill with patter the intervals between the showing of vintage cartoons, doled out as sparingly as if they were some rare elixir—which indeed they were.

In Boston, where I grew up, we had "Boomtown," with Rex Trailer, 7 a handsome singing cowboy, and his faithful, if none-too-bright, sidekick, the sombreroed and serape-clad Pablo. (I was astonished to discover once, when my father took me to one of Rex's "personal appearances," that Pablo was not really Mexican and that he also had extremely bad breath.) The show began with a film clip of Rex galloping to the studio on his handsome palomino, Goldrush—galloping from where was never entirely clear; New Hampshire, perhaps—but the rest, except for the cartoons, was broadcast live. Rex did rope tricks and was occasionally persuaded to take out his guitar, or his "git-fiddle," as he called it, and sing. (One of his tunes, I seem to recall, had a chorus that consisted of the word "hoofbeats," repeated over and over.) Once in a while a visitor dropped by to talk about fire safety or disease prevention.

It was all a little boring and overearnest, and in retrospect it's 8 amazing that "Boomtown" lasted as long as it did, from 1956 to 1976. (Pablo died years ago, but Rex, I was happy to learn recently while trolling through the Internet, has prospered in the new business of video résumés.) Yet the very dullness and predictability was an essential and soothing part of Saturday morning; it slowed time down, after a fashion, and helped stretch out those precious hours into a drowsy prelunch eternity—a kind of Keatsian daze in which the antics of Popeye and

Bluto and Elmer and Woody never staled, no matter how many times we'd seen them before.

Had we known it, we never would have watched, but "Boomtown" 9 was, by today's standards at least, highly "educational." And oddly enough, this show and others like it were in part done in through the efforts of Action for Children's Television and other lobbying groups dedicated to reforming children's programming and reducing its dependency on commercials.

Still, today's Saturday-morning fare, though much maligned, is in a 10 number of essential ways no worse than what we watched as kids. Some of it, in fact, is little altered: the whole inspired Looney Tunes gang (Bugs, Porky, Daffy, Sylvester, Tweety et al.) still turn up; the Lucky Charms leprechaun, ageless and ever-twinkly, still boasts about how many marshmallows his product contains; Franken Berry, Count Chocula, Cocoa Puffs—they're still being hawked, too, the latter newly enhanced with an infusion of Hershey's chocolate. Barbie's still around, of course, and so are those various creatures—dolls, ponies, mermaids, trolls—with long manes in need of curling and brushing. Dolls that urinate have not gone out of fashion, and neither have weapons-laden space vehicles (batteries not included).

There are even some cartoons on now that are better and more 11 sophisticated than anything we ever watched: the darkly ironic "Ren and Stimpy," for example, or "Men in Black" (where the cheesiness of the animation actually contributes to the humor) or, my favorite, the improbable "Pinky and the Brain," about a pair of lab mice that, as the result of an accident at Acme Labs, have been transformed into, on the one hand, an airhead rodent with a high-pitched North London accent and, on the other, a macrocephalic mad-scientist mouse with plans to take over the world. These shows, like the better prime-time cartoons—"The Simpsons" and "King of the Hill"—successfully talk to kids and adults both. They sometimes seem to operate on two simultaneous planes of reference, in fact, and they pay children the great compliment of not dumbing everything down for them. Or maybe they merely recognize that children know more than we think, or wish, they did.

But where the Saturday-morning TV of today differs enormously 12 from the TV most of us watched is in the virtual absence (except in shows like "Captain Kangaroo," for very young children) of adult figures—of the Rexes and Pablos, those benign gatekeepers, or emissaries from the real world, who while seeming to share our delight in cartoons, our near reverence for them, also reminded us of the importance of brushing our teeth and crossing at crosswalks. Grown-ups turn up on Saturday morning now as either idiots, like the crazed geek who does comic spots on "Disney's 1 Saturday Morning," or meanies, like the crotchety, incompetent teachers and principals on the cartoons "Recess" and "Pepper Ann."

Saturday-morning TV, moreover, is nothing like as sweetly 13 languorous as it used to be. Where a show like "Boomtown" used to come on at 6:30 or 7 and stay on the air for several hours, the new programs come, one after the other, at half-hour intervals, further punctuated by promos and advertisements for shows coming up later, and most of these shows leap on the screen with MTV-like logo sequences and rock-inspired theme songs and then lurch from commercial to commercial in short, hyperactive bursts. Many of the newer shows— "The X-Men" and "The New Adventures of Voltron," for example—are inspired by comic books, and with their lantern-jawed, steroidal heroes, stilted dialogue and creaky plots, they employ an aggressive, hard-edged freeze-frame style in which there is seldom a quiet or reflective moment. The violence in these shows, of which there's a fair amount, isn't realistic, exactly—the bad guys tend to be rendered unconscious rather than outright killed or maimed—but neither is it as surreally goofy as the violence in a Road Runner or Tweety and Sylvester episode, say, where bombs and missiles and explosives of every kind go off with thrilling frequency, blowing cats and coyotes sky high and wrecking amazing, if temporary, disfigurement (popping eyeballs, missing digits, smoking ears, anvil-shaped heads) without causing any harm at all.

In the end, the effect of the new, hyper Saturday-morning style, 14 whether deliberate or not, is to make time pass faster and to do away with the old sensation of endlessness, of moments hardly ticking by. As an experiment, on a recent Saturday I watched children's TV for five hours straight, from 7 to noon. (Don't try this at home, parents, without medical supervision.) I was bored much of the time, yet when I closed my eyes and tried to doze, I was invariably jarred awake by some new sound effect or other. But I was astonished by how quickly the hours flew. It was Saturday afternoon before I knew it.

The kids may not mind, however, or even notice, for how many of 15 them get to enjoy the full five-hour orgy anymore? We wake them up before dawn for the long drive to the hockey rink, and then there's band practice, ballet lessons, the math tutor and, if there's time, that play date we penciled in a few weeks ago and that we can confirm now on the car phone on the way to the orthodontist.

Many kids today, if they watch Saturday-morning TV at all, watch it 16 the way grown-ups watch "Today" or "Good Morning America"—on the run, in snatches, while hastily swallowing a vitamin pill. And on those mornings, increasingly rare, when we parents yield to temptation— when, in response to that gentle tugging on our foot or to the tiny hand clamped over our nose, we say, "Mommy and Daddy are tired right now, why don't you turn on TV for a little while?"—we are afterward undone with guilt, certain that we have cost them at least 20 points on the SAT's. For grown-ups as well as children, Saturday morning is quickly becoming a thing of the past, just another slot in the overfull datebook of our lives.

In the grand scheme of things, this may not be the worst fate that has 17 befallen our civilization, but it's regrettable nonetheless. We all of us need some down time, and children especially. There is actually something to be said for doing nothing and for learning how to be bored. There is even more to be said for escapism, for stepping out of time. And this is where children's TV has truly let us down: not in its shameless huckstering or in its shying away from "educational content," whatever that is. The problem is that the sustained quality of the daydreaming it offers is so seldom worth waking up for. Children's TV doesn't need fewer cartoons; it needs better cartoons, better drawn and with better characters. It needs narrative, which is not the same as an action plot. It needs modulation and variety. And it needs, every now and then, the voice of an adult—if for no other reason than to gently remind children that they can't stay in their pajamas forever.

Responding to Reading

1. In paragraph 5, McGrath says, "*All* TV imparts life lessons of a sort—if only lessons in how greedy or manipulative or boring television producers can be. And what we take away from the experience of watching television is more than what the programmers have put there." Do you agree? What lessons do you think television teaches its viewers?
2. How, according to McGrath, was the Saturday morning television of the 1950s like and unlike todays? Given the similarities and differences he identifies, do you agree that the effect of Saturday morning television on children can still be seen as largely positive?
3. McGrath says, "Watching television, even if you watch it alone, is also a social experience" (5). What does he mean? Would Winn (p. 258) agree?

CELEBRITY JOURNALISM, THE PUBLIC, AND PRINCESS DIANA

Joe Saltzman

Veteran journalist Joe Saltzman (1934–) received his B.A. in journalism from the University of Southern California (USC) and his M.S. from the Columbia School of Journalism. After working for several years as a newspaper reporter and editor, Saltzman joined CBS news in 1964 and worked there for the next ten years, producing daily news shows as well as many documentaries, five of them Emmy winners. He created the broadcasting, sequence at USC's School of Journalism in 1974 and served as the school's chair for fourteen years. He is currently associate dean of the Annenberg School of Communication at USC. During his tenure at USC, Saltzman has continued to work as an active journalist, and has also produced segments of Entertainment Tonight and Entertainment This Week. In addition, he is also a columnist for USA Today, where the following article appeared in January 1998.

The stink of the hypocrisy surrounding Princess Diana's death was overwhelming. There were the self-serving politicians grabbing publicity by suggesting legislation they knew was unconstitutional and unnecessary. There were the self-serving actors who rushed to judgment because they have their own axes to grind when it comes to the dark side of tabloid journalism. There were the isolated supermarket managers who self-righteously removed all the tabloids from their stores saying they wanted no part of that kind of business, ignoring other products on their shelves that promise results impossible to achieve. 1

There were the family and friends of the Princess who denounced the media while ignoring the Princess's special history with it and how she knowingly used the news media to create herself anew in her own carefully crafted image. There were the American tabloids themselves who immediately promised that they would never buy or publish pictures of the dying Princess and then congratulated themselves on record sales of issues featuring stories chronicling every detail of her final hours. 2

There were the traditional news media, so quick to condemn the tabloids, and even faster when it came to plastering one photo after another of the Princess in their publications and TV programs. *Time* and *Newsweek* threw together more than 25 pages of photos and text, including a dramatic picture of the wreckage of the car. *People* gave Diana its cover for the 44th time, then produced two later covers offering "The Diana Interviews." CBS gave viewers "48 Hours" in the Princess's life, and every other TV newsmagazine and morning and evening news show treated the event as if it were the biggest news story of the century. 3

And of course there was the public, angrily denouncing the photographers while lapping up their products with so much zeal that paparazzi photographs of Diana repeatedly created record sales for any publication printing them. 4

The key question ignored was why were so many millions of people around the world so interested in Princess Diana? How did they come to know this woman so well and mourn her death so personally? 5

The reason is that the Princess epitomized the sad state of journalism around the world, culminating with the decade's preoccupation 6 with celebrity journalism—journalism that not only creates instant celebrities, but gives them life through the constant repetition of countless personal details. Millions believed they knew the real Diana because they had been reading about every aspect of her royal and private life for years. When every minute detail of a person's life is printed in the press day after day, readers begin to feel as if they know this person intimately. When Princess Diana died, it was for many like losing a member of their family. In fact many believed they knew the Princess better than anyone else in their lives.

The difference between the tabloids and the traditional press and TV 7 coverage is so subtle as to be unrecognizable. Some tabloids do buy pictures secretly taken of celebrities in hiding or snapped after some provocation, but these out-of-focus, blurred shots make up such a small percentage of celebrity coverage that it is almost meaningless. More people read about the Princess in *People* or *Vanity Fair* or favorable gushy tabloid stories. And when networks and national news magazines spend so much time covering the Princess's death, blaming the tabloids and the paparazzi for causing it may well be the worst hypocrisy of all.

The way to stop all this nonsense is to quit pandering to the public's 8 desire for gossip and celebrity stories. Quit publishing pictures of people whose only claim to fame is that they have money or good looks. Redefine news so it omits the bizarre and the unusual. Forget celebrities and freaks and report the news that truly affects us all—news about the economy, about the government, about the environment, about people and issues that affect the way we live and work.

You can find that kind of news buried in the *New York Times*, the *Wall* 9 *Street Journal*, and a handful of other publications. You can see and hear it on PBS television and National Public Radio. An educated minority goes to these sources. But put a key economic issue on the cover of *Newsweek* and who will buy it when *Time* has a picture of some media created celebrity smiling on its cover? Who will watch the *News Hour with Jim Lehrer* instead of a local newscast filled with the murder of the night, sports, weather, and the ever-present entertainment news?

This may be the time to simply change the definition of what is 10 news. News should be events and circumstances that have an important effect on our lives. A discussion in Congress on taxes, any election in any city or state in the nation, attacks on the environment, the distribution of wealth and goods in the country—these are news stories that should be given the banner headlines they deserve.

We live in a society obsessed with celebrity. People care more about 11 how much a new film costs and takes in at the box office than they do about local elections. The only way a politician can get on the evening news is to be caught on camera with a prostitute or a drug dealer. Talk about the issues and no one listens.

As long as you want to find out the latest dirt about a beleaguered 12 princess or a second-rate actor, nothing is going to change much. Because, in the end, after the angry shouting of the mob and the stoning of the messenger, this is the way you want it. You tell the media every day what you want with your purchasing power. When you stop embracing celebrity journalism, when it is no longer profitable to publish pictures of every facet of a celebrity's daily life, then all of this will stop and the media—all the media, from the lowest tabloids to the loftiest national news magazines—will look for something else that you want. And then they'll give it to you.

To complain about the way things are is simply to add more 13 hypocrisy to the stench all around us.

Responding to Reading

1. In paragraph 6, Saltzman states that Princess Diana "epitomized the sad state of journalism around the world." What does he mean? Can you give examples of other public figures whom the media have turned into celebrities? What characteristics do these people share?

2. In paragraph 8, Saltzman offers suggestions for ways to end the practice of "celebrity journalism." Do you think the steps he suggests are likely to solve the problems he identifies?

3. In his last three paragraphs, Saltzman places the blame for the perpetuation of celebrity journalism on "a society obsessed with celebrity" (11)—in other words, on people like his readers. Do you believe this conclusion is accurate? Do you believe it is fair?

SEX, LIES, AND ADVERTISING

Gloria Steinem

Feminist writer, editor, speaker, and political activist Gloria Steinem (1934–   ) was born in Toledo, Ohio. After graduation from Smith College, she became active in the women's movement as an organizer and speaker, worked as a journalist, and founded Ms. magazine in 1971. Steinem came to national prominence with her essay "I Was a Playboy Bunny," a humorous and sarcastic exposé of the harassment she suffered on the job. Her most recent books are Revolution from Within: A Book of Self-Esteem *(1992),* Moving beyond Words *(1993), and* On Self-Esteem *(1995). Of social change, she has said, "When one member of a group changes, it shifts the balance for everyone, and when one group changes, it changes the balance of society." In the following essay, first published in* Ms. *in 1990, Steinem describes the difficulties a serious women's magazine like* Ms. *has in attracting advertisers and explains how advertisers can control a magazine's content.*

About three years ago, as *glasnost*[1] was beginning and *Ms.* seemed 1 to be ending, I was invited to a press lunch for a Soviet official. He entertained us with anecdotes about new problems of democracy in his country. Local Communist leaders were being criticized in their media for the first time, he explained, and they were angry.

"So I'll have to ask my American friends," he finished pointedly, 2 "how more *subtly* to control the press." In the silence that followed, I said, "Advertising."

The reporters laughed, but later, one of them took me aside: How 3 *dare* I suggest that freedom of the press was limited? How dare I imply that his newsweekly could be influenced by ads?

I explained that I was thinking of advertising's media-wide influ- 4 ence on most of what we read. Even newsmagazines use "soft" cover stories to sell ads, confuse readers with "advertorials," and occasionally self-censor on subjects known to be a problem with big advertisers.

But, I also explained, I was thinking especially of women's mag- 5 azines. There, it isn't just a little content that's devoted to attracting ads, it's almost all of it. That's why advertisers, not readers, have always been the problem for *Ms.* As the only women's magazine that didn't supply what the ad world euphemistically describes as "supportive editorial atmosphere" or "complementary copy" (for instance, articles that praise food/fashion/beauty subjects to "support" and "comple-ment" food/fashion/beauty ads), *Ms.* could never attract enough advertising to break even.

"Oh, *women's* magazines," the journalist said with contempt. 6 "Everybody knows they're catalogs—but who cares? They have nothing to do with journalism."

I can't tell you how many times I've had this argument in 25 years 7 of working for many kinds of publications. Except as money-making machines—"cash cows" as they are so elegantly called in the trade—women's magazines are rarely taken seriously. Though changes being made by women have been called more far-reaching than the industrial revolution—and though many editors try hard to reflect some of them in the few pages left to them after all the ad-related subjects have been covered—the magazines serving the female half of this country are still far below the journalistic and ethical standards of news and general interest publications. Most depressing of all, this doesn't even rate an exposé.

---

[1] A policy of greater openness and freedom instituted by the Soviet Union's Communist govern-ment in the late 1980s. [Eds.]

If *Time* and *Newsweek* had to lavish praise on cars in general and   8
credit General Motors in particular to get GM ads, there would be a
scandal—maybe a criminal investigation. When women's magazines
from *Seventeen* to *Lear's* praise beauty products in general and credit
Revlon in particular to get ads, it's just business as usual.

1

When *Ms.* began, we didn't consider *not* taking ads. The most   9
important reason was keeping the price of a feminist magazine low
enough for most women to afford. But the second and almost equal
reason was providing a forum where women and advertisers could talk
to each other and improve advertising itself. After all, it was (and still
is) as potent a source of information in this country as news or TV and
movie dramas.

We decided to proceed in two stages. First, we would convince mak-   10
ers of "people products" used by both men and women but advertised
mostly to men—cars, credit cards, insurance, sound equipment, financial
services, and the like—that their ads should be placed in a women's magazine. Since they were accustomed to the division between editorial and
advertising in news and general interest magazines, this would allow our
editorial content to be free and diverse. Second, we would add the best
ads for whatever traditional "women's products" (clothes, shampoo, fragrance, food, and so on) that surveys showed *Ms.* readers used. But we
would ask them to come in *without* the usual quid pro quo of "complementary copy."

We knew the second step might be harder. Food advertisers have   11
always demanded that women's magazines publish recipes and articles
on entertaining (preferably ones that name their products) in return for
their ads; clothing advertisers expect to be surrounded by fashion
spreads (especially ones that credit their designers); and shampoo,
fragrance, and beauty products in general usually insist on positive
editorial coverage of beauty subjects, plus photo credits besides. That's
why women's magazines look the way they do. But if we could break
this link between ads and editorial content, then we wanted good ads
for "women's products," too.

By playing their part in this unprecedented mix of *all* the things our   12
readers need and use, advertisers also would be rewarded: Ads for
products like cars and mutual funds would find a new growth market;
the best ads for women's products would no longer be lost in oceans of
ads for the same category; and both would have access to a laboratory
of smart and caring readers whose response would help create effective
ads for other media as well.

I thought then that our main problem would be the imagery in 13
ads themselves. Car-makers were still draping blondes in evening
gowns over the hoods like ornaments. Authority figures were almost
always male, even in ads for products that only women used. Sadistic,
he-man campaigns even won industry praise. For instance, *Advertising
Age* had hailed the infamous Silva Thin cigarette theme, "How to Get a
Woman's Attention: Ignore Her," as "brilliant." Even in medical journals, tranquilizer ads showed depressed housewives standing beside
piles of dirty dishes and promised to get them back to work.

Obviously, *Ms.* would have to avoid such ads and seek out the best 14
ones—but this didn't seem impossible. *The New Yorker* had been select-
ing ads for aesthetic reasons for years, a practice that only seemed to
make advertisers more eager to be in its pages. *Ebony* and *Essence* were
asking for ads with positive black images, and though their struggle
was hard, they weren't being called unreasonable.

Clearly, what *Ms.* needed was a very special publisher and ad sales 15
staff. I could think of only one woman with experience on the business
side of magazines—Patricia Carbine, who recently had become a vice
president of *McCall's* as well as its editor in chief—and the reason I
knew her name was a good omen. She had been managing editor at
Look (really *the* editor, but its owner refused to put a female name at the
top of his masthead) when I was writing a column there. After I did an
early interview with Cesar Chavez, then just emerging as a leader of
migrant labor, and the publisher turned it down because he was worried about ads from Sunkist, Pat was the one who intervened. As I
learned later, she had told the publisher she would resign if the interview wasn't published. Mainly because *Look* couldn't afford to lose Pat,
it *was* published (and the ads from Sunkist never arrived).

Though I barely knew this woman, she had done two things I 16
always remembered: put her job on the line in a way that editors often
talk about but rarely do, and been so loyal to her colleagues that she
never told me or anyone outside *Look* that she had done so.

Fortunately, Pat did agree to leave *McCall's* and take a huge cut in 17
salary to become publisher of *Ms.* She became responsible for training
and inspiring generations of young women who joined the *Ms.* ad sales
force, many of whom went on to become "firsts" at the top of publishing. When *Ms.* first started, however, there were so few women with
experience selling space that Pat and I made the rounds of ad agencies
ourselves. Later, the fact that *Ms.* was asking companies to do business
in a different way meant our saleswomen had to make many times the
usual number of calls—first to convince agencies and then client companies besides—and to present endless amounts of research. I was often
asked to do a final ad presentation, or see some higher decision-maker,
or speak to women employees so executives could see the interest of
women they worked with. That's why I spent more time persuading

advertisers than editing or writing for *Ms.* and why I ended up with an unsentimental education in the seamy underside of publishing that few writers see (and even fewer magazines can publish).

Let me take you with us through some experiences, just as they 18 happened:

• Cheered on by early support from Volkswagen and one or two 19 other car companies, we scrape together time and money to put on a major reception in Detroit. We know U.S. car-makers firmly believe that women choose the upholstery, not the car, but we are armed with statistics and reader mail to prove the contrary: A car is an important purchase for women, one that symbolizes mobility and freedom.

But almost nobody comes. We are left with many pounds of shrimp 20 on the table, and quite a lot of egg on our face. We blame ourselves for not guessing that there would be a baseball pennant play-off on the same day, but executives go out of their way to explain they wouldn't have come anyway. Thus begins ten years of knocking on hostile doors, presenting endless documentation, and hiring a full-time saleswoman in Detroit; all necessary before *Ms.* gets any real results.

This long saga has a semihappy ending: foreign and, later, domes- 21 tic car-makers eventually provided *Ms.* with enough advertising to make cars one of our top sources of ad revenue. Slowly, Detroit began to take the women's market seriously enough to put car ads in other women's magazines, too, thus freeing a few pages from the hothouse of fashion-beauty-food ads.

But long after figures showed a third, even a half, of many car 22 models being bought by women, U.S. makers continued to be uncomfortable addressing women. Unlike foreign car-makers, Detroit never quite learned the secret of creating intelligent ads that exclude no one, and then placing them in women's magazines to overcome past exclusion. (*Ms.* readers were so grateful for a routine Honda ad featuring rack and pinion steering, for instance, that they sent fan mail.) Even now, Detroit continues to ask, "Should we make special ads for women?" Perhaps that's why some foreign cars still have a disproportionate share of the U.S. women's market.

• In the Ms. Gazette, we do a brief report on a congressional hear- 23 ing into chemicals used in hair dyes that are absorbed through the skin and may be carcinogenic. Newspapers report this too, but Clairol, a Bristol-Myers subsidary that makes dozens of products—a few of which have just begun to advertise in *Ms.*—is outraged. Not at new papers or news magazines, just at us. It's bad enough that Ms. is the only women's magazine refusing to provide the usual "complementary" articles and beauty photos, but to criticize one of their categories— *that* is going too far.

We offer to publish a letter from Clairol telling its side of the story. 24 In an excess of solicitousness, we even put this letter in the Gazette, not in Letters to the Editors where it belongs. Nonetheless—and in spite of surveys that show *Ms.* readers are active women who use more of almost everything Clairol makes than do the readers of any other women's magazine—*Ms.* gets almost none of these ads for the rest of its natural life.

Meanwhile, Clairol changes its hair-coloring formula, apparently in   25 response to the hearings we reported.

• Our saleswomen set out early to attract ads for consumer   26 electronics: sound equipment, calculators, computers, VCRs, and the like. We know that our readers are determined to be included in the technological revolution. We know from reader surveys that *Ms.* readers are buying this stuff in numbers as high as those of magazines like *Playboy*, or "men 18 to 34," the prime targets of the consumer electronics industry. Moreover, unlike traditional women's products that our readers buy but don't need to read articles about, these are subjects they want covered in our pages. There actually *is* a supportive editorial atmosphere.

"But women don't understand technology," say executives at the   27 end of ad presentations. "Maybe not," we respond, "but neither do men—and we all buy it."

"If women *do* buy it," say the decision-makers, "they're asking their   28 husbands and boyfriends what to buy first." We produce letters from *Ms.* readers saying how turned off they are when salesmen say things like "Let me know when your husband can come in."

After several years of this, we get a few ads for compact sound   29 systems. Some of them come from JVC, whose vice president, Harry Elias, is trying to convince his Japanese bosses that there is something called a women's market. At his invitation, I find myself speaking at huge trade shows in Chicago and Las Vegas, trying to persuade JVC dealers that showrooms don't have to be locker rooms where women are made to feel unwelcome. But as it turns out, the shows themselves are part of the problem. In Las Vegas, the only women around the technology displays are seminude models serving champagne. In Chicago, the big attraction is Marilyn Chambers, who followed Linda Lovelace of *Deep Throat* fame as Chuck Traynor's captive and/or employee. VCRs are being demonstrated with her porn videos.

In the end, we get ads for a car stereo now and then, but no VCRs;   30 some IBM personal computers, but no Apple or Japanese ones. We notice that office magazines like *Working Woman* and *Savvy* don't benefit as much as they should from office equipment ads either. In the electronics world, women and technology seem mutually exclusive. It remains a decade behind even Detroit.

• Because we get letters from little girls who love toy trains, and   31 who ask our help in changing ads and box-top photos that feature little boys only, we try to get toy-train ads from Lionel. It turns out that Lionel executives *have* been concerned about little girls. They made a pink train, and were surprised when it didn't sell.

Lionel bows to consumer pressure with a photograph of a boy *and* a girl—but only on some of their boxes. They fear that, if trains are associated with girls, they will be devalued in the minds of boys. Needless to say, *Ms.* gets no train ads, and little girls remain a mostly unexplored market. By 1986, Lionel is put up for sale. 32

But for different reasons, we haven't had much luck with other kinds of toys either. In spite of many articles on child-rearing; an annual listing of nonsexist, multiracial toys by Letty Cottin Pogrebin; Stories for Free Children, a regular feature also edited by Letty; and other prize-winning features for or about children, we get virtually no toy ads. Generations of *Ms.* saleswomen explain to toy manufacturers that a larger proportion of *Ms.* readers have preschool children than do the readers of other women's magazines, but this industry can't believe feminists have or care about children. 33

• When *Ms.* begins, the staff decides not to accept ads for feminine hygiene sprays or cigarettes: they are damaging and carry no appropriate health warnings. Though we don't think we should tell our readers what to do, we do think we should provide facts so they can decide for themselves. Since the antismoking lobby has been pressing for health warnings on cigarette ads, we decide to take them only as they comply. 34

Philip Morris is among the first to do so. One of its brands, Virginia Slims, is also sponsoring women's tennis and the first national polls of women's opinions. On the other hand, the Virginia Slims theme, "You've come a long way, baby," has more than a "baby" problem. It makes smoking a symbol of progress for women. 35

We explain to Philip Morris that this slogan won't do well in our pages, but they are convinced its success with some women means it will work with *all* women. Finally, we agree to publish an ad for a Virginia Slims calendar as a test. The letters from readers are critical—and smart. For instance: Would you show a black man picking cotton, the same man in a Cardin suit, and symbolize the antislavery and civil rights movements by smoking? Of course not. But instead of honoring the test results, the Philip Morris people seem angry to be proven wrong. They take away ads for *all* their many brands. 36

This costs *Ms.* about $250,000 the first year. After five years, we can no longer keep track. Occasionally, a new set of executives listens to *Ms.* saleswomen, but because we won't take Virginia Slims, not one Philip Morris product returns to our pages for the next 16 years. 37

Gradually, we also realize our naïveté in thinking we *could* decide against taking cigarette ads. They became a disproportionate support of magazines the moment they were banned on television, and few magazines could compete and survive without them; certainly not *Ms.*, which lacks so many other categories. By the time statistics in the 1980s 38 showed that women's rate of lung cancer was approaching men's, the necessity of taking cigarette ads has become a kind of prison.

• General Mills, Pillsbury, Carnation, Del Monte, Dole, Kraft, 39 Stouffer, Hormel, Nabisco: You name the food giant, we try it. But no matter how desirable the *Ms.* readership, our lack of recipes is lethal.

We explain to them that placing food ads *only* next to recipes associ- 40 ates food with work. For many women, it is a negative that works *against* the ads. Why not place food ads in diverse media without recipes (thus reaching more men, who are now a third of the shoppers in supermarkets anyway), and leave the recipes to specialty magazines like *Gourmet* (a third of whose readers are also men)?

These arguments elicit interest, but except for an occasional ad for a 41 convenience food, instant coffee, diet drinks, yogurt, or such extras as avocados and almonds, this mainstay of the publishing industry stays closed to us. Period.

• Traditionally, wines and liquors didn't advertise to women: Men 42 were thought to make the brand decisions, even if women did the buying. But after endless presentations, we begin to make a dent in this category. Thanks to the unconventional Michel Roux of Carillon Importers (distributors of Grand Marnier, Absolut Vodka, and others), who assumes that food and drink have no gender, some ads are leaving their men's club.

Beermakers are still selling masculinity. It takes *Ms.* fully eight years 43 to get its first beer ad (Michelob). In general, however, liquor ads are less stereotyped in their imagery—and far less controlling of the editorial content around them—than are women's products. But given the underrepresentation of other categories, these very facts tend to create a disproportionate number of alcohol ads in the pages of *Ms.* This in turn dismays readers worried about women and alcoholism.

• We hear in 1980 that women in the Soviet Union have been 44 producing feminist *samizdat* (underground, self-published books) and circulating them throughout the country. As punishment, four of the leaders have been exiled. Though we are operating on our usual shoestring, we solicit individual contributions to send Robin Morgan to interview these women in Vienna.

The result is an exclusive cover story that includes the first news of 45 a populist peace movement against the Afghanistan occupation, a prediction of *glasnost* to come, and a grassroots, intimate view of Soviet women's lives. From the popular press to women's studies courses, the response is great. The story wins a Front Page award.

Nonetheless, this journalistic coup undoes years of efforts to get an 46 ad schedule from Revlon. Why? Because the Soviet women on our cover *are not wearing makeup.*

• Four years of research and presentations go into convincing 47 airlines that women now make travel choices and business trips.

United, the first airline to advertise in *Ms.*, is so impressed with the response from our readers that one of its executives appears in a film for our ad presentations. As usual, good ads get great results.

But we have problems unrelated to such results. For instance: 48 Because American Airlines flight attendants include among their labor demands the stipulation that they could choose to have their last names preceded by "Ms." on their name tags—in a long-delayed revolt against the standard, "I am your pilot, Captain Rothgart, and this is your flight attendant, Cindy Sue"—American officials seem to hold the magazine responsible. We get no ads.

There is still a different problem at Eastern. A vice president cancels 49 subscriptions for thousands of copies on Eastern flights. Why? Because he is offended by ads for lesbian poetry journals in the *Ms.* Classified. A "family airline," as he explains to me coldly on the phone, has to "draw the line somewhere."

It's obvious that *Ms.* can't exclude lesbians and serve women. 50 We've been trying to make that point ever since our first issue included an article by and about lesbians, and both Suzanne Levine, our managing editor, and I were lectured by such heavy hitters as Ed Kosner, then editor of *Newsweek* (and now of *New York Magazine*), who insisted that *Ms.* should "position" itself *against* lesbians. But our advertisers have paid to reach a guaranteed number of readers, and soliciting new subscriptions to compensate for Eastern would cost $150,000, plus rebating money in the meantime.

Like almost everything ad-related, this presents an elaborate 51 organizing problem. After days of searching for sympathetic members of the Eastern board, Frank Thomas, president of the Ford Foundation, kindly offers to call Roswell Gilpatrick, a director of Eastern. I talk with Mr. Gilpatrick, who calls Frank Borman, then the president of Eastern. Frank Borman calls me to say that his airline is not in the business of censoring magazines: *Ms.* will be returned to Eastern flights.

• Women's access to insurance and credit is vital, but with the 52 exception of Equitable and a few other ad pioneers, such financial services address men. For almost a decade after the Equal Credit Opportunity Act passes in 1974, we try to convince American Express that women are a growth market—but nothing works.

Finally, a former professor of Russian named Jerry Welsh becomes 53 head of marketing. He assumes that women should be cardholders, and persuades his colleagues to feature women in a campaign. Thanks to this 1980s series, the growth rate for female cardholders surpasses that for men.

For this article, I asked Jerry Welsh if he would explain why 54 American Express waited so long. "Sure," he said, "they were afraid of having a 'pink' card."

- Women of color read *Ms.* in disproportionate numbers. This is a 55
source of pride to *Ms.* staffers, who are also more racially representative
than the editors of other women's magazines. But this reality is
obscured by ads filled with enough white women to make a reader
snowblind.

Pat Carbine remembers mostly "astonishment" when she requested 56
African American, Hispanic, Asian, and other diverse images. Marcia
Ann Gillespie, a *Ms.* editor who was previously the editor in chief of
Essence, witnesses ad bias a second time: Having tried for *Essence* to get
white advertisers to use black images (Revlon did so eventually, but
L'Oréal, Lauder, Chanel, and other companies never did), she sees
similar problems getting integrated ads for an integrated magazine.
Indeed, the ad world often creates black and Hispanic ads only for black
and Hispanic media. In an exact parallel of the fear that marketing a
product to women will endanger its appeal to men, the response is
usually, "But your [white] readers won't identify."

In fact, those we are able to get—for instance, a Max Factor ad made 57
for *Essence* that Linda Wachner gives us after she becomes president—are
praised by white readers, too. But there are pathetically few such images.

- By the end of 1986, production and mailing costs have risen 58
astronomically, ad income is flat, and competition for ads is stiffer than
ever. The 60/40 preponderance of edit over ads that we promised to
readers becomes 50/50; children's stories, most poetry, and some fiction
are casualties of less space; in order to get variety into limited pages, the
length (and sometimes the depth) of articles suffers; and, though we do
refuse most of the ads that would look like a parody in our pages, we
get so worn down that some slip through. Still, readers perform
miracles. Though we haven't been able to afford a subscription mailing
in two years, they maintain our guaranteed circulation of 450,000.

Nonetheless, media reports on *Ms.* often insist that our unprof- 59
itability must be due to reader disinterest. The myth that advertisers
simply follow readers is very strong. Not one reporter notes that other
comparable magazines our size (say, *Vanity Fair* or *The Atlantic*) have
been losing more money in one year than *Ms.* has lost in 16 years. No
matter how much never-to-be-recovered cash is poured into starting a
magazine or keeping one going, appearances seem to be all that matter.
(Which is why we haven't been able to explain our fragile state in public. Nothing causes ad flight like the smell of nonsuccess.)

My healthy response is anger. My not-so-healthy response is 60
constant worry. Also an obsession with finding one more rescue. There
is hardly a night when I don't wake up with sweaty palms and pounding heart, scared that we won't be able to pay the printer or the post
office; scared most of all that closing our doors will hurt the women's
movement.

Out of chutzpah and desperation, I arrange a lunch with Leonard 61
Lauder, president of Estée Lauder. With the exception of Clinique (the
brainchild of Carol Phillips), none of Lauder's hundreds of products has
been advertised in Ms. A year's schedule of ads for just three or four of
them could save us. Indeed, as the scion of a family-owned company
whose ad practices are followed by the beauty industry, he is one of the
few men who could liberate many pages in all women's magazines just
by changing his mind about "complementary copy."

Over a lunch that costs more than we can pay for some articles, I 62
explain the need for his leadership. I also lay out the record of Ms.: more
literary and journalistic prizes won, more new issues introduced into the
mainstream, new writers discovered, and impact on society than any
other magazine; more articles that became books, stories that became
movies, ideas that became television series, and newly advertised products that became profitable; and, most important for him, a place for his
ads to reach women who aren't reachable through any other women's
magazine. Indeed, if there is one constant characteristic of the ever-
changing Ms. readership, it is their impact as leaders. Whether it's waiting until later to have first babies, or pioneering PABA as sun protection
in cosmetics, *whatever* they are doing today, a third to a half of American
women will be doing three to five years from now. It's never failed.

But, he says, Ms. readers are not *our* women. They're not interested 63
in things like fragrance and blush-on. If they were, Ms. would write
articles about them.

On the contrary, I explain, surveys show they are more likely to buy 64
such things than the readers of, say, *Cosmopolitan* or *Vogue*. They're good
customers because they're out in the world enough to need several sets
of everything: home, work, purse, travel, gym, and so on. They just
don't need to read articles about these things. Would he ask a men's
magazine to publish monthly columns on how to shave before he
advertised Aramis products (his line for men)?

He concedes that beauty features are often concocted more for 65
advertisers than readers. But Ms. isn't appropriate for his ads anyway,
he explains. Why? Because Estée Lauder is selling "a kept-woman
mentality."

I can't quite believe this. Sixty percent of the users of his products 66
are salaried, and generally resemble Ms. readers. Besides, his company
has the appeal of having been started by a creative and hardworking
woman, his mother, Estée Lauder.

That doesn't matter, he says. He knows his customers, and they 67
would *like* to be kept women. That's why he will never advertise in Ms.

In November 1987, by vote of the Ms. Foundation for Education 68
and Communication (Ms.'s owner and publisher, the media subsidiary
of the Ms. Foundation for Women), Ms. was sold to a company whose

officers, Australian feminists Sandra Yates and Anne Summers, raised
the investment money in their country that *Ms.* couldn't find in its own.
They also started *Sassy* for teenage women.

In their two-year tenure, circulation was raised to 550,000 by invest- 69
ment in circulation mailings, and, to the dismay of some readers, editorial features on clothes and new products made a more traditional bid for
ads. Nonetheless, ad pages fell below previous levels. In addition, *Sassy*,
whose fresh voice and sexual frankness were an unprecedented success
with young readers, was targeted by two mothers from Indiana who
began, as one of them put it, "calling every Christian organization I
could think of." In response to this controversy, several crucial advertisers pulled out.

Such links between ads and editorial content was a problem in 70
Australia, too, but to a lesser degree. "Our readers pay two times more
for their magazines," Anne explained, "so advertisers have less power
to threaten a magazine's viability."

"I was shocked," said Sandra Yates with characteristic directness. 71
"In Australia, we think you have freedom of the press—but you don't."

Since Anne and Sandra had not met their budget's projections for 73
ad revenue, their investors forced a sale. In October 1989, *Ms.* and *Sassy*
were bought by Dale Lang, owner of *Working Mother, Working Woman*,
and one of the few independent publishing companies left among the
conglomerates. In response to a request from the original *Ms.* staff—as
well as to reader letters urging that *Ms.* continue, plus his own belief
that *Ms.* would benefit his other magazines by blazing a trail—he
agreed to try the ad-free, reader-supported *Ms.* . . . and to give us
complete editorial control.

2

In response to the workplace revolution of the 1970s, traditional 73
women's magazines—that is, "trade books" for women working at
home—were joined by *Savvy, Working Woman*, and other trade books
for women working in offices. But by keeping the fashion/beauty/
entertaining articles necessary to get traditional ads and then adding
career articles besides, they inadvertently produced the antifeminist
stereotype of Super Woman. The male-imitative, dress-for-success
woman carrying a briefcase became the media image of a woman
worker, even though a blue-collar woman's salary was often higher
than her glorified secretarial sister's, and though women at a real
briefcase level are statistically rare. Needless to say, these dress-for-
success women were also thin, white, and beautiful.

In recent years, advertisers' control over the editorial content of 74
women's magazines has become so institutionalized that it is written

into "insertion orders" or dictated to ad salespeople as official policy. The following are recent typical orders to women's magazines:

- Dow's Cleaning Products stipulates that ads for its Vivid and 75 Spray 'n Wash products should be adjacent to "children or fashion editorial"; ads for Bathroom Cleaner should be next to "home furnishing/family" features; and so on for other brands. "If a magazine fails for half the brands or more," the Dow order warns, "it will be omitted from further consideration."

- Bristol-Myers, the parent of Clairol, Windex, Drano, Bufferin, and 76 much more, stipulates that ads be placed next to "a full page of compatible editorial."

- S. C. Johnson & Son, makers of Johnson Wax, lawn and laundry 77 products, insect sprays, hair sprays, and so on, orders that its ads *"should not be opposite extremely controversial features or material antithetical to the nature/copy of the advertised product."* (Italics theirs.)

- Maidenform, manufacturer of bras and other apparel, leaves 78 a blank for the particular product and states: "The creative concept of the _____ campaign, and the very nature of the product itself appeal to the positive emotions of the reader/consumer. Therefore, it is imperative that all editorial agencies reflect that same positive tone. The editorial must not be negative in content or lend itself contrary to the _____ product imagery/message (*e.g., editorial relating to illness, disillusionment, large size fashion, etc.*)." (Italics mine.)

- The De Beers diamond company, a big seller of engagement 79 rings, prohibits magazines from placing its ads with "agencies to hard news or anti- love/romance themed editorial."

- Procter & Gamble, one of this country's most powerful and 80 diversified advertisers, stands out in the memory of Anne Summers and Sandra Yates (no mean feat in this context): Its products were not to be placed in any issue that included *any* material on gun control, abortion, the occult, cults, or the disparagement of religion. Caution was also demanded in any issue covering sex or drugs, even for educational purposes.

Those are the most obvious chains around women's magazines. 81 There are also rules so clear they needn't be written down: for instance, an overall "look" compatible with beauty and fashion ads. Even "real" nonmodel women photographed for a woman's magazine are usually made up, dressed in credited clothes, and retouched out of all reality. When editors do include articles on less-than-cheerful subjects (for instance, domestic violence), they tend to keep them short and unillustrated. The point is to be "upbeat." Just as women in the street are asked, "Why don't you smile, honey?" women's magazines acquire an institutional smile.

Within the text itself, praise for advertisers' products has become so 82 ritualized that fields like "beauty writing" have been invented. One of its frequent practitioners explained seriously that "It's a difficult art. How many new adjectives can you find? How much greater can you make a lipstick sound? The FDA[2] restricts what companies can say on labels, but we create illusion. And ad agencies are on the phone all the time pushing you to get their product in. A lot of them keep the business based on how many editorial clippings they produce every month. The worst are products," like Lauder's as the writer confirmed, "with their own name involved. It's all ego."

Often, editorial becomes one giant ad. Last November, for instance, 83 *Lear's* featured an elegant woman executive on the cover. On the contents page, we learned she was wearing Guerlain makeup and Samsara, a new fragrance by Guerlain. Inside were full-page ads for Samsara and Guerlain antiwrinkle cream. In the cover profile, we learned that this executive was responsible for launching Samsara and is Guerlain's director of public relations. When the *Columbia Journalism Review* did one of the few articles to include women's magazines in coverage of the influence of ads, editor Frances Lear was quoted as defending her magazine because "this kind of thing is done all the time."

Often, advertisers also plunge odd-shaped ads into the text, no mat- 84 ter what the cost to the readers. At *Woman's Day*, a magazine originally founded by a supermarket chain, editor in chief Ellen Levine said, "The day the copy had to rag around a chicken leg was not a happy one."

Advertisers are also adamant about where in a magazine their ads 85 appear. When Revlon was not placed as the first beauty ad in one Hearst magazine, for instance, Revlon pulled its ads from *all* Hearst magazines. Ruth Whitney, editor in chief of *Glamour*, attributes some of these demands to "ad agencies wanting to prove to a client that they've squeezed the last drop of blood out of a magazine." She also is, she says, "sick and tired of hearing that women's magazines are controlled by cigarette ads." Relatively speaking, she's right. To be as censoring as are many advertisers for women's products, tobacco companies would have to demand articles in praise of smoking and expect glamorous photos of beautiful women smoking their brands.

I don't mean to imply that the editors I quote here share my 86 objections to ads: Most assume that women's magazines have to be the way they are. But it's also true that only former editors can be completely honest. "Most of the pressure came in the form of direct product mentions," explains Sey Chassler, who was editor in chief of *Redbook* from the sixties to the eighties. "We got threats from the big guys, the Revlons, blackmail threats. They wouldn't run ads unless we credited them.

"But it's not fair to single out the beauty advertisers because these 87 pressures came from everybody. Advertisers want to know two things:

---

[2] The federal Food and Drug Administration. [Eds.]

What are you going to charge me? What *else* are you going to do for me? It's a holdup. For instance, management felt that fiction took up too much space. They couldn't put any advertising in that. For the last ten years, the number of fiction entries into the National Magazine Awards has declined.

"And pressures are getting worse. More magazines are more bottom- 88 line oriented because they have been taken over by companies with no interest in publishing.

"I also think advertisers do this to women's magazines especially," 89 he concluded, "because of the general disrespect they have for women."

Even media experts who don't give a damn about women's maga- 90 zines are alarmed by the spread of this ad-edit linkage. In a climate *The Wall Street Journal* describes as an unacknowledged Depression for media, women's products are increasingly able to take their low standards wherever they go. For instance: Newsweeklies publish uncritical stories on fashion and fitness. *The New York Times Magazine* recently ran an article on "firming creams," complete with mentions of advertisers. Vanity Fair published a profile of one major advertiser, Ralph Lauren, illustrated by the same photographer who does his ads, and turned the lifestyle of another, Calvin Klein, into a cover story. Even the outrageous *Spy* has toned down since it began to go after fashion ads.

And just to make us really worry, films and books, the last media 91 that go directly to the public without having to attract ads first, are in danger, too. Producers are beginning to depend on payments for displaying products in movies, and books are now being commissioned by companies like Federal Express.

But the truth is that women's products—like women's magazines— 92 have never been the subjects of much serious reporting anyway. News and general interest publications, including the "style" or "living" sections of newspapers, write about food and clothing as cooking and fashion, and almost never evaluate such products by brand name. Though chemical additives, pesticides, and animal fats are major health risks in the United States, and clothes, shoddy or not, absorb more consumer dollars than cars, this lack of information is serious. So is ignoring the contents of beauty products that are absorbed into our bodies through our skins, and that have profit margins so big they would make a loan shark blush.

3

What could women's magazines be like if they were as free as 93 books? as realistic as newspapers? as creative as films? as diverse as women's lives? We don't know.

But we'll only find out if we take women's magazines seriously. If 94
readers were to act in a concerted way to change traditional practices of
all women's magazines and the marketing of *all* women's products, we
could do it. After all, they are operating on our consumer dollars; money
that we now control. You and I could:

- write to editors and publishers (with copies to advertisers) that
  we're willing to pay *more* for magazines with editorial independence, but will *not* continue to pay for those that are just editorial
  extensions of ads;

- write to advertisers (with copies to editors and publishers) that
  we want fiction, political reporting, consumer reporting—whatever is, or is not, supported by their ads;

- put as much energy into breaking advertising's control over
  content as into changing the images in ads, or protesting ads for
  harmful products like cigarettes;

- support only those women's magazines and products that take *us*
  seriously as readers and consumers.

- Those of us in the magazine world can also use the carrot- 95
  and-stick technique. For instance: Pointing out that, if magazines
  were a regulated medium like television, the demands of advertisers would be against FCC[3] rules. Payola and extortion could be
  punished. As it is, there are probably illegalities. A magazine's
  postal rates are determined by the ratio of ad to edit pages, and
  the former costs more than the latter. So much for the stick.

The carrot means appealing to enlightened self-interest. For 96
instance: There are many studies showing that the greatest factor in
determining an ad's effectiveness is the credibility of its surroundings.
The "higher the rating of editorial believability," concluded a 1987
survey by the *Journal of Advertising Research*, "the higher the rating of the
advertising." Thus, an impenetrable wall between edit and ads would
also be in the best interest of advertisers.

Unfortunately, few agencies or clients hear such arguments. Editors 97
often maintain the false purity of refusing to talk to them at all. Instead,
they see ad salespeople who know little about editorial, are trained in
business as usual, and are usually paid by commission. Editors might
also band together to take on controversy. That happened once when all
the major women's magazines did articles in the same month on the
Equal Rights Amendment. It could happen again.

---

[3] The Federal Communications Commission. [Eds.]

It's almost three years away from life between the grindstones of 98
advertising pressures and readers' needs. I'm just beginning to realize
how edges got smoothed down—in spite of all our resistance.

I remember feeling put upon when I changed "Porsche" to "car" in 99
a piece about Nazi imagery in German pornography by Andrea
Dworkin—feeling sure Andrea would understand that Volkswagen, the
distributor of Porsche and one of our few supportive advertisers, asked
only to be far away from Nazi subjects. It's taken me all this time to
realize that Andrea was the one with a right to feel put upon.

Even as I write this, I get a call from a writer for *Elle*, who is doing 100
a whole article on where women part their hair. Why, she wants to
know, do I part mine in the middle?

It's all so familiar. A writer trying to make something of a nothing 101
assignment; an editor laboring to think of new ways to attract ads;
readers assuming that other women must want this ridiculous stuff;
more women suffering for lack of information, insight, creativity, and
laughter that could be on these same pages.

I ask you: Can't we do better than this?   102

Responding to Reading

1. In paragraph 4, Steinem observes, "Even news magazines use 'soft' cover
   stories to sell ads, confuse readers with 'advertorials,' and occasionally
   self-censor on subjects known to be a problem with big advertisers." Do
   you believe such practices are ethical? Does the fact that they are so
   widespread make them more acceptable to you?
2. Why, according to Steinem, are women's magazines particularly vulnerable
   to advertisers' demands? Do you agree with her statement in paragraph 8:
   "If *Time* and *Newsweek* had to lavish praise on cars in general and credit
   General Motors in particular to get GM ads, there would be a scandal—
   maybe a criminal investigation. When women's magazines . . . praise
   beauty products in general and credit Revlon in particular to get ads, it's
   just business as usual"?
3. Do you think Steinem may be overstating her case? If so, what might be
   motivating her?

GRASPING THE DARK IMAGES OF ROCK

Kevin J. H. Dettmar

*Kevin J. H. Dettmar (1959–) received his B.A. in English and psychol-
ogy from the University of California, Davis, and a Ph.D. in British literature
from UCLA. He has taught at Loyola Marymount University and Clemson*

University, and he is currently chair of the Department of English at Southern Illinois University at Carbondale. Much of his scholarly focus is on twentieth-century British and American literature and culture. Among his books are Reading Rock & Roll: Authenticity, Appropriation, Aesthetic *(1999), and he has also published a wide variety of essays on topics ranging from James Joyce to* The Simpsons. *He is currently at work on* Irony in the Public Sphere, *which examines uses of irony since the 1840s in Britain and the United States. The following essay, originally titled "Ironic Literacy," appeared in the* Chronicle of Higher Education *in June 2000.*

A few weeks ago, my 14-year-old daughter, Audrey, came upstairs 1 to tell me that a Columbine High School junior, a basketball star named Greg Barnes, had hanged himself. When his father found him, Blink-182's "Adam's Song" was playing in the background. Currently in heavy rotation on the modern-rock stations, it is a song in which the singer/speaker contemplates suicide.

My daughter learned of the suicide nearly a week after the fact 2 because it was the topic of conversation on the morning show carried by her favorite pop-music radio station. One of the hosts had seen something about the suicide on CNN the previous night, and was outraged that the song had been getting airplay. (The station on which Audrey heard the news doesn't play the song, though it has played other Blink-182 songs.) A lively conversation took place on the air, with telephone callers, and on the "Graffiti Wall" of the show's site on the World Wide Web. Though some callers tried to argue that no one commits suicide because of what he might have heard in a song, a large number agreed with the host's opinion that if a song doesn't express something positive, it shouldn't be played on the radio.

Although a majority of participants in the show's online colloquy 3 voiced their opposition to formal censorship, many expressed a desire for a kind of point-of-purchase censorship, suggesting, for instance, that the parental-advisory label found on a CD like Blink-182's Enemy of the State be turned into a purchase restriction, similar to the PG-13 and R ratings for films. Many listeners spoke in favor of parental supervision, including a teenager who wrote on the show's Web site: "The parents should be well informed of the music that their children listen to. They should take everyone of their kid's CD's or tapes and listen to them, and then decide what to do. My parents do it and I think everyone else's should. My parents has took [sic] away my Eminem CD, my Dr. Dre CD, my Kid Rock CD, and also my Limp Bizkit CD."

Perhaps it's an occupational hazard, but, as an English teacher, I 4 can't help seeing in all this not the issue of censorship, but a parable about the hazards of reading poorly, and about the dangers of a populace just marginally literate when it comes to understanding irony—particularly as it is used in rock music.

Greg Barnes's death followed by just two weeks the one-year 5
anniversary of the mass shooting at Columbine High School.
Rock'n'roll was at the scene of that crime as well, at least by implication:
In the wake of the shooting, investigators discovered that the killers,
Eric Harris and Dylan Klebold, had listened obsessively to the "goth"
music of Marilyn Manson, Rammstein, and KMFDM. A kind of ad-hoc-
cause-and-effect argument was advanced in some quarters that the
music's dark messages were in some way responsible for the boys' dark
acts. Harris, for instance, had posted the lyrics to KMFDM's "Son of a
Gun" on his Web site:

> Shockwave
> Massive attack
> Atomic blast
> Son of a gun is back.

There are certainly sentiments here to give one pause—especially a 6
journalist hot on the scent of a story. But the story that the song actually tells, while hardly sophisticated, is more complicated than those
lines suggest, for the "son of a gun" is later called a "sh— for brains."
Thus the song, while on the surface appearing to glamorize violence,
attempts on another level to question the very values its hero identifies
with.

That narrative strategy—giving voice to views with which one 7
disagrees as a way to expose that position's flaws—is called irony. Rock
'n' roll has deployed irony as a narrative strategy from its earliest days.
But rock's irony has become increasingly sophisticated and under-
stated over time, and with its increasing textual density has come an
increased risk that a certain kind of fan will miss the point of a song
entirely.

Truth be told, rock 'n' roll has never done a good job of presenting 8
the case against suicide, with or without irony. The locus classicus is
David Bowie's "Rock 'N' Roll Suicide," the closing track on The Rise
and Fall of Ziggy Stardust and the Spiders from Mars. Yet, while the
anguish in Bowie's voice on that track is, by the end of the song, almost
unbearable, the argument, finally, is quite mundane:

> Oh no love! you're not alone
> You're watching yourself but you're
> too unfair
> You got your head all tangled up but if
> I could only make you care

"Jumper," a recent hit song by Third Eye Blind, is another good 9
example of the limitations of the genre:

I wish you would step back from that ledge, my friend
You could cut ties with all the lies
That you've been living in

Even one of the most beautifully elegiac albums of the past decade, 10
Neil Young's Sleeps With Angels, finally falls short, as Young tries to
imagine going back in time and persuading Nirvana's front man, Kurt
Cobain, not to take his own life:

When you get weak, and you need to test your will
When life's complete, but there's something missing still
Distracting you from this must be the one you love
Must be the one whose magic touch can change your mind.

Cobain's wife, Courtney Love, no doubt believed herself to be pro- 11
viding just that kind of support when Cobain took his life. Surely resisting suicide involves more than just being distracted from life's
emptiness.

A recent spoken-word piece by Bobby Gaylor called, very simply, 12
"Suicide," takes a less simplistic view. Although it's essentially a novelty record, it touched a number of people with its irreverent, sometimes
vulgar, take on the subject. As the music comes up, Gaylor begins his
perverse "pep talk":

Animals don't have a choice.
If they're not happy with their place in the world . . . too bad.
They have to live the life they've been given.
Humans, on the other hand, don't have to.
We have a choice.
If you don't like your place in the world you can get off any-
    time you want.
Suicide. That's right.

For the first two minutes, the piece maintains that air of cold indif- 13
ference. In the second section, Gaylor begins to think out loud of all the
reasons that suicide might be a good thing, both for the one who ends
his life and for those he leaves behind:

"Now, I'm not saying 'Kill yourself.' But if you're gonna be an
idiot and do it anyway, it's no sweat off of my back. There's a lot of
good that could come from it. A little bit of bad thrown in."

The good part for the narrator: A job will open . . . An apartment 14
will become available . . . There'll be more air for me." The good part for
the person considering suicide: "You'll never get AIDS . . . You won't

have to worry about calories ever . . . . No more Barry Manilow . . . For a few years anyway."

The third and final section, however, slides imperceptibly into the small, everyday joys—and the huge, life-changing ones—that the deceased will never experience: "You'll . . . miss McDonald's French Fries . . . Bugs Bunny . . . The amazing electrifying feeling that surges through your body when you kiss someone for the first time." 15

In the end, Gaylor jeers at the would-be suicide the way a Man-hat-tan cab driver might: "Hey, you were born—Finish what was started." 16

"Suicide" is so broadly ironic that it borders on satire—no reason-ably intelligent person who listens through to the end could remain in doubt about the song's intentions. In an interview on the Virgin Megastore Web site, Gaylor explained his motivation for the song: 17

"I wrote it for a friend who was suicidal, and that's how it all began. I didn't know what to say, you just keep harping on about the usual 'think about your family, and all the people that love you, man. Your friends, I mean, you'd be letting them down. We all love you' and its like, they kind of know that already, and they've already gone beyond that. So I sat down going ok, I'm a creative son of a b—h. I should be able to write something here that can get his attention.' So I did." 18

Listeners who have logged on to the guest book on Gaylor's site, while acknowledging that sometimes "people get pi—d and don't listen to the whole thing," overwhelmingly approve of the song and its strategy. A counselor hoped that teenagers would listen to the song's message. A fan heard the single on the radio and couldn't wait for the CD to come out so he could bring it to his church youth group. One note was posted by the father of a 13-year-old girl who hanged herself two years ago: "I just wish that Jodie would have heard your recording. I hope it helps others . . . " 19

Blink-182's "Adam's Song" attempts a much riskier ironic strategy than Gaylor's "Suicide." The singer, Mark Hoppus, in the voice of a character named Adam, speaks of his despair from the position of one clinging precariously to life. Suicide seems to him like the logical answer. My students and I spent some time discussing the song recently in my graduate seminar on irony in the public sphere. They decided that the song attempts to "say no" to suicide by dramatizing the illogical thought processes of the fictional Adam, and that it suggests, by the song's close, reasons to hold on to life. Hoppus said in an interview that the message of the song is: "Whatever your personal demons are, find the strength to fight them, and realize that there are better things ahead." 20

His intention would seem to be similar to Gaylor's, and yet "Adam's Song" is in the news because it supplied the background music for a suicide. It's important to note, though, that Greg Barnes's 21 suicide, for all its tragedy, was largely ignored by the major news media until the possible link to rock 'n' roll became public knowledge.

One of the most egregious examples of misreading in the context of 22 rock occurred when Kurt Cobain ended his life, on April 5, 1994. His suicide note contained a quotation from the Nell Young song "My My, Hey Hey (Out of the Blue)": "I don't have the passion anymore and so remember, its better to burn out than to fade away."

While I have no interest in either correcting the reading or 23 questioning the motives of a dead man, it must be said that Cobain, whether intentionally or not, gets Young's point badly wrong. Young wrote "My My, Hey Hey" about one of the most outlandish stage creations of the rock era: Johnny Rotten, the character that the singer John Lydon created to front the Sex Pistols ("The king is gone but he's not forgotten/This is the story of Johnny Rotten").

In context, the lines "It's better to burn out/Than to fade away," in 24 the song's opening stanza, refer to Lydon's decision to kill off Johnny Rotten after the Sex Pistols' disastrous U.S. tour in January 1978. The king is dead, but John Lydon is alive and kicking; he went on after the Pistols' demise to found the band Public Image Ltd.

"Young's song is a tribute to Lydon's "public image"; to quote it as 25 a justification of suicide requires either an ignorance of its larger con- text—an ignorance that's difficult to ascribe to an avid punk-rock fan like Cobain—or an active forgetting by someone bent on destroying himself.

Something of this dense textual history finds its way into Blink- 26 182's "Adam's Song." In media reports of the recent Columbine suicide, it's the opening and closing lines of the song's first verse that are always quoted. For instance, the day after the news broke, an article in the The Denver Post—headlined "Song Only Clue to Student's Despair"— suggested that "The only clue as to why Columbine High basketball star Greg Barnes cut short such a promising young life may lie in lyrics found playing over and over in his garage. . . . Adam's Song, by the group Blink-182, was playing when Greg's parents found the body. . . . The lyrics include the phrases, 'I never thought I'd die alone' and 'I'm too depressed to go on. You'll be sorry when I'm gone.'"

Between those lines, however, is a knowing echo of the Nirvana 27 song "Come As You Are." Adam, contemplating suicide, suggests that he has obeyed Cobain's instructions ("Take your time/Hurry up/The choice is yours/Don't be late") in all but one telling detail:

I took my time, I hurried up
The choice was mine I didn't think enough.

"Come As You Are," like almost all of Nirvana's music, is frequently 28 read in the wake of Cobain's suicide as a cry for help:

> And I swear
> That I don't have a gun
> No I don't have a gun.

The grim truth is that Cobain did have a gun, and on the day he 29 died he put its muzzle in his mouth. Hence, as Adam thinks about taking his own life, he seems to see Cobain as a role model who has gone there before him. But by the end of the song, Adam's crisis has passed. That small but important detail seems to have eluded the journalists writing about the Columbine suicide.

> I never conquered, rarely came
> But tomorrow holds such better days
> Days when I can still feel alive
> When I can't wait to get outside.

We'll probably never know whether Greg Barnes failed to hear the 30 song through to the end, or whether, because of his own pain, he wasn't able to hear the entirety of what the song was saying. Some of those writing on the Graffiti Wall of the radio show that my daughter heard testified that "Adam's Song" had helped them out of their own suicidal depressions.

Songs, like any other text, can always be appropriated for inappro- 31 priate ends—by both rock's insiders and its outsiders, by despondent teens and slipshod media pundits. Sarah McLachlan, for instance, recently demanded that her song "I Will Remember You" be removed from a graphic video showing the bloody aftermath of the Columbine High School massacre being sold by the Jefferson County Sheriff's Department. But to the degree that songs like "Adam's Song" and "My My, Hey Hey" (and fiction like *American Psycho* or television programs like *South Park*) are used to justify the very behaviors they seek to condemn—through irony—we as cultural educators have much to answer for.

Responding to Reading

1. In discussing the relationship between teen suicides and song lyrics, Dettmar, an English professor, seems to advocate not censorship but education. Do you agree with him that what he calls poor reading skills are at least partly to blame for the kinds of suicides he discusses?
2. Dettmar reproduces a variety of song lyrics in his essay. What is his purpose in doing so? Do these lyrics convince you that "the music's dark messages"

(5) are linked to violent acts like murder and suicide? Explain.

3. Simply put, irony is language that says one thing and means another. Do you see the song lyrics Dettmar quotes as ironic (as he does), or do you interpret them differently?

Television and African Americans

Kate Tuttle

Harvard graduate Kate Tuttle (1974–) is a freelance writer based in Cambridge, Massachusetts. She is a contributing editor for the Boston Book Review *and has also written for the* Boston Phoenix, *the* Harvard University Gazette, *and the on-line journal* harvard.net news. *Tuttle has also been a frequent contributor to* Africana.com, *an online source of news and cultural reporting focusing on African-American issues. The following appeared in a recent posting of* Africana.com.

From the negative stereotypes in *Beulah* and *Amos 'n' Andy* to the "white Negroes" in *Julia* and *I Spy* to the arguably too-perfect Huxtable family on *The Cosby Show*, the majority of portrayals of African Americans on television have been one-dimensional, distorted, insulting, or sugar-coated. For many viewers, though, even unsatisfactory images seem preferable to the general absence of black television characters during television's early days. The history of the depiction of blacks on television has evolved from near invisibility broken by a parade of stereotypes to greater diversity and realism, but most critics agree that the medium has far to go.

The Early Years

Commercial television was born in 1948 as each of the three major 1 networks, ABC, CBS, and NBC, began broadcasting. 1948 was also a significant year in African American history, with the desegregation of the United States armed forces . . . and an endorsement of civil rights in the presidential platform of the Democratic Party, headed by President Harry S. Truman.

But black presence in the early years of television followed the 2 pattern earlier set by radio. In fact, the first two series starring African Americans both came to television after decades of popularity on radio, and each replaced white radio actors with black actors. *Beulah*, which showcased a supporting character on the popular *Fibber McGee and Molly* show, debuted in 1950. As played by Ethel Waters, Hattie McDaniel, and Louise Beavers on television, Beulah was cast in the stereotypical mold of the happy, overweight, black female "mammy." Cheerfully caring for the white family who employed her as house-keeper, Beulah had little discernible life of her own (although the cultural critic Donald Bogle points out that the interaction between Beulah and her long-time boyfriend provided some of the show's best moments). Beulah ran until 1953, when protests by the National Association for the Advancement of Colored People (NAACP) and other groups forced the network to cancel the series.

Amos 'n' Andy, which ran from 1951 to 1953, was based on the most ₃ listened-to radio show of the 1930s and 1940s. Unlike *Beulah*, *Amos 'n' Andy* portrayed an all-black world in which the shiftless, joking Andy (played by Spencer Williams) and the passive, long-suffering Amos (Alvin Childress) interacted with characters depicting the entire range of stereotypical black images. Its roots in the tradition of minstrelsy caused the NAACP to launch lawsuits and boycott threats that were instrumental in causing the show's cancellation. Speaking in the docu-mentary *Color Adjustment*, written and directed by Marion Riggs, the actress Diahann Carroll remembers being forbidden to watch *Amos 'n' Andy*, which her parents felt was demeaning to blacks. But some modem critics have praised the show's intricate and sophisticated comedy and lauded the actors, many of whom came from the black vaudeville tradition. After the series was cancelled, it continued to appear in syndication until 1966.

Other black images in 1950s television included variety shows, ₄ which occasionally featured African American entertainers. Duke Ellington, Cab Calloway, Paul Robeson, Ella Fitzgerald, Sarah Vaughan, and others appeared on shows hosted by veteran white entertainers such as Ed Sullivan, Milton Berle, and Steve Allen. But no African American had his own national variety show until 1956, when *The Nat "King" Cole Show* premiered. Cole, who had hosted a radio pro-gram in the 1940s, was urbane, elegant, and considered nonthreatening by white viewers. His show featured both white and black entertainers, including Pearl Bailey, Count Basie, and Mahalia Jackson, and was a great source of pride for black viewers starved for positive African American television images. But with the deepening racial tensions of the 1950s, Cole had difficulty attracting corporate sponsors, especially after some white viewers became outraged when Cole touched the arm of a white female guest. The show was cancelled after one season.

Civil Rights and the "White Negro"

One arena in which African Americans appeared on television ₅ beginning in the 1950s, and reaching a peak in the 1960s, was in the serious documentaries about rural poverty, segregation, and the growing

Civil Rights Movement. In addition, as the white segregationist backlash exploded into violence throughout the American South, "images of black people dominated the news," according to the writer and scholar Henry Louis Gates Jr. Seen as a noble, almost saintly figure, the Reverend Martin Luther King Jr., whose marches in Selma, Birmingham, and Montgomery, Alabama, heightened white America's awareness of the Civil Rights Movement, became black America's spokesperson on television in the eyes of many newly sympathetic white viewers. By contrast, some black leaders were treated harshly on television. Malcolm X was the subject of a documentary titled *The Hate That Hate Produced* (1959), which did little to dispel white fears of the Nation of Islam leader.

At the same time, as television news shows began to report seri- 6 ously on racism and the fight for civil rights, television's entertainment programs became even more overwhelmingly white. Since its birth, the medium had avoided controversy, possibly offensive to viewers (and advertisers). During the 1960s, as protests rose against both racism and the Vietnam War, programming became less and less realistic. (For example, some of the most popular shows on television at that time featured witches, genies, and other escapist fantasy). As the cultural critic J. Fred McDonald pointed out, comedies such as *Petticoat Junction* and *The Andy Griffith Show*, both set in the South, portrayed all-white worlds in which prejudice seemingly did not exist.

When black characters did appear, network executives crafted the 7 most inoffensive, blandly perfect images possible. *I Spy* (1965–1968), which starred Bill Cosby and Robert Culp as an interracial team of secret agents, presented Cosby's character, Alexander Scott, as a Rhodes scholar, an elegant sophisticate whose education was superior not only to the vast majority of African Americans but also to nearly all whites. *Julia* (1968–1971) featured Diahann Carroll as a widowed nurse and single mother. Carroll's character was bland, bleached of all evidence of black culture. Derided as a "white Negro" by critics, and suspected of being played by a white actress in darkening makeup, Carroll's Julia never encountered poverty or racism. Still, Julia was, according to African American actress Esther Rolle, "a step above the grinning domestic."

Designed to overcome negative stereotypes, such series presented 8 "fully assimilable black people," according to Gates. In an era that featured so few black representations in the mass media, even positive images were heavily scrutinized by African Americans and usually found wanting. Shows like *I Spy, Julia*, and the action series *Mod Squad* and *Mission Impossible* (each of which featured black costars) clashed with the reality of most African Americans' lives. But attempts to present a more balanced picture, such as the short-lived dramatic series *East Side, West Side* (1963–1964), usually failed quickly. Starring James Earl Jones and Cicely Tyson, *East Side, West Side* featured sophisticated writing and provocative situations depicting both ghetto life and the pain of integration. The show lasted only one season.

Relevance and Roots

By the late 1960s television began to emerge from its fantasy world to 9 present programming more in touch with the reality of the tumultuous times. The first comedy series to deal with race was *All in the Family*, (1971–1979), a show with a mostly white cast. At its head was Archie Bunker (played by Carroll O'Connor), an unrepentant racist, bigot, and homophobe. While some felt that Archie's use of racial slurs amounted to condoning prejudice, most saw the series as an important move toward realism, particularly in terms of race relations, on television (the Bunkers' next door neighbors were a black family whose characters were later featured in a popular spinoff series, *The Jeffersons*, which aired from 1975 to 1985.

One of the most dramatic changes came in children's television, 10 which had been a wasteland in terms of black images. Starting in 1969 the public television series *Sesame Street* showed children and adults of a variety of racial and ethnic backgrounds interacting and learning. *Fat Albert and the Cosby Kids* (1972–1989) was an animated version of children and events from producer Bill Cosby's own Philadelphia childhood. More shows followed, including cartoons based on the adventures of the Jackson Five and the Harlem Globetrotters.

Produced by the *All in the Family* team, *Good Times* (1974–1979) was 11 the first television comedy to focus on a poor black family, one including both father and mother, living in the midst of a vibrant, diverse black community. But social relevance gave way to echoes of the minstrel character Stepin Fetchit, as the show increasingly revolved around the buffoonish character of JJ, the elder son. According to Esther Rolle, the actress who played JJ's mother, "negative images have been quietly slipped in on us" through the clowning, wide-eyed JJ.

Although the 1970s saw a dramatic rise in the number of television 12 shows built around black characters, most made no pretense of seriousness or realism. *Sanford and Son* (1972–1977) starred the veteran comedian Redd Foxx as an irascible junk dealer and Demond Wilson as his long-suffering son. Despite the implied social relevance of its ghetto setting, the show was vintage 1970s escapism. Its wide popularity derived in part from its self-aware use of stereotypical aspects of black humor, elaborate insults, shrill women, scheming men, and it inspired a succession of inferior shows, including *Grady* (1975–1976), *Baby I'm Back* (1978), and *What's Happenin'* (1976–1979), which critics dubbed "the new minstrelsy."

No dramatic series starring a black actor aired until the 1980s. But it 13
was in drama, made-for-television movies and miniseries, that some of
the most significant television images of African Americans emerged in
the 1970s. *The Autobiography of Miss Jane Pittman* (1974), starring Cicely
Tyson, was hailed as "possibly the finest movie ever made for television." The movie, a series of flashbacks, is set in 1962 and traces
Pittman's life from her childhood in slavery to the civil rights era she
lived to see (the character is 110 years old). Its climactic scene features
Pittman bending to take a sip from a whites-only water fountain.

Roots, which aired over eight nights in 1977, was a television event 14
not only for African Americans but for all Americans. The highest-rated
miniseries ever, *Roots*, based on Alex Haley's book about his family's history from freedom in Africa to slavery in the American South, attracted
an estimated 130 million viewers. According to the cultural critic Marion
Riggs, *Roots* was presented as an immigrant tale that white audiences
could relate to, "transforming a national disgrace into an epic triumph of
the family and the American dream." Although carefully crafted to
appeal to the white audience (it was reported that the actor LeVar
Burton, who played Kunta Kinte, was nearly dropped from the project
because producers thought his lips were too large), *Roots* was nonetheless a stirring and powerful drama. It was also a showcase for many
black actors, including Burton, Louis Gossett Jr., and Cicely Tyson.

Material Success

By the late 1970s no obvious color line remained in television. Black 15
actors appeared in soap operas, as costars in dramatic series, and as the
focus of comedies. In the wake of *Roots*, several television movies, including *King* (1978), *Roots: The Next Generations* (1979), and *Attica* (1980), featured African American historical themes, But most depictions of blacks
in television continued to follow the pattern of either high-minded history
lesson or low-rent stereotypic comedy. Rarely allowed to exist as fully
realized human beings, some of the most popular black characters of the
early 1980s were wisecracking black children adopted into white families,
the situation in both *Different Strokes* (1978–1986) and *Webster* (1983–1987),
or, as in earlier television history, loyal sidekicks to white heroes.

When *The Cosby Show* debuted in 1984, it won enthusiastic reviews 16
and a loyal audience, both black and white. Focusing on a loving, intact,
successful African American family, *The Cosby Show* starred Bill Cosby
and Phylicia Rashad as the upper-middle-class parents of five children.
Like the white families in 1950s television, theirs was a caring, supportive unit that blended humor with wisdom. Cosby, who had long criticized the negative portrayals of African Americans in television,

consulted psychiatrist Dr. Alvin Poussaint in writing and producing the program, resulting in a positive, almost educational tone. The top-rated series for many of its nine seasons, *Cosby*, according to critic Patricia Turner, reinforced "the notion that the Civil Rights Movement took care of all the racial inequities of society."

One series that attempted a more balanced depiction was the short- 17 lived *Frank's Place* (1987-1988), about a black professor who inherits a New Orleans restaurant. Tim Reid, who had previously costarred in *WKRP in Cincinnati*, produced and starred in *Frank's Place*, which he said reflected his desire to see blacks portrayed not monolithically but with the full range of humanity. Although the well written show won an Emmy Award, it was cancelled after one season.

Like Cosby and Reid, a rising number of African Americans began 18 working behind the television camera in the late 1980s, resulting in a flowering of black-themed shows. *A Different World*, which spun off from Cosby and was produced by Debbie Allen, depicted life at a historically black university. Others included Quincy Jones's *Fresh Prince of Bel Air*, starring Will Smith, and *In Living Color*, produced by Keenan Ivory Wayans. In Living Color, one of the then-new Fox network's first hits, brought freshness and irreverence to its humor, much of which was based on racial stereotypes (the show's outrageousness reminded some critics of *The Flip Wilson Show*, which ran from 1970 to 1974).

Fox, which also produced *Living Single, Martin*, and *South Central*, 19 was the first network to focus so much energy on attracting black audiences with shows featuring African American actors. Some critics, among them Frank Reid, charged that the Fox shows merely perpetuated the old, negative stereotypes, this time in the lingo of the hip hop generation. (One Fox series, *Roc*, with a brilliant ensemble cast culled mostly from August Wilson's stage play *Fences*, escaped this criticism.) But with the increasing fragmentation of the television audience, caused in part by the growth of cable television, black viewers responded eagerly to the new black shows. Another venue for television geared exclusively to the African American community came of age in the early 1990s. Black Entertainment Television (BET) capitalized on music videos, sports, and reruns of black-focused series to attract a nationwide audience.

Black programming was lucrative because it appealed not only to the 20 black audience but also to whites, especially white youth, increasingly enamored of black culture. Michael Jordan and other basketball stars became some of corporate America's favorite spokespersons, and white teenagers took their fashion and language cues from rap musicians. The success of African Americans Arsenio Hall and Oprah Winfrey in late-night and daytime talk shows led to dozens of imitators, both black and white. In addition, Winfrey produced and acted in *The Women of Brewster Place*, a 1988 miniseries based on Gloria Naylor's novel, and in 1998 produced the television adaptation of Dorothy West's *The Wedding*, among other made-for-television projects. A cultural phenomenon and one of the richest people in America, Winfrey's naturalness, warmth, and pride in her African American culture have found favor with both blacks and whites.

By the late 1990s more African Americans than ever were involved in 21 the television industry, some in executive and production roles. Taboos against interracial sex and other forms of social equality had eroded. But there were still no prime-time dramatic series devoted to telling the stories of black Americans, and many of the images seen by black children (who are estimated to watch television at a rate 64 percent higher than the national average) continued to perpetuate limited stereotypes.

Responding to Reading

1. What stereotypes of African-Americans were perpetuated by television shows of the 1950s?
2. How were African-Americans portrayed on television in the 1960s? How does Tuttle account for this change in the image of blacks on TV?
3. In the last paragraph of her essay, Tuttle comments that in the late 1990s, "there were still no prime-time dramatic series devoted to telling the stories of black Americans, and many of the images seen by black children . . . continued to perpetuate limited stereotypes." Has anything changed since then? What stereotyped images of African-Americans are seen on TV today?

THE GLOBAL VILLAGE[1] FINALLY ARRIVES

Pico Iyer

Born in England to parents who had emigrated from India, Pico Iyer (1957–) attended Oxford University and Harvard. During the 1980s, he was a correspondent for Time *magazine, focusing on international affairs, and he continues to contribute essays and reviews to that magazine as well as to the* Partisan Review, *the* Village Voice, *and the (London)* Times Literary Supplement. *His books include* Video Nights in Kathmandu *and* Other Reports from the Not-So-Far-East *(1988), a humorous look at encounters between Eastern and Western cultures;* Cuba and the Night *(1995), a novel; and* The Global Soul: Jet Lag, Shopping Malls, and the Search for Home *(2000). In the following essay, which was written for* Time *in 1993, Iyer suggests that the blending of international cultures he observes at home in Southern California is becoming the paradigm for the entire world.*

---

[1] The term *global village* was coined in 1967 by Canadian cultural critic Marshall McLuhan to describe an increasingly interdependent world, linked by electronic technology. [Eds.]

This is the typical day of a relatively typical soul in today's diversi- 1
fied world. I wake up to the sound of my Japanese clock radio, put on a
T-shirt sent me by my uncle in Nigeria and walk out into the street, past
German cars, to my office. Around me are English-language students
from Korea, Switzerland and Argentina—all on the Spanish-named road
in this Mediterranean-style town. On TV, I find, the news is in Mandarin;
today's baseball game is being broadcast in Korean. For lunch I can walk
to a sushi bar, a tandoori palace, a Thai café or the newest burrito joint
(run by an old Japanese lady). Who am I, I sometimes wonder, the son of
Indian parents and a British citizen who spends much of his time in Japan
(and therefore—what else?—an American permanent resident)? And
where am I?

I am, as it happens, in Southern California, in a quiet, relatively unin- 2
ternational town, but I could easily be in Vancouver or Sydney or London
or Hong Kong. All the world's a rainbow coalition, more and more; the
whole planet, you might say, is going global. When I fly to Toronto, or
Paris, or Singapore, I disembark in a world as hyphenated as the one I left.
More and more of the globe looks like America, but an America that is
itself looking more and more like the rest of the globe. Los Angeles
famously teaches 82 different languages in its schools. In this respect, the
city seems only to bear out the old adage that what is in California today
is in America tomorrow, and next week around the globe.

In ways that were hardly conceivable even a generation ago, the 3
new world order is a version of the New World writ large: a wide-open
frontier of polygor terms and postnational trends. A common multiculturalism links us all—call it Planet Hollywood. Planet Reebok or the
United Colors of Benetton. *Taxi* and *hotel* and *disco* are the universal
terms now, but so are *karaoke* and *yoga* and *pizza*. For the gourmet alone,
there is *tiramisù* at the Burger King in Kyoto, echt[2] angel hair pasta in
Saigon and enchiladas on every menu in Napal.

But deeper than mere goods, it is souls that are mingling. In 4
Brussels, a center of the new "unified Europe," one new baby in every
four is Arab. Whole parts of the Paraguayan capital of Asunción are
largely Korean. And when the prostitutes of Melbourne distributed
some procondom pamplets, one of the languages they used was
Macedonian.[3] Even Japan, which prides itself on its centuries-old
socially engineered uniculture, swarms with Iranian illegals, Western
executives, Pakistani laborers and Filipina hostesses.

The global village is defined, as we know, by an international youth 5
culture that takes its clues form American pop culture. Kids in Perth
and Prague and New Delhi are all tuning in to Santa Barbara on TV, and
wriggling into 501 jeans, while singing along to Madonna's latest in

---

[2] Real, authentic. [Eds.]
[3] Melbourne is in Australia, Macedonia in eastern Europe. [Eds.]

English. CNN (which has grown 70-fold in 13 years) now reaches more that 140 countries; an American football championship pits London against Barcelona. As fast as the world comes to America, America goes round the world—but it is an America that is itself multi-tongued and many hued, an America of Amy Tan and Janet Jackson and movies with dialogue in Lakota.[4]

For far more than goods and artifacts, the one great influence being   6 broadcast around the world in greater numbers and at greater speed than ever before is people. What were once clear divisions are now tangles of crossed lines: there are 40,000 "Canadians" resident on Hong Kong, Many of whose first language is Cantonese. And with people come customs: while new immigrants from Taiwan and Vietnam and India—some of the so-called Asian Calvinists—all-American values of hard work and family closeness and entrepreneurial energy to America, America is sending its values of upward mobility and individualism and melting-pot hopefulness to Taipei and Saigon and Bombay.

Values, in fact, travel at the speed of fax; by now almost half the   7 world's Mormons live outside the U.S. A diversity of one culture quickly becomes a diversity of many: the "typical American" who goes to Japan today may be a third-generation Japanese American, or the son of a Japanese woman married to a California serviceman, or the off-spring of a Salvadorian father and an Italian mother from San Fransico. When he goes out with a Japanese woman, more than two cultures are brought into play.

None of this, of course, is new: Chinese silks were all the rage in   8 Rome centuries ago, and Alexandria before the time of Christ was a paradigm of the modern universal city. Not even American eclecticism is new: many a small town has long known Chinese restaurants, Indian doctors and Lebanese grocers. But now all these cultures are crossing at the speed of light. And the rising diversity of the planet is something more than mere cosmopolitanism: it is a fundamental recoloring of the very complexion of societies. Cities like Paris, of Hong Kong, have always had a soigné, international air and served as magnets for exiles and émigrés, but now smaller places are multinational too. Marseilles speaks French with a distinctly North African twang. Islamic fundamentalism has one of its strongholds in Bradford, England. It is the sleepy coastal towns of Queensland, Australia, that print their menus in Japanese.

The danger this internationalism presents are evident: not for   9 nothing did the Tower of Babel collapse. As national borders fall, tribal alliances, and new manmade divisions, rise up, and the world learns every day terrible new meanings of the word Balkanization.[5] And while some places are wired for international transmission, others (think of

---

[4] Native American language used in the movie *Dances With Wolves*. [Eds]
[5] Breaking up of a region into smaller, often hostile groups. [Eds.]

Recovering substance abuser Kitty Dukakis once called a press 1
conference to announce her descent into alcoholism and request respect
for her privacy. It was shortly after her husband's defeat in the 1988 presidential race, when she was less newsworthy than the pearls adorning
Barbara Bush's neck. I marveled only briefly at the spectacle of a
woman seeking privacy in a press conference and public confession of
an addiction. Some people, especially famous and formerly famous
ones, seem to enjoy their privacy only in public. Now You Know, Kitty
Dukakis called her book, in case you cared.

Still, millions of readers who don't care about Dukakis and all the 2
other recovering personalities who write books are curious, I guess.
Confessional autobiographies by second-string celebrities are publish-
ing staples (and where would the talk shows be without them?). Ali
MacGraw exposes her sex addiction and the lurid details of her mar-
riage to Steve McQueen. Suzanne Somers chronicles her life as an
ACOA [Adult Child of an Alcoholic]. Former first children Michael
Reagan and Patti Davis reveal their histories of abuse.

"I truly hope my book will help others to heal," the celebrity diarists 3
are likely to say. Or they assure us that writing their books was therapeutic (and if they pay me to read them, I will). But the celebrities don't
really have to explain the decision to go public. In our culture of recovery we take their confessions for granted. Talking about yourself is "part
of the process." Suggesting to someone that she is talking too much
about herself is a form of abuse. If you can't feign interest in someone
else's story, you're supposed to maintain respectful or, better yet,
stunned silence. In recovery, where everyone gets to claim that she's
survived some holocaust of family life, everyone gets to testify.

The tradition of testifying in court, church, or the marketplace for jus- 4
tice, God, or the public good is a venerable one that I would not impugn.
But it is also a tradition I'd rather not debase by confusing testifying with
advertisements for yourself or simple plays for sympathy and attention.
The recovery movement combines the testimonial tradition that serves a
greater good, like justice, with the therapeutic tradition in which talking
about yourself is its own reward. It also borrows liberally from the
revivalist tradition of testifying to save your soul and maybe others: in
recovery, even the most trivial testimony is sanctified.

I'm not impugning therapy or religion either, but I wish that peo- 5
ple would keep them off the streets. Religion has, of course, a complicated, controversial history of public uses and abuses, which are
beyond the scope of this [essay]. But therapy was conceived as a private transaction between doctors and patients (experts and clients) or
between groups of patients, clients, seekers of psychic well-being.
Testimony was public. By blurring the distinction between confession
and testimony, recovery transforms therapy into a public process too.
People even do it on TV.

Most of us do love to talk about ourselves, although I've always 6
regarded it as a slightly illicit pleasure or one you pay for by the hour.
Etiquette books dating back over a century gently admonish readers to
cultivate the art of listening, assuming that, unmannered in their natural
states, most people are braggarts and bores. Success primers have
always stressed that listening skills will help you get ahead: Listen raptly
to someone in power who loves talking about himself in order to impress
him with your perspicacity. Listening is a useful form of flattery, Dale
Carnegie[1] advised, sharing with men what women have always known.
Flirting is a way of listening. (Feminism is women talking.)

For women who were socialized to listen, uncritically, talking too 7
much about themselves may feel like an act of rebellion. Maybe Kitty
Dukakis felt liberated by her book. Personal development passes for
politics, and what might once have been called whining is now exalted
as a process of asserting selfhood; self-absorption is regarded as a form
of self-expression, as if creative acts involved no interactions with the
world. Feminists did say that the personal was political, but they meant
that private relations between the sexes reflected public divisions of
power, that putatively private events, like wife beating, were public
concerns. They didn't mean that getting to know yourself was sufficient
political action. Consciousness raising was supposed to inspire activism.
Feminism is women talking, but it is not women only talking and not
women talking only about themselves.

Talk shows and the elevation of gossip to intellectual discourse are, 8
after all, postfeminist, postmodern phenomena. In academia, where
gossip is now text, poststructural scholars scour history for the private,
particular experiences of ordinary "unempowered" people; and like
denizens of daytime TV, they also talk a lot about themselves, decon-
structing their own class, racial, or ethnic biases in perverse assertions
of solidarity with what are presumed to be other entirely subjective
selves. On talk shows, ordinary people, subject of tomorrow's scholars,
find their voice. Men and mostly women distinguished only by various
and weird infidelities or histories of drug abuse and overeating get
equal time with movie actors, soap stars, and the occasional hair stylist.
Now everyone can hope for sixty minutes of fame, minus some time for
commercials.

I never really wonder anymore why people want to talk about 9
themselves for nearly an hour in front of millions of strangers. They find
it "affirming"; like trees that fall in the forest, they're not sure that they
exist when no one's watching. I've accepted that as postmodern human
nature. I do wonder at the eagerness and pride with which they reveal,
on national television, what I can't help thinking of as intimacies—sexual
and digestive disorders; personal conflicts with parents, children,

---

[1] Author of on of the first succesful series of self-improvement books [Eds.]

spouses, lovers, bosses, and best friends. I wonder even more at the intensity with which the audience listens.

Why aren't they bored? It may be that listening is simply the price 10 they pay for their turn to grab the mike and have their say, offering criticism or advice, just like the experts. But they seem genuinely intrigued by the essentially unremarkable details of other people's lives and other people's feelings. Something in us likes soap operas, I know, but watching the talks is not like watching "Dallas" or "Days of Our Lives." The guests aren't particularly articulate, except on "Geraldo" sometimes, where they seem to be well coached; they rarely finish their sentences, which trail off in vague colloquialisms, you know what I mean? Most guests aren't witty or perceptive or even telegenic. They aren't artful. They are the people you'd ignore if you saw them on line at the supermarket instead of on TV.

I'm not sure how we got to the point of finding anyone else's 11 confessions, obsessions, or advertisements for herself entertaining. I'm not sure why watching other people's home movies became fun; the appeal of "America's Funniest Home Videos" eludes me. But it's clear that the popularity of "real people" television—talk shows and home videos—has little to do with compassion and the desire to connect. If an average person on the subway turns to you, like the ancient mariner, and starts telling you her tale, you turn away or nod and hope she stops, not just because you fear she might be crazy. If she tells her tale on camera, you might listen. Watching strangers on television, even responding to them from a studio audience, we're disengaged—voyeurs collaborating with exhibitionists in rituals of sham community. Never have so many known so much about people for whom they cared so little.

A woman appears on "Oprah Winfrey" to tell the nation that she 12 hates herself for being ugly. Oprah and the expert talk to her about self-esteem and the woman basks, I think, in their attention. The spectacle is painful and pathetic, and watching it, I feel diminished.

Oprah, I suspect, regards her show as a kind of public service. The 13 self-proclaimed ugly woman is appearing on a segment about our obsession with good looks. We live in a society that values pretty people over plain, Oprah explains; and maybe she is exploring a legitimate public issue, by exploiting a private pathology.

Daytime TV, however, is proudly pathological. On "Geraldo" a 14 recovering sex addict shares a story of incest—she was raped by her father and stepfather; her husband and children are seated next to her on the stage. This is family therapy. (The family that reveals together congeals together.) Her daughter talks about being a lesbian. Two sex addiction experts—a man and a woman, "professional and personal partners"—explain and offer commentary on sex and love addictions.

"It's not a matter of frequency," they say in response to questions about how often sex addicts have sex. Anonymous addicts call in with their own tales, boring and lurid: "I do specifically use sex to make myself feel better," one caller confesses. Who doesn't?

Geraldo, his experts, and the members of his audience address the problem of promiscuity with the gravity of network anchors discussing a sub-Saharan famine. If I were a recovering person, I might say that they're addicted to melodrama. In fact, Geraldo does a show on people "addicted to excitement—drama, danger, and self destruction"—people who create crises for themselves. He offers us a self-evaluation tool— eleven questions "to determine whether you're a soap opera queen." Do you get mad at other drivers on the road? Do you talk about your problems with a lot of other people? Questions like these make addicts of us all, as experts must hope. Labeling impatience in traffic a symptom of disease creates a market for the cure; and Joy Davidson, the expert author who identified the "soap opera syndrome" for us is here on "Geraldo," peddling her book.

The audience is intrigued. People stand up to testify to their own experiences with drama and excitement addictions. With the concern of any patient describing her symptoms, one woman says that she often disagrees with her husband for no good reason. Someone else confesses to being a worrier.

No one suggests to Davidson that calling the mundane concerns and frustrations of daily life symptoms of the disease of overdramatizing is, well, overdramatizing. In the language of recovery, we might say that Davidson is an enabler, encouraging her readers to indulge in their melodrama addictions, or we might say that she too is a practicing melodrama addict. One man does point out that there are "people in the ghetto" who don't have to fabricate their crises. But if Davidson gets the point, she successfully eludes it. Yes, she admits, the crises in the ghetto are real, but what matters is the way you deal with them. As Norman Vincent Peale[2] might say, people in crisis have only to develop a happiness habit.

Meanwhile, on daytime TV, middle-class Americans are busy practicing their worry habits, swapping stories of disease and controversial eccentricities. Here is a sampling of "Oprah": Apart from the usual assortment of guests who eat, drink, shop, worry, or have sex too much, there are fathers who sleep with their sons' girlfriends (or try to), sisters who sleep with their sisters' boyfriends, women who sleep with their best friends' sons, women who sleep with their husbands' bosses (to help their husbands get ahead), men who hire only pretty women, and men and

---

[2] Minister, lecuturer, and writer (1898–1993), whose best-selling series fo books beginnig with *The Power of Positive Thinking* (1952) made him one of the first self-help authors. [Eds.]

women who date only interracially. Estranged couples share their grievances while an expert provides on-air counseling: "Why are you so afraid
to let your anger out at her?" he asks a husband. "Why don't you let him
speak for himself," he chides the wife. Couples glare at each other, sometimes the women cry, and the expert keeps advising them to get in touch
with their feelings and build up their self-esteem. The chance to sit in on
someone else's therapy session is part of the appeal of daytime TV. When
Donahue[3] interviews the children of prostitutes, he has an expert on hand
to tell them how they feel.

The number of viewers who are helped by these shows is impossible   19
to know, but it's clear that they're a boon to several industries—publishing, therapy, and, of course, recovery. Commercials often tie in to the
shows. A segment on food addiction is sponsored by weight-loss programs: "It's not what you're eating. It's what's eating you," the ads assure
anxious overeaters. Shows on drug and alcohol abuse are sponsored by
treatment centers, set in sylvan glades. Standing by lakes, leaning on
trees, the pitchmen are soft and just a little somber—elegiac; they might
be selling funeral plots instead of a recovery lifestyle and enhanced
self-esteem.

On almost every show, someone is bound to get around to self   20
esteem; most forms of misconduct are said to be indicative of low
self-esteem. On every other show, someone talks about addiction. The
audiences usually speak fluent recovery. You can talk about your inner
child or your grief work on "Oprah" and no one will ask you what you
mean. "I follow a twelve-step program that helps me deal with the disease concept, the addiction [to overeating]," a man in the audience
announces, and people nod. No one asks, "What's a twelve-step program?" or "What do you mean by addiction?" Oprah testifies too: "I'm
still addicted [to food]. I'll never be free."

On stage, a panel of recovering food addicts, all women, is vowing   21
never to diet again. "We have to allow ourselves to love ourselves," they
say, and Oprah agrees. "I'm never going to weigh another piece of
chicken." Tired of "seeking control," these women want to accept their
weight, not constantly struggle to lose it, and I wish them luck. Beauty
may lack moral value, but it's useful, and what has been labeled
beastly—obesity or really bad skin—is a painful liability, as the women
on "Oprah" make clear. They've apparently spent much of their lives
embarrassed by their bodies; now, in recovery, they talk about the
"shame" of fatness. They find some self-esteem in victimhood. They
aren't gluttons but "victims of a disease process." Being fat is not their
fault. Recovering from obesity "is not about self-control," one woman

---

[3] Among the first to host a day-time talk show focusing on ther personal problems of "average"
people, Phil Donahue was on the air from 1967 to 1996. [Eds.]

says, voicing the ethos of recovery that dispenses with will. "It's about self-love."

But the next day, when Oprah does a show on troubled marriages, 22 some sort of therapist, Dr. Ron, advises a woman who is self-conscious about her small breasts to have implants. He berates her unfaithful husband for not supporting her in this quest for a better body, for her own good, for the sake of her self-esteem, and to help save their marriage: her poor self-image was one of the reasons he strayed. That a woman with small breasts can't be expected to improve her self-esteem without implants is apparently evident to Dr. Ron and everyone else on the show. No one questions his wisdom, not even learning-to-love-herself Oprah, recovering dieter.

I digress, but so do Geraldo, Donahue, and Oprah. Talking about 23 these shows, I find it hard to be entirely coherent, and coherence would not do justice to the kaleidoscope of complaints, opinions, prejudices, revelations, and celebrations they comprise: Geraldo discusses celibacy with a panel of virgins and Helen Gurley Brown. "There are no medical risks associated with virginity," a doctor assures us. Adopted children and their biological parents as well as siblings separated from birth for over twenty years meet, for the first time, on "Geraldo" ("Reunions of the Heart: Finding a Lost Love," the show is called). "Welcome long-lost brother Brian," Geraldo commands, to wild applause, as Brian emerges from backstage, and in a TV minute people are hugging and sobbing on camera as they did years ago on "This Is Your Life." I want someone in the audience to ask them why they're not having their reunions in private, but I already know the answer. "We want to share the love and joy of this moment," they'd say. "We want to inspire other people from broken families not to give up the search." I suspect that the audience knows these answers too. Clapping and crying (even Geraldo is teary), reached for and touched, they offer support and validation: "It's a real blessing to see how you've all been healed of your hurts," one woman in the audience declares. Geraldo makes a plea for open adoption, grappling with an issue, I guess.

Occasionally, I admit, the shows are instructive in ways they intend, 24 not just as portraits of popular culture. Donahue's segment on grandparents who are raising the children of their drug-addicted children manages to be dignified and sad. He talks to obese children without overdramatizing their struggles or exploiting them. (Donahue is good with kids.) Oprah seems likable and shrewd in the midst of her silliest shows, and, once in a while, the testimony illuminates an issue: date rape or racially segregated proms.

This is the new journalism—issues packaged in anecdotes that may 25 or may not be true. As an occasional, alternative approach to news and analysis, it is affecting; as the predominant approach, it is not just trite but

they simply universalized their own experiences: "It worked for me. So it will work for everyone else."

Testifying, as a substitute for thinking, is contagious. You even 37 find it in the halls of academe. Teaching college freshmen, I quickly discovered that my students were interested only in issues that were dramatized—in fiction, memoirs, or popular journalism. Raised on "Donahue" and docudramas, they found mere discussions of ideas "too dry and academic." You can't even be academic in academia anymore. Instead of theory, they sought testimony.

Among graduate students and professors too, subjectivity has been 38 in fashion for several years. The diversification of student populations and concern for multiculturalism have made respect for subjective experiences and points of view political imperatives. Fashions in literary and legal theory and historical research focus on knowledge as a matter of perspective, disdaining the "pretense" of objectivity. Scholars get to talk about themselves. Theory is nothing but testimony.

I'm not suggesting that the dead white males who once held sway 39 and set standards had The Answer or that a multiplicity of perspectives in matters of politics and theory isn't welcome. Nor am I suggesting that analysis should somehow be divorced from experience. I'm only suggesting the obvious—that analysis and experience need to be balanced. There are degrees of objectivity worth trying to acquire.

It should be needless to say that individual preferences are not 40 always the best measures of what is generally good. A tax provision that saves you money may still be generally unfair. Of course, the recovery movement is not analogous to the tax code. It is not imposed on us. It is not a public policy that demands deliberation and debate. I don't want to gloss over the difference between public acts and private experiments with personality development. Indeed, I want to highlight it.

A self-referential evaluation of a self-help movement is probably 41 inevitable and, to some extent, appropriate. A self-referential evaluation of public policies can be disastrous. What is disturbing about watching the talk shows is recognizing in discussions of private problems a solipsism that carries over into discussions of public issues. What you see on "Oprah" is what you see in the political arena. We choose our elected officials and formulate policies on the basis of how they make us feel about ourselves. (Jimmy Carter's biggest mistake was in depressing us.) We even evaluate wars according to their effect on our self-esteem: Vietnam was a downer. The Persian Gulf War, like a good self-help program, cured us of our "Vietnam syndrome" and "gave us back our pride," as General Motors hopes to do with Chevrolets. Norman Schwarzkopf and Colin Powell satisfied our need for heroes, everyone said. The networks stroked us with video montages of handsome young soldiers, leaning on tanks, staring off into the desert, wanting to "get the job done" and go home. By conservative estimates, 150,000 people were killed outright in the war; the number who will die from disease, deprivation, and environmental damage may be incalculable. Whether or not the war was necessary, whether or not the victory was real, we should consider it a great success because it gave us parades and a proud Fourth of July. The culture of recovery is insidious: now the moral measure of a war is how it makes us feel about ourselves.

"Try and put aside your own experiences in recovery and the way 42 it makes you feel," I suggested to the audience on "Oprah." "Think about what the fascination with addiction means to us as a culture. Think about the political implications of advising people to surrender their will and submit to a higher power." People in the audience looked at me blankly. Later, in the limo, one of my copanelists (against codependency) shook his head at me and smiled and said, "That was a PBS comment."

Some two months later I showed my "Oprah" tape to a group of col- 43 lege friends, over a bottle of wine. None of them is involved in the recovery movement or familiar with its programs or jargon. Listening to six panelists and a studio audience compete for air time, in eight-minute segments between commercials, none of them thought the "Oprah" show made any sense. Like the man in the audience who asked, "What are you all recovering from?" they didn't have a clue. "You have to think with your hearts and not your heads," a for-codependency expert exhorted us at the end of the show, as the credits rolled.

Responding to Reading

1. According to Kaminer, what is the difference between "confessing" and "testifying"? What danger does she see in "blurring the distinction between confession and testimony" (5)?

2. In paragraph 11, Kaminer says, "Never have so many known so much about people for whom they cared so little." Why do you suppose so many people are willing "to talk about themselves for nearly an hour in front of millions of strangers" (9)? Why do you think so many viewers of talk shows find them so compelling?

3. "The trouble with talk shows," Kaminer says, "is that they claim to do so much more than entertain; they claim to inform and explain" (31). In paragraph 24, she concedes that talk shows are sometimes "'instructive"; for the most part, though, she is highly critical of these programs, saying, among other things, that they encourage viewers to "substitute sentimentality for thought" (25). Do you think Kaminer is being too hard on talk shows? Do you think she is taking them too seriously? Explain your views.

———————————— FOCUS ————————————

Does Media Violence Hurt?

UNNATURAL KILLERS

John Grisham

Best-selling novelist John Grisham (1955–   ) was born in Jonesboro, Arkansas, and graduated from Mississippi State University. After earning his law degree from the University of Mississippi in 1981, he worked as an attorney until 1990, also serving three terms in the Mississippi state legislature. Although his first novel (A Time to Kill)—written while he was still practicing law—was not an immediate success, with The Firm (1991) Grisham began a string of blockbusters that so far remains unbroken: The Pelican Brief (1992), The Client (1993), The Chamber (1994), The Rainmaker (1995), The Runaway Jury (1996), The Partner (1997), The Street Lawyer (1998), The Brethren (2000), and The Painted House (2001). While most of his books have also been turned into highly successful films, Grisham's relationship with Hollywood is not without strain. Following the senseless murder of a Mississippi friend by a teenage couple apparently influenced by the film Natural Born Killers, Grisham filed a highly publicized lawsuit against the director, Oliver Stone, and the studio that released the film, seeking damages for wrongful death. In the following essay written in 1996 for the Oxford American, Grisham describes the couple's killing spree and argues that lawsuits such as his are the only way to bring Hollywood violence under control.

The town of Hernando, Mississippi has five thousand people, more 1 or less, and is the seat of government for DeSoto County. It is peaceful and quiet, with an old courthouse in the center of the square. Memphis is only fifteen minutes away, to the north, straight up Interstate 55. To the west is Tunica County, now booming with casino fever and drawing thousands of tourists.

For ten years I was a lawyer in Southaven, a suburb to the north, 2 and the Hernando courthouse was my hangout. I tried many cases in the main courtroom. I drank coffee with the courthouse regulars, ate in the small cafes around the square, visited my clients in the nearby jail.

It was in the courthouse that I first met Mr. Bill Savage. I didn't know 3 much about him back then, just that he was soft-spoken, exceedingly polite, always ready with a smile and a warm greeting. In 1983, when I first announced my intentions to seek an office in the state legislature, Mr. Savage stopped me in the second-floor rotunda of the courthouse and offered me his encouragement and good wishes.

A few months later, on election night as the votes were tallied and 4 the results announced to a rowdy throng camped on the courthouse lawn, it became apparent that I would win my race. Mr. Savage found me and expressed his congratulations. "The people have trusted you," he said. "Don't let them down."

He was active in local affairs, a devout Christian and solid citizen 5 who believed in public service and was always ready to volunteer. For thirty years, he worked as the manager of a cotton gin two miles outside Hernando on a highway that is heavily used by gamblers anxious to get to the casinos in Tunica.

Around five p.m., on March 7, 1995, someone entered Bill Savage's 6 office next to the gin, shot him twice in the head at point-blank range, and took his wallet, which contained a few credit cards and two hundred dollars.

There were no witnesses. No one heard gunshots. His body was 7 discovered later by an insurance salesman making a routine call.

The crime scene yielded few clues. There were no signs of a struggle. 8 Other than the bullets found in the body, there was little physical evidence. And since Bill Savage was not the kind of person to create ill will or maintain enemies, investigators had nowhere to start. They formed the opinion that he was murdered by outsiders who'd stopped by for a fast score, then hit the road again, probably toward the casinos.

It had to be a simple robbery. Why else would anybody want to 9 murder Bill Savage?

The townspeople of Hernando were stunned. Life in the shadows 10 of Memphis had numbed many of them to the idea of random violence, but here was one of their own, a man known to all, a man who, as he went about his daily affairs, minding his own business, was killed in his office just two miles from the courthouse.

The next day, in Ponchatoula, Louisiana, three hundred miles south, 11 and again just off Interstate 55, Patsy Byers was working the late shift at a convenience store. She was thirty-five years old, a happily married mother of three, including an eighteen-year-old who was about to graduate from high school. Patsy had never worked outside the home, but had taken the job to earn a few extra dollars to help with the bills.

Around midnight, a young woman entered the convenience store 12 and walked to a rack where she grabbed three chocolate bars. As she approached the checkout counter, Patsy Byers noticed the candy, but she didn't notice the .38. The young woman thrust it forward, pulled the trigger, and shot Patsy in the throat.

The bullet instantly severed Patsy's spinal cord, and she fell to the 13 floor bleeding. The young woman screamed and fled the store, leaving Patsy paralyzed under the cash register.

The girl returned. She'd forgotten the part about the robbery. When 14 she saw Patsy she said, "Oh, you're not dead yet." Patsy began to plead, "Don't kill me," she kept saying to the girl who stepped over her and tried in vain to open the cash register. She asked Patsy how to open it.

Patsy explained it as best she could. The girl fled with $105 in cash, 15 leaving Patsy, once again, to die.

But Patsy did not die, though she will be a quadriplegic for the rest 16 of her life.

The shooting and robbery was captured on the store's surveillance 17 camera, and the video was soon broadcast on the local news. Several full facial shots of the girl were shown.

The girl, however, vanished. Weeks, and then months, passed with- 18 out the slightest hint to her identity making itself known.

Authorities in Louisiana had no knowledge of the murder of Bill 19 Savage, and authorities in Mississippi had no knowledge of the shooting of Patsy Byers, and neither state had reason to suspect the two shootings were committed by the same people.

The crimes, it was clear, were not committed by sophisticated crim- 20 inals. Soon two youths began bragging about their exploits. And then an anonymous informant whispered to officials in Louisiana that a certain young woman in Oklahoma was involved in the shooting of Patsy Byers.

The young woman was Sarah Edmondson, age nineteen, the 21 daughter of a state court judge in Muskogee, Oklahoma. Her uncle is the Attorney General of Oklahoma. Her grandfather once served as Congressman, and her great uncle was Governor and then later a U.S. Senator. Sarah Edmondson was arrested on June 2, 1995, at her parents' home, and suddenly the pieces fell into place.

Sarah and her boyfriend, Benjamin Darras, age eighteen, had drifted 22 south in early March. The reason for the journey has not been made clear. One version has them headed for Florida so that Ben could finally see the ocean. Another has them aiming at New Orleans and Mardi Gras. And a third is that they wanted to see the Grateful Dead concert in Memphis, but, not surprisingly, got the dates mixed-up.

At any rate, they stumbled through Hernando on March 7, and 23 stayed just long enough, Sarah says, to kill and rob Bill Savage. Then they raced deeper south until they ran out of money. They decided to pull another heist. This is when Patsy Byers met them.

Though Sarah and Ben have different socioeconomic backgrounds, 24 they made a suitable match. Sarah, a member of one of Oklahoma's most prominent political families, began using drugs and alcohol at the age of thirteen. At fourteen she was locked up for psychiatric treatment.

She has admitted to a history of serious drug abuse. She managed to finish high school, with honors, but then dropped out of college.

Ben's family is far less prominent. His father was an alcoholic who 25 divorced Ben's mother twice, then later committed suicide. Ben too has a history of drug abuse and psychiatric treatment. He dropped out of high school. Somewhere along the way he met Sarah, and for awhile they lived the great American romance—the young, troubled, mindless drifters surviving on love.

Once they were arrested, lawyers got involved, and the love affair 26 came to a rapid end. Sarah blames Ben for the killing of Bill Savage. Ben blames Sarah for the shooting of Patsy Byers. Sarah has better lawyers, and it appears she will also attempt to blame Ben for somehow controlling her in such a manner that she had no choice but to rob the store and shoot Patsy Byers. Ben, evidently, will have none of this. It looks as if he will claim his beloved Sarah went into the store only to rob it, that he had no idea whatsoever that she planned to shoot anyone, that, as he waited outside in the getaway car, he was horrified when he heard a gunshot. And so on.

It should be noted here that neither Ben nor Sarah have yet been tried 27 for any of these crimes. They have not been found guilty of anything, yet. But as the judicial wheels begin to turn, deals are being negotiated and cut. Pacts are being made.

Sarah's lawyers managed to reach an immunity agreement with the 28 State of Mississippi in the Savage case. Evidently, she will testify against Ben, and in return will not be prosecuted. Her troubles will be confined to Louisiana, and if convicted for the attempted murder of Patsy Byers and the robbing of the store, Sarah could face life in prison. If Ben is found guilty of murdering and robbing Bill Savage, he will most likely face death by lethal injection at the state penitentiary in Parchman, Mississippi. Juries in Hernando are notorious for quick death verdicts.

On January 24, 1996, during a preliminary hearing in Louisiana, 29 Sarah testified, under oath, about the events leading up to both crimes. It is from this reported testimony that the public first heard the appalling details of both crimes.

According to Sarah, she and Ben decided to travel to Memphis to 30 see the Grateful Dead. They packed canned food and blankets, and left the morning of March 6. Sarah also packed her father's .38, just in case Ben happened to attack her for some reason. Shortly before leaving Oklahoma, they watched the Oliver Stone movie *Natural Born Killers*.

For those fortunate enough to have missed *Natural Born Killers*, it is a 31 repulsive story of two mindless young lovers, Mickey (Woody Harrelson) and Mallory (Juliette Lewis), who blaze their way across the Southwest, killing everything in their path while becoming famous. According to the script, they indiscriminately kill fifty-two people before they are caught. It seems like many more. Then they manage to kill at least fifty more as

The wife and children and countless friends of Bill Savage have 52 already begun the healing process, though the loss is beyond measure.

Patsy Byers is a quadriplegic for life, confined to a wheelchair, faced 53 with enormous medical bills, unable to hug her children or do any one of a million things she did before she met Sarah Edmondson. She's already filed a civil suit against the Edmondson family, but her prospects of a meaningful physical recovery are dim.

A question remains: Are there other players in this tragic episode? 54 Can fault be shared?

I think so. 55

Troubled as they were, Ben and Sarah had no history of violence. 56 Their crime spree was totally out of character. They were confused, disturbed, shiftless, mindless—the adjectives can be heaped on with shovels—but they had never hurt anyone before.

Before, that is, they saw a movie. A horrific movie that glamorized 57 casual mayhem and bloodlust. A movie made with the intent of glorifying random murder.

Oliver Stone has said that *Natural Born Killers* was meant to be a 58 satire on our culture's appetite for violence and the media's craving for it. But Oliver Stone always takes the high ground in defending his dreadful movies. A satire is supposed to make fun of whatever it is attacking. But there is no humor in *Natural Born Killers*. It is a relentlessly bloody story designed to shock us and to further numb us to the senselessness of reckless murder. The film wasn't made with the intent of stimulating morally depraved young people to commit similar crimes, but such a result can hardly be a surprise.

Oliver Stone is saying that murder is cool and fun, murder is a high, 59 a rush, murder is a drug to be used at will. The more you kill, the cooler you are. You can be famous and become a media darling with your face on magazine covers. You can get by with it. You will not be punished.

It is inconceivable to expect either Stone or the studio executives to 60 take responsibility for the aftereffects of their movie. Hollywood has never done so; instead, it hides behind its standard pious First Amendment arguments, and it pontificates about the necessities of artistic freedom of expression. Its apologists can go on, ad nauseam, about how meaningful even the most pathetic film is to social reform.

It's no surprise that *Natural Born Killers* has inspired several young 61 people to commit murder. Sadly, Ben and Sarah aren't the only kids now locked away and charged with murder in copycat crimes. Since the release of the movie, at least several cases have been reported in which random killings were executed by troubled young people who claim they were all under the influence, to some degree, of Mickey and Mallory.

Any word from Oliver Stone? 62

Of course not.   63

I'm sure he would disclaim all responsibility. And he'd preach a bit   64
about how important the film is as a commentary on the media's
insatiable appetite for violence. If pressed, he'd probably say that there
are a lot of crazies out there, and he can't be held responsible for what
they might do. He's an *artist* and he can't be bothered with the effects of
what he produces.

I can think of only two ways to curb the excessive violence of a film   65
like *Natural Born Killers*. Both involve large sums of money—the only
medium understood by Hollywood.

The first way would be a general boycott of similar films. If people   66
refused to purchase tickets to watch such an orgy of violence as *Natural
Born Killers*, then similar movies wouldn't be made. Hollywood is pious,
but only to a point. It will defend its crassest movies on the grounds that
they are necessary for social introspection, or that they need to test the
limits of artistic expression, or that they can ignore the bounds of decency
as long as these movies label themselves as satire. This all works fine if
the box office is busy. But let the red ink flow and Hollywood suddenly
has a keen interest in rediscovering what's mainstream.

Unfortunately, boycotts don't seem to work. The viewing public is   67
a large, eclectic body, and there are usually enough curious filmgoers to
sustain a controversial work.

So, forget boycotts.   68

The second and last hope of imposing some sense of responsibility on   69
Hollywood, will come through another great American tradition, the
lawsuit. Think of a movie as a product, something created and brought to
market, not too dissimilar from breast implants, Honda three-wheelers,
and Ford Pintos. Though the law has yet to declare movies to be
products, it is only one small step away. If something goes wrong with
the product, whether by design or defect, and injury ensues, then its
makers are held responsible.

A case can be made that there exists a direct causal link between the   70
movie *Natural Born Killers* and the death of Bill Savage. Viewed another
way, the question should be: Would Ben have shot innocent people *but for*
the movie? Nothing in his troubled past indicates violent propensities.
But once he saw the movie, he fantasized about killing, and his fantasies
finally drove them to their crimes.

The notion of holding filmmakers and studios legally responsible   71
for their products has always been met with guffaws from the industry.

But the laughing will soon stop. It will take only one large verdict   72
against the likes of Oliver Stone, and his production company, and
perhaps the screenwriter, and the studio itself, and then the party will be
over. The verdict will come from the heartland, far away from Southern

California, in some small courtroom with no cameras. A jury will finally say enough is enough; that the demons placed in Sarah Edmondson's mind were not solely of her making.

Once a precedent is set, the litigation will become contagious, and 73 the money will become enormous. Hollywood will suddenly discover a desire to rein itself in.

The landscape of American jurisprudence is littered with the 74 remains of large, powerful corporations which once thought themselves bulletproof and immune from responsibility for their actions. Sadly, Hollywood will have to be forced to shed some of its own blood before it learns to police itself.

Even sadder, the families of Bill Savage and Patsy Byers can only 75 mourn and try to pick up the pieces, and wonder why such a wretched film was allowed to be made.

Responding to Reading

1. Grisham opens his essay by providing background, including an explanation of his relationship to murder victim Bill Savage. Is this background information necessary? Does it help Grisham make his point?
2. Is this essay an attack on one film, *Natural Born Killers,* and its director, Oliver Stone? A critique of Hollywood's values? A call to action designed to encourage readers to hold studios legally responsible for their films? What do you see as Grisham's primary purpose in writing this essay?
3. In paragraph 70, Grisham says, "A case can be made that there exists a direct causal link between the movie *Natural Born Killers* and the death of Bill Savage." Do you agree? Does Grisham make such a case? Explain your conclusions.

HOLLOW CLAIMS
ABOUT FANTASY VIOLENCE
Richard Rhodes

Born in Kansas City, Kansas, in 1937, Richards Rhodes graduated with a B.A. in history from Yale University in 1959. He has been a fellow of the Guggenheim, Ford, MacArthur, and Alfred P. Sloan Foundations and of the National Endowment for the Arts. His 1986 book, The Making of the Atomic Bomb, *won a Pulitzer Prize in general nonfiction and a National Book Award.* Dark Sun: The Making of the Hydrogen Bomb *(1995) was a finalist for the Pulitzer Prize in history. Rhodes also served as correspondent for a one-hour PBS* Frontline *documentary, "Nuclear Reaction," about*

American's fear of nuclear energy. His most recent book is Why They Kill: The
Discoveries of a Maverick Criminologist *(1999). The following essay
appeared on the op-ed page of the* New York Times *in September 2000.*

The moral entrepreneurs are at it again, pounding the entertain- 1
ment industry for advertising its Grand Guignolesque confections to
children. If exposure to this mock violence contributes to the development of violent behavior, then our political leadership is justified in its
indignation at what the Federal Trade Commission has reported about
the marketing of violent fare to children. Senators John McCain and
Joseph Lieberman have been especially quick to fasten on the F.T.C.
report as they make an issue of violent offerings to children.

But is there really a link between entertainment and violent behavior? 2

The American Medical Association, the American Psycological 3
Association, the American Academy of Pediactrics and the National
Institute of Mental Health all say yes. They base their claims on social science research that has been sharply criticized and disputed within the
social science profession, especially outside the Untied States. In fact, no
direct, causal link between exposure to mock violence in the media and
subsequent violent behavior has ever been demonstrated, and the few
claims of modest correlation have been contradicted by other findings,
sometimes in the same studies.

History alone should call such a link into question. Private violence 4
has been declining in the West since the media-barren late Middle Ages,
when homicide rates are estimated to have been 10 times what they are
in Western nations today. Historians attribute the decline to improving
social controls over violence—police forces and commons access to
courts of law—and to a shift away from brutal physical punishment in
child-rearing (a practice that still appears as a common factor in the
background of violent criminals today).

The American Medical Association has based its endorsement of 5
the media violence theory in major part on the studies of Brandon
Centerwall, a psychiatrist in Seattle. Dr. Centerwall compared the murder rates for whites in three countries from 1945 to 1974 with numbers
for television set ownership. Until 1975, television broadcasting was
banned in South Africa, and "white homicide rates remained stable"
there, Dr. Centerwall found, while corresponding rates in Canada and
the United States doubled after television was introduced.

A spectacular finding, but it is meaningless. As Franklin E. Zimring 6
and Gordon Hawkins of the University of California at Berkeley
subsequently pointed out, homicide rates in France, Germany, Italy and
Japan either failed to change with increasing television ownership in the
same period or actually declined, and American homicide rates have
more recently been sharply decling despite a proliferation of popular

media outlets—not only movies and television, but also video games and the Internet.

Other social science that supposedly undergrids the theory, too, is 7 marginal and problematic. Laboratory studies that expose children to selected incidents of televised mock violence and then assess changes in the children's behavior have sometimes found more "aggressive" behavior after the exposure—usually verbal, occasionally physical.

But sometimes the control group, shown incidents judged not to be 8 violent, behaves more aggressively afterward then the test group; somtimes comedy produces the more aggressive behavior; and sometimes there's no change. The only obvious conclusion is that sitting and watching television stimulates subsequent physical activity. Any kid could tell you that.

As for those who claim that entertainment promotes violent behavior 9 by desensitizing people to violence, the British scholar Martin Barker offers this critique: "Their claim is that the materials they judge to be harmful can only influence us by trying to make us be the same as them. So horrible things will make us horrible—not horrified. Terrifying things will make us terrifying—not terrified. To see something aggressive makes us feel aggressive—not aggressed against. This idea is so odd, it is hard to know where to begin in challenging it."

Even more influential on national policy has been a 22-year study 10 by two University of Michigan psychologists, Leonard D. Eron and L. Rowell Huesmann, of boys exposed to so-called violent media. The Telecommunications Act of 1996, which mandated the television V-chip, allowing parents to screen out unwanted programming, invoked these findings, asserting,"Studies have shown that children exposed to violent video programming at a young age have a higher tendency for violent and aggressive behavior later in life than children not so exposed."

Well, not exactly. Following 875 children in upstate New York from 11 third grade through high school, the psychologists found a correlation between a preference for violent television at age 8 and aggressiveness at age 18. The correlation—0.31—would mean television accounted for about 10 percent of the influence that led to this behavior. But the correlation only turned up in one of three measures of aggression: the assessment of students by their peers. It didn't show up in students' reports about themselves of in psychological testing. And for girls, there was no correlation at all.

Despite the lack of evidence, politicians can't resist blaming the 12 media for violence. They can stake out the moral high ground confident that the First Amendment will protect them from having to actually write legislation that would be likely to alienate the entertainment industry. Some use the issue as a smokescreen to avoid having to confront gun control.

But violence isn't learned from mock violence. There is good 13
evidence—casual evidence, not correlational—that it's learned in personal violent encounters, beginning with the brutalization of children
by their parents or their peers.

The money spent on all the social science research I've described was 14
diverted from the National Institute of Mental Health budget by reducing
support for the construction of community mental health centers. To this
day there is no standardized reporting system for emergency-room findings of physical child abuse. Violence is on the decline in America, but if
we want to reduce it even further, protecting children from real violence
in their real lives—not the pale shadow of mock violence—is the place to
begin.

Responding to Reading

1. In paragraph 3, Rhodes states emphatically that "no direct, causal link
   between exposure to mock violence in the media and subsequent violent
   behavior has ever been demonstrated." Why, then, do so many people—
   such as John Grisham (p. 318)—believe that such a link exists?
2. Rhodes is sharply critical of the social science research he summarizes, and
   he often makes irreverent or sarcastic comments such as the following:

   • "A spectacular finding, but it is meaningless" (6).

   • "Any kid could tell you that" (8).

   • (Quoting British scholar Martin Barker) "'This idea is so odd, it is hard to
     know where to begin in challenging it" (9).

   Do statements like these make you less inclined to accept Rhodes's position,
   or does his essay stand on its evidence?
3. Beyond setting the record straight on the question of the link between
   "mock violence" and actual violent acts, what other purpose or purposes
   does Rhodes hope to accomplish in this essay? For example, on whom does
   he place the blame for the misconception he identifies?

WHEN LIFE IMITATES VIDEO

John Leo

John Leo has been a columnist and contributing editor at U.S. News
& World Report *since 1988. Previously, he wrote about social science
issues and cultural trends for* Time *magazine and reported on religion for*
The New York Times. *In addition, Leo served as associate editor at*

Commonweal *magazine, reviewed books for the magazine* Society, *and launched the "Press Clips" column in the* Village Voice. *He is a former deputy commissioner of New York City's Environmental Protection Administration. In 1989, he published a book of political and social humor,* How the Russians Invented Baseball and Other Essays of Enlightenment, *including many of his popular "Ralph & Wanda" dialogues— imaginary conversations between a liberal feminist and her conservative "masculinist" husband, which had previously appeared in* Time *and in* McCall's. *The following essay appeared in* U.S. News *in 1999.*

Was it real life or an acted-out video game?   1

Marching through a large building using various bombs and guns to   2
pick off victims is a conventional video-game scenario. In the Colorado massacre, Dylan Klebold and Eric Harris used pistolgrip shotguns, as in some video-arcade games. The pools of blood, screams of agony, and pleas for mercy must have been familiar—they are featured in some of the newer and more realistic kill-for-kicks games. "With each kill," the *Los Angeles Times* reported, "the teens cackled and shouted as though playing one of the morbid video games they loved." And they ended their spree by shooting themselves in the head, the final act in the game Postal, and, in fact, the only way to end it.

Did the sensibilities created by the modern, video kill games play a   3
role in the Littleton massacre? Apparently so. Note the cool and casual cruelty, the outlandish arsenal of weapons, the cheering and laughing while hunting down victims one by one. All of this seems to reflect the style and feel of the video killing games they played so often.

No, there isn't any direct connection between most murderous games   4
and most murders. And yes, the primary responsibility for protecting children from dangerous games lies with their parents, many of whom like to blame the entertainment industry for their own failings.

But there is a cultural problem here: We are now a society in which   5
the chief form of play for millions of youngsters is making large numbers of people die. Hurting and maiming others is the central funactivity in video games played so addictively by the young. A widely cited survey of 900 fourth-through-eight-grade students found that almost half of the children said their favorite electronic games involve violence. Can it be that all this constant training in make-believe killing has no social effects?

Dress Rehearsal

The conventional argument is that this is a harmless activity among   6
children who know the difference between fantasy and reality. But the games are often played by unstable youngsters unsure about the difference. Many of these have been maltreated or rejected and left alone most of the time (a precondition for playing the games obsessively).

Adolescent feelings of resentment, powerlessness and revenge pour into the killing games. In these children, the games can become a dress rehearsal for the real thing.

Psychologist David Grossman of Arkansas State University, a retired 7 Army officer, thinks "point and shoot" video games have the same effect as military strategies used to break down a soldier's aversion to killing. During World War II, only 15 to 20 percent of all American soldiers fired their weapon in battle. Shooting games in which the target is a man-shaped outline, the Army found, made recruits more willing to "make killing a reflex action."

Video games are much more powerful versions of the military's pri- 8 mitive discovery about overcoming the reluctance to shoot. Grossman says Michael Carneal, the schoolboy shooter in Paducah, Ky., showed the effects of video-game lessons in killing. Carneal coolly shot nine times, hitting eight people, five of them in the head or neck. Head shots pay a bonus in many video games. Now the Marine Corps is adapting a version of Doom, the hyperviolent game played by one of the Littleton killers, for its own training purposes.

More realistic touches in video games help blur the boundary 9 between fantasy and reality—guns carefully modeled on real ones, accurate-looking wounds, screams, and other sound effects, even the recoil of a heavy rifle. Some newer games seem intent on erasing children's empathy and concern for others. Once the intended victims of video slaughter were mostly gangsters or aliens. Now some games invite players to blow away ordinary people who have done nothing wrong—pedestrians, marching bands, an elderly woman with a walker. In these games, the shooter is not a hero, just a violent sociopath. One ad for a Sony game says: "Get in touch with your gun-toting, testosterone-pumping, cold-blooded murdering side."

These killings are supposed to be taken as harmless over-the-top 10 jokes. But the bottom line is that the young are being invited to enjoy the killing of vulnerable people picked at random. This looks like the final lesson in a course to eliminate any lingering resistance to killing.

SWAT teams and cops now turn up as the intended victims of some 11 video-game killings. This has the effect of exploiting resentments toward law enforcement and making real-life shooting of cops more likely. This sensibility turns up in the hit movie *Matrix:* world-saving hero Keanu Reeves, in a mandatory Goth-style, long black coat packed with countless heavy-duty guns, is forced to blow away huge numbers of uniformed law-enforcement people.

"We have to start worrying about what we are putting into the minds 12 of our young," says Grossman. "Pilots train on flight simulators, drivers on driving simulators, and now we have our children on murder simulators." If we want to avoid more Littleton-style massacres, we will begin taking the social effects of the killing games more seriously.

Responding to Reading

1. In paragraph 1, Leo asks a question about the 1999 Littleton, Colorado, massacre: "Was it real life or an acted-out video game?" How would you answer this question? How might John Grisham (p. 318) respond?
2. Leo quotes psychologist David Grossman extensively. What is Grossman's position? Does Leo share this position? Would his essay be more convincing if he cited additional sources?
3. In paragraph 5, Leo identifies a "cultural problem": "We are now," he says, "a society in which the chief form of play for millions of youngsters is making large numbers of people die." In your opinion, *is* this kind of "play" a problem?

──────────── WIDENING THE FOCUS ────────────

- Sharon Olds, "Rite of Passage" (p. 339)

- Barbara Ehreneich, "The Myth of Man as Hunter" (p. 643)

- Geroge Orwell, "Shooting an Elephant" (p. 658)

- Russel Feingold, "The Need for a Moratorium on Executions" (p. 719)

Responding to the Image

1. Look carefully at this photograph. Does is strike you as spontaneous or posed by the photographer? Do you think the photographer intended to make a point about media violence?
2. How do you respond to the photograph? Have you encountered similar situations in your own experience?

———————————————— WRITING ————————————————

Media and Society

1. What do you think the impact of various media discussed in this chapter will be in the years to come? What trends do you see emerging that you believe will change the way you think or the way you live? Write an essay in which you speculate about future trends and their impact. If you like, you may consider essays in Chapter 7, "The Wired Revolution," as well as essays in this chapter.

2. After reading Tuttle's essay about stereotypes of African-Americans on television, write an essay in which you consider the representation of African-Americans and other ethnic and racial minorities in advertising—specifically, in magazine ads and television commercials. Do you believe these individuals are adequately represented? Do you think they are depicted fairly and accurately? Do you think commercial messages stereotype any groups? Read (or reread) Gloria Steinem's "Sex, Lies, and Advertising" (p. 274) before you begin.

3. Keep a daily log of the programs you listen to on the radio and watch on television, the movies you see, and the newspapers and magazines you read. (Don't forget to include material you read online.) After one week, review your log, and consider why you chose what you did and how these different kinds of media informed, provoked, or entertained you. Chart your habits, including the time you spent and what you selected, and write a report evaluating the impact of various media on you.

4. Do films and television shows present an accurate image of your gender, race, religion, or ethnic group? In what ways, if any, is the image you see unrealistic? In what ways, if any, is it demeaning? If possible, include recommendations for improving the media image of the group you discuss. What should be done to challenge—or change—simplistic or negative images? Whose responsibility should it be to effect change?

5. Should the government continue to support public television and radio? What, if anything, do public radio and television provide that commercial programming does not offer? (Before beginning this essay, compare newspaper listings of public and commercial programming, and try to spend a few hours screening public television and radio programs if you are not familiar with them.)

6. What kind of "family values" are promoted on television and in popular films? Would you say that these media are largely "profamily" or "antifamily"? Using the essays in this chapter by

Winn, McGrath, and Kaminer for background, choose several films and television programs that support your position. Then, write an essay that takes a strong stand on this issue. (Be sure to define exactly what you mean by *family* and *family values*)

7. To what extent, if any, should sexual content—for example, obscenity in music lyrics or explicitly sexual images in magazine ads or on the Internet—be censored? Write an essay in which you take a stand on this issue.

8. What danger, if any, do you see for young people in the seductive messages of the music they listen to? Do you believe that parents and educators are right to be concerned about the effect the messages in rock and rap music have on teenagers and young adults, or do you think they are overreacting? Support your position with quotations from popular music. If you like, you can also interview friends and relatives and use their responses to help you develop your argument.

9. In "Celebrity Journalism, the Public, and Princess Diana," Joe Saltzman defines *news* as "the events and circumstances that have an important effect on our lives" (10). Write an essay in which you compare the specific kinds of newspaper, magazine, and television news reports that conform to Saltzman's definition of *news* with those kinds of reports that do not. Then, try to draw some conclusions about how the media's definition of *news* differs from Saltzman's. Be sure to give examples from all three media.

10. Does media violence hurt? If so, whom does it hurt most? After reading the three essays in the Focus section of this chapter, write an essay that answers these questions.

11. **For Internet research:** A number of online resources deal with the effects of media violence. Among these are sites by the Center for Media Studies and Public Affairs at: <http://www.cmpa.com/tvent/violence.htm> and by the National Coalition on Television Violence at: <http://www.nctv.org/>. Other pertinent sites include <http://www.lionlamb.org/links.html> and http://www.mediachannel.org/atissue/sample3/>. The 1999 Senate report "Children, Violence, and the Media" can be found at <http.//www.senate.gov/~judiciary/mediavio.htm>. You may use these resources to supplement the Focus readings as you write on the essay topic suggested in number 10 above.

5

GENDER AND SOCIETY

——————— PREPARING TO READ AND WRITE ———————

Attitudes about gender have changed dramatically over the past thirty years, and they continue to change. For some, these changes have resulted in confusion and anger as well as liberation. One reason for this confusion is that people can no longer rely on fixed roles to tell them how to behave in public and how to function within their families. Still, many men and women—uncomfortable with the demands of confining gender roles and unhappy with the expectations those roles create— yearn for even less rigidity, for an escape from stereotypes into a society where roles are not defined solely by gender.

Unfortunately, many people still tend to see men and women in terms of outdated and unrealistic stereotypes. Men are strong, tough, and brave, and women are weak, passive, and in need of protection. Men understand mathematics and science and have a natural aptitude for mechanical tasks. They also have the drive, the aggressiveness, the competitive edge, and the power to succeed. They are never sentimental and never cry. Women are better at small, repetitive tasks and shy away from taking bold, decisive actions. They enjoy, and are good at, domestic activities, and they have a natural aptitude for nurturing. They may like their jobs, but they will leave them to devote themselves to husband and children.

As we read the preceding list of stereotypes, some of us may react neutrally (or even favorably), while others may react with annoyance; how we react tells us something about our society and something about ourselves. But as a number of writers in this section point out, stereotypes are not just inaccurate; they also limit the way people think, the roles they chose to assume, and, ultimately, the positions they occupy in society.

As the Focus section of this chapter, "Who Has It Harder, Women or Men?" (p. 372) illustrates, both men and women have had problems living up to the images they believe they should conform to and filling the roles that have been set for them. Some believe that the emphasis in recent years on improving the self-image of young girls has been largely unsuccessful, and that "Generation X" is a generation of girls who hate themselves and their bodies. Others believe that it is boys who have suffered, for as parents and teachers have focused on girls, they have neglected the needs of boys. Some blame the feminist movement for the problems faced by girls *and* boys; others blame society. The central questions seem to be "Who (if anyone) is suffering?" "Who is at fault?" Beyond those questions, of course, lies the more important question: "What can be done to improve the lives of women and of men?"

As you read and prepare to write about the essays in this chapter, you may consider the following questions:

- Is the writer male or female? Are you able to determine the author's gender without reading the author's name or the headnote? Does the writer's gender really matter?

- Is the writer's focus on males, on females, or on both sexes?

- When was the essay written? Does the date of publication affect its content?

- Does the essay seem fair? Balanced?

- Does the writer discuss gender as a sexual, political, economic, or social issue?

- What does the writer suggest are the specific advantages or disadvantages of being male? Of being female?

- Does the writer support the status quo, or does he or she suggest that change is necessary? Possible? Inevitable?

- Does the writer recommend specific changes? What are they?

- Is your interpretation of the issue the same as the interpretation presented in the essay?

- Does the writer express the view that men and women are fundamentally different? If so, does he or she suggest that these differences can (or should) be overcome, or at least lessened?

- Does the writer see gender differences as the result of environment or of heredity?

- Does the essay challenge any of your ideas about male-female roles?

- In what ways is the essay like other essays in this chapter?

We could easily kill a two-year-old,
he says in his clear voice. The other
men agree, they clear their throats
like Generals, they relax and get down to
playing war, celebrating my son's life.

25

Responding to Reading

1. What is a "rite of passage"? Why do you think Olds gives her poem the title she does?
2. What does Olds refer to the children at her son's birthday party as "men"?
3. What comment does Olds make about what it means to be male in contemporay American society?

PROFESSIONS FOR WOMEN

Virginia Woolf

Virginia Woolf was born in London, England, in 1882 to a highly literary family. Largely self-educated, she began writing criticism for the Times Literary Supplement *when she was in her early twenties and published her first novel,* The Voyage Out, *in 1915. In later novels, including* Mrs. Dalloway *(1925),* To the Lighthouse *(1927), and* The Waves *(1931), she experimented with formal conventions, creating some of the most innovative works of the twentieth century. She was also a noted essayist, publishing two collections titled* The Common Reader *in 1925 and 1932 and two feminist arguments,* A Room of One's Own *(1929) and* Three Guineas *(1938). Troubled by mental illness from an early age, Woolf took her life in 1941. Her husband, Leonard, edited several posthumously published collections, including* The Death of the Moth and Other Essays *(1942), where the following essay appeared. It was originally composed as a speech delivered in 1931 to a British women's organization, the Women's League of Service.*

When your secretary invited me to come here, she told me that your 1
Society is concerned with the employment of women and she suggested that I might tell you something about my own professional experiences. It is true I am a woman; it is true I am employed, but what professional experiences have I had? It's difficult to say. My profession is literature; and in that profession there are fewer experiences for women than in any other, with the exception of the stage—fewer, I mean, that are peculiar to women. For the road was cut many years ago—by Fanny Burney,

by Aphra Behn, by Harriet Martineau, by Jane Austen, by George Eliot—many famous women, and many more unknown and forgotten, have been before me, making the path smooth, and regulating my steps. Thus, when I came to write, there were very few material obstacles in my way. Writing was a reputable and harmless occupation. The family peace was not broken by the scratching of a pen. No demand was made upon the family purse. For ten and sixpence one can buy paper enough to write all the plays of Shakespeare—if one has a mind that way. Pianos and models, Paris, Vienna and Berlin, masters and mistresses, are not needed by a writer. The cheapness of writing paper is, of course, the reason why women have succeeded as writers before they have succeeded in the other professions.

But to tell you my story—it is a simple one. You have only got to fig- 2 ure to yourselves a girl in a bedroom with a pen in her hand. She had only to move that pen from left to right—from ten o'clock to one. Then it occurred to her to do what is simple and cheap enough after all—to slip a few of those pages into an envelope, fix a penny stamp in the corner, and drop the envelope in the red box at the corner. It was thus that I became a journalist; and my effort was rewarded on the first day of the following month—a very glorious day it was for me—by a letter from an editor containing a check for one pound ten shillings and sixpence. But to show you how little I deserve to be called a professional woman, how little I know of the struggles and difficulties of such lives, I have to admit that instead of spending that sum upon bread and butter, rent, shoes and stockings, or butcher's bills, I went out and bought a cat—a beautiful cat, a Persian cat, which very soon involved me in bitter disputes with my neighbors.

What could be easier than to write articles and to buy Persian cats 3 with the profits? But wait a moment. Articles have to be about something. Mine, I seem to remember, was about a novel by a famous man. And while I was writing this review, I discovered that if I were going to review books I should need to do battle with a certain phantom. And the phantom was a woman, and when I came to know her better I called her after the heroine of a famous poem, The Angel in the House. It was she who used to come between me and my paper when I was writing reviews. It was she who bothered me and wasted my time and so tormented me that at last I killed her. You who come of a younger and happier generation may not have heard of her—you may not know what I mean by the Angel in the House. I will describe her as shortly as I can. She was intensely sympathetic. She was immensely charming. She was utterly unselfish. She excelled in the difficult arts of family life. She sacrificed herself daily. If there was chicken, she took the leg; if there was a draught she sat in it—in short she was so constituted that she never had a mind or a wish of her own, but preferred to sympathize always with the minds and wishes of others. Above all—I need not say it—she was pure. Her purity was supposed to be her chief beauty—her blushes, her great grace. In those days—the last of Queen Victoria—every house had its Angel. And when I came to write I encountered her with the very first words. The shadow of her wings fell on my page; I heard the rustling of her skirts in the room. Directly, that is to say, I took my pen in hand to review that novel by a famous man, she slipped behind me and whispered: "My dear, you are a young woman. You are writing about a book that has been written by a man. Be sympathetic; be tender; flatter; deceive; use all the arts and wiles of our sex. Never let anybody guess that you have a mind of your own. Above all, be pure." And she made as if to guide my pen. I now record the one act for which I take some credit to myself, though the credit rightly belongs to some excellent ancestors of mine who left me a certain sum of money—shall we say five hundred pounds a year?—so that it was not necessary for me to depend solely on charm for my living. I turned upon her and caught her by the throat. I did my best to kill her. My excuse, if I were to be had up in a court of law, would be that I acted in self-defense. Had I not killed her she would have killed me. She would have plucked the heart out of my writing. For, as I found, directly I put pen to paper, you cannot review even a novel without having a mind of your own, without expressing what you think to be the truth about human relations, morality, sex. And all these questions, according to the Angel in the House, cannot be dealt with freely and openly by women; they must charm, they must conciliate, they must—to put it bluntly—tell lies if they are to succeed. Thus, whenever I felt the shadow of her wing or the radiance of her halo upon my page, I took up the inkpot and flung it at her. She died hard. Her fictitious nature was of great assistance to her. It is far harder to kill a phantom than a reality. She was always creeping back when I thought I had despatched her. Though I flatter myself that I killed her in the end, the struggle was severe; it took much time that had better have been spent upon learning Greek grammar; or in roaming the world in search of adventures. But it was a real experience; it was an experience that was bound to befall all women writers at that time. Killing the Angel in the House was part of the occupation of a woman writer.

But to continue my story. The Angel was dead; what then remained? 4 You may say that what remained was a simple and common object—a young woman in a bedroom with an inkpot. In other words, now that she had rid herself of falsehood, that young woman had only to be herself. Ah, but what is "herself"? I mean, what is a woman? I assure you, I do not know. I do not believe that you know. I do not believe that anybody can know until she has expressed herself in all the arts and professions open to human skill. That indeed is one of the reasons why I have come here—out of respect for you, who are in process of showing us by your experiments what a woman is, who are in process of providing us, by your failures and successes, with that extremely important piece of information.

But to continue the story of my professional experiences. I made one pound ten and six by my first review; and I bought a Persian cat with the proceeds. Then I grew ambitious. A Persian cat is all very well, I said; but a Persian cat is not enough. I must have a motor car. And it was thus that I became a novelist—for it is a very strange thing that people will give you a motor car if you will tell them a story. It is a still stranger thing that there is nothing so delightful in the world as telling stories. It is far pleasanter than writing reviews of famous novels. And yet, if I am to obey your secretary and tell you my professional experiences as a novelist, I must tell you about a very strange experience that befell me as a novelist. And to understand it you must try first to imagine a novelist's state of mind. I hope I am not giving away professional secrets if I say that a novelist's chief desire is to be as unconscious as possible. He has to induce in himself a state of perpetual lethargy. He wants life to proceed with the utmost quiet and regularity. He wants to see the same faces, to read the same books, to do the same things day after day, month after month, while he is writing, so that nothing may break the illusion in which he is living—so that nothing may disturb or disquiet the mysterious nosings about, feelings round, darts, dashes and sudden discoveries of that very shy and illusive spirit, the imagination. I suspect that this state is the same both for men and women. Be that as it may, I want you to imagine me writing a novel in a state of trance. I want you to figure to yourselves a girl sitting with a pen in her hand, which for minutes, and indeed for hours, she never dips into the inkpot. The image that comes to my mind when I think of this girl is the image of a fisherman lying sunk in dreams on the verge of a deep lake with a rod held out over the water. She was letting her imagination sweep unchecked round every rock and cranny of the world that lies submerged in the depths of our unconscious being. Now came the experience, the experience that I believe to be far commoner with women writers than with men. The line raced through the girl's fingers. Her imagination had rushed away. It had sought the pools, the depths, the dark places where the largest fish slumber. And then there was a smash. There was an explosion. There was foam and confusion. The imagination had dashed itself against something hard. The girl was roused from her dream. She was indeed in a state of the most acute and difficult distress. To speak without figure she had thought of something, something about the body, about the passions which it was unfitting for her as a woman to say. Men, her reason told her, would be shocked. The consciousness of what men will say of a woman who speaks the truth about her passions had roused her from her artist's state of unconsciousness. She could write no more. The trance was over. Her imagination could work no longer. This I believe to be a very common experience with women writers—they are impeded by the extreme conventionality of the other sex. For though men sensibly allow themselves great freedom in these respects, I doubt that they realize or can control the extreme severity with which they condemn such freedom in women.

These then were two very genuine experiences of my own. These 6 were two of the adventures of my professional life. The first—killing the Angel in the House—I think I solved. She died. But the second, telling the truth about my own experiences as a body, I do not think I solved. I doubt that any woman has solved it yet. The obstacles against her are still immensely powerful—and yet they are very difficult to define. Outwardly, what is simpler than to write books? Outwardly, what obstacles are there for a woman rather than for a man? Inwardly, I think, the case is very different; she has still many ghosts to fight, many prejudices to overcome. Indeed it will be a long time still, I think, before a woman can sit down to write a book without finding a phantom to be slain, a rock to be dashed against. And if this is so in literature, the freest of all professions for women, how is it in the new professions which you are now for the first time entering?

Those are the questions that I should like, had I time, to ask you. 7 And indeed, if I have laid stress upon these professional experiences of mine, it is because I believe that they are, though in different forms, yours also. Even when the path is nominally open—when there is nothing to prevent a woman from being a doctor, a lawyer, a civil servant—there are many phantoms and obstacles, as I believe, looming in her way. To discuss and define them is I think of great value and importance; for thus only can the labor be shared, the difficulties be solved. But besides this, it is necessary also to discuss the ends and the aims for which we are fighting, for which we are doing battle with these formidable obstacles. Those aims cannot be taken for granted; they must be perpetually questioned and examined. The whole position, as I see it— here in this hall surrounded by women practicing for the first time in history I know not how many different professions—is one of extraordinary interest and importance. You have won rooms of your own in the house hitherto exclusively owned by men. You are able, though not without great labor and effort, to pay the rent. You are earning your five hundred pounds a year. But this freedom is only a beginning; the room is your own, but it is still bare. It has to be furnished; it has to be decorated; it has to be shared. How are you going to furnish it, how are you going to decorate it? With whom are you going to share it, and upon what terms? These, I think, are questions of the utmost importance and interest. For the first time in history you are able to ask them; for the first time you are able to decide for yourselves what the answers should be. Willingly would I stay and discuss those questions and answers—but not tonight. My time is up; and I must cease.

Responding to Reading

1. In paragraph 3, Woolf describes her stuggle to kill "the Angel in the House." Who or what is this "angel" Woolf is struggling against, and why must Woolf kill her?
2. Why, according to Woolf, do women writers find it difficult to remain in the "artist's state of unconsciousness" (5)? Is this a problem Woolf believes she herself has—or can—overcome?
3. What message do you think Woolf wants her audience to take away from her lecture? Do you think the message applies to twenty-first-century women as well? Do you think it applies to men?

THE MEN WE CARRY IN OUR MINDS

Scott Russell Sanders

Scott Russell Sanders (1945–) was born in Memphis, Tennessee, and received his B.A. from Brown University and his Ph.D. from Cambridge University in England. A professor of creative writing at Indiana University, he is the author of novels, children's books, science fiction stories, and collections of personal essays, including The Paradise of Bombs *(1988),* Staying Put: Making a Home in a Restless World *(1993), and* The Forces of Spirit *(2000). An ardent environmentalist, Sanders has said, "If my writing does not help my neighbors to live more alertly, pleasurably, or wisely, then it is worth little." In "The Men We Carry in Our Minds," he recalls how he— a poor rural boy at an elite Ivy League college—first encountered women who railed at the "joys and privileges of men," privileges that did not apply to the working-class men of his experience.*

When I was a boy, the men I knew labored with their bodies. They 1 were marginal farmers, just scraping by, or welders, steelworkers, carpenters; they swept floors, dug ditches, mined coal, or drove trucks, their forearms ropy with muscle; they trained horses, stoked furnaces, built tires, stood on assembly lines wrestling parts onto cars and refrigerators. They got up before light, worked all day long whatever the weather, and when they came home at night they looked as though somebody had been whipping them. In the evenings and on weekends they worked on their own places, tilling gardens that were lumpy with clay, fixing broken-down cars, hammering on houses that were always too drafty, too leaky, too small.

The bodies of the men I knew were twisted and maimed in ways 2 visible and invisible. The nails of their hands were black and split, the hands tattooed with scars. Some had lost fingers. Heavy lifting had given many of them finicky backs and guts weak from hernias. Racing why some marriages were happy and others were not. What *did* contribute to happiness was the husband's willingness to do the work at home. Whether they were traditional or more egalitarian in their relationship, couples were happier when the men did a sizable share of housework and child care.

In one study of 600 couples filing for divorce, researcher George 5 Levinger found that the second most common reason women cited for wanting to divorce—after "mental cruelty"—was their husbands' "neglect of home or children." Women mentioned this reason more often than financial problems, physical abuse, drinking, or infidelity.

A happy marriage is supported by a couple's being economically 6 secure, by their enjoying a supportive community, and by their having compatible needs and values. But these days it may also depend on a shared appreciation of the work it takes to nurture others. As the role of the homemaker is being abandoned by many women, the homemaker's work has been continually devalued and passed on to low-paid housekeepers, baby-sitters, or day-care workers. Long devalued by men, the contribution of cooking, cleaning, and care-giving is now being devalued as mere drudgery by many women, too.

In the era of the stalled revolution, one way to make housework and 7 child care more valued is for men to share in that work. Many working mothers are already doing all they can at home. Now it's time for men to make the move.

If more mothers of young children are working at full-time jobs 8 outside the home, and if most couples can't afford household help, who's doing the work at home? Adding together the time it takes to do a paid job and to do housework and child care and using estimates from major studies on time use done in the 1960s and 1970s, I found that women worked roughly 15 more hours each week than men. Over a year, they worked an extra month of 24-hour days. Over a dozen years, it was an extra year of 24-hour days. Most women without children spend much more time that men on housework. Women with children devote more time to both housework and child care. Just as there is a wage gap between men and women in the workplace, there is a "leisure gap" between them at home. Most women work one shift at the office or factory and a "second shift" at home.

In my research, I interviewed and observed 52 couples over an 9 eight-year period as they cooked dinner, shopped, bathed their children, and in general struggled to find enough time to make their complex lives work. The women I interviewed seemed to be far more deeply torn between the demands of work and family than were their husbands. They talked more about the abiding conflict between work and family. They felt the second shift was *their* issue, and most of their husbands agreed. When I telephoned one husband to arrange an interview with him, explaining that I wanted to ask him how he managed work and family life, he replied genially, "Oh, this will *really* interest my *wife*."

Men who shared the load at home seemed just as pressed for time   10 as their wives, and as torn between the demands of career and small children. But of the men I surveyed, the majority did not share the load at home. Some refused outright. Others refused more passively, often offering a loving shoulder to lean on, or an understanding ear, as their working wife faced the conflict they both saw as hers. At first it seemed to me that the problem of the second shift *was* hers. But I came to realize that those husbands who helped very little at home were often just as deeply affected as their wives—through the resentment their wives felt toward them and through their own need to steel themselves against that resentment.

A clear example of this phenomenon is Evan Holt, a warehouse   11 furniture salesman who did very little housework and played with his four-year-old son, Joey, only at his convenience. His wife, Nancy, did the second shift, but she resented it keenly and half-consciously expressed her frustration and rage by losing interest in sex and becoming overly absorbed in Joey.

Even when husbands happily shared the work, their wives *felt* more   12 responsible for home and children. More women than men kept track of doctor's appointments and arranged for kids playmates to come over. More mothers than fathers worried about a child's Halloween costume or a birthday present for a school friend. They were more likely to think about their children while at work and to check in by phone with the baby-sitter.

Partly because of this, more women felt torn between two kinds of   13 urgency, between the need to soothe a child's fear of being left at day-care and the need to show the boss she's "serious" at work. Twenty percent of the men in my study shared housework equally. Seventy percent did a substantial amount (less than half of it, but more than a third), and 10 percent did less than a third. But even when couples more equitably share the work at home, women do two thirds of the daily jobs at home, such as cooking and cleaning up—jobs that fix them into a rigid routine. Most women cook dinner, for instance, while men change the oil in the family car. But, as one mother pointed out, dinner needs to be prepared every evening around six o'clock, whereas the car oil needs to be changed every six months, with no particular deadline. Women do more child care than men, and men repair more household appliances. A child needs to be tended to daily, whereas the repair of household appliances can often wait, said the men, "until I have time." Men thus have more control over when they make their contributions than women do. They may be very busy with family chores, but, like the executive who tells his secretary to "hold my calls," the man has more control over his time.

In his book *Megatrends,* John Naisbitt reports that 83 percent of corporate executives believed that more men feel the need to share the responsibilities of parenting; yet only 9 percent of corporations offer paternity leave.

Public strategies are linked to private ones. Economic and cultural 24 trends bear on family relations in ways it would be useful for all of us to understand. The happiest two-job marriages I saw during my research were ones in which men and women shared the housework and parenting. What couples called good communication often meant that they were good at saying thanks to one another for small aspects of taking care of the family. Making it to the school play, helping a child read, cooking dinner in good spirit, remembering the grocery list, taking responsibility for cleaning up the bedrooms—these were the silver and gold of the marital exchange. Until now, couples committed to an equal sharing of housework and child care have been rare. But, if we as a culture come to see the urgent need of meeting the new problems posed by the second shift, and if society and government begin to shape new policies that allow working parents more flexibility then we will be making some progress toward happier times at home and work. And as the young learn by example, many more women and men will be able to enjoy the pleasure that arises when family life is family life, and not a second shift.

Responding to Reading

1. Hochschild coined the terms "second shift" and "stalled revolution." Define each of these terms. Are they appropriate for what they denote? Would other terms—for example, *late shift* or *swing shift* and *postponed revolution* or *failed revolution*—be more appropriate? Explain.
2. According to Hochschild, women *feel* that they are "under more strain than men" (14) even when their husbands do their share of housework and child care. How does Hochschild account for this?
3. Beginning with paragraph 18, Hochschild recommends changes that she believes will ease the strain on working families—because, as she says in paragraph 23, "public strategies are linked to private ones." Given what Hochschild has said about the basic differences in men's and women's approaches to their family roles, do you believe that government and corporations can solve the problem she identifies? Explain your reasoning.

SEX AND THE SOLDIER

Stephanie Gutmann

Stephanie Gutmann (1960–   ) was born in Chicago, Illinois, and holds a B.A. from Roosevelt University there and an M.S. from the Columbia University School of Journalism. She has been on the staffs of the Wilkes-Barre (Pennsylvania) Times Leader, *the* Los Angeles Times, *and the* New York Post, *serving as a features writer, entertainment critic, and reporter. She has also written for* The New York Times, Playboy, Cosmopolitan, *and the* Washington Post, *among other publications. Her book* The Kinder, Gentler Military: Can America's Gender Neutral Fighting Force Still Win Wars? *was published in 2000. In the following essay, which first appeared in the* New Republic *in 1997, Gutmann takes a critical look at current attempts to integrate women recruits into the U.S. military forces.*

February 4, 1997, and an all-too-familiar looking headline—"TOP 1 ENLISTED MAN IN THE ARMY STANDS ACCUSED OF SEX ASSAULT"—occupies a prime corner of the front page of The New York Times. Just a few weeks earlier, the papers had been reporting charges of inappropriate hazing of female cadets at the Citadel. And just a few months before that, several female recruits at the Army's Aberdeen Proving Ground had accused drill instructors of rape and sexual harassment, unleashing a torrent of similar accusations from female soldiers around the country. In this latest case, as in so many of the others, blame will be difficult to affix. Once more it will come down to "he said, she said." Once more there will be op-eds, hand-wringing and counselors; once more the Army will have to deploy its investigatory troops. This, just as the Army digs out from Aberdeen—where there are still over 200 criminal charges to investigate, and a hot-line brings in new complaints every day.

What no one is publicly saying (but what everyone in the military 2 knows) is that incidents like these are bound to recur. In a military that is dedicated to the full integration of women, and to papering over the implications of that integration as best it can, sex and sexual difference will continue to be a disruptive force. And regulating sex will become an ever more important military sideline, one whose full costs in money, labor and morale we will not really know until the forces are called on to do what they are assembled to do: fight.

The military's sex problems begin with the simple anatomical 3 differences between men and women. Racial integration, to which the integration of women is ceaselessly compared, took the military about a century to achieve (quite successfully in the end) and that involved differences that are only skin deep. An effective fighting force depends on a steady supply of known quantities; it needs "units" made up of interchangeable elements called soldiers. Once one got over skin color, racial integration was still about integrating the same body.

But what happens when you try to absorb a population that is not, 4 in unit terms, interchangeable? What happens when you try to integrate into a cohesive whole two populations with radically different bodies? In the elemental, unremittingly physical world of the soldier, sex differences—masked by technology in the civilian world—stand out in high relief. Consider the female soldier not in political terms, but in the real, inescapable terms of physical structure. She is, on average, about five inches shorter than the male soldier, has half the upper body strength, lower aerobic capacity and 37 percent less muscle mass. She has a lighter skeleton, which may mean, for instance, that she won't be able to "pull G forces" as reliably in a fighter plane. She cannot pee standing up, a problem that may seem trivial, but whose impact on long marches was the subject of an entire Army research study; under investigation was a device called the "Freshette Complete System," which would allow women to pee standing up in places where foliage doesn't supply ample cover. She tends, particularly if she is under the age of 30 (as are 60 percent of military personnel), to get pregnant.

One would expect that such a sweeping social experiment (and one 5 so expensive—just refitting the *U.S.S. Eisenhower* to accommodate 400 new female sailors cost $1 million, for example) would hit some rough patches. But don't expect to hear about them from the military brass. Afflicted by a kind of "Vietnam syndrome" about the possibility of winning an ideological battle against the civilians who increasingly influence military policy, the brass now seem mostly concerned with trying to prove how well, as one officer put it, they "get it" where women are concerned. This week, when Army Chief of Staff General Dennis J. Reimer said he thought the service should re-examine whether the advantages of jointly training men and women outweigh the drawbacks, it was something of a bombshell. In general, the military has maintained a virtual silence about problems with the new influx of female soldiers, and, in the ranks, negative comments about integration are considered "career killers." Those who don't "get it" talk about it in the barracks and on the Internet, which has become a haven for military samizdat[1] about sex and other dicey matters. As one soldier wrote in a typical online exchange, "examples of these latest 'revelations' [about sex between subordinates and their immediate superiors] are known to nearly everyone who has served. But we were never allowed to discuss . . . our concerns openly because it would raise issues about the

---

[1] A clandestine network for thoughts and ideas. [Eds.]

efficacy of mixing girls and boys and that was politically incorrect, a career- ending taboo."

In general, the military's response to the problems of gender inte- 6 gration has been to recruit more women. The more women, the more feminized the culture, the fewer problems with sex, goes the thinking. (One corollary of this may be the recent decline in male enlistment. In focus groups, young men tend to cite, among other reasons for not joining up, fear of purges like the one after Tailhook and the increased presence of females in the ranks.)

The big recruitment drive has brought the percentage of women in 7 the force to 14 percent, which may not seem like much but is up from 2 percent at the close of the Vietnam War. Women now make up 20 percent of new recruits—compared to 12 percent a decade ago. And the effort to recruit still more women is relentless. In 1991, when the Marines replaced their slogan "A FEW GOOD MEN" with "THE FEW, THE PROUD, THE MARINES," the idea was to sound more female-friendly. Nowadays, much of a military recruiter's time is consumed with trying to cajole women to enlist. And in practice, unfortunately, this often means adapting—which is to say, lowering—standards without exactly admitting to doing so.

The goal for a young Marine recruiter named C. J. Chivers, for exam- 8 ple, became just "'Get 'em on the plane.' If there were any problems, boot camp could sort it out." Chivers, whose stint as a recruiter lasted from 1992–94, adds that "invariably we would fill up the white male quotas almost immediately. So it became any woman that came in there that met the minimums, we gotta hire. What that did was take all the subjectivity out of it, an enormous part of the evaluation process. I couldn't say 'I got a bad vibe' the way I could with a guy." A recruiter also had to work hard to maintain what Chivers calls an "informal double standard" on strength differences: "Invariably the guys went down to Officer Candidate School with a near-perfect physical score while the women just cleared the minimum"—even using what military brass call "gender-normed" test results and "dual," i.e. lower, standards: for example, in the Marines, fitness for women is tested with a flexed arm hang instead of pull-ups, half the number of sit-ups and a slower run.

Women have also been lured into the service with the promise of a 9 more important role. Since 1994 more than 80,000 new jobs have been opened in positions that were formerly off-limits. Rescinding the combat exclusion law and the risk rule has allowed women to qualify to fly combat planes and to serve on combat ships. Women are still not allowed to serve on submarines, but *Navy Times* reports that "a review underway to examine future submarine designs may include a study on including women crew members."

And ever since the Gulf war, when women served in combat 10 support roles, the possibility of taking that last step—of knocking down barriers to the infantry—has been very much in the air. Ground combat,

renamed the "confidence course" and moved indoors to comprise "an indoor labyrinth of pipes to crawl through, monkey bars to swing from, ladders to climb up and balance beams to sidestep over."

And at Fort Jackson, South Carolina—where, in 1995, boys and   17 girls shared barracks—an *Army Times* reporter recently found that grunts no longer have to do pushups to a count. Instead, they are asked to perform "a timed exercise in which soldiers do the best they can in a set period." One drill instructor has solved the male/female strength discrepancy problem by putting young recruits in "ability groups" for their morning run. "You're not competing with the rest of the company," Colonel Byron D. Greene, the director of Plans, Training and Mobilization, told *Army Times*. "You are competing against yourself and your own abilities."

But life—especially military life—does not ignore physical differ-   18 ences. When young soldiers leave training, they are assigned jobs (called Military Occupational Specialities or MOSs), and the physical requirements of these jobs are not nearly as forgiving as a "New Army" drill instructor. A typical Army MOS, the kind of combat support MOS a young woman might request, could involve lots of lifting and loading, of shell casings, for instance. Pat Schroeder can say what she likes, but "a shell casing," groused an Army physiologist, "is always gonna weigh ninety pounds. There's nothing we can do about that."

Female soldiers themselves know this. A 1987 Army Research   19 Institute survey found that women are more likely than men to report that insufficient upper body strength interferes with their job perfor- mance. Twenty-six percent of female light wheel vehicle mechanics, for example, said they found it "very difficult" to do their job, as opposed to 9 percent of the men in that specialty who were polled.

And, according to Army physiologist Everett Harman, "[Command   20 Reports] have indicated that many soldiers are not physically capable of meeting the demands of their military occupational specialities. Unfor- tunately women fall disproportionately into this category." Attrition is particularly high, Harman said, in "heavy" (requiring 100-pound lift- ing) and "very heavy" (over 100 pounds) MOSs like Food Service Specialist, Motor Transport Operator and Unit Supply Specialist. Retraining and reassigning a soldier has been estimated to cost about $16,000, but advising a female soldier that she may have trouble with an MOS she is considering is, sources say, one of those "career-killing" statements that bureaucratically wise officers have learned to avoid.

There have been two attempts made in the past fifteen years to   21 establish "gender-neutral" strength standards and a qualifying pre-test for each MOS, but as *Army Times* reported, "on both occasions, the requirements were eventually abandoned when studies showed most women couldn't meet the standards proposed for nearly 70 percent of the Army specialties." In 1995, a group of military researchers were set to try again, but this time the project didn't even reach the partial implementation stage because funding was denied. Funding was also recently denied to Harman, who had applied for a grant to do a second study of "remedial strength training for women," after his first had shown promising results. Harman believes the brass do not like his approach because it admits that female soldiers are not strong enough to perform basic military tasks, which is contrary to the military's line. "At the highest level, I think they feel that if we show that women can get stronger, then the onus would be on the women to get stronger," he says, "while it is the jobs that should be made easier."

But can the jobs be made easier? Can weapons get lighter (as some 22 advisers are urging)—without reducing lethality? Proponents of the change-the-equipment-not-the-people view point to the highly auto-mated Air Force. But the Air Force is not the Army, and it is not the Marines. "If you have a plane sitting on the runway and you have to load it with supplies—bombs, whatever, you can have machines that drive out there, that raise the stuff on a little elevator," Harman points out. "But out in the woods and fields a lot has to get done by hand. Even in the kitchen there are big pots weighing about 100 pounds or so. It would take a tremendous amount of research to make certain jobs lighter, because you're talking about re-engineering the whole thing. Carrying a tool box, changing a truck tire; there are certain jobs, for instance, where you have to carry a toolbox that might weigh a few hundred pounds and put it up on the wing of a plane."

Online, where military folk often say impolitic things, there is a 23 sense of foreboding about the danger of ignoring the strength issue: "Nothing is more demoralizing," wrote one Marine, "than to have to turn your formation around to go pick up the females. This is only training. I can even put the females on remedial training and they still hold up my formations. I would hate to see how many Marines I would lose if we were in combat and had to be somewhere fast."

There is one respect, though, in which the stubborn physical reali- 24 ties of integrating women cannot be easily denied—and that is their capacity for childbearing. A recent article in *Stars and Stripes* reported that a woman had to be evacuated for pregnancy approximately every three days in the Bosnian theater from December 20, 1995, when the deployment began, until July 19, 1996. Army public relations people in Bosnia don't dispute that claim, but they also say pregnancy is no particular problem for the Army, "no different than appendicitis."

It is clearly not a problem anymore in a career sense. All branches and 25 some of the service academies have softened policies on pregnancies and made it clear that their official stance is now completely accepting. Unfurling one such policy in February, 1995, Navy Secretary John H. Dalton told reporters that "Navy leadership recognize that pregnancy is a natural event that can occur in the lives of Navy servicewomen . . . and is not a presumption of medical incapacity." The Army has followed suit, stating that "Pregnancy does not normally adversely affect the career of a soldier."

In fact, pregnancy is now so "non-adverse" that soldiers say it's 26 sometimes used to get out of "hell tours" like Bosnia, to go home. "I know other females that have done things . . . probably to get out of going somewhere," Specialist Carrie Lambertus told *Army Times*. "It happens all the time."

A woman who turns up pregnant in Bosnia is shipped in short 27 order to the U.S. or Germany. Then, according to an Army spokesman, "female soldiers have the option of either staying on active duty or applying for release [with an honorable discharge] from active duty." Those who decide to stay in the military get six weeks maternity leave. The new Navy policy also provides for help in locating a runaway dad and in establishing paternity.

In the Navy, pregnancy rates run about 8 percent of the force at any 28 given time. A pregnant woman is allowed to stay onboard ship up to her fifth month; then she gets reassigned to shore duty to avoid the heavy lifting that is a sailor's lot, not to mention the hazardous chemicals in engine rooms. Of the 400 women on the first gender-integrated warship, the *U.S.S. Eisenhower*, twenty-four were "non-deployable" due to pregnancy at the start of a Persian Gulf tour and another fifteen were evacuated once on the water. On the *U.S.S. Acadia*—dubbed "the Love Boat" by the press—thirty-six out of a total 360 female sailors aboard had to be evacuated during a Gulf tour.

And no matter how determinedly the military defines pregnancy as 29 a non-issue, the facts of pregnancy cannot be altered. A pregnant soldier is—or soon will be—a non-deployable soldier. A General Accounting Office study of soldiers called up to go to the Persian Gulf showed that women were four times more non-deployable than men—because of the pregnancy and recovery numbers. As Lambertus puts it, "If you're in a platoon where they're moving equipment or digging, setting up tents, [pregnant soldiers] are not going to be doing anything, except maybe sitting there and answering the phone all day. That really does cause some resentment." If her commanders had wanted to make sure the unit was truly deployable "they'll have to reclassify me and send me somewhere else, which would take more money, more time. So actually, it would be cheaper for them just to wait and keep me [here]."

Then there is the matter of how one gets pregnant in the first place— 30 the matter of what happens when you take men and women, aged on average 18 to 25, away from what are generally small-town homes, ship them to exotic ports of call, house them in the catacomb-like berthing areas of ships, in coed tents or in crowded barracks and then subject them to loneliness, boredom and high stress. The fantasy of civilian activists like Pat Schroeder is that the result will look something like the bustling, efficient bridge of the *Starship Enterprise*. The reality is apt to look more like "a big high school"—which is the way a sailor named Elizabeth Rugh described her ship, the newly integrated *U.S.S. Samuel Gompers*.

Troops in Bosnia and Herzegovina (there were 1,500 female troops in   31 the first deployment) generally live in coed tents with eight to ten people. Ranks are mixed, privates bedded down next to superiors. Troops are not allowed to drink alcohol or eat in restaurants, but they *are* allowed to have sex—as long as they are single and not doing it with a subordinate (or superior) in their chain of command. In a solemn statement provided to *Stars and Stripes*, Army spokesman Captain Ken Clifton wrote that "the Army does not prohibit heterosexual relations among consenting single soldiers . . . but it does not provide facilities for sexual relations."

Lack of official facilities does not seem to be a great obstacle.   32 "Where there's a will there's a way!" Captain Chris Scholl told *Stars and Stripes*. Favorite locations, he said, include the backs of Humvees parked on a deserted air strip, tents, latrines, even underground bunkers—if you can hack standing up to your ankles in icy water. "It's going on all over the place," said Scholl. "They've locked us down so what else is there to do?"

And there is, of course, the problem of nonconsensual sex. A   33 Defense Department spokesman says "there is no way to get a good number" on the frequency of rapes and sexual assaults in the armed forces, because each service keeps its own numbers and defines things slightly differently. Still, it is clear that the Aberdeen case was not an isolated incident. The Army recorded twenty-four incidents it categorized as "sexual assaults" involving U.S. soldiers in the Gulf war; these cases range from that of a 24-year-old specialist who had been on overnight guard duty in the desert with a male soldier and awoke to find him fondling her under the blanket they had shared for warmth to that of a 21-year-old private who was raped at knifepoint by a sergeant.

The making of a soldier is a rough, hands-on, invasive process—a   34 preparation for what may be a very rough end. "[T]he training, the discipline, the daily humiliations, the privileges of 'brutish' sergeants, the living en masse like schools of fish," wrote James Jones in his essay "The Evolution of a Soldier," "are all directed toward breaking down the sense of sanctity of the physical person, and toward hardening the awareness that a soldier is the chattel (hopefully the proud chattel but a chattel all the same) of the society he serves."

Soldiers abuse each other—in training, in command, in hazing ritu-   35 als. It is a self-regulating mechanism; finding the weak links, then shaming them or bullying them to come up to par, is one way a unit ensures, or tries to ensure, its own survival, since on the battlefield one's life depends on one's buddies' performance.

Meanwhile, the brass attempt to operate on both tracks, to honor   36 the standards of both the civilian and the military world. They know they must encourage "cohesion" in their mixed-gender units, but they know, too, that they must avoid the wrong kind of cohesion—the kind that could stimulate jealousies, lovers' spats and . . . babies. So they end up sending a rather scrambled message, something like "Women are different but they're not different"; "We have the same expectations for women but you cannot treat them the same."

"Cry havoc and let slip the dogs of war," roared Shakespeare's Marc   37 Antony. Something tells me he wasn't talking about 19-year-old girls. "Let the dogs loose," read a piece of locker-room samizdat (observed by writer Kathy Dobie) at a coed basic training program in Florida. Men ache to unleash their dogs of war. Women generally have to be exhorted or trained to—then, good students and employees that they are, they can probably manage a semblance of dogginess at least for a while. But do we really want them to? Can a man of say, 35, be trained not to stay his hand when he needs to send a 20-year-old girl onto a mortar-strafed field? Can the impulse which, still, impels men to try to protect women be overridden? Do we want it to be? Won't sex always gum up the works? Would we really prefer if it didn't?

Responding to Reading

1. According to Gutmann, why will women never be successfully integrated into the armed forces? What evidence does she offer to support her position? How convincing a case does she make?
2. At several points Gutmann addresses the arguments against her position. Summarize these arguments. How effective are Gutmann's responses?
3. Is there an intermediate position that Gutmann does not consider? For example, could women perform some kinds of combat duties but not others? Should she have discussed such a compromise position? Why or why not?

MARKED WOMEN

Deborah Tannen

A professor of linguistics at Georgetown University in Washington, D.C., Deborah Tannen (1945–   ) has written both scholarly and popular books examining the problems people encounter communicating across cultural and gender lines. Her three bestsellers—That's Not What I Meant:

How Conversational Style Makes or Breaks Your Relationships *(1987)*,
You Just Don't Understand: Women and Men in Conversation *(1990)*,
and Talking from 9 to 5 *(1994)—have given her readers a new perspective
on how communication style affects how a message is perceived. Her most
recent book is* The Argument Culture *(1998). The following essay, written
in 1993, is something of a departure from Tannen's usual work. Here she
focuses not on different communication styles, but on the striking contrast
she finds between the neutral way men in our culture are able to present
themselves to the world and the more message-laden way women must generally do so.*

Some years ago I was at a small working conference of four women 1
and eight men. Instead of concentrating on the discussion I found
myself looking at the three other women at the table, thinking how each
had a different style and how each style was coherent.

One woman had dark brown hair in a classic style, a cross between 2
Cleopatra and Plain Jane. The severity of her straight hair was softened
by wavy bangs and ends that turned under. Because she was beautiful,
the effect was more Cleopatra than plain.

The second woman was older, full of dignity and composure. Her 3
hair was cut in a fashionable style that left her with only one eye, thanks
to a side part that let a curtain of hair fall across half her face. As she
looked down to read her prepared paper, the hair robbed her of bifocal
vision and created a barrier between her and the listeners.

The third woman's hair was wild, a frosted blond avalanche falling 4
over and beyond her shoulders. When she spoke she frequently tossed
her head, calling attention to her hair and away from her lecture.

Then there was makeup. The first woman wore facial cover that 5
made her skin smooth and pale, a black line under each eye and mascara that darkened already dark lashes. The second wore only a light
gloss on her lips and a hint of shadow on her eyes. The third had blue
bands under her eyes, dark blue shadow, mascara, bright red lipstick
and rouge; her fingernails flashed red.

I considered the clothes each woman had worn during the three 6
days of the conference: In the first case, man-tailored suits in primary
colors with solid-color blouses. In the second, casual but stylish black
T-shirts, a floppy collarless jacket and baggy slacks or a skirt in neutral
colors. The third wore a sexy jump suit; tight sleeveless jersey and tight
yellow slacks; a dress with gaping armholes and an indulged tendency
to fall off one shoulder.

Shoes? No. 1 wore string sandals with medium heels; No. 2, sensible, 7
comfortable walking shoes; No. 3, pumps with spike heels. You can fill
in the jewelry, scarves, shawls, sweaters—or lack of them.

As I amused myself finding coherence in these styles, I suddenly 8
wondered why I was scrutinizing only the women. I scanned the eight

I have never been inclined toward biological explanations of gender 24 differences in language, but I was intrigued to see Ralph Fasold bring biological phenomena to bear on the question of linguistic marking in his book "The Sociolinguistics of Language." Fasold stresses that language and culture are particularly unfair in treating women as the marked case because biologically it is the male that is marked. While two X chromosomes make a female, two Y chromosomes make nothing. Like the linguistic markers *s, es* or *ess,* the Y chromosome doesn't "mean" anything unless it is attached to a root form—an X chromosome.

Developing this idea elsewhere, Fasold points out that girls are 25 born with fully female bodies, while boys are born with modified female bodies. He invites men who doubt this to lift up their shirts and contemplate why they have nipples.

In his book, Fasold notes "a wide range of facts which demonstrates 26 that female is the unmarked sex." For example, he observes that there are a few species that produce only females, like the whiptail lizard. Thanks to parthenogenesis, they have no trouble having as many daughters as they like. There are no species, however, that produce only males. This is no surprise, since any such species would become extinct in its first generation.

Fasold is also intrigued by species that produce individuals not 27 involved in reproduction, like honeybees and leaf-cutter ants. Reproduction is handled by the queen and a relatively few males; the workers are sterile females. "Since they do not reproduce," Fasold says, "there is no reason for them to be one sex or the other, so they default, so to speak, to female."

Fasold ends his discussion of these matters by pointing out that if 28 language reflected biology, grammar books would direct us to use "she" to include males and females and "he" only for specifically male referents. But they don't. They tell us that "he" means "he or she," and that "she" is used only if the referent is specifically female. This use of "he" as the sex-indefinite pronoun is an innovation introduced into English by grammarians in the 18th and 19th centuries, according to Peter Mühlhäusler and Rom Harré in "Pronouns and People." From at least about 1500, the correct sex-indefinite pronoun was "they," as it still is in casual spoken English. In other words, the female was declared by grammarians to be the marked case.

Writing this article may mark me not as a writer, not as a linguist, 29 not as an analyst of human behavior, but as a feminist—which will have positive or negative, but in any case powerful, connotations for readers. Yet I doubt that anyone reading Ralph Fasold's book would put that label on him.

I discovered the markedness inherent in the very topic of gender after 30 writing a book on differences in conversational style based on geographical region, ethnicity, class, age and gender. When I was interviewed, the vast majority of journalists wanted to talk about the differences between women and men. While I thought I was simply describing what I observed—something I had learned to do as a researcher—merely mentioning women and men marked me as a feminist for some.

When I wrote a book devoted to gender differences, in ways of 31 speaking, I sent the manuscript to five male colleagues, asking them to alert me to any interpretation, phrasing or wording that might seem unfairly negative toward men. Even so, when the book came out, I encountered responses like that of the television talk show host who, after interviewing me, turned to the audience and asked if they thought I was male-bashing.

Leaping upon a poor fellow who affably nodded in agreement, 32 she made him stand and asked, "Did what she said accurately describe you?" "Oh, yes," he answered. "That's me exactly." "And what she said about women—does that sound like your wife?" "Oh yes," he responded. "That's her exactly." "Then why do you think she's male-bashing?" He answered, with disarming honesty, "Because she's a woman and she's saying things about men."

To say anything about women and men without marking oneself as 33 either feminist or anti-feminist, male-basher or apologist for men seems as impossible for a woman as trying to get dressed in the morning without inviting interpretations of her character.

Sitting at the conference table musing on these matters, I felt sad to 34 think that we women didn't have the freedom to be unmarked that the men sitting next to us had. Some days you just want to get dressed and go about your business. But if you're a woman, you can't, because there is no unmarked woman.

Responding to Reading

1. Tannen notes that men "can choose styles that are marked, but they don't have to" (12); however, she believes that women do not have the "option of being unmarked." What does she mean? Can you give some examples of women's styles that you believe are unmarked? (Note that in paragraph 16, Tannen says there are no such styles.)
2. In paragraph 33, Tannen says, "To say anything about women and men without marking oneself as either feminist or anti-feminist, male-basher or apologist for men seems as impossible for a woman as trying to get dressed in the morning without inviting interpretations of her character." Do you agree?
3. In paragraphs 24–28, Tannen discusses Ralph Fasold's book *The Sociolinguistics of Language*. Why does she include this material? Could she have made her point as effectively without it?

---------------------------------- FOCUS ----------------------------------

Who Has It Harder,
Women or Men?

THE GIRLS OF GEN X

Barbara Dafoe Whitehead

Born in Appleton, Wisconsin, in 1944, Barbara Dafoe Whitehead did her undergraduate work at the University of Wisconsin and earned her M.A. and Ph.D. from the University of Chicago. A frequent lecturer on issues related to the family, she codirects the Marriage Project, a research and public education organization. Her 1993 Haper's *magazine article, "Dan Quayle Was Right," sparked considerable debate over the effects of single-parent households on children. She continued her argument that two-parent families produce more well-adjusted children in* The Divorce Culture: Rethinking Our Commitments to Marriage and Family *(1997). Whitehead's most recent book is* Goodbye to Girlhood: What's Troubling Girls and What We Can Do about It *(1999). The following essay was published online by the American Enterprise Institute in 1998.*

All is not well with the women of Generation X.   1

Consider the evidence: Close to 40 percent of college women are fre-   2
quent binge drinkers, a behavior related to date rapes and venereal disease. Young women suffer higher levels of depression, suicidal thoughts and attempts than men from early adolescence on. Between 1980 and '92, the rate of completed suicides more than tripled among white girls and doubled among black girls. For white women between 15 and 24, suicide is the third leading cause of death. And there is evidence that young women are less happy today the 20 years ago. Using data from a survey of high school seniors, sociologist Norval D. Glenn has tracked the trends of reported happiness for young men and women. Since 1977, the "happiness index" has been trending downward for young women. Moreover, this decline is specific to girls. Young men's reported happiness has risen slightly over the same Time. Gen X women seem to experience the greatest discontent in two areas: Men, and their own bodies. Young women can find sex easily, but they have a hard time finding a caring and sexually faithful partner who will share their lives. Marline Pearson, who teaches at a large community college in Madison, Wisconsin, recently asked her women students to identify the greatest obstacle facing women today. The difficulty of "finding and keeping a

loving partner" topped the list, outranking obstacles such as job discrimination, sexual harassment in the workplace, and domestic violence. In addition to being disappointed in their intimate relationships with men, women are discontented with their own bodies. Healthy young women of normal weight describe themselves as fat or "gross." At puberty or even earlier, girls begin restricting what they eat. Two-thirds of ninth-grade girls report attempts to lose weight in the previous month. Of course, dieting is not new, but Gen X women do more than watch calories. Some starve themselves. Others eat but are afraid to keep food in their body. Instead, they chew their food and spit it out, vomit it up, or purge it with laxatives. Even more widespread than eating disorders is disordered eating, the restrictive and obsessive monitoring of food consumption. According to some experts, most college women today suffer from disordered eating. Indeed, it is the rare college or university today that does not have at least one specialist in eating disturbances on its counseling staff. According to one survey, the number-one wish among young women, outranking the desire to end homelessness, poverty, or racism, is to get and stay thin.

These conditions afflict some of the most privilege young women of 3 the generation. This comes as a shock to older, baby-boom women. After all, college-educated Gen X women—the first full beneficiaries of the achievements of the women's movement—have grown up with more freedom, opportunity and choice than their mothers or grandmothers. More to the point, they have been the beneficiaries of what might be called the girlhood project: the systematic and self-conscious effort to change the culture and prepare girls for lives as liberated, self-determined individuals with successful careers, sexual freedoms, and nearly limitless personal choice.

As a mother raising daughters in the 1970s and '80s, I remember the 4 heady sense of possibility that accompanied the girlhood project. Sons were sons, but daughters were a social experiment. We gave them books like Marlo Thomas's *Free To Be You and Me* and read them stories in *Ms.* like "The Princess Who Could Stand on Her Own Two Feet." We dressed them in jeans and sneakers. We fought for their right to play Little League baseball. We pushed for more sex education in the schools. We urged them to please themselves rather than to please men.

Given our optimistic expectations, it is bitterly disappointing to 5 reach the '90s only to discover that young women's happiness index is falling, not rising. What is happening to our bright and talented daughters?

Several feminist writers have grappled with this question. Therapist 6 Mary Pipher was the first to describe the dark side of American girlhood in her best-selling book *Revivng Ophelia*. Pipher's case histories present a disturbing portrait of depressed and angry adolescent girls, self-mutilating, self-starving, self-loathing. Two more recent books offer a thoughtful analysis and criticism of the changing nature of American girlhood. In *Promiscuities*, her memoir of growing up fast and sexy in the '70s, Naomi Wolf describes the confused sexual awakening of privileged girls raised by self-absorbed parents too busy sampling the pleasures of the sexual revolution themselves to guide or protect their daughters. Historian Joan Jacobs Brumberg's *The Body Project: An Intimate History of Girlhood* meticulously documents the downward slide of girls' aspirations and ambitions over the past century, from improving one's character through good works to improving one's body through grueling workouts.

All three accounts point to one source of trouble: the passage between 7 girlhood and womanhood. Growing up has never been easy for girls, of course, but it is more prolonged and perilous than ever before. Puberty can begin as early as eight; first sexual intercourse commonly occurs between 15 and 17; and women remain single and sexually active into their middle or late twenties. Forty-five percent of women who came of age in the 1950s and '60s were still virgins at age 19, and for many of those 19-year-old women, their first sexual intercourse occurred on their wedding night. But only 17 percent of women who came of age in the 1970s and '80s were virgins at 19. Since many Gen X women postpone marriage until their late twenties, few are likely to be virgins on their wedding night. As a consequence, girls are exposed to the problems associated with unmarried sex at an earlier age and for a longer period of time than a generation ago.

A rough consensus exists on some key factors that make coming of 8 age more difficult for girls today: a cultural emphasis on thinness which makes the normal weight gains of puberty a source of anxiety and self-loathing; a media saturated with sexually explicit images and misogynistic messages; the sexual revolution and the availability of the Pill; which relieved men of any significant burden of responsibility for the negative consequences of unmarried sex; the high rate of family breakup and dysfunction; and the erosion of adult supervision. Puberty is now fraught with danger and anxiety.

Young girls are now at greater risk for early and traumatic sexual- 9 ization, often by adult men. According to Brumberg, there have also been dramatic shifts in the social controls governing the sexuality of adolescent girls. Professional providers of contraceptive and abortion services have replaced mothers as the main source of authority on sexual matters. This shift has contributed to the demoralization of female sexuality and the decline in chastity.

At age 15, Naomi Wolf tells us, she followed the responsible, 10 "healthy," medically approved approach to getting rid of her virginity. With her boyfriend, she went to a clinic to be fitted for a diaphragm, a business "easier than getting a learner's permit to drive a car." Yet as she prepared for the procedure, she missed a sense of occasion. "It was weird to have these adults just hand you the keys to the kingdom, ask 'Any questions?,' wave and return to their paperwork. . . . The end of our virginity passed unmarked." she writes, "neither mourned or celebrated."

Both Brumberg and Wolf are critical of the medicalization of girls' 11 sexuality, with its emphasis on sexual health and self-management. (In the words of one sex education book, the goal for girls is to stay "healthy, safe, and in charge.") This places an unsupportable burden on young girls to protect themselves from predatory males. It also neglects girls' emotional needs for affiliation and affection, as well as their desire to have their sexuality invested with some larger meaning.

These revisionist-feminist writers seek to remoralize girlhood, but 12 not with the morals of yesteryear. Instead, they call upon older women to take responsibility for (and pride in) younger womens' sexuality, and they look to senior women and especially mothers to instruct girls more actively. This advice overlooks at least one crucial point. Older women are already involved in shaping the passage to womanhood and have been for more than 20 years. It is feminist women who write and edit books and magazines for teen girls. It is feminist women who have fought for abortion rights and the end to parental consent laws for girls. It is feminist women who have championed the right of girls to be as sexually free as boys. In short, these older women are the authors of the girlhood project. Are they now the right parties to repair the damage done?

The girlhood project was rooted in rebellion against traditional 13 conceptions of girlhood. According to feminist critics, earlier generations of girls were raised primarily to be wives and mothers. From puberty on, parents taught daughters to be modest, nice, nurturing, accomplished in the domestic arts, and virginal. Since a young woman's virginity was a moral as well as a physical condition, family and church conspired to keep women pure.

Whether this is actually a fair summary of prevailing American sex 14 roles prior to the 1960s is dubious. Even in the 1830s, Alexis de Tocqueville commented that Americans "have calculated that there was little chance of repressing in woman the most tyrannical passions of the human heart and that it was a safer policy to teach her to control them herself. Unable to prevent her chastity from being often in danger, they want her to know how to defend herself, and they count on the strength of her free determination more than on safeguards which have been shaken or overthrown. . . . Unable or unwilling to keep a girl in perpetual ignorance, they are in a hurry to give her precocious knowledge of everything."

In any case, the activists who undertook the girlhood project 15 declared war on what they viewed as Victorian double standards for boys and girls, which they blamed for unhappy marriages and unfulfilled female desires. Feminists called instead for a new single sexual standard—based on traditional boyhood. In their play and pursuits, little girls were to be made more like boys. Among liberal elites, a traditionally feminine daughter became a mild social embarrassment, while a feisty tomboy daughter was a source of pride.

In everything from sports to sex, girls gained experiences that were 16 once off-limits. Twenty-five years ago, only one in 27 high school girls participated in team sports. By 1994, one in three did. A copy-the-boys approach was also applied to sexuality. Increasingly, the timing of girls' sexual awakening resembled boys. Today, the most frequent age of first intercourse is 17 for girls, 16 for boys. In frequency of intercourse and number of sexual partners, the traditional gender gap is closing as well. Modesty has also disappeared. Girls can be as profane, sexually frank, and "horny" as the guys. "Girls talk in the casual, expletive-laced manner stereotypically attributed to men," one 18-year-old college male writes. "Sex is discussed in all its variations, and bizarre or deviant sexual practices are often explored. This sort of talk is considered 'flirting'."

Amidst its success at ending different standards for the sexes, the 17 girlhood project has created new discontents. For one thing, it contributes to girls' unhappiness with their bodies. The tomboy ideal is demanding. It favors the few girls who are naturally wiry and athletic, and leaves the majority of girls displeased with their own shapes. The rapturous acclaim for tiny Olympic gymnasts and lithe skaters gives nonathletic girls still another reason to feel disappointed in their normal forms.

The more masculine body ideal shifts the locus of body shame from 18 sexual organs to more visible body parts. Today's college women know how to find their clitoris in a mirror, but they can't bear to look at their "thunder thighs." Fashion magazines, which girls begin to read at age nine or ten and continue to consult well into their 20s, provoke body shame. Virtually all these magazines send one clear message: Your body is a mess. For example, the cover of the December 1997 *Jump*, a magazine for young teens, features stories entitled, "Body Bummers: How to go from feeling flawed to fab" and "Sizing up boobs." Such magazines tell girls to like themselves, whatever their size or shape, but they only feature flat-chested models who are six feet tall and 105 pounds. Indeed, a recurrent rumor among teenage girls is that these models are really boys.

Girls respond to body shame with rigid technocratic monitoring of 19 their bodies. Again. the strenuous pursuit of feminine virtue has not disappeared but shifted location. The virtue of staying sexually pure has been replaced by the virtue of staying physically fit. In my corner of western Massachusetts, swarms of college women descend on the local health club each fall. They work out in the weight room or on the treadmills, their pony tails bobbing, their arms pumping, their faces sweaty and serious. Some read fashion magazines as they work out.

It does not take a degree in cultural anthropology to figure out that 20 more is going on here than mere exercise. In girl culture today, "working out" is the new self-purification ritual, deeply invested with positive moral meaning. Good girls work out. Bad girls let themselves go. In the same way, eating has become a means of self-purification, and food itself has been moralized. There are good foods that one takes into the body and bad foods that one avoids or throws up. This helps explain why so many college women see "bad" foods as far more dangerous than drugs or alcohol, and why young women who drink and take recreational drugs will simultaneously refuse to eat anything but "pure" pesticide free, fat-free organic food. Food is entirely divorced from pleasure and sociability while the other ingested substances are not.

If the girlhood project leads young women on a quest for a mas- 21 culinized body, it also sets them on the path toward a more masculinized emotional life. There is now a single sex standard for men and women, but it favors Hugh Hefner, not Betty Friedan.

As much as young women's sexual lives resemble men's in the tim- 22 ing of first sex and the number of sex partners, their reasons for having sex remain very different. The nation's most comprehensive and up-to date sex survey reports that 48 percent of women have intercourse for the first time out of "affection for their partner," compared to only 25 percent of men. The researchers add, "Young women often go along with intercourse the first time, finding little physical pleasure in it, and a substantial number report being forced to have intercourse. These facts reflect the dramatic costs for young women, and they seem to be increasing as young women have intercourse earlier in the life course."

Even when young women deliberately set out to lose their virginity, 23 they often experience feelings of sadness, emptiness, and disappointment afterward. Women may want affection, tenderness, and commitment in their relationships, but what they actually get is "more naked, loss-filled sex," says Warren Schumacher, who teaches courses in marriage and the family at the University of Massachusetts. Thus, though the girlhood project prepares girls for sex, it says nothing to them about love.

With the decoupling of sex and love, intense passion and romance 24 are vanishing. Loveless sex has become a routine pleasure of the single life, on a par with a good movie. Sexless love is also part of singlehood. According to psychologist Joanna Gutmann, a counselor at the University of Chicago, asexual couplings are increasingly common. Gen X men and women may share beds without ever having sex, or they may start out in a sexual relationship and then eventually shift to a comfy, asexual living-together relationship for the sake of companionship and convenience. Passionate, romantic love between young men and women is increasingly rare, says Gutmann.

By the time they reach their late twenties, many educated women in 25 urban areas complain that all the good men are "taken" (or not available because they are gay). Some single women find it easier to hook up with different people for different purposes. "It doesn't make sense to rely on one person to meet all your needs," one 28-year-old woman told me. "Our generation diversifies. We might have one person for sex, one to go out club-hopping, another to share thoughts and feelings." Comradeship has replaced courtship and marriage as the preferred path to intimacy. To use a political metaphor, the aspiration to union has been abandoned for the more modest goal of confederacy.

Two decades after the girlhood project began, it may be judged not 26 only by its aspirations but also by its decidedly mixed results. In important respects, it has improved the lot of girls. Adolescent girls now receive more serious mentoring attention from important men in their lives, including fathers, teachers, and coaches. Their participation in sports prepares them for a work world still largely shaped by male codes of conduct rooted in competition, combat, and conquest. More importantly, they are no longer bound by the marriage-and-motherhood script. They are free to follow their own desires as they make choices about their work and private lives.

At the same time, the girlhood project has shortchanged young 27 women. The passage from girlhood to womanhood now entails a remarkably strenuous effort to transcend biology. Most girls are not cut out to be to be tomboys forever. Too often now, normal female physical and psychological maturation is taken as a problem, a worrisome sign that girls are "falling behind boys."

Today, all that is naturally womanly—especially anything related 28 to childbearing—is treated by elites as something to be managed, minimized, and somehow overcome. Nearly all women still want motherhood, but they have grown up with the idea that it is a trauma that must be "worked into" a career. The only trouble-free times in the female life course are now defined as the periods when women are least connected to their womanliness: in childhood and again in old age. A woman's life between ages 10 and 60 has been medicalized and problematized, with a host of products and technologies like birth control and abortion, hormone replacement therapy, and cosmetic surgery being offered to ward off or manage what is natural. Is it any wonder that Gen X women look at adult life with a measure of fear and trembling?

The attempt to remake American girlhood is deeply connected to 29 feminist aspirations. So how are feminists responding to signs of trouble popping up among Generation Xers? Many are ringing alarm bells—and blaming society or men. Others are urging their fellow feminists to offer more personal guidance to the young. Liberal women, say Brumberg and others, must make a new commitment to girl advocacy.

More mentoring is a worthwhile goal, but the state of American girl- 30 hood won't improve unless older feminists acknowledge their own responsibility for creating some of the difficulties today's young women face. To begin, women may have to confront their own anxieties about body image. Many American girls now grow up with mothers who are dieting, working out, and always complaining about their bodies. Indeed, it is often mothers who feel shame over their daughters' weight gains in puberty and rush their 11-year-olds to a fat camp or a pediatrician for a medically supervised diet.

Older feminist women, not the patriarchy, also edit the fashion mag- 31 azines girls so eagerly consult. Nowhere else on a newsstand will you find as much body worship and emphasis on dress and dieting, or as many models made up like drug-addled prostitutes, or as many articles romanticizing casual sex. The same magazines are obsessed with money, things, and the trappings of celebrity. They assume every girl is focused on her self and her sex life, rather than her family and community, and they ignore any topic of civic, religious, or intellectual seriousness.

In addition, the firsthand models that today's girls grow up with are 32 too often no more responsible or inspiring than this magazine fare. Revisionist feminists themselves acknowledge that it is the nice progressive parents of Gen Xers who turned self-actualization, divorce, live-in lovers, the drug habit (stretching from pot to Prozac), latch-key childhood, New Age therapies, and feel-good morals into mass phenomena.

Older women who aspire to be advocates to today's girls ought to 33 consult the desires of the girls themselves. They will find that, more than sex, girls are interested in love and the business of finding a male worthy of love. Contemporary liberal institutions give these girls hundreds of books and articles devoted to the mechanics of sex, and many warnings about the dangers of penises not wearing condoms, but almost no information about how to make a life with the boys attached to them.

Older women must recognize that their feminist critique of 1950s 34 girlhood, which inspired the effort to remake female upbringing, may not fit the realities of girls' lives now. Maybe the problem then was the tyranny of the feminine mystique. But the solution today is not a more unnatural and therefore even more tyrannical masculine mystique.

Responding to Reading

1. In paragraph 6, Whitehead introduces three feminist writers—Mary Pipher, Naomi Wolf, and Joan Jacobs Brumberg—whose theories and findings she refers to later in her essay. How does she evaluate the ideas of these writers? Does she accept their views?

2. What is the "girlhood project"? What problems does Whitehead believe this "project" has caused?

3. Why, according to Whitehead, do "Gen X women look at adult life with a measure of fear and trembling" (28)? Whom does she blame for the problems faced by Gen X women? Where does she believe the solution to these problems lies? Do you agree with her?

The performance gap between boys and girls in high school leads 9
directly to the growing gap between male and female admissions to college. The Department of Education reports that in 1996 there were 8.4
million women but only 6.7 million men enrolled in college. It predicts
that women will hold on to and increase their lead well into the next
decade, and that by 2007 the numbers will be 9.2 million women and 6.9
million men.

Deconstructing the Test-Score Gap

Feminists cannot deny that girls get better grades, are more engaged 10
academically, and are now the majority sex in higher education. They
argue, however, that these advantages are hardly decisive. Boys, they
point out, get higher scores than girls on almost every significant standardized test—especially the Scholastic Assessment Test and law school,
medical school, and graduate school admissions tests.

In 1996 I wrote an article for *Education Week* about the many ways in 11
which girl students were moving ahead of boys. Seizing on the test-score
data that suggest boys are doing better than girls, David Sadker, a professor of education at American University and a co-author with his wife,
Myra, of *Failing at Fairness: How America's Schools Cheat Girls* (1994), wrote,
"If females are soaring in school, as Christina Hoff Sommers writes, then
these tests are blind to their flight." On the 1998 SAT boys were thirty-five
points (out of 800) ahead of girls in math and seven points ahead in
English. These results seem to run counter to all other measurements of
achievement in school. In almost all other areas boys lag behind girls.
Why do they test better? Is Sadker right in suggesting that this is a mani-
festation of boys' privileged status?

The answer is no. A careful look at the pool of students who take the 12
SAT and similar tests shows that the girls' lower scores have little or
nothing to do with bias or unfairness. Indeed, the scores do not even
signify lower achievement by girls. First of all, according to *College
Bound Seniors*, an annual report on standardized-test takers published
by the College Board, many more "at risk" girls than "at risk" boys take
the SAT—girls from lower-income homes or with parents who never
graduated from high school or never attended college. "These characteristics," the report says, "are associated with lower than average SAT
scores." Instead of wrongly using SAT scores as evidence of bias against
girls, scholars should be concerned about the boys who never show up
for the tests they need if they are to move on to higher education.

Another factor skews test results so that they appear to favor boys. 13
Nancy Cole, the president of the Educational Testing Service, calls it the
"spread" phenomenon. Scores on almost any intelligence or achievement test are more spread out for boys than for girls—boys include

more prodigies and more students of marginal ability. Or, as the political scientist James Q. Wilson once put it, "There are more male geniuses and more male idiots."

Boys also dominate dropout lists, failure lists, and learning-disability lists. Students in these groups rarely take college-admissions tests. On the other hand, exceptional boys who take school seriously show up in disproportionately high numbers for standardized tests. Gender-equity activists like Sadker ought to apply their logic consistently: if the shortage of girls at the high end of the ability distribution is evidence of unfairness to girls, then the excess of boys at the low end should be deemed evidence of unfairness to boys.   14

Suppose we were to turn our attention away from the highly motivated, self-selected two fifths of high school students who take the SAT and consider instead a truly representative sample of American schoolchildren. How would girls and boys then compare? Well, we have the answer. The National Assessment of Educational Progress started in 1969 and mandated by Congress, offers the best and most comprehensive measure of achievement among students at all levels of ability. Under the NAEP program 70,000 to 100,000 students, drawn from forty-four states, are tested in reading, writing, math, and science at ages nine, thirteen, and seventeen. In 1996, seventeen-year-old boys outperformed seventeen-year-old girls by five points in math and eight points in science, whereas the girls outperformed the boys by fourteen points in reading and seventeen points in writing. In the past few years girls have been catching up in math and science while boys have continued to lag far behind in reading and writing.   15

In the July, 1995, issue of *Science*, Larry V. Hedges and Amy Nowell, researchers at the University of Chicago, observed that girls' deficits in math were small but not insignificant. These deficits, they noted, could adversely affect the number of women who "excel in scientific and technical occupations." Of the deficits in boys' writing skills they wrote, "The large sex differences in writing . . . are alarming . . . . The data imply that males are, on average, at a rather profound disadvantage in the performance of this basic skill." They went on to warn,   16

> The generally larger numbers of males who perfom near the bottom of the distribution on reading comprehension and writing also have policy implications. It seems likely that individuals with such poor literacy skills will have difficulty finding employment in an increasingly information-driven economy. Thus, some intervention may be required to enable them to participate constructively.

Hedges and Nowell were describing a serious problem of national scope, but because the focus elsewhere has been on girls' deficits, few Americans know much about the problem or even suspect that it exists.

Indeed, so accepted has the myth of girls in crisis become that even 17
teachers who work daily with male and female students tend to reflexively dismiss any challenge to the myth, or any evidence pointing to the
very real crisis among boys. Three years ago Scarsdale High School, in
New York, held a gender-equity workshop for faculty members. It was
the standard girls-are-being-shortchanged fare, with one notable difference. A male student gave a presentation in which he pointed to evidence
suggesting that girls at Scarsdale High were well ahead of boys. David
Greene, a social-studies teacher, thought the student must be mistaken,
but when he and some colleagues analyzed department grading patterns,
they discovered that the student was right. They found little or no difference in the grades of boys and girls in advanced- placement social-studies classes. But in standard classes the girls were doing a lot better.

And Greene discovered one other thing: few wanted to hear about 18
his startling findings. Like schools everywhere, Scarsdale High has been
strongly influenced by the belief that girls are systematically deprived.
That belief prevails among the school's gender-equity committee and
has led the school to offer a special senior elective on gender equity.
Greene has tried to broach the subject of male underperformance with
his colleagues. Many of them concede that in the classes they teach, the
girls seem to be doing better than the boys, but they do not see this as
part of a larger pattern. After so many years of hearing about silenced,
diminished girls, teachers do not take seriously the suggestion that boys
are not doing as well as girls even if they see it with their own eyes in
their own classrooms.

Responding to Reading

1. In paragraph 4, Sommers states her essay's thesis: "That girls are treated as
   the second sex in school and consequently suffer, that boys are accorded
   privileges and consequently benefit—these are things everyone is presumed to know. But they are not true." Do you agree that the supposed
   privileged position of boys is "something everyone is presumed to know"?
   Do you accept it as true?
2. Paragraph 6 of this essay presents a long list of areas in which "girls outshine
   boys." Compare this paragraph with the first three paragraphs of Barbara
   Dafoe Whitehead's pessimistic portrait of the women of Generation X
   (p. 372). Is it possible that both writers' observations are accurate? Explain.
3. Sommers believes that "the myth of girls in crisis" is so entrenched that
   "even teachers who work daily with male and female students tend to
   reflexively dismiss any challenge" (to it). If what she says is true, would you
   expect this belief among teachers to benefit boys or girls in the long run?
   Why?

THE FUTURE OF MEN

Susan Faludi

Susan Faludi (1959–   ) majored in history and literature at Harvard University and was managing editor of the campus newspaper, the Harvard Crimson, *when it broke a major story involving sexual harassment on campus. Later, working for the* Wall Street Journal, *Faludi won a Pulizer Prize for journalism for a story on price gouging by a supermarket chain. An ardent feminist, Faludi wrote the highly controversial 1991 book* Backlash: The Undeclared War on Women, *in which she argued that the strides women had been making toward equality were being deliberately undercut by politicians and the media. Most recently, she published* Stiffed: The Betrayal of the American Man *(1999), a look at how contemporary society has short-changed working-class men. The following essay, published online by* MSN, *is adapted from that book.*

Angry White Males. Deadbeat Dads. Boys Behaving Badly. Road 1 Rage. A man shoots up a day-trading brokerage. Another man shoots up a Jewish day-care center. Some boys shoot up schoolyards across the country. Men's suicide rate climbs; their incomes stagnate; and Madison Avanue aims magazines and cosmetics to what advertisers call "the new Neanderthal." What's the matter with men, anyway?

That seem to be the question on the media's mind. And the media— 2 along with pundits, politicans and pop psychologists—have offered one reason over and over. It's women's fault. Or, more specifically, it's those feminists who "took men's power away." Boys behaving badly? That's because the campaign to lift girls' self-confidence has "damaged" boys' self-esteem. (Feminists attitudes can "create boys that are either murderous of suicidal," the authors of *Raising a Son* warn typically.) Deadbeat dads? That's because women are taking away the man's "right" to rule the roost. (Get rid of those "feminist" laws that make divorce too easy, conservatives urge.) Men going postal? That's because the p.c. police give all the good jobs to gals. (Let's ban affirmative action, some opinion-makers clamor.

No wonder so many men conclude women are the enemy. "The 3 male gender has taken a back seat across the board," James Lawrence, a laid-off aerospace engineer, said to me. "Women have taken a very masculine role in American society." His view is widely shared. You hear it from the left when New Age men's movement members fret that feminists have created the "soft male." You hear it on right, when "angry white male" voters blame their troubles on feminism led by that superfeminist, Hiliary Clinton. Some conspiracy-minded militiamen I talked to even fault the president's wife for the fiery deaths of the Branch Dividians in Waco, Texas.

When someone starts seeing enemies everywhere, even in the most 4
unlikely places, it's a sure sign he's in crisis. Mark Barton, the day trader
who went on a murderous rampage in Atlanta the summer after he lost
more than $100,000 in the stock market, left a note saying he bludgeoned
his wife "because she was one of the main reasons for my demise." But,
as he conceded in the same note, he knew she wasn't the source of his
agony.

By the same token, women's independence isn't the cause of most 5
men's problems. Working women aren't hogging the best jobs: Two-
thirds are still in service, sales or clerical posts. Women aren't flinging
off wedding rings to become high-flying careerists: Single mothers suffer a poverty rate three times the national rate, and 61 percent of ex
homemakers live at or below the poverty line. Boys aren't bringing guns
to school because feminists created "Take Our Daughters to Work Day."
And let's get real, Hiliary Clinton did not snatch away an entire nation's
manhood.

Yet, men do feel "feminized," as many men I interviewed put it. 6
And with good reason. They have been feminized—just not by women.
The source of their troubles lies elswhere: in a celebrity-driven, con-
sumer culture that has stripped them of an old-fashioned masculinity.

American manhood has traditionally been defined by proving one- 7
self useful to society—from Daniel Boone building a wilderness community, to G.I.s restoring democracy, to the average man plying an essential
craft that gave him a sense of honor. But we are passing from a utilitarian
society, where people's public service is needed and so valued, to a consumer, celebrity-saturated culture where people's credit cards, display
value and marketable fame seem to be all that's recognized.

So many men feel useless, trapped in an ornamental world where 8
only the most marketable "brand name" wins. That's why many men
feel, as one sports fan termed it to me, "stiffed." He and his fellow Cleveland Browns fans once were useful boosters, supporting their team with
their loyalty; now they were just props in a television marketing spectacle, and when the team got a richer deal from another city, the loyal fans
go jilted. The few men who succeed in the new ornamental game don't
feel much better—they suspect they've been feminized, too. Even that
bulging-pecs icon of ornamental masculinity, Sylvester Stallone, tried to
quit doing action in films because, as he told me, he felt imprisoned in the
"feminine mystique," where "everything is a display."

Men's crisis, ironically, is the same one that beset women after World 9
War II, when they were booted from the workplace and told to find true
womanhood by shopping, decorating and sporting the New Look.
Women finally revolted—with a movement that demanded useful roles
for their sex, liberating millions to pursue work and public service meaningful to them and society. The last great revival of the women's movement in the '60 and '70s was largely a response to the onslaught of

commercial, consumer culture that told women they should define themselves by ads for hair spray and Lemon Pledge and feminie hygiene products.

When men say they feel "feminized," they mean they are being 10 increasingly confined by that ornamental surface femininity that women rebelled against. Which is why, far from being men's worst enemy, feminism could be men's greatest ally. Because the most recent wave of feminism was women's attempt to fight the forces that now have men by the throat, feminists have experienced lessons that they can impart to their brothers. As the one movement based on the recognition that useful, public roles are essential to being fully human, feminism may be men's best hope to restore a meaningful, thriving manhood.

Responding to Reading

1. According to Faludi, who or what do the media and politicians blame for the depressing picture of men she presents in paragraph 1? Does Faludi agree with this interpretation? Do you? Would Christina Hoff Sommers (p. 380)?

2. In paragraph 6, Faludi asserts that many men feel "feminized"; in paragraph 8, she states that many men feel "stiffed." What does she mean by the terms *feminized* and *stiffed*? How does she account for these feelings?

3. How, according to Faludi, can feminism be "men's greatest ally" (10)? Do you think she is right, or do you think she is being too optimistic? Do you see another solution to the problems men face?

more powerful and hopeful than yours. But why should I mourn at the untimely fate of my people? Tribe follows tribe, and nation follows nation, like the waves of the sea. It is the order of nature, and regret is useless. Your time of decay may be distant, but it will surely come, for even the White Man whose God walked and talked with him as friend with friend cannot be exempt from the common destiny. We may be brothers after all. We will see. . . .

Every part of this soil is sacred in the estimation of my people. 6 Every hillside, every valley, every plain and grove, has been hallowed by some sad or happy event in days long vanished. The very dust upon which you now stand responds more lovingly to their footsteps than to yours, because it is rich with the blood of our ancestors and our bare feet are conscious of the sympathetic touch. Even the little children who lived here and rejoiced here for a brief season will love these somber solitudes and at eventide they greet shadowy returning spirits. And when the last Red Man shall have perished, and the memory of my tribe shall have become a myth among the White Men, these shores will swarm with the invisible dead of my tribe, and when your children's children think themselves alone in the field, the store, the shop, upon the highway, or in the silence of the pathless woods, they will not be alone. At night when the streets of your cities and villages are silent and you think them deserted, they will throng with the returning hosts that once filled and still love this beautiful land. The White Man will never be alone.

Let him be just and deal kindly with my people, for the dead are not 7 powerless. Dead, did I say? There is no death, only a change of worlds.

Responding to Reading

1. The point is made in paragraph 2 that Native Americans and whites are "two distinct races with separate origins and separate destinies." What differences are then identified? Are there any similarities?

2. Is the speech's tone primarily hopeful, resigned, conciliatory, angry, or bitter? What dreams, if any, does the speech suggest for Chief Seattle's people? Do you think these dreams have been realized?

3. Paragraph 5 offers the observation, "We may be brothers after all. We will see." What do you suppose Chief Seattle means?

WHY THE AMERICANS ARE SO RESTLESS IN THE MIDST OF THEIR PROSPERITY

Alexis de Tocqueville

Historian and political scientist Alexis de Tocqueville (1805–1859) was born in Verneuil, France. After studying law, he entered politics and later went on to serve in the Chamber of Deputies and as minister of foreign affairs. In 1831, the French government sent him on a mission to the United States to draft a report on the penal system. His stay led him to write an important book about life in early America, De la Démocratie en Amerique *(1835), which was translated as* Democracy in America *and published here between 1835 and 1840. In this book, de Tocqueville examined American political and social institutions of the time, as well as what he saw as the character of the American people. Long considered a classic of political science, the book continues to be an important source for scholars and politicians. The following essay, Chapter 13 of* Democracy in America, *suggests why de Tocqueville's work continues to be so relevant.*

In certain remote corners of the Old World you may still sometimes 1 stumble upon a small district that seems to have been forgotten amid the general tumult, and to have remained stationary while everything around it was in motion. The inhabitants, for the most part, are extremely ignorant and poor; they take no part in the business of the country and are frequently oppressed by the government, yet their countenances are generally placid and their spirits light.

In America I saw the freest and most enlightened men placed in the 2 happiest circumstances that the world affords; it seemed to me as if a cloud habitually hung upon their brow, and I thought them serious and almost sad, even in their pleasures.

The chief reason for this contrast is that the former do not think of the 3 ills they endure, while the latter are forever brooding over advantages they do not possess. It is strange to see with what feverish ardor the Americans pursue their own welfare, and to watch the vague dread that constantly torments them lest they should not have chosen the shortest path which may lead to it.

A native of the United States clings to this world's goods as if he 4 were certain never to die; and he is so hasty in grasping at all within his reach that one would suppose he was constantly afraid of not living long enough to enjoy them. He clutches everything, he holds nothing fast, but soon loosens his grasp to pursue fresh gratifications.

In the United States a man builds a house in which to spend his old 5 age, and he sells it before the roof is on; he plants a garden and lets it just as the trees are coming into bearing; he brings a field into tillage and leaves other men to gather the crops; he embraces a profession and gives it up; he settles in a place, which he soon afterwards leaves to carry his changeable longings elsewhere. If his private affairs leave him any leisure, he instantly plunges into the vortex of politics; and if at the end of a year of unremitting labor he finds he has a few days' vacation, his eager curiosity whirls him over the vast extent of the United States, and he will travel fifteen hundred miles in a few days to shake off his happiness. Death at length overtakes him, but it is before he is weary of his bootless chase of that complete felicity which forever escapes him.

At first sight there is something surprising in this strange unrest of so many happy men, restless in the midst of abundance. The spectacle itself, however, is as old as the world; the novelty is to see a whole people furnish an exemplification of it. 6

Their taste for physical gratifications must be regarded as the original source of that secret disquietude which the actions of the Americans betray and of that inconstancy of which they daily afford fresh examples. He who has set his heart exclusively upon the pursuit of worldly welfare is always in a hurry, for he has but a limited time at his disposal to reach, to grasp, and to enjoy it. The recollection of the shortness of life is a constant spur to him. Besides the good things that he possesses, he every instant fancies a thousand others that death will prevent him from trying if he does not try them soon. This thought fills him with anxiety, fear, and regret and keeps his mind in ceaseless trepidation, which leads him perpetually to change his plans and his abode. 7

If in addition to the taste for physical well-being a social condition be added in which neither laws nor customs retain any person in his place, there is a great additional stimulant to this restlessness of temper. Men will then be seen continually to change their track for fear of missing the shortest cut to happiness. 8

It may readily be conceived that if men passionately bent upon physical gratifications desire eagerly, they are also easily discouraged; as their ultimate object is to enjoy, the means to reach that object must be prompt and easy or the trouble of acquiring the gratification would be greater than the gratification itself. Their prevailing frame of mind, then, is at once ardent and relaxed, violent and enervated. Death is often less dreaded by them than perseverance in continuous efforts to one end. 9

The equality of conditions leads by a still straighter road to several of the effects that I have here described. When all the privileges of birth and fortune are abolished, when all professions are accessible to all, and a man's own energies may place him at the top of any one of them, an easy and unbounded career seems open to his ambition and he will readily persuade himself that he is born to no common destinies. But this is an erroneous notion, which is corrected by daily experience. The same equality that allows every citizen to conceive these lofty hopes renders all the citizens less able to realize them; it circumscribes their powers on every side, while it gives freer scope to their desires. Not 10 only are they themselves powerless, but they are met at every step by immense obstacles, which they did not at first perceive. They have swept away the privileges of some of their fellow creatures which stood in their way, but they have opened the door to universal competition; the barrier has changed its shape rather than its position. When men are nearly alike and all follow the same track, it is very difficult for any one individual to walk quickly and cleave a way through the dense throng that surrounds and presses on him. This constant strife between the inclination springing from the equality of condition and the means it supplies to satisfy them harasses and wearies the mind.

It is possible to conceive of men arrived at a degree of freedom that should completely content them; they would then enjoy their independence without anxiety and without impatience. But men will never establish any equality with which they can be contented. Whatever efforts a people may make, they will never succeed in reducing all the conditions of society to a perfect level; and even if they unhappily attained that absolute and complete equality of position, the inequality of minds would still remain, which, coming directly from the hand of God, will forever escape the laws of man. However democratic, then, the social state and the political constitution of a people may be, it is certain that every member of the community will always find out several points about him which overlook his own position; and we may foresee that his looks will be doggedly fixed in that direction. When inequality of conditions is the common law of society, the most marked inequalities do not strike the eye; when everything is nearly on the same level, the slightest are marked enough to hurt it. Hence the desire of equality always becomes more insatiable in proportion as equality is more complete.

Among democratic nations, men easily attain a certain equality of condition, but they can never attain as much as they desire. It perpetually retires from before them, yet without hiding itself from their sight, and in retiring draws them on. At every moment they think they are about to grasp it; it escapes at every moment from their hold. They are near enough to see its charms, but too far off to enjoy them; and before they have fully tasted its delights, they die.

To these causes must be attributed that strange melancholy which often haunts the inhabitants of democratic countries in the midst of their abundance, and that disgust at life which sometimes seizes upon them in the midst of calm and easy circumstances. Complaints are made in France that the number of suicides increases; in America suicide is rare, but insanity is said to be more common there than anywhere else. These are all different symptoms of the same disease. The Americans do not put an end to their lives, however disquieted they may be, because their religion forbids it; and among them materialism may be said hardly to exist, notwithstanding the general passion for physical gratification. The will resists, but reason frequently gives way.

an ambition was beyond my capabilities. Well-to-do Negroes lived in a world that was almost as alien to me as the world inhabited by whites.

What, then, was there? I held my life in my mind, in my conscious- 95 ness each day, feeling at times that I would stumble and drop it, spill it forever. My reading had created a vast sense of distance between me and the world in which I lived and tried to make a living, and that sense of distance was increasing each day. My days and nights were one long, quiet, continuously contained dream of terror, tension, and anxiety. I wondered how long I could bear it.

Responding to Reading

1. In what sense did access to books bring Wright closer to achieving the American Dream? What new obstacles did books introduce?
2. In paragraph 74, Wright mentions his "Jim Crow station in life." The term *Jim Crow*, derived from a character in a minstrel show, refers to laws enacted in southern states that legalized racial segregation. What is Wright's "station in life"? In what ways does he adapt his behavior to accommodate this Jim Crow image? In what ways does he defy this stereotype?
3. After World War II, Wright left the United States to live in Paris. Given what you have read in this essay, does his decision surprise you? Do you think he made the right choice?

AMERICAN DREAMER
Bharati Mukherjee

Novelist and short-story writer Bharati Mukherjee (1940–   ) was born in Calcutta, India, and attended the university there. In 1961, she came to the United States to attend the University of Iowa, where she received an M.F.A. degree in creative writing. In 1963, she married a fellow student, an American of Canadian parentage, thus gaining U.S. citizenship. She and her husband lived in Canada for fourteen years, where she taught at McGill University. A U.S. resident since then, she is currently on the faculty at the University of California at Berkeley. Much of Mukherjee's fiction deals with the conflicts faced by Indian immigrants in North America as they attempt to embrace a new culture that does not always embrace them in return. Among her novels are Tiger's Daughter *(1972),* Wife *(1975),* Jasmine *(1989),* The Holder of the World *(1993), and* Leave It to Me *(1997). Her short-story collection* The Middleman and Other Stories *(1988) won the National Book Critics Circle Award. An avowed assimilationist, Mukherjee has written, "My books have often been read as unapologetic (and in some quarters overenthusiastic) texts for cultural and psychological*

'mongrelization.' It's a word I celebrate." In the following essay, written in
1997, she celebrates her "American dream" of diverse cultures coming
together "as a constantly reforming, transmogrifying 'we.'"

The United States exists as a sovereign Nation. "America," in con- 1
trast, exists as a myth of democracy and equal opportunity to live by, or
as an ideal goal to reach.

I am a naturalized U.S. citizen, which means that, unlike native-born 2
citizens, I had to prove to the U.S. government that I merited citizenship.
What I didn't have to disclose was that I desired "America," which to me
is the stage for the drama of self-transformation.

I was born in Calcutta and first came to the United States—to Iowa 3
City, to be precise—on a summer evening in 1961. I flew into a small airport surrounded by cornfields and pastures, ready to carry out the two
commands my father had written out for me the night before I left
Calcutta: Spend two years studying creative writing at the Iowa Writers'
Workshop, then come back home and marry the bridegroom he selected
for me from our caste and class.

In traditional Hindu families like ours, men provided and women 4
were provided for. My father was a patriarch and I a pliant daughter.
The neighborhood I'd grown up in was homogeneously Hindu,
Bengali-speaking, and middle-class. I didn't expect myself to ever disobey or disappoint my father by setting my own goals and taking
charge of my future.

When I landed in Iowa 35 years ago, I found myself in a society in 5
which almost everyone was Christian, white, and moderately well-off.
In the women's dormitory I lived in my first year, apart from six international graduate students (all of us were from Asia and considered
"exotic"), the only non-Christian was Jewish, and the only nonwhite an
African-American from Georgia. I didn't anticipate then, that over the
next 35 years, the Iowa population would become so diverse that it
would have 6,931 children from non-English-speaking homes registered as students in its schools, nor that Iowans would be in the grip of
a cultural crisis in which resentment against immigrants, particularly
refugees from Vietnam, Sudan, and Bosnia, as well as unskilled
Spanish-speaking workers, would become politicized enough to cause
the Immigration and Naturalization Service to open an "enforcement"
office in Cedar Rapids in October for the tracking and deporting of
undocumented aliens.

In Calcutta in the '50s, I heard no talk of "identity crisis"—communal 6
or individual. The concept itself—of a person not knowing who he or she
is—was unimaginable in our hierarchical, classification-obsessed society. One's identity was fixed, derived from religion, caste, patrimony, and
mother tongue. A Hindu Indian's last name announced his or her forefathers' caste and place of origin. A Mukherjee could *only* be a Brahmin

harsh, the overwhelming local sentiment was that vandalism was an "American" crime, and that flogging Fay would deter Singapore youths from becoming "Americanized."

Conversely, in 1994, in Tavares, Florida, the Lake County School 19 Board announced its policy (since overturned) requiring middle school teachers to instruct their students that American culture, by which the board meant European-American culture, is inherently "superior to other foreign or historic cultures." The policy's misguided implication was that culture in the United States has not been affected by the American Indian, African-American, Latin-American, and Asian-American segments of the population. The sinister implication was that our national identity is so fragile that it can absorb diverse and immigrant cultures only by recontextualizing them as deficient.

Our nation is unique in human history in that the founding idea of 20 "America" was in opposition to the tenet that a nation is a collection of like-looking, like-speaking, like-worshiping people. The primary criterion for nationhood in Europe is homogeneity of culture, race, and religion—which has contributed to blood-soaked balkanization[2] in the former Yugoslavia and the former Soviet Union.

America's pioneering European ancestors gave up the easy homo- 21 geneity of their native countries for a new version of utopia. Now, in the 1990s, we have the exciting chance to follow that tradition and assist in the making of a new American culture that differs from both the enforced assimilation of a "melting pot" and the Canadian model of a multicultural "mosaic."

The multicultural mosaic implies a contiguity of fixed, self- 22 sufficient, utterly distinct cultures. Multiculturalism, as it has been practiced in the United States in the past 10 years, implies the existence of a central culture, ringed by peripheral cultures. The fallout of official multiculturalism is the establishment of one culture as the norm and the rest as aberrations. At the same time, the multiculturalist emphasis on race- and ethnicity-based group identity leads to a lack of respect for individual differences within each group, and to vilification of those individuals who place the good of the nation above the interests of their particular racial or ethnic communities.

We must be alert to the dangers of an "us" vs. "them" mentality. In 23 California, this mentality is manifesting itself as increased violence between minority, ethnic communities. The attack on Korean-American merchants in South Central Los Angeles in the wake of the Rodney King beating trial is only one recent example of the tragic side effects of this mentality. On the national level, the politicization of ethnic identities has encouraged the scapegoating of legal immigrants, who are blamed

---

[2] A breakdown into smaller, often hostile, units. [Eds.]

for economic and social problems brought about by flawed domestic and foreign policies.

We need to discourage the retention of cultural memory if the aim of that retention is cultural balkanization. We must think of American culture and nationhood as a constantly reforming, transmogrifying "we." 24

In this age of diasporas, one's biological identity may not be one's only identity. Erosions and accretions come with the act of emigration. The experience of cutting myself off from a biological homeland and settling in an adopted homeland that is not always welcoming to its dark-complexioned citizens has tested me as a person, and made me the writer I am today. 25

I choose to describe myself on my own terms, as an American, rather than as an Asian-American. Why is it that hyphenation is imposed only on nonwhite Americans? Rejecting hyphenation is my refusal to categorize the cultural landscape into a center and its peripheries; it is to demand that the American nation deliver the promises of its dream and its Constitution to all its citizens equally. 26

My rejection of hyphenation has been misrepresented as race treachery by some India-born academics on U.S. campuses who have appointed themselves guardians of the "purity" of ethnic cultures. Many of them, though they reside permanently in the United States and participate in its economy, consistently denounce American ideals and institutions. They direct their rage at me because, by becoming a U.S. citizen and exercising my voting rights, I have invested in the present and not the past; because I have committed myself to help shape the future of my adopted homeland, and because I celebrate racial and cultural mongrelization. 27

What excites me is that as a nation we have not only the chance to retain those values we treasure from our original cultures but also the chance to acknowledge that the outer forms of those values are likely to change. Among Indian immigrants, I see a great deal of guilt about the inability to hang on to what they commonly term "pure culture." Parents express rage or despair at their U.S.-born children's forgetting of, or indifference to, some aspects of Indian culture. Of those parents I would ask: What is it we have lost if our children are acculturating into the culture in which we are living? Is it so terrible that our children are discovering or are inventing homelands for themselves? 28

Some first-generation Indo-Americans, embittered by racism and by unofficial "glass ceilings," construct a phantom identity, more-Indian-than-Indians-in-India, as a defense against marginalization. I ask: Why don't you get actively involved in fighting discrimination? Make your voice heard. Choose the forum most appropriate for you. If you are a 29 citizen, let your vote count. Reinvest your energy and resources into revitalizing your city's disadvantaged residents and neighborhoods. Know your constitutional rights, and when they are violated, use the agencies of redress the Constitution makes available to you. Expect change, and when it comes, deal with it!

As a writer, my literary agenda begins by acknowledging that 30 America has transformed me. It does not end until I show that I (along with the hundreds of thousands of immigrants like me) am minute by minute transforming America. The transformation is a two-way process: It affects both the individual and the national-cultural identity.

Others who write stories of migration often talk of arrival at a new 31 place as a loss, the loss of communal memory and the erosion of an original culture. I want to talk of arrival as gain.

Responding to Reading

1. As a self-described "transient with conflicting loyalties to two very different cultures" (9), the newly married Mukherjee found herself in the midst of an "identity crisis." Has she been able to resolve this crisis? If so, how? Do you think it is possible for a native-born American to suffer a similar identity crisis?
2. In what sense has Mukherjee's immigration been a loss? In what sense has it been a gain? Is she speaking primarily for herself in this essay, or does she mean to speak for immigrants in general? How can you tell?
3. In paragraph 18, Mukherjee says, "Americans see themselves as the embodiments of liberty, openness, and individualism, even as the world judges them for drugs, crime, violence, bigotry, militarism, and homelessness." What is your reaction to this statement? Do you think it is true? Do you think it is fair?

THE MYTH OF THE LATIN WOMAN: I JUST MET A GIRL NAMED MARIA

Judith Ortiz Cofer

Born in Puerto Rico and raised in Paterson, New Jersey, Judith Ortiz Cofer (1952–) is an award-winning poet and novelist as well as an essayist. Her books include the novel The Line of the Sun *(1989);* Silent Dancing *(1990), a collection of biographical essays;* The Latin Deli: Prose and Poetry *(1993); and* The Year of Our Revolution *(1998), a collection for young adult readers. A teacher of creative writing at the University of Georgia, she has said that she began writing because "as a native speaker of Spanish, I first perceived of language, especially the English language, as a barrier, a challenge to be met with the same kind of closed-eyed bravado that prompted me to jump into the deep end of the pool before taking my first swimming lesson." In the following essay from* The Latin Deli, Cofer *describes the stereotypes she has confronted as a Latina.*

On a bus trip to London from Oxford University where I was earn- 1
ing some graduate credits one summer, a young man, obviously fresh
from a pub, spotted me and as if struck by inspiration went down on his
knees in the aisle. With both hands over his heart he broke into an Irish
tenor's rendition of "Maria" from *West Side Story*.[1] My politely amused
fellow passengers gave his lovely voice the round of gentle applause it
deserved. Though I was not quite as amused, I managed my version of
an English smile: no show of teeth, no extreme contortions of the facial
muscles—I was at this time of my life practicing reserve and cool. Oh,
that British control, how I coveted it. But "Maria" had followed me to
London, reminding me of a prime fact of my life: you can leave the
island, master the English language, and travel as far as you can, but if
you are a Latina, especially one like me who so obviously belongs to
Rita Moreno's[2] gene pool, the island travels with you.

This is sometimes a very good thing—it may win you that extra 2
minute of someone's attention. But with some people, the same things
can make *you* an island—not a tropical paradise but an Alcatraz, a place
nobody wants to visit. As a Puerto Rican girl living in the United States[3]
and wanting like most children to "belong," I resented the stereotype
that my Hispanic appearance called forth from many people I met.

Growing up in a large urban center in New Jersey during the 1960s, 3
I suffered from what I think of as "cultural schizophrenia." Our life was
designed by my parents as a microcosm of their *casas*[4] on the island. We
spoke in Spanish, ate Puerto Rican food bought at the *bodega*,[5] and practiced strict Catholicism at a church that allotted us a one-hour slot each
week for mass, performed in Spanish by a Chinese priest trained as a
missionary for Latin America.

As a girl I was kept under strict surveillance by my parents, since 4
my virtue and modesty were, by their cultural equation, the same as
their honor. As a teenager I was lectured constantly on how to behave
as a proper *senorita*. But it was a conflicting message I received, since the
Puerto Rican mothers also encouraged their daughters to look and act
like women and to dress in clothes our Anglo friends and their mothers
found too "mature" and flashy. The difference was, and is, cultural; yet

---

[1] A popular Broadway musical, loosely based on *Romeo and Juliet*, about two rival street gangs, one
Anglo and one Puerto Rican, in New York City.
[2] Puerto Rico–born actress who won an Oscar for her role in the 1960 movie version of *West Side
Story*. [Eds.]
[3] Although it is an island, Puerto Rico is part of the United States (it is a self-governing common-
wealth). [Eds.]
[4] Homes. [Eds.]
[5] Small grocery store. [Eds.]

crossing back and forth between the black and the white worlds. In the fol-
lowing essay, which originally appeared in Ms. *in 1986, Staples talks person-*
ally about white people's images of black men and how he deals with them.

My first victim was a woman—white, well dressed, probably in her   1
early twenties. I came upon her late one evening on a deserted street in
Hyde Park, a relatively affluent neighborhood in an otherwise mean,
impoverished section of Chicago. As I swung onto the avenue behind her,
there seemed to be a discreet, uninflammatory distance between us. Not
so. She cast back a worried glance. To her, the youngish black man—a
broad six feet two inches with a beard and billowing hair, both hands
shoved into the pockets of a bulky military jacket—seemed menacingly
close. After a few more quick glimpses, she picked up her pace and was
soon running in earnest. Within seconds she disappeared into a cross
street.

That was more than a decade ago. I was 22 years old, a graduate stu-   2
dent newly arrived at the University of Chicago. It was in the echo of that
terrified woman's footfalls that I first began to know the unwieldy inher-
itance I'd come into—the ability to alter public space in ugly ways. It was
clear that she thought herself the quarry of a mugger, a rapist, or worse.
Suffering a bout of insomnia, however, I was stalking sleep, not defense-
less wayfarers. As a softy who is scarcely able to take a knife to a raw
chicken—let alone hold it to a person's throat—I was surprised, embarrassed, and dismayed all at once. Her flight made me feel like an accom-
plice in tyranny. It also made it clear that I was indistinguishable from the
muggers who occasionally seeped into the area from the surrounding
ghetto. That first encounter, and those that followed, signified that a vast,
unnerving gulf lay between nighttime pedestrians—particularly
women—and me. And I soon gathered that being perceived as dangerous
is a hazard in itself. I only needed to turn a corner into a dicey situation,
or crowd some frightened, armed person in a foyer somewhere, or make
an errant move after being pulled over by a policeman. Where fear and
weapons meet—and they often do in urban America—there is always the
possibility of death.

In that first year, my first away from my hometown, I was to   3
become thoroughly familiar with the language of fear. At dark, shadowy intersections in Chicago, I could cross in front of a car stopped at a
traffic light and elicit the *thunk, thunk, thunk, thunk* of the driver—black,
white, male, or female—hammering down the door locks. On less traveled streets after dark, I grew accustomed to but never comfortable with
people who crossed to the other side of the street rather than pass me.
Then there were the standard unpleasantries with police, doormen,
bouncers, cab drivers, and others whose business it is to screen out troublesome individuals *before* there is any nastiness.

I moved to New York nearly two years ago and I have remained an 4 avid night walker. In central Manhattan, the near-constant crowd cover minimizes tense one-on-one street encounters. Elsewhere—visiting friends in SoHo, where sidewalks are narrow and tightly spaced buildings shut out the sky—things can get very taut indeed.

Black men have a firm place in New York mugging literature. 5 Norman Podhoretz in his famed (or infamous) 1963 essay, "My Negro Problem—And Ours," recalls growing up in terror of black males; they "were tougher than we were, more ruthless," he writes—and as an adult on the Upper West Side of Manhattan, he continues, he cannot constrain his nervousness when he meets black men on certain streets. Similarly, a decade later, the essayist and novelist Edward Hoagland extols a New York where once "Negro bitterness bore down mainly on other Negroes." Where some see mere panhandlers, Hoagland sees "a mugger who is clearly screwing up his nerve to do more than just *ask* for money." But Hoagland has "the New Yorker's quickhunch posture for broken-field maneuvering," and the bad guy swerves away.

I often witness that "hunch posture," from women after dark on the 6 warrenlike streets of Brooklyn where I live. They seem to set their faces on neutral and, with their purse straps strung across their chests bandolier style, they forge ahead as though bracing themselves against being tackled. I understand, of course, that the danger they perceive is not a hallucination. Women are particularly vulnerable to street violence, and young black males are drastically overrepresented among the perpetrators of that violence. Yet these truths are no solace against the kind of alienation that comes of being ever the suspect, against being set apart, a fearsome entity with whom pedestrians avoid making eye contact.

It is not altogether clear to me how I reached the ripe old age of 22 7 without being conscious of the lethality nighttime pedestrians attributed to me. Perhaps it was because in Chester, Pennsylvania, the small, angry industrial town where I came of age in the 1960s, I was scarcely noticeable against a backdrop of gang warfare, street knifings, and murders. I grew up one of the good boys, had perhaps a half-dozen fist fights. In retrospect, my shyness of combat has clear sources.

Many things go into the making of a young thug. One of those 8 things is the consummation of the male romance with the power to intimidate. An infant discovers that random flailings send the baby bottle flying out of the crib and crashing to the floor. Delighted, the joyful babe repeats those motions again and again, seeking to duplicate the feat. Just so, I recall the points at which some of my boyhood friends were finally seduced by the perception of themselves as tough guys. When a mark cowered and surrendered his money without resistance, myth and reality merged—and paid off. It is, after all, only manly to embrace the power to frighten and intimidate. We, as men, are not supposed to give an inch of our lane on the highway; we are to seize the fighter's edge in work and in play and even in love; we are to be valiant in the face of hostile forces.

Unfortunately, poor and powerless young men seem to take all this 9 nonsense literally. As a boy, I saw countless tough guys locked away; I have since buried several, too. They were babies, really—a teenage cousin, a brother of 22, a childhood friend in his mid-twenties—all gone down in episodes of bravado played out in the streets. I came to doubt the virtues of intimidation early on. I chose, perhaps even unconsciously, to remain a shadow—timid, but a survivor.

The fearsomeness mistakenly attributed to me in public places often 10 has a perilous flavor. The most frightening of these confusions occurred in the late 1970s and early 1980s when I worked as a journalist in Chicago. One day, rushing into the office of a magazine I was writing for with a deadline story in hand, I was mistaken for a burglar. The office manager called security and, with an ad hoc posse, pursued me through the labyrinthine halls, nearly to my editor's door. I had no way of proving who I was. I could only move briskly toward the company of someone who knew me.

Another time I was on assignment for a local paper and killing time 11 before an interview. I entered a jewelry store on the city's affluent Near North Side. The proprietor excused herself and returned with an enormous red Doberman pinscher straining at the end of a leash. She stood, the dog extended toward me, silent to my questions, her eyes bulging nearly out of her head. I took a cursory look around, nodded, and bade her good night. Relatively speaking, however, I never fared as badly as another black male journalist. He went to nearby Waukegan, Illinois, a couple of summers ago to work on a story about a murderer who was born there. Mistaking the reporter for the killer, police hauled him from his car at gunpoint and but for his press credentials would probably have tried to book him. Such episodes are not uncommon. Black men trade tales like this all the time.

In "My Negro Problem—And Ours," Podhoretz writes that the 12 hatred he feels for blacks makes itself known to him through a variety of avenues—one being his discomfort with that "special brand of paranoid touchiness" to which he says blacks are prone. No doubt he is speaking here of black men. In time, I learned to smother the rage I felt at so often being taken for a criminal. Not to do so would surely have led to madness—via that special "paranoid touchiness" that so annoyed Podhoretz at the time he wrote the essay.

I began to take precautions to make myself less threatening. I move 13 about with care, particularly late in the evening. I give a wide berth to nervous people on subway platforms during the wee hours, particularly when I have exchanged business clothes for jeans. If I happen to be entering a building behind some people who appear skittish, I may walk by, letting them clear the lobby before I return, so as not to seem to be following them. I have been calm and extremely congenial on those rare occasions when I've been pulled over by the police.

And on late-evening constitutionals along streets less traveled by, I 14 employ what has proved to be an excellent tension-reducing measure: I whistle melodies from Beethoven and Vivaldi and the more popular classical composers. Even steely New Yorkers hunching toward night-time destinations seem to relax, and occasionally they even join in the tune. Virtually everybody seems to sense that a mugger wouldn't be warbling bright, sunny selections from Vivaldi's *Four Seasons*. It is my equivalent of the cowbell that hikers wear when they know they are in bear country.

Responding to Reading

1. Staples speaks quite matter-of-factly of the fear he inspires. Does your experience support his assumption that black men have the "ability to alter public space (2)"? Why or why not? Do you believe white men also have this ability? Explain.
2. In paragraph 13, Staples suggests some strategies that he believes make him "less threatening." What else, if anything, do you think he could do? Do you believe he *should* adopt such strategies? Explain your position.
3. Although Staples says he arouses fear in others, he also admits that he himself feels fearful. Why? Do you think he has reason to be fearful? What does this sense of fear say about his access to the American Dream?

ON DUMPSTER DIVING

Lars Eighner

When Lars Eighner (1948–) was eighteen years old, his mother threw him out of her house because she found out he was gay. Then a student at the University of Texas at Austin, Eighner began a series of part-time and dead-end jobs that ended in 1988 when he was fired from his position at an Austin mental hospital and soon after evicted from his apartment. At that point he headed for Los Angeles, spending three years homeless on the streets, shuttling between California and Texas with Lizbeth, his Labrador retriever. During his travels, he began to keep a journal, and these entries, along with letters he wrote to a friend, resulted in the remarkable document Travels with Lizbeth: Three Years on the Road and on the Streets *(1993), portions of which had been published previously in several different magazines and journals. In the following chapter from that book, originally published in the* Threepenny Review *in 1991, Eighner takes readers on a graphic yet lyrical voyage through the process of scavenging Dumpsters for food and other necessities.*

This chapter was composed while the author was homeless. The present tense has been preserved.

Long before I began Dumpster diving I was impressed with 1
Dumpsters, enough so that I wrote the Merriam-Webster research service to discover what I could about the word *Dumpster*. I learned from
them that it is a proprietary word belonging to the Dempsey Dumpster
company. Since then I have dutifully capitalized the word, although it
was lowercased in almost all the citations Merriam-Webster photo-
copied for me. Dempsey's word is too apt. I have never heard these
things called anything but Dumpsters. I do not know anyone who
knows the generic name for these objects. From time to time I have
heard a wino or hobo give some corrupted credit to the original and call
them Dipsy Dumpsters.

I began Dumpster diving about a year before I became homeless.   2

I prefer the word *scavenging* and use the word *scrounging* when I 3
mean to be obscure. I have heard people, evidently meaning to be
polite, use the word *foraging*, but I prefer to reserve that word for gathering nuts and berries and such which I do also according to the season
and the opportunity. *Dumpster diving* seems to me to be a little too cute
and, in my case, inaccurate because I lack the athletic ability to lower
myself into the Dumpsters as the true divers do, much to their increased
profit.

I like the frankness of the word *scavenging*, which I can hardly think 4
of without picturing a big black snail on an aquarium wall. I live from
the refuse of others. I am a scavenger. I think it a sound and honorable
niche, although if I could I would naturally prefer to live the comfortable consumer life, perhaps—and only perhaps—as a slightly less
wasteful consumer, owing to what I have learned as a scavenger.

While Lizbeth and I were still living in the shack on Avenue B as my 5
savings ran out, I put almost all my sporadic income into rent. The
necessities of daily life I began to extract from Dumpsters. Yes, we
ate from them. Except for jeans, all my clothes came from Dumpsters.
Boom boxes, candles, bedding, toilet paper, a virgin male love doll,
medicine, books, a typewriter, dishes, furnishings, and change, sometimes amounting to many dollars—I acquired many things from the
Dumpsters.

I have learned much as a scavenger. I mean to put some of what I 6
have learned down here, beginning with the practical art of Dumpster
diving and proceeding to the abstract.

What is safe to eat?   7

After all, the finding of objects is becoming something of an urban 8 art. Even respectable employed people will sometimes find something tempting sticking out of a Dumpster or standing beside one. Quite a number of people, not all of them of the bohemian type, are willing to brag that they found this or that piece in the trash. But eating from Dumpsters is what separates the dilettanti from the professionals. Eating safely from the Dumpsters involves three principles: using the senses and common sense to evaluate the conditions of the found materials, knowing the Dumpsters of a given area and checking them regularly, and seeking always to answer the question "Why was this discarded?"

Perhaps everyone who has a kitchen and a regular supply of gro- 9 ceries has, at one time or another, made a sandwich and eaten half of it before discovering mold on the bread or got a mouthful of milk before realizing the milk had turned. Nothing of the sort is likely to happen to a Dumpster diver because he is constantly reminded that most food is discarded for a reason. Yet a lot of perfectly good food can be found in Dumpsters.

Canned goods, for example, turn up fairly often in the Dumpsters I 10 frequent. All except the most phobic people would be willing to eat from a can, even if it came from a Dumpster. Canned goods are among the safest of foods to be found in Dumpsters but are not utterly foolproof.

Although very rare with modern canning methods, botulism is 11 a possibility. Most other forms of food poisoning seldom do lasting harm to a healthy person, but botulism is most certainly fatal and often the first symptom is death. Except for carbonated beverages, all canned goods should contain a slight vacuum and suck air when first punctured. Bulging, rusty, and dented cans and cans that spew when punctured should be avoided, especially when the contents are not very acidic or syrupy.

Heat can break down the botulin, but this requires much more 12 cooking than most people do to canned goods. To the extent that botulism occurs at all, of course, it can occur in cans on pantry shelves as well as in cans from Dumpsters. Need I say that home-canned goods are simply too risky to be recommended.

From time to time one of my companions, aware of the source of my 13 provisions, will ask, "Do you think these crackers are really safe to eat?" For some reason it is most often the crackers they ask about.

This question has always made me angry. Of course I would not 14 offer my companion anything I had doubts about. But more than that, I wonder why he cannot evaluate the condition of the crackers for himself. I have no special knowledge and I have been wrong before. Since he knows where the food comes from, it seems to me he ought to assume some of the responsibility for deciding what he will put in his mouth. For myself I have few qualms about dry foods such as crackers, cookies, cereal, chips, and pasta if they are free of visible contaminants and still dry and crisp. Most often such things are found in the original packaging, which is not so much a positive sign as it is the absence of a negative one.

Raw fruits and vegetables with intact skins seem perfectly safe to 15 me, excluding of course the obviously rotten. Many are discarded for minor imperfections that can be pared away. Leafy vegetables, grapes, cauliflower, broccoli, and similar things may be contaminated by liquids and may be impractical to wash.

Candy, especially hard candy, is usually safe if it has not drawn 16 ants. Chocolate is often discarded only because it has become discolored as the cocoa butter de-emulsified. Candying, after all, is one method of food preservation because pathogens do not like very sugary substances.

All of these foods might be found in any Dumpster and can be eval- 17 uated with some confidence largely on the basis of appearance. Beyond these are foods that cannot be correctly evaluated without additional information.

I began scavenging by pulling pizzas out of the Dumpster behind a 18 pizza delivery shop. In general, prepared food requires caution, but in this case I knew when the shop closed and went to the Dumpster as soon as the last of the help left.

Such shops often get prank orders; both the orders and the products 19 made to fill them are called *bogus*. Because help seldom stays long at these places, pizzas are often made with the wrong topping, refused on delivery for being cold, or baked incorrectly. The products to be discarded are boxed up because inventory is kept by counting boxes: A boxed pizza can be written off; an unboxed pizza does not exist.

I never placed a bogus order to increase the supply of pizzas and I 20 believe no one else was scavenging in this Dumpster. But the people in the shop became suspicious and began to retain their garbage in the shop overnight. While it lasted I had a steady supply of fresh, sometimes warm pizza. Because I knew the Dumpster I knew the source of the pizza, and because I visited the Dumpster regularly I knew what was fresh and what was yesterday's.

The area I frequent is inhabited by many affluent college students. 21 I am not here by chance; the Dumpsters in this area are very rich. Students throw out many good things, including food. In particular they tend to throw everything out when they move at the end of a semester, before and after breaks, and around midterm, when many of them despair of college. So I find it advantageous to keep an eye on the academic calendar.

Students throw food away around breaks because they do not 22 know whether it has spoiled or will spoil before they return. A typical discard is a half jar of peanut butter. In fact, nonorganic peanut butter does not require refrigeration and is unlikely to spoil in any reasonable time. The student does not know that, and since it is Daddy's money, the student decides not to take a chance. Opened containers require caution and some attention to the question "Why was this discarded?" But in the case of discards from student apartments, the answer may be that the item was thrown out through carelessness, ignorance, or wastefulness. This can sometimes be deduced when the item is found with many others, including some that are obviously perfectly good.

Some students, and others, approach defrosting a freezer by chuck- 23 ing out the whole lot. Not only do the circumstances of such a find tell the story, but also the mass of frozen goods stays cold for a long time and items may be found still frozen or freshly thawed.

Yogurt, cheese, and sour cream are items that are often thrown out 24 while they are still good. Occasionally I find a cheese with a spot of mold, which of course I just pare off, and because it is obvious why such a cheese was discarded, I treat it with less suspicion than an apparently perfect cheese found in similar circumstances. Yogurt is often discarded, still sealed, only because the expiration date on the carton had passed. This is one of my favorite finds because yogurt will keep for several days, even in warm weather.

Students throw out canned goods and staples at the end of semesters 25 and when they give up college at midterm. Drugs, pornography, spirits, and the like are often discarded when parents are expected—Dad's day, for example. And spirits also turn up after big party weekends, presumably discarded by the newly reformed. Wine and spirits, of course, keep perfectly well even once opened, but the same cannot be said of beer.

My test for carbonated soft drinks is whether they still fizz vigor- 26 ously. Many juices or other beverages are too acidic or too syrupy to cause much concern, provided they are not visibly contaminated. I have discovered nasty molds in vegetable juices, even when the product was found under its original seal; I recommend that such products be decanted slowly into a clear glass. Liquids always require some care. One hot day I found a large jug of Pat O'Brien's Hurricane mix. The jug had been opened, but it was still ice cold. I drank three large glasses before it became apparent to me that someone had added the rum to the mix, and not a little rum. I never tasted the rum, and by the time I began to feel the effects I had already ingested a very large quantity of the beverage. Some divers would have considered this a boon, but being suddenly intoxicated in a public place in the early afternoon is not my idea of a good time.

I have heard of people maliciously contaminating discarded food 27 and even handouts, but mostly I have heard of this from people with vivid imaginations who have had no experience with Dumpsters themselves. Just before the pizza shop stopped discarding its garbage at night, jalapeños began showing up on most of the discarded pizzas. If indeed this was meant to discourage me it was a wasted effort because I am native Texan.

For myself, I avoid game, poultry, pork, and egg-based foods, whe- 28 ther I find them raw or cooked. I seldom have the means to cook what I find, but when I do I avail myself of plentiful supplies of beef, which is often in very good condition. I suppose fish becomes disagreeable before it becomes dangerous. Lizbeth is happy to have any such thing that is past its prime and, in fact, does not recognize fish as food until it is quite strong.

Home leftovers, as opposed to surpluses from restaurants, are very 29 often bad. Evidently, especially among students, there is a common type of personality that carefully wraps up even the smallest leftover and shoves it into the back of the refrigerator for six months or so before discarding it. Characteristic of this type are the reused jars and margarine tubs to which the remains are committed. I avoid ethnic foods I am unfamiliar with. If I do not know what it is supposed to look like when it is good, I cannot be certain I will be able to tell if it is bad.

No matter how careful I am I still get dysentery at least once a 30 month, oftener in warm weather. I do not want to paint too romantic a picture. Dumpster diving has serious drawbacks as a way of life.

I learned to scavenge gradually, on my own. Since then I have initi- 31 ated several companions into the trade. I have learned that there is a predictable series of stages a person goes through in learning to scavenge.

At first the new scavenger is filled with disgust and self-loathing. 32 He is ashamed of being seen and may lurk around, trying to duck behind things, or he may try to dive at night. (In fact, most people instinctively look away from a scavenger. By skulking around, the novice calls attention to himself and arouses suspicion. Diving at night is ineffective and needlessly messy.)

Every grain of rice seems to be a maggot. Everything seems to stink. 33 He can wipe the egg yolk off the found can, but he cannot erase from his mind the stigma of eating garbage.

That stage passes with experience. The scavenger finds a pair of 34 running shoes that fit and look and smell brand-new. He finds a pocket calculator in perfect working order. He finds pristine ice cream, still frozen, more than he can eat or keep. He begins to understand: People throw away perfectly good stuff, a lot of perfectly good stuff.

At this stage, Dumpster shyness begins to dissipate. The diver, after 35 all, has the last laugh. He is finding all manner of good things that are his for the taking. Those who disparage his profession are the fools, not he.

He may begin to hang on to some perfectly good things for which he 36 has neither a use nor a market. Then he begins to take note of the things that are not perfectly good but are nearly so. He mates a Walkman with broken earphones and one that is missing a battery cover. He picks up things that he can repair.

At this stage he may become lost and never recover. Dumpsters are 37 full of things of some potential value to someone and also of things that never have much intrinsic value but are interesting. All the Dumpster divers I have known come to the point of trying to acquire everything they touch. Why not take it, they reason, since it is all free? This is, of course, hopeless. Most divers come to realize that they must restrict themselves to items of relatively immediate utility. But in some cases the diver simply cannot control himself. I have met several of these pack-rat types. Their ideas of the values of various pieces of junk verge on the psychotic. Every bit of glass may be a diamond, they think, and all that glistens, gold.

I tend to gain weight when I am scavenging. Partly this is because I 38 always find far more pizza and doughnuts than water-packed tuna, nonfat yogurt, and fresh vegetables. Also I have not developed much faith in the reliability of Dumpsters as a food source, although it has been proven to me many times. I tend to eat as if I have no idea where my next meal is coming from. But mostly I just hate to see food go to waste and so I eat much more than I should. Something like this drives the obsession to collect junk.

As for collecting objects, I usually restrict myself to collecting one 39 kind of small object at a time, such as pocket calculators, sunglasses, or campaign buttons. To live on the street I must anticipate my needs to a certain extent: I must pick up and save warm bedding I find in August because it will not be found in Dumpsters in November. As I have no access to health care, I often hoard essential drugs, such as antibiotics and antihistamines. (This course can be recommended only to those with some grounding in pharmacology. Antibiotics, for example, even when indicated are worse than useless if taken in insufficient amounts.) But even if I had a home with extensive storage space, I could not save everything that might be valuable in some contingency.

I have proprietary feelings about my Dumpsters. As I have men- 40 tioned, it is no accident that I scavenge from ones where good finds are common. But my limited experience with Dumpsters in other areas suggests to me that even in poorer areas, Dumpsters, if attended with sufficient diligence, can be made to yield a livelihood. The rich students discard perfectly good kiwifruit; poorer people discard perfectly good apples. Slacks and Polo shirts are found in the one place; jeans and T-shirts in the other. The population of competitors rather than the affluence of the dumpers most affects the feasibility of survival by scavenging. The large number of competitors is what puts me off the idea of trying to scavenge in places like Los Angeles.

Curiously, I do not mind my direct competition, other scavengers, 41 so much as I hate the can scroungers.

People scrounge cans because they have to have a little cash. I have 42
tried scrounging cans with an able-bodied companion. Afoot a can
scrounger simply cannot make more than a few dollars a day. One can
extract the necessities of life from the Dumpsters directly with far less
effort than would be required to accumulate the equivalent value in
cans. (These observations may not hold in places with container
redemption laws.)

Can scroungers, then, are people who must have small amounts of 43
cash. These are drug addicts and winos, mostly the latter because the
amounts of cash are so small. Spirits and drugs do, like all other commodities, turn up in Dumpsters and the scavenger will from time to
time have a half bottle of a rather good wine with his dinner. But the
wino cannot survive on these occasional finds; he must have his daily
dose to stave off the DTs. All the cans he can carry will buy about three
bottles of Wild Irish Rose.

I do not begrudge them the cans, but can scroungers tend to tear up 44
the Dumpsters, mixing the contents and littering the area. They become
so specialized that they can see only cans. They earn my contempt by
passing up change, canned goods, and readily hockable items.

There are precious few courtesies among scavengers. But it is com- 45
mon practice to set aside surplus items: pairs of shoes, clothing, canned
goods, and such. A true scavenger hates to see good stuff go to waste,
and what he cannot use he leaves in good condition in plain sight.

Can scroungers lay waste to everything in their path and will stir 46
one of a pair of good shoes to the bottom of a Dumpster, to be lost or
ruined in the muck. Can scroungers will even go through individual
garbage cans, something I have never seen a scavenger do.

Individual garbage cans are set out on the public easement only on 47
garbage days. On other days going through them requires trespassing
close to a dwelling. Going through individual garbage cans without
scattering litter is almost impossible. Litter is likely to reduce the public's tolerance of scavenging. Individual cans are simply not as produc-
tive as Dumpsters; people in houses and duplexes do not move so often
and for some reason do not tend to discard as much useful material.
Moreover, the time required to go through one garbage can that serves
one household is not much less than the time required to go through a
Dumpster that contains the refuse of twenty apartments.

But my strongest reservation about going through individual 48
garbage cans is that this seems to me a very personal kind of invasion
to which I would object if I were a householder. Although many things
in Dumpsters are obviously meant never to come to light, a Dumpster
is somehow less personal.

I avoid trying to draw conclusions about the people who dump in 49
the Dumpsters I frequent. I think it would be unethical to do so,

although I know many people will find the idea of scavenger ethics too funny for words.

Dumpsters contain bank statements, correspondence, and other 50 documents, just as anyone might expect. But there are also less obvious sources of information. Pill bottles, for example. The labels bear the name of the patient, the name of the doctor, and the name of the drug. AIDS drugs and antipsychotic medicines, to name but two groups, are specific and are seldom prescribed for any other disorders. The plastic compacts for birth-control pills usually have complete label information.

Despite all of this sensitive information, I have had only one apart- 51 ment resident object to my going through the Dumpster. In that case it turned out the resident was a university athlete who was taking bets and who was afraid I would turn up his wager slips.

Occasionally a find tells a story. I once found a small paper bag con- 52 taining some unused condoms, several partial tubes of flavored sexual lubricants, a partially used compact of birth-control pills, and the torn pieces of a picture of a young man. Clearly she was through with him and planning to give up sex altogether.

Dumpster things are often sad—abandoned teddy bears, shredded 53 wedding books, despaired-of sales kits. I find many pets lying in state in Dumpsters. Although I hope to get off the streets so that Lizbeth can have a long and comfortable old age, I know this hope is not very realistic. So I suppose when her time comes she too will go into a Dumpster. I will have no better place for her. And after all, it is fitting, since for most of her life her livelihood has come from the Dumpster. When she finds something I think is safe that has been spilled from a Dumpster, I let her have it. She already knows the route around the best ones. I like to think that if she survives me she will have a chance of evading the dog catcher and of finding her sustenance on the route.

Silly vanities also come to rest in the Dumpsters. I am a rather accom- 54 plished needleworker. I get a lot of material from the Dumpsters. Evidently sorority girls, hoping to impress someone, perhaps themselves, with their mastery of a womanly art, buy a lot of embroider-by-number kits, work a few stitches horribly, and eventually discard the whole mess. I pull out their stitches, turn the canvas over, and work an original design. Do not think I refrain from chuckling as I make gifts from these kits.

I find diaries and journals. I have often thought of compiling a book 55 of literary found objects. And perhaps I will one day. But what I find is hopelessly commonplace and bad without being, even unconsciously, camp. College students also discard their papers. I am horrified to discover the kind of paper that now merits an A in an undergraduate course. I am grateful, however, for the number of good books and magazines the students throw out.

In the area I know best I have never discovered vermin in the 56 Dumpsters, but there are two kinds of kitty surprise. One is alley cats whom I meet as they leap, claws first, out of Dumpsters. This is especially thrilling when I have Lizbeth in tow. The other kind of kitty surprise is a plastic garbage bag filled with some ponderous, amorphous mass. This always proves to be used cat litter.

City bees harvest doughnut glaze and this makes the Dumpster at 57 the doughnut shop more interesting. My faith in the instinctive wisdom of animals is always shaken whenever I see Lizbeth attempt to catch a bee in her mouth, which she does whenever bees are present. Evidently some birds find Dumpsters profitable, for birdie surprise is almost as common as kitty surprise of the first kind. In hunting season all kinds of small game turn up in Dumpsters, some of it, sadly, not entirely dead. Curiously, summer and winter, maggots are uncommon.

The worst of the living and near-living hazards of the Dumpsters 58 are the fire ants. The food they claim is not much of a loss, but they are vicious and aggressive. It is very easy to brush against some surface of the Dumpster and pick up half a dozen or more fire ants, usually in some sensitive area such as the underarm. One advantage of bringing Lizbeth along as I make Dumpster rounds is that, for obvious reasons, she is very alert to ground-based fire ants. When Lizbeth recognizes a fire-ant infestation around our feet, she does the Dance of the Zillion Fire Ants. I have learned not to ignore this warning from Lizbeth, whether I perceive the tiny ants or not, but to remove ourselves at Lizbeth's first pas de bourrée.[1] All the more so because the ants are the worst in the summer months when I wear flip-flops if I have them. (Perhaps someone will misunderstand this. Lizbeth does the Dance of the Zillion Fire Ants when she recognizes more fire ants than she cares to eat, not when she is being bitten. Since I have learned to react promptly, she does not get bitten at all. It is the isolated patrol of fire ants that falls in Lizbeth's range that deserves pity. She finds them quite tasty.)

By far the best way to go through a Dumpster is to lower yourself 59 into it. Most of the good stuff tends to settle at the bottom because it is usually weightier than the rubbish. My more athletic companions have often demonstrated to me that they can extract much good material from a Dumpster I have already been over.

To those psychologically or physically unprepared to enter a 60 Dumpster, I recommend a stout stick, preferably with some barb or hook at one end. The hook can be used to grab plastic garbage bags. When I find canned goods or other objects loose at the bottom of a Dumpster, I lower a bag into it, roll the desired object into the bag, and then hoist the bag out—a procedure more easily described than executed. Much Dumpster diving is a matter of experience for which nothing will do except practice.

---

[1] A short walking or running step in ballet. [Eds.]

Dumpster diving is outdoor work, often surprisingly pleasant. It is 61 not entirely predictable; things of interest turn up every day and some days there are finds of great value. I am always very pleased when I can turn up exactly the thing I most wanted to find. Yet in spite of the element of chance, scavenging more than most other pursuits tends to yield returns in some proportion to the effort and intelligence brought to bear. It is very sweet to turn up a few dollars in change from a Dumpster that has just been gone over by a wino.

The land is now covered with cities. The cities are full of Dumpsters. 62 If a member of the canine race is ever able to know what it is doing, then Lizbeth knows that when we go around to the Dumpsters, we are hunting. I think of scavenging as a modern form of self-reliance. In any event, after having survived nearly ten years of government service, where everything is geared to the lowest common denominator, I find it refreshing to have work that rewards initiative and effort. Certainly I would be happy to have a sinecure again, but I am no longer heartbroken that I left one.

I find from the experience of scavenging two rather deep lessons. 63 The first is to take what you can use and let the rest go by. I have come to think that there is no value in the abstract. A thing I cannot use or make useful, perhaps by trading, has no value however rare or fine it may be. I mean useful in a broad sense—some art I would find useful and some otherwise.

I was shocked to realize that some things are not worth acquiring, 64 but now I think it is so. Some material things are white elephants that eat up the possessor's substance. The second lesson is the transience of material being. This has not quite converted me to a dualist,[2] but it has made some headway in that direction. I do not suppose that ideas are immortal, but certainly mental things are longer lived than other material things.

Once I was the sort of person who invests objects with sentimental 65 value. Now I no longer have those objects, but I have the sentiments yet.

Many times in our travels I have lost everything but the clothes I 66 was wearing and Lizbeth. The things I find in Dumpsters, the love letters and rag dolls of so many lives, remind me of this lesson. Now I hardly pick up a thing without envisioning the time I will cast it aside. This I think is a healthy state of mind. Almost everything I have now has already been cast out at least once, proving that what I own is valueless to someone.

Anyway, I find my desire to grab for the gaudy bauble has been 67 largely sated. I think this is an attitude I share with the very wealthy— we both know there is plenty more where what we have came from.

---

[2] One who believes that material things also exist as spiritual ideals or abstractions. [Eds.]

Between us are the rat-race millions who nightly scavenge the cable channels looking for they know not what.

I am sorry for them.

Responding to Reading

1. In paragraph 6, Eighner explains, "I have learned much as a scavenger. I mean to put some of what I have learned down here, beginning with the practical art of Dumpster diving and proceeding to the abstract." Do you think Eighner's purpose goes beyond educating his readers? What other purpose do you think he might have?
2. What surprised you most about Eighner's essay? Did any information embarrass you? Repulse you? Make you feel guilty? Arouse your sympathy? Arouse your pity? Explain your response. Do you think Eighner intended you to feel the way you do?
3. How do you suppose Eighner would define the American Dream? What do you think he might have to say about its limits?

HOW IT FEELS TO BE COLORED ME

Zora Neale Hurston

Folklorist and writer Zora Neale Hurston (1901–1969) grew up in Eatonville, Florida, the first incorporated African-American community in the United States, and Hurston herself was the first African-American woman admitted to Barnard College in New York City. There she developed an interest in anthropology, and she studied with Columbia University's famous anthropologist Franz Boas. Mules and Men *(1935) is her book of folklore about voodoo among southern blacks. During the Harlem Renaissance of the 1920s and 1930s, Hurston wrote stories celebrating the hope and joy of African-American life, music, and stories. Her most notable novel is* Their Eyes Were Watching God *(1937). The essay below, which features Hurston's strong personal voice, is from the collection* I Love Myself When I Am Laughing *(1979), edited by Alice Walker.*

I am colored but I offer nothing in the way of extenuating circum- 1 stances except the fact that I am the only Negro in the United States whose grandfather on the mother's side was *not* an Indian chief.

I remember the very day that I became colored. Up to my thir- 2 teenth year I lived in the little Negro town of Eatonville, Florida. It is exclusively a colored town. The only white people I knew passed through the town going to or coming from Orlando. The native whites rode dusty horses, the Northern tourists chugged down the sandy village road in automobiles. The town knew the Southerners and never stopped cane chewing[1] when they passed. But the Northerners were something else again. They were peered at cautiously from behind curtains by the timid. The more venturesome would come out on the porch to watch them go past and got just as much pleasure out of the tourists as the tourists got out of the village.

The front porch might seem a daring place for the rest of the town, 3 but it was a gallery seat for me. My favorite place was atop the gate-post. Proscenium[2] box for a born first-nighter. Not only did I enjoy the show, but I didn't mind the actors knowing that I liked it. I usually spoke to them in passing. I'd wave at them and when they returned my salute, I would say something like this: "Howdy-do-well-I-thank-you- where-you-goin'?" Usually the automobile or the horse paused at this, and after a queer exchange of compliments, I would probably "go a piece of the way" with them, as we say in farthest Florida. If one of my family happened to come to the front in time to see me, of course negotiations would be rudely broken off. But even so, it is clear that I was the first "welcome-to-our-state" Floridian, and I hope the Miami Chamber of Commerce will please take notice.

During this period, white people differed from colored to me only 4 in that they rode through town and never lived there. They liked to hear me "speak pieces" and sing and wanted to see me dance the parse-mela, and gave me generously of their small silver for doing these things, which seemed strange to me for I wanted to do them so much that I needed bribing to stop. Only they didn't know it. The colored people gave no dimes. They deplored any joyful tendencies in me, but I was their Zora nevertheless. I belonged to them, to the nearby hotels, to the county—everybody's Zora.

But changes came in the family when I was thirteen, and I was sent 5 to school in Jacksonville. I left Eatonville, the town of the oleanders,[3] as Zora. When I disembarked from the river-boat at Jacksonville, she was no more. It seemed that I had suffered a sea change. I was not Zora of Orange County any more, I was now a little colored girl. I found it out in certain ways. In my heart as well as in the mirror, became a fast brown—warranted not to rub nor run.

But I am not tragically colored. There is no great sorrow dammed 6 up in my soul, nor lurking behind my eyes. I do not mind at all. I do not belong to the sobbing school of Negrohood who hold that nature somehow has given them a lowdown dirty deal and whose feelings are all hurt about it. Even in the helter-skelter skirmish that is my life, I have

---

[1] Chewing sugar cane. [Eds.]

[2] In the ancient Greek theater, the stage; in the modern theater, the opening that frames the stage area. [Eds.]

[3] Tropical flowers. [Eds.]

seen that the world is to the strong regardless of a little pigmentation more or less. No, I do not weep at the world—I am too busy sharpening my oyster knife.[4]

Someone is always at my elbow reminding me that I am the grand- 7 daughter of slaves. It fails to register depression with me. Slavery is sixty years in the past. The operation was successful and the patient is doing well, thank you. The terrible struggle[5] that made me an American out of a potential slave said "On the line!" The Reconstruction[6] said "Get set!"; and the generation before said "Go!" I am off to a flying start and I must not halt in the stretch to look behind and weep. Slavery is the price I paid for civilization, and the choice was not with me. It is a bully adventure and worth all that I have paid through my ancestors for it. No one on earth ever had a greater chance for glory. The world to be won and nothing to be lost. It is thrilling to think—to know that for any act of mine, I shall get twice as much praise or twice as much blame. It is quite exciting to hold the center of the national stage, with the spectators not knowing whether to laugh or to weep.

The position of my white neighbor is much more difficult. No brown 8 specter pulls up a chair beside me when I sit down to eat. No dark ghost thrusts its leg against mine in bed. The game of keeping what one has is never so exciting as the game of getting.

I do not always feel colored. Even now I often achieve the uncon- 9 scious Zora of Eatonville before the Hegira.[7] I feel most colored when I am thrown against a sharp white background.

For instance at Barnard. "Beside the waters of the Hudson" I feel 10 my race. Among the thousand white persons, I am a dark rock surged upon, and overswept, but through it all, I remain myself. When covered by the waters, I am; and the ebb but reveals me again.

Sometimes it is the other way around. A white person is set down 11 in our midst, but the contrast is just as sharp for me. For instance, when I sit in the drafty basement that is The New World Cabaret with a white person, my color comes. We enter chatting about any little nothing that we have in common and are seated by the jazz waiters. In the abrupt way that jazz orchestras have, this one plunges into a number. It loses no time in circumlocutions, but gets right down to business. It constricts the thorax and splits the heart with its tempo and narcotic harmonies. This orchestra grows rambunctious, rears on its hind legs and attacks the tonal veil with primitive fury, rending it, clawing it until it breaks through to the jungle beyond. I follow those heathen—follow them

---

[4] Reference is to the expression "The world is my oyster." [Eds.]
[5] The Civil War. [Eds.]
[6] The period immediately following the Civil War. [Eds.]
[7] The flight of Muhammad from Mecca in A.D. 622. [Eds.]

exultingly. I dance wildly inside myself; I yell within, I whoop; I shake my assegai[8] above my head, I hurl it true to the mark *yeeeeooww!* I am in the jungle and living in the jungle way. My face is painted red and yellow and my body is painted blue. My pulse is throbbing like a war drum. I want to slaughter something—give paid, give death to what, I do not know. But the piece ends. The men of the orchestra wipe their lips and rest their fingers. I creep back slowly to the veneer we call civilization with the last tone and find the white friend sitting motionless in his seat, smoking calmly.

"Good music they have here," he remarks, drumming the table   12
with his fingertips.

Music. The great blobs of purpose and red emotion have not   13
touched him. He has only heard what I felt. He is far away and I see him but dimly across the ocean and the continent that have fallen between us. He is so pale with his whiteness then and I am so colored.

At certain times I have no race, I am *me*. When I set my hat at a cer-   14
tain angle and saunter down Seventh Avenue, Harlem City, feeling as snooty as the lions in front of the Forty-Second Street Library, for instance. So far as my feelings are concerned, Peggy Hopkins Joyce[9] on the Boule Mich with her gorgeous raiment, stately carriage, knees knocking together in a most aristocratic manner, has nothing on me. The cosmic Zora emerges. I belong to no race nor time. I am the eternal feminine with its string of beads.

I have no separate feeling about being an American citizen and col-   15
ored. I am merely a fragment of the Great Soul that surges within the boundaries. My country, right or wrong.

Sometimes, I feel discriminated against, but it does not make me   16
angry. It merely astonishes me. How *can* any deny themselves the pleasure of my company? It's beyond me.

But in the main, I feel like a brown bag of miscellany propped against   17
a wall. Against a wall in company with other bags, white, red and yellow. Pour out the contents, and there is discovered a jumble of small things priceless and worthless. A first-water diamond, an empty spool, bits of broken glass, lengths of string, a key to a door long since crumbled away, a rusty knife-blade, old shoes saved for a road that never was and never will be, a nail bent under the weight of things too heavy for any nail, a dried flower or two still a little fragrant. In your hand is the brown bag. On the ground before you is the jumble it held—so much like the jumble in the bags, could they be emptied, that all might be dumped in a single heap and the bags refilled without altering the contents of any greatly. A

---

[8] South African hunting spear. [Eds.]

[9] American known for setting trends in beauty and fashion in the 1920s. The Boule Mich (also Boul' Mich), short for *Boulevard St. Michel,* is a street on Paris's Left Bank. [Eds.]

bit of colored glass more or less would not matter. Perhaps that is how the Great Stuffer of Bags filled them in the first place—who knows?

Responding to Reading

1. How, according to Hurston, does it feel to be "colored"? How do her feelings about her color change as she grows older? Why do they change?
2. In what sense does Hurston see herself as fundamentally different from the white people she encounters? Does she see this difference as a problem? Does her reaction surprise you?
3. When Hurston says, "At certain times I have no race, I am *me*" (14), does she mean that she feels assimilated into the larger society, or does she mean something else? Do you think it is possible to be only yourself and not a member of any particular racial or ethnic group? Explain.

THE TELLTALE HEART: APOLOGY, REPARATION, AND REDRESS

Charles R. Lawrence III and Mari Matsuda

Charles R. Lawrence (1943–   ) and Mari Matsuda (1956–   ) are professors at Georgetown University Law School. Their book We Won't Go Back: Making the Case for Affirmative Action *(1997) argues that affirmative action programs are still necessary to provide educational and professional opportunities for members of groups that have historically been limited by discrimination. It includes not only the authors' own reasoning but also testimony from people who have experienced discrimination and benefited from affirmative action. In the following chapter from the book, Lawrence and Matsuda suggest that affirmative action as reparation for past injustice can bring "balance to all our lives—not just the material balance of integration, but the emotional and spiritual balance of healthy souls."*

I tremble for my country, when I reflect that God is just.

—Thomas Jefferson

They shall build up the ancient ruins,
they shall raise up the former devastations;
they shall repair the ruined cities,
the devastations of many generations.

—Isaiah 61:4

One sunny day, on the island of Yap, in part of the Pacific island   1
group of Micronesia, I was running a course designed to teach the common law of torts to Micronesian judges. I posed a hypothetical designed to illustrate the master rule of fault-based liability in tort. "What if," I asked, "a little boy runs out from behind the high brush, into the road, and is hit by a car? The driver was driving carefully and could not have stopped in time to avoid the accident. The child is killed instantly."

This was the easy case, the first of a series of hypotheticals designed   2
to show that once fault is unclear, liability becomes unclear. To the judges, however, it was not an easy case. It was a false case. No one could respond to it justly without more facts.

One of the judges, enjoying the Socratic method[1] and intending to   3
teach me a thing or two, asked for more facts. How many sons, he asked, in the family of the driver? How many sons in the family of the injured child? How did the family of the injured child learn of the injury? How soon, and from whom?

"Okay," I said, "I give up. You tell me how you would decide the   4
case."

What the judges learned that day was the peculiar habit, in Western   5
law, of limiting the relevant facts. All an American jurist would want to know is whether the driver was at fault in the accident; there would be no liability if the driver was exercising ordinary care.

What I learned from the judges that day is that there is a universe   6
of relevant questions to ask after an accident if one lives on a tiny, isolated island, and if it is an absolute imperative to live in peace.

Fault is irrelevant, the judges explained. If your driving hurts some-   7
one, you should make sure you go immediately to the family to tell of the tragedy and of your grief. They should not hear the news first from someone else. Your remorse must meet the test of sincerity. Your kin should come quickly with food and gifts to show their intent to make amends. If you are lucky, you will have a son to work the taro fields of the family who lost a son. Your son will work for them all of his days, as part of your apology, and the apology, sanctified by elders and sacred ritual, must find a gracious welcome in the wounded family. If they allow their loss to overcome them, such that your sincere apology is received insincerely, they will lose status in the community.

This system of repairing great loss is not about account keeping. It   8
is part of the sacred, in a culture that does not separate the sacred from the secular. The longstanding customs that govern reactions to the tragedy of an automobile accident guarantee the spiritual wholeness of all citizens. When either side—what we would call in Western law the plaintiff or the defendant—fails to comport itself according to custom, the well-being of the entire community is in jeopardy.

---

[1] Educational method that involves the use of probing questions. [Eds.]

If the judges' system works in the idealized way they described, it 9
achieves something the American legal system does not: both the plaintiff and the defendant walk away at peace.

In another part of the Pacific, Native Hawaiians speak matter-of- 10
factly about the payback for human failings. Traditional Hawaiians
place value in the concept of *pono*, the state of being that is peace,
repose, goodness. Upsetting *pono*, disrupting the rhythms of the land
and its people, is a wrong—not only to fellow human beings, but to the
cosmology. The price is illness, misfortune, cataclysm. When the vol-
cano erupts, taking out roads and villages, the Hawaiians look around
for someone who acted against *pono*—perhaps the developer who bull-
dozed old burial grounds, or the politician who acted out of greed, or a
family whose feud was left to fester.

In the Judeo-Christian tradition, the Lord says, "Vengeance is mine." 11
There is a wisdom beyond human comprehension that determines what
pain to exact for human transgression. Few cultures exist that do not have
some notion of judgment. Actions have consequences. This is a law of
physics we transmute to a law of our lives.

Those cultures which make active use of apology rituals are often 12
the ones that acknowledge the importance of community cohesion.
Apology rituals, within societies that depend on the clan or village to
provide a social safety net, are essential for survival. A dispute resolution mechanism that results in one party's walking home happy and the
other's walking away from the village forever is an utter failure. To
make the community whole, to erase the bad feelings of the past, to
come jointly once again to the table, is imperative. In the Jalé villages of
New Guinea, for instance, elders require feuding clan members to come
together to feast on pig, each tearing the best morsel from the bone to
place in the mouth of the former foe. This is what makes the elders smile.
An apology in such communities leads to a gain, not a loss, in status.

This approach contrasts with the modern Western view that an 13
apology diminishes status. Typically, in American society, when someone confesses an error or wrongdoing, he is seen as weak and van-
quished, disempowered and vulnerable. Ask an American lawyer what
to do at the scene of an accident, whether a car crash or a nuclear meltdown, and the first rule is "Don't apologize."

In America we have no comparable clan, no network of kin and 14
near kin with whom we must maintain peace, with whom we must cer-
emoniously share our food even when we don't want to. The failure to
know that the globe is our village, that every act of disregard for the
planet and its inhabitants sets in motion disruptions of the good, is the
curse of modernism. It is what makes us unable to see affirmative action
as bringing balance to all our lives—not just the material balance of integration, but the emotional and spiritual balance of healthy souls.

The case for affirmative action includes notions of reparation, recti- 15
fication, and redress: the deliberate effort to identify and make amends
for past wrong. Reparation is not all there is to affirmative action. It is
neither the most compelling nor the most persuasive reason for it, but it
is a reason worth considering, for there are costs in the refusal, ever, to
apologize.

As the fiftieth anniversary of the end of the Second World War 16
approached, refusal to apologize became a leitmotif. The Smithsonian
canceled the Enola Gay exhibit because some felt it focused too much on
the horror and not enough on the military rationale for dropping the
atomic bomb. Meanwhile, the Japanese government was persistently
embarrassed by the claims of its victims: brave women in Korea and the
Philippines who came forward to tell how they were raped, imprisoned,
tortured, and forced into prostitution, as well as POW survivors of
death marches and horrific abuse. No one in a position of power in
either country could say he was sorry for the lives lost and damaged in
the horror of war, or suggest publicly that some of the loss was unnecessary, wrong, or evil.

Whatever the record of history will bear, and I believe it will show 17
that the bombing of Hiroshima was racist, as were the many atrocities
committed by the Japanese army, there is a social code that stands in the
way of even asking the factual questions that might lead to the need for
an apology. We don't need to look back at American military action, this
code tells us. The war is over, the cause was just, we will only hurt ourselves, our prestige, and the honor of those who sacrificed all by asking,
Was there anything we could have done differently, more justly, with
more care?

What does it do, to a nation and the world, to refuse to look back? 18
When someone else, someday, is making the decision about dropping the
bomb on me, I want him to face a record of history that judges the United
States wrong for what happened to civilians in 1945. When someone,
someday, is preparing new internment camps for citizens rounded up
without habeas corpus,[2] I want him to know the judgment of both courts
and Congress: the World War II internment of Japanese Americans was
unconstitutional. This historical memory, the careful judgment made on
the record of history, is the only inoculation we have against future harm.
This is not endless, useless guilt; it is judgment with utility. It takes past
harm as the teaching that will shelter future citizens.

The way to imprint that teaching is through reparation. To the 19
extent that at least part of the justification for affirmative action is reparation, affirmative action rests on a notion that is alien to modern

---

[2] Legal term referring to the formal writ required to arrest a person. [Eds.]

jurisprudence. Oliver Wendell Holmes—seen by some as the architect of modern American legal thought—saw as his life's greatest work his distillation of the common law into its basic principles. At the core of his conceptualized system of justice was the notion of objectively determined, fault-based liability: if a person does something that is unreasonable under society's objective rules of behavior, that person is at fault and must pay compensation to the victim.

Reparation, affirmative action, and the remediation of past injustice [20] look like nothing Holmes envisioned. Rather than defying societal norms, the perpetrators of racial and gender injustice acted precisely in accordance with those norms. They had no particular victim in mind, nor a comprehensive plan, for example, to perpetrate the genocide of Native Americans. It was just something that happened on their way to achieving a destiny made manifest by their casual belief in superiority and entitlement.

The standard liberal legal ideology, which focuses on individual [21] fault, clashes with the ideology supporting reparation. A standard legal claim pits an individual victim against a perpetrator of recent wrongdoing, whereas a claim in reparation pits victim group members against perpetrator descendants and current beneficiaries of past injustice.

A reparations claim lacks the logic and efficiency paramount in the [22] Holmesean world view. It is out of control. In reparations, the lines delineating liability are fuzzy, the exact identities of parties in action are unknowable, and the costs are potentially bankrupting. Under a regime of reparations, no individual actor could calculate in advance the parameters of potential liability.

The logic of reparation lies beyond the logic of the law, raising pre- [23] dictable objections. First, critics claim that reparations are politically untenable: divisive, obsessive, distracting from real issues. Second, they argue that the historical basis of the claim is invalid: either the past harm did not occur, or it was somehow justifiable. Third, the imprecise outlines of both the victim and the perpetrator class render reparation claims fatally imprecise. Fourth, the passage of time renders connection between the original wrong and present effects of that wrong vague and unprovable. Fifth, damages for past wrong are impossible to calculate and to distribute fairly. Finally, to the extent that reparation is aimed toward a group rather than an individual, it raises the ethical objection of disregard of the individual.

We reject these arguments. Correcting past wrongs, such as dis- [24] crimination, through programs like affirmative action is divisive because it just might work. It may open the doors of opportunity and break down barriers to power sharing. It is, indeed, less divisive to let power and privilege stay where they are. The uneasy peace gained from silence in the face of oppression is a known quantity, one that even the disenfranchised sometimes choose over the unknown.

Every movement for progressive social change is called "too divi- 25 sive," which often translates as "Keep the status quo."[3] The objection that reparations set up a hierarchy of suffering, however, merits a thoughtful response. We are leery of proclamations that some wrongs are worse than others or that some people are particularly privileged in their pain. Experienced seekers of justice usually conclude that ranking oppressions is a useless exercise. At the same time, asserting the pure equality of pain deprecates human experience. In our own lives we know that some losses are greater than others, some pain easily surmounted, other pain a lifetime's burden. In an account of justice that takes history seriously, we do need to say, with caution, that there are losses of such magnitude that we, as Americans, need to recognize them as our particular obligation to address.

In the United States, a key question is whether a certain historical 26 wrong bears any relation to our ongoing culture of subordination. The enslavement of African Americans and the genocide of Native Americans are parts of American history that gave rise to particular forms of current American racism. This is not the same as saying that only members of these two groups are the victims of racism, nor is it the same as making the moral evaluation that what happened in these cases was the worst thing ever experienced by any group of human beings. Rather, these events loom large in the origin of our constitutional order, our economic development, and our shared culture. The slave ships brought to the United States an institution that indelibly shaped our understanding of race. Similarly, the massacres of Native Americans required a rationalization and a psychology of denial that mark American colonialism. White supremacy, sometimes expressed explicitly, and just as often denied vehemently, is the legacy of these events.

The record of broken bodies is on the ground we tread; the narra- 27 tive traditions of native people and of African Americans tell us that something extraordinary happened on this land, in a time close to ours. Some 90 percent of the estimated hundred million American Indians who lived at the time of European contact were decimated, in what one author called "a demographic disaster [that] has no equal in history." That number is significant enough to call extraordinary, and to suggest an extraordinary care as we consider our responsibilities to American Indians today.

Edgar Allan Poe, an American who lived in the time of slavery, 28 understood the dark side. He wrote of a man who murdered his tormentor and hid the victim's heart under the floorboards. The investigators arrived, and the murderer proceeded with his calm rendition of a coverup. Somewhere in the background he heard a noise and realized

---

[3] Latin for "the existing state of affairs." [Eds.]

the heart was beating. Surely the constables heard it, he thought as he escalated his professions of innocence. Unable to bear the noise, he ripped open the floorboards and revealed his guilt to the astonished onlookers.

Like the telltale heart beating beneath the floorboards in Poe's story, 29 the weeping at the 1890 Wounded Knee[4] massacre and the moans of the Middle Passage[5] make a persistent pounding when we speak of liberty and equality and the greatness of our America. The casual superiority of a rich and free nation is something we maintain only by speaking loudly, drowning out the sounds that grow ever larger as our frantic efforts to deny and explain escalate. What Myrdal[6] called the American dilemma, what Du Bois[7] called the color line, and what present commentators call the race relations problem are all part of our national culture. Until we speak the truth about it, we cannot know the truth about our own condition.

Keeping the telltale heart under the floorboards is a preoccupation 30 of the postrevisionist historians who argue that dredging up past wrongs is false history. When Pete Wilson[8] announced his soon-to-fail bid for the presidency of the United States, he chose as a central theme the evil of negative history. We've got to stop talking about slavery and Native Americans and emphasize what is good about America, he said. This echoes the view of professional historians, like Lynne Cheney and Arthur Schlesinger. Why all this talk about victims? Why not admit the greatness of the United States? Why this compulsion to look for the bad?

Other detractors of reparation try to deny or justify past harm. The 31 argument that no harm occurred presents factual claims that are refuted elsewhere. We note, however, that a denial of the harm is often not a factual claim at all, but a form of assault designed to perpetuate the harm itself.

Unlike the claim that no wrong occurred, various attempts at justi- 32 fication try to explain or deflect the wrong. A common explanation for slavery, for example, is that within the culture of that era, the inferiority of Africans was taken for granted. To condemn acts from the vantage point of the present is "ahistoric" or "anachronistic." It is precisely because there were many people in the time of slavery who knew it was wrong that we are able to judge it as wrong today. The truth about slavery was made plain by the enslaved Africans themselves, who in narra-

---

[4] Almost two hundred unarmed Sioux men, women, and children were shot by U.S. Cavalry troops at Wounded Knee, South Dakota. [Eds.]

[5] The "Middle Passage" refers to the triangular route of African slave trade, from ports in Europe, to the African coast, to the Americas, and back. [Eds.]

[6] Swedish economist and sociologist Gunnar Myrdal (1898–1987) wrote The American Dilemma (1944, 1962), a detailed study of race relations in the United States which concluded that racial problems are inextricably entwined with the democratic functioning of American society. [Eds.]

[7] W. E. B. Du Bois (1868–1963) was an early civil rights leader who demanded both economic and political equality for blacks. [Eds.]

[8] Republican California governor from 1990 to 1998. [Eds.]

tives and song left a contemporaneous text of condemnation. This truth was not held exclusively by the enslaved; the international antislavery movement brought together many, educated and uneducated, rich and poor, black and white, who studied the evils of slavery and condemned the institution in its time. It is not only from our present vantage point, but also in wise eyes of the past, including Thomas Jefferson's, that slavery is unmitigated evil.

Similarly, when feminists condemn the sexism of past political lead-   33
ers and social institutions, we are warned that we are using the distorting lens of the present. This argument ignores the many noted women and some men who have condemned patriarchy for over a hundred years, as well as the anonymous women of generations earlier who sang their versions of the blues, telling us that "hard is the fortune of al womankind."

In the end, however, the argument over whether what happened in   34
American history was justified or explainable, given past realities, does not answer the call for reparation. Whether the wrong was somehow "understandable in context" does not mean it was just, and justice requires attention to harm regardless of the parameters of blame.

Regardless of past transgressions, some argue, present remedies are   35
impossible because of imprecision. If the *res*, the thing, is stolen and the thief caught, the law returns it to the rightful owner. This is the paradigm of what the law does, and among the oldest writs are those for the return of the *res*. What if the thing that is stolen, however, is not a *res*, but rather freedom, sovereignty, dignity? What if there is no clearly identifiable thief and no single owner, but multitudes who benefit and multitudes who suffer because of some historic wrong? Lack of precision in the law weakens a claim. Those who come before the law are expected to make a coherent case against a fixed defendant: Who did this to you? How were you harmed? What was the price of your loss? If the answer to any of these is "I cannot say with certainty," then the claimant is not worthy in the eyes of the law.

In today's world, in the interests of justice, we make some excep-   36
tions to this demand for precision. When poisonous pollution enters the river from sources unknown, for instance, affecting millions of downstream users and planting in some communities the seeds of cancer that will become evident only years in the future, a so-called Superfund problem arises. The solution may be to tax all producers of the poison and create a fund for possible future harms. Though the details about perpetrator and victim are not known, there is often a sense that the law should respond in some way to the disaster, typically through legislation.

Similarly, in the world of antitrust and commercial law, it some-   37
times happens that a great way to make money is to bilk a million people out of a dollar apiece. The victims may never know of their loss, and identifying all who were cheated and proving their loss is a logistical impossibility. Class action suits or class remedies are possible solutions.

If everyone who used a teller machine at Cheatum Savings was illegally deprived of a dollar in one year, for example, a court might require a dollar discount on fees to everyone who banks there the next year. Not everyone who benefits from the discount is someone who lost out during the period of cheating, but the fit is close enough, and the inability to identify the victims with precision is not a reason to let Cheatum off the hook. We allow this imprecision in order to uphold standards of the marketplace that are seen as critical to consumer confidence. Obsession with precision puts the demands of arithmetic before the demands of justice, ignoring the more central goals of stability and fairness.

Along with imprecision, there is the problem of time. According to 38 American jurisprudence, as time passes, regardless of right or wrong, claims are put to rest. For an ordinary negligence claim, states typically set the limit at two to six years. After that, it is too late for a plaintiff to bring a claim. The time bar, or statute of limitations, is said to promote settled expectations and business planning; we need to know the outer limits of our liability so that we can go on with the business of commerce.

If seven years is too long ago for a civil law suit, what are we to 39 make of a hundred years? In most nations a hundred years is not so long ago. A theory of reparation focuses on the magnitude of harm done and its continuing effects, weighed against the passage of time. When the evidence of continuing effect is strong, the passage of time is not a reason to waive the wrong. While dwelling on the past is not always a good thing, in some cases forgiving and forgetting are impossible, particularly if the old wrongs continue to give rise to new harms.

Reflective adults ponder and regret the mistakes of their lives and 40 recall the traumas done to them. Victims of childhood abuse or neglect may well spend hours trying to understand how their past shapes their present attitudes, relations, and personality. A common survival strategy for the most egregious abuse is to forget or diminish what happened. There is no real forgetting, however. The anxiety, flashback, depression, and other symptoms of repressed trauma remain. The body remembers, calling out with a range of illnesses and behaviors the words we cannot say: something terrible happened to me, and I am in pain. A person stuck in the past, reciting a list of grievances over and over without resolution, is not whole; but neither is the person who cannot see the past, who does not know she is sad today because she was raised yesterday by someone who saw no joy in life.

"Forgive and forget" is too simple a solution for the complex harms 41 human beings inflict on one another. The abused child must remember, confront, and express anger before any forgiveness is mentally healthy. On a larger scale, national healing, something politicians seek in platitudinous addresses, will not come cheap. The forgiveness that is close to godliness is a deep forgiveness, the one that comes when the work is done, the past confronted, the pain acknowledged and expressed. This task is not about feeling guilty, pointing fingers, extracting vengeance. It is about liberation. . . .

No one wants to confront that which hurts the most; no one wants 42 to open up the carefully cabined places of forgetting; but some wise souls learn that hiding from what is hard gives no shelter. The past, whether personal or geopolitical, is ours, and acknowledging our origins is what enables us to make our lives better than what the past alone might have predicted.

What is the price of peace? The story of the Native Hawaiians is 43 illustrative. Native Hawaiians have long protested the loss of their sovereign nation, their lands, and much of their culture as a result of the U.S.–backed takeover of Hawaii in 1893. One of the specific claims relates to native lands, ceded to the State of Hawaii by the United States government, and held in trust for Native Hawaiians. The state, the Native Hawaiians claim, is in breach of the terms of that trust. They would like to sue the state to force it to use the ceded lands, as required by law, for the benefit of Native Hawaiians. There is one problem, however. State law does not give Hawaiians the right of legal action. They cannot sue in state court.

For years, the Hawaiians have lobbied the state legislature for 44 a "right to sue" bill, which would allow their claims to come to court. In opposing the bill, the state has argued that if it is sued, it will go bankrupt. If the Hawaiians could sue, they could very well win, and the actual damages, for years of misdirection of benefits that were intended for Hawaiians, could surpass the revenues and assets of the state.

Making up for past wrong, in short, should not happen, according to 45 the state, because it would cost too much. This argument against reparation trumps all the others. Instead of saying it didn't happen or it was too long ago, it says if the harm caused is too large, there is no remedy. The argument is somewhat disingenuous. The practical reality is that no litigant will ever collect full damages if they will bankrupt the state. At some point, the political process will have to allow for compromise. When Japanese Americans sought redress for their internment during World War II, for example, most recognized that no monetary amount could compensate them for what they lost: careers, education, land, businesses, hand-built farm houses, loved ones lost to poor medical care, a lifetime's possessions left behind for the junkman, the comfort of familiar streets and faces gone—so much, tangible and intangible, that was irreplaceable. Most significant of all, though, was the loss of rights and the shattering of expectations about freedom and citizenship. A million dollars would not have made whole what each person lost. No one asked for a million dollars. What they asked for, and got, was an amount large enough to constitute a genuine apology but small enough to pass through the legislative process. Reparations exact not a pound of flesh, but, rather, sixteen ounces of mutual sorrow over loss.

Reparation, to the extent that it recognizes group harm and group   46
responsibility, rings of collectivism, something feared by Red baiters and derogated by those classical philosophers who ground their ethics in the individual. Although the criticism of dehumanizing individualism is implicit throughout this book, we do not reject the belief that each human being is sacred, unique, and entitled to individual recognition before the law. A simple choice that puts either individuals or groups first is not enough to resolve the reparations debate, for groups are made up of individuals. Any philosophy giving primacy either to individual rights or to the group must confront that fact of human life. The relations of individuals to groups and groups to other groups are something we cannot avoid in defining what is just.

Reparation, like affirmative action, is for everyone. The direct ben-   47
eficiaries, as deserving as they may be, are not the center of reparation. All of the objections to reparation come down to one thing: the failure to see individual interest as tied inextricably to community interest. Making peace with the past, so that we can live and work together in a peaceful future, is what will ultimately save all individuals. The person free to invent himself or herself and walk unfettered, the person whose individual choices are paramount in the political philosophies of the modern age, that individual is revealed only when the legacy of past oppressions is wiped away.

Reparation is only one part of affirmative action. . . . Affirmative   48
action is required in order to institute equality today. Nonetheless, part of the justification for affirmative action is and should be the correction of past injustice.

When affirmative action is defined strictly as a remedy for past injus-   49
tice, it is easy to attack. Some argue that a focus on the past detracts from the issues or problems of the present; people become mired in past grievances and are sapped of the will to struggle around current injustice. Some, like the majority of the present Supreme Court, are skeptical of claims that past wrongs, such as the enslavement of African Americans, are connected to present disadvantage. The unstated message is "Get over it; it was a long time ago." Others feel that if past wrongdoing is the basis for affirmative action, then only African Americans, and not other minorities, should benefit from affirmative action. This leads to a no-win game of comparing oppressions—whose suffering was the most egregious, whose claim for compensation the most compelling—and it oversimplifies the goals of affirmative action into a settling of accounts: "Let's find the true historical wrong, the clear victim, the price of their pain, and then fix it up with a direct payment."

This notion of affirmative action as simple payback for past wrong 50
misunderstands the social function of history in our lives. We are made
by our past; we can't live, breathe, act, or invent apart from it. Confronting and knowing our collective history is important because it is
what shapes present circumstances; we are racist today because we
were racist yesterday. The forms and the dynamics of that racism will
change over time, but the root is connected to the branch in a way that
is present in the here and now.

Of course, the fight for affirmative action of the 1960s and beyond 51
was not a fight merely for acknowledgment of past wrong; it was a passionate struggle to improve present conditions, to gain jobs, education,
and political participation today.

Acknowledging this doesn't remove the element of reparation from 52
affirmative action, however. There is a past-based part of the original
demand: this country must know and acknowledge past wrong if it is
to progress on the road to justice. We cannot end racism without knowing where it came from and how it works in our culture. In this sense,
the inability to say "We were wrong, we are sorry, we will right this
wrong" means that we are stuck in time. If we refuse to confront the
past, we become bound to it and cannot move forward.

What this means for affirmative action, and for progressive politics 53
in general, is that we have to do two things at once. We should . . . live
in the present, focusing on present need and expanding affirmative
action programs to reach all people who, for whatever reason, are excluded from education, jobs, and participation in the democratic
process. At the same time, we can recognize our particular responsibility for correcting the past wrongs in our history. It was right for this
nation to issue a formal apology to the thousands of Japanese Americans who were incarcerated in America's concentration camps. The
healing of the Japanese Americans required this, as did our self-percep-
tion as a good and free country. There are apologies we have not made;
atrocities carried out in our name that continue to debase our most
sacred symbols of democracy. We must confront our horrors and pledge
that they will not happen again.

As this . . . was written, the Truth Commission, charged with find- 54
ing out what happened to the thousands of South Africans who were
victims of atrocities during the struggle to end apartheid, began its
work in South Africa, that nation determined to remember and move
forward from a bloody past. One by one the witnesses came before the
commissioners. The tortured whispered their survivors' stories; the parents wept describing their murdered children; some of the murderers
wept, too, holding out their killing hands as an entire nation watched.

There is no more powerful process a nation can undertake. The 55
commissioners had to halt the proceedings at times when neither they

nor the witnesses could bear to continue. Counselors were called on to help the commissioners confront their own traumas at hearing one story after another of human suffering.

Nothing that happens before the Truth Commission can restore a 56 peaceful heart to grieving parents, nor absolve the eternal guilt of the torturer. Nothing will happen except confrontation with truth, and out of that beginning the new South Africa will start its healing.

The living struggle to give meaning to the loss of the dead; the 57 grieving heart seeks reasons. The freedom fighters of South Africa knew they risked all for their people's liberation. They did not know, when they joined their cause, that they were bringing an additional gift to the larger world. In its search to uncover the past and thereby move forward to healing, South Africa is setting an example while the world watches. No nation, great or small, past or present, has undertaken this level of collective confrontation with its own evil as part of a peaceful transition to a free and equal society.

May they find their peace, and, someday, may we find ours.   58

Responding to Reading

1. Lawrence and Matsuda defend affirmative action because they believe it is needed to make amends for past injustices—that is, to offer "apology, reparation, and redress." Are you swayed by their arguments in favor of the importance of "apology rituals" (12), do you consider such arguments irrelevant? Do you see affirmative action as an essential ingredient of the American Dream? Explain.

2. Reread paragraphs 28–29, in which Lawrence and Matsuda draw an analogy between Poe's "telltale heart" and the sad and shameful secrets in U.S. history. Do you find this analogy convincing? Why or why not? What other events do you think have created a similar kind of "persistent pounding"? Do you believe it is possible to make amends for such events? Explain.

3. In recent years, the U.S. government has issued apologies for past "mistakes"—for example, the Tuskegee syphilis experiments and the institution of slavery. In addition, the government has paid reparations to the Japanese-Americans interned during World War II. How do you think Lawrence and Matsuda feel about these practices?

FOCUS

What Is the American Dream?

THE DECLARATION OF INDEPENDENCE

Thomas Jefferson

Thomas Jefferson (1743-1826) was a lawyer, statesman, diplomat, architect, scientist, politician, writer, education theorist, and musician. During his impressive political life, Jefferson served as governor of Virginia, member of the Continental Congress, secretary of state, vice president, and then president for two terms beginning in 1801. He collected nearly ten thousand books, and his library later became the basis of the Library of Congress. The Declaration of Independence, drafted by Jefferson and amended by the Continental Congress, reflects Jefferson's belief in reason and the natural rights of individuals.

In Congress, July 4, 1776: The Unanimous Declaration of the Thirteen United States of America

When in the Course of human events it becomes necessary for one 1 people to dissolve the political bands which have connected them with another, and to assume among the powers of the earth, the separate and equal station to which the Laws of Nature and of Nature's God entitle them, a decent respect to the opinions of mankind requires that they should declare the causes which impel them to the separation.

We hold these truths to be self-evident, that all men are created 2 equal, that they are endowed by their Creator with certain unalienable Rights, that among these are Life, Liberty and the pursuit of Happiness. That to secure these rights, Governments are instituted among Men, deriving their just powers from the consent of the governed. That whenever any Form of Government becomes destructive of these ends, it is the Right of the People to alter or to abolish it, and to institute new Government, laying its foundation on such principles and organizing its powers in such form, as to them shall seem most likely to effect their Safety and Happiness. Prudence, indeed, will dictate that Governments long established should not be changed for light and transient causes; and accordingly all experience hath shewn, that mankind are more disposed to suffer, while evils are sufferable, than to right themselves by abolishing the forms to which they are accustomed. But when a long train of abuses and usurpations, pursuing invariably the same Object, evinces a design to reduce them under absolute Despotism, it is their right, it is their duty, to throw off such Government, and to provide new Guards for their future security. Such has been the patient sufferance of these Colonies; and such is now the necessity which constrains them to alter their former Systems of Governors. The history of the present King of Great Britain is a history of repeated injuries and usurpations, all having in direct object the establishment of an absolute Tyranny over these States. To prove this, let Facts be submitted to a candid world.

He has refused his Assent to Laws, the most wholesome and necessary for the public good. 3

He has forbidden his Governors to pass laws of immediate and pressing importance, unless suspended in their operation till his Assent should be obtained; and when so suspended, he has utterly neglected to attend to them. 4

He has refused to pass other Laws for the accommodation of large districts of people, unless those people would relinquish the right of Representation in the Legislature, a right inestimable to them and formidable to tyrants only. 5

He has called together legislative bodies at places unusual, uncomfortable, and distant from the depository of their Public Records, for the sole purpose of fatiguing them into compliance with his measures. 6

He has dissolved Representative Houses repeatedly, for opposing with manly firmness his invasions on the rights of the people. 7

He has refused for a long time, after such dissolutions, to cause others to be elected; whereby the Legislative Powers, incapable of Annihilation, have returned to the People at large for their exercise; the State remaining in the mean time exposed to all the dangers of invasion from without, and convulsions within. 8

He has endeavored to prevent the population of these States; for that purpose obstructing the Laws for Naturalization of Foreigners; refusing to pass others to encourage their migration hither, and raising the conditions of new Appropriations of Lands. 9

He has obstructed the Administration of Justice, by refusing his Assent to Laws for establishing Judiciary Powers. 10

He has made Judges dependent on his Will alone, for the tenure of their offices, and the amount and payment of their salaries. 11

He has erected a multitude of New Offices, and sent hither swarms of Officers to harass our people, and eat out their substance. 12

He has kept among us, in times of peace, Standing Armies without the Consent of our legislatures. 13

He has affected to render the Military independent of and superior to the Civil Power. 14

He has combined with others to subject us to a jurisdiction foreign to our constitution, and unacknowledged by our laws; giving his Assent to their Acts of pretended Legislation: For quartering large bodies of armed 15 troops among us: For protecting them, by a mock Trial, from punishment for any Murders which they should commit on the Inhabitants of these States: For cutting off our Trade with all parts of the world: For imposing Taxes on us without our Consent: For depriving us in many cases, of the benefits of Trial by Jury; For transporting us beyond Seas to be tried for pretended offenses: For abolishing the free System of English Laws in a neighboring Province, establishing therein an Arbitrary government, and enlarging its Boundaries so as to render it at once an example and fit instrument for introducing the same absolute rule into these Colonies: For taking away our Charters, abolishing our most valuable Laws and altering fundamentally the Forms of our Governments: For suspending our own Legislatures, and declaring themselves invested with power to legislate for us in all cases whatsoever.

He has abdicated Government here, by declaring us out of his 16 Protection and waging War against us.

He has plundered our seas, ravaged our Coasts, burnt our towns, 17 and destroyed the lives of our people.

He is at this time transporting large Armies of foreign Mercenaries 18 to complete the works of death, desolation and tyranny, already begun with circumstances of Cruelty & Perfidy scarcely paralleled in the most barbarous ages, and totally unworthy the Head of a civilized nation.

He has constrained our fellow Citizens taken Captive on the high 19 Seas to bear Arms against their Country, to become the executioners of their friends and Brethren, or to fall themselves by their Hands.

He has excited domestic insurrections amongst us, and has endeav- 20 ored to bring on the inhabitants of our frontiers, the merciless Indian Savages, whose known rule of warfare, is an undistinguished destruction of all ages, sexes, and conditions.

In every stage of these Oppressions We have Petitioned for Redress in 21 the most humble terms: Our repeated Petitions have been answered only by repeated injury. A Prince, whose character is thus marked by every act which may define a Tyrant, is unfit to be the ruler of a free people.

Nor have We been wanting in attention to our British brethren. We 22 have warned them from time to time of attempts by their legislature to extend an unwarrantable jurisdiction over us. We have reminded them of the circumstances of our emigration and settlement here. We have appealed to their native justice and magnanimity, and we have conjured them by the ties of our common kindred to disavow these usurpations, which would inevitably interrupt our connections and correspondence. They too have been deaf to the voice of justice and of consanguinity. We must, therefore, acquiesce in the necessity, which denounces our Separation, and hold them, as we hold the rest of mankind, Enemies in War, in Peace Friends.

We, THEREFORE, the Representatives of the UNITED STATES OF 23 AMERICA, in General Congress, Assembled, appealing to the Supreme

Judge of the world for the rectitude of our intentions, do, in the Name, and by Authority of the good People of these Colonies, solemnly publish and declare, That these United Colonies are, and of Right ought to be FREE AND INDEPENDENT STATES; that they are Absolved from all Allegiance to the British Crown, and that all political connection between them and the State of Great Britain, is and ought to be totally dissolved; and that as Free and Independent States, they have full Power to levy War, conclude Peace, contract Alliances, establish Commerce, and to do all other Acts and Things which Independent States may of right do. And for the support of this Declaration, with a firm reliance on the protection of Divine Providence, we mutually pledge to each other our Lives, our Fortunes, and our sacred Honor.

Respond To Reading

1. The Declaration of Independence was written in the eighteenth century, a time when logic and reason were thought to be the supreme achievements of human beings. Do you think this document is as resonable as it seems to be on the surface, or does it also include appeals to the emotions? Explain.
2. Paragraphs 3 through 20 consist of a litany of grievances, expressed in forceful parallel language. How is this use of parallelism similar to (or different from) the language used by Kennedy (p. 453) and King (p. 457)?
3. Do you think it is fair, as some have done, to accuse the framers of the Declaration of Independence of being racist? Sexist?

THE NEW COLOSSUS

Emma Lazarus

Born in New York City, Emma Lazarus (1849-1887) was one of the foremost poets of her day. Her collections included Admetus and Other Poems (1871) and Songs of a Semite (1882), and she was also well known for her essays, translations, and a verse play. Today, however, she is little more than a footnote, remembered almost exclusively for her poem "The New Colossus." Written in 1883, as part of an effort to raise funds for the Statue of Liberty, the sonnet was later inscribed on the statue's base. It remains a vivid reminder of the immigrant's dream of America.

Not like the brazen giant of Greek fame,
With conquering limbs astride from land to land;
Here at our sea-washed, sunset gates shall stand
A mighty woman with a torch, whose flame
Is the imprisoned lightning, and her name   5
Mother of Exiles. From her beacon-hand
Glows world-wide welcome; her mild eyes command
The air-bridged harbor that twin cities frame.
"Keep, ancient lands, your storied pomp!" cries she
With silent lips. "Give me your tired, your poor,   10
Your huddled masses yearning to breathe free,
The wretched refuse of your teeming shore.
Send these, the homeless, tempest-tost to me,
I lift my lamp beside the golden door!"

Responding to Reading

1. The Colossus of Rhodes, an enormous statue of the Greek god Apollo, was considered one of the seven wonders of the world. Why do you think this poem is called "The New Colossus"?
2. Who is the poem's speaker? Who is being addressed?
3. What is the "golden door" to which the last line refers?

INAUGURAL ADDRESS

John F. Kennedy

John Fitzgerald Kennedy was born in Brookline, Massachusetts, in 1917. After receiving a degree from Harvard University, he enlisted in the U.S. Navy in 1941, serving as a PT boat commander in the South Pacific. A highly charismatic politician, he was elected to the U.S. House of Representatives in 1947 and entered the Senate in 1953. In 1960, he defeated the Republican candidate, Richard Nixon, for the presidency, becoming both the youngest man elected president and the first Roman Catholic to do so. During his tenure, the government adopted policies promoting racial equality, aid to the poor and to education, and increased availability of medical care; the Peace Corps was established as well. But as president, Kennedy was also responsible for involving the country further in the doomed Vietnam conflict. He was assassinated in November 1963, a year before the end of his first term. Laying out his optimistic goals for the future, Kennedy delivered the following address when he was sworn in as president.

Vice President Johnson, Mr. Speaker, Mr. Chief Justice, President 1
Eisenhower, Vice President Nixon, President Truman, Reverend Clergy,
fellow citizens:

We observe today not a victory of party but a celebration of 2
freedom—symbolizing an end as well as a beginning—signifying re-
newal as well as change. For I have sworn before you and Almighty
God the same solemn oath our forebears prescribed nearly a century
and three-quarters ago.

The world is very different now. For man holds in his mortal hands 3
the power to abolish all forms of human poverty and all forms of human
life. And yet the same revolutionary beliefs for which our forebears
fought are still at issue around the globe—the belief that the rights of man
come not from the generosity of the state but from the hand of God.

We dare not forget today that we are the heirs of that first revolution. 4
Let the word go forth from this time and place, to friend and foe alike,
that the torch has been passed to a new generation of Americans—born
in this century, tempered by war, disciplined by a hard and bitter peace,
proud of our ancient heritage—and unwilling to witness or permit the
slow undoing of those human rights to which this nation has always been
committed, and to which we are committed today at home and around
the world.

Let every nation know, whether it wishes us well or ill, that we shall 5
pay any price, bear any burden, meet any hardship, support any friend,
oppose any foe to assure the survival and the success of liberty.

This much we pledge—and more.   6

To those old allies whose cultural and spiritual origins we share, we 7
pledge the loyalty of faithful friends. United there is little we cannot do
in a host of cooperative ventures. Divided there is little we can do—for
we dare not meet a powerful challenge at odds and split asunder.

To those new states whom we welcome to the ranks of the free, we 8
pledge our word that one form of colonial control shall not have passed
away merely to be replaced by a far more iron tyranny. We shall not
always expect to find them supporting our view. But we shall always
hope to find them strongly supporting their own freedom—and to
remember that, in the past, those who foolishly sought power by riding
the back of the tiger ended up inside. To those people in the huts and
villages of half the globe struggling to break the bonds of mass misery,
we pledge our best efforts to help them help themselves, for whatever
period is required—not because the communists may be doing it, not
because we seek their votes, but because it is right. If a free society cannot help the many who are poor, it cannot save the few who are rich.

To our sister republics south of our border, we offer a special 9
pledge—to convert our good words into good deeds—in a new alliance
for progress—to assist free men and free governments in casting off the

chains of poverty. But this peaceful revolution of hope cannot become the prey of hostile powers. Let all our neighbors know that we shall join with them to oppose aggression or subversion anywhere in the Americas. And let every other power know that this Hemisphere intends to remain the master of its own house.

To that world assembly of sovereign states, the United Nations, our 10 last best hope in an age where the instruments of war have far outpaced the instruments of peace, we renew our pledge of support—to prevent it from becoming merely a forum for invective—to strengthen its shield of the new and the weak—and to enlarge the area in which its writ may run.

Finally, to those nations who would make themselves our adver- 11 sary, we offer not a pledge but a request: that both sides begin anew the quest for peace, before the dark powers of destruction unleashed by science engulf all humanity in planned or accidental self-destruction.

We dare not tempt them with weakness. For only when our arms 12 are sufficient beyond doubt can we be certain beyond doubt that they will never be employed.

But neither can two great and powerful groups of nations take com- 13 fort from our present course—both sides overburdened by the cost of modern weapons, both rightly alarmed by the steady spread of the deadly atom, yet both racing to alter that uncertain balance of terror that stays the hand of mankind's final war.

So let us begin anew—remembering on both sides that civility is not 14 a sign of weakness, and sincerity is always subject to proof. Let us never negotiate out of fear. But let us never fear to negotiate.

Let both sides explore what problems unite us instead of belaboring 15 those problems which divide us.

Let both sides, for the first time, formulate serious and precise pro- 16 posals for the inspection and control of arms and bring the absolute power to destroy other nations under the absolute control of all nations.

Let both sides seek to invoke the wonders of science instead of its 17 terrors. Together let us explore the stars, conquer the deserts, eradicate disease, tap the ocean depths and encourage the arts and commerce.

Let both sides unite to heed in all corners of the earth the command 18 of Isaiah—to "undo the heavy burdens . . . (and) let the oppressed go free."

And if a beachhead of cooperation may push back the jungle of sus- 19 picion, let both sides join in creating a new endeavor, not a new balance of power, but a new world of law, where the strong are just and the weak secure and the peace preserved.

All this will not be finished in the first one hundred days. Nor will it 20 be finished in the first one thousand days, nor in the life of this Administration, nor even perhaps in our lifetime on this planet. But let us begin.

In your hands, my fellow citizens, more than mine, will rest the 21
final success or failure of our course. Since this country was founded,
each generation of Americans has been summoned to give testimony to
its national loyalty. The graves of young Americans who answered the
call to service surround the globe.

Now the trumpet summons us—again not as a call to bear arms, 22
though arms we need—not as a call to battle, though embattled we
are—but a call to bear the burden of a long twilight struggle, year in and
year out, "rejoicing in hope, patient in tribulation"—a struggle against
the common enemies of man: tyranny, poverty, disease and war itself.
Can we forge against these enemies a grand and global alliance, North
and South, East and West, that can assure a more fruitful life for all
mankind? Will you join in that historic effort?

In the long history of the world, only a few generations have been 23
granted the role of defending freedom in its hour of maximum danger.
I do not shrink from this responsibility—I welcome it. I do not believe
that any of us would exchange places with any other people or any
other generation. The energy, the faith, the devotion which we bring to
this endeavor will light our country and all who serve it—and the glow
from that fire can truly light the world. And so, my fellow Americans:
ask not what your country can do for you—ask what you can do for
your country. My fellow citizens of the world: ask not what America
will do for you, but what together we can do for the freedom of man.

Finally, whether you are citizens of America or citizens of the world, 24
ask of us here the same high standards of strength and sacrifice which
we ask of you. With a good conscience our only sure reward, with history the final judge of our deeds, let us go forth to lead the land we love,
asking His blessing and His help, but knowing that here on earth God's
work must truly be our own.

Responding to Reading

1. At the beginning of his speech, Kennedy alludes to the "revolutionary
   beliefs" of Jefferson and asserts, "We are the heirs of that first revolution"
   (4). What does he mean? Do you think his speech offers adequate support
   for this statement?
2. What, according to Kennedy, must we still achieve in order to fulfill
   Jefferson's dreams? Can you think of other problems that must still be
   solved before we can consider the American Dream a reality?
3. Near the end of his speech, Kennedy says, "And so, my fellow Americans:
   ask not what your country can do for you—ask what you can do for your
   country" (23). What does this famous, often-quoted passage actually mean
   in practical terms? Do you think this exhortation is realistic? Do you think
   it is fair? Explain.

I HAVE A DREAM
Martin Luther King, Jr.

One of the greatest civil rights leaders and orators of this century, Martin Luther King, Jr. (1929–1968), was also a Baptist minister and winner of the 1964 Nobel Peace Prize. He was born in Atlanta, Georgia, and earned degrees from four institutions. Influenced by Thoreau and Gandhi, King altered the spirit of African-American protest in the United States by advocating nonviolent civil disobedience to achieve racial equality. King's books include Letter From Birmingham Jail *(1963) and* Where Do We Go from Here: Chaos or Community? *(1967). King was assassinated on April 4, 1968. He delivered the following speech from the steps of the Lincoln Memorial during the March on Washington on August 28, 1963.*

I am happy to join with you today in what will go down in history as the greatest demonstration for freedom in the history of our nation.

Fivescore years ago, a great American, in whose symbolic shadow we stand today, signed the Emancipation Proclamation. This momentous decree came as a great beacon light of hope to millions of Negro slaves who had been seared in the flames of withering injustice. It came as a joyous daybreak to end the long night of their captivity.

But one hundred years later, the Negro still is not free; one hundred years later, the life of the Negro is still sadly crippled by the manacles of segregation and the chains of discrimination; one hundred years later, the Negro lives on a lonely island of poverty in the midst of a vast ocean of material prosperity; one hundred years later, the Negro is still languishing in the corners of American society and finds himself in exile in his own land.

So we've come here today to dramatize a shameful condition. In a sense we've come to our nation's capital to cash a check. When the architects of our republic wrote the magnificent words of the Constitution and the Declaration of Independence, they were signing a promissory note to which every American was to fall heir. This note was the promise that all men, yes, black men as well as white men, would be guaranteed the unalienable rights of life, liberty, and the pursuit of happiness.

It is obvious today that America has defaulted on this promissory note in so far as her citizens of color are concerned. Instead of honoring this sacred obligation, America has given the Negro people a bad check; a check which has come back marked "insufficient funds." We refuse to believe that there are insufficient funds in the great vaults of opportunity of this nation. And so we've come to cash this check, a check that will give us upon demand the riches of freedom and the security of justice.

We have also come to this hallowed spot to remind America of the fierce urgency of now. This is no time to engage in the luxury of cooling off or to take the tranquilizing drug of gradualism. Now is the time to make real the promises of democracy; now is the time to rise from the dark and desolate valley of segregation to the sunlit path of racial justice; now is the time to lift our nation from the quicksands of racial injustice to the solid rock of brotherhood; now is the time to make justice a reality for all God's children. It would be fatal for the nation to overlook the urgency of the moment. This sweltering summer of the Negro's legitimate discontent will not pass until there is an invigorating autumn of freedom and equality.

Nineteen sixty-three is not an end, but a beginning. And those who 7 hope that the Negro needed to blow off steam and will now be content, will have a rude awakening if the nation returns to business as usual.

There will be neither rest nor tranquility in America until the Negro 8 is granted his citizenship rights. The whirlwinds of revolt will continue to shake the foundations of our nation until the bright day of justice emerges.

But there is something that I must say to my people who stand on 9 the warm threshold which leads into the palace of justice. In the process of gaining our rightful place we must not be guilty of wrongful deeds.

Let us not seek to satisfy our thirst for freedom by drinking from the 10 cup of bitterness and hatred. We must forever conduct our struggle on the high plane of dignity and discipline. We must not allow our creative protest to degenerate into physical violence. Again and again we must rise to the majestic heights of meeting physical force with soul force.

The marvelous new militancy which has engulfed the Negro com- 11 munity must not lead us to a distrust of all white people, for many of our white brothers, as evidenced by their presence here today, have come to realize that their destiny is tied up with our destiny and they have come to realize that their freedom is inextricably bound to our freedom. This offense we share mounted to storm the battlements of injustice must be carried forth by a biracial army. We cannot walk alone.

And as we walk, we must make the pledge that we shall always 12 march ahead. We cannot turn back. There are those who are asking the devotees of civil rights, "When will you be satisfied?" We can never be satisfied as long as the Negro is the victim of the unspeakable horrors of police brutality.

We can never be satisfied as long as our bodies, heavy with fatigue 13 of travel, cannot gain lodging in the motels of the highways and the hotels of the cities. We cannot be satisfied as long as the Negro's basic mobility is from a smaller ghetto to a larger one.

We can never be satisfied as long as our children are stripped of 14 their selfhood and robbed of their dignity by signs stating "for whites only." We cannot be satisfied as long as a Negro in Mississippi cannot vote and a Negro in New York believes he has nothing for which to vote. No, we are not satisfied, and we will not be satisfied until justice rolls down like waters and righteousness like a mighty stream.

I am not unmindful that some of you have come here out of exces- 15 sive trials and tribulation. Some of you have come fresh from narrow jail cells. Some of you have come from areas where your quest for freedom left you battered by the storms of persecution and staggered by the winds of police brutality. You have been the veterans of creative suffering. Continue to work with the faith that unearned suffering is redemptive.

Go back to Mississippi; go back to Alabama; go back to South 16 Carolina; go back to Georgia; go back to Louisiana; go back to the slums and ghettos of the northern cities, knowing that somehow this situation can, and will be changed. Let us not wallow in the valley of despair.

So I say to you, my friends, that even though we must face the dif- 17 ficulties of today and tomorrow, I still have a dream. It is a dream deeply rooted in the American dream that one day this nation will rise up and live out the true meaning of its creed—we hold these truths to be self-evident, that all men are created equal.

I have a dream that one day on the red hills of Georgia, sons of for- 18 mer slaves and sons of former slave-owners will be able to sit down together at the table of brotherhood.

I have a dream that one day, even the state of Mississippi, a state 19 sweltering with the heat of injustice, sweltering with the heat of oppression, will be transformed into an oasis of freedom and justice.

I have a dream my four little children will one day live in a nation 20 where they will not be judged by the color of their skin but by the content of their character. I have a dream today!

I have a dream that one day, down in Alabama, with its vicious 21 racists, with its governor having his lips dripping with the words of interposition and nullification, that one day, right there in Alabama, little black boys and black girls will be able to join hands with little white boys and white girls as sisters and brothers. I have a dream today!

I have a dream that one day every valley shall be exalted, every hill 22 and mountain shall be made low, the rough places shall be made plain, and the crooked places shall be made straight and the glory of the Lord will be revealed and all flesh shall see it together.

This is our hope. This is the faith that I go back to the South with. 23

With this faith we will be able to hew out of the mountain of despair 24 a stone of hope. With this faith we will be able to transform the jangling discords of our nation into a beautiful symphony of brotherhood.

With this faith we will be able to work together, to pray together, to 25 struggle together, to go to jail together, to stand up for freedom together, knowing that we will be free one day. This will be the day when all of God's children will be able to sing with new meaning—"my country 'tis of thee; sweet land of liberty; of thee I sing; land where my fathers died, land of the pilgrim's pride; from every mountain side, let freedom ring"—and if America is to be a great nation, this must become true.

So let freedom ring from the prodigious hilltops of New Hampshire.   26

Let freedom ring from the mighty mountains of New York.   27

Let freedom ring from the heightening Alleghenies of Pennsylvania.   28

Let freedom ring from the snow-capped Rockies of Colorado.   29

Let freedom ring from the curvaceous slopes of California.   30

But not only that.   31

Let freedom ring from Stone Mountain of Georgia.   32

Let freedom ring from Lookout Mountain of Tennessee.   33

Let freedom ring from every hill and molehill of Mississippi, from every mountainside, let freedom ring.   34

And when we allow freedom to ring, when we let it ring from every village and hamlet, from every state and city, we will be able to speed up that day when all of God's children—black men and white men, Jews and Gentiles, Catholics and Protestants—will be able to join hands and to sing in the words of the old Negro spiritual, "Free at last, free at last; thank God Almighty, we are free at last."   35

Responding to Reading

1. What exactly is King's dream? Do you believe it has come true in any sense?
2. Speaking as a representative of his fellow African-American citizens, King tells his audience that African Americans find themselves "in exile in [their] own land" (3). Do you believe this is still true of African-Americans? Of members of other minority groups? Which groups? Why?
3. Jefferson wrote in the eighteenth century; King, in the twentieth. Jefferson wrote as an insider, a man of privilege; King, as an outsider. What do their dreams have in common? How did each man intend to achieve his dream?

──────────── WIDENING THE FOCUS ────────────

- Jonathan Kozol, "Savage Inequalites" (p. 112)

- Martin Luther King, Jr., "Letter from Birmingham Jail" (p. 457)

- Russell Feingold. "The Need for a Moratorium on Executions" (p. 719)

Responding to the Image

1. What does this photograph suggest to you about the power of the American Dream? How might this little girl—or her parents—define the American Dream?
2. Compare the expression on the little girl's face with that of the model of the Statue of Liberty she is looking at. What point do you think the photographer intended to make with this picture?

--- **WRITING** ---

The American Dream

1. Write an essay in which you support the idea that the strength of the United States comes from its ability to assimilate many different groups. In your essay, discuss specific contributions your own ethnic group and others have made to American society.

2. Both Judith Ortiz Cofer and Bharati Mukherjee identify strongly with a culture that is not part of the U.S. mainstream. Compare and contrast their views about assimilation into the dominant "American" culture. Before you begin, read Pico Iyer's "The Global Village Finally Arrives" in Chapter 4.

3. Some of the writers in this chapter respond to their feelings of being excluded from American society with anger and protest; others respond with resignation and acceptance. Considering several different writers and situations, write an essay in which you contrast these two kinds of responses. Under what circumstances, if any, does each kind of response make sense?

4. What do you see as the greatest obstacle to full access to the American Dream? (You might, for example, consider the limitations posed by gender, race, religion, language, social class, ethnicity, physical handicap, lack of education, or poverty.) Support your thesis with references to several selections in this chapter—and, if you like, to your own experiences.

5. In paragraph 22 of her essay "American Dreamer," Bharati Mukherjee discusses the limitations of the "multicultural mosaic" metaphor; later in her essay, she explains why she rejects hypenation, preferring to see herself "as an American rather than as an Asian-American" (p. 462, paragraph 26). Choose several of the writers represented in this chapter, and consider how they would react to Mukherjee's position.

6. Is the United States still a land of opportunity? Support your position on this issue with references to readings in this chapter and elsewhere in this book. Be sure to explain what you mean by *opportunity*.

7. Using the readings in this chapter as source material, write a manifesto that sets forth the rights and responsibilities of all Americans. (Begin by reading Kennedy's inaugural address.)

8. Read the essay by Charles R. Lawrence III and Mari Matsuda. Then, considering their arguments as well as your own experiences and observations as a student, try to formulate a position on the issue of affirmative action. Are affirmative action programs necessary to provide full access to the American Dream for all? Are certain

groups owed compensation for past mistreatment—and, if so, which ones? Or are affirmative action programs inherently unfair, discriminating against some groups even as they help others? For additional background, you may read Jonathan Kozol's "Savage Inequalities" or Maya Angelou's "Graduation" in Chapter 2.

9. Most of the writers whose works appear in this chapter are Americans, people who view the American Dream as something of their own. De Toqueville, however, was clearly an outsider, looking at American institutions and aspirations from an objective point of view. What special insights did his outsider status give him? Which of the writers in this chapter might benefit from de Toqueville's insights?

10. Read the selections by Jefferson, Lazarus, Kennedy, and King in the Focus section of this chapter. Then, try to answer the question "What is the American Dream?"

11. **For Internet research:** A prime on-line source of documents relating to the American Dream is provided by the Library of Congress (<http://memory.loc.gov>), but its sheer size makes it difficult to maneuver. Smaller sites affiliated with universities include <http://odur.let.rug.nl/~usa/01>, <http://www.law.ou.edu/hist/#ind>, and <http://luminet.net/~tgovt/docs.htm>. For documents relating to African-American history, see <http://www.watson.org/lisa/blackhistory> and <http://www.Africana.com>. For women's history resources, see <http://www.germantownacademy.org/Academics/US/history/Herstory/WomensHistory.htm>. Another informative site is that of the U.S. Immigaration and Naturalization Service, <http://www.ins.usdoj.gov/graphics/aboutins/history/index.htm>. Any of these could help you develop an essay defining the American Dream, as suggested in number 10 above.

7

THE WIRED REVOLUTION

———— PREPARING TO READ AND WRITE ————

By now, it is clear that the computer has profoundly changed both our world and us. No other technological advance—except possibly the invention of the printing press—has had such an impact on the way we gather and process information. No longer limited to a specific library, students can instantly access a world of books and articles from an electronic database or the Internet. With e-mail, people separated by thousands of miles are no more than a keystroke away. Even the way we do business has changed—perhaps forever. In the future, online catalogs and interactive websites may well take the place of stores, banks, and even college classrooms.

For all their potential for good, computers also have a dark side. In one sense, computers have linked people together; in another sense, they have isolated people who sit alone in front of their computers accessing a virtual reality. Another concern is whether we are up to the challenge of the information age. Will people ever be able to process all the information—some of it reliable and some of it highly questionable—that computers make available? Still another concern is whether the hundreds of millions of dollars being spent to wire American classrooms have been invested wisely. Do computers actually improve the learning skills of students, or do they simply distract both teachers and students from the business of education?

The Focus section in this chapter (p. 499) addresses the question "Is There Equality in Cyberspace?" The essays in this section examine the fact that not all groups have access to the Internet. The result of this inequality is a "digital divide" that has the potential for being every bit as destructive as forced segregation was in the past.

As you read and prepare to write about the essays in this chapter, you may consider the following questions:

- How does the writer approach computers? With an open mind or with a set of preconceived ideas?

- What technical background does the writer expect readers to have?

- On what issue does the writer focus?

- What position does the writer take on this issue? Do you agree or agree disagree with his or her position?

- Does the writer focus on the positive or the negative effects of technology?

- If the essay focuses on a problem, does it concentrate on finding a solution, speculating on long-term effects, or warning about future consequences?

- Is the writer optimistic or pessimistic about the future of computers?

- What areas of common concern do the writers explore?

- How are the writers' views on computers alike? How are their views different?

TWO VIEWS OF TECHNOLOGY'S PROMISE

Ashley Dunn

A native of California, Ashley Dunn attended the University of California at Santa Cruz, where he studied journalism. From 1996 to 1998, he wrote the "Mind and Machine" column for the "Cybertimes" section of the New York Times. *He is currently a staff writer with the* Los Angeles Times, *focusing on technology. The following essay originally appeared in* the New York Times.

After a night of chasing dogs and cursing antiquarians in 1909, a 1
32-year-old Italian poet by the name of Filippo Tommaso Marinetti
scribbled out an exuberant paean to the technology of the new century
titled, "The Joy of Mechanical Force."

"Let's go! . . . Friends, away!" wrote Marinetti, whose piece appeared 2
in the February 20, 1909 issue of *Le Figaro*, the Paris newspaper. "Let's go!
Mythology and the Mystic Ideal are defeated at last. We're about to see
the Centaur's birth and, soon after, the first flight of Angels! . . . We must
shake at the gates of life, test the bolts and hinges. Let's go! Look there,
on the earth, the very first dawn! There's nothing to match the splendor

of the sun's red sword, slashing for the first time through our millennial gloom!"

For Marinetti, the technology of the new century brought a liberation. 3 Within his essay, he penned a Manifesto of Futurism, in which he hailed the glories of machines, war and the chaos of the twentieth-century city, to incite the artistic community of his time.

"We will sing of the great crowds excited by work, by pleasure and 4 by riot; we will sing of the multicolored, polyphonic tides of revolution in the modern capitals; we will sing of the vibrant nightly fervor of arsenals and shipyards blazing with the violent electric moons; greedy railway stations that devour smoke-plumed serpents; factories hung on clouds by the crooked lines of their smoke."

The Futurist movement lasted only a few years before mutating 5 into other forms. Some of its early proponents died in the mechanized brutality of World War I. Others migrated to different artistic movements. Marinetti himself became a Fascist poet, the court darling of Mussolini.

Despite its dubious credentials, the Manifesto of Futurism still stands 6 as one of the defining documents on the allure of technology.

Since Marinetti's time, the excitement over technological progress 7 has been considerably muddied. While the same exhilaration is felt in pondering the possibilities of future microprocessors or the ultimate expansion of the Internet, it has also been joined by a sense of grim oppression.

It is a modern vision of technology that has been shaped by a group 8 of thinkers, including Jean Baudrillard and Paul Virilio, who have focused on the distorting power of the computer.

In a 1995 essay titled "Red Alert in Cyberspace," Virilio, wrote: 9 "What is now under way is a disturbance of the perception of the real: a trauma. And we need to concentrate on this. Because no technology has ever been developed that has not had to struggle against its own specific negativity."

The essay, published in French in *Le Monde Diplomatique* and in 10 English in the British journal *Radical Philosophy*, went on to warn: "The specific negativity of information superhighways is precisely this disorientation of alterity, of our relation to the other and to the world. It is quite clear that this disorientation, the 'de-situation,' will bring about a profound disturbance with consequences for society and, in turn, for democracy."

Virilio, Baudrillard and Marinetti form a set of bookends to our 11 century that mark a shifting vision of technology from a force of individual liberation at the beginning of the century to one of collective oppression at the terminus. How did we find ourselves in this place?

Marinetti wrote his manifesto at a particular moment of industrial 12 development that for the first time, put the power of the machine in the hands of individuals. For a century before Marinetti, the machine largely had been only an oppressive force—the ceaseless devices of the industrial revolution. But the automobile marked a significant turning point for Marinetti. Now individuals could partake of the same amplification of labor that factory owners had enjoyed. Even today, the automobile, along with its lesser cousins—the leaf blower, lawn mower and weed wacker—remains the most important labor amplifying device that individuals own.

But since Marinetti's time, technology has reached another turning 13 point, driven by devices like television and computers, which affect the senses. For Baudrillard and Virilio, these new types of devices have led to a perceptual distortion of reality that they believe can be used to oppress.

Their writings are difficult, and I can only offer a rough approxima- 14 tion of their views. But even in their crudest form they are a fascinating expression of modern concerns about technology.

For Jean Baudrillard the key is an idea that he calls "simulation." In 15 his vision, past reality was dominated by real objects, which could be reproduced—the foundation of industrial society. The material nature of things meant that what you saw was what you got.

But the computer and other devices opened a new world in which 16 objects could be created that had no material counterpart. It seems like a small point, but these simulations, Baudrillard says, are the pieces of a new type of reality—"hyper-reality"—an artificial world with artificial rules.

Like a computer program that rejects unknown or improper inputs, 17 hyper-reality demands its own type of perfection and orderliness. The systems that create these simulations have a "surgical compulsion" to "excise negative characteristics and remodel things synthetically into ideal forms." What he is trying to say is that in hyper-reality, real people and real things look like errors that must be remodeled or removed.

There are numerous examples of how this has become an oppressive 18 power. For example, credit bureaus have a digital version of your identity in storage. It's not really you by any stretch of the imagination, but for banks, business owners or perhaps employers, that digital simulation of you carries enormous power.

For Baudrillard, hyper-reality is quickly overwhelming material 19 reality, driven by our own preference for the neatness of simulation over the chaos of reality. It's why Disneyland can be so seductive.

Paul Virilio strikes at this same issue of oppression from a different 20 perspective but maintains the same sense of foreboding in the gap that is developing between material reality and virtual reality.

Virilio argues that the development of information devices has 21 created a world dominated by instantaneous and immediate interaction. Again, this would seem to be a good thing, in the sense that we can now just pick up a phone and talk to other people, or watch live events on television. For Virilio, however, this is a formula for disaster.

A world of "real time" has begun to displace our old world based 22 on real space, locality and proximity.

"We face the prospect in the twenty-first century of the invention 23 of a perspective based on real time, replacing the spatial perspective, the perspective based on real space, discovered by Italian artists of the quatrocento," Virilio wrote in "Red Alert in Cyberspace." "Perhaps we forget how much the cities, politics, wars and economies of the Medieval world were transformed by the invention of perspective.

"Perceived reality is being split into the real and the virtual, and 24 we are getting a kind of stereo-reality in which existence loses its reference points. To be is to be *in situ*, here and now, *hic et nunc*. But cyberspace and instantaneous, globalized information are throwing all that into total confusion."

The result of this speed gap between the real and virtual worlds is a 25 disorientation of the individual that can be manipulated by those who control the flow of information—typically governments and businesses.

The ideas of Baudrillard and Virilio crystallize what most Net users 26 have grasped in their own ways. But what is ultimately jarring about their thoughts—as well as about the writings of Marinetti—is that they seem so distant to the ordinary experience of virtuality.

The computer and other information devices clearly can be used to 27 oppress, but they have also been used in myriad ways to liberate and energize, in the same sense that Marinetti articulated 90 years ago.

As for Marinetti's exuberance, there is an aura of magic about 28 advanced technology, but at the same time, there is a plainness and neutrality of many devices that we use every day without thought, like a fax machine or a programmable videocassette recorder. For all the philosophizing, there is a part of technological devices that make them no different from hammers.

Humans share a propensity for gazing on advanced technology in 29 an almost magical light. But at the same time, the "surgical compulsion" of technology to remodel the world in its own image drives a counterforce that constantly turns the once exotic into the commonplace.

Once the devices become common, the magic is gone and they 30 stand in more realistic terms—a mix of complexity and triviality, power and stupidity. Then, we ponder their existence less and less—or at least we ponder them in very different ways.

Today, people sing the glories of the automobile in magazines like 31 *Motor Trend* or *Road and Track*. Their admiration is paraded in the streets of Los Angeles in the form of Volkswagens festooned with toilet seats or dented Impalas that smoke down the freeway.

The impact of technology is not easily wrapped in a single bundle. 32 Even as Marinetti was careening down the streets of Milan, Marxists were gathering strength elsewhere to bring down the oppressive system of the factory. As Baudrillard and Virilio warn of imminent doom, the CyberUtopians and Extropians hail the technological leaps that they hope will push mankind to another level of development.

For us commoners, the cycle is not nearly so refined or exclusive but is more a mix of the many ways that technology has improved or worsened our lot in life. So much of technology cannot even be categorized as good or bad anymore. 33

Consider the flashing red lights on my son's shoes. A few hundred years ago, they would have been revered as magic. Today, they are simply what comes with kids [*sic*] shoes, whether you want them or not. 34

My son's shoes make me think that perhaps there is no linear path toward doom or salvation, but rather cycles of exotic-to-common that never end and constantly overlap. In the same world that produced Marinetti's machines of liberation and Baudrillard and Virilio's wired doom, there are also these shoes. They blink with beautiful predictability and precision, for no purpose at all. 35

Responding to Reading

1. According to Dunn, what are the two views of technology's promise? In what way do they serve as "bookends" to the twentieth century?
2. What is Dunn's view of technology? In what way is his view different from that of Baudrillard and Vitrilio?
3. In paragraph 25, Dunn says that the gap between the real and the virtual worlds disorients individuals and enables them to be "manipulated by those who control the flow of information—typically governments and businesses." What does he mean? Do you agree?

An Age of Optimism

Nicholas Negroponte

One of the so-called founders of the Internet, Nicholas Negroponte (1943–) was pursuing graduate studies in architecture at the Massachusetts Institute of Technology when he became interested in how computers could be designed for most efficient use. He joined the faculty of MIT in 1966 and while there started the Architecture Machine group to further the study of human- computer interface. Now Jerome B. Weisner Professor of media technology, Negroponte also heads MIT's Media Laboratory, a think tank funded by private corporations to direct research into the future of human communication. He has also been involved in the financing of several computer-related ventures, including Wired *magazine, to which he contributes a monthly column. Following is the final chapter of his book* Being Digital *(1995), in which he speculates about how computer technology will affect the future.*

I am optimistic by nature. However, every technology or gift of science has a dark side. Being digital is no exception. 1

The next decade will see cases of intellectual-property abuse and 2 invasion of our privacy. We will experience digital vandalism, software piracy, and data thievery. Worst of all, we will witness the loss of many jobs to wholly automated systems, which will soon change the white-collar workplace to the same degree that it has already transformed the factory floor. The notion of lifetime employment at one job has already started to disappear.

The radical transformation of the nature of our job markets, as we 3 work less with atoms and more with bits, will happen at just about the same time the 2 billion-strong labor force of India and China starts to come on-line (literally). A self-employed software designer in Peoria will be competing with his or her counterpart in Pohang. A digital typographer in Madrid will do the same with one in Madras. American companies are already outsourcing hardware development and software production to Russia and India, not to find cheap manual labor but to secure a highly skilled intellectual force seemingly prepared to work harder, faster, and in a more disciplined fashion than those in our own country.

As the business world globalizes and the Internet grows, we will start 4 to see a seamless digital workplace. Long before political harmony and long before the GATT[1] talks can reach agreement on the tariff and trade of atoms (the right to sell Evian water in California), bits will be borderless, stored and manipulated with absolutely no respect to geopolitical boundaries. In fact, time zones will probably play a bigger role in our digital future than trade zones. I can imagine some software projects that literally move around the world from east to west on a twenty-four-hour cycle, from person to person or from group to group, one working as the other sleeps. Microsoft will need to add London and Tokyo offices for software development in order to produce on three shifts.

As we move more toward such a digital world, an entire sector of the 5 population will be or feel disenfranchised. When a fifty-year-old steelworker loses his job, unlike his twenty-five-year-old son, he may have no digital resilience at all. When a modern-day secretary loses his job, at least he may be conversant with the digital world and have transferable skills.

---

[1]General Agreement on *Tariffs* and *Trade,* an international free trade agreement. [Eds.]

Bits are not edible; in that sense they cannot stop hunger. Computers 6
are not moral; they cannot resolve complex issues like the rights to life
and to death. But being digital, nevertheless, does give much cause for
optimism. Like a force of nature, the digital age cannot be denied or
stopped. It has four very powerful qualities that will result in its ultimate
triumph: decentralizing, globalizing, harmonizing, and empowering

The decentralizing effect of being digital can be felt no more strongly 7
than in commerce and in the computer industry itself. The so-called management
information systems (MIS) czar, who used to reign over a glass-
enclosed and air-conditioned mausoleum, is an emperor with no clothes,
almost extinct. Those who survive are usually doing so because they out-
rank anybody able to fire them, and the company's board of directors is
out of touch or asleep or both.

Thinking Machines Corporation, a great and imaginative supercom- 8
puter company started by electrical engineering genius Danny Hillis, disappeared after ten years. In that short space of time it introduced the
world to massively parallel computer architectures. Its demise did not
occur because of mismanagement or sloppy engineering of their so-called
Connection Machine. It vanished because parallelism could be decentralized; the very same kind of massively parallel architectures have suddenly become possible by threading together low-cost, mass-produced
personal computers.

While this was not good news for Thinking Machines, it is an impor- 9
tant message to all of us, both literally and metaphorically. It means the
enterprise of the future can meet its computer needs in a new and scal-
able way by populating its organization with personal computers that,
when needed, can work in unison to crunch on computationally intensive problems. Computers will literally work both for individuals and
for groups. I see the same decentralized mind-set growing in our society,
driven by young citizenry in the digital world. The traditional centralist
view of life will become a thing of the past.

The nation-state itself is subject to tremendous change and global- 10
ization. Governments fifty years from now will be both larger and
smaller. Europe finds itself dividing itself into smaller ethnic entities
while trying to unite economically. The forces of nationalism make it too
easy to be cynical and dismiss any broad-stroke attempt at world unification. But in the digital world, previously impossible solutions become
viable.

Today, when 20 percent of the world consumes 80 percent of its 11
resources, when a quarter of us have an acceptable standard of living and
three-quarters don't, how can this divide possibly come together? While
the politicians struggle with the baggage of history, a new generation is
emerging from the digital landscape free of many of the old prejudices.
These kids are released from the limitation of geographic proximity as the

sole basis of friendship, collaboration, play, and neighborhood. Digital technology can be a natural force drawing people into greater world harmony.

The harmonizing effect of being digital is already apparent as previ- 12
ously partitioned disciplines and enterprises find themselves collab rating, not competing. A previously missing common language emerges, allowing people to understand across boundaries. Kids at school today experience the opportunity to look at the same thing from many perspectives. A computer program, for example, can be seen simultaneously as a set of computer instructions or as concrete poetry formed by the indentations in the text of the program. What kids learn very quickly is that to know a program is to know it from many perspectives, not just one.

But more than anything, my optimism comes from the empowering 13
nature of being digital. The access, the mobility, and the ability to effect change are what will make the future so different from the present. The information superhighway may be mostly hype today, but it is an understatement about tomorrow. It will exist beyond people's wildest predictions. As children appropriate a global information resource, and as they discover that only adults need learner's permits, we are bound to find new hope and dignity in place where very little existed before.

My optimism is not fueled by an anticipated invention or discovery. 14
Finding a cure for cancer and AIDS, finding an acceptable way to control population, or inventing a machine that can breathe our air and drink our oceans and excrete unpolluted forms of each are dreams that may or may not come about. Being digital is different. We are not waiting on any invention. It is here. It is now. It is almost genetic in its nature, in that each generation will become more digital than the preceding one. The control bits of that digital future are more than ever before in the hands of the young. Nothing could make me happier.

Responding to Reading

1. Negroponte begins by saying, "I am optimistic by nature" (1). He then goes on to point out "the dark side" of digital technology. Why does Negroponte begin his essay with a discussion of the drawbacks of digital technology?

2. According to Negroponte, digital technology will create "greater world harmony" (11). How will this be accomplished? Do you agree with his prediction?

3. In paragraph 13, Negroponte says that his optimism "comes from the empowering nature of being digital." In what way does he think being digital is empowering? Is Negroponte being realistic, or is he being overly optimistic?

COMPUTERS

Lewis Thomas

Lewis Thomas (1913–1993), born in Flushing, New York, was a doctor, researcher, and teacher affiliated with Johns Hopkins University, New York University, and the Memorial Sloan-Kettering Cancer Center. Thomas began writing a column called "Notes of a Biology Watcher" for the New England Journal of Medicine *in 1971 and gained popularity with new readers when some of these columns were collected in* Lives of a Cell *(1974), which won the National Book Award. Other collections of his essays are* The Medusa and the Snail: More Notes of a Biology Watcher *(1979),* Late Night Thoughts on Listening Mahler's Ninth Symphony *(1983), and* Fragile Specie *(1992). Thomas was known for his optimistic views of relationships in the natural world, and for combining scientific observation with lyrical prose. "Computers" first appeared in the* New England Journal of Medicine *in 1974.*

You can make computers that are almost human. In some respects 1 they are superhuman; they can beat most of us at chess, memorize whole telephone books at a glance, compose music of a certain kind and write obscure poetry, diagnose heart ailments, send personal invitations to vast parties, even go transiently crazy. No one has yet programmed a computer to be of two minds about a hard problem, or to burst out laughing, but that may come. Sooner or later, there will be real human hardware, great whirring, clicking cabinets intelligent enough to read magazines and vote, able to think rings around the rest of us.

Well, maybe, but not for a while anyway. Before we begin organiz- 2 ing sanctuaries and reservations for our software selves, lest we vanish like the whales, here is a thought to relax with.

Even when technology succeeds in manufacturing a machine as big 3 as Texas to do everything we recognize as human, it will still be, at best, a single individual. This amounts to nothing, practically speaking. To match what we can do, there would have to be 3 billion of them with more coming down the assembly line, and I doubt that anyone will put up the money, much less make room. And even so, they would all have to be wired together, intricately and delicately, as we are communicating with each other, talking incessantly, listening. If they weren't at each other this way, all their waking hours, they wouldn't be anything like human, after all. I think we're safe, for a long time ahead.

It is in our collective behavior that we are most mysterious. We 4 won't be able to construct machines like ourselves until we've understood this, and we're not even close. All we know is the phenomenon: we spend our time sending messages to each other, talking and trying to listen at the same time, exchanging information. This seems to be our most urgent biological function; it is what we do with our lives. By the time we reach the end, each of us has taken in a staggering store, enough to exhaust any computer, much of it incomprehensible, and we generally manage to put out even more than we take in. Information is our source of energy; we are driven by it. It has become a tremendous enterprise, a kind of energy system on its own. All 3 billion of us are being connected by telephones, radios, television sets, airplanes, satellites, harangues on public-address systems, newspapers, magazines, leaflets dropped from great heights, words got in edgewise. We are becoming a grid, a circuitry around the earth. If we keep at it, we will become a computer to end all computers, capable of fusing all the thoughts of the world into a syncytium.

Already, there are no closed, two-way conversations. Any word you 5 speak this afternoon will radiate out in all directions, around town before tomorrow, out and around the world before Tuesday, accelerating to the speed of light, modulating as it goes, shaping new, and unexpected messages, emerging at the end as an enormously funny Hungarian joke, a fluctuation in the money market, a poem, or simply a long pause in someone's conversation in Brazil.

We do a lot of collective thinking, probably more than any other so- 6 cial species, although it goes on in something like secrecy. We don't acknowledge the gift publicly, and we are not as celebrated as the insects, but we do it. Effortlessly, without giving it a moment's thought, we are capable of changing our language, music, manners, morals, entertainment, even the way we dress, all around the earth in a year's turning. We seem to do this by general agreement, without voting or even polling. We simply think our way along, pass information around, exchange codes disguised as art, change our minds, transform ourselves.

Computers cannot deal with such levels of improbability, and it is 7 just as well. Otherwise, we might be tempted to take over the control of ourselves in order to make long-range plans, and that would surely be the end of us. It would mean that some group or other, marvelously intelligent and superbly informed, undoubtedly guided by a computer, would begin deciding what human society ought to be like, say, over the next five hundred years or so, and the rest of us would be persuaded, one way or another, to go along. The process of social evolution would then grind to a standstill, and we'd be stuck in today's rut for a millennium.

Much better we work our way out of it on our own, without gover- 8 nance. The future is too interesting and dangerous to be entrusted to any predictable, reliable agency. We need all the fallibility we can get. Most of all, we need to preserve the absolute unpredictability and total improbability of our connected minds. That way we can keep open all the options, as we have in the past.

It would be nice to have better ways of monitoring what we're up to 9 so that we could recognize change while it is occurring, instead of waking up as we do now to the astonished realization that the whole century just past wasn't what we thought it was, at all. Maybe computers can be used to help in this, although I rather doubt it. You can make simulation models of cities, but what you learn is that they seem to be beyond the reach of intelligent analysis; if you try to use common sense to make predictions, things get more botched up than ever. This is interesting, since a city is the most concentrated aggregation of humans, all exerting whatever influence they can bring to bear. The city seems to have a life of its own. If we cannot understand how this works, we are not likely to get very far with human society at large.

Still, you'd think there would be some way in. Joined together, the 10 great mass of human minds around the earth seems to behave like a coherent, living system. The trouble is that the flow of information is mostly one-way. We are all obsessed by the need to feed information in, as fast as we can, but we lack sensing mechanisms for getting anything much back. I will confess that I have no more sense of what goes on in the mind of mankind than I have for the mind of an ant. Come to think of it, this might be a good place to start.

Responding to Reading

1. In what ways are human beings different from computers? According to Thomas, will computers ever be like human beings?
2. In paragraph 4, Thomas says, "It is in our collective behavior that we are most mysterious." What does he mean? Do you agree with his assessment?
3. Thomas wrote this essay in 1974. What point was he making? In your opinion, is this point still relevant today? Would another title have conveyed his point more effectively?

PREGNANT WITH POSSIBILITY
Gregory J. E. Rawlins

Gregory J. E. Rawlins (1958–   ) received his bachelor's degree in mathematics from the University of the West Indies and his doctorate in computer science from the University of Waterloo. Currently a professor of computer science at Indiana University, he is the author of numerous scholarly articles, as well as the textbooks Foundations of Genetic Algorithms *(1991) and* Compared to What? An Introduction to the Analysis of Algorithms *(1992). A popular speaker on issues of electronic publishing, Rawlins has also published two books on technology for a general audience:* Moths to the

Flame: The Seductions of Computer Technology (1996) and Slaves of the Machine: The Quickening of Computer Technology (1997). The following selection from Moths to the Flame *argues that computer technology has the grim potential to increase the divisions among the world's citizens in terms of money and power relationships.*

Only connect! That was the whole of her sermon. Only connect the prose and the passion, and both will be exalted, and human love will be seen at its highest.

—E. M. Forster, *Howards End*

Today's computer technology is rapidly turning us into three completely new races: the superpoor, the rich, and the superrich. The superpoor are perhaps eight thousand in every ten thousand of us. The rich —me and you—make up most of the remaining two thousand, while the superrich are perhaps the last two of every ten thousand. Roughly speaking, the decisions of two superrich people control what almost two thousand of us do, and our decisions, in turn, control what the remaining eight thousand do. These groups are really like races since the group you're born into often determines which group your children will be born into.

Only the rich and superrich have the opportunity, education, and resources to own and use computer technology. It's hard to get excited about computers when you're busy starving to death; or living in a tense matrix of drugs and crime and fear; or being forced to prostitute yourself for food and shelter; or being repressed by your own government.

A boy in Bangladesh, a girl in Somalia, or—perhaps saddest of all— many ghetto children in the world's richest countries, might never be able to step onto the world stage that is the net. Working their way among the destroyed buildings and equally destroyed social structures of their environment, they are permanently disenfranchised from the world many of us take for granted. Computers alone cannot erode that mountain of destitution.

Today, we number nearly six thousand million people, but we have only five hundred million telephones—one for each twelve of us. Half of us have never placed a single telephone call in our lives. There are already well over a hundred million computers, and over sixteen million more are added each year—with the number rising rapidly. In a decade or two, five hundred million of us may be connected to a computer network. That connection might eventually make the difference between being an information-starved peon and a global villager.

It is often said that computers will destroy ancient power centers and enfranchise greater masses of people. It is true that in America over a third of all households already have computers. Yet that proportion jumps to well over half for homes with university graduates and to three quarters for homes with incomes above seventy-five thousand dollars. If that pattern is repeated in the world as a whole, computers might merely ensure that the ancient pyramid of power extends into a thin sharp spike, with a tiny few determining the fate of the millions.

By the time that happens, however, there should be a few hundred 6 million people active on the net. (Just think, a global electronic community of a hundred million gossipers.) Perhaps among them will be enough people both connected to the rest of us and compassionate enough to speak for the dispossessed. Perhaps.

Every new communication medium is special. But the net is extra 7 special, because we, the users, are the ones making it, not some faceless corporation. It's growing as fast as it is because it merges two hugely endowed technologies: computers and communications. But it's also growing rapidly because the more people who get on it, the more valuable access to it becomes. Like telephones and fax machines, tennis clubs and bars, the net becomes more attractive as more of us join it. So it's likely that everyone who can afford to will be on the net in fairly short order.

We're gregarious, gossipy creatures, continually talking to each 8 other to find out what others think—or what we should think. Out of that reliance we build community, whether in a pub, at the laundromat, or on the net. Without that communication, that bonding, human society would cease to be. But the net presents numerous dangers too. The search for communion could easily turn into a flight from community. Don't like your neighbors? No problem; turn off, tune in, and drop into a whole other world of people you never have to actually touch. Further, as its demographics broaden and it goes commercial, the net's content will inevitably become more splintered, more trivialized, and perhaps more acrimonious. That's the way of things.

Computers won't bring about a better world—perhaps nothing can 9 do that. But they certainly can change the world: in some ways for the better; in others, for the worse. That's the nature of today's new technology. By changing things in fundamental ways right before our eyes, it lets us see more clearly who we really are by showing us what we truly value. Sometimes, perhaps far more often than necessary, what we see is an ugly side of human nature.

Still, the net today is a glorious experiment. Considering that no one 10 planned it and no one controls it, it shows us that we can make very complex systems work despite our many flaws. As it quickly commercializes, and changes drastically, we should work to preserve some of its more democratic and humane characteristics. Because that's something to be proud of.

Only connect. 11

Responding to Reading

1. Why does Rawlins open and close his essay with a reference to E. M. Forster's phrase "Only connect"? What does this phrase mean?
2. In the opening paragraphs of his essay, Rawlins discusses the gap (technological as well as economic) between "the superpoor, the rich, and the superrich" (1). He concludes, "Computers alone cannot erode [the] mountain of destitution" poor people confront (3). Do you think the fact that they do not have access to the technology so many others take for granted could actually make poor people's lives *worse*? Explain.
3. Would you describe Rawlins's attitude as essentially optimistic or pessimistic? On what issues would he and Ted Gup, who wrote the following essay, agree?

THE END OF SERENDIPITY

Ted Gup

Born in Lima, Ohio, Ted Gup (1950–   ) attended Brandeis University, as well as Trinity College in Dublin, Ireland. He also holds a law degree from Case Western Reserve University. He was a staff writer at the Washington Post *for ten years and, later, a correspondent for* Time *magazine. Currently a professor of journalism at Case Western Reserve, Gup has published articles and essays on a variety of topics as well as* The Book of Honor: Covert Lives and Classified Deaths at the CIA *(2000). The following essay appeared in the* Chronicle of Higher Education *in 1997.*

When I was a young boy, my parents bought me a set of *The World* 1 *Book Encyclopedia.* The 22 burgundy-and-gold volumes lined the shelves above my bed. On any given day or night I would reach for a book and lose myself for hours in its endless pages of maps, photographs, and text. Even when I had a purpose in mind—say, for instance, a homework assignment on salamanders—I would invariably find myself reading instead of Salem and its witch hunts or of Salamis, where the Greeks routed the Persians in the fifth century B.C. Like all encyclopedias of the day, it was arranged alphabetically, based on sound and without regard to subject. As a child, I saw it as a system wondrously whimsical and exquisitely inefficient. Perfect for exploration. The "S" volume alone could lead me down 10,000 unconnected highways.

The world my two young sons inherit is a very different place. That 2 same encyclopedia now comes on cd-rom. Simply drop the platinum disk into the A-drive and type in a key word. In a flash the subject appears on the screen. The search is perfected in a single keystroke—no flipping of pages, no risk of distraction, no unintended consequences. And therein lies the loss.

My boys belong to an age vastly more efficient in its pursuit of 3 information but oblivious to the pleasures and rewards of serendipity. From Silicon Valley to M.I.T., the best minds are dedicated to refining our search for answers. Noble though their intentions may be, they are inadvertently smothering the opportunity to find what may well be the more important answers—the ones to questions that have not yet even occurred to us. I wish, then, to write on behalf of random epiphanies and the virtues of accidental discovery—before they, too, go the way of my old Remington manual[1].

My boys are scarcely aware that they are part of a grand experiment 4 in which the computer, the Internet, and the World-Wide Web are redefining literacy and reshaping the architecture of how they learn. These innovations are ushering in a world that, at least to my tastes, is entirely too purposeful—as devoid of romance as an arranged marriage. Increasingly, we hone our capacity to target the information that we seek. More ominous still, we weed out that which we deem extraneous. In a world of information overload, this ability to filter what reaches us has been hailed as an unqualified good. I respectfully disagree.

Consider, for example, those of my sons' generation who are learn- 5 ing to read the newspaper on a computer screen. They do not hold in their hands a cumbersome front page but instead see a neat menu that has sliced and diced the news into user-friendly categories. They need not read stories but merely scan topical headings—sports, finance, entertainment. The risk that they or any readers will inadvertently be drawn into a story afield from their peculiar interests, or succumb to some picture or headline, grows ever more remote. The users define their needs while the computer, like an overly eager waiter, stands ready to deliver, be it the latest basketball scores, updates of a personal stock portfolio, or tomorrow's weather. In my youth, information was a smorgasbord. Walking past so irresistible an array of dishes, I found it impossible not to fill my plate. Today, everything is à la carte.

There are moral consequences to being able to tailor the information 6 that reaches us. Like other journalists, I have spent much of my life writing stories that I knew, even as I worked on them, would not be welcomed by my readers. Accounts of war, of hardship or want seldom are.

---

[1] A manual—that is, nonelectric—typewriter. [Eds.]

But those stories found their way first into readers' hands and then into their minds. They were read sometimes reluctantly, sometimes with resentment, and, most often, simply because they appeared on the printed page. Doubtless the photo of a starving child or a string of refugees stretching above the morning's shredded wheat and orange juice may be viewed as an unsightly intrusion, but it is hard to ignore.

In cyberspace, such intrusions will become less frequent. There will 7 be fewer and fewer uninvited guests. Nothing will come unless summoned. Unless the mouse clicks on the story, the account will not materialize. And who will click on the story headlined "Rwandans Flee," "Inner-City Children Struggle," or even "Endangered Butterflies Fight for Survival"? If the mouse is a key, it is also a padlock to keep the world out.

Those already on the margins of our consciousness—the homeless, 8 the weak, the disenfranchised—are being pushed right off the page, exiled into cyberspace and the ever-expanding domain of the irrelevant. Already the phrase "That's not on my screen" has found its way into common parlance. In the end, self-interest may be the most virulent form of censorship, inimical to compassion and our sense of community. It is the ultimate V-chip, this power to sanitize reality, to bar unpleasantries. "Technology," the Swiss playwright Max Frisch once observed, is "the knack of so arranging the world that we don't have to experience it."

It would be ironic if the computer, this great device of interconnec- 9 tivity, should engender a world of isolationists. Yet increasingly we use its powers to read about ourselves and to feed our own parochial self-interests. Instead of a global village, we risk a race of cyber-hermits. And the World-Wide Web, the promised badge to that which is beyond ourselves, may be yet another moat to protect the self-absorbed.

A friend of mine recently joined Microsoft. He was struck by the 10 youthfulness of those around him and the absolute faith they had that every question had an answer, every problem a solution. It is the defining character of the Microsoft Culture, its celebration of answers. Within that church, there are few Luthers[2] to challenge its orthodoxy. So much energy is spent to produce the right answers that little time is left to ponder the correctness of the questions.

I find it amusing that Bill Gates, shrewd investor that he is, has 11 emerged as one of the world's premier art collectors, acquiring the notebooks of Leonardo da Vinci, the consummate figure of the Renaissance. I wonder: Does he identify with that genius, or, perhaps recognizing the peril in which that humanistic traditon is now placed, is he simply attempting to corner the market on its artifacts?

---

[2] The reference is to Martin Luther (1483–1546), the religious reformer who broke with the Catholic Church. [Eds.]

This is not a revolution but an evolution. In ancient caves can be 12
found flakes of flint left by early humans, evidence of the first impulse
to put a point on our tools, to refine them. The computer, with its search
engines, is simply an extension of that primal urge. From the Olduvai
Gorge[3] to Silicon Valley, we have always been obsessed with bringing
our tools to a perfect point. But where knowledge of the world is concerned, I suspect there is some virtue to possessing a blunter instrument. Sometimes a miss produces more than a hit.

Ironically, we continue to call entrées to cyberspace "Web browers," 13
but increasingly they are used not to browse but to home in on a narrow
slice of the universe. We invoke mystery with corporate names such as
"Oracle," but we measure progress in purely quantitative terms—giga-
bits and megahertz, capacity and speed. Our search engines carry
names such as "Yahoo" and "Excite," but what they deliver is ever more
predictable. The parameters of the universe shrink, defined by key
words and Boolean filters, sieves that—with each improvement in
search engines—increasingly succeed in siphoning off anything less
than responsive to our inquiries. The more precise the response, the
more the process is hailed as a success.

What has been billed as the information superhighway has, like all 14
superhighways, come with a price. We have shortened the time
between departure and arrival, but gone is all scenery in between,
reduced to a Pentium blur. We settle for information at the expense of
understanding and mistake retrieval for exploration. The vastness of
the Internet's potential threatens to shrink into yet another utility. As the
technology matures, the adolescent exuberance of surfing the Web
yields to the drudgery of yet another commute.

One need not be a Luddite[4] or technophobe to sound a cautionary 15
word in the midst of euphoria over technology. I have a fantasy that one
day I will produce a computer virus and introduce it into my own desktop, so that when my sons put in their key word—say, "salamander"—
the screen will erupt in a brilliant but random array of maps and
illustrations and text that will divert them from their task. This I will do
so that they may know the sheer joy of finding what they have not
sought. I might even wish for this virus to spread from computer to
computer. And I would name this virus for that which ought not to be
lost—serendipity.

---

[3] Site in Tanzania where the fossilized remains of many protohumans have been discovered. [Eds.]
[4] Name given to groups of laborers who rioted in 1811 and 1816 in parts of England, destroying
knitting machines—a new technology—which they believed were responsible for unemployment;
more generally, a term for one who opposes new technology. [Eds].

Responding to Reading

1. According to Gup, how is browsing the web different from browsing through a print encyclopedia? What does he feel has been lost? Do you think he is right?
2. Explain the "moral consequences" Gup discusses in paragraphs 6 through 8. Do you think he is an alarmist, or do you agree that our ability to block unpleasant "intrusions" and "uninvited guests"(7) has potentially serious social implications?
3. In paragraph 9, Gup observes that more and more often, we seem to be using the powers of the computer "to read about ourselves and to feed our own parochial self-interests. " He continues, "Instead of a global village, we risk a race of cyber-hermits." Do you agree? Would Nicholas Negroponte (p. 469)?

IF JOHN DEWEY WERE ALIVE TODAY, HE'D BE A WEBHEAD

Peshe Kuriloff

A graduate of Radcliffe College with a Ph.D. from Bryn Mawr, Peshe Kuriloff has been on the English faculty of the University of Pennsylvania for more than fifteen years. Specializing in creative nonfiction, writing across the curriculum, and teacher training, Kuriloff currently directs the Mellon Writing Project, which focuses on learning in an electronic environment and on new ways of teaching writing online. She has published numerous academic articles as well as pieces for magazines and newspapers, and she also works as a professional communications consultant for businesses and corporations. The following essay originally appeared in the Chronicle of Higher Education *in April 2000.*

When my husband brought home our first Macintosh computer in 1986, and told our children—who were then 12, 8, and 5—not to touch it until he had read the directions, they naturally ignored him. Long before he found time to go through the instructions, they had the machine out of the box, up and running, with software installed, and were pleading for games and other enhancements. They never worried, as he did, about breaking the computer or making sure it was operating correctly. They wanted results, and they learned from experience. They tried various strategies to make the machine work. When they made mistakes, they corrected them. In a short time, they knew how to make the computer do what they wanted. Their learning process was straight out of John Dewey.

Not so much as a premonition of a technology-enhanced universe 2 appears in the writings of Dewey, the educational theorist who has inspired generations of education reformers since he began presenting his thinking at the end of the 19th century. Yet Dewey's dedication to experience as the foundation of education has startling relevance to the debate raging over the value of online teaching and learning. Although the absence of face-to-face interaction unquestionably changes the character of education, the experience of computer-based learning has advantages that we are only beginning to appreciate.

In *Experience and Education*, published in 1938, Dewey offered this 3 summary of the state of education: "Conservatives as well as radicals in education are profoundly discontented with the present educational situation taken as a whole. There is at least this much agreement among intelligent persons of both schools of educational thought. The educational system must move one way or another, either backward to the intellectual and moral standards of a pre-scientific age or forward to ever greater utilization of scientific method in the development of the possibilities of growing, expanding experience."

Although I would hesitate to argue that nothing has changed in the 4 past 62 years, or that the scientific method has not been employed pervasively as the route to learning, Dewey's point still seems well taken. The value of experience as a learning tool has yet to receive wide acceptance outside the natural sciences. Dewey's thinking continues to suggest new ways to conceptualize education. In particular, his insistence on "trying" or "undergoing" as the source of knowledge can help to guide us toward more scientific thinking about, and evaluation of, the uses of instructional technology.

Computer manufactures and software developers are already fol- 5 lowing Dewey's lead. They don't even bother to provide detailed instructions for their products. We are supposed to learn by doing. If we get stuck and can't figure something out on our own, we can call for help. But the self-starters who persist and learn on their own quickly become tomorrow's technological elite.

If we look at the skills required to use computers effectively, not 6 even the most vehement opponent of technology should object to their value as learning tools. Gaining control over the technology fosters a sense of mastery that empowers learners in concrete ways. Acquisition of a skill, such as installing programs, or thorough knowledge of a single program opens the door to numerous possibilities for new learning and experience. The lure of mastery seduces students to experiment, take risks, fail, and try again. Few of the courses that I have taught capture the sense of adventure my students experience in their quest for new knowledge about and control over technology.

The introduction of new instructional technologies is creating a pre-   7
cious opportunity to develop new pedagogies and enhance learning in
ways that will better meet the needs of our society in the 21st century. The
failures of our educational system at all levels have been widely publicized. Even college students often lack literacy and quantitative skills.

To date, solutions have focused on raising standards and giving   8
students more—more reading, more testing—but not on changing our
methods of instruction and our expectations for learning. As Linda
Darling-Hammond, of Stanford University, and many other educators
have pointed out, however, our current educational system was designed
for a different era. We no longer need managers to oversee the Industrial
Revolution; instead, we need adventurers prepared to explore cyberspace, the newest frontier.

It is not by accident that the new technological experts have   9
become so successful and amassed so much power in such a short time.
Like the explorers who navigated the earth to discover new continents,
these adventurers have defined spaces we didn't know existed, and
have registered their claims to that territory.

Yet, the basic curiosity that prompts even young children to pick up   10
a computer mouse and explore cyberspace is in short supply in conventional college classrooms. In recent years, I have often heard my colleagues complain about passive students, devoid of intellectual curiosity.
Computer enthusiasts, however, show a great deal of initiative and routinely take learning into their own hands. Instead of requiring students
to memorize facts or give the prescribed answers to the questions we
pose, we should encourage them to search the Internet for new information and ideas. The skills involved in that process are the same skills that
will help them find solutions for today's social, economic, and political
problems.

Technology is advancing at a relentless pace. As educators, we must   11
exploit our students' experiences with computers to nurture the skills
that will enable them to control, rather than react to, the changes that
new technology will bring.

The rapid pace of change demands flexible thinkers, who view   12
learning and relearning, changing direction, and trying new approaches
as part of everyday life. A great deal of what students learn in college
becomes obsolete before they graduate. We have changed our ideas
about what constitutes the core of a good education. Learning how to
learn has become the most fundamental skill that an educated person
needs to master, and the instrument that enables learning in almost
every field is the computer.

Learning how to learn does no occur simply as a result of knowing   13
how to use a computer to access information. Open-ended searches
help us teach students how to learn. Such searches are a common feature of Internet navigation, because the Net's structure is nonlinear, and

its contents change all the time. The logical thinking that helped previous generations solve problems doesn't work well in the electronic environment. Logic is just one, limited tool for finding answers; intuition plays a critical role, too. Furthermore, learning by reading may well eventually take a back seat to learning from multimedia sources. Successful learners from now on will rely on a more varied repertoire of strategies for absorbing and applying new information—skills we sorely need.

The difficulty of the problems we face in our society demands patience, persistence, and a willingness to make mistakes and try again, traits that are also essential for anyone attempting to develop computer literacy. Open-minded, independent thinkers are more likely to try the multiple strategies needed to make a software program work, or to solve a social problem. They are also better equipped to deal with the absence of authority in cyberspace, and to communicate effectively with a wide range of stakeholders in the real world.   14

As Dewey emphasized, however, not all experience has equal educational value. Although undirected exploration of the Internet, for example, is informative, it does not constitute a good education. Students left to learn on their own may accept as truth the kind of un-examined thinking that proliferates on the Internet. We need to guide them, to teach them to think critically and analyze information. With our help, students can learn to gather appropriate information and to reach thoughtful conclusions.   15

Computers have revolutionized learning in ways that we have barely begun to appreciate. We have experienced enough, however, to recognize the need to change our thinking about the purposes, methods, and outcome of higher education. Rather than resisting or postponing change, we need to anticipate and learn from it. We must harness the technology and use it to educate our students more effectively than we have been doing. Otherwise, we will surrender our authority to those who can.   16

Responding to Reading

1. In the first part of her essay, Kuriloff discusses John Dewey's "dedication to experience as the foundation for education" (2). According to Kuriloff, in what way are "computer manufacturers and software developers following Dewey's lead" (5)?

2. What are the shortcomings of the American education system? Up until now, why have efforts to reform it failed? According to Kuriloff, how could the use of computers change this situation?

3. This essay originally appeared in a publication aimed at teachers at colleges and universities. What concerns does Kuriloff assume her readers have about the role of computers in education? How does she address these concerns?

INFORMING OURSELVES TO DEATH

Neil Postman

Neil Postman who holds an Ed.D from Columbia University has been on the faculty of New York University for almost forty years. Currently, he is a professor in the School of Education and chair of the Department of Culture and Communication there. Among his many books are Amusing Ourselves to Death: Public Discourse in the Age of Show Business *(1985),* Technopoly: The Surrender of Culture to Technology *(1992), and* The End of Education: Redefining the Value of School *(1995). A sharp critic of the effects of the media and of those who tout the "wonders" of new technology, Postman has shared his views in a wide variety of popular periodicals. The following essay was first delivered as a speech to a meeting of information specialists sponsored by IBM in 1990.*

The great English playwright and social philosopher George Bernard 1 Shaw once remarked that all professions are conspiracies against the common folk. He meant that those who belong to elite trades—physicians, lawyers, teachers, and scientists—protect their special status by creating vocabularies that are incomprehensible to the general public. This process prevents outsiders from understanding what the profession is doing and why—and protects the insiders from close examination and criticism. Professions, in other words, build forbidding walls of technical gobbledygook over which the prying and alien eye cannot see.

Unlike George Bernard Shaw, I raise no complaint against this, for I 2 consider myself a professional teacher and appreciate technical gobbledygook as much as anyone. But I do not object if occasionally someone who does not know the secrets of my trade is allowed entry to the inner halls to express an untutored point of view. Such a person may sometimes give a refreshing opinion or, even better, see something in a way that the professionals have overlooked. I believe I have been invited to speak at this conference for just such a purpose.

I do not know very much more about computer technology than the 3 average person—which isn't very much. I have little understanding of what excites a computer programmer or scientist, and in examining the descriptions of the presentations at this conference, I found each one more mysterious than the next. So, I clearly qualify as an outsider.

But I think that what you want here is not merely an outsider but 4 an outsider who has a point of view that might be useful to the insiders. And that is why I accepted the invitation to speak. I believe I know something about what technologies do to culture, and I know even more about what technologies undo in a culture. In fact, I might say, at the start, that what a technology undoes is a subject that computer experts apparently know very little about. I have heard many experts in computer technology speak about the advantages that computers will bring. With one exception—namely, Joseph—I have never heard anyone speak seriously and comprehensively about the disadvantages of computer technology, which strikes me as odd, and makes me wonder if the profession is hiding something important. That is to say, what seems to be lacking among computer experts is a sense of technological modesty.

After all, anyone who has studied the history of technology knows 5 that technological change is always a Faustian bargain: Technology giveth and technology taketh away, and not always in equal measure. A new technology sometimes creates more than it destroys. Sometimes, it destroys more than it creates. But it is never one-sided.

The invention of the printing press is an excellent example. Printing 6 fostered the modern idea of individuality but it destroyed the medieval sense of community and social integration. Printing created prose but made poetry into an exotic and elitist form of expression. Printing made modern science possible but transformed religious sensibility into an exercise in superstition. Printing assisted in the growth of the nation-state but, in so doing, made patriotism into a sordid if not a murderous emotion.

Another way of saying this is that a new technology tends to favor 7 some groups of people and harms other groups. School teachers, for example, will, in the long run, probably be made obsolete by television, as blacksmiths were made obsolete by the automobile, as balladeers were made obsolete by the printing press. Technological change, in other words, always results in winners and losers.

In the case of computer technology, there can be no disputing that 8 the computer has increased the power of large-scale organizations like military establishments or airline companies or banks or tax collecting agencies. And it is equally clear that the computer is now indispensable to high-level researchers in physics and other natural sciences. But to what extent has computer technology been an advantage to the masses of people? To steel workers, vegetable store owners, teachers, automobile mechanics, musicians, bakers, brick layers, dentists and most of the rest into whose lives the computer now intrudes? These people have had their private matters made more accessible to powerful institutions. They are more easily tracked and controlled; they are subjected to more examinations, and are increasingly mystified by the decisions made about them. They are more often reduced to mere numerical objects. They are being buried by junk mail. They are easy targets for advertising agencies and political organizations. The schools teach their children to operate computerized systems instead of teaching things that are more valuable to children. In a word, almost nothing happens to the losers that they need, which is why they are losers.

It is to be expected that the winners—for example, most of the speak- 9 ers at this conference—will encourage the losers to be enthusiastic about computer technology. That is the way of winners, and so they sometimes tell the losers that with personal computers the average person can balance a checkbook more neatly, keep better track of recipes, and make more logical shopping lists. They also tell them that they can vote at home, shop at home, get all the information they wish at home, and thus make community life unnecessary. They tell them that their lives will be conducted more efficiently, discreetly neglecting to say from whose point of view or what might be the costs of such efficiency.

Should the losers grow skeptical, the winners dazzle them with the 10 wondrous feats of computers, many of which have only marginal relevance to the quality of the losers' lives but which are nonetheless impressive. Eventually, the losers succumb, in part because they believe that the specialized knowledge of the masters of a computer technology is a form of wisdom. The masters, of course, come to believe this as well. The result is that certain questions do not arise, such as, to whom will the computer give greater power and freedom, and whose power and freedom will be reduced?

Now, I have perhaps made all of this sound like a well planned con- 11 spiracy, as if the winners know all too well what is being won and what lost. But this is not quite how it happens, for the winners do not always know what they are doing, and where it will all lead. The Benedictine monks who invented the mechanical clock in the 12th and 13th centuries believed that such a clock would provide a precise regularity to the seven periods of devotion they were required to observe during the course of the day. As a matter of fact, it did. But what the monks did not realize is that the clock is not merely a means of keeping track of the hours but also of synchronizing and controlling the actions of men. And so, by the middle of the 14th century, the clock had moved outside the walls of the monastery, and brought a new and precise regularity to the life of the workman and the merchant. The mechanical clock made possible the idea of regular production, regular working hours, and a standardized product. Without the clock, capitalism would have been quite impossible. And so, here is a great paradox: the clock was invented by men who wanted to devote themselves more rigorously to God; and it ended as the technology of greatest use to men who wished to devote themselves to the accumulation of money. Technology always has unforeseen consequences, and it is not always clear, at the beginning, who or what will win, and who or what will lose.

I might add, by way of another historical example, that Johann 12 Gutenberg was by all accounts a devoted Christian who would have been horrified to hear Martin Luther, the accursed heretic, declare that printing is "God's highest act of grace, whereby the business of the Gospel is driven forward." Gutenberg thought his invention would advance the cause of the Holy Roman See, whereas in fact, it turned out to bring a revolution which destroyed the monopoly of the Church.

We may well ask ourselves, then, is there something that the masters 13
of computer technology think they are doing for us which they and we
may have reason to regret? I believe there is, and it is suggested by the
title of my talk, "Informing Ourselves to Death." In the time remaining, I
will try to explain what is dangerous about the computer, and why. And
I trust you will be open enough to consider what I have to say. Now, I
think I can begin to get at this by telling you of a small experiment I have
been conducting, on and off, for the past several years. There are some
people who describe the experiment as an exercise in deceit and exploitation but I will rely on your sense of humor to pull me through.

Here's how it works: It is best done in the morning when I see a col- 14
league who appears not to be in possession of a copy of *The New York
Times*. "Did you read *The Times* this morning?," I ask. If the colleague
says yes, there is no experiment that day. But if the answer is no, the
experiment can proceed. "You ought to look at Page 23, I say. "There's
a fascinating article about a study done at Harvard University."
"Really? What's it about?" is the usual reply. My choices at this point are
limited only by my imagination. But I might say something like this:
"Well, they did this study to find out what foods are best to eat for losing weight, and it turns out that a normal diet supplemented by chocolate eclairs, eaten six times a day, is the best approach. It seems that
there's some special nutrient in the eclairs—economical dioxin—that
actually uses up calories at an in-credible rate."

Another possibility, which I like to use with colleagues who are 15
known to be health conscious is this one: "I think you'll want to know
about this," I say. "The neuro-physiologists at the University of Stuttgart
have uncovered a connection between jogging and reduced intelligence.
They tested more than 1200 people over a period of five years, and found
that as the number of hours people jogging increased, there was a corresponding decrease in their intelligence. They don't know exactly why but
there it is."

I'm sure, by now, you understand what my role is in the experi- 16
ment: to report something that is quite ridiculous—one might say,
beyond belief. Let me tell you, then, some of my results: Unless this is
the second or third time I've tried this on the same person, most people
will believe or at least not disbelieve what I have told them. Sometimes
they say: "Really? Is that possible?" Sometimes they do a double-take,
and reply, "Where'd you say that study was done?" And sometimes
they say, "You know, I've heard something like that."

Now, there are several conclusions that might be drawn from these 17
results, one of which was expressed by H. L. Mencken fifty years ago
when he said, there is no idea so stupid that you can't find a professor
who will believe it. This is more of an accusation than an explanation
but in any case I have tried this experiment on non-professors and get
roughly the same results. Another possible conclusion is one expressed

by George Orwell—also about fifty years ago—when he remarked that the average person today is about as naive as was the average person in the Middle Ages. In the Middle Ages people believed in the authority of their religion, no matter what. Today, we believe in the authority of our science, no matter what.

But I think there is still another and more important conclusion to [18] be drawn, related to Orwell's point but rather off at a right angle to it. I am referring to the fact that the world in which we live is very nearly incomprehensible to most of us. There is almost no fact—whether actual or imagined—that will surprise us for very long, since we have no comprehensive and consistent picture of the world which would make the fact appear as an unacceptable contradiction. We believe because there is no reason not to believe. No social, political, historical, metaphysical, logical or spiritual reason. We live in a world that, for the most part, makes no sense to us. Not even technical sense. I don't mean to try my experiment on this audience, especially after having told you about it, but if I informed you that the seats you are presently occupying were actually made by a special process which uses the skin of a Bismark herring, on what grounds would you dispute me? For all you know—indeed, for all I know—the skin of a Bismark herring could have made the seats on which you sit. And if I could get an industrial chemist to confirm this fact by describing some incomprehensible process by which it was done, you would probably tell someone tomorrow that you spent the evening sitting on a Bismark herring.

Perhaps I can get a bit closer to the point I wish to make with anal- [19] ogy: If you opened a brand-new deck of cards, and started turning the cards over, one by one you would have a pretty good idea of what their order is. After you had gone from the ace of spades through the nine of spades, you would expect a ten of spades to come up next. And if a three of diamonds showed up instead, you would be surprised and wonder what kind of deck of cards this is. But if I gave you a deck that had been shuffled twenty times, and then asked you to turn the cards over, you would not expect any card in particular—a three of diamonds would be just as likely as a ten of spades. Having no basis for assuming a given order, you would have no reason to react with disbelief or even surprise to whatever card turns up.

The point is that, in a world without spiritual or intellectual order, [20] nothing is unbelievable; nothing is predictable, and therefore, nothing comes as a particular surprise.

In fact, George Orwell was more than a little unfair to the average [21] person in the Middle Ages. The belief system of the Middle Ages was rather like my brand-new deck of cards. There existed an ordered, comprehensible world-view, beginning with the idea that all knowledge and goodness come from God. What the priests had to say about the world was derived from the logic of their theology. There was nothing arbitrary about the things people were asked to believe, including the fact that the world itself was created at 9 A.M. on October 23 in the year 4004 B.C. That could be explained, and was, quite lucidity, to the satisfaction of anyone. So could the fact that 10,000 angels could dance on the head of a pin. It made quite good sense, if you believed that the Bible is the revealed word of God and that the universe is populated with angels. The medieval world was, to be sure, mysterious and filled with wonder, but it was not without a sense of order. Ordinary men and women might not clearly grasp how the harsh realities of their lives fit into the grand and benevolent design, but they had no doubt that there was such a design, and their priests were well able, by deduction from a handful of principles, to make it, if not rational, at least coherent.

The situation we are presently in is much different. And I should 22 say, sadder and more confusing and certainly more mysterious. It is rather like the shuffled deck of cards I referred to. There is no consistent, integrated conception of the world which serves as the foundation on which our edifice of belief rests. And therefore, in a sense, we are more naive than those of the Middle Ages, and more frightened, for we can be made to believe almost anything. The skin of a Bismark herring makes about as much sense as a vinyl alloy or encomial dioxin.

Now, in a way, none of this is our fault. If I may turn the wisdom of 23 Cassius on its head: the fault is not in ourselves but almost literally in the stars. When Galileo turned his telescope toward the heavens, and allowed Kepler to look as well, they found no enchantment or authorization in the stars, only geometric patterns and equations. God, it seemed, was less of a moral philosopher than a master mathematician. This discovery helped to give impetus to the development of physics but did nothing but harm to theology. Before Galileo and Kepler, it was possible to believe that the Earth was the stable center of the universe, and that God took a special interest in our affairs. Afterward, the Earth became a lonely wanderer in an obscure galaxy in a hidden corner of the universe, and we were left to wonder if God had any interest in us at all. The ordered, comprehensible world of the Middle Ages began to unravel because people no longer saw in the stars the face of a friend.

And something else, which once was our friend, turned against us, 24 as well. I refer to information. There was a time when information was a source that helped human beings to solve specific and urgent problems of their environment. It is true enough that in the Middle Ages, there was a scarcity of information but its very scarcity made it both important and usable. This began to change, as everyone knows, in the late 15th century when a goldsmith named Gutenberg, from Mainz, converted an old wine press into a printing machine, and in so doing, created what we now call an information explosion. Forty years after the invention of the press, there were printing machines in 110 different countries; 50 years after, more than eight million books had been printed, almost all of them filled with information that had previously not been available to the average person.

Nothing could be more misleading than the idea that computer 25 technology introduced the age of information. The printing press began that age, and we have not been free of it since. But what started out as a liberating stream has turned into a deluge of chaos. If I may take my own country as an example, here is what we are faced with: In America, there are 260,000 billboards; 11,520 newspapers; 11,556 periodicals; 27,000 video outlets for renting tapes; 362 million TV sets; and over 400 million radios. There are 40,000 new book titles published every year (300,000 world-wide) and every day in America 41 million photographs are taken, and just for the record, over 60 billion pieces of advertising junkmail come into our mail boxes every year. Everything from telegraphy and photography in the nineteenth century to the silicon chip in the twentieth has amplified the din of information, until matters have reached such proportions today that for the average person, information no longer has any relation to the solution of problems.

The tie between information and action has been severed. Inform- 26 ation is now a commodity that can be sought and sold, or used as a form of entertainment, or worn like a garment to enhance one's status. It comes indiscriminately, directed at no one in particular, disconnected from usefulness; we are glutted with information, drowning in information, have no control over it, don't know what to do with it. And there are two reasons we do not know what to do with it. First, as I have said, we no longer have a coherent conception of ourselves, and our universe, and our relation to one another and our world. We no longer know, as the Middle Ages did, where we come from, and where we are going, or why. That is, we don't know what information is relevant, and what information is irrelevant to our lives. Second, we have directed all of our energies and intelligence to inventing machinery that does nothing but increase the supply of information. As a consequence, our defenses against information glut have broken down; our information immune system is inoperable. We don't know how to filter it out, we don't know how to reduce it; we don't know to use it. We suffer from a kind of cultural AIDS.

Now, into this situation comes the computer. The computer, as we 27 know, has a quality of universality, not only because its uses are almost infinitely various but also because computers are commonly integrated into the structure of other machines. Therefore it would be fatuous of me to warn against every conceivable use of a computer. But there is no denying that the most prominent uses of computers have to do with information. When people talk about "information sciences," they are talking about computers—how to store information, how to retrieve information, how to organize information. The computer is an answer to the questions, How can I get more information, faster, and in a more usable form? These would appear to be reasonable questions. But now I should like to put some other questions to you that seem to me more reasonable. Did Iraq invade Kuwait because of a lack of information? If a hideous war should ensue between Iraq and the U.S., will it happen because of a lack of information? If children die of starvation in Ethiopia, does it occur because of a lack of information? Does racism in South Africa exist because of a lack of information? If criminals roam the streets of New York City, do they do so because of a lack of information?

Or, let us come down to a more personal level: If you and your 28 spouse are unhappy together, and end your marriage in divorce, will it happen because of a lack of information? If your children misbehave and bring shame to your family, does it happen because of a lack of information? If someone in your family has a mental breakdown, will it happen because of a lack of information?

I believe you will have to concede that what ails us, what causes us 29 the most misery and pain—at both cultural and personal levels—has nothing to do with the sort of information made accessible by computers. The computer and its information cannot answer any of the fundamental questions we need to address to make our lives more meaningful and humane. The computer cannot provide an organizing moral framework. It cannot tell us what questions are worth asking. It cannot provide a means of understanding why we are here or why we fight each other or why decency eludes us so often, especially when we need it the most. The computer is, in a sense, a magnificent toy that distracts us from facing what we most needed to confront—spiritual emptiness, knowledge of ourselves, usable conceptions of the past and future. Does one blame the computer for this? Of course not. It is, after all, only a machine. But it is presented to us, with trumpets blaring, as at this conference, as a technological messiah.

Through the computer, the heralds say, we will make education bet- 30 ter, religion better, politics better, our minds better—best of all, ourselves better. This is, of course, nonsense, and only the young or the ignorant or the foolish could believe it. I said a moment ago that computers are not to blame for this. And that is true, at least in the sense that we do not blame an elephant for its huge appetite or a stone for being hard or a cloud for hiding the Sun. That is their nature, and we expect nothing different from them. But the computer has a nature, as well. True, it is only a machine but a machine designed to manipulate and generate information. That is what computers do, and therefore they have an agenda and an unmistakable message. The message is that through more and more information, more conveniently packaged, more swiftly delivered, we will find solutions to our problems. And so all the brilliant young men and women, believing this, create ingenious things for the computer to do, hoping that in this way, we will become wiser and more decent and more noble. And who can blame them? By becoming masters of this wondrous technology, they will acquire prestige and power and some will even become famous.

In a world populated by people who believe that through more and more information, paradise is attainable, the computer scientist is king. But I maintain that all of this is a monumental and dangerous waste of human talent and energy. Imagine what might be accomplished if this talent and energy were turned to philosophy, to theology, to the arts, to imaginative literature or to education? Who knows what we could learn from such people—perhaps why there are wars, and hunger, and homelessness and mental illness and danger. As things stand now, the geniuses of computer technology will give us Star Wars, and tell us that is the answer to nuclear war. They will give us artificial intelligence, and tell us that this is the way to self-knowledge. They will give us instantaneous global communication, and tell us this is the way to mutual understanding. They will give us Virtual Reality and tell us this is the answer to spiritual poverty. But that is only the way of the technician, the fact-monger, the information junkie, and the technological idiot. 31

Here is what Henry David Thoreau told us: "All our inventions are but improved means to an unimproved end." Here is what Goethe told us: "One should, each day, try to hear a little song read a good poem, see a fine picture, and, if it is possible, speak a few reasonable words." And here is what Socrates told us: "The unexamined life is not worth living." And here is what the prophet Micah told us: "What does the Lord require of thee but to do justly, and to love mercy and to walk humbly with thy God?" And I can tell you—if I had the time (although you all know it well enough)—what Confucius, Isaiah, Jesus, Mohammed, the Buddha, Spinoza and Shakespeare told us. It is all the same: There is no escaping from ourselves. The human dilemma is as it has always been, and we solve nothing fundamental by cloaking ourselves in technological glory. Even the humblest cartoon character knows this, and I shall close by quoting the wise old possum named Pogo, created by the cartoonist, Walt Kelley. I commend his words to all the technological utopians and messiahs present. "We have met the enemy," Pogo said, "and he is us." 32

Responding to Reading

1. In paragraph 7 Postman says, "a new technology tends to favor some groups of people and harms other groups"? What examples does he present to support this assertion? How convincing are these examples?
2. What does Postman mean when he says, "Nothing could be more misleading than the idea that computer technology introduced the age of information" (25)?

3. According to Postman, computers cannot address the most pressing problems human beings face. For this reason, says Postman, all effort devoted to computers is a "dangerous waste of talent and energy" (31). Do you agree? How would Pesche Kuriloff (p. 482) respond to Postman's statement?

BARDS OF THE INTERNET: IF E-MAIL REPRESENTS THE RENAISSANCE OF PROSE, WHY IS SO MUCH OF IT AWFUL?

Philip Elmer-Dewitt

Born in Boston and a graduate of Oberlin College and the Columbia University Graduate School of Journalism, Philip Elmer-Dewitt joined Time *magazine as an assistant in 1979 and became a staff writer in 1983, covering science and technology and heading up a new "Computers" column. Later a senior editor and currently assistant managing editor of science, medicine, and technology, Elmer-Dewitt has written over 450 stories for* Time *and has written or edited more than 50 cover stories. The following essay appeared in* Time *magazine.*

One of the unintended side effects of the invention of the telephone 1 was that writing went out of style. Oh, sure, there were still full-time scribblers—journalists, academics, professional wordsmiths. And the great centers of commerce still found it useful to keep on hand people who could draft a memo, a brief, a press release or a contract. But given a choice between picking up a pen or a phone, most folks took the easy route and gave their fingers—and sometimes their mind—a rest.

Which makes what's happening on the computer networks all 2 the more startling. Every night, when they should be watching television, millions of computer users sit down at their keyboards; dial into CompuServe, Prodigy, America Online or the Internet; and start typing—e-mail, bulletin-board postings, chat messages, rants, diatribes, even short stories and poems. Just when the media of McLuhan were supposed to render obsolete the medium of Shakespeare, the online world is experiencing the greatest boom in letter writing since the eighteenth century.

"It is my overwhelming belief that e-mail and computer conferenc- 3 ing are teaching an entire generation about the flexibility and utility of prose," writes Jon Carroll, a columnist at the *San Francisco Chronicle*. Patrick Nielsen Hayden, an editor at Tor Books, compares electronic bulletin boards with the "scribblers' compacts" of the late eighteenth and early nineteenth centuries, in which members passed letters from hand to hand, adding a little more at each turn. David Sewall, an associate editor at the University of Arizona, likens netwriting to the literary scene Mark Twain discovered in San Francisco in the 1860s, "when people were reinventing journalism by grafting it onto the tall-tale folk tradition." Others hark back to Tom Paine and the Revolutionary War pamphleteers, or even to the Elizabethan era, when, thanks to Gutenberg, a generation of English writers became intoxicated with language.

But such comparisons invite a question: if online writing today rep- 4 resents some sort of renaissance, why is so much of it so awful? For it can be very bad indeed: sloppy, meandering, puerile, ungrammatical, poorly spelled, badly structured and at times virtually content free. "HEY!!!1? reads an all too typical message on the Internet, "I THINK METALLICA IZ REEL KOOL DOOD!1!!!"

One reason, of course, is that e-mail is not like ordinary writing. 5 "You need to think of this as 'written speech'," says Gerard Van der Leun, a literary agent based in Westport, Connecticut, who has emerged as one of the pre-eminent stylists on the Net. "These things are little more considered than coffeehouse talk and a lot less considered than a letter. They're not to have and hold; they're to fire and forget." Many online postings are composed "live" with the clock ticking, using rudimentary word processors on computer systems that charge by the minute and in some cases will shut down without warning when an hour runs out.

That is not to say that with more time every writer on the Internet 6 would produce sparkling copy. Much of the fiction and poetry is second-rate or worse, which is not surprising given that the barriers to entry are so low. "In the real world," says Mary Anne Mohanraj, a Chicago- based poet, "it takes a hell of a lot of work to get published, which naturally weeds out a lot of the garbage. On the Net, just a few keystrokes sends your writing out to thousands of readers."

But even among the reams of bad poetry, gems are to be found. Mike 7 Godwin, a Washington-based lawyer who posts under the pen name "mnemonic," tells the story of Joe Green, a technical writer at Cray Research who turned a moribund discussion group called rec.arts.poems into a real poetry workshop by mercilessly critiquing the pieces he found there. "Some people got angry and said if he was such a god of poetry, why didn't he publish his poems to the group?" recalls Godwin. "He did, and blew them all away." Green's Well Met in Minnesota, a mock-epic account of a face-to-face meeting with a fellow network scribbler, is now revered on the Internet as a classic. It begins, "The truth is that when I met Mark I was dressed as the Canterbury Tales. Rather difficult to do as you might suspect, but I wanted to make a certain impression."

The more prosaic technical and political discussion groups, mean- 8
while, have become so crowded with writers crying for attention that a
Darwinian survival principle has started to prevail. "It's so competitive
that you have to work on your style if you want to make any impact,"
says Jorn Baraer, a software designer in Chicago. Good writing on the
Net tends to be clear, vigorous, witty and above all brief. "The medium
favors the terse," says Crawford Kilian, a writing teacher at Capilano
College in Vancouver, British Columbia. "Short paragraphs, bulleted
lists and one-liners are the units of thought here."

Some of the most successful netwriting is produced in computer 9
conferences, where writers compose in a kind of collaborative heat,
knocking ideas against one another until they spark. Perhaps the best
examples of this are found on the WELL, a Sausalito, California, bulletin
board favored by journalists. The caliber of discussion is often so high
that several publications—including the *New York Times* and the *Wall
Street Journal*—have printed excerpts from the WELL.

Curiously, what works on the computer networks isn't necessarily 10
what works on paper. Netwriters freely lace their prose with stage
acronyms and "smileys," the little faces constructed with punctuation
marks and intended to convey the winks, grins and grimaces of ordinary
conversations. Somehow it all flows together quite smoothly. On the
other hand, polished prose copied onto bulletin boards from books and
magazines often seems long-winded and phony. Unless they adjust to
the new medium, professional writers can come across as self-important
blowhards in debates with more nimble networkers. Says Brock Meeks,
a Washington-based reporter who covers the online culture for *Communications Daily*: "There are a bunch of hacker kids out there who can
string a sentence together better than their blue-blooded peers simply
because they log on all the time and write, write, write."

There is something inherently democratizing—perhaps even revolu- 11
tionary—about the technology. Not only has it enfranchised thousands of
would-be writers who otherwise might never have taken up the craft, but
it has also thrown together classes of people who hadn't had much
direct contact before: students, scientists, senior citizens, computer
geeks, grassroots (and often blue-collar) bulletin-board enthusiasts and
most recently the working press.

"It's easy to make this stuff look foolish and trivial," says Tor Books' 12
Nielsen Hayden. "After all, a lot of everyone's daily life is foolish and
trivial. I mean, really, smileys? Housewives in Des Moines who log on
as VIXEN?"

But it would be a mistake to dismiss the computer-message boards 13
or to underestimate the effect a lifetime of dashing off e-mail will have
on a generation of young writers. The computer networks may not be
Brook Farm or the Globe Theatre, but they do represent, for millions of

people, a living, breathing life of letters. One suspects that the Bard himself, confronted with the Internet, might have dived right in and never logged off.

Responding to Reading

1. Elmer-Dewitt begins his essay by comparing the telephone to the computer. What point does Elmer-Dewitt hope to make with this comparison? Is he successful?

2. Elmer-Dewitt concedes that much online writing is "sloppy, meandering, puerile, ungrammatical, poorly spelled, badly structured and at times virtually content free" (4). Even so, he thinks that it represents a kind of cultural renaissance in writing. Do you agree? Should he have spent more time addressing the arguments against his position?

3. In paragraph 11, Elmer-Dewitt says that computer technology has "thrown together classes of people who hadn't much direct contact before." What classes of people does he list? What classes does he omit? How serious are these omissions?

---------------------------------- FOCUS ----------------------------------

Is There Equality in Cyberspace?

ONE INTERNET, TWO NATIONS
Henry Louis Gates, Jr.

Henry Louis Gates, Jr., (1950–   ) grew up in rural West Virginia and went on to receive degrees from Yale and Cambridge universities. He now holds an endowed chair at Harvard University and chairs the Department of Afro-American Studies there. A prolific author, Gates has contributed articles to a wide variety of publications, including the New Yorker *and the* New York Times, *and has written, edited, and coedited numerous books ranging from anthologies of African-American writers to literary criticism to his memoir,* Colored People *(1994). Recent works include* Thirteen Ways of Looking at a Black Man *(1997),* Wonders of the African World *(1999), and (as coeditor)* Africana: The Encyclopedia of the African and African-American Experience *(1999). He also hosted a 1999 PBS documentary series about life in Africa. The following essay appeared on the op-ed page of the* New York Times *in 1999.*

After the Stono Rebellion of 1739 in South Carolina—the largest 1 uprising of slaves in the colonies before the American Revolution—legislators there responded by banishing two forms of communication among the slaves: the mastery of reading and writing, and the mastery of "talking drums," both of which had been crucial to the capacity to rebel.

For the next century and a half, access to literacy became for the 2 slaves a hallmark of their humanity and an instrument of liberation, spiritual as well as physical. The relation between freedom and literacy became the compelling theme of the slave narratives, the great body of printed books that ex-slaves generated to assert their common humanity with white Americans and to indict the system that had oppressed them.

In the years since the abolition of slavery, the possession of literacy 3 has been a cardinal value of the African-American tradition. It is no accident that the first great victory in the legal battle over segregation was fought on the grounds of education—of equal access to literacy.

Today, blacks are failing to gain access to the new tools of literacy: 4 the digital "knowledge economy." And while the dilemma that our ancestors confronted was imposed by others, this cybersegregation is, to a large degree, self-imposed.

The Government's latest attempt to understand why low-income 5 African-Americans and Hispanics are slower to embrace the Internet and the personal computer than whites—the Commerce Department study "Falling Through the Net"—suggests that income alone can't be blamed for the so-called digital divide. For example, among families earning $15,000 to $35,000 annually, more than 33 percent of whites own computers, compared with only 19 percent of African-Americans—a gap that has widened 64 percent over the past five years despite declining computer prices.

The implications go far beyond online trading and chat rooms. Net 6 promoters are concerned that the digital divide threatens to become a twenty-first century poll tax that, in effect, disenfranchises a third of the nation. Our children, especially, need access not only to the vast resources that technology offers for education, but also to the rich cultural contexts that define their place in the world.

Today we stand at the brink of becoming two societies, one largely 7 white and plugged in and the other black and unplugged.

One of the most tragic aspects of slavery was the way it destroyed 8 social connections. In a process that the sociologist Orlando Patterson calls "social death," slavery sought to sever blacks from their history and culture, from family ties and a sense of community. And, of course, de jure segregation after the Civil War was intended to disconnect blacks from equal economic opportunity, from the network of social contacts that enable upward mobility and, indeed, from the broader world of ideas.

Despite the dramatic growth of the black middle class since affirma- 9 tive action programs were started in the late 60's, new forms of disconnectedness have afflicted black America. Middle-class professionals often feel socially and culturally isolated from their white peers at work and in the neighborhood and from their black peers left behind in the underclass. The children of the black underclass, in turn, often lack middle-class role models to help them connect to a history of achievement and develop their analytical skills.

It would be a sad irony if the most diverse and decentralized elec- 10 tronic medium yet invented should fail to achieve ethnic diversity among its users. And yet the Commerce Department study suggests that the solution will require more than cheap PC's. It will involve content.

Until recently, the African-American presence on the Internet was 11 minimal, reflecting the chicken-and-egg nature of Internet economics. Few investors have been willing to finance sites appealing to a PC-scarce community. Few African-Americans have been compelled to sign on to a medium that offers little to interest them. And educators interested in diversity have repeatedly raised concerns about the lack of minority-oriented educational software.

Consider the birth of the recording industry in the 1920's. Blacks 12 began to respond to this new medium only when mainstream companies like Columbia Records introduced so-called race records, blues and jazz discs aimed at a nascent African-American market. Blacks who would never have dreamed of spending hard-earned funds for a record by Rudy Vallee or Kate Smith would stand in lines several blocks long to purchase the new Bessie Smith or Duke Ellington hit.

New content made the new medium attractive. And the growth of 13 Web sites dedicated to the interests and needs of black Americans can play the same role for the Internet that race records did for the music industry.

But even making sites that will appeal to a black audience can only 14 go so far. The causes of poverty are both structural and behavioral. And it is the behavioral aspect of this cybersegregation that blacks themselves are best able to address. Drawing on corporate and foundation support, we can transform the legion of churches, mosques, and community centers in our inner cities into after-school centers that focus on redressing the digital divide and teaching black history. We can draw on the many examples of black achievement in structured classes to re-establish a sense of social connection.

The Internet is the twenty-first century's talking drum, the very 15 kind of grass-roots communication tool that has been such a powerful source of education and culture for our people since slavery. But this talking drum we have not yet learned to play. Unless we master the new information technology to build and deepen the forms of social connection that a tragic history has eroded, African-Americans will face a form of cybersegregation in the next century as devastating to our aspirations as Jim Crow segregation was to those of our ancestors. But this time, the fault will be our own.

Responding to Reading

1. What is the connection between the denial of literacy to African-Americans after the Stono Rebellion and the failure of African-Americans to gain access to the Internet? What is the difference between these two situations?
2. According to Gates, "Today we stand on the brink of becoming two societies, one largely white and plugged in and the other black and unplugged." (7) What does Gates say can be done to solve this problem?
3. Gates ends his essay by saying, "But this time, the fault will be our own" (15). What does he mean? What will happen if African-Americans fail to close the "digital divide"? Do you think Gates is being overly pessimistic?

WOMEN AND COMPUTERS:
IS THERE EQUITY IN CYBERSPACE?

Paula Span

Paula Span, a graduate of Boston University, is the New York–based style writer for the Washington Post *and has also contributed articles to publications such as* Esquire, Glamour, Redbook, *the* Wall Street Journal, *and a variety of alternative presses. She is an adjunct professor at the Columbia University School of Journalism and has also served as the McGaw Professor of Writing at Princeton University. Span wrote the following piece for the* Washington Post *in 1994.*

The love affair between men and computers was something I knew 1 about but didn't really get, until that morning at the local coffee shop. My pal Pam and I were gabbing in the front booth when in walked Michael, a friend and journalist about to take a leave from his newspaper to write a book. His first step, naturally, was to sink a significant chunk of his book advance into a shiny new computer. It was a beauty: worked faster than a speeding locomotive, boasted many megabytes of RAM, brewed cappuccino, etc.

Pam and I exchanged glances. This sounded familiar. She had writ- 2 ten several books on an Apple so antediluvian that the company no longer manufactures it, and abandoned it only when it got damaged by clumsy movers. Yet her husband was about to invest in a pricey new CD-ROM rig, making unconvincing noises about how useful their daughter would find it for schoolwork. My own husband, as it happened, was also taking advantage of a new work assignment and plunging computer prices to replace the system he'd purchased just two years before, though his new machine wasn't as powerful as Michael's. ("Mike could fly to Chicago with that thing" he would later remark, wistfully.)

More speed. Better performance. With names like Quadra and 3 Performa, computers even sound like cars these days. (Quick, is it a fastback or a sedan?) The women I know, who all primarily use these things for work, don't give them two seconds' thought unless they encounter some problem. On the other hand, a lot of the men I know ogle weird software in the MacWarehouse catalogue and always seem to require some new $200 gizmo that quacks.

"It's guy thing," Pam and I decided, virtually in unison. Women 4 treat computers like reliable station wagons: Learn how to make them take you where you want to go, and as long as they're functioning properly, who cares about pistons and horsepower? Computers are useful but unexciting. When something goes wrong, you call a mechanic.

Whereas guys, even those who never learned how to change an oil 5
filter, are enamored of computers, want to play with them, upgrade
them, fix them when they falter, compare theirs with the other guys'.

As an admitted technoklutz, I initially figured this observation 6
might simply reflect my own prejudice, not to mention a small sample
size. Computers, after all, were initially thought to be a field in which
women would triumph. Computers had no history of discrimination.
They had no history at all. They did not require biceps. They wouldn't
be, to adopt the social science term, gendered.

Well. It turned out—as I started looking into the whole evolving 7
subject of women, computers, on-line communications and other matters I had previously been unconcerned about—that computing is even
more of a guy thing than I knew. That's worth paying attention to, not
only for women but for our daughters (mine's 12). Yet I would also
learn, as I ventured hesitantly into the computer communications realm
dubbed cyberspace, that things don't have to stay this way.

Warning: The following article contains assorted generalizations 8
and risks gender stereotyping.

For there are, no question, numerous males who are phobic about 9
or merely uninterested in computing. And there are plenty of techie
females, women who know their algorithms, who run major software
companies, and who can clean the cat hair out of a trackball in 30 seconds or less.

But it's hard to overlook the stats. Who studies computer science? 10
The Chronicle of Higher Education's latest numbers show that fewer
than 30 percent of the people getting bachelor's and master's degrees
are women and that fewer than one in seven doctorates is earned by a
woman.

Who works in the industry? The Bureau of Labor Statistics reports 11
that the percentage of women who are computer systems analysts
and scientists has barely budged in a decade. It's still under 30 percent,
even though nearly half a million more people have entered the field.
Fewer than a third of computer programmers are women, as well,
another statistic little changed since 1983.

Who pants over those fat, glossy computer magazines (PC World, 12
Byte, MacUser) whose lust-inspiring displays of software and laptops
have been dubbed, by writer James Fallows, compuporn? Eighty percent of their readers are male, says the research firm Simmons MRI. (So
are 85 percent of those who buy the newer and hipper Wired.)

Millions of women use computers at their jobs, of course, though 13
often in routinized ways that leave the machines' more intriguing possibilities unexplored. But home computers, which after several years of
significant growth still are found in only 31 percent of American homes

This, at least, is the theme developed by well-known MIT sociologist 20
Sherry Turkle in an essay that's part of a 1988 collection called Technology and Women's Voices. Basing her analysis on interviews with college
women who were doing well in computer courses but resisted identifying themselves as "computer science types," Turkle says that women
"observe [the hackers'] obsessions, observe their anti-sensuality, observe
the ways in which they have put things rather than people at the center
of their lives and count themselves out."

It's not hard to understand why an adolescent boy might find com- 21
puting seductive. At a time when sexual pressures and social demands
loom threateningly large, the hacker culture offers autonomy, mastery,
safety. "The hook is the feeling of power that it gives you: You control a
world of your own making," says my friend Steve Adamczyk, an MIT
grad who owns a software company called the Edison Design Group.
(I'd call Steve a former nerd except that, he explains, "it's like being an
alcoholic: You're always a nerd but you're a recovering nerd.") Staying
up all night coding software in FORTRAN, as Steve did in high school,
was "terrifically appealing to people who don't do so well at controlling
the real world, maintaining relationships and all that."

Girls, though of course also buffeted by adolescence, have by that 22
point been culturally programmed to maintain relationships. And those
who withdraw generally seem to find safe havens other than computer
labs.

As a small but influential cadre, hackers are also something of an 23
alien species to non-nerd men. But men, Turkle writes, are apt to view
hackers' achievements with admiration. Women, however many magazine stories they read about Bill Gates's net-worth, are more likely, to
bolt.

The good news is that unlike some stubborn power imbalances 24
requiring generations to redress (the composition of the U.S. Congress
comes to mind), computer attitudes appear to be rather dramatically
revisable. And such attempts are underway: This year, the National
Science Foundation has more than tripled its funding for programs
aimed at pulling girls and women into science, math and engineering.
The boys-will-be-nerds paradigm "is just a throwback to separate
spheres, simply a vestigial anachronism," announces Jo Sanders, of the
Center for Advanced Study, City University of New York.

Sanders ran the NSF-funded Computer Equity Expert Project. A 25
30-month-long guerrilla campaign to increase girls' participation in
math, science and technology by, well, gently but firmly smashing sexism. Sanders convened 200 teachers and administrators, representing
every state, for week-long seminars on the causes and consequences of
the gender gap and strategies for closing it. Back in their middle and
high schools, these people taught computer equity workshops to their

remain largely a male preserve. (And a middle-class preserve, but that's another story.) LINK Resources, a New York consulting firm, has found that in only a quarter of those homes is the primary user a woman.

As for cyberspace, about which more later, no one's hung a "No 14 Girls Allowed" sign on the door. It's often a male clubhouse nonetheless, one girls can enter provided they are willing and able to scramble through the briers, shinny up the tree, ignore the skinned knees and announce that they can spit a watermelon seed just as far as the guys inside can. Figuratively speaking.

All of this reflects attitudes toward computers that form at unnerv- 15 ingly young ages.

Ten years ago, not long after *Time* magazine had declared the com- 16 puter its Person of the Year, education journals started to fill with reports about the way schoolaged boys embraced computers while girls avoided them. Boys were more likely to have home computers and use them, to enroll in computer camps and summer programs, to take advantage of school computer labs, to elect high school computer courses. Academics who pay attention to these things say they haven't seen much dramatic change since.

So much for parents' assuring themselves that kids who've grown 17 up in the Super Mario Era won't inherit their elders' anxieties and biases. The old patterns show considerable staying power. As early as first grade, according to a 1990 study in the Journal of Research and Development in Education, computer use is seen, by both boys and girls, as masculine. Reading and writing, on the other hand, have no perceived gender associations.

Researchers offer various explanations, including the well- 18 documented aversion that many girls develop to math and science, the ever-popular lack-of-role-models theory, and the fact that many boys are introduced to computers through those kill-and-maim computer and video games that girls very sensibly disdain. (Who dubbed the control a joystick, anyway?) The disparity, however triggered, intensifies with age: by high school, girls may use computers to write their term papers (test show that they're as competent at it as the guys), but deeper interest is suspect.

Computing's male aura may be one of the enduring legacies of the 19 mythic hackers and nerds who patched together the early personal computers, hammered out breakthrough programs and invented computer bulletin boards. (A notorious few also dabbled in phone and credit-card fraud.) They were true trailblazers. In addition, they and their descendants are, as a subculture, so unappetizing—pale geeks without social skills who lose themselves in binary code, sci-fi sagas and chess gambits—that women develop "computational reticence" in response.

own faculties and recruited girls with everything from guest speakers to pizza parties.

The project, which ended last year, got results with startling 26 speed. Reports flooded in: Within a year, an all-male advanced PASCAL class in Virginia turned 50 percent female and an all-male elective computer course in Oklahoma was nearly a third female, while a West Virginia computer club increased its female membership tenfold. "When you change attitudes," Sanders concludes, "the resistance just evaporates."

As for us grown-up women no longer facing math and science 27 requirements, our resistance is also susceptible to change. What has been missing until recently, however, isn't just spine-stiffening; it's a motivation, some reason to acquire or cozy up to a computer, an incentive to struggle past the inevitable glitches.

For years, if you didn't need a computer for work, it has been hard 28 to see what it would do for you. No one really needs to make that sort of investment in time and money to balance her checkbook, file her recipes (to cite one early personal-computer application that was supposed to turn us on) or handle ordinary correspondence. The love of gadgetry and tinkering that draws some men to computers as a hobby hasn't had much measurable impact on women.

What's been missing is the Killer App.

That's the term Silicon Valley types use for the breakthrough use, 30 the irresistible application that finally makes a technological advance not just a toy but a useful tool, so that ordinary people look at it and say, "We need one of those." The Killer App for the desktop computer itself was the Lotus 1-2-3 spreadsheet. The Killer App for microwave ovens, now in 80 percent of homes, was probably reheating leftovers, or maybe popping corn.

The Killer App that draws women into computer use in significant 31 numbers, researchers tell me will be communication. With a cheap modem and a few commands that connect you to a network, you can reach out and touch people you know and hundreds of thousands of people you don't and discuss everything from breastfeeding to foreign policy. This isn't technology, this is expression, relationships, community, all the things women are taught to be skilled at.

Cyberspace isn't as brave-new-world as the name makes it sound. 32 Reva Basch, whom I've recently met-by-modem on a computer conferring system called the WELL, told me this story: "My mother-in-law, who's 80, was visiting and expressed curiosity about the WELL. I showed it to her, showed her some of the conferences. She said, 'Why, honey, it's just talking, isn't it? She got it."

My daughter, Emma, was my guide at first. Growing up with par- 33 ents who use computers (however rudimentary) and encourage her to do likewise, plus hours of playing Nintendo and computer games with

friends who are boys, seems to have immunized her against com-
puter-aversion. She's not fascinated by the things, exactly, but she's
entirely unthreatened by them. So, six weeks before I began writing this
essay, I nervously sat down at the Macintosh bequeathed to her when
my husband, partly for that very reason, bought his latest. She patiently
showed me now to log on to America Online, the country's third largest
computer communications system.

America Online is easy to use, even for a neophyte. It has a welcom- 34
ing "interface," a display of onscreen symbols to point to and click at, so
that you can read highlights from USA Today and the Atlantic, send electronic mail ("E-mail") to friends and strangers, scroll through 406 messages from fans of Smashing Pumpkins and add your own in the
RockLink Forum, or join as many as 22 other users all typing away at each
other in "real time" in each of dozens of "lobbies" and "chat areas." It's
gotten so popular and grown so fast that the system grew temporarily
choked and sluggish this winter from overuse by its 600,000 subscribers.

I found AOL reassuringly simple but not particularly impatico and 35
so, two weeks later, I logged onto the WELL, a Sausalito-based network
founded in 1985 by the folks who published the Whole Earth Catalogue.
This was not simple, and resulted in the humiliation of repeatedly having to dash down two flights of stairs to ask my husband (already a
WELLbeing), "How do you get to an OK prompt?," then dash back up.
But I've figured out enough to be able to send and receive E-mail and
join in the conversation. I've entered cyberspace.

It's become part of the daily routine: I brush my teeth; I go to my 36
aerobics class; I dial the WELL. Once there, I check my E-mail box (an
on-line friend from Massachusetts says revisions on her novel are going
well; an on-line friend and new dad in California says the baby slept
five hours last night). I usually visit Women on the WELL first (no guys
allowed) to learn the latest depressing or exhilarating details of the lives
of women I've never met but am coming to know anyway, to commis-
erate or cheer them on, to complain that I've gained three pounds.

Then I venture out to see who's arguing about what topic in the 37
media conference and who's soliciting advice in the parenting conference. If I care to, I add my own comments stories, jokes, requests for
information and general two cents worth. If I had hours to spend at this,
as some folks seem to, I could join conferences where people are
yakking about politics, bicycling, sex, Judaism, AIDS, the Grateful Dead
and a zillion other passions and problems.

I haven't yet dared the next step, which is using the WELL to access 38
the Internet, the vast global aggregation of computer networks that
would allow me to use countless libraries and databases, join hundreds
more conferences, and tell *millions* of people that I've gained three
pounds. But I could. And someday, depending on how much of the prat-
tling about the "information superhighway" and its services one chooses

to believe, I'll use a computer (attached discreetly to my television) to make rental movies pop up on my TV screen, buy everything from groceries to mutual funds, take the courses I need to finish my master's degree. It all looks quite prosaic at this point—just lines of text appearing on my screen—but it feels very exciting.

At the moment, cyberspace is populated primarily by—did you guess this?—men. The WELL has only about 15 to 18 percent women among its 8,000 subscribers, its managers believe, a proportion considered representative of most conferencing or "bulletin board" systems (BBSs). Even the big on-line services that spend bundles on advertising and direct mail have drawn few female subscribers (though they believe that many women and children log on using men's accounts). Most of CompuServe's 1.5 million subscribers are guys (90 percent) and so are most of America Online's (85 percent); Prodigy claims to be the most egalitarian of the big on-line services with a 30 percent female membership. 39

Yet these are numbers that could change quickly and dramatically, as women learn that even those who don't know bauds from broads can use a BBS (believe me when I tell you) and—more significantly—learn that there are reasons to. 40

I give you Sarah Randolph, the poet who co-hosts the WELL's writers conference, who lives in a small seaside town and was "just really hungry for conversation and life" when she bought a modem and joined this odd little community. Through it she's made friends, picked up writing jobs, and learned how to increase her garden's broccoli yield. It isn't a substitute for having real people around, yet it has its own rewards. "In the real world, there's your body. Your body is shy and needs something to hold on to at a party," she muses. On-line, "I feel fairly transparent . . . I feel like I can go anywhere in that world." 41

I give you Patrizia DiLucchio, who read about the WELL a few years ago while writing her dissertation "on an extremely dry topic" and thought "it sounded like having pen pals . . . like putting messages in bottles and sending them out to alien shores." Now, because she lives in the San Francisco area, the WELL's home port, "half the people I hang out with in real life I met on the WELL." She also had a heavy-duty romance of several years' duration with a fellow WELLperson, and she's hardly the only one: "To some extent, all bulletin boards are interactive personals ads." 42

I give you Ellen Pack, president of a new on-line service that reverses the usual stats (10 percent of its members are male) called Women's Wire. Along with the databases on women's health, the updates on legislation and such, Women's Wire lets Pack, a San Franciscan, stay in touch with her parents and sisters in New York via E-mail. "My mom is 65 and not particularly computer-literate, but I got her a Mac and now she logs on," Pack reports. "It doesn't replace face-to-face or the occasional phone call, but I communicate with them 43 so much more now because it's sooo easy." E-mail is cheaper and more convenient than long distance telephoning, and Pack points out, "it lets you have all the incremental communications, things you wouldn't pick up the phone for."

I give you, moreover, my friend Pam, who sallied into cyberspace 44 about the same time I did and is busily researching her new book via America Online. We agree that our most serious current problem with computer networks is that work and family obligations can really cut into the time we spend on-line.

And yet. The thing about cyberspace is that although sometimes it 45 feels like a sophisticated graduate seminar or a good-natured pub, it can also, for women, feel like a walk past a construction site or a wrong turn down a dark street. Like life itself, it requires tactical decisions about how to proceed in a not-always-welcoming sphere: Do you opt for a strategic retreat into protected bunkers? Lobby for reform? Take a deep breath and wade in swinging?

For cyberspace is not an alternate, genderless universe. College 46 women report dopey sexist limericks and images of breasts sent via computer nets. Women can be publicly propositioned or stalked by E-mail suitors who hurl abuse when they get rejected. My daughter, visiting an America Online gathering called Teen That, is regularly invited by the teenaged boys who predominate therein to enter a private "room." Sometimes she sees whether they have anything interesting to say. Sometimes she Just Types No.

I have watched as someone named Stacey logged onto an AOL 47 book discussion group, introduced herself as a newcomer, then disappeared from the screen for a while. She came back long enough to type out, "What are all these messages?" She'd been flooded "with IMs—instant messages directed only to her. The other women in the group pointed out that her female ID had made her a target for attention. It was at this point that, although I had not encountered such treatment, I changed my own ID to something offering no gender clues. The problem, hardly limited to American Online, is widely reported. "You seek out your friends and places you know are safe and harassment-free," an AOL subscriber named Citywoman tells me via E-mail.

You don't have to sit still for such annoyances, of course. Many on- 48 line systems have some sort of recourse, hosts or monitors who chastise offenders, or policies that can toss a persistent harasser off the net. On the WELL, a "bozofilter" command allows you to simply never hear from a given user again, an option I'd find useful in everyday existence. You can change in ID like Citywoman to a string of numbers or to JackSpratt. You can confront jerks.

Still, if cyberspace were a workplace, this stuff would qualify as cre- 49 ating a hostile environment. "Hearing that incidents happen probably discourages some women who haven't even tried going on-line," worries Reva Basch, who co-hosts the cozy Women on the WELL conference. "They'll say, 'Oooh, you'll get cruised and hit on. Who needs it? I get enough of that on my job.'"

It was Basch who alerted the WELL at large to another way in which cyberspace can mirror life: the discovery last summer that a "cybercad" had been romancing several WELLwomen simultaneously, exchanging erotic E-mail with each of them without the others' knowledge, going so far as to visit one woman using a plane ticket she helped pay for. The incident, first reported in this newspaper, sparked weeks of heated discussion about whether and how this sort-of community should respond. The cad eventually resigned his account voluntarily, but left behind a lot of unanswered questions about what the differences between behavior on-line and behavior IRL (in real life) are and ought to be.

And if it's tough to figure out what to do about virtual knavery, what to do about a virtual rape? It happened in a computer-generated environment developed by Xerox researchers in Palo Alto, Calif., reachable through the Internet and called LambdaMOO. In this fantasy domain, a kind of multi-authored fictional work-in-progress known to its denizens as "the MOO," a motley array of characters glide through many rooms, doing and saying what users sitting at their terminals (mostly college and graduate students in their late teens and early twenties, three-fourths of them male) tell them to do and say. Last year, in a incident vividly reported in the Village Voice, a crude jester named Mr. Bungle sexually assaulted several other LambdaMOO characters in a rampage of intensifying verbal violence. The ensuing sociopolitical debate was fierce and prolonged.

Civilization—as designed by Pavel Curtis, who heads the Xerox Social Virtual Reality Project—has now come to the MOO. An arrangement of petitions and ballots allows users to modify the system, request arbitration, seek justice. In the on-line world, Curtis concludes, "the medium is different, but the people are the same."

Less dramatic than rape or harassment, but a deterrent nevertheless to bringing women into cyberspace, is the matter of style. Here again, the hackers of yore have left their fingerprints all over the world they helped create. Hackers were known for a strong anti-authoritarian streak, a libertarian philosophy that resisted rules, controls, the restrictive codes of real life. They also adopted online a style of expression that reflected all the maturity, nuance and nurturing qualities of 17-year-old boys. (A recent press release about a book on women and information technology, for example, posted on a University of Illinois network, brought immediate and snarky attacks on the woman who'd written the release, "Who is she, a cow who belongs to NOW?" "A member of Dykes on Bikes?")

This is the clubhouse atmosphere that greets the tentative new- 54
comer of either gender. Nets and conferences have their own varying
personalities, but many of them offer no-holds-barred arguments and
aggressive put-downs, a rambunctious interplay (known as "flaming")
in which women, vastly outnumbered, find their contributions derided
or simply ignored. Academics analyzing "netiquette" have pointed out
that both men and women respond more to men's messages. Some
women charge in and give as good as they get: others retreat.

The WELL, for instance, seems a reasonably civil place with an egal- 55
itarian tradition, where conflict-avoidance abbreviations like "imho" (in
my humble opinion) and "YMMV" (your mileage may vary) abound.
Yet even here, there are women who feel more comfortable in the supportive confines of the women's conference and rarely leave it (though
others find it earnest and too polite and rarely enter). During an on-line
flap about "male discourse," a woman named Tigereye kept the history
conference at a boil for weeks with remarks about the "traditional male
style of communication involving gratuitous oneupmanship, insult and
posturing we can readily observe on the WELL."

What if women dominated the net and set the tone? To find out, 56
Nancy Baym, a University of Illinois doctoral candidate, has immersed
herself in a Usenet group called re.arts.tv.soaps, devoted to discussion
of soap operas. (And referred to as RATS, which is why Baym hopes to
title her dissertation "Of RATS and Women.") Its participants are largely
female engineers, techies and academics who like to break up their
workdays with discussions on such topics as, "Is Dixie a Ho?"

Wading through 7,000 posted messages on the subject of "All My 57
Children," Baym found a language of elaborate courtesy. "They use a
lot of politeness strategies to make disagreement nonthreatening," she
reports. "They'll try to build the esteem of the person they're disagreeing with: 'Jane, I see your point of view, but I must say . . .' Alternately,
they'll diminish the force of their disagreement, qualify things: 'I could
be wrong but . . .' In the soap group, the netiquette is, don't insult people. If you look at groups discussing 'Star Trek,' they'll say, 'Stay off the
'Net, you Nazi!'"

Groans all around. Somewhere between enforcing Nice Networks for 58
women, and having women set upon by wolf packs roaming the Internet,
there must be a workable middle ground. I count myself among the optimists, partly because there are systems that demonstrate the possibility of
egalitarianism. It doesn't happen by accident, but it does happen.

ECHO, a New York-based bulletin board, is more than 50 percent 59
female, an achievement attributed to its founder's determination to lure
women in by means of tutorials, a mentoring program and reduced
rates. Arlington's Metasystems Design Group operates the Meta
Network, a conferencing system that is also more than half female—and
aspires to be a no-flame zone.

"We do all the things good moderators do in person," says 60
Metasystems partner Lisa Kimball. On the Meta Net, new members get
buddies, flamers get a private talking-to, welcomes are issued the first
time someone speaks up online, yet the opinions fly. "It's like arriving
at a big party with lots of people," Kimball says. "One issue is finding
out were the bar is, but it's even better when the hostess says, 'I'm so
glad you're here. There's someone over on the other side of the room I
think you'd like to meet'."

One of the elders of cyberspace, who has founded bulletin boards 61
in many places, is Dave Hughes, a k a the Cursor Cowboy. He now runs
the Old Colorado City Electronic Cottage, based in Colorado Springs,
from which perspective he can see the analogy between that onetime
frontier and this one. "It's the same as going into the gold rush towns,"
the Cowboy observes. "Males jump onto their horses, set up these rois-
tering places, saloons and all. As soon as you begin to approach one-.
third to one-half of the population being women . . . you still have the
saloons and the hoop-de-doo, but you also have the schools.

"It's the same in the on-line world, dominated by men, their 62
language, their interests. . . . The moment a woman goes on-line, she's a
target for all sorts of things, like the gal that came into town on the
stage. . . . [On-line women] have to be like frontier women, a little
tougher-skinned. . . . They have to master all kinds of skills they didn't
know before. But as the numbers increase, the language changes, the
subjects begin to reflect a more balanced society.

Does it matter? I vote yes. 63

True, people of either gender can still live meaningful lives without 64
computers. If I never progressed beyond the half-dozen commands necessary to send my stories to *The Washington Post*, I might suffer little
handicap. I don't think that will be true for my daughter, though, or any
of our daughters. They're entering a world in which card catalog drawers have already vanished from the public library, replaced by terminals
and keyboards.

Perhaps they won't need to he whiz-bang programmers (though it 65
wouldn't hurt). But they can't afford to see computers as toys for boys,
to see ignorance as feminine, to wring their hands over the keyboard
and worry that they'll break something.

"A sense of yourself as a technologically competent person is no 66
small shakes in this world," Jo Sanders of City University says. "It builds
confidence in yourself as a problem-solver. It's important on a résumé
whether or not the job you're interested in uses computers. . . . It's proof
that you are able to learn things, a certificate of capability."

I recall, 20 years ago—as women were trying to free themselves 67
from a set of social expectations that has already changed startlingly—
a brief vogue for feminist courses in auto repair. Whether or not you

could afford to have someone change your oil or your tire, a sense of independence and mastery of the world demanded that you take on the guy things. You wanted to demonstrate to yourself and others that you could change spark plugs even if, once having proven it, you went back to dropping your VW Bug off at the local garage.

More and more, the computer world feels like that. Women have to 68 be in it because incompetence is an unattractive trait. Women have to be in it because decisions about language and culture and access are being made and we should be involved in making them. Women have to be in it because, although nobody really knows what form all this technology will take, there shouldn't be any clubhouse we're afraid to climb into.

I think that because of timely early intervention, Emma will handle 69 the clubhouse just fine.

As for myself, I'm not afraid of the guys inside, but I dread the tech- 70 nical challenge of climbing the tree. Still, a couple of weeks ago, I logged on and typed in "support" and ordered the WELL User's Manual, Version 5.1a. It arrived recently, a fat and daunting volume that tells you when to use "lsz-a*" as opposed to "lxm stky my*." I'm sure there are dozens of elegant functions in it that I don't need and may never master, just as I doubt that I'll ever drool over the compu-porn in Byte or order RAM-doublers by mail.

But I need to know how to download. I've got to learn how to move 71 files around. So I'm going to wade in. It was sort of a kick, late the other night, when Tigereye taught me, via E-mail how to extract. It wasn't so difficult; I just typed "!extract -u tigereye history" and the stuff poured forth in waves.

Responding to Reading

1. Why, according to Span, is computing "a guy thing" (7)? What evidence does she present to support her contention?
2. Span's essay contains the following disclaimer: "Warning: The following article contains assorted generalizations and risks gender stereotyping" (8). Is this statement necessary? Do generalizations and gender stereotyping undercut Span's points?
3. According to Span, what rules should be followed in cyberspace? How would these rules make cyberspace more attractive to women? Do you agree?

GOVERNMENT AND THE INTERNET: HAVES AND HAVE-NOTS

Matthew Symonds

Matthew Symonds is the Internet technology and communications editor for The Economist *magazine and was winner of the 2000 Wincott Award for senior financial journalism. He is the author of* The Culture of Anxiety: The Middle Class Crisis *(1998).*

E-government is not just e-business on a larger scale. One of the most fundamental differences is that whereas businesses can, by and large, choose their customers, government cannot. The debate over the so-called "digital divide" is like the ghost at the e-government feast. For e-government to succeed fully, the dream of internet access for all has to become a reality.

Governments are well aware that large and expensive e-projects will command little support if only a privileged minority benefits. As David Agnew of the Toronto-based Governance in the Digital Economy Project, which is supported by eight big IT firms and 20 national and local governments, argues, "If putting government online is just a way of reinforcing access for people who probably already have more opportunity to access government and decision-makers, then it hasn't really been much of an advance after all."

When Arizona's Democrats held their state presidential primary online in March, it nearly did not happen—not because of security and authentication problems (although there were plenty of those), but because a pressure group called the Voting Integrity Project tried to have it banned. It almost persuaded a court that the vote would disenfranchise the state's minorities, so should be ruled illegal.

Raise the specter of the digital divide with the technology vendors and e-government champions within the public sector, and their brows furrow with concern—but not for long. They are, after all, professional technology optimists. But they also genuinely believe that many of the barriers to near-universal internet access are falling, at least in economically advanced countries (though it is worth remembering that half the world has never even made a telephone call). Survey after survey has found that the main barriers to access are the fear that it is too expensive, that computers are too complicated and that somehow the whole thing is not really relevant or useful. Those optimists argue that, one by one, each of those perfectly legitimate anxieties is being overcome.

What's the problem?

Too expensive? Internet-ready rcs can be bought for little more than $300—less than the price of most televisions, a device that has found its way into 99% of all American homes. Some Internet service providers (isps) are even giving rcs away in return for two or three years' subscription, and other firms offer free ecs to users who agree to be bombarded by advertisements while online. True, access fees and telephone call charges remain high in some countries, but unmetered local calls are spreading from America to Europe, and free isps are evolving a range of different business models.

not valid now

Too complicated and unreliable? That will soon be fixed by the proliferation of non-rc devices which provide access to the web. Among them will be simple terminals that do nothing more than run a browser and take all their applications from the web. These will be found in places such as schools, community centers, libraries and anywhere else that needs a robust machine and has an "always on" connection. An even simpler version is the kind of web kiosk with a touch-screen that is springing up in cities such as Singapore and Toronto.

Access in libraries — kiosks

Many people will be able to do as much business as they need over the Internet with inexpensive smart mobile phones, some of which will soon take the form of a wrist-watch that can be activated by speech rather than via a fiddly keypad. Many new mobile phones are already being loaded with wnr software and microbrowsers. Another way of getting online is by interactive digital television. Early services, such as BSkyB's Open in Britain, are still clunky, but the technology will improve, and the set-top box decoders will often come free.

mobile phones digital TV HD TV assume literate?

The more extreme technology optimists, such as Adam Thierer of the conservative Heritage Foundation in Washington, DC, say that the rapidly falling price of both computing power and bandwidth will in fact create a "digital deluge," so any policies aimed at giving access to the "Information-poor" are quite unnecessary and may be counterproductive. It is a comforting view, but probably quite wrong.

The latest release of the U.S. Department of Commerce's survey "Falling Through the Net" paints a disturbing picture in which the digital divide between rich and poor, white and non-white, well educated and under-schooled seems, if anything, to have widened significantly during the five years in which this information has been collected. Among the examples of the digital divide today, the survey found that:

People with a college degree are eight times more likely to have a rc at home and 16 times more likely to have Internet access at home than those with an elementary school education.

A high-income household in an urban area is 20 times more likely to have Internet access than a rural, low-income household.

A child in a low-income white family is three times more likely to have Internet access than a child in a comparable black family, and four times more likely than if he were Hispanic.

A wealthy household of Asian descent is 34 times more likely to have Internet access than a poor black household.

A child in a two-parent white household is twice as likely to have 15 Internet access as a child in a single-parent household. If the child is black, he is four times more likely to have Internet access than his single-parent counterpart.

Disabled people are nearly three times less likely to have home access 16 to the Internet than people without disabilities.

In other words, although Internet penetration has risen across all 17 demographic groups, the digital divide remains only too real. It has also become a poignant proxy for almost every other kind of disadvantage and inequality in society.

Chalk and cheese

It would be hard to find a better real-life symbol for the digital divide 18 than the gulf between Silicon Valley's leafy Palo Alto, home to dot.com millionaires, where the average house sells for nearly $700,000, and East Palo Alto, the desperate little town on the other side of Highway 101 that not long ago claimed America's highest murder rate. Palo Alto's website has 251 sections and is a paragon of e-government. Among many other things, it allows users to send forms to the planning department and search the city's library catalogue. During storms, it even provides live video footage of flood-prone San Francisquito Creek. East Palo Alto's site, by contrast, has only three pages, containing little more than outdated population figures and the address of City Hall.

The digital divide is not so much a question of access but of educa- 19 tion. As Esther Dyson, an Internet pundit, puts it "You can put computers in community centers, but only the literate people are likely to go use them." Simpler, cheaper ways of getting on to the web will help, as will content that seems relevant to those who shun the Internet today—after all, the mobile phone has conquered all social classes, thanks to its sheer usefulness and simplicity. But even with enlightened policies such as America's "e-rate," which gives cut-price web access to schools and libraries, and the growing number of private-public partnerships to spread both technology and training in its use, there is a danger that the "digital deluge" may reach only those parts where the grass is already green. The same people who have wired rcs today will collect all the fancy new web gadgets that are coming in, and the rest will continue to go without.

So what does this mean for e-government architects? First, as IBM's 20 Todd Ramsey points out, they have to accept that some people, especially the elderly, will never want to deal with government—or indeed anyone else—online. That means some off line channels will almost certainly have to be kept open for year after everything has moved on to the web. Second, they must find ways to allow even those diehards to benefit from the e-government transformation by improving the quality of the off line channels and targeting them better. Not all the savings from electronic service delivery will be bankable.

Third, they need to think up incentives for those on the wrong side of the digital divide to take the leap. Government may be able to act as a catalyst in a way that the private sector cannot. What persuades most people to try the Internet is the promise that they will find something relevant to them. If the most convenient way of getting welfare benefits is online, a lot of people who had never thought of using the web will have a go.

Responding to Reading

1. In paragraph 2, Symonds quotes David Agnew of the Governance in the Digital Economy Project. What does Agnew mean when he says, "If putting government online is just a way of reinforcing access for people who probably already have more opportunity to access government decision-makers, then it hasn't really been much of an advance after all"? Do you agree?

2. What barriers make it difficult for poor people to access the Internet? What evidence does Symonds present to support the existence of a digital divide between "rich and poor, white and non-white, well educated and under-schooled" (10)?

3. According to Symonds, what should be done to persuade people to try the Internet? How do his suggestions differ from those of Henry Lewis Gates, Jr. (p. 499)?

WIDENING THE FOCUS

- Maya Angelou, "Graduation" (p. 102)
- Jonathan Kozol, 'The Human Cost of an Illiterate Society" (p. 112).
- Pico Iyer, 'The Global Village Finally Arrives" (p. 303)

Responding to the Image

1. Do you think this photograph is an accurate representation of who is most likely to be doing high-powered computing in the workplace, that is, using computers in ways that go beyond relatively simple functions such as data entry and word processing? Is there anything surprising to you about this photograph?
2. A 1997 study showed that only 17 percent of those taking advanced placement tests in computer science were female. How does that figure affect your interpretation of the photograph?

WRITING

The Wired Revolution

1. Write an essay in which you examine the ways in which the computer has made your life easier or more difficult. Use your own experience as well as any of the essays in this chapter to support your points.
2. Reread Ashley Dunn's essay "Two Views of Technology's Promise." Then, write an essay in which you discuss which view of technology's future you hold. You can refer to Dunn's essay, the ideas of Nicholas Negroponte, Lewis Thomas, Gregory J. E. Rawlins, or Ted Gup.
3. Write a proposal to ensure that all people have access to the Internet. What specific actions would you recommend? How would these actions enfranchise the groups that are currently on the wrong side of the "digital divide"? Be sure to refer to one or more of the essays in the Focus section of this chapter.
4. According the Philip Elmer-Dewitt, e-mail, computer conferencing, and computer-messaging boards are responsible for a boom in writing. Discuss the effect that the computer has had on your writing. Has it been a positive or a negative force—or has it been both positive and negative?
5. In 1994, then-Vice President Al Gore made a speech in which he said that the Internet would spread participatory democracy around the world. Do you agree? Do you think that the presence of the Internet in a country makes democracy more or less likely? To support your points, refer to some of the essays in this chapter.
6. Can you think of a technological advance other than computers that has had a profound impact on society? Write an essay in which you select a relatively recent innovation—cell phones or cable television, for example—and discuss the impact of this advance on yourself or on society.
7. At various times, the government has tried to regulate the Internet. For example, in 1997, the Supreme Court of the United States decided that a law that attempted to protect children from sexually explicit material was unconstitutional. Do you think that the Internet should be regulated? In what areas should the government intervene? In what areas should it let the Internet regulate itself?
8. In a recent poll, teachers in the United States thought teaching computer skills was more important than teaching European history, biology, chemistry, and physics. Do you agree with this assessment? Do you think that computers in the classroom improve the quality of education? In your essay, consider the ideas of Ted Gup, Peshe Kuriloff, or Neil Postman.

9. One of the criticisms of the Internet is that the people who access it have a difficult time determining what information is reliable and what information is not. Write a pamphlet that high school students could use to assess the information they get from the Internet. Be sure to discuss the techniques that you use to evaluate material from websites, newsgroups, or computer bulletin boards.

10. In his essay "One Internet, Two Nations," Henry Lewis Gates, Jr., says that the digital divide threatens to disenfranchise a third of the nation. Do you, like Gates, believe that not having access to the Internet is the same as not having the vote? If so, why? If not, why not? Refer to the other essays in the Focus section when you prepare your answer.

11. **For Internet research:** The site <http://www.digitaldivide.gov> offers information about government action being taken to increase the computer and Internet access of poor, rural, and minority groups; the site <http://www.speakout.com/Issues/Briefs/1154> provides links to various pertinent articles and documents. A site devoted to increasing access to African-Americans is <http://www.digitalsojourn.org>, and further information about such access can be found at <http://racerelations.about.com/cs/index.htm>. Use these sites as well as other sources you may find to write an essay exploring the kinds of actions that need to be taken to ensure equality in cyberspace.

8

MEDICINE AND
HUMAN VALUES

───────── PREPARING TO READ AND WRITE ─────────

Because medical science has made such great advances, it is easy to forget that until the 1930s, doctors could do little more than diagnose most diseases. With the discovery of sulfa drugs and penicillin, the situation changed, and physicians were actually able to cure diseases that had decimated human populations for centuries. Since the mid-1970s, medical science has made tremendous advances toward understanding basic biological processes and prolonging human life. Recently, however, new diseases and new forms of old diseases have threatened to wipe out these gains. For example, AIDS, a disease almost unheard of twenty-five years ago, afflicts millions of people worldwide, and tuberculosis in new drug-resistant forms (ironically, caused in part by the medications used to cure tuberculosis) is making a deadly comeback in American cities. Thus, scientists could once again face the uncomfortable fact that in the near future, epidemics might be as common as they were a hundred years ago.

Like our gains against disease, our advances in medical technology have proved to be a mixed blessing. Although doctors are armed with an array of high-tech equipment, they must face problems this technology has created. For example, how far should doctors go to preserve human life? At what point, if any, does a life become not worth saving? The writers in this chapter struggle with these and other questions. In some cases, they simply define the issues and acknowledge their difficulty. In other cases, they offer answers that at best are tentative or incomplete. Still, writers—along with doctors, ethicists, and theologians—continue to search for answers.

The Focus section in this chapter (p. 581) addresses the question "Whose Life Is It Anyway?" The essays in this section examine the issue of assisted suicide. For example, do patients who are suffering from a terminal disease have the right to ask doctors to put an end to their suffering? If the answer is yes, under what conditions should they be able to do so? If the answer is no, what other options should they have?

As you read and prepare to write about the essays in this chapter, you may consider the following questions:

- Is the writer a physician? A scientist? A layperson? Does the writer's background make you more or less receptive to his or her ideas?

- On what issue does the writer focus?

- What position does the writer take on the issue? Do you agree or disagree with this position?

- Is the writer's emphasis on the theory or on the practice of medicine?

- What preconceptions do you have about the issue? Does the essay reinforce or contradict your preconceptions?

- What background in science or medicine does the writer assume readers have?

- Is the writer optimistic or pessimistic about the future of medicine? About the future in general?

- Is the writer's purpose to educate? To make readers think about a provocative idea? To persuade them? To warn them?

- In what ways is the essay similar to or different from others in this chapter?

THE BLACK DEATH

Barbara Tuchman

Historical writer and journalist Barbara Tuchman (1912–1989) won Pulitzer Prizes for two of her books: The Guns of August *(1962) and* Stillwell and the American Experience in China, 1911–1945 *(1971). Known for both her literary approach and her factual accuracy, Tuchman once described herself as "a writer whose subject is history." Some of her many works are* The Proud Tower: A Portrait of the World before the War, 1890–1914 *(1966),* A Distant Mirror: The Calamitous Fourteenth Century *(1978), and a collection of essays,* Practicing History *(1981). Tuchman was awarded the American Academy of Arts and Sciences gold medal for history in 1978. In the following excerpt from* A Distant Mirror,

she graphically describes the Black Death (or bubonic plague) without senti-
mentality or melodrama, using a variety of different sources to document this
plague's horrifying effects.

In October 1347, two months after the fall of Calais, Genoese trad- 1
ing ships put into the harbor of Messina in Sicily with dead and dying
men at the oars. The ships had come from the Black Sea port of Caffa
(now Feodosiya) in the Crimea, where the Genoese maintained a trading post. The diseased sailors showed strange black swellings about the
size of an egg or an apple in the armpits and groin. The swellings oozed
blood and pus and were followed by spreading boils and black blotches
on the skin from internal bleeding. The sick suffered severe pain and
died quickly within five days of the first symptoms. As the disease
spread, other symptoms of continuous fever and spitting of blood
appeared instead of the swellings or buboes. These victims coughed
and sweated heavily and died even more quickly, within three days or
less, sometimes in 24 hours. In both types everything that issued from
the body—breath, sweat, blood from the buboes and lungs, bloody
urine, and blood-blackened excrement—smelled foul. Depression and
despair accompanied the physical symptoms, and before the end
"death is seen seated on the face."

The disease was bubonic plague, present in two forms: one that 2
infected the bloodstream, causing the buboes and internal bleeding, and
was spread by contact; and a second, more virulent pneumonic type
that infected the lungs and was spread by respiratory infection. The
presence of both at once caused the high mortality and speed of contagion. So lethal was the disease that cases were known of persons going
to bed well and dying before they woke, of doctors catching the illness
at a bedside and dying before the patient. So rapidly did it spread from
one to another that to a French physician, Simon de Covino, it seemed
as if one sick person "could infect the whole world." The malignity of
the pestilence appeared more terrible because its victims knew no prevention and no remedy.

The physical suffering of the disease and its aspect of evil mystery 3
were expressed in a strange Welsh lament which saw "death coming
into our midst like black smoke, a plague which cuts off the young, a
footless phantom which has no mercy for fair countenance. Woe is me
of the shilling in the armpit! It is seething, terrible . . . a head that gives
pain and causes a loud cry . . . a painful angry knob. . . . Great is its
seething like a burning cinder . . . a grievous thing of ashy color." Its erup-
tion is ugly like the "seeds of black peas, broken fragments of brittle
sea-coal . . . the early ornaments of black death, cinders of the peelings of
the cockle weed, a mixed multitude, a black plague like halfpence, like
berries. . . ."

Rumors of a terrible plague supposedly arising in China and 4
spreading through Tartary (Central Asia) to India and Persia,
Mesopotamia, Syria, Egypt, and all of Asia Minor had reached Europe
in 1346. They told of a death so devastating that all of India was said to
be depopulated, whole territories covered by dead bodies, other areas
with no one left alive. As added up by Pope Clement VI at Avignon, the
total of reported dead reached 23,840,000. In the absence of a concept of
contagion, no serious alarm was felt in Europe until the trading ships
brought their black burden of pestilence into Messina while other
infected ships from the Levant carried it to Genoa and Venice.

By January 1348 it penetrated France via Marseille, and North 5
Africa via Tunis. Shipborne along coasts and navigable rivers, it spread
westward from Marseille through the ports of Languedoc to Spain and
northward up the Rhône to Avignon, where it arrived in March. It
reached Narbonne, Montpellier, Carcassonne, and Toulouse between
February and May, and at the same time in Italy spread to Rome
and Florence and their hinterlands. Between June and August it reached
Bordeaux, Lyon, and Paris, spread to Burgundy and Normandy, and
crossed the Channel from Normandy into southern England. From Italy
during the same summer it crossed the Alps into Switzerland and
reached eastward to Hungary.

In a given area the plague accomplished its kill within four to six 6
months and then faded, except in the larger cities, where, rooting into
the close-quartered population, it abated during the winter, only to
reappear in spring and rage for another six months.

In 1349 it resumed in Paris, spread to Picardy, Flanders, and the 7
Low Countries, and from England to Scotland and Ireland as well as to
Norway, where a ghost ship with a cargo of wool and a dead crew
drifted offshore until it ran aground near Bergen. From there the plague
passed into Sweden, Denmark, Prussia, Iceland, and as far as
Greenland. Leaving a strange pocket of immunity in Bohemia, and
Russia unattacked until 1351, it had passed from most of Europe by
mid-1350. Although the mortality rate was erratic, ranging from one
fifth in some places to nine tenths or almost total elimination in others,
the overall estimate of modern demographers has settled—for the area
extending from India to Iceland—around the same figure expressed in
Froissart's casual words: "a third of the world died." His estimate, the
common one at the time, was not an inspired guess but a borrowing of
St. John's figure for mortality from plague in Revelation, the favorite
guide to human affairs of the Middle Ages.

A third of Europe would have meant about 20 million deaths. No 8
one knows in truth how many died. Contemporary reports were an
awed impression, not an accurate count. In crowded Avignon, it was
said, 400 died daily; 7,000 houses emptied by death were shut up; a

single graveyard received 11,000 corpses in six weeks; half the city's inhabitants reportedly died, including 9 cardinals or one third of the total, and 70 lesser prelates. Watching the endlessly passing death carts, chroniclers let normal exaggeration take wings and put the Avignon death toll at 62,000 and even at 120,000, although the city's total population was probably less than 50,000.

When graveyards filled up, bodies at Avignon were thrown into the 9 Rhône until mass burial pits were dug for dumping the corpses. In London in such pits corpses piled up in layers until they overflowed. Everywhere reports speak of the sick dying too fast for the living to bury. Corpses were dragged out of homes and left in front of doorways. Morning light revealed new piles of bodies. In Florence the dead were gathered up by the Compagnia della Misericordia—founded in 1244 to care for the sick—whose members wore red robes and hoods masking the face except for the eyes. When their efforts failed, the dead lay putrid in the streets for days at a time. When no coffins were to be had, the bodies were laid on boards, two or three at once, to be carried to graveyards or common pits. Families dumped their own relatives into the pits, or buried them so hastily and thinly "that dogs dragged them forth and devoured their bodies."

Amid accumulating death and fear of contagion, people died with- 10 out last rites and were buried without prayers, a prospect that terrified the last hours of the stricken. A bishop in England gave permission to laymen to make confession to each other as was done by the Apostles, "or if no man is present then even to a woman," and if no priest could be found to administer extreme unction, "then faith must suffice." Clement VI found it necessary to grant remissions of sin to all who died of the plague because so many were unattended by priests. "And no bells tolled," wrote a chronicler of Siena, "and nobody wept no matter what his loss because almost everyone expected death. . . . And people said and believed, 'this is the end of the world.'"

In Paris, where the plague lasted through 1349, the reported death 11 rate was 800 a day, in Pisa 500, in Vienna 500 to 600. The total dead in Paris numbered 50,000 or half the population. Florence, weakened by the famine of 1347, lost three to four fifths of its citizens, Venice two thirds, Hamburg and Bremen, though smaller in size, about the same proportion. Cities, as centers of transportation, were more likely to be affected than villages, although once a village was infected, its death rate was equally high. At Givry, a prosperous village in Burgundy of 1,200 to 1,500 people, the parish register records 615 deaths in the space of fourteen weeks, compared to an average of thirty deaths a year in the previous decade. In three villages of Cambridgeshire, manorial records show a death rate of 47 percent, 57 percent, and in one case 70 percent. When the last survivors, too few to carry on, moved away, a deserted village sank back into the wilderness and disappeared from the map altogether, leaving only a grass-covered ghostly outline to show where mortals once had lived.

In enclosed places such as monasteries and prisons, the infection of 12 one person usually meant that of all, as happened in the Franciscan convents of Carcassonne and Marseille, where every inmate without exception died. Of the 140 Dominicans at Montpellier only seven survived. Petrarch's[1] brother Gherardo, member of a Carthusian monastery, buried the prior and 34 fellow monks one by one, sometimes three a day, until he was left alone with his dog and fled to look for a place that would take him in. Watching every comrade die, men in such places could not but wonder whether the strange peril that filled the air had not been sent to exterminate the human race. In Kilkenny, Ireland, Brother John Clyn of the Friars Minor, another monk left alone among dead men, kept a record of what had happened lest "things which should be remembered perish with time and vanish from the memory of those who come after us." Sensing "the whole world, as it were, placed within the grasp of the Evil One," and waiting for death to visit him too, he wrote, "I leave parchment to continue this work, if perchance any man survive and any of the race of Adam escape this pestilence and carry on the work which I have begun." Brother John, as noted by another hand, died of the pestilence, but he foiled oblivion.

The largest cities of Europe, with populations of about 100,000, 13 were Paris and Florence, Venice and Genoa. At the next level, with more than 50,000, were Ghent and Bruges in Flanders, Milan, Bologna, Rome, Naples, and Palermo, and Cologne. London hovered below 50,000, the only city in England except York with more than 10,000. At the level of 20,000 to 50,000 were Bordeaux, Toulouse, Montpellier, Marseille, and Lyon in France, Barcelona, Seville, and Toledo in Spain, Siena, Pisa, and other secondary cities in Italy, and the Hanseatic[2] trading cities of the Empire. The plague raged through them all, killing anywhere from one third to two thirds of their inhabitants. Italy, with a total population of 10 to 11 million, probably suffered the heaviest toll. Following the Florentine bankruptcies, the crop failures and workers' riots of 1346-47, the revolt of Cola di Rienzi that plunged Rome into anarchy, the plague came as the peak of successive calamities. As if the world were indeed in the grasp of the Evil One, its first appearance on the European mainland in January 1348 coincided with a fearsome earthquake that carved a path of wreckage from Naples up to Venice. Houses collapsed, church towers toppled, villages were crushed, and the destruction reached as

---

[1] Italian poet (1304–1374). [Eds.]

[2] A league of medieval German market towns. [Eds.]

far as Germany and Greece. Emotional response, dulled by horrors, underwent a kind of atrophy epitomized by the chronicler who wrote, "And in these days was burying without sorrowe and wedding without friendschippe."

In Siena, where more than half of the inhabitants died of the plague, [14] work was abandoned on the great cathedral, planned to be the largest in the world, and never resumed, owing to loss of workers and master masons and "the melancholy and grief" of the survivors. The cathedral's truncated transept still stands in permanent witness to the sweep of death's scythe. Agnolo di Tura, a chronicler of Siena, recorded the fear of contagion that froze every other instinct. "Father abandoned child, wife husband, one brother another," he wrote, "for this plague seemed to strike through the breath and sight. And so they died. And no one could be found to bury the dead for money or friendship. . . . And I, Agnolo di Tura, called the Fat, buried my five children with my own hands, and so did many others likewise."

There were many to echo his account of inhumanity and few to bal- [15] ance it, for the plague was not the kind of calamity that inspired mutual help. Its loathsomeness and deadliness did not herd people together in mutual distress, but only prompted their desire to escape each other. "Magistrates and notaries refused to come and make the wills of the dying," reported a Franciscan friar of Piazza in Sicily; what was worse, "even the priests did not come to hear their confessions." A clerk of the Archbishop of Canterbury reported the same of English priests who "turned away from the care of their benefices from fear of death." Cases of parents deserting children and children their parents were reported across Europe from Scotland to Russia. The calamity chilled the hearts of men, wrote Boccaccio[3] in his famous account of the plague in Florence that serves as introduction to the *Decameron.* "One man shunned another . . . kinsfolk held aloof, brother was forsaken by brother, oftentimes husband by wife; nay, what is more, and scarcely to be believed, fathers and mothers were found to abandon their own children to their fate, untended, unvisited as if they had been strangers." Exaggeration and literary pessimism were common in the 14th century, but the Pope's physician, Guy de Chauliac, was a sober, careful observer who reported the same phenomenon: "A father did not visit his son, nor the son his father. Charity was dead."

Yet not entirely. In Paris, according to the chronicler Jean de Venette, [16] the nuns of the Hôtel Dieu or municipal hospital, "having no fear of death, tended the sick with all sweetness and humility." New nuns repeatedly took the places of those who died, until the majority "many

---

[3] Italian writer (1313–1375) whose *Decameron* is a collection of one hundred stories told by a group of plague survivors who flee to a country estate to escape contagion. [Eds.]

times renewed by death now rest in peace with Christ as we may piously believe."

When the plague entered northern France in July 1348, it settled first 17 in Normandy and, checked by winter, gave Picardy a deceptive interim until the next summer. Either in mourning or warning, black flags were flown from church towers of the worst-stricken villages of Normandy. "And in that time," wrote a monk of the abbey of Fourcarment, "the mortality was so great among the people of Normandy that those of Picardy mocked them." The same unneighborly reaction was reported of the Scots, separated by a winter's immunity from the English. Delighted to hear of the disease that was scourging the "southrons," they gathered forces for an invasion, "laughing at their enemies." Before they could move, the savage mortality fell upon them too, scattering some in death and the rest in panic to spread the infection as they fled.

In Picardy in the summer of 1349 the pestilence penetrated the cas- 18 tle of Coucy to kill Enguerrand's[4] mother, Catherine, and her new husband. Whether her nine-year-old son escaped by chance or was perhaps living elsewhere with one of his guardians is unrecorded. In nearby Amiens, tannery workers, responding quickly to losses in the labor force, combined to bargain for higher wages. In another place villagers were seen dancing to drums and trumpets, and on being asked the reason, answered that, seeing their neighbors die day by day while their village remained immune, they believed that they could keep the plague from entering "by the jollity that is in us. That is why we dance." Further north in Tournai on the border of Flanders, Gilles li Muisis, Abbot of St. Martin's, kept one of the epidemic's most vivid accounts. The passing bells rang all day and all night, he recorded, because sextons were anxious to obtain their fees while they could. Filled with the sound of mourning, the city became oppressed by fear, so that the authorities forbade the tolling of bells and the wearing of black and restricted funeral services to two mourners. The silencing of funeral bells and of criers' announcements of deaths was ordained by most cities. Siena imposed a fine on the wearing of mourning clothes by all except widows.

Flight was the chief recourse of those who could afford it or arrange 19 it. The rich fled to their country places like Boccaccio's young patricians of Florence, who settled in a pastoral palace "removed on every side from the road" with "wells of cool water and vaults of rare wines." The urban poor died in their burrows, "and only the stench of their bodies informed neighbors of their death." That the poor were more heavily afflicted than the rich was clearly remarked at the time, in the north as in the south. A Scottish chronicler, John of Fordun, stated flatly that the

---

[4] Throughout *A Distant Mirror*, the book from which this excerpt is taken, Tuchman traces the impact of events on the life a French nobleman named Enguerrand de Coucy. [Eds.]

pest "attacked especially the meaner sort and common people—seldom the magnates." Simon de Covino of Montpellier made the same observation. He ascribed it to the misery and want and hard lives that made the poor more susceptible, which was half the truth. Close contact and lack of sanitation was the unrecognized other half. It was noticed too that the young died in greater proportion than the old; Simon de Covino compared the disappearance of youth to the withering of flowers in the fields.

In the countryside peasants dropped dead on the roads, in the fields, 20 in their houses. Survivors in growing helplessness fell into apathy, leaving ripe wheat uncut and livestock untended. Oxen and asses, sheep and goats, pigs and chickens ran wild and they too, according to local reports, succumbed to the pest. English sheep, bearers of the precious wool, died throughout the country. The chronicler Henry Knighton, canon of Leicester Abbey, reported 5,000 dead in one field alone, "their bodies so corrupted by the plague that neither beast nor bird would touch them," and spreading an appalling stench. In the Austrian Alps wolves came down to prey upon sheep and then, "as if alarmed by some invisible warning, turned and fled back into the wilderness." In remote Dalmatia bolder wolves descended upon a plague-stricken city and attacked human survivors. For want of herdsmen, cattle strayed from place to place and died in hedgerows and ditches. Dogs and cats fell like the rest.

The dearth of labor held a fearful prospect because the 14th century 21 lived close to the annual harvest both for food and for next year's seed. "So few servants and laborers were left," wrote Knighton, "that no one knew where to turn for help." The sense of a vanishing future created a kind of dementia of despair. A Bavarian chronicler of Neuberg on the Danube recorded that "Men and women . . . wandered around as if mad" and let their cattle stray "because no one had any inclination to concern themselves about the future." Fields went uncultivated, spring seed unsown. Second growth with nature's awful energy crept back over cleared land, dikes crumbled, salt water reinvaded and soured the lowlands. With so few hands remaining to restore the work of centuries, people felt, in Walsingham's words, that "the world could never again regain its former prosperity."

Though the death rate was higher among the anonymous poor, the 22 known and the great died too. King Alfonso XI of Castile was the only reigning monarch killed by the pest, but his neighbor King Pedro of Aragon lost his wife, Queen Leonora, his daughter Marie, and a niece in the space of six months. John Cantacuzene, Emperor of Byzantium, lost his son. In France the lame Queen Jeanne and her daughter-in-law Bonne de Luxemburg, wife of the Dauphin, both died in 1349 in the same phase that took the life of Enguerrand's mother. Jeanne, Queen of Navarre, daughter of Louis X, was another victim. Edward III's second daughter, Joanna, who was on her way to marry Pedro, the heir of

Castile, died in Bordeaux. Women appear to have been more vulnerable than men, perhaps because, being more housebound, they were more exposed to fleas. Boccaccio's mistress Fiammetta, illegitimate daughter of the King of Naples, died, as did Laura, the beloved—whether real or fictional—of Petrarch. Reaching out to us in the future, Petrarch cried, "Oh happy posterity who will not experience such abysmal woe and will look upon our testimony as a fable."

In Florence Giovanni Villani, the great historian of his time, died at 23 68 in the midst of an unfinished sentence: ". . . *e dure questo pistolenza fino a . . .* (in the midst of this pestilence there came to an end . . .)." Siena's master painters, the brothers Ambrogio and Pietro Lorenzetti, whose names never appear after 1348, presumably perished in the plague, as did Andrea Pisano, architect and sculptor of Florence. William of Ockham and the English mystic Richard Rolle of Hampole both disappear from mention after 1349. Francisco Datini, merchant of Prato, lost both his parents and two siblings. Curious sweeps of mortality afflicted certain bodies of merchants in London. All eight wardens of the Company of Cutters, all six wardens of the Hatters, and four wardens of the Goldsmiths died before July 1350. Sir John Pulteney, master draper and four times Mayor of London, was a victim, likewise Sir John Montgomery, Governor of Calais.

Among the clergy and doctors the mortality was naturally high 24 because of the nature of their professions. Out of 24 physicians in Venice, 20 were said to have lost their lives in the plague, although, according to another account, some were believed to have fled or to have shut themselves up in their houses. At Montpellier, site of the leading medieval medical school, the physician Simon de Covino reported that, despite the great number of doctors, "hardly one of them escaped." In Avignon, Guy de Chauliac confessed that he performed his medical visits only because he dared not stay away for fear of infamy, but "I was in continual fear." He claimed to have contracted the disease but to have cured himself by his own treatment; if so, he was one of the few who recovered.

Clerical mortality varied with rank. Although the one-third toll of 25 cardinals reflects the same proportion as the whole, this was probably due to their concentration in Avignon. In England, in strange and almost sinister procession, the Archbishop of Canterbury, John Stratford, died in August 1348, his appointed successor died in May 1349, and the next appointee three months later, all three within a year. Despite such weird vagaries, prelates in general managed to sustain a higher survival rate than the lesser clergy. Among bishops the deaths have been estimated at about one in twenty. The loss of priests, even if many avoided their fearful duty of attending the dying, was about the same as among the population as a whole.

Government officials, whose loss contributed to the general chaos, 26 found, on the whole, no special shelter. In Siena four of the nine members of the governing oligarchy died, in France one third of the royal notaries, in Bristol 15 out of the 52 members of the Town Council or almost one third. Tax-collecting obviously suffered, with the result that Philip VI was unable to collect more than a fraction of the subsidy granted him by the Estates in the winter of 1347–48.

Lawlessness and debauchery accompanied the plague as they had during the great plague of Athens of 430 B.C., when according to Thucydides,[5] men grew bold in the indulgence of pleasure: "For seeing how the rich died in a moment and those who had nothing immediately inherited their property, they reflected that life and riches were alike transitory and they resolved to enjoy themselves while they could." Human behavior is timeless. When St. John had his vision of plague in Revelation, he knew from some experience or race memory that those who survived "repented not of the work of their hands. . . . Neither repented they of their murders, nor of their sorceries, nor of their fornication, nor of their thefts." 27

Responding to Reading

1. Many passages of Tuchman's essay include unpleasant descriptions of the plague victims' symptoms. Is this kind of descriptive detail—for example, "the dead lay putrid in the streets" (9)—necessary? Why do you think Tuchman includes it?

2. Which kinds of support do you find most compelling in Tuchman's essay: statistics, quotations from contemporary sources, anecdotes, victims' names, or summaries of historical sources? What do you think Tuchman would gain by adding other kinds of support, such as artists' re-creations of the scenes, quotations from modern-day historians, analysis by modern-day medical professionals, or a case study of one family?

3. What point is Tuchman trying to make with this essay? What revelance does an essay about the plague in the fourteenth century have for contemporary readers?

---

[5] Ancient Greek historian. [Eds.]

IMELDA

Richard Selzer

A surgeon as well as an accomplished writer, Richard Selzer (1928–   )
was born in Troy, New York, where his father had a family medical practice
until his death when Selzer was twelve. Following in his father's footsteps,
he attended Albany Medical College and Yale Medical School, later serving
on the faculty there as a professor of surgery. Influenced by his artistic
mother, Selzer also took an early interest in literature but didn't himself
begin writing for publication until he was in his forties. Since then he has
published essays and stories in a variety of magazines and journals, and his
collections include Mortal Lessons *(1977),* Letters to a Young Doctor
(1982), and Imagine a Woman *(1991). A memoir,* Raising the Dead: A
Doctor's Encounter with His Own Mortality, *was published in 1994. Of*
his two professions, Selzer has written, "The surgeon sutures together the
tissues of the body to make whole what is sick or injured; the writer sews
words into sentences to fashion a new version of human experience." Selzer's
work often focuses on the complex relationship between doctor and patient;
in the following essay, he recalls a surgeon he worked under in medical school
whose compassionate gesture toward a young patient has remained with
Selzer all his life.

I heard the other day that Hugh Franciscus had died. I knew him   1
once. He was the Chief of Plastic Surgery when I was a medical student
at Albany Medical College. Dr. Franciscus was the archetype of the professor of surgery—tall, vigorous, muscular, as precise in his technique as
he was impeccable in his dress. Each day a clean lab coat monkishly
starched, that sort of thing. I doubt that he ever read books. One book
only, that of the human body, took the place of all others. He never raised
his eyes from it. He read it like a printed page as though he knew that in
the calligraphy there just beneath the skin were all the secrets of the
world. Long before it became visible to anyone else, he could detect the
first sign of granulation at the base of a wound, the first blue line of new
epithelium at the periphery that would tell him that a wound would heal,
or the barest hint of necrosis that presaged failure. This gave him the
appearance of a prophet. "This skin graft will take," he would say, and
you must believe beyond all cyanosis, exudation and inflammation that
it would.

He had enemies, of course, who said he was arrogant, that he ex-   2
alted activity for its own sake. Perhaps. But perhaps it was no more than
the honesty of one who knows his own worth. Just look at a scalpel,
after all. What a feeling of sovereignty, megalomania even, when you
know that it is you and you alone who will make certain use of it. It was
said, too, that he was a ladies' man. I don't know about that. It was all
rumor. Besides, I think he had other things in mind than mere living.

Hugh Franciscus was a zealous hunter. Every fall during the season he drove upstate to hunt deer. There was a glass-front case in his office where he showed his guns. How could he shoot a deer? we asked. But he knew better. To us medical students he was someone heroic, someone made up of several gods, beheld at a distance, and always from a lesser height. If he had grown accustomed to his miracles, we had not. He had no close friends on the staff. There was something a little sad in that. As though once long ago he had been flayed by friendship and now the slightest breeze would hurt. Confidences resulted in dishonor. Perhaps the person in whom one confided would scorn him, betray. Even though he spent his days among those less fortunate, weaker than he—the sick, after all—Franciscus seemed aware of an air of personal harshness in his environment to which he reacted by keeping his own counsel, by a certain remoteness. It was what gave him the appearance of being haughty. With the patients he was forthright. All the facts laid out, every question anticipated and answered with specific information. He delivered good news and bad with the same dispassion.

I was a third-year student, just turned onto the wards for the first time, and clerking on Surgery. Everything—the operating room, the 3 morgue, the emergency room, the patients, professors, even the nurses—was terrifying. One picked one's way among the mines and booby traps of the hospital, hoping only to avoid the hemorrhage and perforation of disgrace. The opportunity for humiliation was everywhere.

It all began on Ward Rounds. Dr. Franciscus was demonstrating a 4 cross-leg flap graft he had constructed to cover a large fleshy defect in the leg of a merchant seaman who had injured himself in a fall. The man was from Spain and spoke no English. There had been a comminuted fracture of the femur, much soft tissue damage, necrosis. After weeks of debridement and dressings, the wound had been made ready for grafting. Now the patient was in his fifth postoperative day. What we saw was a thick web of pale blue flesh arising from the man's left thigh, and which had been sutured to the open wound on the right thigh. When the surgeon pressed the pedicle with his finger, it blanched; when he let up, there was a slow return of the violaceous color.

"The circulation is good," Franciscus announced. "It will get bet- 5 ter." In several weeks, we were told, he would divide the tube of flesh at its site of origin, and tailor it to fit the defect to which, by then, it would have grown more solidly. All at once, the webbed man in the bed reached out, and gripping Franciscus by the arm, began to speak rapidly, pointing to his groin and hip. Franciscus stepped back at once to disengage his arm from the patient's grasp.

"Anyone here know Spanish? I didn't get a word of that."   6

"The cast is digging into him up above," I said. "The edges of the 7 plaster are rough. When he moves, they hurt."

Without acknowledging my assistance, Dr. Franciscus took a plas- 8
ter shears from the dressing cart and with several large snips cut away
the rough edges of the cast.

"*Gracias, gracias.*" The man in the bed smiled. But Franciscus had 9
already moved on to the next bed. He seemed to me a man of immense
strength and ability, yet without affection for the patients. He did not
want to be touched by them. It was less kindness that he showed them
than a reassurance that he would never give up, that he would bend
every effort. If anyone could, he would solve the problems of their flesh.

Ward Rounds had disbanded and I was halfway down the corridor 10
when I heard Dr. Franciscus's voice behind me.

"You speak Spanish." It seemed a command. 11

"I lived in Spain for two years," I told him. 12

"I'm taking a surgical team to Honduras next week to operate on 13
the natives down there. I do it every year for three weeks, somewhere.
This year, Honduras. I can arrange the time away from your duties here
if you'd like to come along. You will act as interpreter. I'll show you how
to use the clinical camera. What you'd see would make it worthwhile."

So it was that, a week later, the envy of my classmates, I joined the 14
mobile surgical unit—surgeons, anesthetists, nurses and equipment—
aboard a Military Air Transport plane to spend three weeks performing
plastic surgery on people who had been previously selected by an
advance team. Honduras. I don't suppose I shall ever see it again. Nor
do I especially want to. From the plane it seemed a country made of
clay—burnt umber, raw sienna, dry. It had a deadweight quality, as
though the ground had no buoyancy, no air sacs through which a breeze
might wander. Our destination was Comayagua, a town in the Central
Highlands. The town itself was situated on the edge of one of the flat-
lands that were linked in a network between the granite mountains.
Above, all was brown, with only an occasional Spanish cedar tree;
below, patches of luxuriant tropical growth. It was a day's bus ride from
the airport. For hours, the town kept appearing and disappearing with
the convolutions of the road. At last, there it lay before us, panting and
exhausted at the bottom of the mountain.

That was all I was to see of the countryside. From then on, there was 15
only the derelict hospital of Comayagua, with the smell of spoiling bananas and the accumulated odors of everyone who had been sick there for
the last hundred years. Of the two, I much preferred the frank smell of the
sick. The heat of the place was incendiary. So hot that, as we stepped from
the bus, our own words did not carry through the air, but hung limply at
our lips and chins. Just in front of the hospital was a thirsty courtyard
where mobs of waiting people squatted or lay in the meager shade, and
where, on dry days, a fine dust rose through which untethered goats
shouldered. Against the walls of this courtyard, gaunt, dejected men
stood, their faces, like their country, preternaturally solemn, leaden. Here

no one looked up at the sky. Every head was bent beneath a wide-brimmed straw hat. In the days that followed, from the doorway of the dispensary, I would watch the brown mountains sliding about, drinking the hospital into their shadow as the afternoon grew later and later, flattening us by their very altitude.

The people were mestizos, of mixed Spanish and Indian blood. 16 They had flat, broad, dumb museum feet. At first they seemed to me indistinguishable the one from the other, without animation. All the vitality, the hidden sexuality, was in their black hair. Soon I was to know them by the fissures with which each face was graven. But, even so, compared to us, they were masked, shut away. My job was to follow Dr. Franciscus around, photograph the patients before and after surgery, interpret and generally act as aide-de-camp. It was exhilarating. Within days I had decided that I was not just useful, but essential. Despite that we spent all day in each other's company, there were no overtures of friendship from Dr. Franciscus. He knew my place, and I knew it, too. In the afternoon he examined the patients scheduled for the next day's surgery. I would call out a name from the doorway to the examining room. In the courtyard someone would rise. I would usher the patient in, and nudge him to the examining table where Franciscus stood, always, I thought, on the verge of irritability. I would read aloud the case history, then wait while he carried out his examination. While I took the "before" photographs, Dr. Franciscus would dictate into a tape recorder:

"Ulcerating basal cell carcinoma of the right orbit—six by eight cen- 17 timeters—involving the right eye and extending into the floor of the orbit. Operative plan: wide excision with enucleation of the eye. Later, bone and skin grafting." The next morning we would be in the operating room where the procedure would be carried out.

We were more than two weeks into our tour of duty—a few days to 18 go—when it happened. Earlier in the day I had caught sight of her through the window of the dispensary. A thin, dark Indian girl about fourteen years old. A figurine, orange-brown, terra-cotta, and still attached to the unshaped clay from which she had been carved. An older, sun-weathered woman stood behind and somewhat to the left of the girl. The mother was short and dumpy. She wore a broad-brimmed hat with a high crown, and a shapeless dress like a cassock. The girl had long, loose black hair. There were tiny gold hoops in her ears. The dress she wore could have been her mother's. Far too big, it hung from her thin shoulders at some risk of slipping down her arms. Even with her in it, the dress was empty, something hanging on the back of a door. Her breasts made only the smallest imprint in the cloth, her hips none at all. All the while, she pressed to her mouth a filthy, pink, balled-up rag as though to stanch a flow or buttress against pain. I knew that what she had come to show us, what we were there to see, was hidden beneath that pink cloth. As I watched, the woman handed down to her a gourd from which the girl drank, lapping like a dog. She was the last patient of the day. They had been waiting in the courtyard for hours.

"Imelda Valdez," I called out. Slowly she rose to her feet, the cloth [19] never leaving her mouth, and followed her mother to the examining-room door. I shooed them in.

"You sit up there on the table," I told her. "Mother, you stand over [20] there, please." I read from the chart:

"This is a fourteen-year-old girl with a complete, unilateral, left- [21] sided cleft lip and cleft palate. No other diseases or congenital defects. Laboratory tests, chest X ray—negative."

"Tell her to take the rag away," said Dr. Franciscus. I did, and the [22] girl shrank back, pressing the cloth all the more firmly.

"Listen, this is silly," said Franciscus. "Tell her I've got to see it. [23] Either she behaves, or send her away."

"Please give me the cloth," I said to the girl as gently as possible. [24] She did not. She could not. Just then, Franciscus reached up and, taking the hand that held the rag, pulled it away with a hard jerk. For an instant the girl's head followed the cloth as it left her face, one arm still upflung against showing. Against all hope, she would hide herself. A moment later, she relaxed and sat still. She seemed to me then like an animal that looks outward at the infinite, at death, without fear, with recognition only.

Set as it was in the center of the girl's face, the defect was utterly [25] hideous—a nude rubbery insect that had fastened there. The upper lip was widely split all the way to the nose. One white tooth perched upon the protruding upper jaw projecting through the hole. Some of the bone seemed to have been gnawed away as well. Above the thing, clear almond eyes and long black hair reflected the light. Below, a slender neck where the pulse trilled visibly. Under our gaze the girl's eyes fell to her lap where her hands lay palms upward, half open. She was a beautiful bird with a crushed beak. And tense with the expectation of more shame.

"Open your mouth," said the surgeon. I translated. She did so, and [26] the surgeon tipped back her head to see inside.

"The palate, too. Complete," he said. There was a long silence. At [27] last he spoke.

"What is your name?" The margins of the wound melted until she [28] herself was being sucked into it.

"Imelda." The syllables leaked through the hole with a slosh and a [29] whistle.

"Tomorrow," said the surgeon, "I will fix your lip. *Mañana*." [30]

It seemed to me that Hugh Franciscus, in spite of his years of expe- [31] rience, in spite of all the dreadful things he had seen, must have been awed by the sight of this girl. I could see it flit across his face for an instant. Perhaps it was her small act of concealment, that he had had to demand that she show him the lip, that he had had to force her to show it to him. Perhaps it was her resistance that intensified the disfigurement. Had she brought her mouth to him willingly, without shame, she would have been for him neither more nor less than any other patient.

He measured the defect with calipers, studied it from different 32 angles, turning her head with a finger at her chin.

"How can it ever be put back together?" I asked. 33

"Take her picture," he said. And to her, "Look straight ahead." 34 Through the eye of the camera she seemed more pitiful than ever, her humiliation more complete.

"Wait!" The surgeon stopped me. I lowered the camera. A strand of 35 her hair had fallen across her face and found its way to her mouth, becoming stuck there by saliva. He removed the hair and secured it behind her ear.

"Go ahead," he ordered. There was the click of the camera. The girl 36 winced.

"Take three more, just in case." 37

When the girl and her mother had left, he took paper and pen and 38 with a few lines drew a remarkable likeness of the girl's face.

"Look," he said. "If this dot is A, and this one B, this, C, and this, D, 39 the incisions are made A to B, then C to D. CD must equal AB. It is all equilateral triangles." All well and good, but then came X and Y and rotation flaps and the rest.

"Do you see?" he asked. 40

"It is confusing," I told him. 41

"It is simply a matter of dropping the upper lip into a normal posi- 42 tion, then crossing the gap with two triangular flaps. It is geometry," he said.

"Yes," I said. "Geometry." And relinquished all hope of becoming a 43 plastic surgeon.

In the operating room the next morning the anesthesia had already 44 been administered when we arrived from Ward Rounds. The tube emerging from the girl's mouth was pressed against her lower lip to be kept out of the field of surgery. Already, a nurse was scrubbing the face which swam in a reddish-brown lather. The tiny gold earrings were included in the scrub. Now and then, one of them gave a brave flash. The face was washed for the last time, and dried. Green towels were placed over the face to hide everything but the mouth and nose. The drapes were applied.

"Calipers!" The surgeon measured, locating the peak of the dis- 45 torted Cupid's bow.

"Marking pen!" He placed the first blue dot at the apex of the bow. 46 The nasal sills were dotted; next, the inferior philtral dimple, the vermilion line. The A flap and the B flap were outlined. On he worked, peppering the lip and nose, making sense of chaos, realizing the lip that lay waiting in that deep essential pink, that only he could see. The last dot and line were placed. He was ready.

"Scalpel!" He held the knife above the girl's mouth.   47

"O.K. to go ahead?" he asked the anesthetist.   48

"Yes."   49

He lowered the knife.   50

"No! Wait!" The anesthetist's voice was tense, staccato. "Hold it!"   51

The surgeon's hand was motionless.   52

"What's the matter?"   53

"Something's wrong. I'm not sure. God, she's hot as a pistol.   54
Blood pressure is way up. Pulse one eighty. Get a rectal temperature."
A nurse fumbled beneath the drapes. We waited. The nurse retrieved
the thermometer.

"One hundred seven . . . no . . . eight." There was disbelief in her   55
voice.

"Malignant hyperthermia," said the anesthetist. "Ice! Ice! Get lots of   56
ice!" I raced out the door, accosted the first nurse I saw.

"Ice!" I shouted. "*Hielo!*[1] Quickly! *Hielo!*" The woman's expression   57
was blank. I ran to another. "*Hielo! Hielo!* For the love of God, ice."

"*Hielo?*" She shrugged. "*Nada.*"[2] I ran back to the operating room.   58

"There isn't any ice." I reported. Dr. Franciscus had ripped off his   59
rubber gloves and was feeling the skin of the girl's abdomen. Above the
mask his eyes were the eyes of a horse in battle.

"The EKG is wild . . ."   60

"I can't get a pulse . . ."   61

"What the hell . . ."   62

The surgeon reached for the girl's groin. No femoral pulse.   63

"EKG flat. My God! She's dead!"   64

"She can't be."   65

"She is."   66

The surgeon's fingers pressed the groin where there was no pulse to   67
be felt, only his own pulse hammering at the girl's flesh to be let in.

It was noon, four hours later, when we left the operating room. It   68
was a day so hot and humid I felt steamed open like an envelope. The
woman was sitting on a bench in the courtyard in her dress like a cassock. In one hand she held the piece of cloth the girl had used to conceal
her mouth. As we watched, she folded it once neatly, and then again,
smoothing it, cleaning the cloth which might have been the head of the
girl in her lap that she stroked and consoled.

"I'll do the talking here," he said. He would tell her himself, in   69
whatever Spanish he could find. Only if she did not understand was I

---

[1] Ice. [Eds.]

[2] Nothing. [Eds.]

to speak for him. I watched him brace himself, set his shoulders. How could he tell her? I wondered. What? But I knew he would tell her everything, exactly as it had happened. As much for himself as for her, he needed to explain. But suppose she screamed, fell to the ground, attacked him, even? All that hope of love . . . gone. Even in his discomfort I knew that he was teaching me. The way to do it was professionally. Now he was standing above her. When the woman saw that he did not speak, she lifted her eyes and saw what he held crammed in his mouth to tell her. She knew, and rose to her feet.

"*Señora*," he began, "I am sorry." All at once he seemed to me 70 shorter than he was, scarcely taller than she. There was a place at the crown of his head where the hair had grown thin. His lips were stones. He could hardly move them. The voice dry, dusty.

"No one could have known. Some bad reaction to the medicine for 71 sleeping. It poisoned her. High fever. She did not wake up." The last, a whisper. The woman studied his lips as though she were deaf. He tried, but could not control a twitching at the corner of his mouth. He raised a thumb and forefinger to press something back into his eyes.

"*Muerte*,"[3] the woman announced to herself. Her eyes were human, 72 deadly.

"*Sí, muerte*." At that moment he was like someone cast, still alive, as 73 an effigy for his own tomb. He closed his eyes. Nor did he open them until he felt the touch of the woman's hand on his arm, a touch from which he did not withdraw. Then he looked and saw the grief corroding her face, breaking it down, melting the features so that eyes, nose, mouth ran together in a distortion, like the girl's. For a long time they stood in silence. It seemed to me that minutes passed. At last her face cleared, the features rearranged themselves. She spoke, the words coming slowly to make certain that he understood her. She would go home now. The next day her sons would come for the girl, to take her home for burial. The doctor must not be sad. God has decided. And she was happy now that the harelip had been fixed so that her daughter might go to Heaven without it. Her bare feet retreating were the felted pads of a great bereft animal.

The next morning I did not go to the wards, but stood at the gate 74 leading from the courtyard to the road outside. Two young men in striped ponchos lifted the girl's body wrapped in a straw mat onto the back of a wooden cart. A donkey waited. I had been drawn to this place as one is drawn, inexplicably, to certain scenes of desolation—executions, battlefields. All at once, the woman looked up and saw me. She had taken off her hat. The heavy-hanging coil of her hair made her head seem larger, darker, noble. I pressed some money into her hand.

---

[3] Dead. [Eds.]

"For flowers," I said. "A priest." Her cheeks shook as though minutes ago a stone had been dropped into her navel and the ripples were just now reaching her head. I regretted having come to that place. 75

"*Sí, sí,*" The woman said. Her own face was stitched with flies. "The doctor is one of the angels. He has finished the work of God. My daughter is beautiful." 76

What could she mean! The lip had not been fixed. The girl had died before he would have done it. 77

"Only a fine line that God will erase in time," she said. 78

I reached into the cart and lifted a corner of the mat in which the girl had been rolled. Where the cleft had been there was now a fresh line of tiny sutures. The Cupid's bow was delicately shaped, the vermilion border aligned. The flattened nostril had now the same rounded shape as the other one. I let the mat fall over the face of the dead girl, but not before I had seen the touching place where the finest black hairs sprang from the temple. 79

"*Adiós, adiós. . . .*" And the cart creaked away to the sound of hooves, a tinkling bell. 80

There are events in a doctor's life that seem to mark the boundary between youth and age, seeing and perceiving. Like certain dreams, they illuminate a whole lifetime of past behavior. After such an event, a doctor is not the same as he was before. It had seemed to me then to have been the act of someone demented, or at least insanely arrogant. An attempt to reorder events. Her death had come to him out of order. It should have come after the lip had been repaired, not before. He could have told the mother that, no, the lip had not been fixed. But he did not. He said nothing. It had been an act of omission, one of those strange lapses to which all of us are subject and which we live to regret. It must have been then, at that moment, that the knowledge of what he would do appeared to him. The words of the mother had not consoled him; they had hunted him down. He had not done it for her. The dire necessity was his. He would not accept that Imelda had died before he could repair her lip. People who do such things break free from society. They follow their own lonely path. They have a secret which they can never reveal. I must never let on that I knew. 81

How often I have imagined it. Ten o'clock at night. The hospital of Comayagua is all but dark. Here and there lanterns tilt and skitter up and down the corridors. One of these lamps breaks free from the others and descends the stone steps to the underground room that is the morgue of the hospital. This room wears the expression as if it had waited all night for someone to come. No silence so deep as this place with its cargo of newly dead. Only the slow drip of water over stone. The door closes gassily and clicks shut. The lock is turned. There are four tables, each with a body encased in a paper shroud. There is no mistaking her. She is the smallest. The surgeon takes a knife from his pocket and slits open the 82 paper shroud, that part in which the girl's head is enclosed. The wound seems to be living on long after she has died. Waves of heat emanate from it, blurring his vision. All at once, he turns to peer over his shoulder. He sees nothing, only a wooden crucifix on the wall.

He removes a package of instruments from a satchel and arranges [83] them on a tray. Scalpel, scissors, forceps, needle holder. Sutures and gauze sponges are produced. Stealthy, hunched, engaged, he begins. The dots of blue dye are still there upon her mouth. He raises the scalpel, pauses. A second glance into the darkness. From the wall a small lizard watches and accepts. The first cut is made. A sluggish flow of dark blood appears. He wipes it away with a sponge. No new blood comes to take its place. Again and again he cuts, connecting each of the blue dots until the whole of the zigzag slice is made, first on one side of the cleft, then on the other. Now the edges of the cleft are lined with fresh tissue. He sets down the scalpel and takes up scissors and forceps, undermining the little flaps until each triangle is attached only at one side. He rotates each flap into its new position. He must be certain that they can be swung without tension. They can. He is ready to suture. He fits the tiny curved needle into the jaws of the needle holder. Each suture is placed precisely the same number of millimeters from the cut edge, and the same distance apart. He ties each knot down until the edges are apposed. Not too tightly. These are the most meticulous sutures of his life. He cuts each thread close to the knot. It goes well. The vermilion border with its white skin roll is exactly aligned. One more stitch and the Cupid's bow appears as if by magic. The man's face shines with moisture. Now the nostril is incised around the margin, released, and sutured into a round shape to match its mate. He wipes the blood from the face of the girl with gauze the he has dipped in water. Crumbs of light are scattered on the girl's face. The shroud is folded once more about her. The instruments are handed into the satchel. In a moment the morgue is dark and a lone lantern ascends the stairs and is extinguished.

Six weeks later I was in the darkened amphitheater of the Medical [84] School. Tiers of seats rose in a semicircle above the small stage where Hugh Franciscus stood presenting the case material he had encountered in Honduras. It was the highlight of the year. The hall was filled. The night before he had arranged the slides in the order in which they were to be shown. I was at the controls of the slide projector.

"Next slide!" he would order from time to time in that military [85] voice which had called forth blind obedience from generations of medical students, interns, residents and patients.

"This is a fifty-seven-year-old man with a severe burn contracture of [86] the neck. You will notice the rigid webbing that has fused the chin to the presternal tissues. No motion of the head on the torso is possible. . . . Next slide!"

"Click," went the projector.   [87]

"Here he is after the excision of the scar tissue and with the head in 88 full extension for the first time. The defect was then covered. . . . Next slide!"

"Click." 89

". . . with full-thickness drums of skin taken from the abdomen with 90 the Padgett dermatome. Next slide!"

"Click." 91

And suddenly there she was, extracted from the shadows, sus- 92 pended above and beyond all of us like a resurrection. There was the oval face, the long black hair unbraided, the tiny gold hoops in her ears. And that luminous gnawed mouth. The whole of her life seemed to have been summed up in this photograph. A long silence followed that was the surgeon's alone to break. Almost at once, like the anesthetist in the operating room in Comayagua, I knew that something was wrong. It was not that the man would not speak as that he could not. The audience of doctors, nurses and students seemed to have been infected by the black, limitless silence. My own pulse doubled. It was hard to breathe. Why did he not call out for the next slide? Why did he not save himself? Why had he not removed this slide from the ones to be shown? All at once I knew that he had used his camera on her again. I could see the long black shadows of her hair flowing into the darker shadows of the morgue. The sudden blinding flash . . . The next slide would be the one taken in the morgue. He would be exposed.

In the dim light reflected from the slide, I saw him gazing up at her, 93 seeing not the colored photograph, I thought, but the negative of it where the ghost of the girl was. For me, the amphitheater had become Honduras. I saw again that courtyard littered with patients. I could see the dust in the beam of light from the projector. It was then that I knew that she was his measure of perfection and pain—the one lost, the other gained. He, too, had heard the click of the camera, had seen her wince and felt his mercy enlarge. At last he spoke.

"Imelda." It was the one word he had heard her say. At the sound 94 of his voice I removed the next slide from the projector. "Click" . . . and she was gone. "Click" again, and in her place the man with the orbital cancer. For a long moment Franciscus looked up in my direction, on his face an expression that I have given up trying to interpret. Gratitude? Sorrow? It made me think of the gaze of the girl when at last she understood that she must hand over to him the evidence of her body.

"This is a sixty-two-year-old man with a basal cell carcinoma of the 95 temple eroding into the bony orbit . . ." he began as though nothing had happened.

At the end of the hour, even before the lights went on, there was loud 96 applause. I hurried to find him among the departing crowd. I could not. Some weeks went by before I caught sight of him. He seemed vaguely convalescent, as though a fever had taken its toll before burning out.

Hugh Franciscus continued to teach for fifteen years, although he 97 operated a good deal less, then gave it up entirely. It was as though he had grown tired of blood, of always having to be involved with blood, of having to draw it, spill it, wipe it away, stanch it. He was a quieter, softer man, I heard, the ferocity diminished. There were no more expeditions to Honduras or anywhere else.

I, too, have not been entirely free of her. Now and then, in the years 98 that have passed, I see that donkey-cart cortège, or his face bent over hers in the morgue. I would like to have told him what I now know, that his unrealistic act was one of goodness, one of those small, persevering acts done, perhaps, to ward off madness. Like lighting a lamp, boiling water for tea, washing a shirt. But, of course, it's too late now.

Responding to Reading

1. What motivated Dr. Franciscus to repair Imelda's lip after she had died? Does Selzer think he did the right thing?
2. What were Dr. Franciscus's good qualities? What were his shortcomings as a physician? Overall, does Selzer consider him a good doctor? Do you?
3. What does Selzer learn from the story of Imelda? What does he mean when he says, "I too, have not been entirely free of her" (98)? Is the true subject of the essay Imelda, Dr. Franciscus, or Richard Selzer? Explain.

What Nurses Stand For

Suzanne Gordon

Suzanne Gordon (1945–   ) was born in New York City and received her B.A. from Cornell University and her M.A. from Johns Hopkins. A freelance writer and editor, she writes frequently about social issues and health care. She is coeditor of Caregiving: Readings in Knowledge, Practice, Ethics, and Politics *(1996), author of* Life Support: Three Nurses on the Front Lines *(1997), and coauthor of* From Silence to Voice: What Nurses Know and Must Communicate to the Public *(2000). The following excerpt from* Life Support *appeared in the* Atlantic Monthly; *in it, Gordon explains that nurses play a far greater role in medical caregiving than most people realize.*

At four o'clock on a Friday afternoon the hematology-oncology 1 clinic at Boston's Beth Israel Hospital is quiet. Paddy Connelly and Frances Kiel, two of the eleven nurses who work in the unit, sit at the nurses' station—an island consisting of two long desks equipped with phones, which ring constantly, and computers. They are encircled by thirteen blue-leather reclining chairs, in which patients may spend only a brief time, for a short chemotherapy infusion, or an entire afternoon, to receive more complicated chemotherapy or blood products. At one of the chairs Nancy Rumplik is starting to administer chemotherapy to a man in his mid-fifties who has colon cancer.

Rumplik is forty-two and has been a nurse on the unit for seven years. She stands next to the wan-looking man and begins to hang the intravenous [IV] drugs that will treat his cancer. As the solution drips through the tubing and into his vein, she sits by his side, watching to make sure that he has no adverse reaction.

Today she is acting as triage nurse—the person responsible for patients who walk in without an appointment, for patients who call with a problem but can't reach their primary nurse, for the smooth functioning of the unit, and, of course, for responding to any emergencies. Rumplik's eyes thus constantly sweep the room to check on the other patients. She focuses for a moment on a heavy-set African-American woman in her mid-forties, dressed in a pair of navy slacks and a brightly colored shirt, who is sitting in the opposite corner. Her sister, who is younger and heavier, is by her side. The patient seems fine, so Rumplik returns her attention to the man next to her. Several minutes later she looks up again, checks the woman, and stiffens. There is now a look of anxiety on the woman's face. Rumplik, leaning forward in her chair, stares at her.

"What's she getting?" she mouths to Kiel.

Looking at the patient's chart, Frances Kiel names a drug that has been known to cause severe allergic reactions. In that brief moment, as the two nurses confer, the woman suddenly clasps her chest. Her look of anxiety turns to terror. Her mouth opens and shuts in silent panic. Rumplik leaps up from her chair, as do Kiel and Connelly, and sprints across the room.

"I can't breathe," the woman sputters when Rumplik is at her side. Her eyes bulging, she grasps Rumplik's hand tightly; her eyes roll back as her head slips to the side. Realizing that the patient is having an anaphylactic reaction (her airway is swelling and closing), Rumplik immediately turns a small spigot on the IV tubing to shut off the drip. At the same instant Kiel calls a physician and the emergency-response team. By this time the woman is struggling for breath.

Kiel slips an oxygen mask over the woman's head and wraps a blood-pressure cuff around her arm. Connelly administers an antihistamine to stop the allergic reaction, and cortisone to decrease the inflammation blocking her airway. The physician, an oncology fellow, arrives within minutes. He assesses the situation and then notices the woman's sister standing paralyzed, watching the scene. "Get out of here!" he commands sharply. The woman moves away as if she had been slapped.

Just as the emergency team arrives, the woman's breathing returns 8 to normal and the look of terror fades from her face. Taking Rumplik's hand again, she looks up and says, "I couldn't breathe. I just couldn't breathe." Rumplik gently explains that she has had an allergic reaction to a drug and reassures her that it has stopped.

After a few minutes, when the physician is certain that the patient 9 is stable, he and the emergency-response team walk out of the treatment area, but the nurses continue to comfort the shaken woman. Rumplik then crosses the room to talk with her male patient, who is ashen-faced at this reminder of the potentially lethal effects of the medication that he and others are receiving. Responding to his unspoken fears, Rumplik says quietly, "It's frightening to see something like that. But it's under control."

He nods silently, closes his eyes, and leans his head back against 10 the chair. Rumplik goes over to the desk where Connelly and Kiel are breathing a joint sigh of relief. One of the nurses comments on the physician's treatment of the patient's sister. "Did you hear him? He just told her to get out."

Wincing with distress, Rumplik looks around for the sister. She goes 11 into the waiting room, where the woman is sitting in a corner, looking bereft and frightened. Rumplik sits down next to her, explains what happened, and suggests that the patient could probably benefit from some overnight company. Then she adds, "I'm sorry the doctor talked to you like that. You know, it's a very anxious time for all of us."

At this gesture of respect and recognition the woman, who has 12 every strike—race, class, and sex—against her when dealing with elite white professionals in this downtown hospital, smiles solemnly. "I understand. Thank you."

Nancy Rumplik returns to her patient.   13

"I Am Ready to Die"

It is 6:00 P.M. Today Jeannie Chaisson, a clinical nurse specialist, 14 arrived at her general medical unit at seven in the morning and cared for patients until three-thirty in the afternoon. At home now, she makes herself a pot of coffee and sits down in the living room, cradling her cup. Just as she is shedding the strain of the day, the phone rings.

It's the husband of one of Chaisson's patients—a sixty-three-year-old 15 woman suffering from terminal multiple myeloma, a cancer of the bone marrow. When Chaisson left the hospital, she knew the family was in crisis. Having endured the cancer for several years, the woman is exhausted from the pain, from the effects of the disease and failed treatments, and from the pain medication on which she has become increasingly dependent. Chaisson knows she is ready to let death take her. But her husband and daughter are not.

Now the crisis that was brewing has exploded. Chaisson's caller is 16 breathless, frantic with anxiety, as he relays his wife's pleas. She wants to die. She is prepared to die. She says the pain is too much. "You've got to do something," he implores Chaisson. "Keep her going—stop her from doing this."

Chaisson knows that it is indeed time for her to do something—but, 17 sadly, not what the anguished husband wishes. "Be calm," she tells him. "Please hold on. We'll all talk together. I'm coming right in." Leaving a note for her family, she gets into her car and drives back to the hospital.

When Chaisson walks into the patient's room, she is not surprised 18 by what she finds. Seated next to the bed is the visibly distraught husband. Behind him the patient's twenty-five-year-old daughter paces in front of a picture window with a view across Boston. The patient is lying in a state somewhere between consciousness and coma, shrunken by pain and devoured by the cancer's progress. Chaisson has seen scenes like this many times before in her fifteen-year career as a nurse.

As she looks at the woman, she can understand why her husband 19 and her daughter are so resistant. They remember her as she first appeared to Chaisson, three years ago—a bright, feisty sixty-year-old woman, her nails tapered and polished, her hair sleekly sculpted into a perfect silver pouf. Chaisson remembers the day, during the first of many admissions to the unit, when she asked the woman if she wanted her hair washed.

The woman replied in astonishment, "I do not wash my hair. I have 20 it done. Once a week."

Now her hair is unkempt, glued to her face with sweat. Her nails 21 are no longer polished. Their main work these days is to dig into her flesh when the pain becomes too acute. The disease has slowly bored into her bones. Simply to stand is painful and could even be an invitation to a fracture. Her pelvis is disintegrating. The nurses have inserted an indwelling catheter, because having a bedpan slipped underneath her causes agony, but she has developed a urinary-tract infection. Because removing the catheter will make the infection easier to treat, doctors suggest this course of action. Yet if the catheter is removed, the pain will be intolerable each time she has to urinate.

When the residents and interns argued that failure to treat the infec- 22 tion could mean the patient would die, Chaisson responded, "She's dying anyway. It's her disease that is killing her, not a urinary tract infection." They relented.

Now the family must confront this reality.   23

Chaisson goes to the woman's bed and gently wakes her. Smiling at 24
her nurse, the woman tries to muster the energy to explain to her husband and her daughter that the pain is too great and she can no longer attain that delicate balance, so crucial to dying patients, between fighting off pain and remaining alert for at least some of the day. Only when she is practically comatose from drugs can she find relief.

"I am ready to die," she whispers weakly. 25

Her husband and daughter contradict her—there is still hope. 26

Jeannie Chaisson stands silent during this exchange and then inter- 27
venes, asking them to try to take in what their loved one is telling them. Then she repeats the basic facts about the disease and its course. "At this point there is no treatment for the disease," she explains, "but there is treatment for the pain, to make the patient comfortable and ease her suffering." Chaisson spends another hour sitting with them, answering their questions and allowing them to feel supported. Finally the family is able to heed the patient's wishes—leave the catheter in and do not resuscitate her if she suffers a cardiac arrest. Give her enough morphine to stop the pain. Let her go.

The woman visibly relaxes, lies back, and closes her eyes. Chaisson 28
approaches the husband and the daughter, with whom she has worked for so long, and hugs them both. Then she goes out to talk to the medical team.

Before leaving for home, Chaisson again visits her patient. The hus- 29
band and the daughter have gone for a cup of coffee. The woman is quiet. Chaisson sits down at the side of her bed and takes her hand. The woman opens her eyes. Too exhausted to say a word, she merely squeezes the nurse's hand in gratitude. For the past three years Chaisson has helped her to fight her disease and live as long as possible. Now she is here to help her die.

The Endangered RN

When we hear the word "hospital," technology and scientific inven- 30
tion spring to mind: mechanical ventilators, dialysis machines, intravenous pumps, biomedical research, surgery, medication. These, many believe, are the life supports in our health-care system. This technology keeps people alive, and helps to cure and heal them.

In fact there are other, equally important life supports in our health 31
care system: the 2.2 million nurses who make up the largest profession in health care, the profession with the highest percentage of women, and the second largest profession after teaching. These women and men weave a tapestry of care, knowledge, and trust that is critical to patients' survival.

Nancy Rumplik and Jeannie Chaisson have between them more 32
than a quarter century's experience caring for the sick. They work in an
acute-care hospital, one of Harvard Medical School's teaching hospitals.
Beth Israel not only is known for the quality of its patient care but also
is world-renowned for the quality of its nursing staff and its institutional commitment to nursing.

The for-profit, market-driven health care that is sweeping the 33
nation is threatening this valuable group of professionals. To gain an
advantage in the competitive new health-care marketplace, hospitals all
over the country are trying to cut their costs. One popular strategy is to
lay off nurses and replace them with lower-paid, less-skilled workers.

American hospitals already use 20 percent fewer nurses than their 34
counterparts in other industrialized countries. Nursing does provide
attractive middle-income salaries. In 1992 staff nurses earned, on average, $33,000 a year. Clinical nurse specialists, who have advanced edu-
cation and specialize in a particular field, earned an average of $41,000,
and nurse practitioners, who generally have a master's degree and provide primary-care services, earned just under $44,000. Yet RN salaries and
benefits altogether represent only about 16 percent of total hospital costs.

Nevertheless, nurses are a major target of hospital "restructuring" 35
plans, which in some cases have called for a reduction of 20 to 50 percent in registered nursing staff.

The process of job elimination, deskilling, and downgrading seri- 36
ously erodes opportunities for stable middle-class employment in nursing as in other industries. However, as the late David Gordon
documented in his book *Fat and Mean: The Corporate Squeeze of Working
Americans and the Myth of Managerial "Downsizing,"* reduced "head
counts" among production or service workers don't necessarily mean
that higher-level jobs (and the pay and perquisites associated with
them) are being chopped as well. In fact, Gordon argued, many headline grabbing exercises in corporate cost-cutting leave executive compensation untouched, along with other forms of managerial "bloat."

Even in this era of managed-care limits on physicians' compensation, 37
nurses' pay is relatively quite modest. And the managers of care themselves—particularly hospital administrators and health-maintenance
-organization executives—are doing so well that even doctors look
underpaid by comparison.

According to the business magazine *Modern Healthcare's* 1996 38
physician-compensation report, the average salary in family practice
is $128,096, in internal medicine $135,755, in oncology $164,621, in
anesthesiology $193,242, and in general surgery $199,342. Some specialists earn more than a million dollars a year.

A survey conducted in 1995 by *Hospitals & Health Networks*, the 39
magazine of the American Hospital Association, found that the average

total cash compensation for hospital CEOs was $188,500. In large hospitals the figure went up to $280,900, and in for-profit chains far higher. In 1995, at age forty-three, Richard Scott, the CEO of Columbia/Healthcare Corporation, received a salary of $2,093,844. He controlled shares in Columbia/HCA worth $359.5 million.

In 1994 compensation for the CEOs of the seven largest for-profit 40 HMOs averaged $7 million. Even those in the not-for-profit sector of insurance earn startling sums: in 1995 John Burry Jr., the chairman and CEO of Ohio Blue Cross and Blue Shield, was paid $1.6 million.

According to a report in *Modern Healthcare*, a proposed merger with 41 the for-profit Columbia/HCA would have paid him $3 million "for a decade-long no-compete contract . . . [and] up to $7 million for two consulting agreements."

At the other end of the new health-care salary spread are "unli- 42 censed assistive personnel" (UAPs), who are now being used instead of nurses. They usually have little background in health care and only rudimentary training. Yet UAPs may insert catheters, read EKGs, suction tracheotomy tubes, change sterile dressings, and perform other traditional nursing functions. To keep patients from becoming unduly alarmed about—or even aware of—this development, some hospitals now prohibit nurses from wearing any badges that identify them as RNs. Thus everyone at the bedside is some kind of generic "patient-care technician"—regardless of how much or how little training and experience she or he has.

In some health-care facilities other nonprofessional staff—janitors, 43 housekeepers, security guards, and aides—are also being "cross-trained" and transformed into "multi-skilled" workers who can be assigned to nursing duties. One such employee was so concerned about the impact of this on patient care that he recently wrote a letter to Timothy McCall, M.D., a critic of multi-skilling, after reading a magazine article the latter had written on the subject.

> I am an employee of a 95-bed, long-term care facility. My position is that of a security guard. Ninety-five percent of my job consists of maintenance, housekeeping, admitting persons into clinical lab to pick-up & leave specimens. Now a class, 45 minutes, is being given so employees can feed, give bedpans & move patients. My expertise is in law enforcement & security, 25 years. I am not trained or licensed in patient care, maintenance, lab work, etc. . . . This scares me. Having untrained, unlicensed people performing jobs, in my opinion, is dangerous.

Training of RN replacements is indeed almost never regulated by 44 state licensing boards. There are no minimum requirements governing the amount of training that aides or cross-trained workers must have before they can be redeployed to do various types of nursing work. Training periods can range from a few hours to six weeks. One 1994 study cited in a 1996 report by the Institute of Medicine on nursing staffing found that

> 99 percent of the hospitals in California reported less than 120 hours of on-the-job training for newly hired ancillary nursing person-nel. Only 20 percent of the hospitals required a high school diploma. The majority of hospitals (59 percent) provided less than 20 hours of classroom instruction and 88 percent provided 40 hours or less of instruction time.

Because the rapidly accelerating UAP trend is so new, its impact on 45 patient care has not yet been fully documented. However, in a series of major studies over the past twenty years researchers have directly linked higher numbers and greater qualifications of registered nurses on hospital units to lower mortality rates and decreased lengths of hospital stay. Reducing the number of expert nurses in the hospital, the community, and homes endangers patients' lives and wastes scarce resources. Choosing to save money by reducing nursing care aggravates the impersonality of a medical system that tends to turn human beings into their diseases and the doctors who care for them into sophisticated clinical machines. When they're sick, patients do not ask only what pills they should take or what operations they should have. They are preoccupied with questions such as Why me? Why now? Nurses are there through this day-by-day, minute-by-minute attack on the soul. They know that for the patient not only a sick or infirm body but also a life, a family, a community, a society, needs to heal.

Media Stereotypes

Although nurses help us to live and die, in the public depiction of 46 health care patients seem to emerge from hospitals without ever having benefited from their assistance. Whether patients are treated in an emergency room in a few short hours or on a critical-care unit for months on end, we seem to assume that physicians are responsible for all the successes—and failures—in our medical system. In fact, we seem to believe that they are responsible not only for all of the curing but also for much of the caring.

Nurses remain shadowy figures moving mysteriously in the back- 47 ground. In television series they often appear as comic figures. On TV's short-lived *Nightingales*, on the sitcom *Nurses*, and on the medical drama *Chicago Hope* nurses are far too busy pining after doctors or racing off to aerobics classes to care for patients.

ER gives nurses more prominence than many other hospital shows, 48
but doctors on *ER* are constantly barking out commands to perform the
simplest duties—get a blood pressure, call the OR—to experienced emergency-room nurses. In reality the nurses would have thought of all this
before the doctor arrived. In an emergency room as busy and sophisticated as the one on *ER*, the first clinician a patient sees is a triage nurse,
who assesses the patient and dictates what he needs, who will see him,
and when. Experienced nurses will direct less-experienced residents (and
have sometimes done so on *ER*), suggesting a medication, a test, consultation with a specialist, or transfer to the operating room. The great irony
of *ER* is that Carol Hathaway, the nurse in charge, is generally relegated
to comforting a child or following a physician's orders rather than, as
would occur in real life, helping to direct the staff in saving lives.

Not only do doctors dominate on television but they are the focus of 49
most hard-news health-care coverage. Reporters rarely cover innovations
in nursing, use nurses as sources, or report on nursing research. The
health-care experts whom reporters or politicians consult are invariably
physicians, representatives of physician organizations, or policy specialists who tend to look at health care through the prism of economics.
"Who Counts in News Coverage of Health Care?," a 1990 study by the
Women, Press & Politics Project, in Cambridge, Massachusetts, of health-
care coverage in *The New York Times*, the *Los Angeles Times*, and *The
Washington Post*, found that out of 908 quotations that appeared in three
months' worth of health-care stories, nurses were the sources for ten.

The revolution in health care has become big news. Occasionally 50
reporters will turn their attention to layoffs in nursing, but the story is
rarely framed as an important public-health issue. Rather, it is generally
depicted as a labor-management conflict. Nursing unions are battling
with management. Nurses say this; hospital administrators claim that.
Whom can you believe?

Worse still, this important issue may be couched in the stereotypes 51
of nursing or of women's work in general. A typical example appeared
on *NBC Nightly News* in September of 1994. The show ran a story
that involved a discussion of the serious problems, including deaths,
resulting from replacing nurses with unlicensed aides. The anchor introduced it as "a new and controversial way of administering TLC."[1]
Imagine how the issue would be characterized if 20 to 50 percent of staff
physicians were eliminated in thousands of American hospitals. Would
it not be front-page news, a major public-health catastrophe? Patients all
over the country would be terrified to enter hospitals. Yet we learn
about the equivalent in nursing with only a minimum of concern. If laying

---

[1] That is, "tender, loving care." [Eds.]

off thousands of nurses results only in the loss of a little TLC, what difference does it make if an aide replaces a nurse?

Nursing is not simply a matter of TLC. It's a matter of life and 52 death. In hospitals, which employ 66 percent of America's nurses, nurses monitor a patient's condition before, during, and after high-tech medical procedures. They adjust medication, manage pain and the side effects of treatment, and instantly intervene if a life-threatening change occurs in a patient's condition.

In our high-tech medical system nurses care for the body and the 53 soul. No matter how sensitive, caring, and attentive physicians are, nurses are often closer to the patient's needs and wishes. That's not because they are inherently more caring but because they spend far more time with patients and are likely to know them better. This time and knowledge allows them to save lives. Nurses also help people to adjust to the lives they must live after they have recovered. And when death can no longer be delayed, nurses help patients confront their own mortality with at least some measure of grace and dignity.

The Stigma of Sickness

There is another reason that nurses' work so often goes unrecog- 54 nized. Even some of the patients who have benefited the most from nurses' critical care are unable to credit its importance publicly. Because nurses observe and cushion what the physician and writer Oliver Sacks has called human beings' falling "radically into sickness," they are a reminder of the pain, fear, vulnerability, and loss of control that adults find difficult to tolerate and thus to discuss. A man who has had a successful heart bypass will boast of his surgeon's accomplishments to friends at a dinner party. A woman who has survived a bone-marrow transplant will extol her oncologist's triumph in the war against cancer to her friends and relatives. But what nurses did for those two patients will rarely be mentioned. It was a nurse who bathed the cardiac patient and comforted him while he struggled with the terror of possible death. It was a nurse who held the plastic dish under the cancer patient's lips as she was wracked with nausea, and who wiped a bottom raw from diarrhea. As Claire Fagin and Donna Diers have explained in an eloquent essay titled "Nursing as Metaphor," nurses stand for intimacy. They are our secret sharers. Even though they are lifelines during illness, when control is restored the residue of our anxiety and mortality clings to them like dust, and we flee the memory.

At one moment a nurse like Nancy Rumplik or Jeannie Chaisson 55 may be involved in a sophisticated clinical procedure that demands expert judgment and advanced training in the latest technology. The next moment she may do what many people consider trivial or menial work, such as emptying a bedpan, giving a sponge bath, administering medication, or feeding or walking a patient.

The fact that nurses' work incorporates many so-called menial tasks 56 that don't demand total attention is not a reason to replace nurses with less-skilled workers. This hands-on care allows nurses to explore patients' physical condition *and* to register their anxiety and fear. It allows them to save lives *and* to ascertain when it's appropriate to help patients die. It is only in watching nurses weave the tapestry of care that we grasp its integrity and its meaning for a society that too easily forgets the value of things that are beyond price.

Responding to Reading

1. Gordon begins her essay with two long narratives. What does each of these stories illustrate? How do they help Gordon make her point about nurses? How is this section of the essay different from the rest of the essay?
2. What new positions have for-profit health care corporations created to save money? (For example, what are "unlicensed assistive personnel," or UAPs, and "multiskilled" workers?) According to Gordon, how are the actions of these corporations compromising health care in the United States?
3. According to Gordon, why does the work of nurses so often go unnoticed? In what way do the media contribute to this situation? In what way do people's attitudes toward "nurses' work" add to the problem?

THE TURBID EBB AND FLOW OF MISERY

Margaret Sanger

Margaret Higgins Sanger (1883–1966) was born in Corning, New York, and worked for many years as a public health nurse in New York City. The conditions she witnessed among the city's poor led her to become an early advocate for birth control, based on the belief that having fewer children would improve the health and economic condition of poor families. Her outspoken views sparked considerable controversy, and she was arrested in 1916 for operating a birth control clinic in Brooklyn. Through her work as president of the National Committee on Federal Legislation for Birth Control, Sanger was instrumental in the adoption of laws that legalized medically supervised birth control throughout the United States. The following is a chapter from her 1938 autobiography.

> Every night and every morn
> Some to misery are born.
> Every morn and every night

Some are born to sweet delight.
Some are born to sweet delight,
Some are born to endless night.

—William Blake

During these years [about 1912] in New York trained nurses were in   1
great demand. Few people wanted to enter hospitals; they were afraid
they might be "practiced" upon, and consented to go only in desperate
emergencies. Sentiment was especially vehement in the matter of having babies. A woman's own bedroom, no matter how inconveniently
arranged, was the usual place for her lying-in. I was not sufficiently free
from domestic duties to be a general nurse, but I could ordinarily manage obstetrical cases because I was notified far enough ahead to plan my
schedule. And after serving my two weeks I could get home again.

Sometimes I was summoned to small apartments occupied by   2
young clerks, insurance salesmen, or lawyers, just starting out, most of
them under thirty and whose wives were having their first or second
baby. They were always eager to know the best and latest method in
infant care and feeding. In particular, Jewish patients, whose lives cen-
tered around the family, welcomed advice and followed it implicitly.

But more and more my calls began to come from the Lower East   3
Side, as though I were being magnetically drawn there by some force
outside my control. I hated the wretchedness and hopelessness of the
poor, and never experienced that satisfaction in working among them
that so many noble women have found. My concern for my patients
was now quite different from my earlier hospital attitude. I could see
that much was wrong with them which did not appear in the physiological or medical diagnosis. A woman in childbirth was not merely a
woman in childbirth. My expanded outlook included a view of her
background, her potentialities as a human being, the kind of children
she was bearing, and what was going to happen to them.

The wives of small shopkeepers were my most frequent cases, but I   4
had carpenters, truck drivers, dishwashers, and pushcart vendors. I
admired intensely the consideration most of these people had for their
own. Money to pay doctor and nurse had been carefully saved months in
advance—parents-in-law, grandfathers, grandmothers, all contributing.

As soon as the neighbors learned that a nurse was in the building   5
they came in a friendly way to visit, often carrying fruit, jellies, or
gefüllter fish made after a cherished recipe. It was infinitely pathetic to
me that they, so poor themselves, should bring me food. Later they
drifted in again with the excuse of getting the plate, and sat down for a
nice talk; there was no hurry. Always back of the little gift was the question, "I am pregnant (or my daughter, or my sister is). Tell me something
to keep from having another baby. We cannot afford another yet."

I tried to explain the only two methods I had ever heard of among 6 the middle classes, both of which were invariably brushed aside as unacceptable. They were of no certain avail to the wife because they placed the burden of responsibility solely upon the husband—a burden which he seldom assumed. What she was seeking was self-protection she could herself use, and there was none.

Below this stratum of society was one in truly desperate circum- 7 stances. The men were sullen and unskilled, picking up odd jobs now and then, but more often unemployed, lounging in and out of the house at all hours of the day and night. The women seemed to slink on their way to market and were without neighborliness.

These submerged, untouched classes were beyond the scope of orga- 8 nized charity or religion. No labor union, no church, not even the Salvation Army reached them. They were apprehensive of everyone and rejected help of any kind, ordering all intruders to keep out; both birth and death they considered their own business. Social agents, who were just beginning to appear, were profoundly mistrusted because they pried into homes and lives, asking questions about wages, how many were in the family, had any of them ever been in jail. Often two or three had been there or were now under suspicion of prostitution, shoplifting, purse snatching, petty thievery, and, in consequence, passed furtively by the big blue uniforms on the corner.

The utmost depression came over me as I approached this surrepti- 9 tious region. Below Fourteenth Street I seemed to be breathing a differ- ent air, to be in another world and country where the people had habits and customs alien to anything I had ever heard about.

There were then approximately ten thousand apartments in New 10 York into which no sun ray penetrated directly; such windows as they had opened only on a narrow court from which rose fetid odors. It was seldom cleaned, though garbage and refuse often went down into it. All these dwellings were pervaded by the foul breath of poverty, that moldy, indefinable, indescribable smell which cannot be fumigated out, sickening to me but apparently unnoticed by those who lived there. When I set to work with antiseptics, their pungent sting, at least tem- porarily, obscured the stench.

I remember one confinement case to which I was called by the doctor 11 of an insurance company. I climbed up the five flights and entered the airless rooms, but the baby had come with too great speed. A boy of ten had been the only assistant. Five flights was a long way; he had wrapped the placenta in a piece of newspaper and dropped it out the window into the court.

Many families took in "boarders," as they were termed, whose small 12 contributions paid the rent. These derelicts, wanderers, alternately work- ing and drinking, were crowded in with the children; a single room sometimes held as many as six sleepers. Little girls were accustomed to dressing and undressing in front of the men, and were often violated, occasionally by their own fathers or brothers, before they reached the age of puberty.

Pregnancy was a chronic condition among the women of this class. 13 Suggestions as to what to do for a girl who was "in trouble" or a married woman who was "caught" passed from mouth to mouth—herb teas, turpentine, steaming, rolling downstairs, inserting slippery elm, knitting needles, shoe-hooks. When they had word of a new remedy they hurried to the drugstore, and if the clerk were inclined to be friendly he might say, "Oh, that won't help you, but here's something that may." The younger druggists usually refused to give advice because, if it were to be known, they would come under the law; midwives were even more fearful. The doomed women implored me to reveal the "secret" rich people had, offering to pay me extra to tell them; many really believed I was holding back information for money. They asked everybody and tried anything, but nothing did them any good. On Saturday nights I have seen groups of from fifty to one hundred with their shawls over their heads waiting outside the office of a five-dollar abortionist.

Each time I returned to this district, which was becoming a recur- 14 rent nightmare, I used to hear that Mrs. Cohen "had been carried to a hospital, but had never come back," or that Mrs. Kelly "had sent the children to a neighbor and had put her head into the gas oven." Day after day such tales were poured into my ears—a baby born dead, great relief—the death of an older child, sorrow but again relief of a sort—the story told a thousand times of death from abortion and children going into institutions. I shuddered with horror as I listened to the details and studied the reasons back of them—destitution linked with excessive childbearing. The waste of life seemed utterly senseless. One by one worried, sad, pensive, and aging faces marshaled themselves before me in my dreams, sometimes appealingly, sometimes accusingly.

These were not merely "unfortunate conditions among the poor" 15 such as we read about. I knew the women personally. They were living, breathing, human beings, with hopes, fears, and aspirations like my own, yet their weary, misshapen bodies, "always ailing, never failing," were destined to be thrown on the scrap heap before they were thirty-five. I could not escape from the facts of their wretchedness; neither was I able to see any way out. My own cozy and comfortable family existence was becoming a reproach to me.

Then one stifling mid-July day of 1912 I was summoned to a Grand 16 Street tenement. My patient was a small, slight Russian Jewess, about twenty-eight years old, of the special cast of feature to which suffering lends a madonna-like expression. The cramped three-room apartment was in a sorry state of turmoil. Jake Sachs, a truck driver scarcely older than his wife, had come home to find the three children crying and her unconscious from the effects of a self-induced abortion. He had called the nearest doctor, who in turn had sent for me. Jake's earnings were trifling, and most of them had gone to keep the none-too-strong children clean and properly fed. But his wife's ingenuity had helped them to save a little, and this he was glad to spend on a nurse rather than have her go to a hospital.

The doctor and I settled ourselves to the task of fighting the septicemia. Never had I worked so fast, never so concentratedly. The sultry days and nights were melted into a torpid inferno. It did not seem possible there could be such heat, and every bit of food, ice, and drugs had to be carried up three flights of stairs.   17

Jake was more kind and thoughtful than many of the husbands I had encountered. He loved his children, and had always helped his wife wash and dress them. He had brought water up and carried garbage down before he left in the morning, and did as much as he could for me while he anxiously watched her progress.   18

After a fortnight Mrs. Sachs' recovery was in sight. Neighbors, ordinarily fatalistic as to the results of abortion, were genuinely pleased that she had survived. She smiled wanly at all who came to see her and thanked them gently, but she could not respond to their hearty congratulations. She appeared to be more despondent and anxious than she should have been, and spent too much time in meditation.   19

At the end of three weeks, as I was preparing to leave the fragile patient to take up her difficult life once more, she finally voiced her fears, "Another baby will finish me, I suppose?"   20

"It's too early to talk about that," I temporized.   21

But when the doctor came to make his last call, I drew him aside. "Mrs. Sachs is terribly worried about having another baby."   22

"She well may be," replied the doctor, and then he stood before her and said, "Any more such capers, young woman, and there'll be no need to send for me."   23

"I know, doctor," she replied timidly, "but," and she hesitated as though it took all her courage to say it, "what can I do to prevent it?"   24

The doctor was a kindly man, and he had worked hard to save her, but such incidents had become so familiar to him that he had long since lost whatever delicacy he might once have had. He laughed good-naturedly. "You want to have your cake and eat it too, do you? Well, it can't be done."   25

Then picking up his hat and bag to depart he said, "Tell Jake to sleep on the roof."   26

I glanced quickly at Mrs. Sachs. Even through my sudden tears I could see stamped on her face an expression of absolute despair. We simply looked at each other, saying no word until the door had closed behind the doctor. Then she lifted her thin, blue-veined hands and clasped them beseechingly. "He can't understand. He's only a man. But   27 you do, don't you? Please tell me the secret, and I'll never breathe it to a soul. *Please!"*

What was I to do? I could not speak the conventionally comforting 28 phrases which would be of no comfort. Instead, I made her as physically easy as I could and promised to come back in a few days to talk with her again. A little later, when she slept, I tiptoed away.

Night after night the wistful image of Mrs. Sachs appeared before 29 me. I made all sorts of excuses to myself for not going back. I was busy on other cases; I really did not know what to say to her or how to convince her of my own ignorance; I was helpless to avert such monstrous atrocities. Time rolled by and I did nothing.

The telephone rang one evening three months later, and Jake Sachs' 30 agitated voice begged me to come at once; his wife was sick again and from the same cause. For a wild moment I thought of sending someone else, but actually, of course, I hurried into my uniform, caught up my bag, and started out. All the way I longed for a subway wreck, an explosion, anything to keep me from having to enter that home again. But nothing happened, even to delay me. I turned into the dingy doorway and climbed the familiar stairs once more. The children were there, young little things.

Mrs. Sachs was in a coma and died within ten minutes. I folded her 31 still hands across her breast, remembering how they had pleaded with me, begging so humbly for the knowledge which was her right. I drew a sheet over her pallid face. Jake was sobbing, running his hands through his hair and pulling it out like an insane person. Over and over again he wailed, "My God! My God! My God!"

I left him pacing desperately back and forth, and for hours I myself 32 walked and walked and walked through the hushed streets. When I finally arrived home and let myself quietly in, all the household was sleeping. I looked out my window and down upon the dimly lighted city. Its pains and griefs crowded in upon me, a moving picture rolled before my eyes with photographic clearness: women writhing in travail to bring forth little babies; the babies themselves naked and hungry, wrapped in newspapers to keep them from the cold; six-year-old children with pinched, pale, wrinkled faces, old in concentrated wretchedness, pushed into gray and fetid cellars, crouching on stone floors, their small scrawny scuttling through rags, making lamp shades, artificial flowers; white coffins, black coffins, coffins, coffins interminably passing in never-ending succession. The scenes piled one upon another on another. I could bear it no longer.

As I stood there the darkness faded. The sun came up and threw its 33 reflection over the house tops. It was the dawn of a new day in my life also. The doubt and questioning, the experimenting and trying, were now to be put behind me. I knew I could not go back merely to keeping people alive.

I went to bed, knowing that no matter what it might cost, I was fin- 34
ished with palliatives and superficial cures; I was resolved to seek out
the root of evil, to do something to change the destiny of mothers whose
miseries were vast as the sky.

Responding to Reading

1. What social classes does Sanger discuss? According to Sanger, what are the
   characteristics of each social class? Which is most needy? Why?
2. Why does Sanger tell the story of Mrs. Sachs? How did her situation change
   the direction of Sanger's life?
3. What attitudes does Sanger have toward her patients? Does she see them as
   her equals, or does she think she is better than they are? At any point in the
   essay does she seem as if she is condescending?

A PLEA FOR THE CHIMPS

Jane Goodall

*English-born Jane Goodall (1934–   ) has spent most of her adult life
studying the behavior of wild chimpanzees in the jungles of Tanzania.
Shortly after graduating high school, she visited Kenya, where she met nat-
uralist and paleontologist Louis Leakey. Impressed by her love of wildlife,
Leakey arranged for her to conduct a six-month field study of chimpanzees
on a Tanzanian reserve, a project which has stretched to almost four decades.
Goodall has described her fascinating observations in a number of popular
books, including* In the Shadow of Man *(1971; revised 1988),* The
Chimpanzees of Gombe: Patterns of Behavior *(1986), and* Through a
Window: My Thirty Years with the Chimpanzees of Gombe *(1990). As
she has said, "Animals are like us. They feel pain like we do. We want people
to understand that every chimp is an individual, with the same kinds of intellectual abilities." In the following 1987 article, Goodall makes the case for
more humane treatment of chimpanzees used for medical research.*

The chimpanzee is more like us, genetically, than any other animal. 1
It is because of similarities in physiology, in biochemistry, in the
immune system, that medical science makes use of the living bodies of
chimpanzees in its search for cures and vaccines for a variety of human
diseases.

There are also behavioral, psychological and emotional similarities 2
between chimpanzees and humans, resemblances so striking that they
raise a serious ethical question: are we justified in using an animal so
close to us—an animal, moreover, that is highly endangered in its
African forest home—as a human substitute in medical experimentation?

In the long run, we can hope that scientists will find ways of explor- 3
ing human physiology and disease, and of testing cures and vaccines,
that do not depend on the use of living animals of any sort. A number
of steps in this direction already have been taken, prompted in large
part by a growing public awareness of the suffering that is being
inflicted on millions of animals. More and more people are beginning to
realize that nonhuman animals—even rats and guinea pigs—are not
just unfeeling machines but are capable of enjoying their lives, and of
feeling fear, pain and despair.

But until alternatives have been found, medical science will con- 4
tinue to use animals in the battle against human disease and suffering.
And some of those animals will continue to be chimpanzees.

Because they share with us 99 percent of their genetic material, 5
chimpanzees can be infected with some human diseases that do not
infect other animals. They are currently being used in research on the
nature of hepatitis non-A non-B, for example, and they continue to play
a major role in the development of vaccines against hepatitis B.

Many biomedical laboratories are looking to the chimpanzee to 6
help them in the race to find a vaccine against acquired immune defi-
ciency syndrome. Chimpanzees are not good models for AIDS research;
although the AIDS virus stays alive and replicates within the chimpanzee's bloodstream, no chimp has yet come down with the disease
itself. Nevertheless, many of the scientists involved argue that only by
using chimpanzees can potential vaccines be safely tested.

Given the scientists' professed need for animals in research, let us 7
turn aside from the sensitive ethical issue of whether chimpanzees *should*
be used in medical research, and consider a more immediate *issue*: how
are we treating the chimpanzees that are actually being used?

Just after Christmas I watched, with shock, anger and anguish, a 8
videotape—made by an animal-rights group during a raid—revealing
the conditions in a large biomedical research laboratory, under contract
to the National Institutes of Health, in which various primates, including chimpanzees, are maintained. In late March, I was given permission
to visit the facility.

It was a visit I shall never forget. Room after room was lined with 9
small, bare cages, stacked one above the other, in which monkeys circled round and round and chimpanzees sat huddled, far gone in
depression and despair.

Young chimpanzees, 3 or 4 years old, were crammed, two together, 10
into tiny cages measuring 22 inches by 22 inches and only 24 inches
high. They could hardly turn around. Not yet part of any experiment,
they had been confined in these cages for more than three months.

The chimps had each other for comfort, but they would not remain 11
together for long. Once they are infected, probably with hepatitis, they
will be separated and placed in another cage. And there they will

remain, living in conditions of severe sensory deprivation, for the next several years. During that time, they will become insane.

A juvenile female rocked from side to side, sealed off from the out- 12 side world behind the glass doors of her metal isolation chamber. She was in semidarkness. All she could hear was the incessant roar of air rushing through vents into her prison.

In order to demonstrate the "good" relationship the lab's caretaker 13 had with this chimpanzee, one of the scientists told him to lift her from the cage. The caretaker opened the door. She sat, unmoving. He reached in. She did not greet him—nor did he greet her. As if drugged, she allowed him to take her out. She sat motionless in his arms. He did not speak to her, she did not look at him. He touched her lips briefly. She did not respond. He returned her to her cage. She sat again on the bars of the floor. The door closed.

I shall be haunted forever by her eyes, and by the eyes of the other 14 infant chimpanzees I saw that day. Have you ever looked into the eyes of a person who, stressed beyond endurance, has given up, succumbed utterly to the crippling helplessness of despair? I once saw a little African boy, whose whole family had been killed during the fighting in Burundi. He too looked out at the world, unseeing, from dull, blank eyes.

Though this particular laboratory may be one of the worst, from 15 what I have learned, most of the other biomedical animal-research facilities are not much better. Yet only when one has some understanding of the true nature of the chimpanzee can the cruelty of these captive conditions be fully understood.

Chimpanzees are very social by nature. Bonds between individuals, 16 particularly between family members and close friends, can be affectionate, supportive, and can endure throughout their lives. The accidental separation of two friendly individuals may cause them intense distress. Indeed, the death of a mother may be such a psychological blow to her child that even if the child is 5 years old and no longer dependent on its mother's milk, it may pine away and die.

It is impossible to overemphasize the importance of friendly physi- 17 cal contact for the well-being of the chimpanzee. Again and again one can watch a frightened or tense individual relax if she is patted, kissed or embraced reassuringly by a companion. Social grooming, which provides hours of close contact, is undoubtedly the single most important social activity.

Chimpanzees in their natural habitat are active for much of the day. 18 They travel extensively within their territory, which can be as large as 50 square kilometers for a community of about 50 individuals. If they hear other chimpanzees calling as they move through the forest, or anticipate arriving at a good food source, they typically break into excited charging displays, racing along the ground, hurling sticks and rocks and shaking the vegetation. Youngsters, particularly, are full of energy, and spend long hours playing with one another or by themselves, leaping through the branches and gamboling along the ground. Adults sometimes join these games. Bunches of fruit, twigs and rocks may be used as toys.

Chimpanzees enjoy comfort. They construct sleeping platforms each 19 night, using a multitude of leafy twigs to make their beds soft. Often, too, they make little "pillows" on which to rest during a midday siesta.

Chimps are highly intelligent. They display cognitive abilities that 20 were, until recently, thought to be unique to humans. They are capable of cross-model transfer of information—that is, they can identify by touch an object they previously have only seen, and vice versa. They are capable of reasoned thought, generalization, abstraction and symbolic representation. They have some concept of self. They have excellent memories and can, to some extent, plan for the future. They show a capacity for intentional communication that depends, in part, on their ability to understand the motives of the individuals with whom they are communicating.

Chimpanzees are capable of empathy and altruistic behavior. They 21 show emotions that are undoubtedly similar, if not identical, to human emotions—joy, pleasure, contentment, anxiety, fear and rage. They even have a sense of humor.

The chimpanzee child and the human child are alike in many ways; 22 in their capacity for endless romping and fun; their curiosity; their ability to learn by observation, imitation and practice; and, above all, in their need for reassurance and love. When young chimpanzees are brought up in a human home and treated like human children, they learn to eat at table, to help themselves to snacks from the refrigerator, to sort and put away cutlery, to brush their teeth, to play with dolls, to switch on the television and select a program that interests them and watch it.

Young chimpanzees can easily learn over 200 signs of the American 23 language of the deaf and use these signs to communicate meaningfully with humans and with one another. One youngster, in the laboratory of Dr. Roger S. Fouts, a psychologist at Central Washington University, has picked up 68 signs from four older signing chimpanzee companions, with no human teaching. The chimp uses the signs in communication with other chimpanzees and with humans.

The chimpanzee facilities in most biomedical research laboratories 24 allow for the expression of almost none of these activities and behaviors. They provide little—if anything—more than the warmth, food and water, and veterinary care required to sustain life. The psychological and emotional needs of these creatures are rarely catered to, and often not even acknowledged.

In most labs the chimpanzees are housed individually, one chimp to 25
a cage, unless they are part of a breeding program. The standard size of
each cage is about 25 feet square and about 6 feet high. In one facility, a
cage described in the catalogue as "large," designed for a chimpanzee
of up to 25 kilograms (55 pounds), measures 2 feet 6 inches by 3 feet 8
inches, with a height of 5 feet 4 inches. Federal requirements for cage
size are dependent on body size; infant chimpanzees, who are the most
active, are often imprisoned in the smallest cages.

In most labs, the chimpanzees cannot even lie with their arms 26
and legs outstretched. They are not let out to exercise. There is seldom
anything for them to do other than eat, and then only when food is
brought. The caretakers are usually too busy to pay much attention to
individual chimpanzees. The cages are bleak and sterile, with bars
above, bars below, bars on every side. There is no comfort in them, no
bedding. The chimps, infected with human diseases, will often feel sick
and miserable.

What of the human beings who administer these facilities—the 27
caretakers, veterinarians and scientists who work at them? If they are
decent, compassionate people, how can they condone, or even tolerate,
the kind of conditions I have described?

They are, I believe, victims of a system that was set up long before 28
the cognitive abilities and emotional needs of chimpanzees were understood. Newly employed staff members, equipped with a normal measure of compassion, may well be sickened by what they see. And, in
fact, many of them do quit their jobs, unable to endure the suffering
they see inflicted on the animals yet feeling powerless to help.

But others stay on and gradually come to accept the cruelty, believ- 29
ing (or forcing themselves to believe) that it is an inevitable part of the
struggle to reduce human suffering. Some become hard and callous in
the process, in Shakespeare's words, "all pity choked with custom of fell
deeds."

A handful of compassionate and dedicated caretakers and veteri- 30
narians are fighting to improve the lots of the animals in their care. Vets
are often in a particularly difficult position, for if they stand firm and try
to uphold high standards of humane care, they will not always be welcome in the lab.

Many of the scientists believe that a bleak, sterile and restricting 31
environment is necessary for their research. The cages must be small,
the scientists maintain, because otherwise it is too difficult to treat the
chimpanzees—to inject them, to draw their blood or to anesthetize
them. Moreover, they are less likely to hurt themselves in small cages.

The cages must also be barren, with no bedding or toys, say the sci- 32
entists. This way, the chimpanzees are less likely to pick up diseases or
parasites. Also, if things are lying about, the cages are harder to clean.

And the chimpanzees must be kept in isolation, the scientists believe, 33
to avoid the risk of cross-infection, particularly in hepatitis research.

Finally, of course, bigger cages, social groups and elaborate fur- 34
nishings require more space, more caretakers—and more money. Perhaps, then, if we are to believe these researchers, it is not possible to
improve conditions for chimpanzees imprisoned in biomedical research
laboratories.

I believe not only that it is possible, but that improvements are 35
absolutely necessary. If we do not do something to help these creatures,
we make a mockery of the whole concept of justice.

Perhaps the most important way we can improve the quality of life 36
for the laboratory chimps is to increase the number of carefully trained
caretakers. These people should be selected for their understanding of
animal behavior and their compassion and respect for, and dedication
to, their charges. Each caretaker, having established a relationship of
trust with the chimpanzees in his care, should be allowed to spend time
with the animals over and above that required for cleaning the cages
and providing the animals with food and water.

It has been shown that a chimpanzee who has a good relationship 37
with his caretaker will cooperate calmly during experimental procedures, rather than react with fear or anger. At the Dutch Primate
Research Center, at Rijswijk, for example, some chimpanzees have been
trained to leave their group cage on command and move into small, single cages for treatment. At the Stanford Primate Center in California, a
number of chimpanzees were taught to extend their arms for the drawing of blood. In return they were given a food reward.

Much can be done to alleviate the pain and stress felt by younger 38
chimpanzees during experimental procedures. A youngster, for example, can be treated when in the presence of a trusted human friend.
Experiments have shown that young chimps react with high levels of
distress if subjected to mild electric shocks when alone, but show almost
no fear or pain when held by a sympathetic caretaker.

What about cage size? Here we should emulate the animal protec- 39
tion regulations that already exist in Switzerland. These laws stipulate
that a cage must be, at minimum, about 20 meters square and 3 meters
high for pairs of chimpanzees.

The chimpanzees should never be housed alone unless this is an 40
essential part of the experimental procedure. For chimps in solitary
confinement, particularly youngsters, three to four hours of friendly
interaction with a caretaker should be mandatory. A chimp taking part
in hepatitis research, in which the risk of cross-infection is, I am told,
great, can be provided with a companion of a compatible species if it
doesn't infringe on existing regulations—a rhesus monkey, for example,
which cannot catch or pass on the disease.

For healthy chimpanzees there should be little risk of infection from 41 bedding and toys. Stress and depression, however, can have deleterious effects on their health. It is known that clinically depressed humans are more prone to a variety of physiological disorders, and heightened stress can interfere with immune function. Given the chimpanzee's similarities to humans, it is not surprising that the chimp in a typical laboratory, alone in his bleak cage, is an easy prey to infections and parasites.

Thus, the chimpanzees also should be provided with a rich and 42 stimulating environment. Climbing apparatus should be obligatory. There should be many objects for them to play with or otherwise manipulate. A variety of simple devices designed to alleviate boredom could be produced quite cheaply. Unexpected food items will elicit great pleasure. If a few simple buttons in each cage were connected to a computer terminal, it would be possible for the chimpanzees to feel they at least have some control over their world—if one button produced a grape when pressed, another a drink, or another a video picture. (The Canadian Council of Animal Care recommends the provision of television for primates in solitary confinement, or other means of enriching their environment.)

Without doubt, it will be considerably more costly to maintain 43 chimpanzees in the manner I have outlined. Should we begrudge them the extra dollars? We take from them their freedom, their health and often their lives. Surely, the least we can do is try to provide them with some of the things that could make their imprisonment more bearable.

There are hopeful signs. I was immensely grateful to officials of the 44 National Institutes of Health for allowing me to visit the primate facility, enabling me to see the conditions there and judge them for myself. And I was even more grateful for the fact that they gave me a great deal of time for serious discussions of the problem. Doors were opened and a dialogue begun. All who were present at the meetings agreed that, in light of present knowledge, it is indeed necessary to give chimpanzees a better deal in the labs.

Plans are now under way for a major conference to discuss ways 45 and means of bringing about such change. Sponsored by the N.I.H. and organized by Roger Fouts (who toured the lab with me) and myself, this conference—which will be held in mid-December at the Jane Goodall Institute in Tucson, Ariz.—will bring together for the first time administrators, scientists and animal technicians from various primate facilities around the country and from overseas. The conference will, we hope, lead to the formulation of new, humane standards for the maintenance of chimpanzees in the laboratory.

I have had the privilege of working among wild, free chimpan- 46 zees for more than 26 years. I have gained a deep understanding of chimpanzee nature. Chimpanzees have given me so much in my life. The least

I can do is to speak out for the hundreds of chimpanzees who, right now, sit hunched, miserable and without hope, staring out with dead eyes from their metal prisons. They cannot speak for themselves.

Responding to Reading

1. Goodall says in paragraph 7 that she doesn't want to discuss the issue of whether chimpanzees should be used in medical research. Does she successfully sidestep this issue in her essay, or does she indirectly address it? Explain.
2. What arguments against Goodall's proposals could scientists who use chimpanzees in experiments make? Does Goodall address any of these arguments in her essay? Should she have?
3. Some proponents of animal rights say that animals should not be used in experiments where human beings would not be used. Do you agree? Would Goodall agree with this position?

MY WORLD NOW

Anna Mae Halgrim Seaver

The following essay originally appeared as a "My Turn" column in Newsweek *magazine in June 1994. Anna Mae Halgrim Seaver (1919–1994) had recently died at the nursing home where she had been confined for some time, and her son discovered these notes in her room after her death.*

This is my world now; it's all I have left. You see, I'm old. And, I'm 1 not as healthy as I used to be. I'm not necessarily happy with it but I accept it. Occasionally, a member of my family will stop in to see me. He or she will bring me some flowers or a little present, maybe a set of slippers—I've got 8 pair. We'll visit for awhile and then they will return to the outside world and I'll be alone again.

Oh, there are other people here in the nursing home. Residents, 2 we're called. The majority are about my age. I'm 84. Many are in wheelchairs. The lucky ones are passing through—a broken hip, a diseased heart, something has brought them here for rehabilitation. When they're well they'll be going home.

Most of us are aware of our plight—some are not. Varying stages of 3 Alzheimer's have robbed several of their mental capacities. We listen to endlessly repeated stories and questions. We meet them anew daily, hourly or more often. We smile and nod gracefully each time we hear a retelling. They seldom listen to my stories, so I've stopped trying.

The help here is basically pretty good, although there's a large 4 turnover. Just when I get comfortable with someone he or she moves on to another job. I understand that. This is not the best job to have.

I don't much like some of the physical things that happen to us. I 5 don't care much for a diaper. I seem to have lost the control acquired so diligently as a child. The difference is that I'm aware and embarrassed but I can't do anything about it. I've had 3 children and I know it isn't pleasant to clean another's diaper. My husband used to wear a gas mask when he changed the kids. I wish I had one now.

Why do you think the staff insists on talking baby talk when speak- 6 ing to me? I understand English. I have a degree in music and am a certified teacher. Now I hear a lot of words that end in "y." Is this how my kids felt? My hearing aid works fine. There is little need for anyone to position their face directly in front of mine and raise their voice with those "y" words. Sometimes it takes longer for a meaning to sink in; sometimes my mind wanders when I am bored. But there's no need to shout.

I tried once or twice to make my feelings known. I even shouted 7 once. That gained me a reputation of being "crotchety." Imagine me, crotchety. My children never heard me raise my voice. I surprised myself. After I've asked for help more than a dozen times and received nothing more than a dozen condescending smiles and a "Yes, deary, I'm working on it," something begins to break. That time I wanted to be taken to a bathroom.

I'd love to go out for a meal, to travel again. I'd love to go to my 8 own church, sing with my own choir. I'd love to visit my friends. Most of them are gone now or else they are in different "homes" of their children's choosing. I'd love to play a good game of bridge but no one here seems to concentrate very well.

My children put me here for my own good. They said they would 9 be able to visit me frequently. But they have their own lives to lead. That sounds normal. I don't want to be a burden. They know that. But I would like to see them more. One of them is here in town. He visits as much as he can.

Something else I've learned to accept is loss of privacy. Quite often 10 I'll close my door when my roommate—imagine having a roommate at my age—is in the TV room. I do appreciate some time to myself and believe that I have earned at least that courtesy. As I sit thinking or writing, one of the aides invariably opens the door unannounced and walks in as if I'm not there. Sometimes she even opens my drawers and begins rummaging around. Am I invisible? Have I lost my right to respect and dignity? What would happen if the roles were reversed? I am still a human being. I would like to be treated as one.

The meals are not what I would choose for myself. We get variety 11
but we don't get a choice. I am one of the fortunate ones who can still
handle utensils. I remember eating off such cheap utensils in the Great
Depression. I worked hard so I would not have to ever use them again.
But here I am.

Did you ever sit in a wheelchair over an extended period of time? 12
It's not comfortable. The seat squeezes you into the middle and applies
constant pressure on your hips. The armrests are too narrow and my
arms slip off. I am luckier than some. Others are strapped into their
chairs and abandoned in front of the TV. Captive prisoners of daytime
television; soap operas, talk shows and commercials.

One of the residents died today. He was a loner who, at one time, 13
started a business and developed a multimillion-dollar company. His
children moved him here when he could no longer control his bowels.
He didn't talk to most of us. He often snapped at the aides as though
they were his employees. But he just gave up; willed his own demise.
The staff has made up his room and another man has moved in.

A typical day. Awakened by the woman in the next bed wheezing— 14
a former chain smoker with asthma. Call an aide to wash me and place
me in my wheelchair to wait for breakfast. Only 67 minutes until breakfast. I'll wait. Breakfast in the dining area. Most of the residents are in
wheelchairs. Others use canes or walkers. Some sit and wonder what
they are waiting for. First meal of the day. Only 3 hours and 26 minutes
until lunch. Maybe I'll sit around and wait for it. What is today? One
day blends into the next until day and date mean nothing.

Let's watch a little TV. Oprah and Phil and Geraldo and who cares 15
if some transvestite is having trouble picking a color-coordinated
wardrobe from his husband's girlfriend's mother's collection. Lunch.
Can't wait. Dried something with puréed peas and coconut pudding.
No wonder I'm losing weight.

Back to my semiprivate room for a little semiprivacy or a nap. I do 16
need my beauty rest, company may come today. What is today, again?
The afternoon drags into early evening. This used to be my favorite time
of the day. Things would wind down. I would kick off my shoes. Put my
feet up on the coffee table. Pop open a bottle of Chablis and enjoy the
fruits of my day's labor with my husband. He's gone. So is my health.
This is my world.

Responding to Reading

1. Seaver's son compiled this essay from notes left in his mother's room after
    her death. Perhaps for this reason, it seems to jump from one subject to
    another. Are there any advantages to this choppy structure? Would a
    smoother, more unified structure have been more effective?

2. What picture of life in a nursing home does Seaver present? How does she characterize the people who live there?
3. In paragraph 9 Seaver says "My children put me here for my own good. . . . But they have their own lives to lead. . . . I don't want to be a burden." Do you think Seaver means what she says? What do you think her son hoped to accomplish by publishing her notes?

Do Not Go Gentle into That Good Night

Dylan Thomas

Born in Swansea, Wales, in 1914, Dylan Thomas was one of the most popular poets of his day. His first collection, Eighteen Poems *(1934), was both hailed and condemned for its earthy vigor, but it immediately made his reputation. Later collections include* Twenty-Five Poems *(1936),* Deaths and Entrances *(1946), and* In Country Sleep and Other Poems *(1952). He also published several volumes of whimsical prose, including* Portrait of the Artist as a Young Dog *(1940), and the drama* Under Milkwood *(1954). Famous for his dramatic public readings of his work, Thomas made several highly successful tours of the United States. He died in New York City in 1953 at the age of thirty-nine of complications arising from alcoholism.*

Do not go gentle into that good night,
Old age should burn and rave at close of day;
Rage, rage against the dying of the light.

Though wise men at their end know dark is right,
Because their words had forked no lightning they   5
Do not go gentle into that good night.

Good men, the last wave by, crying how bright
Their frail deeds might have danced in a green bay,
Rage, rage against the dying of the light.

Wild men who caught and sang the sun in flight,   10
And learn, too late, they grieved it on its way,
Do not go gentle into that good night.

Grave men, near death, who see with blinding sight
Blind eyes could blaze like meteors and be gay,
Rage, rage against the dying of the light.   15

And you, my father, there on the sad height,
Curse, bless, me now with your fierce tears, I pray,
Do not go gentle into that good night.
Rage, rage against the dying of the light.

Responding to Reading

1. What is the speaker's attitude toward death? How does he want people to act as they face death?
2. What different kinds of men are discussed in this poem? How does each of these types of men face death? What type of man is the speaker's father?
3. How realistic are the speaker's wishes? What is your opinion of him? Is he concerned about his father? Himself? Something else?

ON THE FEAR OF DEATH
Elisabeth Kübler-Ross

Born in Zurich, Switzerland, psychologist and physician Elisabeth Kübler-Ross (1917–   ) has made a distinguished career of her interest in dying patients and their families. She established a pioneering interdisciplinary seminar in the care of the terminally ill when she taught at the University of Chicago, and for many years, she headed a center for terminal patients in rural Virginia. Her first book on the subject was On Death and Dying *(1969), and she also wrote* Death: The Final State *(1974),* On Childhood and Death *(1985), and* AIDS: The Ultimate Challenge *(1987). In recent years she has turned her attention to what happens after death, the subject of* On Life after Death *(1991). Her most recent books are* The Wheel of Life: A Memoir of Living and Dying *(1997) and* Remember the Secret *(2000), a book for children. In the following excerpt from* On Death and Dying, *Kübler-Ross argues that we should confront death directly to reduce our fear of it.*

Let me not pray to be sheltered from dangers but to be fear-
    less in facing them.
Let me not beg for the stilling of my pain but for the heart to
    conquer it.
Let me not look for allies in life's battlefield but to my own
    strength.
Let me not crave in anxious fear to be saved but hope for the
    patience to win my freedom.

Grant me that I may not be a coward, feeling your mercy in
my success alone; but let me find the grasp of your hand
in my failure.

Rabindranath Tagore, *Fruit-Gathering*

Epidemics have taken a great toll of lives in past generations. Death 1
in infancy and early childhood was frequent and there were few families
who didn't lose a member of the family at an early age. Medicine has
changed greatly in the last decades. Widespread vaccinations have practically eradicated many illnesses, at least in western Europe and the
United States. The use of chemotherapy, especially the antibiotics, has
contributed to an ever decreasing number of fatalities in infectious diseases. Better child care and education have effected a low morbidity and
mortality among children. The many diseases that have taken an impressive toll among the young and middle-aged have been conquered.
The number of old people is on the rise, and with this fact come the number of people with malignancies and chronic diseases associated more
with old age.

Pediatricians have less work with acute and life-threatening situa- 2
tions as they have an ever increasing number of patients with psychoso-
matic disturbances and adjustment and behavior problems. Physicians
have more people in their waiting rooms with emotional problems than
they have ever had before, but they also have more elderly patients who
not only try to live with their decreased physical abilities and limitations
but who also face loneliness and isolation with all its pains and anguish.
The majority of these people are not seen by a psychiatrist. Their needs
have to be elicited and gratified by other professional people, for instance,
chaplains and social workers. It is for them that I am trying to outline the
changes that have taken place in the last few decades, changes that are
ultimately responsible for the increased fear of death, the rising number
of emotional problems, and the greater need for understanding of and
coping with the problems of death and dying.

When we look back in time and study old cultures and people, we 3
are impressed that death has always been distasteful to man and will
probably always be. From a psychiatrist's point of view this is very
understandable and can perhaps best be explained by our basic knowledge that, in our unconscious, death is never possible in regard to ourselves. It is inconceivable for our unconscious to imagine an actual
ending of our own life here on earth, and if this life of ours had to end,
the ending is always attributed to a malicious intervention from the outside by someone else. In simple terms, in our unconscious mind we can
only be killed; it is inconceivable to die of a natural cause or of old age.
Therefore death in itself is associated with a bad act, a frightening happening, something that in itself calls for retribution and punishment.

One is wise to remember these fundamental facts as they are essen- 4
tial in understanding some of the most important, otherwise unintelli-
gible communications of our patients.

The second fact that we have to comprehend is that in our uncon- 5
scious mind we cannot distinguish between a wish and a deed. We are
all aware of some of our illogical dreams in which two completely
opposite statements can exist side by side—very acceptable in our
dreams but unthinkable and illogical in our wakening state. Just as our
unconscious mind cannot differentiate between the wish to kill somebody in anger and the act of having done so, the young child is unable
to make this distinction. The child who angrily wishes his mother to
drop dead for not having gratified his needs will be traumatized greatly
by the actual death of his mother—even if this event is not linked
closely in time with his destructive wishes. He will always take part or
the whole blame for the loss of his mother. He will always say to himself—rarely to others—"I did it, I am responsible, I was bad, therefore
Mommy left me." It is well to remember that the child will react in the
same manner if he loses a parent by divorce, separation, or desertion.
Death is often seen by a child as an impermanent thing and has therefore little distinction from a divorce in which he may have an opportunity to see a parent again.

Many a parent will remember remarks of their children such as, "I 6
will bury my doggy now and next spring when the flowers come up
again, he will get up." Maybe it was the same wish that motivated the
ancient Egyptians to supply their dead with food and goods to keep
them happy and the old American Indians to bury their relatives with
their belongings.

When we grow older and begin to realize that our omnipotence is 7
really not so omnipotent, that our strongest wishes are not powerful enough to make the impossible possible, the fear that we have
contributed to the death of a loved one diminishes—and with it the
guilt. The fear remains diminished, however, only so long as it is not
challenged too strongly. Its vestiges can be seen daily in hospital corridors and in people associated with the bereaved.

A husband and wife may have been fighting for years, but when the 8
partner dies, the survivor will pull his hair, whine and cry louder and
beat his chest in regret, fear and anguish, and will hence fear his own
death more than before, still believing in the law of talion—an eye for
an eye, a tooth for a tooth—"I am responsible for her death, I will have
to die a pitiful death in retribution."

Maybe this knowledge will help us understand many of the old 9
customs and rituals which have lasted over the centuries and whose
purpose is to diminish the anger of the gods or the people as the case
may be, thus decreasing the anticipated punishment. I am thinking of
the ashes, the torn clothes, the veil, the *Klage Weiber*[1] of the old days—

they are all means to ask you to take pity on them, the mourners, and are expressions of sorrow, grief, and shame. If someone grieves, beats his chest, tears his hair, or refuses to eat, it is an attempt at self-punishment to avoid or reduce the anticipated punishment for the blame that he takes on the death of a loved one.

This grief, shame, and guilt are not very far removed from feelings 10 of anger and rage. The process of grief always includes some qualities of anger. Since none of us likes to admit anger at a deceased person, these emotions are often disguised or repressed and prolong the period of grief or show up in other ways. It is well to remember that it is not up to us to judge such feelings as bad or shameful but to understand their true meaning and origin as something very human. In order to illustrate this I will again use the example of the child—and the child in us. The five-year-old who loses his mother is both blaming himself for her disappearance and being angry at her for having deserted him and for no longer gratifying his needs. The dead person then turns into something the child loves and wants very much but also hates with equal intensity for this severe deprivation.

The ancient Hebrews regarded the body of a dead person as some- 11 thing unclean and not to be touched. The early American Indians talked about the evil spirits and shot arrows in the air to drive the spirits away. Many other cultures have rituals to take care of the "bad" dead person, and they all originate in this feeling of anger which still exists in all of us, though we dislike admitting it. The tradition of the tombstone may originate in this wish to keep the bad spirits deep down in the ground, and the pebbles that many mourners put on the grave are left-over symbols of the same wish. Though we call the firing of guns at military funerals a last salute, it is the same symbolic ritual as the Indian used when he shot his spears and arrows into the skies.

I give these examples to emphasize that man has not basically 12 changed. Death is still a fearful, frightening happening, and the fear of death is a universal fear even if we think we have mastered it on many levels.

What has changed is our way of coping and dealing with death and 13 dying and our dying patients.

Having been raised in a country in Europe where science is not so 14 advanced, where modern techniques have just started to find their way into medicine, and where people still live as they did in this country half a century ago, I may have had an opportunity to study a part of the evolution of mankind in a shorter period.

I remember as a child the death of a farmer. He fell from a tree and 15 was not expected to live. He asked simply to die at home, a wish that was granted without questioning. He called his daughters into the bedroom

---

[1] Wailing wives. [Eds.]

and spoke with each one of them alone for a few moments. He arranged his affairs quietly, though he was in great pain, and distributed his belongings and his land, none of which was to be split until his wife should follow him in death. He also asked each of his children to share in the work, duties, and tasks that he had carried on until the time of the accident. He asked his friends to visit him once more, to bid good-bye to them. Although I was a small child at the time, he did not exclude me or my siblings. We were allowed to share in the preparations of the family just as we were permitted to grieve with them until he died. When he did die, he was left at home, in his own beloved home which he had built, and among his friends and neighbors who went to take a last look at him where he lay in the midst of flowers in the place he had lived in and loved so much. In that country today there is still no make-believe slumber room, no embalming, no false makeup to pretend sleep. Only the signs of very disfiguring illnesses are covered up with bandages and only infectious cases are removed from the home prior to the burial.

Why do I describe such "old-fashioned" customs? I think they are 16 an indication of our acceptance of a fatal outcome, and they help the dying patient as well as his family to accept the loss of a loved one. If a patient is allowed to terminate his life in the familiar and beloved environment, it requires less adjustment for him. His own family knows him well enough to replace a sedative with a glass of his favorite wine; or the smell of a home-cooked soup may give him the appetite to sip a few spoons of fluid which, I think, is still more enjoyable than an infusion. I will not minimize the need for sedatives and infusions and realize full well from my own experience as a country doctor that they are sometimes life-saving and often unavoidable. But I also know that patience and familiar people and foods could replace many a bottle of intravenous fluids given for the simple reason that it fulfills the physiological need without involving too many people and/or individual nursing care.

The fact that children are allowed to stay at home where a fatality 17 has stricken and are included in the talk, discussions, and fears gives them the feeling that they are not alone in the grief and gives them the comfort of shared responsibility and shared mourning. It prepares them gradually and helps them view death as part of life, an experience which may help them grow and mature.

This is in great contrast to a society in which death is viewed as 18 taboo, discussion of it is regarded as morbid, and children are excluded with the presumption and pretext that it would be "too much" for them. They are then sent off to relatives, often accompanied with some unconvincing lies of "Mother has gone on a long trip" or other unbelievable stories. The child senses that something is wrong, and his distrust in adults will only multiply if other relatives add new variations of the story, avoid his questions or suspicions, shower him with gifts as a meager substitute for a loss he is not permitted to deal with. Sooner or later the child will become aware of the changed family situation and, depending on the age and personality of the child, will have an unresolved grief and regard this incident as a frightening, mysterious, in any case very traumatic experience with untrustworthy grownups, which he has no way to cope with.

It is equally unwise to tell a little child who lost her brother that God 19 loved little boys so much that he took little Johnny to heaven. When this little girl grew up to be a woman she never solved her anger at God, which resulted in a psychotic depression when she lost her own little son three decades later.

We would think that our great emancipation, our knowledge of 20 science and of man, has given us better ways and means to prepare ourselves and our families for this inevitable happening. Instead the days are gone when a man was allowed to die in peace and dignity in his own home.

The more we are making advancements in science, the more we 21 seem to fear and deny the reality of death. How is this possible?

We use euphemisms, we make the dead look as if they were asleep, 22 we ship the children off to protect them from the anxiety and turmoil around the house if the patient is fortunate enough to die at home, we don't allow children to visit their dying parents in the hospitals, we have long and controversial discussions about whether patients should be told the truth—a question that rarely arises when the dying person is tended by the family physician who has known him from delivery to death and who knows the weaknesses and strengths of each member of the family.

I think there are many reasons for this flight away from facing death 23 calmly. One of the most important facts is that dying nowadays is more gruesome in many ways, namely, more lonely, mechanical, and dehumanized; at times it is even difficult to determine technically when the time of death has occurred.

Dying becomes lonely and impersonal because the patient is often 24 taken out of his familiar environment and rushed to an emergency room. Whoever has been very sick and has required rest and comfort especially may recall his experience of being put on a stretcher and enduring the noise of the ambulance siren and hectic rush until the hospital gates open. Only those who have lived through this may appreciate the discomfort and cold necessity of such transportation which is only the beginning of a long order—hard to endure when you are well, difficult to express in words when noise, light, pumps, and voices are all too much to put up with. It may well be that we might consider more the patient under the sheets and blankets and perhaps stop our well-meant efficiency and rush in order to hold the patient's hand, to smile, or to listen to a question. I include the trip to the hospital as the first episode in dying, as it is for many. I am putting it exaggeratedly in contrast to the sick man who is left at home—not to say that lives should not be saved if they can be saved by a hospitalization but to keep the focus on the patient's experience, his needs and his reactions.

When a patient is severely ill, he is often treated like a person with no right to an opinion. It is often someone else who makes the decision if and when and where a patient should be hospitalized. It would take so little to remember that the sick person too has feelings, has wishes and opinions, and has—most important of all—the right to be heard. 25

Well, our presumed patient has now reached the emergency room. He will be surrounded by busy nurses, orderlies, interns, residents, a lab technician perhaps who will take some blood, an electrocardiogram technician who takes the cardiogram. He may be moved to X ray and he will overhear opinions of his condition and discussions and questions to members of the family. He slowly but surely is beginning to be treated like a thing. He is no longer a person. Decisions are made often without his opinion. If he tries to rebel he will be sedated and after hours of waiting and wondering whether he has the strength, he will be wheeled into the operating room or intensive treatment unit and become an object of great concern and great financial investment. 26

He may cry for rest, peace, and dignity, but he will get infusions, transfusions, a heart machine, or tracheotomy[2] if necessary. He may want one single person to stop for one single minute so that he can ask one single question—but he will get a dozen people around the clock, all busily preoccupied with his heart rate, pulse, electrocardiogram or pulmonary functions, his secretions or excretions but not with him as a human being. He may wish to fight it all but it is going to be a useless fight since all this is done in the fight for his life, and if they can save his life they can consider the person afterwards. Those who consider the person first may lose precious time to save his life! At least this seems to be the rationale or justification behind all this—or is it? Is the reason for this increasingly mechanical, depersonalized approach our own defensiveness? Is this approach our own way to cope with and repress the anxieties that a terminally or critically ill patient evokes in us? Is our concentration on equipment, on blood pressure, our desperate attempt to deny the impending death which is so frightening and discomforting to us that we displace all our knowledge onto machines, since they are less close to us than the suffering face of another human being which would remind us once more of our lack of omnipotence, our own limits and failures, and last but not least perhaps our own mortality? 27

Maybe the question has to be raised: Are we becoming less human or more human? . . . It is clear that whatever the answer may be, the patient is suffering more—not physically, perhaps, but emotionally. 28

---

[2] An incision in the trachea in the neck to allow the insertion of a breathing tube. [Eds.]

And his needs have not changed over the centuries, only our ability to gratify them.

Responding to Reading

1. Despite advances in medical science over the centuries, Kübler-Ross says, death remains "a fearful, frightening happening, and the fear of death is a universal fear even if we think we have mastered it on many levels" (12). Do you think she is correct?
2. To what extent do you agree with Kübler-Ross that we should confront the reality of death directly—for example, by being honest with children, keeping terminally ill patients at home, and allowing dying patients to determine their own treatment? What arguments are there against each of her suggestions?
3. Instead of quoting medical authorities, Kübler-Ross supports her points with anecdotes. Do you find this support convincing? Would hard scientific data be more convincing? Explain.

MISPLACED PRIORITIES: A FOCUS ON GUNS

Robert L. Borosage

Robert L. Borosage (1944–) holds a bachelor's degree from Michigan State University, a law degree from Yale, and a master's degree in international affairs from George Washington University. He has served as an adviser to such politicians as Senator Barbara Boxer, and Jesse Jackson, and he is currently codirector of the Campaign for America's Future, an organization founded to put forth a populist economic agenda for the United States. Borosage has written about political, economic, and national security issues for publications including the New York Times, *the* Washington Post, *and* The Nation. *He is also a frequent commentator on National Public Radio, C-SPAN, and other broadcast news media. The following essay originally appeared in the* Los Angeles Times *in the summer of 2000 following an international AIDS conference held in South Africa.*

The AIDS epidemic, as former South African President Nelson 1 Mandela said at the global AIDS conference last week, "is a tragedy of unprecedented proportions." A U.S. National Intelligence Estimate now projects that one out of four people in southern Africa is likely to die of the disease and warns that unimaginable toll may be repeated, if not

across the world. When an Iraqi division heads south in the desert, it is tracked instantly and can trigger an immediate deployment of air, sea and ground forces. But the spread of AIDS can threaten the lives of one in four people in sub-Saharan Africa, destabilize governments, set off a regional depression and still have trouble gaining attention, much less any serious commitment, from U.S. policymakers.

The administration is not solely at fault. It faces a Republican Con- 12 gress that routinely assails foreign assistance. When Clinton declared AIDS a security threat, Senate Majority Leader Trent Loot (R-Miss.) dismissed it as gesture for "special interest," meaning, presumably, African American voters. Our allies have also been slow to react to the AIDS crisis, waiting for Washington to take the lead.

The U.S. military is so powerful that we now wage wars without tak- 13 ing casualties. Our economy is so strong that we look on Russia's misery or Africa's horror at a far remove. The challenge of meeting the global AIDS crisis is forbidding. So perhaps it should not surprise us that U.S. response to this human disaster is slow and halting. Yet, one thing is certain: If there were a way to strafe or bomb AIDS, we'd be there. But we don't do plagues.

Responding to Reading

1. What does Borosage mean when he says that in the United States, "We don't do plagues; we do guns" (1)? Why does he think that the United States has been so slow to respond to the AIDS epidemic in Africa?
2. In his essay, Borosage concentrates mainly on what the United States should do to address the AIDS epidemic in Africa (he briefly mentions our allies in paragraph 12). Why doesn't he discuss the role of other countries? Is he implying that the AIDS epidemic is mainly the United States's responsibility? Do you agree?
3. According to Borosage, how is the AIDS epidemic in Africa like the bubonic plague in fourteenth-century Europe? How is it different? How would Barbara Tuchman (p. 522) respond to this comparison?

─────────────────── FOCUS ───────────────────

Whose Life Is It Anyway?

THE ETHICS OF EUTHANASIA
Lawrence J. Schneiderman

Born in New York City, Lawrence J. Schneiderman (1932–   ) received his M.D. from Harvard Medical School in 1957 and has been on the staffs of Boston City Hospital, the National Institutes of Health, and Stanford University School of Medicine. Since 1970, he has been a professor at the University of California-San Diego School of Medicine, where he is direc-tor of the program in medical ethics. In addition to his contributions to med-ical journals, Schneiderman is the author of Wrong Medicine: Doctors, Patients, *and* Futile Treatments *(1995). In the following essay, which orig-inally appeared in the* Humanist *in 1990, he considers the complex question "What will become of a society that permits—indeed promotes—death as a social good?"*

Should physicians be permitted to offer death among their thera- 1
peutic options? Should they be licensed to kill—not inadvertently or negligently but willfully, openly, and compassionately? This, on the most superficial level, is the euthanasia debate.

In California, a petition to put this matter before the voters failed to 2
gain sufficient signatures. Perhaps this was because too many of those life-affirming hedonists cringed at the thought of signing their own death warrants, or—more likely in this land where almost everything has a price—because the sponsoring Hemlock Society[1] did not hire enough solicitors.

In any case, euthanasia is being performed.   3

As a medical ethicist, when I give talks on this subject to physicians, 4
I always ask: "How many of you have ever hastened death to alleviate the suffering of your patients?" Many hands are raised—uneasily; I can offer them no legal immunity. Of all the humane acts physicians per-form, euthanasia is the one we do most furtively.

But this is an old story. In 1537, while serving in the army of 5
Francis I, the troubled surgeon Ambroise Paré confided in his diary:

─────────

[1] Organization devoted to the individual's right to suicide. [Eds.]

We thronged into the city and passed over the dead bodies and some that were not yet dead, hearing them cry under the feet of our horses, which made a great pity in my heart, and truly I repented that I had gone forth from Paris to see so pitiful a spectacle. Being in the city, I entered a stable, thinking to lodge my horse and that of my man, where I found four dead soldiers and three who were propped against the wall, their faces wholly disfigured, and they neither saw, nor heard, nor spoke, and their clothes yet flaming from the gun powder, which had burnt them. Beholding them with pity there came an old soldier who asked me if there was any means of curing them. I told him no. At once he approached them and cut their throats gently and without anger. Seeing this great cruelty I said to him that he was an evil man. He answered me that he prayed God that when he should be in such a case, he might find someone that would do the same for him, to the end that he might not languish miserably.

Today, the euthanasia debate takes place under the shadow of Nazi 6 doctors who appropriated the term to describe the "special treatment" given first to the physically and mentally handicapped, then to the weak and elderly, and, finally, to Jews, gypsies, and other "undesirables" as part of the Final Solution—all in the name of social hygiene. In that monstrous orgy of evil, numbers replaced names, bodies replaced souls; all were hauled by the trainload to work or to death, then converted to ashes or merely dumped in such profusion that the very earth bubbled. That was no *euthanasia*—no easy, pleasant death. That was ugly, debasing death.

But we are different, are we not? Not like *them*. And yet, and 7 yet . . . didn't we American physicians commit atrocities of our own, such as allowing untreated blacks to succumb to the "natural course" of syphilis; misleading Spanish-speaking women into thinking they were obtaining contraceptives, when in fact they were receiving inactive dummy tablets to distinguish drug side-effects, resulting in unwanted pregnancies; and injecting cancer cells into unwitting elderly patients? All for the sake of medical progress . . . we can only look back and shake our heads.

Worthy colleagues—with whom I respectfully disagree—are so 8 fearful of the "Naziness" in us all that they oppose withholding life-sustaining treatment from *anyone*: the malformed newborn with no hope of survival, the permanently unconscious patient, the terminal cancer patient who begs to be allowed to die. Who would be next? they argue. The physically and mentally handicapped? The weak and the elderly? And then? And then? This, of course, is the familiar "slippery slope" argument. Start with one exception and you inevitably skid down the moral slope of ever more exceptions. This also is the euthanasia debate, on a deeper level. What will become of a society that permits—indeed promotes—death as a social good?

An ethics consultation is where we ponder such questions at the 9
bedside of a patient who perhaps is hopelessly ill. Not infrequently,
back in the doctor's conference room, a harried resident will burst out:
"What good is it for us to keep him alive anyway?" I don't regard this as a
callous question for the simple reason that it is phrased intimately and
in the singular: Why do *we* keep *him* alive? In contrast, you'd be surprised how often decent people who possess the most humane and
compassionate sensibilities demand: "Why do *they* keep *them* alive?"
That question, in my view, is morally indistinguishable from: "Why do
they let *them* die?"

For, you see, the first question arises from *this* patient, this special 10
case, *here*. The second question arises from a state of mind—those people. *There*. It is a state of mind that provides a dehumanizing abstraction
appealing to both extremes of the political spectrum, and it has been
applied to both ends of life. It can lead to the demand that *all* handicapped newborns be kept alive without regard to their specific agonies
and that life-prolonging treatment be denied to *all* the elderly beyond a
certain age.

What is so special about the special case? For those of us in medi- 11
cine, it exerts a palpable moral power; the special case is our daily news,
our gossip, a shaping force in our culture. Case studies and case reports
are basic teaching tools. *Case* (from *casus*, "happening," "accident") in
its original meaning refers to a unique person in unique circumstances.
Physicians are molded by their particular autobiography of cases, by
their own singular distressing experiences. My first physical diagnosis
teacher said, "Make sure you examine the neck veins. Always. Once I
missed a patient with congestive heart failure because I neglected to do
so." Since then, I have heard many such honest confessions—covertly,
for in the litigious world of contemporary medicine, it is almost treachery to reveal that this is how we learn best, by being wrong. To help my
compulsively driven and terrified students get on with their duties, I
tell them that, if it is true you learn from your mistakes, someday I will
know everything.

And we do learn from our special cases, one by one—sometimes 12
badly and incompletely, but each time the lesson is so painful that ultimately we do learn. For example, as a medical student, I was monitoring
the blood pressure of a man dying of acute pulmonary edema and
myocardial infarction.[2] The end of a gala evening for him. Next to me was
the man's wife—coiffed and elegantly gowned, cradling his head and
crooning her love while the man blanched into death. It was a good
death, since his physician, who was controlling the intravenous infusion
on the other side of the bed, had made sure that the man was heavily
sedated with morphine. It was a lesson I took with me to my internship,

---

[2] In layperson's terms, a severe heart attack. [Eds.]

become *why* (the motive) and *how* (the method). One can have the cruelest motive and employ the kindest method; for example, slipping Gramps an overdose of sleeping medicine to get rid of him and get at his money. Or, one can have the kindest motive and employ the cruelest method: letting him "languish miserably" (in the words of Paré) out of a loving reluctance to hasten his death. Neither of these acts is as morally defensible, in my opinion, as the bloody dagger-thrust performed "gently and without anger" by that old unknown soldier.

And so, while the cautious Dutch carry on, several states—including California, once again—are preparing euthanasia initiatives.[5] And the difficult questions will have to be faced. Can we be both merciful and just in matters of medically administered death? How? Do we keep the laws the way they are and grant no exceptions, thus publicly condemning (while at the same time insidiously perpetuating) unsupervised euthanasia? Or should we change the laws? And if we do so, can we craft them in such a way so as not to destroy hallowed and fragile values? Should we explicitly define and sanction certain acts of humane suicide assisted by physicians? Should we allow patients direct legal access to the necessary drugs? Or should we not attempt to change the laws but only openly acknowledge (as in the Netherlands) certain permissible violations—thus cautioning physicians to weigh each act as one they may have to defend in criminal court? The approach we take will reveal much about ourselves as a society. Are our moral cousins the Nazis or the Dutch? Can we keep our anguish fresh each time we contemplate the end of a fellow human being? Or will our anguish grow stale, allowing us to slide down the slope from "easy death" to "useful death," heaping *them* into nameless, faceless piles, saying there go *they*, not *I*, and discovering too late—as others have before—that if yesterday *they* were the retarded, the handicapped, the Jews, the blacks; and if today *they* are the elderly, the AIDS patient; then tomorrow *they* will be ourselves, wondering where all the others are—common waste requiring special treatment rather than special cases sharing a common fate.

Responding to Reading

1. Should physicians be able to "offer death among their therapeutic options" (1)? Or should doctors maintain life at all costs? How would you respond to the "slippery slope" argument (8) offered by opponents of euthanasia?
2. What does Schneiderman mean when he says, "This, I submit, is what the euthanasia debate is about: theoretical and statistical abstractions versus the anguishing, messy particulars of the special case" (17)? Do you agree that this is indeed "what the debate is all about"?

---

[5] In late 1997, doctor-assisted suicide became legal in Oregon. [Eds.]

3. Both Schneiderman and Jack Kevorkian (below) are physicians, but they take different positions on euthanasia. How would Schneiderman react to Kevorkian's statement that he "acted openly, ethically, legally, with complete and uncompromising honesty" (14) when he assisted in a suicide?

A CASE OF ASSISTED SUICIDE
Jack Kevorkian

Popularly known as "Dr. Death," Jack Kevorkian (1928–   ) has had a long interest in death and dying, which some critics trace to the fact that most of his Armenian family was annihilated by German soldiers during World War II. Trained in pathology at the University of Michigan, he was one of the earliest advocates of executing criminals by lethal injection, a practice that is followed in many states today. He has also argued in favor of using condemned criminals in medical experiments that will eventually kill them. Kevorkian's greatest notoriety, however, stems from his publicly acknowledged assistance in the suicides of over one hundred people with terminal or debilitatingly painful illnesses, actions for which he was convicted of second-degree murder in 1999, following three mistrials and one acquittal. He is currently serving a ten- to twenty-five-year sentence in a Michigan prison. In the following chapter from his book Prescription Medicide: The Goodness of Planned Death *(1991), Kevorkian describes in detail the first suicide in which he assisted using his "Mercitron," the device he invented for this purpose.*

Amid the flurry of telephone calls in the fall of 1989 was one from a   1 man in Portland, Oregon, who learned of my campaign from an item in *Newsweek* (November 13, 1989). Ron Adkins's rich, baritone, matter-of-fact voice was tinged with a bit of expectant anxiety as he calmly explained the tragic situation of his beloved wife. Janet Adkins was a remarkable, accomplished, active woman—wife, mother, grandmother, revered friend, teacher, musician, mountain climber, and outdoorsperson —who, for some time, had noticed (as did her husband) subtle and gradually progressive impairment of her memory. The shock of hearing the diagnosis of Alzheimer's disease four months earlier was magnified by the abrupt and somewhat callous way her doctor announced it. The intelligent woman knew what the diagnosis portended, and at that instant decided she would not live to experience the horror of such a death.

Knowing that Janet was a courageous fighter, Ron and their three   2 sons pleaded with her to reconsider and at least give a promising new therapy regimen a try. Ron explained to me that Janet was eligible to take part in an experimental trial using the newly developed drug Tacrine® or THA at the University of Washington in Seattle. I concurred that Janet should enroll in the program because any candidate for the

Mercitron must have exhausted every potentially beneficial medical intervention, no matter how remotely promising.

I heard nothing more from the Adkinses until April 1990. Ron called ₃ again, after Janet and he saw me and my device on a nationally televised talk show. Janet had entered the experimental program in January, but it had been stopped early because the new drug was ineffective. In fact, her condition got worse; and she was more determined than ever to end her life. Even though from a physical standpoint Janet was not imminently terminal, there seemed little doubt that mentally she was— and, after all, it is one's mental status that determines the essence of one's existence. I asked Ron to forward to me copies of Janet's clinical records, and they corroborated what Ron had said.

I then telephoned Janet's doctor in Seattle. He opposed her planned ₄ action and the concept of assisted suicide in general. It was his firm opinion that Janet would remain mentally competent for at least a year (but from Ron's narrative I concluded that her doctor's opinion was wrong and that time was of the essence). Because Janet's condition was deteriorating and there was nothing else that might help arrest it, I decided to accept her as the first candidate—a qualified, justifiable candidate if not "ideal"—and well aware of the vulnerability to criticism of picayune and overly emotional critics.

A major obstacle was finding a place to do it. Because I consider ₅ medicide to be necessary, ethical, and legal, there should be nothing furtive about it. Another reason to pursue the practice above-board is to avert the harassment or vindictiveness of litigation. Consequently, when searching for a suitable site I always explained that I planned to assist a suffering patient to commit suicide. That posed no problem for helping a Michigan resident in his or her own residence. But it was a different matter for an out-of-state guest who must rent temporary quarters.

And I soon found out how difficult a matter it could be. My own ₆ apartment could not be used because of lease constraints, and the same was true of my sister's apartment. I inquired at countless motels, funeral homes, churches of various denominations, rental office buildings, clinics, doctors' offices for lease, and even considered the futile hope of renting an emergency life-support ambulance. Many owners, proprietors, and landlords were quite sympathetic but fearful and envisioned the negative public reaction that could seriously damage and even destroy their business enterprises. In short, they deemed it bad for public relations. More dismaying yet was the refusal of people who are known supporters and active campaigners for euthanasia to allow Janet and me the use of their homes.

Finally, a friend agreed to avail us of his modest home in Detroit; ₇ I immediately contacted Ron to finalize plans. My initial proposal was to carry out the procedure at the end of May 1990, but Ron and Janet preferred to avoid the surge of travel associated with the Memorial Day weekend. The date was postponed to Monday, June 4th.

In the meantime, my friend was warned by a doctor, in whom he 8 confided, not to make his home available for such a purpose. Soon thereafter the offer was quickly withdrawn. With the date set and airline tickets having been purchased by Janet, Ron, and a close friend of Janet's, I had to scamper to find another site. The device required an electrical outlet, which limited the possibilities.

I had made a Herculean effort to provide a desirable, clinical set- 9 ting. Literally and sadly, there was "no room at the inn." Now, having been refused everywhere I applied, the *only alternative* remaining was my 1968 camper and a suitable campground.

As expected, the owners of a commercial site refused permission, 10 even though they were sympathetic to the proposed scheme. They then suggested the solution by recommending that I rent space at a public camping site not too far away. The setting was pleasant and idyllic.

As with many other aspects of this extraordinary event, I was aware 11 of the harsh criticism that would be leveled at the use of a "rusty old van." In the first place, the twenty-two-year-old body may have been rusting on the outside, but its interior was very clean, orderly, and comfortable. I have slept in it often and not felt degraded. But carping critics missed the point: the essence and significance of the event are far more important than the splendor of the site where it takes place. If critics are thus deluded into denouncing the exit from existence under these circumstances, then why not the same delusional denunciation of entrance into existence when a baby is, of necessity, born in an old taxicab? On the contrary, the latter identical scenario seems to arouse only feelings of sentimental reverence and quaint joy.

But the dishonesty doesn't stop there. I have been repeatedly criti- 12 cized for having assisted a patient after a short personal acquaintance of two days. Overlooked or ignored is my open avowal to be the first practitioner in this country of a new and as yet officially unrecognized specialty. Because of shameful stonewalling by her own doctors, Janet was forced to refer herself to me. And acting as a unique specialist, of necessity self-proclaimed, solitary, and independent, I was obligated to scrutinize Janet's clinical records and to consult with her personal doctor. The latter's uncooperative attitude (tacitly excused by otherwise harsh critics) impaired but did not thwart fulfillment of my duties to a suffering patient and to my profession.

It is absurd even to imply, let alone to protest outright, that a med- 13 ical specialist's competence and ethical behavior are contingent upon some sort of time interval, imposed arbitrarily or by fiat. When a doctor refers a patient for surgery, in many cases the surgical specialist performs his *ultimate* duty after personal acquaintance with the patient from a mere hour or two of prior consultation (in contrast to my having spent at least twelve hours in personal contact with Janet). In a few instances the surgeon operates on a patient seen for the first time on the operating table—and anesthetized to unconsciousness.

Moreover, in sharp contrast to the timorous, secretive, and even 14 deceitful intention and actions of other medical euthanasists on whom our so-called bioethicists now shower praise, I acted openly, ethically, legally, with complete and uncompromising honesty, and—even more important—I remained in personal attendance during the second most meaningful medical event in a patient's earthly existence. Were he alive today, it's not hard to guess what Hippocrates[1] would say about all this.

My two sisters, Margo and Flora, and I met with Ron, Janet, and 15 Janet's close friend Carroll Rehmke in their motel room on Saturday afternoon, 2 June 1990. After getting acquainted through a few minutes of conversation, the purpose of the trip was thoroughly discussed. I had already prepared authorization forms signifying Janet's intent, determination, and freedom of choice, which she readily agreed to sign. Here again, while she was resolute in her decision, and absolutely mentally competent, her impaired memory was apparent when she needed her husband's assistance in forming the cursive letter "A." She could print the letter but not write it, and the consent forms required that her signature be written. So her husband showed her on another piece of paper how to form the cursive "A," and Janet complied. At this time, Ron and Carroll also signed a statement attesting to Janet's mental competence. Following this signing session, I had Flora videotape my interview with Janet and Ron. The forty-five-minute taping reinforced my own conviction that Janet was mentally competent but that her memory had failed badly. However, the degree of memory failure led me to surmise that within four to six months she would be too incompetent to qualify as a candidate. It should be pointed out that in medical terms loss of memory does not automatically signify mental incompetence. Any rational critic would concede that a mentally sound individual can be afflicted with even total amnesia.

Around 5:30 P.M. that same day all six of us had dinner at a well- 16 known local restaurant. Seated around the same table for many hours, our conversation covered many subjects, including the telling of jokes. Without appearing too obvious, I constantly observed Janet's behavior and assessed her moods as well as the content and quality of her thoughts. There was absolutely no doubt that her mentality was intact and that she was not the least depressed over her impending death. On the contrary, the only detectable anxiety or disquieting demeanor was among the rest of us to a greater or lesser degree. Even in response to

---

[1] Ancient Greek physician, called the father of medicine, who gave his name to the Hippocratic oath taken by all medical doctors. [Eds.]

jokes, Janet's appropriately timed and modulated laughter indicated clear and coherent comprehension. The only uneasiness or distress she exhibited was due to her embarrassment at being unable to recall aspects of the topic under discussion at the time. And that is to be expected of intelligent, sensitive, and diligent individuals.

We left the restaurant at 12:30 A.M. Sunday. Janet and Ron enjoyed 17 their last full day by themselves.

At 8:30 A.M. the next day, Monday, 4 June 1990, I drove into a rented 18 space at Groveland Park in north Oakland County, Michigan. At the same time, my sisters drove to the motel to fetch Janet, who had composed (and submitted to my sister) a brief and clear note reiterating her genuine desire to end her life and exonerating all others in this desire and the actual event. For the last time, Janet took tearful leave of her grieving husband and Carroll, both of whom were inconsolable. It was Janet's wish that they not accompany her to the park.

The day began cold, damp, and overcast. I took a lot of time in set- 19 ting up the Mercitron and giving it a few test runs. In turning to get a pair of pliers in the cramped space within the van, I accidentally knocked over the container of thiopental solution, losing a little over half of it. I was fairly sure that the remainder was enough to induce and maintain adequate unconsciousness, but I chose not to take the risk. I drove the forty-five miles home and got some more.

In the meantime, at about 9:30 A.M. my sisters and Janet had arrived 20 at the park. They were dismayed to learn of the accidental spill and opted to accompany me on the extra round trip, which required two and one-half hours. We reentered the park at approximately noontime. Janet remained in the car with Margo while Flora helped me with minor tasks in the van as I very carefully prepared and tested the Mercitron. Everything was ready by about 2:00 P.M., and Janet was summoned.

She entered the van alone through the open sliding side door and 21 lay fully clothed on the built-in bed covered with freshly laundered sheets. Her head rested comfortably on a clean pillow. The windows were covered with new draperies. With Janet's permission I cut small holes in her nylon stockings at the ankles, attached ECG electrodes to her ankles and wrists, and covered her body with a light blanket. Our conversation was minimal. In accordance with Janet's wish, Flora read to her a brief note from her friend Carroll, followed by a reading of the Lord's prayer. I then repeated my earlier instructions to Janet about how the device was to be activated, and asked her to go through the motions. In contrast to my sister and me, Janet was calm and outwardly relaxed.

I used a syringe with attached needle to pierce a vein near the 22 frontal elbow area of her left arm. Unfortunately, her veins were delicate and fragile; even slight movement of the restrained arm caused the needle to penetrate through the wall of the vein resulting in leakage. Two more attempts also failed, as did a fourth attempt on the right side.

supporters of what has come to be called the "right to die" are even now battling their way through the implications. The moral questions raised by assisted suicide are weighty, but our ability as a society to deal with them has been seriously weakened by the judicial rush to enshrine one side's moral answer in the framework of constitutional rights.

The two cases presented the same basic question, but the courts dealt 7 with it in very different ways. In March, the Court of Appeals for the Ninth Circuit, based in San Francisco, decided the case of Compassion in Dying v. State of Washington, resting the right to assisted suicide for the terminally ill on the due process clause of the 14th Amendment, the same provision in which the courts have located the abortion right. The right to choose how to end one's own life, the court explained, was a direct descendant of the right to choose whether to bear a child, and, as with abortion, the state must have a very strong reason before it may interfere.

Then, less than a month later, the Second Circuit struck down New 8 York's assisted-suicide ban in the case of Quill v. Vacco. The Second Circuit rejected the due process argument, pointing out that the United States Supreme Court has limited that approach to cases in which the state is interfering with a fundamental liberty "deeply rooted in this Nation's history and tradition," like the freedom to marry or procreate. The right to obtain assistance in suicide, the court sensibly concluded, does not fit this definition. But the Quill court found a rationale of its own: the right to assisted suicide is supported, said the judges, by another part of the 14th Amendment—the equal protection clause. Why? Because New York allows mentally competent terminally ill patients on life support to direct the removal of the supporting apparatus, even when the removal will hasten or directly cause their deaths, but prohibits those who do not need life support from obtaining drugs to hasten or directly cause their deaths. So the state is discriminating, in the court's terms, by allowing some of the terminally ill, but not others, to die quickly.

The logic of Quill, although more attractive than that of Com- 9 passion in Dying, seems terribly forced, not least because the state allows many other distinctions among the terminally ill—for example, wealthier patients often have access to experimental drugs and therapies that others do not. These distinctions may not always seem sensible or fair but they hardly rise to the level of constitutional concern.

And there is a larger analytical problem with both decisions. If the 10 right to choose suicide with the help of a physician is of constitutional dimension, it is difficult to discern how it can be limited to those who are terminally ill. Terminal illness is not a legal category—it is a medical category, and one that even doctors sometimes have trouble defining. Some of us who teach constitutional law—the old-fashioned types, I suppose—still tell our students that constitutional rights arise by virtue of citizenship, not circumstance. This implies that each of us (each who is a competent adult, at least) possesses an identical set of rights. So if there is indeed a constitutional right to suicide, assisted or not, it must attach to all citizens.

If the right to pursue assistance in suicide attaches to all citizens, 11 then the Constitution is at present being violated by all the state laws permitting the involuntary hospitalization of individuals who try suicide. Instead of locking them up, we should be asking them if they would like assistance in their task. In fact, the Second Circuit has matters precisely backward: if everybody except the terminally ill were allowed to seek the assistance of physicians in suicide, the equal protection claim might have merit. If, on the other hand, the terminally ill are allowed to seek suicide, the court's concern for equality might suggest that everybody should be allowed to do it, lest the state discriminate between two groups who want to die, those who desire to commit suicide because they are terminally ill and those who desire to commit suicide because they are dreadfully unhappy.

Except in emergencies, a court decision is the worst way to resolve 12 a moral dilemma. Constitutional rights, as they mature, have a nagging habit of bursting from the analytical confinements in which they are spawned. When the Supreme Court struck down organized classroom prayer in 1962, nobody other than a few opponents of the rulings, dismissed as cranks, envisioned a future in which courts would order traditional religious language and symbols stripped from official buildings and state seals. And did the justices who voted to legalize abortion in 1973 really imagine that two decades later, the United States would be home to 1.5 million abortions a year?

In the case of the right to assisted suicide, the risks are many. For 13 example, it is far from obvious that the right can be limited to adults. The abortion right isn't. The Supreme Court has ruled that pregnant minors must be allowed to demonstrate to a judge that they are mature enough to make up their own minds about abortion. It does not take much of a stretch to imagine a judge concluding that a young person mature enough to decide that a child should not come into the world is also mature enough to decide that her (or his) own life is not worth living.

And there are other, more ominous difficulties. Some worried med- 14 ical ethicists have predicted that a right to assisted suicide might lead exhausted families to encourage terminally ill relatives to kill themselves. Moreover, women are more likely than men to try suicide, but men succeed much more often than women. With the help of health care workers, women, too, might begin to succeed at a high rate. Is this form of gender equality what we are looking for?

But the biggest problem with the idea of a constitutional right to 15 assisted suicide is that the courts (if the decisions stand) are preempting a moral debate that is, for most Americans, just beginning. To criticize the constitutional foundation for the recent decisions is not at all to suggest that the policy questions are easy ones. There are strong, thoughtful voices—and plausible moral arguments—on both sides of the assisted-suicide debate, as there are in the larger euthanasia debate. The questions are vital ones: Do our mortal lives belong to us alone or do they belong to the communities or families in which we are embedded? Will this new right give the dying a greater sense of control over their circumstances, or will it weaken our respect for life?

These are, as I said, weighty questions, and the policy arguments on either side are the stuff of which public political and moral debates are made. And a thoughtful, well-reasoned debate over assisted suicide is precisely what we as a nation need; we do not need judicial intervention to put a decisive end to a conversation that we as a people have scarcely begun. Because the arguments on both sides carry such strong moral plausibility—and because the claim of constitutional right is anything but compelling—the questions should be answered through popular debate and perhaps legislation, not through legal briefs and litigation. In an ideal world, the Supreme Court would swiftly overturn Quill and Compassion in Dying, allowing the rest of us the space and time for the moral reflection that the issue demands.

Responding to Reading

1. What does Carter mean when he says, "The moral questions raised by assisted suicide are weighty, but our ability as a society to deal with them has been seriously weakened by the judicial rush to enshrine one side's moral answer in the framework of constitutional rights" (6)?

2. Carter argues against making the "right to die" a constitutional right by identifying the problems that would occur if such a right were granted. What are these problems? According to Carter, how should society handle the issue of assisted suicide?

3. Carter criticizes two Supreme Court decisions: *Compassion in Dying v. State of Washington* and *Quill v. Vacco*. How would Jack Kevorkian (p. 587) respond to these decisions? Is Carter sidestepping the moral issue by focusing on the Constitution?

Widening the Focus

- Robert Frost, "The Road Not Taken" (p. 652)

- Sally Thane Christensen, "Is a Tree Worth a Life?" (p. 629)

- Garrett Hardin, "Lifeboat Ethics: The Case Against 'Aid' That Harms" (p. 697)

Responding to the Image

1. This is a photograph of Jack Kevorkian along with television interviewer Barbara Walters wearing a mask connected to a device similar to Kevorkian's Mercitron, the machine he used in numerous assisted suicides (see the selection by Kevorkian on p. 587). Do you feel that Walters in any way trivializes the issue by trying on the mask? Do you see this as legitimate journalism? Why do you think so?

2. Kevorkian has been nicknamed "Dr. Death" by the media. Does this seem to you a legitimate characterization?

––––––––––––––––––––––––– WRITING –––––––––––––––––––––––––

Medicine and Human Values

1. In a 1993 editorial in *Forbes* magazine, publisher Malcolm S. Forbes, Jr., called Dr. Jack Kevorkian a "serial killer" who should be "tried for murder—or at least manslaughter." Write an essay in which you side with either Forbes or Kevorkian, referring to the other essays in the Focus section to support your position. (Keep in mind that Kevorkian is now serving a ten- to twenty-five-year sentence for murder.)

2. What obligation (if any) does the government have to provide health care to people? For example, in what situations should the government provide free medical care? When should the cost of health care be borne by individuals? How should the government pay for the care that you think it should provide? In your essay, refer to Robert Borosage's "Misplaced Priorities: A Focus on Guns" (p. 577) as well as to Garrett Hardin's "Lifeboat Ethics: The Case against 'Aid' That Harms" (p. 697).

3. Assume you are either an animal rights activist or a person who believes that animal experimentation is necessary. Write an editorial for your local newspaper in which you present your case, citing information in Jane Goodall's essay. If you like, you may also refer to Claire McCarthy's "Dog Lab" in Chapter 10 (p. 707).

4. Go to the library or to the Internet and find some information about Margaret Sanger; specifically, consider the public's reaction to her ideas. Then, assume you are Sanger's supervisor. Write a report in which you assess Sanger's actions as a visiting nurse, and decide whether or not you support her decision to discuss birth control with her patients. Keep in mind that to do so in 1912 was against the law.

5. In "What Nurses Stand For," Suzanne Gordon says that the public's lack of concern about the layoffs of nurses "may be couched in the stereotypes of nursing or of women's work in general" (51). Interview several of your friends and family members about their attitudes toward nurses. Find out whether they see them as highly trained professionals or as people who do menial tasks. Then, write an essay in which you discuss your findings.

6. In "Imelda," Richard Selzer considers the limitations of medical science. Choose a medical problem and discuss how it presents challenges for both medical personnel and the general public. If you like, you may refer to the essays by Selzer and Kübler-Ross.

7. Identify a medical advance that has changed either your own life or the life of someone you know. Write an essay in which you discuss

how this development has affected you or the person you know—and, possibly, society as a whole.

8. Assume you are the new director of Anna Mae Halgrim Seaver's nursing home. Write a memo in which you outline changes that would make life in the nursing home better for its residents. In your memo, respond specifically to the points Seaver mentions in her essay.

9. Some people have compared the current AIDS epidemic to the bubonic plague that Barbara Tuchman describes in "The Black Death." Write an essay in which you compare the two diseases. In what ways are they the same, and in what ways are they different? For example, are our attitudes toward AIDS different from those of the people who lived in the fourteenth century toward the bubonic plague? In addition to Tuchman's essay, you may also refer to Robert L. Borosage's "Misplaced Priorities: A Focus on Guns."

10. Do you think a person has a right to die? Under what circumstances? In what way? Who, if anyone, should "assist" the patient? Write an essay in which you discuss these issues. Include information from Dylan Thomas's "Do Not Go Gentle Into That Good Night," Lawrence J. Schneiderman's "The Ethics of Euthanasia," Stephen L. Carter's "Rush to Lethal Judgment," and Jack Kevorkian's "A Case of Assisted Suicide."

11. **For Internet research:** The site <http://www.euthanasia.com> offers extensive information arguing against euthanasia; the site <http://www.choice.org> is devoted to choice in dying. In addition, you can find information about euthanasia laws at <http://www.about.com/msub26.htm>. Use these sites and other sources you find to help you write a news-magazine-style article exploring both sides of this issue.

9

NATURE AND THE
ENVIRONMENT

Over a hundred years ago, essayist Henry David Thoreau, already sensing the dangers of industrialism and expansionism, decided to move into the woods next to Walden Pond to reestablish his connections with nature. To one degree or another, *Walden*, Thoreau's account of his retreat, has influenced many of the writers in this section. Like Thoreau, they are concerned with examining the complex relationship between human beings and the environment; most believe that by ignoring this relationship, human beings help to eliminate scores of species each year, destroy thousands of acres of rain forest, and, ultimately, risk the extinction of all life on earth.

Today, we live in a technological culture, yet nature, with all its majesty, endures. By such phenomena as grass pushing up through cracks in the pavement or dead animals littering the roads, nature reminds us that another, larger world exists outside our limited human sphere. Of course, the price we pay for living in society is our estrangement from the natural environment. We are not estranged in the literal sense of the word, for we are surrounded by the trees in our parks, the animals we keep as pets or in zoos, and the gardens we maintain in our yards. Still, the nature with which we have become familiar has become so domesticated that we have ceased to see it as alien or exotic.

Despite the gulf that seems to separate many contemporary men and women from nature, one thing remains clear: nature continues to affect us in subtle and mysterious ways. As Chief Seattle says in "Letter to President Pierce, 1855," humankind cannot break its contact with nature, for "whatever happens to the beasts also happens to man. All things are connected. Whatever befalls the earth befalls the sons of the earth." In many ways, we are dependent upon our natural environment, and we have a responsibility—perhaps even a duty—to preserve it.

The Focus section in this chapter (p. 637) addresses the question "Who Owns the Land?" The essays in this section examine the complex relationship between human beings and the natural world and raises some troubling questions. For example, do we have the right to exploit the environment for our own benefit, or do we have the obligation to protect and preserve nature for future generations? These questions have no easy answers, yet as the essays in this section illustrate, they are the starting points for most discussions about the environment.

As you read and prepare to write about the essays in this chapter, you may consider the following questions:

- What is the writer's attitude toward nature?

- Is nature seen as hostile or friendly?

- Does the writer present an objective or subjective description of nature?

- Do you think the writer is being realistic or idealistic? Reasonable or unreasonable? Practical or romantic?

- What relationship does the writer think people have with nature? What relationship does he or she think people *ought* to have with nature?

- What does the writer see as the consequences of being separated from nature?

- What effect does interaction with nature have on the writer?

- What preconceived ideas does the writer think people have about nature? Does the writer support or challenge these ideas?

- What effect does the writer think civilization has on nature? Do you agree with the writer?

- In what ways is the essay similar to or different from other essays in this chapter?

LETTER TO PRESIDENT PIERCE, 1855

Chief Seattle

This selection is an 1855 letter to U.S. President Franklin Pierce from Native American Chief Seattle (see p. 392), who served as a mediator between his tribes and the first white settlers in the area around Puget Sound; here, Seattle warns the conquering white nation, "Continue to contaminate your bed, and you will one night suffocate in your own waste."

We know that the white man does not understand our ways. One portion of the land is the same to him as the next, for he is a stranger who comes in the night and takes from the land whatever he needs. The earth is not his brother, but his enemy, and when he has conquered it, he moves on. He leaves his fathers' graves, and his children's birthright is forgotten. The sight of your cities pains the eyes of the red man. But perhaps it is because the red man is a savage and does not understand.

There is no quiet place in the white man's cities. No place to hear the leaves of spring or the rustle of insect's wings. But perhaps because I am a savage and do not understand, the clatter only seems to insult the ears. The Indian prefers the soft sound of the wind darting over the face of the pond, the smell of the wind itself cleansed by a mid-day rain, or scented with the piñon pine. The air is precious to the red man. For all things share the same breath—the beasts, the trees, the man. Like a man dying for many days, he is numb to the stench.

What is man without the beasts? If all the beasts were gone, men would die from great loneliness of spirit, for whatever happens to the beasts also happens to man. All things are connected. Whatever befalls the earth befalls the sons of the earth.

It matters little where we pass the rest of our days; they are not many. A few more hours, a few more winters, and none of the children of the great tribes that once lived on this earth, or that roamed in small bands in the woods, will be left to mourn the graves of a people once as powerful and hopeful as yours.

The whites, too, shall pass—perhaps sooner than other tribes. Continue to contaminate your bed, and you will one night suffocate in your own waste. When the buffalo are all slaughtered, the wild horses all tamed, the secret corners of the forest heavy with the scent of many men, and the view of the ripe hills blotted by talking wires,[1] where is the thicket? Gone. Where is the eagle? Gone. And what is it to say goodby to the swift and the hunt, the end of living and the beginning of survival? We might understand if we knew what it was that the white man dreams, what he describes to his children on the long winter nights, what visions he burns into their minds, so they will wish for tomorrow. But we are savages. The white man's dreams are hidden from us.

Responding to Reading

1. What relationship does Chief Seattle say Native Americans have to the land? In what way does this relationship differ from that of other Americans? Do you think Chief Seattle's assessment of nature is accurate?

---

[1] Telegraph wires. [Eds.]

2. At the end of his letter Chief Seattle says, "But we are savages. The white man's dreams are hidden from us" (5). Why does Chief Seattle call himself a savage? Do you think he wants to be taken literally?
3. How do you think Chief Seattle would react to Al Gore's essay below? Would he be encouraged or discouraged? Explain.

THE WASTELAND

Al Gore

A graduate of Harvard University, Albert Gore (1948–   ) attended both the School of Religion and the School of Law at Vanderbilt University. He was an investigative reporter at the Nashville Tennessean before following his father's footsteps and entering politics. He served Tennessee as a member of the U.S. House of Representatives (1977–1985) and Senator (1985–1993), before assuming the vice presidency, (1993–2001). In 2000, he ran unsuccessfuly for president. The following is an excerpt from Earth in the Balance (1992), Gore's best-selling examination of a wide range of environmental problems. In this excerpt Gore looks specifically at the extent to which we are today "suffocating in our own waste," as Seattle predicted.

One of the clearest signs that our relationship to the global environment is in severe crisis is the floodtide of garbage spilling out of our cities and factories. What some have called the "throwaway society" has been based on the assumptions that endless resources will allow us to produce an endless supply of goods and that bottomless receptacles (i.e., landfills and ocean dumping sites) will allow us to dispose of an endless stream of waste. But now we are beginning to drown in that stream. Having relied for too long on the old strategy of "out of sight, out of mind," we are now running out of ways to dispose of our waste in a manner that keeps it out of either sight or mind.

In an earlier era, when the human population and the quantities of waste generated were much smaller and when highly toxic forms of waste were uncommon, it was possible to believe that the world's absorption of our waste meant that we need not think about it again. Now, however, all that has changed. Suddenly, we are disconcerted— even offended—when the huge quantities of waste we thought we had thrown away suddenly demand our attention as landfills overflow, incinerators foul the air, and neighboring communities and states attempt to dump their overflow problems on us.

The American people have, in recent years, become embroiled in debates about the relative merits of various waste disposal schemes, from dumping it in the ocean to burying it in a landfill to burning it or taking it elsewhere, anywhere, as long as it is somewhere else. Now, however, we must confront a strategic threat to our capacity to dispose of—or even recycle—the enormous quantities of waste now being produced. Simply put, the way we think about waste is leading to the production of so much of it that no method for handling it can escape being completely overwhelmed. There is only one way out: we have to change our production processes and dramatically reduce the amount of waste we create in the first place and ensure that we consider thoroughly, ahead of time, just how we intend to recycle or isolate that which unavoidably remains. But first we have to think clearly about the complexities of the predicament.

Waste is a multifaceted problem. We think of waste as whatever is 4 useless, or unprofitable according to our transitory methods of calculating value, or sufficiently degraded so that the cost of reclamation seems higher than the cost of disposal. But anything produced in excess— nuclear weapons, for example, or junk mail—also represents waste. And in modern civilization, we have come to think of almost any natural resource as "going to waste" if we have failed to develop it, which usually means exploiting it for commercial use. Ironically, however, when we do transform natural resources into something useful, we create waste twice—once when we generate waste as part of the production process and a second time when we tire of the thing itself and throw it away.

Perhaps the most visible evidence of the waste crisis is the problem 5 of how to dispose of our mountains of municipal solid waste, which is being generated at the rate of more than five pounds a day for every citizen of this country, or approximately one ton per person per year. But two other kinds of waste pose equally difficult challenges. The first is the physically dangerous and politically volatile material known as hazardous waste, which accompanied the chemical revolution of the 1930s and which the United States now produces in roughly the same quantities as municipal solid waste. (This is a conservative estimate, one that would double if we counted all the hazardous waste that is currently exempted from regulation for a variety of administrative and political reasons.) Second, one ton of industrial solid waste is created each week for every man, woman, and child—and this does not even count the gaseous waste steadily being vented into the atmosphere. (For example, each person in the United States also produces an average of twenty tons of CO_2[1] each year.) Incredibly, taking into account all three of these conservatively defined categories of waste, every person in the United States produces *more than twice his or her weight in waste every day.*

---

[1] Carbon dioxide. [Eds.]

It's easy to discount the importance of such a statistic, but we can   6
no longer consider ourselves completely separate from the waste we
help to produce at work or the waste that is generated in the process of
supplying us with the things we buy and use.

Our cavalier attitude toward this problem is an indication of how   7
hard it will be to solve. Even the words we use to describe our behavior
reveal the pattern of self-deception. Take, for example, the word *con-*
sumption, which implies an almost mechanical efficiency, suggesting that
all traces of whatever we consume magically vanish after we use it. In
fact, when we consume something, it doesn't go away at all. Rather, it is
transformed into two very different kinds of things: something "useful"
and the stuff left over, which we call "waste." Moreover, anything we
think of as useful becomes waste as soon as we are finished with it, so
our perception of the things we consume must be considered when
deciding what is and isn't waste. Until recently, none of these issues has
seemed terribly important; indeed, a high rate of consumption has often
been cited as a distinguishing characteristic of an advanced society. Now,
however, this attitude can no longer be considered in any way healthy,
desirable, or acceptable.

The waste crisis is integrally related to the crisis of industrial   8
civilization as a whole. Just as our internal combustion engines have
automated the process by which our lungs transform oxygen into carbon dioxide (CO_2), our industrial apparatus has vastly magnified the
process by which our digestive system transforms raw material (food)
into human energy and growth—and waste. Viewed as an extension of
our own consumption process, our civilization now ingests enormous
quantities of trees, coal, oil, minerals, and thousands of substances
taken from their places of discovery, then transforms them into "products" of every shape, kind, and description—and into vast mountain
ranges of waste.

The chemical revolution has burst upon the world with awesome   9
speed. Our annual production of organic chemicals soared from 1 million
tons in 1930 to 7 million tons in 1950, 63 million in 1970, and half a billion
in 1990. At the current rate, world chemical production is now doubling
in volume every seven to eight years. The amount of chemical waste
dumped into landfills, lakes, rivers, and oceans is staggering. In the
United States alone, there are an estimated 650,000 commercial and
industrial sources of hazardous waste; the Environmental Protection
Agency (EPA) believes that 99 percent of this waste comes from only 2
percent of the sources, and an estimated 64 percent of all hazardous waste
is managed at only ten regulated facilities. Two thirds of all hazardous
waste comes from chemical manufacturing and almost one quarter from
the production of metals and machinery. The remaining 11 percent is

divided between petroleum refining (3 percent) and a hundred other smaller categories. According to the United Nations Environment Programme, more than 7 million chemicals have now been discovered or created by humankind, and several thousand new ones are added each year. Of the 80,000 now in common use in significant quantities, most are produced in a manner that also creates chemical waste, much of it hazardous. While many kinds of hazardous chemical waste can be managed fairly easily, other kinds can be extremely dangerous to large numbers of people in even minute quantities. Unfortunately, there is such a wide range of waste labeled "hazardous" that the public is often misled about what is really dangerous and what is not. Most troubling of all, many of the new chemical waste compounds are never tested for their potential toxicity.

In addition, we now produce significant quantities of heavy metal 10 contaminants, like lead and mercury, and medical waste, including infectious waste. Nuclear waste, of course, is the most dangerous of all, since it is highly toxic and remains so for thousands of years. Indeed, the most serious waste problems appear to be those created by federal facilities involved in nuclear weapons production. These problems may have received less attention in the past because most federal facilities are somewhat isolated from their communities. In contrast, the public has become outraged by the dumping of hazardous waste into landfills, because numerous studies and disastrous events have shown that the practice is simply not safe. Basically, the technology for disposing of waste hasn't caught up with the technology of producing it.

Few communities want to serve as a dumping ground for toxic 11 waste; studies have noted the disproportionate number of landfills and hazardous waste facilities in poor and minority areas. For example, a major study, *Toxic Wastes and Race in the United States*, by the United Church of Christ, came to the following conclusion:

> Race proved to be the most significant among variables tested in association with the location of commercial hazardous waste facilities. This represented a consistent national pattern. Communities with the greatest number of commercial hazardous waste facilities had the highest composition of racial and ethnic residents. In communities with two or more facilities or one of the nation's five largest landfills, the average minority percentage of the population was more than three times that of communities without facilities (38% vs. 12%).

It's practically an American tradition: waste has long been dumped 12 on the cheapest, least desirable land in areas surrounded by less fortunate citizens. But the volume of hazardous waste being generated is now so enormous that it is being transported all over the country by haulers who are taking it wherever they can. A few years ago, some were actually dumping it on the roads themselves, opening a faucet underneath the truck and letting the waste slowly drain out as they crossed the countryside. In other cases, hazardous waste was being turned over to unethical haulers controlled by organized crime who dumped the waste on the side of the road in rural areas or into rivers in the middle of the night. There is some evidence that we have made progress in addressing these parts of the problem.

However, the danger we face as a result of improper waste hauling 13 is nothing compared to what happens in most older cities in America every time it rains heavily: huge quantities of raw, untreated sewage are dumped directly into the nearest river, creek, or lake. Since the so-called storm water sewers in these cities were built to connect to the sewer system (before the combined pipes reach the processing plant), the total volume of water during a hard rain is such that the processing plant would be overwhelmed if it didn't simply open the gates, forget about treating the raw sewage, and just dump it directly into the nearest large body of water. This practice is being allowed to continue indefinitely because local officials throughout the country have convinced Congress that the cost of separating the sewers that carry human waste from the sewers that carry rainwater would be greater than the cost of continuing to poison the rivers and oceans. But no effort has been made to calculate the cost of the growing contamination. Could it be because Congress, and indeed this generation of voters, seem to feel that this practice is acceptable because the cost of handling the waste properly will be borne by us, and much of the cost for fouling the environment can be shunted off on our children and their children?

Though federal law purports to prohibit the dumping of municipal 14 sewage and industrial waste into the oceans by 1991, it is obvious that the increasing volumes being generated and the enormous cost of the steps required to prevent ocean dumping will make that deadline laughably irrelevant. Currently, our coastal waters receive 2.3 trillion gallons of municipal effluent and 4.9 billion gallons of industrial wastewater each year, most of which fails to pass muster under the law. Nor are we the only nation guilty of this practice. Germany's river system carries huge quantities of waste toward the sea each day. Most rivers throughout Asia and Europe, Africa and Latin America, are treated as open sewers, especially for industrial waste and sewage. And, the first major tragedy involving chemical waste in the water was in Japan in the 1950s, at Minimata. International cooperative efforts have focused on regional ocean pollution problems, such as the Mediterranean, the North Sea, and the Caribbean.

The disposal of hazardous waste has received a good deal of atten- 15 tion in recent years, though there is still much to be done. For one thing, how do we know which waste is truly hazardous and which isn't? We

can see water, or some kind of liquid, dripping out the bottom of the cars, and some of them contain pure New York garbage." As it turned out, the mayor had agreed to let the hauling company, Tuckasee Inc., bring trash from New York, New Jersey, and Pennsylvania to a landfill thirty-five miles from the railroad siding for a fee of $5 per boxcar, which looked like a good deal for a city whose annual budget is less than $50,000.

Small communities like Mitchellville throughout the Southeast and   23 Midwest are being deluged with shipments of garbage from the Northeast. Rural areas of the western United States are receiving garbage from large cities on the Pacific coast. No wonder that bands of vigilantes have formed to patrol the highways and backroads in areas besieged by trucks of garbage from larger population centers. One of my favorite spoofs on *Saturday Night Live* was a mock commercial for a product called the Yard-a-Pult, a scaled-down model of a medieval catapult, just large enough for the backyard patio, suitable for the launching of garbage bags into your neighbor's property. No need for recycling, incineration, or landfills. The Yard-a-Pult is the ultimate in "out of sight, out of mind" convenience. Unfortunately, the fiction is disturbingly like the reality of our policy for dealing with waste.

Sometimes truth is even stranger than fiction. One of the most   24 bizarre and disturbing consequences of this considerable shipment of waste is the appearance of a new environmental threat called backhauling. Truckers take loads of chemical waste and garbage in one direction and food and bulk liquids (like fruit juice) in the opposite direction—in the same containers. In a lengthy report, the *Seattle Post-Intelligencer* found hundreds of examples of food being carried in containers that had been filled with hazardous waste on the first leg of the journey. Although the trucks were typically washed between loads, the drivers (at some threat to their jobs) described lax inspections, totally inadequate washouts, and the use of liquid deodorizers, themselves dangerous, to mask left-over chemical smells. In 1990, Senators Jim Exon, Slade Gorton, and I joined with Congressman Bill Clinger to pass legislation prohibiting this practice.

But no legislation, by itself, can stop the underlying problem. When   25 one means of disposal is prohibited, the practice continues underground or a new method is found. And what used to be considered unthinkable becomes commonplace because of the incredible pressure from the mounting volumes of waste.

Responding to Reading

1. How does Gore explain why America is called a "throwaway society" (1)? Do you think this characterization is accurate? Has the situation improved since Gore's book was published in 1992?

2. According to Gore, what has changed in recent years that has forced us to reconsider how we dispose of waste? What does he think should be done to alleviate this problem?

3. Much of Gore's essay is devoted to defining the scope of the problem of waste disposal. What examples does Gore use to make his point? How effective are these examples? Does Gore seem optimistic or pessimistic about people's ability to live in harmony with the environment?

MY WOOD

E. M. Forster

British novelist, essayist, and short-story writer E. M. Forster (1879–1969) first won wide recognition with his 1924 novel A Passage to India, *and his novels' popularity has continued, partly because of film versions of* A Passage to India *and* Howards End. *Forster also wrote biographies, literary criticism, and accounts of his travels, as well as* Two Cheers for Democracy, *a 1951 collection of essays. In the following essay from his book* Abinger Harvest *(1936), Forster takes an ironic look at the effect of property ownership on individuals and on society.*

A few years ago I wrote a book which dealt in part with the difficul-   1
ties of the English in India. Feeling that they would have had no difficulties in India themselves, the Americans read the book freely. The more they read it the better it made them feel, and a cheque to the author was the result. I bought a wood with the cheque. It is not a large wood—it contains scarcely any trees, and it is intersected, blast it, by a public footpath. Still, it is the first property that I have owned, so it is right that other people should participate in my shame, and should ask themselves, in accents that will vary in horror, this very important question: What is the effect of property upon the character? Don't let's touch economics; the effect of private ownership upon the community as a whole is another question—a more important question, perhaps, but another one. Let's keep to psychology. If you own things, what's their effect on you? What's the effect on me of my wood?

In the first place, it makes me feel heavy. Property does have this   2
effect. Property produces men of weight, and it was a man of weight who failed to get into the Kingdom of Heaven. He was not wicked, that unfortunate millionaire in the parable, he was only stout; he stuck out in front, not to mention behind, and as he wedged himself this way and that in the crystalline entrance and bruised his well-fed flanks, he saw beneath him a comparatively slim camel passing through the eye of a needle and being woven into the robe of God. The Gospels all through couple stoutness and slowness. They point out what is perfectly obvious,

yet seldom realized: that if you have a lot of things you cannot move about a lot, that furniture requires dusting, dusters require servants, servants require insurance stamps, and the whole tangle of them makes you think twice before you accept an invitation to dinner or go for a bathe in the Jordan. Sometimes the Gospels proceed further and say with Tolstoy that property is sinful; they approach the difficult ground of asceticism here, where I cannot follow them. But as to the immediate effects of property on people, they just show straightforward logic. It produces men of weight. Men of weight cannot, by definition, move like the lightning from the East unto the West, and the ascent of a fourteen-stone bishop into a pulpit is thus the exact antithesis of the coming of the Son of Man. My wood makes me feel heavy.

In the second place, it makes me feel it ought to be larger.   3

The other day I heard a twig snap in it. I was annoyed at first, for   4 I thought that someone was blackberrying, and depreciating the value of the undergrowth. On coming nearer, I saw it was not a man who had trodden on the twig and snapped it, but a bird, and I felt pleased. My bird. The bird was not equally pleased. Ignoring the relation between us, it took fright as soon as it saw the shape of my face, and flew straight over the boundary hedge into a field, the property of Mrs. Henessy, where it sat down with a loud squawk. It had become Mrs. Henessy's bird. Something seemed grossly amiss here, something that would not have occurred had the wood been larger. I could not afford to buy Mrs. Henessy out, I dared not murder her, and limitations of this sort beset me on every side. Ahab did not want that vineyard—he only needed it to round off his property, preparatory to plotting a new curve—and all the land around my wood has become necessary to me in order to round off the wood. A boundary protects. But—poor little thing—the boundary ought in its turn to be protected. Noises on the edge of it. Children throw stones. A little more, and then a little more, until we reach the sea. Happy Canute! Happier Alexander! And after all, why should even the world be the limit of possession? A rocket containing a Union Jack, will, it is hoped, be shortly fired at the moon. Mars. Sirius. Beyond which . . . But these immensities ended by saddening me. I could not suppose that my wood was the destined nucleus of universal dominion—it is so very small and contains no mineral wealth beyond the blackberries. Nor was I comforted when Mrs. Henessy's bird took alarm for the second time and flew clean away from us all, under the belief that it belonged to itself.

In the third place, property makes its owner feel that he ought to do   5 something to it. Yet he isn't sure what. A restlessness comes over him, a vague sense that he has a personality to express—the same sense which, without any vagueness, leads the artist to an act of creation. Sometimes I think I will cut down such trees as remain in the wood, at other times I want to fill up the gaps between them with new trees. Both impulses are pretentious and empty. They are not honest movements towards money-making or beauty. They spring from a foolish desire to express myself and from an inability to enjoy what I have got. Creation, property, enjoyment form a sinister trinity in the human mind. Creation and enjoyment are both very, very good, yet they are often unattainable without a material basis, and at such moments property pushes itself in as a substitute, saying, "Accept me instead—I'm good enough for all three." It is not enough. It is, as Shakespeare said of lust, "The expense of spirit in a waste of shame": it is "Before, a joy proposed; behind, a dream." Yet we don't know how to shun it. It is forced on us by our economic system as the alternative to starvation. It is also forced on us by an internal defect in the soul, by the feeling that in property may lie the germs of self-development and of exquisite or heroic deeds. Our life on earth is, and ought to be, material and carnal. But we have not yet learned to manage our materialism and carnality properly; they are still entangled with the desire for ownership, where (in the words of Dante) "Possession is one with loss."

And this brings us to our fourth and final point: the blackberries.   6

Blackberries are not plentiful in this meager grove, but they are eas-   7
ily seen from the public footpath which traverses it, and all too easily gathered. Foxgloves, too—people will pull up the foxgloves, and ladies of an educational tendency even grub for toadstools to show them on the Monday in class. Other ladies, less educated, roll down the bracken in the arms of their gentlemen friends. There is paper, there are tins. Pray, does my wood belong to me or doesn't it? And, if it does, should I not own it best by allowing no one else to walk there? There is a wood near Lyme Regis, also cursed by a public footpath, where the owner has not hesitated on this point. He had built high stone walls each side of the path, and has spanned it by bridges, so that the public circulate like termites while he gorges on the blackberries unseen. He really does own his wood, this able chap. Dives in Hell did pretty well, but the gulf dividing him from Lazarus could be traversed by vision, and nothing traverses it here. And perhaps I shall come to this in time. I shall wall in and fence out until I really taste the sweets of property. Enormously stout, endlessly avaricious, pseudo-creative, intensely selfish, I shall weave upon my forehead the quadruple crown of possession until those nasty Bolshies come and take it off again and thrust me aside into the outer darkness.

Responding to Reading

1. According to Forster, what are the effects on him of owning his wood? Would you say that these effects are positive or negative?

2. What does this essay reveal about Forster's attitudes toward owning property? Toward individual freedom? Toward nature?
3. How convincing are Forster's conclusions? Do think that Forster could be accused of overstating his case? Explain.

THE OBLIGATION TO ENDURE

Rachel Carson

Naturalist and environmentalist Rachel Carson (1907–1964) was a specialist in marine biology. She won the National Book Award for The Sea around Us *(1951), which, like her other books, appeals to scientists and laypeople alike. While working as an aquatic biologist for the U.S. Fish and Wildlife Service, Carson became concerned about ecological hazards and wrote* Silent Spring *(1962), in which she warned readers about the indiscriminate use of pesticides. This book influenced President John F. Kennedy to begin investigations into this and other environmental problems. In the selection from* Silent Spring *that follows, Carson urges us to question the use of chemical pesticides.*

The history of life on earth has been a history of interaction between living things and their surroundings. To a large extent, the physical form and the habits of the earth's vegetation and its animal life have been molded by the environment. Considering the whole span of earthly time, the opposite effect, in which life actually modifies its surroundings, has been relatively slight. Only within the moment of time represented by the present century has one species—man—acquired significant power to alter the nature of his world.

During the past quarter century this power has not only increased to one of disturbing magnitude but it has changed in character. The most alarming of all man's assaults upon the environment is the contamination of air, earth, rivers, and sea with dangerous and even lethal materials. This pollution is for the most part irrecoverable; the chain of evil it initiates not only in the world that must support life but in living tissues is for the most part irreversible. In this now universal contamination of the environment, chemicals are the sinister and little-recognized partners of radiation in changing the very nature of the world—the very nature of its life. Strontium 90, released through nuclear explosions into the air, comes to earth in rain or drifts down in fallout, lodges in soil, enters into the grass or corn or wheat grown there, and in time takes up its abode in the bones of a human being, there to remain until his death. Similarly, chemicals sprayed on croplands or forests or gardens lie long in soil, entering into living organisms, passing from one to another in a chain of poisoning and death. Or they pass mysteriously by underground streams until they emerge and, through the alchemy of air and sunlight, combine into new forms that kill vegetation, sicken cattle, and work unknown harm on those who drink from once pure wells. As Albert Schweitzer[1] has said, "Man can hardly even recognize the devils of his own creation."

It took hundreds of millions of years to produce the life that now 3 inhabits the earth—eons of time in which that developing and evolving and diversifying life reached a state of adjustment and balance with its surroundings. The environment, rigorously shaping and directing the life it supported, contained elements that were hostile as well as supporting. Certain rocks gave out dangerous radiation; even within the light of the sun, from which all life draws its energy, there were shortwave radiations with power to injure. Given time—time not in years but in millennia—life adjusts, and a balance has been reached. For time is the essential ingredient; but in the modern world there is no time.

The rapidity of change and the speed with which new situations are 4 created follow the impetuous and heedless pace of man rather than the deliberate pace of nature. Radiation is no longer merely the background radiation of rocks, the bombardment of cosmic rays, the ultraviolet of the sun that have existed before there was any life on earth; radiation is now the unnatural creation of man's tampering with the atom. The chemicals to which life is asked to make its adjustment are no longer merely the calcium and silica and copper and all the rest of the minerals washed out of the rocks and carried in rivers to the sea; they are the synthetic creations of man's inventive mind, brewed in his laboratories, and having no counterparts in nature.

To adjust to these chemicals would require time on the scale that is 5 nature's; it would require not merely the years of a man's life but the life of generations. And even this, were it by some miracle possible, would be futile, for the new chemicals come from our laboratories in an endless stream; almost five hundred annually find their way into actual use in the United States alone. The figure is staggering and its implications are not easily grasped—500 new chemicals to which the bodies of men and animals are required somehow to adapt each year, chemically totally outside the limits of biologic experience.

Among them are many that are used in man's war against nature. 6 Since the mid-1940s over 200 basic chemicals have been created for use in killing insects, weeds, rodents, and other organisms described in the modern vernacular as "pests"; and they are sold under several thousand different brand names.

---

[1] Prominent theologian (1875–1965) honored for his work as a scientist, humanitarian, musician, and religious thinker. In 1952, he was awarded the Nobel Peace Prize. [Eds.]

Another factor in the modern insect problem is one that must be   17
viewed against a background of geologic and human history: the spreading of thousands of different kinds of organisms from their native homes
to invade new territories. This worldwide migration has been studied
and graphically described by the British ecologist Charles Elton in his
recent book *The Ecology of Invasions*. During the Cretaceous Period, some
hundred million years ago, flooding seas cut many land bridges between
continents and living things found themselves confined in what Elton
calls "colossal separate nature reserves." There, isolated from others of
their kind, they developed many new species. When some of the land
masses were joined again, about 15 million years ago, these species began
to move out into new territories—a movement that is not only still in
progress but is now receiving considerable assistance from man.

The importation of plants is the primary agent in the modern   18
spread of species, for animals have almost invariably gone along with
the plants, quarantine being a comparatively recent and not completely
effective innovation. The United States Office of Plant Introduction
alone has introduced almost 200,000 species and varieties of plants from
all over the world. Nearly half of the 180 or so major insect enemies of
plants in the United States are accidental imports from abroad, and
most of them have come as hitchhikers on plants.

In new territory, out of reach of the restraining hand of the natural   19
enemies that kept down its numbers in its native land, an invading
plant or animal is able to become enormously abundant. Thus it is no
accident that our most troublesome insects are introduced species.

These invasions, both the naturally occurring and those dependent   20
on human assistance, are likely to continue indefinitely. Quarantine and
massive chemical campaigns are only extremely expensive ways of
buying time. We are faced, according to Dr. Elton, "with a life-and-death
need not just to find new technological means of suppressing this plant
or that animal"; instead we need the basic knowledge of animal populations and their relations to their surroundings that will "promote an
even balance and damp down the explosive power of outbreaks and
new invasions."

Much of the necessary knowledge is now available but we do not   21
use it. We train ecologists in our universities and even employ them in
our governmental agencies but we seldom take their advice. We allow
the chemical death rain to fall as though there were no alternative,
whereas in fact there are many, and our ingenuity could soon discover
many more if given opportunity.

Have we fallen into a mesmerized state that makes us accept as   22
inevitable that which is inferior or detrimental, as though having lost
the will or the vision to demand that which is good? Such thinking, in
the words of the ecologist Paul Shepard, "idealizes life with only its
head out of water, inches above the limits of toleration of the corruption

of its own environment. . . . Why should we tolerate a diet of weak poisons, a home in insipid surroundings, a circle of acquaintances who are not quite our enemies, the noise of motors with just enough relief to prevent insanity? Who would want to live in a world which is just not quite fatal?"

Yet such a world is pressed upon us. The crusade to create a chem- 23 ically sterile, insect-free world seems to have engendered a fanatic zeal on the part of many specialists and most of the so-called control agencies. On every hand there is evidence that those engaged in spraying operations exercise a ruthless power. "The regulatory entomologists[2] . . . function as prosecutor, judge and jury, tax assessor and collector and sheriff to enforce their own orders," said Connecticut entomologist Neely Turner. The most flagrant abuses go unchecked in both state and federal agencies.

It is not my contention that chemical insecticides must never be 24 used. I do contend that we have put poisonous and biologically potent chemicals indiscriminately into the hands of persons largely or wholly ignorant of their potentials for harm. We have subjected enormous numbers of people to contact with these poisons, without their consent and often without their knowledge. If the Bill of Rights contains no guarantee that a citizen shall be secure against lethal poisons distributed either by private individuals or by public officials, it is surely only because our forefathers, despite their considerable wisdom and foresight, could conceive of no such problem.

I contend, furthermore, that we have allowed these chemicals to be 25 used with little or no advance investigation of their effect on soil, water, wildlife, and man himself. Future generations are unlikely to condone our lack of prudent concern for the integrity of the natural world that supports all life.

There is still very limited awareness of the nature of the threat. This 26 is an era of specialists, each of whom sees his own problem and is unaware of or intolerant of the larger frame into which it fits. It is also an era dominated by industry, in which the right to make a dollar at whatever cost is seldom challenged. When the public protests, confronted with some obvious evidence of damaging results of pesticide applications, it is fed little tranquilizing pills of half truth. We urgently need an end to these false assurances, to the sugar coating of unpalatable facts. It is the public that is being asked to assume the risks that the insect controllers calculate. The public must decide whether it wishes to continue on the present road, and it can do so only when in full possession of the facts. In the words of Jean Rostand, "The obligation to endure gives us the right to know."

---

[2] Scientists who study insects. [Eds.]

Responding to Reading

1. After this essay was written, DDT was banned. Recently, however, some scientists have suggested that because some insects have developed resistance to safer insecticides, spraying of DDT should be reinstituted on a limited basis. How would Carson respond to this suggestion? Do you think health considerations and the need for food should outweigh the environmental hazards of spraying DDT?

2. In paragraph 9 of her essay, Carson says that along with the possibility of nuclear extinction, "the central problem of our age has . . . become the contamination of man's total environment." Is she exaggerating? Is her assessment accurate?

3. Should Carson have devoted more time to describing the "interaction between living things and their surroundings" (1)—for example, by showing what we have lost and what we have to lose? What in particular could she have described?

Recycling: No Panacea

William Rathje and Cullen Murphy

Anthropologist William Rathje (1945–   ) was born in South Bend, Indiana, and graduated from the University of Arizona, later receiving his doctorate from Harvard. Since 1971, he has taught at the University of Arizona, where he directs the Garbage Project; students working with the project analyze public landfills as though they were archaeological digs, quantifying the contents as a way of evaluating the kinds of waste generated by Americans and of providing solutions for reducing this waste. Cullen Murphy (1952–   ) was born in New Rochelle, New York, and received his B.A. from Amherst College. He is the managing editor of the Atlantic Monthly, *and for many years, he has also written the text for the "Prince Valiant" comic strip (his father is the artist). A collection of his essays,* Just Curious, *was published in 1995. Rathje and Cullen joined forces to write* Rubbish! The Archaeology of Garbage *(1992), based on Rathje's work with the Garbage Project. The book, according to one critic, "put[s] important garbage issues in perspective; it demolishes myths that hamper our ability to act sensibly; as a nice bonus, it entertains as it goes about its business." In the following section from* Rubbish! *the authors argue that many environmentally conscious Americans put far too much faith in recycling as a cure for our environmental woes.*

Recycling is a necessary component of a sound solid-waste-manage-   1
ment program. Properly conceived and executed, a recycling program can make good economic sense, can help save natural resources, can help reduce pollution, and can divert some tributaries of the solid-waste

stream away from landfills. These are all essential goals. There is no reason, however, for recycling to become an individual or social obsession. Indeed, when recycling does become an obsession in a society, it is sometimes a sign that important aspects of that society have gone seriously awry; as they have, for example, in the Soviet Union, where the scarcity of even the most basic consumer goods has driven the populace to the most desperate frenzies of recycling imaginable. Still, without becoming obsessed by recycling there are useful, pragmatic steps that Americans can and should take to bolster the recycling enterprise—in particular by fostering demand for recycled materials. These steps include buying consumer goods that have truly been made from recycled materials (beware of misleading claims on the packaging) and buying consumer goods that, once discarded, will have the most resale value for the recyclers. . . .

In the meantime it must be remembered that while recycling is one 2 valuable way of coping with America's—or any society's—solid waste, it is by no means a panacea. Yes, from a narrow, technical perspective almost anything that one might find in municipal solid waste *could* be thought of as being somehow recyclable or reusable; the problem is finding significant outlets for such recycled or reused products that also make economic, political, environmental, and psychological sense.

For one thing, it is not farfetched to think that recycling may one day 3 be met with antagonism by its erstwhile middle-class allies. Despite the virtuous public image that recycling possesses when considered in the abstract, in the real world recycling could find its reputation tarnished. There have already been reports, for example, of inroads into the recycling business by organized crime. On a more mundane level, garbage-sorting centers and recycling centers, like any public-works projects, are increasingly becoming objects of NIMBY-type opposition.[1] Most recycling centers and plants are nothing more than enclosed spaces where presorted cans, bottles, and newspapers are temporarily stored or, at worst, where mixed recyclables passing by on conveyer belts are separated by human hands. They do not belch noxious fumes. The work being done inside them may very well be God's. But, BUT, they bear the unholy taint of garbage. And don't forget all those trucks coming and going all day long. As the collection and sorting of garbage for recycling become a growing and regular part of our lives, so will protests against conducting these activities anyplace nearby.

The large-scale composting of municipal solid waste is touted by 4 many as one way of recycling the 5 to 20 percent of household garbage that consists of yard waste and food waste. (The yard-waste volume varies considerably by region.) But composting also confronts NIMBY problems, and environmental concerns of other kinds as well.

---

[1] NIMBY is an acronym for "not in my back yard." [Eds.]

Composting is an ancient practice—there is evidence that composting pits were in use at Knossos, in Crete, some four thousand years ago—and in theory composting seems compelling and attractive. Yard waste has been banned from landfills in more than ten states precisely in order to encourage small-scale composting at home, and a number of companies now sell small plastic "green cones" for this purpose. Large-scale composting of municipal solid waste is something of a different proposition. The enormous volume of rich humus that results from large-scale composting has a variety of commercial uses, and the Europeans began resorting to a significant amount of composting years ago. But composting is expensive. Composting yards are also big, and they can smell; siting them may not prove to be as difficult as siting landfills, but doing so will still take a lot of work. Moreover, if precautions are not taken to prevent certain kinds of biodegradable garbage from joining the compost piles, the compost can become tainted with hazardous elements, such as the heavy metals in inks and pigments. Yard waste may contain traces of pesticides and herbicides. Composting is only just getting under way in the United States, and there are as yet fewer than a hundred composting plants planned or in operation, most of them small. A lot of thought is being given by composting proponents to ways of dampening potential opposition (such as making sure that the composting piles are physically enclosed, to contain "fugitive odors"). But this industry, if such it becomes, is starting out with some handicaps.

Recycling of other kinds exacts an environmental price. The reuse 5 of paper, for example, involves processes that generate a considerable amount of hazardous waste. In order to recycle newspapers, magazines, and, indeed, any printed paper, the paper must first be de-inked. At the end of the de-inking process one is left with essentially two products: on the one hand, de-inked fiber that will be turned into new paper; and on the other, a large quantity of toxic sludge. The recycling of iron and steel, of aluminum, and of plastics, for their part, also result in the production of various kinds of toxic waste and in air emissions that may be hazardous. A 1988 U.S. Office of Technology Assessment report on solid waste observed bluntly of recycling that "it is usually not clear whether secondary manufacturing produces less pollution per ton of material processed than primary manufacturing."

Another vexing reality that communities must confront is that recy- 6 cling can be expensive. A myth was once abroad that recycling was not only an environmentally sound garbage-disposal option but also a potential money-maker or at least money-saver. That this was going to be the case was at least implicitly the notion that lay behind the various "zero-net-cost" recycling schemes many communities adopted. The idea here is that when a city (for example) considers bids from independent recyclers for handling its recycling program, the amount the city finally agrees to pay per ton must be no greater than the cheapest available disposal method other than recycling (which is usually landfilling, the high cost of which in some places is what makes recycling attractive to begin with). The assumption, of course, was that the recycling agency would earn enough from sales of recyclables to more than offset the difference, if any, between city fees and the actual cost of operations. This frequently has turned out not to be the case for private recyclers of household-level commodities, and the same economic realities that bedevil them, of course, also bedevil recycling programs operated by communities themselves. From the start, recyclers have been beset by slumps in commodities prices. The cost of collection programs is high to begin with—think of the capital investment required for new kinds of trucks. There have also been unexpected problems. One major glitch collection programs have faced: the inability of many consumers to sort their recyclables properly prior to pickup, resulting in "contaminated" deliveries that may be rejected by buyers or must be sold for reduced prices. Most cities have had to set up costly labor-intensive or mechanical sorting operations to sort once more the garbage that households have already sorted.

The problem of improper sorting by households is pervasive. The 7 Garbage Project last year sampled the sorting behavior of twenty randomly selected households in a middle-income neighborhood in Tucson. Under the rules of the local curbside recycling program, residents were to separate out all recyclables and place them in a special blue bag. The rest of the garbage was to go into the traditional garbage can. What is and is not recyclable depends, of course, on what the community has decided to recycle, and all participants in the recycling program were given clear definitions of what should and should not go into the blue bag. The results of the Garbage Project's survey of the contents of the twenty blue bags and the garbage cans that went with them were not really unexpected. Taken together, the discards in the blue bags weighed 318 pounds, but fifty of those pounds were taken up by nonrecyclables. Every household made mistakes, either by contaminating the recyclable bag or throwing recyclables into the garbage cans. Indeed, fully half of all the aluminum cans thrown away were found not in the recyclable bag but in the garbage can.

This is why materials-recovery facilities (MRFs) are needed. Once 8 again the American consumer has proved capable of dashing the fondest of hopes. The inevitable consequence of this and other developments is that, far from being a gold mine, recycling will be a procedure—a worthwhile procedure—for which communities must pay considerable sums, often unexpectedly, perhaps consoling themselves with the recognition that resources have been conserved and that some garbage has been kept out of landfills and incinerators.

A further reality that will become apparent with time is that some 9 significant elements of the solid-waste stream that are without question recyclable will prove resistant, for a variety of reasons, to all attempts to recycle them. Rubber tires have so far proved to be a case in point. Tires are every landfill manager's nightmare. They possess a peculiar property: Bury them in a landfill and over time they will slowly rise and eventually emerge onto the surface, as if all the raisins in a loaf of bread had ascended to the top. (One explanation given for this phenomenon is that landfill compactors initially compress the hollow, newly arrived tires, but that over time the tires expand back into the original shape; the act of expansion gradually takes them upwards because the garbage above them is always less compact than the garbage below. An alternative explanation—which also explains how rocks rise to the surface of a pasture—attributes the phenomenon to temperature fluctuations that cause the tire to expand and contract, with small particles drifting into the tiny void that forms under the tire after each contraction; slowly but surely the tire works its way to the surface.) Periodically landfill operators skim the landfill surface with a special vehicle that picks up the latest crop; this is the source of those large tire islands that one sees alongside most landfills, and that every so often ignite uncontrollably and blacken the skies for weeks. In theory, tires would seem an ideal candidate for recycling. There are lots of them—200 million are thrown away every year. They are relatively homogeneous. They even, as we have seen, eerily separate themselves from all the other garbage. And yet nothing that has yet been tried—not using them to make road surfaces or airport runways, not burning them (along with coal) as fuel, not using them for artificial reefs—has made anyone terribly excited (or made anyone much money).

Finally, to repeat, recycling can be a surpassingly fragile enterprise. 10 There are many variables, and their configuration from place to place must dictate strategy and tactics. Some kinds of recycling, such as of aluminum cans, probably make sense everywhere. Other kinds, such as of newsprint, may not. Homogeneity of materials may be a necessity when it comes to recycling, but homogeneity of policy across geographical boundaries ought not to be the watchword with respect to how much of what kinds of garbage America's communities should be recycling. The key is to maintain a tautness between supply and demand, a task that is not always easy and, frankly, not always possible. It may become increasingly difficult as the many collection programs that have been enacted into law begin to take hold, and the volume of recyclables on the market suddenly doubles or triples. What may seem like "success" in the eyes of those who run local recycling programs—an outpouring of public cooperation, an Everest of sorted trash—can at times spell failure for the system as a whole, dooming truckloads of recyclables to be dumped into landfills (as some are even now), driving local programs bankrupt, and, depending on the degree of overabundance of this or that, and its effect on prices, even threatening the health of scrap dealers. Too many communities around the country are now reading headlines like this one from a Boston-area newspaper, *The Enterprise* (Brockton): "RECYCLING WORKING TOO WELL; Industry Can't Handle Glut of Materials." Too many are now reading headlines like this one from *The New York Times:* "Our Towns: When Recycling Means Too Much of a Good Thing." Or this one from Waste Age: "Recyclers Brace for Office Paper Oversupply." It would be an ironic consequence indeed if recycling were undermined by the best of intentions.

The messages to recycling activists: Pay attention to these market 11 factors. Make sure that people in local communities understand the sometimes fickle dynamics of the recycling process. And make sure they understand that recycling has not happened until the loop has been closed.

Responding to Reading

1. What mistaken ideas do Rathje and Murphy assume their readers have about recycling? Where in their essay do they address these misconceptions? What do they gain by discussing them at this point?
2. Rathje and Murphy say that recycling may one day "be met with antagonism by its erstwhile middle-class allies"(3). Why? What can be done to prevent this reaction?
3. What do Rathje and Murphy mean when they say that "recycling has not happened until the loop has been closed" (11)?

SHADES OF GREEN

Jedediah Purdy

Jedidiah Purdy (1976–   ) grew up in rural West Virginia, the child of parents who had been part of the countercultural movement. Home-schooled until his teens, Purdy attended Phillips Exeter Academy and later graduated from Harvard University, with a major in social studies, and from the Yale School of Law. His 1999 book, For Common Things: Irony, Trust, and Commitment in America, *drew considerable attention, in part because of its thesis regarding the decline of commitment to principle in the United States and in part because Purdy was only twenty-three at the time. He is currently a senior correspondent for* The American Prospect *magazine and is researching issues of agriculture, environmental sustainability, and the role of work in American life. The following essay appeared in the* American Prospect *in January 2000.*

More than two-thirds of Americans call themselves environmental- 1 ists. Their rank includes every serious presidential candidate, a growing list of corporate executives, some of the country's most extreme radicals, and ordinary people from just about every region, class, and ethnic group. Even allowing for some hypocrisy, finding consensus so tightly overlaid on division is reason for a closer look.

In fact, there are several environmentalisms in this country, and there 2 have been for a long time. They are extensions of some of the most persistent strands of American thought and political culture. They stand for different and sometimes conflicting policy agendas, and their guiding concerns are often quite widely divergent. Recently, though, they have begun to contemplate a set of issues that promises to transform each of them and to expand environmental politics from its traditional concern with a limited number of wild places and species to a broader commitment to the environment as the place where we all live, all the time.

The oldest and most familiar version of environmental concern might 3 be called romantic environmentalism. Still a guiding spirit of the Sierra Club and the soul of the Wilderness Society and many regional groups, this environmentalism arises from love of beautiful landscapes: the highest mountains, deepest canyons, and most ancient forests. As a movement, it began in the late nineteenth century when America's wealthy discovered outdoor recreation and, inspired by writers like Sierra Club founder John Muir, developed a reverence for untamed places. For these American romantics, encounters with the wild promised to restore bodies and spirits worn down by civilized life.

Today's romantic environmentalists blend this ambition with a 4 delight in whales, wolves, and distant rain forests. More than any other environmentalists, they—still disproportionately white and prosperous—feel a spiritual attachment to natural places.

Muir's environmentalism contains the idea that our true selves await 5 us in the wild. Another type, managerial environmentalism, puts the wild at our service. This approach is a direct descendant of the Progressive era's hopeful reformism, specifically of Teddy Roosevelt's forestry policies; it makes its basic task the fitting together of ecology and economy to advance human ends. Pragmatic, market oriented, but respectful of public institutions, managerial environmentalists design trading schemes for pollution permits at the Natural Resources Defense Council, head up programs at the Environmental Protection Agency (EPA) to collaborate with businesses in developing clean technologies, and envision global environmental standards advancing alongside free trade accords. In their wildeyed moments, they imagine environmental standards advancing alongside free trade accords. In their wildeyed moments, they imagine a high-tech economy that follows nature in producing no waste or, like *The New Republic's* senior editor Gregg Easterbrook, genetic engineering that will turn carnivores into grass eaters and bring lion and lamb together at last. Although it began among policy makers, this managerial attitude is gaining ground in the optimistic culture of Silicon Valley and has many adherents younger than 35.

The environmental justice movement is another thing entirely. Only 6
an idea a decade ago, this effort to address the relationships among race,
poverty, and environmental harm has come to rapid prominence.
Grass-roots projects in inner cities and industrial areas around the country have drawn attention to urban air pollution, lead paint, transfer
stations for municipal garbage and hazardous waste, and other environmental dangers that cluster in poor and minority neighborhoods. Eight
years ago, romantic environmentalism was virtually the only movement
that engaged students on college campuses; now young activists are
equally likely to talk about connections between the environment and
social justice, or on an international scale, the environment and human
rights.

Environmental justice follows the tradition of social inclusion and 7
concern for equity that had its last great triumphs during the civil rights
movement and the War on Poverty. Some of its landmark moments are
court cases ruling that federal projects can be challenged when they
concentrate environmental harm in minority areas, which have begun
to extend the principles of civil rights to environmental policy.

The environmental justice movement also reflects the populist 8
streak that emerges in American politics wherever an isolated community finds itself up against big and anonymous institutions. Activists
and community members tend to mistrust big business and government alike. The constituency of the environmental justice movement
often perceives the gap between the prosperous and the poor, between
whites and minorities, between mainstream culture and their own communities, as much more basic than the difference between the EPA and
Monsanto. All outsiders are on the other side of that gap—an impression that has been reinforced where some local Sierra Club chapters
have ignored community health issues and have endorsed proposals to
put waste dumps in poor neighborhoods rather than in pristine valleys.

Environmental justice advocates have little patience for romantic 9
environmentalism, and their culture of perpetual embattlement is
worlds away from managerial optimism. When "environmentalists" of
such different experiences and sensibilities address the same issue, it is
no surprise that misunderstanding and acrimony sometimes result.
This tension was evident two years ago when the Sierra Club came close
to endorsing strict controls on immigration to slow development and
resource use in this country. The organization's justice-oriented members were outraged, as they had been over the waste-siting disputes a
few years earlier. For the pure romantics, the concerns about poor communities and international equity didn't seem "environmental" at all.
Meanwhile, the impassioned dispute was all rather alien to the measured rationality of the managerial environmentalists' plans for efficient
resource use.

But our several environmentalisms are learning from their interac- 10 tions, and it is possible that the lessons will be good for them all. Romantic environmentalism has long withheld itself from cities, suburbs, and factories, sometimes following Muir in treating these as fallen places where nothing beautiful will grow. The other environmentalisms have challenged this idea by insisting that "the environment" means the space where we live and work, that the built environment of Manhattan and the industrial environment of the lower Mississippi matter as much as the ecosystem of Yellowstone.

The change brings environmental concern home to cities and neigh- 11 borhoods, where people live. This domesticated environmentalism is crystallized in the debates about sprawl, "smart growth," and the design of communities.

It is powered by the recognition that the way we now pursue the 12 things we seem to want—space, light, some trees, a little peace and quiet—can leave us feeling overcrowded and isolated, spending too much time in our cars, living and working in spaces that do not inspire our affection. Communities that decide to make walking or bicycling easy, develop dense housing in return for set-asides of open space, and foster neighborhoods where living, working, and shopping all happen on the same block, are addressing an environmental problem with an environmental solution. This is an environmentalism that urges not just setting aside a piece of wilderness for occasional visits but changing the way we live every day—the way we spend our money, build our homes, and move from place to place.

Attention to these domesticated environmental concerns thus cor- 13 rects a huge blind spot in romantic environmentalism's sometimes exclusive commitment to wilderness. It can also help to bridge a basic gap in the policy proposals of managerial environmentalism. Those proposals concentrate on technological innovation: taxing greenhouse gases, devising permit systems for pollution, and otherwise inventing better devices for living as we already do. The paradox that dogs the managers is that because their policy proposals generally cost money to ordinary people, big industry, or both, they stand little chance without a ground swell of popular support; yet they are just the thing to induce a fit of napping in the average citizen, whose visceral concern for the environment does not carry over into an interest in the tax code. Policies that foster, say, responsible logging, farming for stewardship, or sustainable grazing on public lands have more appeal when they come not as insights of microeconomic analysis and resource management but as part of a proposal that the work we do in nature is more appealing and honorable when it respects nature's requirements. Most of us care little about supply and demand curves, but a fair amount about where we live and how we work. Because it is close to the grain of everyday experience, the language of livable communities and environmentally responsible work can make environmental policy-designers more politically effective.

As for the environmental justice movement, it fits here as the Alabama bus boycotts fit into the 1964 Civil Rights Act. It fights against particular, sometimes quite outrageous, injustices. Its work is right and necessary but not usually connected with a broader agenda for sustaining dignified communities. Yet such an agenda needs not just constituents who are suburbanites upset by sprawl, but the people who suffer most from poor policies on toxics, land use, and transportation: the urban and rural poor. Moreover, a systematic response to the systematic problems those communities face is the only just way to end their thousands of brushfire struggles.

So one possible result of the present trends in environmental politics is a broader, more effective environmental movement. Such a movement might propose that we should need neither to withdraw our innermost selves to the woods nor to experience our neighborhoods as a species of oppression. It would make the human environment a complete and honored portion of environmental politics. Pursuing such goals would require romantics to bring some of their aspirations home from the wilderness, policy specialists to get their hands dirty in a political culture that does not yield to economists' graphs, and environmental justice activists to find reason to turn their populist anger to projects on common ground. None of our several environmentalisms will go away, and none should, but they are all better off with the recognition that the environment is very much a political, cultural, and human affair.

Responding to Reading

1. What are the "several environmentalisms" that Purdy discusses? In what ways are they different from one another?
2. According to Purdy, "Environmental justice advocates have little patience for romantic environmentalism, and their culture of perpetual embattlement is worlds away from managerial optimism" (9). What tensions exist among the advocates of the different environmental movements? Does Purdy think this tension is good or bad?
3. What kind of environmental movement would Purdy like to see in the future? How realistic do his ideas seem?

IS A TREE WORTH A LIFE?

Sally Thane Christensen

A native of Missoula, Montana, and a federal attorney who represents the U.S. Forest Service, Sally Thane Christensen (1954–1992) contributed the following essay to Newsweek *magazine's "My Turn" column in 1991. "My Turn" provides a forum in which readers offer their personal perspectives on a variety of social, cultural, political, and ethical issues. In her column, Christensen describes the potential cancer-fighting substance provided by the bark of the Pacific yew tree and argues that it is wrong for environmentalists to block harvesting of the tree out of a misplaced concern that it may be endangered.*

For most of the last decade, federal timberlands in the West have 1 been held hostage in a bitter fight between environmental groups and the timber industry. The environmentalists want to save the forests and their wildlife occupants. The timber industry wants to cut trees and provide jobs in a depressed economy. Caught in the middle is the United States Forest Service, which must balance the conflicting concepts of sustained yield and multiple use of national forest land.

The latest pawn in this environmental chess match is the Pacific yew 2 tree, a scrubby conifer found from southern Alaska to central California and in Washington, Oregon, Idaho and Montana. Historically the yew has not been harvested for value but often has been treated as logging slash and wasted. Not any longer. An extract of the bark of the Pacific yew known as taxol has been found to have cancer-fighting properties, particularly with ovarian cancer. As many as 30 percent of those treated with taxol have shown significant response. Some researchers call taxol the most significant new cancer drug to emerge in 15 years.

For the first time, the environmental debate over the use of a natural 3 resource involves more than a question of the priority of the resource versus economic considerations. At stake is the value of a species of tree and the habitat it provides for wildlife as opposed to the value of the greatest of all natural resources, human life.

When I was first diagnosed three years ago, no one had an inkling 4 that I would become caught in the center of what may become the most significant environmental debate of my generation. Although as early as 1979 researchers had discovered that taxol killed cancer in a unique way, imprisoning malignant cells in a cage of scaffoldlike rods called microtubules, lab tests on animals were inconclusive. By 1985, however, a woman with terminal ovarian cancer was treated with taxol and had a dramatic response. Six years later, the once lowly yew tree is at the threshold of a controversy that challenges the fundamental precepts of even the most entrenched environmentalist.

It takes about three 100-year-old Pacific yew trees, or roughly 60 5 pounds of bark, to produce enough taxol to treat one patient. When the bark is removed, the tree dies. Environmental groups like the Oregon Natural Resources Council and the Audubon Society are concerned that the Pacific yew as a species may be decimated by the demand for taxol. But this year alone, 12,000 women will die from ovarian cancer. Breast cancer will kill 45,000 women. Is preservation of the Pacific yew worth the price?

It is sublimely ironic that my fate hinges so directly on the Pacific 6 yew. As a federal attorney representing the Forest Service, I have witnessed the environmental movement in the West from its embryonic stages. I have seen such diverse groups as the National Wildlife Federation and the Sierra Club challenge the Forest Service's ability to sell and harvest its trees. Win or lose, the forests are often locked up during the lengthy legal process.

The viability of the national forests does not rise or fall with the 7 Pacific yew. But, unfortunately for cancer victims, the tree is most abundant on national-forest lands which are subject to environmental review by the public. Already challenges to the federal harvest of the yew have begun. In Montana, the Save the Yaak Committee has protested the Kootenai National Forest's intention to harvest yew trees and make them available for experimental use. The committee contends that the yew may be endangered by overharvesting.

I have news for the Save the Yaak Committee. I am endangered, too. 8 I've had four major abdominal surgeries in two years. I've had the conventional chemotherapy for ovarian cancer, and it didn't work. Though I was in remission for almost a year, last August my cancer returned with a vengeance. Taxol may be my last hope.

Because of the scarcity of supply, taxol is not commercially avail- 9 able. It is available only in clinical trials at a number of institutions. Bristol-Myers, working with the National Cancer Institute in Bethesda, Md., is asking the Forest Service to provide 750,000 pounds of bark for clinical studies this year.

The ultimate irony of my story is that I am one of the lucky ones. 10 This May I was accepted by the National Cancer Institute for one of its clinical trials. On May 8 I was infused with my first treatment of taxol. Hospitalized in intensive care at NCI, I watched the precious, clear fluid drip into my veins and prayed for it to kill the cancer that has ravaged my body. I thought about the thousands of women who will die of cancer this year, who will not have my opportunity.

Every effort should be made to ensure that the yew tree is made 11 available for the continued research and development of taxol. Environmental groups, the timber industry and the Forest Service must recognize that the most important value of the Pacific yew is as a treatment for cancer. At the same time, its harvest can be managed in a way that allows for the production of taxol without endangering the continued survival of the yew tree.

The yew may be prime habitat for spotted owls. It may be esthetically appealing. But certainly its most critical property is its ability to treat a fatal disease. Given a choice between trees or people, people must prevail. No resource can be more valuable or more important than a human life. Ask my husband. Ask my two sons. Ask me.   12

Responding to Reading

1. Christensen points out that before taxol, the Pacific yew tree had not been of much value. In what way does this information support environmentalist arguments that endangered habitats and species should be preserved?
2. Christensen makes a compelling case in favor of harvesting the Pacific yew. What would be the short-term and long-term effects of her proposal?
3. Christensen ends her essay by appealing to her readers' emotions: "No resource can be more valuable or more important than a human life. Ask my husband. Ask my two sons. Ask me" (12). What does she gain by ending with this appeal? Would a less emotional conclusion have been more effective?

TOP OF THE FOOD CHAIN

T. Coraghessan Boyle

T. Coraghessan Boyle (1946–   ) received his bachelor's degree from the State University of New York at Potsdam, an M.F.A. from the University of Iowa's Writers Workshop, and a Ph.D. in British literature from the University of Iowa. He is currently a member of the English department at the University of Southern California. He has published some fourteen novels and collections of short stories, including Greasy Lake *(1985),* The Road to Wellville *(1993),* Riven Rock *(1998), and* A Friend of the Earth *(2000), and his work has appeared in virtually every major literary magazine. Boyle has won numerous awards, notably three O'Henry awards for short fiction. The following story appears in his 1998 collected stories.*

The thing was, we had a little problem with the insect vecter there,   1
and believe me, your tamer stuff, your Malathion and pyrethrum and the rest of the so-called environmentally safe products didn't begin to make a dent in it, not a dent. I mean it was utterly useless—we might as well have been spraying with Chanel No. 5 for all the good it did. And you've got to realize these people were literally covered with insects day and night—and the fact that they hardly wore any clothes just compounded the problem. Picture if you can, gentlemen, a naked little two-year-old boy so black with flies and mosquitoes it looks like he's

wearing long johns, or the young mother so racked with the malarial shakes she can't even lift a diet Coke to her lips—it was pathetic, just pathetic, like something out of the Dark Ages. . . . Well, anyway, the decision was made to go with DDT. In the short term. Just to get the situation under control, you understand.

Yes, that's right. Senator. *DDT*: Dichlorodiphenyltrichloroethane.   2

Yes, I'm well aware of that fact, sir. But just because *we* banned it   3
domestically, under pressure from the birdwatching contingent and the hopheads down at the EPA, it doesn't necessarily follow that the rest of the world—especially the developing world—is about to jump on the bandwagon. And that's the key word here, Senator: *developing*. You've got to realize this is Borneo we're talking about here, not Port Townsend or Enumclaw. These people don't know from square one about sanitation, disease control, pest eradication—or even personal hygiene, if you want to come right down to it. It rains a hundred and twenty inches a year, minimum. They dig up roots in the jungle. They've still got head-hunters along the Rajang River, for god's sake.

And please don't forget, they *asked* us to come in there, practically   4
begged us—and not only the World Health Organization, but the Sultan of Brunei and the government in Sarawak too. We did what we could to accommodate them and reach our objective in the shortest period of time and by the most direct and effective means. We went to the air. Obviously. And no one could have foreseen the consequences, no one, not even if we'd gone out and generated a hundred environmental-impact statements—it was just one of those things, a freak occurrence, and there's no defense against that. Not that I know of, anyway. . . .

Caterpillars? Yes, Senator, that's correct. That was the first sign: 5

But let me backtrack a minute here. You see, out in the bush they   6
have these roofs made of thatched palm leaves—you'll see them in the towns too, even in Bintulu or Brunei—and they're really pretty effective, you'd be surprised. A hundred and twenty inches of rain, they've got to figure a way to keep it out of the hut, and for centuries, this was it. Palm leaves. Well, it was about a month after we sprayed for the final time and I'm sitting at my desk in the trailer thinking about the drainage project at Kuching, enjoying the fact that for the first time in maybe a year I'm not smearing mosquitoes all over the back of my neck, when there's a knock at the door. It's this elderly gentleman, tattooed from head to toe, dressed only in a pair of running shorts—they love those shorts, by the way, the shiny material and the tightmachine-stitch-ing, the whole country, men and women and children, they can't get enough of them. . . . Anyway he's the headman of the local village and he's very excited, something about the roots—*atap*, they call them. That all he can say, *atap, atap*, over and over again.

It's raining, of course. It's always raining. So I shrug into my rain   7
slicker, start up the 4×4 and go have a look. Sure enough, all the *atap* roofs

are collapsing, not only in his village, but throughout the target area. The people are all huddled there in their running shorts, looking pretty miserable, and one after another the roofs keep falling in, it's bewildering, and gradually I realize the headman's diatribe has begun to feature a new term I was unfamiliar with at the time—the word caterpillar, as it turns out, in the Iban dialect. But who was to make the connection between three passes with the crop duster and all these staved-in roofs?

Our people finally sorted it out a couple weeks later. The chemical, which, by the way, the cut down the number of mosquitoes exponentially, had the unfortunate side effect of killing off this little wasp—I've got the scientific name for it somewhere in my report here, if you're interested—that preyed on a type of caterpillar that in turn ate palm leaves. Well, with the wasps gone, the caterpillars hatched out with nothing to keep them in check and chewed the roofs to pieces, and that was unfortunate, we admit it, and we had a real cost overrun on replacing those roofs with tin . . . but the people were happier, I think, in the long run, because let's face it, no matter how tightly you weave those palm leaves, they're just not going to keep the water out like tin. Of course, nothing's perfect, and we had a lot of complaints about the rain drumming on the panels, people unable to sleep and what-have-you. . . . 8

Yes, sir, that's correct—the flies were next. 9

Well, you got to understand the magnitude of the fly problem in Borneo, there's nothing like it here to compare it with, except maybe a garbage strike in New York. Every minute of every day you've got flies everywhere, up your nose, in your mouth, your ears, your eyes, flies in your rice, your Coke, your Singapore sling and your gin rickey. It's enough to drive you to distraction, not to mention the disease, these things carry, from dysentery to typhoid to cholera and back round the loop again. And once the mosquito population was down, the flies seemed to breed up to fill in the gap—Borneo wouldn't be Borneo without some damned insect blackening the air. 10

Of course, this was before our people had tracked down the problem with the caterpillars and the wasps and all of that, and so we figured we'd had a big success with the mosquitoes, why not a series of ground sweeps, mount a fogger in the back of a Suzuki Brat and sanitize the huts, not to mention the open sewers, which as you know are nothing but a breeding ground for flies, chiggers and biting insects of every sort. At least it was an error of commission rather than omission. At least we were trying. 11

I watched the flies go down myself. One day they were so thick in the trailer I couldn't even *find* my paperwork, let alone attempt to get through it, and the next they were collecting on the windows, bumbling around like they were drunk. A day later they were gone. Just like that. From a million flies in the trailer to none. . . . 12

Well, no one could have foreseen that, Senator. 13

The geckos ate the flies, yes. You're all familiar with geckos, I 14
assume, gentlemen? These are the lizards you've seen during your trips
to Hawaii, very colorful, patrolling the houses for roaches and flies,
almost like pets, but of course they're wild animals, never lose sight of
that, and just about as unsanitary as anything I can think of, except
maybe flies.

Yes, well don't forget, sir, we're viewing this with twenty-twenty 15
hindsight, but at the time no one gave a thought to geckos or what they
ate—they were just another fact of life in the tropics. Mosquitoes, lizards,
scorpions, leeches—you name it, they've got it. When the flies began piling up on the windowsills like drift, naturally the geckos feasted on them,
stuffing themselves till they looked like sausages crawling up the walls.
Where before they moved so fast you could never be sure you'd seen
them, now they waddled across the floor, laid around in the corners,
clung to the air vents like magnets—and even then no one paid much
attention to them till they started turning belly-up in the streets. Believe
me, we confirmed a lot of things there about the buildup of these products as you move up the food chain and the efficacy—or lack thereof—of
certain methods, no doubt about that. . . .

The cats? That's where it got sticky, really sticky. You see, nobody 16
really lost any sleep over a pile of dead lizards—though we did the tests
routinely and the tests confirmed what we'd expected, that is, the product had been concentrated in the geckos because of the sheer number of
contaminated flies they'd consumed. But lizards are one thing and cats
are another. These people really have an affection for their cats—no
house, no hut, no matter how primitive, is without at least a couple of
them. Mangy-looking things, long-legged and scrawny, maybe, not at
all the sort of animal you'd see here, but there it was: they loved their
cats. Because the cats were functional, you understand—without them,
the place would have been swimming in rodents inside of a week.

You're right there, Senator, yes—that's exactly what happened. 17

You see, the cats had a field day with these feeble geckos—you can 18
imagine, if any of you have ever owned a cat, the kind of joy these animals must have experienced to see their nemesis, this ultra-quick lizard,
and it's just barely creeping across the floor like a bug. Well, to make a
long story short, the cats ate up every dead and dying gecko in the
country, from snout to tail, and then the cats began to die . . . which to
my mind would have been no great loss if it wasn't for the rats.
Suddenly there were rats everywhere—you couldn't drive down the
street without running over half-a-dozen of them at a time. They fouled
the grain supplies, fell in the wells and died, bit infants as they slept in
their cradles. But that wasn't the worst, not by a long shot. No, things
really went down the tube after that. Within the month we were getting
scattered reports of bubonic plague, and of course we tracked them all

it to the shed, a cool and comfortingly square shelter that held phantas-
magoric metal parts; they smelled good, like dirt and grease. I had played
a long time in this shed before some maternal shriek made me lift up on
my haunches to listen to those urgent, possessive sounds that were my
name. Rearing up, my head bumped into something hanging in the dark;
gleaming white, it felt sleek and cold against my cheek. Its smell was
dense and musty and not unlike the slabs of my grandmother's great
arms after her cool, evening sponge baths. In that shed I looked up and
saw the flensed body of a doe; it swung gently, slapping my face. I felt
then as I do even now when eating game: horror and awe and kinship.

Growing up those first years on a Plumas National Forest station 3
high in the Sierra Nevada near Oregon was somewhat like belonging to
a white tribe. The men hiked off every day into their forest and the
women stayed behind in the circle of official cabins, breeding. So far
away from a store, we ate venison and squirrel, rattlesnake and duck.
My first rattle, in fact, was from a diamondback rattler my father killed
as we watched, by snatching it up with a stick and winding it, whiplike,
around a redwood sapling. Rattlesnake tastes just like chicken, but has
many fragile bones to slither one's way through. We also ate rainbow
trout, rabbit, and geese galore. The game was accompanied by such
daily garden dainties as fried okra, mustard greens, corn fritters, wilted
lettuce (our favorite because of that rare, blackened bacon), new pota-
toes and peas, stewed tomatoes, barbecued butter beans.

I was four before I ever had a beef hamburger, and I remember 4
being disappointed by its fatty, nothing taste and the way it fell apart at
the seams whenever my teeth sank into it. Smoked pork shoulder came
much later, in the South; and I was twenty-one, living in New York City,
before I ever tasted leg of lamb. I approached that glazed rack of meat
with a certain guilty self-consciousness, as if I unfairly stalked those
sweet-tempered white creatures myself. But how would I explain
my squeamishness to those urban sophisticates? How explain that I was
shy with mutton when I had been bred on wild things?

Part of it, I suspect, had to do with the belief I'd also been bred 5
on: we become the spirit and body of animals we eat. As a child
eating venison, I liked to think of myself as lean and lovely just like the
deer. I would never be caught dead just grazing while some man who
wasn't even a skillful hunter crept up and conked me over the head. If
someone wanted to hunt me, he must be wily and outwitting. He must
earn me.

My father had also taught us as children that animals were our 6
brothers and sisters under their skin. They died so that we might live.
And of this sacrifice we must be mindful. "God make us grateful for
what we are about to receive," took on new meaning when we imagined the animal's surrender to our own appetites. We also used all the
animal, so that an elk became elk steaks, stew, salami, and sausage. His

head and horns went on the wall to watch us more earnestly than any
baby-sitter, and every Christmas Eve we had a ceremony of making our
own moccasins for the new year out of whatever Father had tanned.
"Nothing wasted," my father would always say, or, as we munched on
sausage cookies made from moosemeat or venison, "Think about who
you're eating." We thought of ourselves as intricately linked to the food
chain. We knew, for example, that a forest fire meant, at the end of the
line, we'd suffer too. We'd have buck stew instead of venison steak, and
the meat would be stringy, withered-tasting, because in the animal kingdom, as it seemed with humans, only the meanest and leanest and
orneriest survived losing their forests.

Once when I was in my early teens, I went along on a hunting trip as   7
the "main cook and bottle-washer," though I don't remember any bottles;
none of these hunters drank alcohol. There was something else coursing
through their veins as they rose long before dawn and disappeared,
returning to my little camp most often dragging a doe or pheasant or rabbit. We ate innumerable cornmeal-fried fish, had rabbit stew seasoned
only with blood and black pepper.

This hunting trip was the first time I remember eating game as a   8
conscious act. My father and Buddy Earl shot a big doe and she lay with
me in the back of the tarp-draped station wagon all the way home. It
was not the smell I minded, it was the glazed great, dark eyes and the
way that head flopped around crazily on what I knew was once a graceful neck. I found myself petting this doe, murmuring all those graces
we'd been taught long ago as children. Thank you for the sacrifice,
thank you for letting us be like you so that we can grow up strong as
game. But there was an uneasiness in me that night as I bounced along
in the back of the car with the deer.

What was uneasy is still uneasy—perhaps it always will be. It's not   9
easy when one really starts thinking about all this: the eating game, the
food chain, the sacrifice of one for the other. It's never easy when one
begins to think about one's most basic actions, like eating. Like becoming what one eats: lean and lovely and mortal.

Why should it be that the purchase of meat at a butcher shop is   10
somehow more righteous than eating something wild? Perhaps it has to
do with our collective unconscious that sees the animal bred for slaughter as doomed. But that wild doe or moose might make it without the
hunter. Perhaps on this primitive level of archetype and unconscious
knowing we even believe that what's wild lives forever.

My father once told this story around a hunting campfire. His own   11
father, who raised cattle during the Great Depression on a dirt farm in
the Ozarks, once fell on such hard times that he had to butcher the pet
lamb for supper. My father, bred on game or their own hogs all his life,
took one look at the family pet on that meat platter and pushed his plate
away. His siblings followed suit. To hear my grandfather tell it, it was

the funniest thing he'd ever seen. "They just couldn't eat Bo-Peep," Grandfather said. And to hear my father tell it years later around that campfire, it was funny, but I saw for the first time his sadness. And I realized that eating had become a conscious act for him that day at the dinner table when Bo-Peep offered herself up.

Now when someone offers me game, I will eat it with all the qualms 12 and memories and reverence with which I grew up eating it. And I think I will always have this feeling of horror and awe and kinship. And something else—full knowledge of what I do, what I become.

Responding to Reading

1. What is Peterson's purpose in writing this essay? To tell people about her childhood? To explore issues about which she feels uncomfortable? To convince people not to eat meat? Something else? Explain.
2. In paragraph 7, Peterson tells about a hunting trip that she went on with her father. What is the purpose of this anecdote? In what way does it reinforce the main point of her essay?
3. In paragraph 2, Peterson tells about the "horror and awe and kinship" she feels whenever she eats game. She uses this phrase again in her conclusion. What does she mean by this phrase? How do you think Barbara Ehrenreich (p. 643) would respond to it?

OUR ANIMAL RITES

Anna Quindlen

Journalist and novelist Anna Quindlen (1953–) was born in Philadelphia, where she received what she calls "a liberal Catholic education." She attended college at Barnard and started her career as a reporter at Time *magazine in 1977. In the early 1980s, she moved to the* New York Times, *where she eventually wrote the widely syndicated personal opinion columns "Life in the 30's" (1986–1988) and "Public and Private" (1990–1994); some of these columns have been collected in the books* Living Out Loud *(1988) and* Thinking Out Loud *(1993). In 1992, she won a Pulitzer Prize for journalism for her "Public and Private" columns. The success of Quindlen's first two novels—*Object Lessons *(1991) and* One True Thing *(1994)—led her to retire from the* Times *and concentrate on fiction writing. Since then she has published a third novel,* Black and Blue *(1998); a children's book,* Happily Ever After *(1995); and a nonfiction work,* A Short Guide to a Happy Life *(2000). Of her nonfiction she has said, "Whenever my response to an important subject is rational and completely cerebral, I know there is something wrong with it. I have always been governed by my gut." In the following 1990 "Public and Private" column, Quindlen looks at the relationship between humans and the wild animals whose territory we are overtaking.*

The bear had the adenoidal breathing of an elderly man with a pas- 1
sion for cigars and a tendency toward emphysema. My first thought,
when I saw him contemplating me through tiny eyes from a rise just
beyond the back porch, was that he looked remarkably bearlike, like a
close-up shot from a public television nature program.

I screamed. With heavy tread—pad, pad, pad, harrumph, har- 2
rumph—the bear went off into the night, perhaps to search for garbage
cans inexpertly closed and apiaries[1] badly lighted. I sat on the porch,
shaking. Everyone asks, "Was he big?" My answer is, "Compared to
what?"

What I leave out when I tell the story is my conviction that the bear 3
is still watching. At night I imagine he is staring down from the hillside
into the lighted porch, as though he had a mezzanine seat for a performance on which the curtain had already gone up. "A nice female, but
not very furry," I imagine him thinking, "I see the cubs have gone to the
den for the night."

Sometimes I suspect I think this because the peace and quiet of the 4
country have made me go mad, and if only I could hear a car alarm, an
ambulance siren, the sound of a boom box playing "The Power" and its
owner arguing with his girlfriend over whether or not he was flirting
with Denise at the party, all that would drive the bear clear out of my
head.

Sometimes I think it is because instead of feeling that the bear is tres- 5
passing on my property, in my heart I believe that I am trespassing on his.

That feeling is not apparent to city people, although there is some- 6
thing about the sight of a man cleaning up after a sheepdog with a sheet
of newspaper that suggests a kind of horrible atonement. The city is a
place built by the people, for the people. There we say people are acting
like animals when they do things with guns and bats and knives that
your ordinary bear would never dream of doing. There we condescend
to our animals, with grooming parlors and cat carriers, using them to
salve our loneliness and prepare us for parenthood.

All you who lost interest in the dog after the baby was born, you 7
know who you are.

But out where the darkness has depth, where there are no street 8
lights and the stars leap out of the sky, condescension, a feeling of
supremacy, what the animal-rights types call speciesism, is impossible.
Oh, hunters try it, and it is pathetic to consider the firepower they
require to bring down one fair-sized deer. They get three bear days in
the autumn, and afterward there is at least one picture in the paper of a
couple of smiling guys in hats surrounding the carcass of an animal that
looks, though dead, more dignified than they do.

---

[1] Bee farms. [Eds.]

Each spring, after the denning and the long, cold drowse, we wait 9 to see if the bear that lives on the hill above our house beat the bullets. We discover his triumph through signs: a pile of bear dung on the lawn, impossible to assign to any other animal unless mastodons still roam the earth. A garbage box overturned into the swamp, the cole slaw container licked clean. Symmetrical scratch marks five feet up on a tree.

They own this land. Once, long ago, someone put a house on it. That 10 was when we were tentative interlopers, when we put a farmhouse here and a barn there. And then we went nuts, built garden condos with pools and office complexes with parking garages and developments with names that always included the words Park, Acres, or Hills. You can't stop progress, especially if it's traveling 65 miles an hour. You notice that more this time of year, when the possums stiffen by the side of the road.

Sometimes the animals fight back. I was tickled by the people who 11 bought a house with a pond and paid a good bit of money for a little dock from which to swim. It did not take long for them to discover that the snapping turtles were opposed to the addition to their ecosystem of humans wearing sunscreen. An exterminator was sent for. The pond was dredged. A guest got bit. The turtles won.

I've read that deer use the same trails all their lives. Someone comes 12 along and puts a neo-Colonial house in the middle of their deer paths, and the deer will use the paths anyway, with a few detours. If you watch, you can see that it is the deer that belong and the house which does not. The bats, the groundhogs, the weasels, the toads—a hundred years from now, while our family will likely be scattered, their descendants might be in this same spot. Somewhere out there the bear is watching, picking his nits and his teeth, breathing his raggedy bear breath, and if he could talk, maybe he'd say, "I wonder when they're going back where they belong."

Responding to Reading

1. Do you think human beings are guilty of "speciesism" (8)?
2. Is Quindlen romanticizing nature? Do you think she attributes more insight and dignity to animals than they actually possess or deserve? Explain.
3. Quindlen spends much of her essay discussing a bear she encountered near her house. Are her sentiments about the bear in this essay similar to or different from those expressed by William Stafford about the deer in "Traveling through the Dark"(p. 645)?

THE MYTH OF MAN AS HUNTER
Barbara Ehrenreich

An unabashed "feminist, populist, socialist, and secular humanist,"
Barbara Ehrenreich (1941–   ) was born in Butte, Montana, to a family of
self-avowed "free-thinkers" and "fourth- or fifth-generation atheists." Now a
resident of Long Island, she holds a Ph.D. from Rockefeller University and is
one of the country's most controversial social critics, offering a decidedly lib-
eral perspective on many political and economic issues. Her books of social
criticism include Fear of Falling: The Inner Life of the Middle Class
(1989), The Worst Years of Our Lives: Irreverent Notes on a Decade of
Greed *(1990),* The Snarling Citizen *(1995), and* Blood Rites: The Origins
and History of the Passions of War *(1997). She is also the author of a novel,*
Kipper's Game *(1993). She is a featured essayist for* Time *magazine, where*
the following piece originally appeared in 1993. Here Ehrenreich suggests that
while early humans may have successfully made the transition from prey to
predators, we are still prey to many enemies, including others of our own
species.

It must seem odd to the duck and deer populations that Americans   1
have paid more than $255 million this summer for the experience of
being prey. In *Jurassic Park* we had the supreme thrill of being hunted
for food by creatures far larger, faster, and —counting teeth and claws—
better armed than we are. With the raptors closing in, we saw how vulnerable the human body is—no claws, no exoskeleton, no blinding
poison sprays. Take away our guns and high-voltage fences and we are,
from a typical predator perspective, tasty mounds of unwrapped meat.

If the experience resonates to the most ancient layers of our brains,   2
it's probably because we spent our first million years or so not just hunting and gathering, but being hunted and gathered. *T. Rex* had been gone
for 60 million years when our progenitors came along, but there were
saber-toothed tigers, lions, cougars, leopards, bears, wolves and wild
boars waiting at the edge of every human settlement and campground.

The myth of "man the hunter" has flatteringly obscured our true   3
prehistory as prey. According to the myth, "man" climbed down from
the trees one day, strode out into the savanna with a sharpened stick in
his hand and started slaughtering the local ungulates.[1] After that, supposedly, the only violence prehumans had to worry about was from
other stick-wielding bipeds like themselves. Thus some punctured aus-
tralopithecine skulls found in Africa were at first chalked up to "intentional armed assault"—until someone pointed out that the punctures
precisely fit the tooth gap of the leopard.

---

[1] Hooved animals. [Eds.]

once said that writing is like fishing in that the writer must be willing to fail.
Some of his many collections of verse are Allegiances *(1970),* The Design
of the Oriole *(1977), and* An Oregon Message *(1987). From* Stories That
Could Be True *(1960) comes his poem "Traveling through the Dark," about
an encounter between nature and technology.*

Traveling through the dark I found a deer
dead on the edge of the Wilson River road.
It is usually best to roll them into the canyon:
that road is narrow; to swerve might make more dead.

By glow of the tail-light I stumbled back of the car   5
and stood by the heap, a doe, a recent killing;
she had stiffened already, almost cold.
I dragged her off; she was large in the belly.

My fingers touching her side brought me the reason—
her side was warm; her fawn lay there waiting,   10
alive, still, never to be born.
Beside that mountain road I hesitated.

The car aimed ahead its lowered parking lights;
under the hood purred the steady engine.
I stood in the glare of the warm exhaust turning red;   15
around our group I could hear the wilderness listen.

I thought hard for us all—my only swerving—
then pushed her over the edge into the river.

Responding to Reading

1. In line 3, the speaker says, "It is usually best to roll them into the canyon."
   What information does this statement give you? Does it make it easier or
   more difficult for you to explain the speaker's initial hesitation? To understand his final action?
2. How does each of the following statements reveal the speaker's view of
   nature?

   • "Beside that mountain road I hesitated" (12)

   • "I could hear the wilderness listen" (16)

   • "I thought hard for us all" (17)

3. After hesitating, the speaker in this poem pushes the pregnant deer into the
   river. Why does he hesitate? Does he feel any of the "horror and awe and
   kinship" that Peterson (p. 637) speaks about in her essay? If so, why does
   he act the way he does?

WIDENING THE FOCUS

- Jane Goodall , "A Plea for the Chimps" (p. 559)
- Annie Dillard, " The Deer at Providencia"(p. 654)
- Claire McCarthy, "Dog Lab"(p. 707)

Responding to the Image

1. How do you respond to this image? Is your response primarily emotional or intellectual? How do you account for this response?
2. This photograph was shot by a newspaper photographer on the opening day of firearm deer season in Marquette, Michigan. What do you think might have been the photographer's purpose? Is this photograph news-worthy, in your opinion? Why or why not?

--- WRITING ---

Nature and the Environment

1. In recent years, the Mediterranean fruit fly has damaged fruit in California and Florida. In an effort to stop the damage, both states have aggressively sprayed malathion, an insecticide with relatively low toxicity to plants and animals. At the present time, however, these efforts have not ended the infestation. Write an essay in which you discuss how Rachel Carson and Barbara Ehrenreich would address this problem.

2. Al Gore and Rachel Carson discuss ways in which the environment can be preserved. Write an essay in which you discuss how a specific change in government policy, social behavior, or industrial policy could improve the environment.

3. In "My Wood," E.M. Forster makes a definite point about private property and ownership. Write an essay in which you agree or disagree with Forster's conclusions. Make sure you use your own ideas as well as the ideas of Chief Seattle in "Letter to President Pierce, 1855" and Anna Quindlen in "Our Animal Rites."

4. In "Growing Up Game," Brenda Peterson deals with the subject of eating. In what ways does she see the act of eating as having important social and political consequences? Compare her sentiments with those expressed by Annie Dillard in "The Deer at Providencia" in Chapter 10 (p. 654).

5. What responsibility do you believe each individual has for doing his or her part to save the planet? Consider what in particular is worth saving in the natural world and what forces you see as working to destroy it. In your answer, refer to two of the following essays: "The Obligation to Endure" by Rachel Carson, "Recycling: No Panacea" by William Rathje and Cullen Murphy, and "Shades of Green" by Jedediah Purdy.

6. In "Our Animal Rites," Anna Quindlen makes an effort to confront an animal on its own terms. Ultimately she fails, describing the bear in human terms and imagining what the bear would say if it could talk. Write an essay in which you discuss some of the writers in this chapter who are objective about animals in their natural settings and some who are not. What are the strengths and weaknesses of each approach?

7. A number of writers in this chapter suggest what individuals can do to improve the environment. Focus on two who seem to take different positions—T. Coraghessan Boyle and Sally Thane Christensen, for example—and compare their approaches. What are the strengths

and weaknesses of each writer's views? Which writer's plan seems most feasible?

8. Chief Seattle says that one day the whites will "suffocate in [their] own waste" (5). Write a letter from Al Gore to Chief Seattle agreeing or disagreeing with this statement. Be specific, and refer to both essays.

9. In "Is a Tree Worth a Life?" Sally Thane Christensen says, "Given a choice between trees or people, people must prevail" (12). In "Our Animal Rites," Anna Quindlen says that human beings are interlopers on land owned by animals. With whom do you agree? Could both be correct? Write an essay in which you consider whether the welfare of plants or animals should ever take precedence over the welfare of human beings. Support your points with references to Christensen's and Quindlen's essays as well as to any other essay in this chapter or elsewhere in this text.

10. Write an essay in which you affirm (or deny) a person's right to hunt. Refer to the essays in the Focus section of this chapter to help you support your position. In addition, make sure you address the major arguments against your position.

11. **For Internet research:** A site devoted to links raising arguments against hunting can be found at <http://arrs.envirolink.org/ar_issues/hunting.html>. The Citizens' Committee for the Right to Keep and Bear Arms offers prohunting links at <http://www.ccrkba.org>, and further prohunting links can be found at http:// www.links.hunters.com>. Using these, the Focus readings, and other sources you might find, write an informative essay exploring the various sides in the debate over hunting for sport.

10

MAKING CHOICES

As Robert Frost suggests in his poem "The Road Not Taken" (p. 652), making choices is fundamental to our lives. The ability—and, in fact, the need—to make complex decisions is part of what makes us human. On a practical level, we choose friends, mates, careers, and places to live. On a more theoretical level, we struggle to make the moral and ethical choices that people have struggled with for thousands of years.

Many times, complex questions have no easy answers; occasionally, they have no answers at all. For example, should we abide by a law even if we believe it to be morally wrong? Should we stand up to authority even if our stand puts us at risk? Should we help less fortunate individuals if such help threatens our own social or economic position? Should we act to save an endangered species if that action may put people out of work? Should we tell the truth even if the truth may hurt us—or hurt someone else? Which road should we take, the easy one or the hard one?

Most of the time, the choice we (and the writers whose works appear in this chapter) face is the same: to act or not to act. To make a decision, we must understand both the long- and short-term consequences of acting in a particular way or of choosing not to act. We must struggle with the possibility of compromise, and with the possibility of making a morally or ethically objectionable decision. And, perhaps most important, we must learn to take responsibility for our decisions.

The writers whose essays are included in the Focus section of this chapter, "Are All Ideas Created Equal?" (p. 754), address the issue of choice as it relates to the free expression of ideas. What is the role in a free society of those who espouse what many people consider nonsense? For example, some people assert that the Holocaust never happened, that evolution is a myth, or that HIV does not cause AIDS. Do such "nonsense," ideas that prominent scientists and historians discount, have a place in public discourse? Should we have the right to decide for ourselves which ideas are "nonsense," or are some messages so repellent—or so dangerous—that they should not be heard? And does denying such ideas a public forum give them additional credibility? Does it make our society as a whole less free? In other words, is it ultimately more dangerous to air such ideas or to censor them? These are difficult questions to answer, but they represent choices that a free society like ours must struggle with—now, in the age of the Internet, more than ever.

As you read and prepare to write about the selections in this chapter, you may consider the following questions:

- On what specific choice or choices does the essay focus? Is the decision to be made moral? Ethical? Political?

- Does the writer introduce a *dilemma*, a choice between two equally problematic alternatives?

- Does the choice the writer presents apply only to one specific situation or case, or does it also have a wider application?

- Is the writer emotionally involved with the issue he or she is discussing? Does this involvement (or lack of involvement) make the selection more or less convincing?

- What social, political, or religious ideas influence the writer? How can you tell? Are these ideas similar to or different from your own views?

- Does the decision under discussion cause the writer to examine his or her own values? The values of others? The values of the society at large? Does the selection lead you to examine your own values?

- Does the writer offer a solution? Do you find it reasonable?

- What choice or choices do you believe should be made? Why?

- Which writers' views seem most alike? Which seem most different?

THE ROAD NOT TAKEN

Robert Frost

Robert Frost (1874–1963), four-time Pulitzer Prize–winning poet of rural New England, lived most of his life in New Hampshire and taught at Amherst College and Dartmouth College. His language is familiar and accessible—but not simple—and his poems are often rich in symbols and allusions. Frost read a poem, "The Gift Outright," that he composed for the occasion at the inauguration of President John F. Kennedy. Some of Frost's more famous poems are "Birches," "Mending Wall," and "Stopping by Woods on a Snowy Evening." "The Road Not Taken" is about uncertainty and the difficulty of choice.

Two roads diverged in a yellow wood,
And sorry I could not travel both
And be one traveller, long I stood
And looked down one as far as I could
To where it bent in the undergrowth;   5

Then took the other, as just as fair,
And having perhaps the better claim,
Because it was grassy and wanted wear;
Though as for that the passing there
Had worn them really about the same,   10

And both that morning equally lay
In leaves no step had trodden black.
Oh, I kept the first for another day!
Yet knowing how way leads on to way,
I doubted if I should ever come back.   15

I shall be telling this with a sigh
Somewhere ages and ages hence:
Two roads diverged in a wood, and I—
I took the one less travelled by,
And that has made all the difference.   20

Responding to Reading

1. What is the difference between the two paths Frost's speaker considers? Why does he make the choice he does?
2. Is "The Road Not Taken" simply about two paths in the wood, or does it suggest more? What makes you think so? To what larger choices might the speaker be alluding?
3. What does the speaker mean by "that has made all the difference" (20)?

ETHICS

Linda Pastan

Poet Linda Pastan (b. 1932) won the Mademoiselle *poetry award as a senior at Radcliffe (the runner-up that year was Sylvia Plath), but she gave up writing when she married in 1953 and did not resume her writing until*

*her children entered school. The winner of numerous prizes, Pastan often
focuses in her work on the complexity of domestic life, using intense imagery
to bring a sense of mystery to everyday matters. Her collections include*
Waiting for My Life *(1981),* PM/AM: New and Selected Poems *(1983),
and* An Early Afterlife *(1995). "Ethics," from* Waiting for My Life, *raises
an ethical question that the speaker suggests cannot really be resolved.*

In ethics class so many years ago
our teacher asked this question every fall:
if there were a fire in a museum
which would you save, a Rembrandt painting
or an old woman who hadn't many   5
years left anyhow? Restless on hard chairs
caring little for pictures or old age
we'd opt one year for life, the next for art
and always half-heartedly. Sometimes
the woman borrowed my grandmother's face   10
leaving her usual kitchen to wander
some drafty, half imagined museum.
One year, feeling clever, I replied
why not let the woman decide herself?
Linda, the teacher would report, eschews   15
the burdens of responsibility.
This fall in a real museum I stand
before a real Rembrandt, old woman,
or nearly so, myself. The colors
within this frame are darker than autumn,   20
darker even than winter—the browns of earth,
though earth's most radiant elements burn
through the canvas. I know now that woman
and painting and season are almost one
and all beyond saving by children.   25

Responding to Reading

1. What choice actually confronts Pastan's speaker? What answer do you
   think the teacher expects the students to give?
2. Do you agree with the teacher that refusing to choose means avoiding
   responsibility? Does Frost's speaker (p. 632) have the option not to choose?
3. When the speaker says that "woman/and painting and season are almost
   one" (23–24), what does she mean? Does she imply that the teacher's question really has no answer? That the children who would "opt one year for
   life, the next for art" (8) are right?

After the fish and meat we ate bananas fried in chunks and served 11
on a tray; they were sweet and full of flavor. I felt terrific. My shirt was
wet and cool from swimming; I had had a night's sleep, two decent
walks, three meals, and a swim—everything tasted good. From time to
time each one of us, separately, would look beyond our shaded roof to
the sunny spot where the deer was still convulsing in the dust. Our
meal completed, we walked around the deer and back to the boats.

That night I learned that while we were watching the deer, the oth- 12
ers were watching me.

We four North Americans grew close in the jungle in a way that was 13
not the usual artificial intimacy of travelers. We liked each other. We
stayed up all that night talking, murmuring, as though we rocked on
hammocks slung above time. The others were from big cities: New
York, Washington, Boston. They all said that I had no expression on my
face when I was watching the deer—or at any rate, not the expression
they expected.

They had looked to see how I, the only woman, and the youngest, 14
was taking the sight of the deer's struggles. I looked detached, apparently, or hard, or calm, or focused, still. I don't know. I was thinking. I
remember feeling very old and energetic. I could say like Thoreau that
I have traveled widely in Roanoke, Virginia.[3] I have thought a great deal
about carnivorousness; I eat meat. These things are not issues; they are
mysteries.

Gentlemen of the city, what surprises you? That there is suffering 15
here, or that I know it?

We lay in the tent and talked, "If it had been my wife," one man said 16
with special vigor, amazed, "she wouldn't have cared what was going
on; she would have dropped *everything* right at that moment and gone
in the village from here to there to there, she would not have *stopped*
until that animal was out of its suffering one way or another. She could-
n't *bear* to see a creature in agony like that."

I nodded.   17

Now I am home. When I wake I comb my hair before the mirror 18
above my dresser. Every morning for the past two years I have seen in
that mirror, beside my sleep-softened face, the blackened face of a burnt
man. It is a wire-service photograph clipped from a newspaper and
taped to my mirror. The caption reads: "Alan McDonald in Miami hospital bed." All you can see in the photograph is a smudged triangle of
face from his eyelids to his lower lip; the rest is bandages. You cannot
see the expression in his eyes; the bandages shade them.

The story, headed MAN BURNED FOR SECOND TIME, begins: 19

---

[3] In *Walden*, Henry David Thoreau (see p. 664) says, "I have traveled a good deal in Concord."
[Eds.]

"Why does God hate me?" Alan McDonald asked from his hospital bed.

"When the gunpowder went off, I couldn't believe it," he said. "I just couldn't believe it. I said, 'No, God couldn't do this to me again.'"

He was in a burn ward in Miami, in serious condition. I do not even 20 know if he lived. I wrote him a letter at the time, cringing.

He had been burned before, thirteen years previously, by flaming 21 gasoline. For years he had been having his body restored and his face remade in dozens of operations. He had been a boy, and then a burnt boy. He had already been stunned by what could happen, by how life could veer.

Once I read that people who survive bad burns tend to go crazy; 22 they have a very high suicide rate. Medicine cannot ease their pain; drugs just leak away, soaking the sheets, because there is no skin to hold them in. The people just lie there and weep. Later they kill themselves. They had not known, before they were burned, that the world included such suffering, that life could permit them personally such pain.

This time a bowl of gunpowder had exploded on McDonald.   23

"I didn't realize what had happened at first," he recounted. "And then I heard that sound from 13 years ago. I was burning. I rolled to put the fire out and I thought, 'Oh God, not again.'

"If my friend hadn't been there, I would have jumped into a canal with a rock around my neck."

His wife concludes the piece, "Man, it just isn't fair."   24

I read the whole clipping again every morning. This is the Big Time 25 here, every minute of it. Will someone please explain to Alan McDonald in his dignity, to the deer at Providencia in his dignity, what is going on? And mail me the carbon.

When we walked by the deer at Providencia for the last time, I said 26 to Pepe, with a pitying glance at the deer, "*Pobrecito*"—"poor little thing." But I was trying out Spanish. I knew at the time it was a ridiculous thing to say.

Responding to Reading

1. Could Dillard have done anything to free the deer? Why do you think she chose to do nothing? Does she regret her decision not to act? Do you think she *should* regret it?

2. In paragraph 14 , Dillard says, "I have thought a great deal about carnivorousness; I eat meat. These things are not issues; they are mysteries." What does she mean? Do you find this statement a satisfactory explanation of her ability to enjoy deer meat while she watches the trapped deer "convulsing in the dust" (11)? Why or why not?

3. What connection does Dillard see between Alan McDonald and the deer at Providencia? Do you see this as a reasonable association, or do you believe Dillard has exploited (or even invented) a connection?

SHOOTING AN ELEPHANT

George Orwell

This detailed account of a cruel incident with an elephant in Burma is George Orwell's (see also p. 220) most powerful criticism of imperialism and the impossible position of British police officers—himself among them—in the colonies. Orwell says about the incident, "It was perfectly clear to me what I ought to do," but then he thinks of "the watchful yellow faces behind," and he realizes that his choice is not so simple.

In Moulmein, in lower Burma, I was hated by large numbers of peo- 1
ple—the only time in my life that I have been important enough for this to happen to me. I was sub-divisional police officer of the town, and in an aimless, petty kind of way anti-European feeling was very bitter. No one had the guts to raise a riot, but if a European woman went through the bazaars alone somebody would probably spit betel juice over her dress. As a police officer I was an obvious target and was baited whenever it seemed safe to do so. When a nimble Burman tripped me up on the football field and the referee (another Burman) looked the other way, the crowd yelled with hideous laughter. This happened more than once. In the end the sneering yellow faces of young men that met me everywhere, the insults hooted after me when I was at a safe distance, got badly on my nerves. The young Buddhist priests were the worst of all. There were several thousands of them in the town and none of them seemed to have anything to do except stand on street corners and jeer at Europeans.

All this was perplexing and upsetting. For at that time I had already 2
made up my mind that imperialism was an evil thing and the sooner I chucked up my job and got out of it the better. Theoretically—and secretly, of course—I was all for the Burmese and all against their oppressors, the British. As for the job I was doing, I hated it more bitterly than I can perhaps make clear. In a job like that you see the dirty work of Empire at close quarters. The wretched prisoners huddling in the stinking cages of the lock-ups, the grey, cowed faces of the long-term convicts, the scarred buttocks of the men who had been flogged with bamboos—all these oppressed me with an intolerable sense of guilt. But I could get nothing into perspective. I was young and ill-educated and I had had to think out my problems in the utter silence that is imposed

on every Englishman in the East. I did not even know that the British Empire is dying, still less did I know that it is a great deal better than the younger empires that are going to supplant it.[1] All I knew was that I was stuck between my hatred of the empire I served and my rage against the evil-spirited little beasts who tried to make my job impossible. With one part of my mind I thought of the British Raj[2] as an unbreakable tyranny, as something clamped down, in *saecula saeculorum*,[3] upon the will of prostrate peoples; with another part I thought that the greatest joy in the world would be to drive a bayonet into a Buddhist priest's guts. Feelings like these are the normal by-products of imperialism; ask any Anglo-Indian official, if you can catch him off duty.

One day something happened which in a roundabout way was 3 enlightening. It was a tiny incident in itself, but it gave me a better glimpse than I had had before of the real nature of imperialism—the real motives for which despotic governments act. Early one morning the sub-inspector at a police station the other end of the town rang me up on the phone and said that an elephant was ravaging the bazaar. Would I please come and do something about it? I did not know what I could do, but I wanted to see what was happening and I got on to a pony and started out. I took my rifle, an old .44 Winchester and much too small to kill an elephant, but I thought the noise might be useful in *terrorem*. Various Burmans stopped me on the way and told me about the elephant's doings. It was not, of course, a wild elephant, but a tame one which had gone "must." It had been chained up, as tame elephants always are when their attack of "must"[4] is due, but on the previous night it had broken its chain and escaped. Its mahout,[5] the only person who could manage it when it was in that state, had set out in pursuit, but had taken the wrong direction and was now twelve hours' journey away, and in the morning the elephant had suddenly reappeared in the town. The Burmese population had no weapons and were quite helpless against it. It had already destroyed somebody's bamboo hut, killed a cow, and raided some fruit-stalls and devoured the stock; also it had met the municipal rubbish van and, when the driver jumped out and took to his heels, had turned the van over and inflicted violences upon it.

The Burmese sub-inspector and some Indian constables were waiting 4 for me in the quarter where the elephant had been seen. It was a very poor quarter, a labyrinth of squalid bamboo huts, thatched with palm-leaf, winding all over a steep hillside. I remember that it was a cloudy, stuffy morning at the beginning of the rains. We began questioning the people

---

[1] This essay was written in 1936, three years before the start of World War II; Stalin and Hitler were in power. [Eds.]
[2] Sovereignty. [Eds.]
[3] From time immemorial. [Eds.]
[4] Frenzy. [Eds.]
[5] Keeper. [Eds.]

as to where the elephant had gone and, as usual, failed to get any definite information. That is invariably the case in the East; a story always sounds clear enough at a distance, but the nearer you get to the scene of events the vaguer it becomes. Some of the people said that the elephant had gone in one direction, some said that he had gone in another, some professed not even to have heard of any elephant. I had almost made up my mind that the whole story was a pack of lies, when we heard yells a little distance away. There was a loud, scandalized cry of "Go away, child! Go away this instant!" and an old woman with a switch in her hand came round the corner of a hut, violently shooing away a crowd of naked children. Some more women followed, clicking their tongues and exclaiming; evidently there was something that the children ought not to have seen. I rounded the hut and saw a man's dead body sprawling in the mud. He was an Indian, a black Dravidian coolie,[6] almost naked, and he could not have been dead many minutes. The people said that the elephant had come suddenly upon him round the corner of the hut, caught him with its trunk, put its foot on his back, and ground him into the earth. This was the rainy season and the ground was soft, and his face had scored a trench a foot deep and a couple of yards long. He was lying on his belly with arms crucified and head sharply twisted to one side. His face was coated with mud, the eyes wide open, the teeth bared and grinning with an expression of unendurable agony. (Never tell me, by the way, that the dead look peaceful. Most of the corpses I have seen looked devilish.) The friction of the great beast's foot had stripped the skin from his back as neatly as one skins a rabbit. As soon as I saw the dead man I sent an orderly to a friend's house nearby to borrow an elephant rifle. I had already sent back the pony, not wanting it to go mad with fright and throw me if it smelt the elephant.

The orderly came back in a few minutes with a rifle and five cartridges, and meanwhile some Burmans had arrived and told us that the elephant was in the paddy fields below, only a few hundred yards away. As I started forward practically the whole population of the quarter flocked out of the houses and followed me. They had seen the rifle and were all shouting excitedly that I was going to shoot the elephant. They had not shown much interest in the elephant when he was merely ravaging their homes, but it was different now that he was going to be shot. It was a bit of fun to them, as it would be to an English crowd; besides they wanted the meat. It made me vaguely uneasy. I had no intention of shooting the elephant—I had merely sent for the rifle to defend myself if necessary—and it is always unnerving to have a crowd following you. I marched down the hill, looking and feeling a fool, with the rifle over my shoulder and an ever-growing army of people jostling at my heels.

5

---

[6] An unskilled laborer. [Eds.]

At the bottom, when you got away from the huts, there was a metalled road and beyond that a miry waste of paddy fields a thousand yards across, not yet ploughed but soggy from the first rains and dotted with coarse grass. The elephant was standing eight yards from the road, his left side towards us. He took not the slightest notice of the crowd's approach. He was tearing up bunches of grass, beating them against his knees to clean them and stuffing them into his mouth.

I had halted on the road. As soon as I saw the elephant I knew with perfect certainty that I ought not to shoot him. It is a serious matter to shoot a working elephant—it is comparable to destroying a huge and costly piece of machinery—and obviously one ought not to do it if it can possibly be avoided. And at that distance, peacefully eating, the elephant looked no more dangerous than a cow. I thought then and I think now that his attack of "must" was already passing off; in which case he would merely wander harmlessly about until the mahout came back and caught him. Moreover, I did not in the least want to shoot him. I decided that I would watch him for a little while to make sure that he did not turn savage again, and then go home.

But at that moment I glanced round at the crowd that had followed me. It was an immense crowd, two thousand at the least and growing every minute. It blocked the road for a long distance on either side. I looked at the sea of yellow faces above the garish clothes—faces all happy and excited over this bit of fun, all certain that the elephant was going to be shot. They were watching me as they would watch a conjurer about to perform a trick. They did not like me, but with the magical rifle in my hands I was momentarily worth watching. And suddenly I realized that I should have to shoot the elephant after all. The people expected it of me and I had got to do it; I could feel their two thousand wills pressing me forward, irresistibly. And it was at this moment, as I stood there with the rifle in my hands, that I first grasped the hollowness, the futility of the white man's dominion in the East. Here was I, the white man with his gun, standing in front of the unarmed native crowd—seemingly the leading actor of the piece; but in reality I was only an absurd puppet pushed to and fro by the will of those yellow faces behind. I perceived in this moment that when the white man turns tyrant it is his own freedom that he destroys. He becomes a sort of hollow, posing dummy, the conventionalized figure of a sahib.[7] For it is the condition of his rule that he shall spend his life in trying to impress the "natives," and so in every crisis he has got to do what the "natives" expect of him. He wears a mask, and his face grows to fit it. I had got to shoot the elephant. I had committed myself to doing it when I sent for the rifle. A sahib has got to act like a sahib; he has got to appear resolute, to know his own mind and do definite things. To come all that way, rifle in hand, with two thousand people

---

[7] Term used by natives of colonial India when referring to a European of rank. [Eds.]

marching at my heels, and then to trail feebly away, having done nothing—no, that was impossible. The crowd would laugh at me. And my whole life, every white man's life in the East, was one long struggle not to be laughed at.

But I did not want to shoot the elephant. I watched him beating his 8 bunch of grass against his knees, with that preoccupied grand-motherly air that elephants have. It seemed to me that it would be murder to shoot him. At that age I was not squeamish about killing animals, but I had never shot an elephant and never wanted to. (Somehow it always seems worse to kill a *large* animal.) Besides, there was the beast's owner to be considered. Alive, the elephant was worth at least a hundred pounds; dead, he would only be worth the value of his tusks, five pounds, possibly. But I had got to act quickly. I turned to some experienced looking Burmans who had been there when we arrived, and asked them how the elephant had been behaving. They all said the same thing: he took no notice of you if you left him alone, but he might charge if you went too close to him.

It was perfectly clear to me what I ought to do. I ought to walk up 9 to within, say, twenty-five yards of the elephant and test his behavior. If he charged, I could shoot; if he took no notice of me, it would be safe to leave him until the mahout came back. But also I knew that I was going to do no such thing. I was a poor shot with a rifle and the ground was soft mud into which one would sink at every step. If the elephant charged and I missed him, I should have about as much chance as a toad under a steam-roller. But even then I was not thinking particularly of my own skin, only of the watchful yellow faces behind. For at that moment, with the crowd watching me, I was not afraid in the ordinary sense, as I would have been if I had been alone. A white man mustn't be frightened in front of "natives"; and so, in general, he isn't frightened. The sole thought in my mind was that if anything went wrong those two thousand Burmans would see me pursued, caught, trampled on, and reduced to a grinning corpse like that Indian up the hill. And if that happened it was quite probable that some of them would laugh. That would never do. There was only one alternative. I shoved the cartridges into the magazine and lay down on the road to get a better aim.

The crowd grew very still, and a deep, low, happy sigh, as of people 10 who see the theatre curtain go up at last, breathed from innumerable throats. They were going to have their bit of fun after all. The rifle was a beautiful German thing with cross-hair sights. I did not then know that in shooting an elephant one would shoot to cut an imaginary bar running from ear-hole to ear-hole. I ought, therefore, as the elephant was sideways on, to have aimed straight at his ear-hole; actually I aimed several inches in front of this, thinking the brain would be further forward.

When I pulled the trigger I did not hear the bang or feel the kick— 11 one never does when a shot goes home—but I heard the devilish roar of glee that went up from the crowd. In that instant, in too short a time, one would have thought, even for the bullet to get there, a mysterious, terrible change had come over the elephant. He neither stirred nor fell, but every line of his body had altered. He looked suddenly stricken, shrunken, immensely old, as though the frightful impact of the bullet had paralysed him without knocking him down. At last, after what seemed a long time—it might have been five seconds, I dare say—he sagged flabbily to his knees. His mouth slobbered. An enormous senility seemed to have settled upon him. One could have imagined him thousands of years old. I fired again into the same spot. At the second shot he did not collapse but climbed with desperate slowness to his feet and stood weakly upright, with legs sagging and head dropping. I fired a third time. That was the shot that did for him. You could see the agony of it jolt his whole body and knock the last remnant of strength from his legs. But in falling he seemed for a moment to rise, for as his hind legs collapsed beneath him he seemed to tower upward like a huge rock toppling, his trunk reaching skywards like a tree. He trumpeted, for the first and only time. And then down he came, his belly towards me, with a crash that seemed to shake the ground even where I lay.

I got up. The Burmans were already racing past me across the mud. 12 It was obvious that the elephant would never rise again, but he was not dead. He was breathing very rhythmically with long rattling gasps, his great mound of a side painfully rising and falling. His mouth was wide open—I could see far down into caverns of pale pink throat. I waited a long time for him to die, but his breathing did not weaken. Finally I fired my two remaining shots into the spot where I thought his heart must be. The thick blood welled out of him like red velvet, but still he did not die. His body did not even jerk when the shots hit him, the tortured breathing continued without a pause. He was dying, very slowly and in great agony, but in some world remote from me where not even a bullet could damage him further. I felt that I had got to put an end to that dreadful noise. It seemed dreadful to see the great beast lying there, powerless to move and yet powerless to die, and not even to be able to finish him. I sent back for my small rifle and poured shot after shot into his heart and down his throat. They seemed to make no impression. The tortured gasps continued as steadily as the ticking of a clock.

In the end I could not stand it any longer and went away. I heard 13 later that it took him half an hour to die. Burmans were bringing dahs[8] and baskets even before I left, and I was told they had stripped his body almost to the bones by the afternoon.

Afterwards, of course, there were endless discussions about the 14 shooting of the elephant. The owner was furious, but he was only an Indian and could do nothing. Besides, legally I had done the right thing,

---

[8] Large knives. [Eds.]

for a mad elephant has to be killed, like a mad dog, if its owner fails to control it. Among the Europeans opinion was divided. The older men said I was right, the younger men said it was a damn shame to shoot an elephant for killing a coolie, because an elephant was worth more than any damn Coringhee coolie. And afterwards I was very glad that the coolie had been killed; it put me legally in the right and it gave me a sufficient pretext for shooting the elephant. I often wondered whether any of the others grasped that I had done it solely to avoid looking a fool.

Responding to Reading

1. The central focus of this essay is Orwell's struggle to decide how to control the elephant. Do you think he really has a choice? Explain.
2. Orwell says that his encounter with the elephant, although "a tiny incident in itself," gave him an understanding of "the real nature of imperialism—the real motives for which despotic governments act" (3). In light of this statement, do your think his purpose in this essay is to explore something about himself or something about the nature of British colonialism—or both?
3. In paragraphs 5–6, Orwell introduces the elephant as peaceful and innocent; in paragraphs 11–12, he describes the animal's misery. What do these paragraphs contribute to the essay?

CIVIL DISOBEDIENCE
Henry David Thoreau

American essayist, journalist, and intellectual Henry David Thoreau (1817–1862) was a social rebel who loved nature and solitude. A follower of transcendentalism, a philosophic and literary movement that flourished in New England, he contributed to the Dial, *a publication that gave voice to the movement's romantic, idealistic, and individualistic beliefs. For three years, Thoreau lived in a cabin near Walden Pond in Concord, Massachusetts; his experiences there are recorded in his most famous book,* Walden *(1854). He left Walden, however, because, according to him, he had "several more lives to live and could not spare any more for that one." A canoe excursion in 1839 resulted in the chronicle* A Week on the Concord and Merrimack Rivers, *and other experiences produced books about Maine and Cape Cod. The following impassioned and eloquent defense of civil disobedience, published in 1849, has influenced such leaders as Gandhi and Martin Luther King, Jr.*

I heartily accept the motto,—"That government is best which 1 governs least;" and I should like to see it acted up to more rapidly and systematically. Carried out, it finally amounts to this, which also I believe,—"That government is best which governs not at all"; and when men are prepared for it, that will be the kind of government which they will have. Government is at best but an expedient; but most governments are usually, and all governments are sometimes, inexpedient. The objections which have been brought against a standing army, and they are many and weighty, and deserve to prevail, may also at last be brought against a standing government. The standing army is only an arm of the standing government. The government itself, which is only the mode which the people have chosen to execute their will, is equally liable to be abused and perverted before the people can act through it. Witness the present Mexican war,[1] the work of comparatively a few individuals using the standing government as their tool; for, in the outset, the people would not have consented to this measure.

This American Government,—what is it but a tradition, though a recent one, endeavoring to transmit itself unimpaired to posterity, but each instant losing some of its integrity? It has not the vitality and force of a single living man; for a single man can bend it to his will. It is a sort of wooden gun to the people themselves. But it is not the less necessary for this; for the people must have some complicated machinery or other, and hear its din, to satisfy that idea of government which they have. Governments show thus how successfully men can be imposed on, even impose on themselves, for their own advantage. It is excellent, we must all allow. Yet this government never of itself furthered any enterprise, but by the alacrity with which it got out of its way. *It* does not keep the country free. *It* does not settle the West. *It* does not educate. The character inherent in the American people has done all that has been accomplished; and it would have done somewhat more, if the government had not sometimes got in its way. For government is an expedient by which men would fain succeed in letting one another alone; and, as has been said, when it is most expedient, the governed are most let alone by it. Trade and commerce, if they were not made of India-rubber, would never manage to bounce over the obstacles which legislators are continually putting in their way; and, if one were to judge these men wholly by the effects of their actions and not partly by their intentions, they would deserve to be classed and punished with those mischievous persons who put obstructions on the railroads.

But, to speak practically and as a citizen, unlike those who call themselves no-government men, I ask for, not at once no government, but *at once* a better government. Let every man make known what kind of government would command his respect, and that will be one step toward obtaining it.

---

[1] In December 1845, the U.S. annexation of Texas, lead to a war between the United States and Mexico (1846–1848). Thoreau opposed this war, thinking it served the interests of slaveholders, who believed that the land won from Mexico would be slave territory. In protest, he refused to pay the Massachusetts poll tax and was arrested for his act of civil disobedience. [Eds.]

After all, the practical reason why, when the power is once in the hands of the people, a majority are permitted, and for a long period continue, to rule is not because they are most likely to be in the right, nor because this seems fairest to the minority, but because they are physically the strongest. But a government in which the majority rule in all cases cannot be based on justice, even as far as men understand it. Can there not be a government in which majorities do not virtually decide right and wrong, but conscience?—in which majorities decide only those questions to which the rule of expediency is applicable? Must the citizen ever for a moment, or in the least degree, resign his conscience to the legislator? Why has every man a conscience, then? I think that we should be men first, and subjects afterward. It is not desirable to cultivate a respect for the law, so much as for the right. The only obligation which I have a right to assume is to do at any time what I think right. It is truly enough said, that a corporation has no conscience; but a corporation of conscientious men is a corporation *with* a conscience. Law never made men a whit more just; and, by means of their respect for it, even the well-disposed are daily made the agents of injustice. A common and natural result of any undue respect for law is, that you may see a file of soldiers, colonel, captain, corporal, privates, powder-monkeys, and all, marching in admirable order over hill and dale to the wars, against their wills, ay, against their common sense and consciences, which makes it very steep marching indeed, and produces a palpitation of the heart. They have no doubt that it is a damnable business in which they are concerned; they are all peaceably inclined. Now, what are they? Men at all? or small movable forts and magazines, at the service of some unscrupulous man in power? Visit the Navy-Yard, and behold a marine, such a man as an American government can make, or such as it can make a man with its black arts,—a mere shadow and reminiscence of humanity, a man laid out alive and standing, and already, as one may say, buried under arms with funeral accompaniments, though it may be,—

> "Not a drum was heard, not a funeral note,
> As his corse to the rampart we hurried;
> Not a soldier discharged his farewell shot
> O'er the grave where our hero we buried."[2]

The mass of men serve the state thus, not as men mainly, but as machines, with their bodies. They are the standing army, and the militia, jailers, constables, posse comitatus, etc. In most cases there is no free exercise whatever of the judgment or of the moral sense; but they put themselves on a level with wood and earth and stones; and wooden men can perhaps be manufactured that will serve the purpose as well.

---

[2] From "The Burial of Sir John Moore at Corunna," by Irish poet Charles Wolfe (1791–1823). [Eds.]

Such command no more respect than men of straw or a lump of dirt. They have the same sort of worth only as horses and dogs. Yet such as these even are commonly esteemed good citizens. Others—as most legislators, politicians, lawyers, ministers, and office-holders—serve the state chiefly with their heads; and, as they rarely make any moral distinctions, they are as likely to serve the Devil, without *intending* it, as God. A very few, as heroes, patriots, martyrs, reformers in the great sense, and *men*, serve the state with their consciences also, and so necessarily resist it for the most part; and they are commonly treated as enemies by it. A wise man will only be useful as a man, and will not submit to be "clay," and "stop a hole to keep the wind away,"[3] but leave that office to his dust at least:—

"I am too high-born to be propertied,
To be a secondary at control,
Or useful serving-man and instrument
To any sovereign state throughout the world."[4]

He who gives himself entirely to his fellow-men appears to them 6 useless and selfish; but he who gives himself partially to them is pronounced a benefactor and philanthropist.

How does it become a man to behave toward this American government to-day? I answer, that he cannot without disgrace be associated 7 with it. I cannot for an instant recognize that political organization as *my* government which is the *slave's* government also.

All men recognize the right of revolution; that is, the right to refuse 8 allegiance to, and to resist, the government, when its tyranny or its inefficiency are great and unendurable. But almost all say that such is not the case now. But such was the case, they think, in the Revolution of '75. If one were to tell me that this was a bad government because it taxed certain foreign commodities brought to its ports, it is most probable that I should not make an ado about it, for I can do without them. All machines have their friction; and possibly this does enough good to counterbalance the evil. At any rate, it is a great evil to make a stir about it. But when the friction comes to have its machine, and oppression and robbery are organized, I say, let us not have such a machine any longer. In other words, when a sixth of the population of a nation which has undertaken to be the refuge of liberty are slaves, and a whole country is unjustly overrun and conquered by a foreign army, and subjected to military law, I think that it is not too soon for honest men to rebel and revolutionize. What makes this duty the more urgent is the fact that the country so overrun is not our own, but ours is the invading army.

---

[3] From *Hamlet* (act V, scene i) by William Shakespeare. [Eds.]
[4] From *King John* (act V, scene ii) by William Shakespeare. [Eds.]

Paley,[5] a common authority with many on moral questions, in his   9
chapter on the "Duty of Submission to Civil Government," resolves all
civil obligation into expediency; and he proceeds to say, "that so long as
the interest of the whole society requires it, that is, so long as the established government cannot be resisted or changed without public incon-
veniency, it is the will of God that the established government be
obeyed, and no longer. . . . This principle being admitted, the justice of
every particular case of resistance is reduced to a computation of the
quantity of the danger and grievance on the one side, and of the probability and expense of redressing it on the other." Of this, he says, every
man shall judge for himself. But Paley appears never to have contemplated those cases to which the rule of expediency does not apply, in
which a people, as well as an individual, must do justice, cost what it
may. If I have unjustly wrested a plank from a drowning man, I must
restore it to him though I drown myself. This, according to Paley, would
be inconvenient. But he that would save his life, in such a case, shall lose
it. This people must cease to hold slaves, and to make war on Mexico,
though it cost them their existence as a people.

In their practice, nations agree with Paley; but does any one think   10
that Massachusetts does exactly what is right at the present crisis?

"A drab of state, a cloth-o'-silver slut,
To have her train borne up, and her soul trail in the dirt."[6]

Practically speaking, the opponents to a reform in Massachusetts   11
are not a hundred thousand politicians at the South, but a hundred
thousand merchants and farmers here, who are more interested in commerce and agriculture than they are in humanity, and are not prepared
to do justice to the slave and to Mexico, *cost what it may.* I quarrel not
with far-off foes, but with those who, near at home, coöperate with, and
do the bidding of, those far away, and without whom the latter would
be harmless. We are accustomed to say, that the mass of men are unprepared; but improvement is slow, because the few are not materially
wiser or better than the many. It is not so important that many should
be as good as you, as that there be some absolute goodness somewhere;
for that will leaven the whole lump. There are thousands who are *in
opinion* opposed to slavery and to the war, who yet in effect do nothing
to put an end to them; who, esteeming themselves children of
Washington and Franklin, sit down with their hands in their pockets,
and say that they know not what to do, and do nothing; who even postpone the question of freedom to the question of free-trade, and quietly
read the prices-current along with the latest advices from Mexico, after

---

[5] William Paley (1743–1805), English clergyman and philosopher. [Eds.]

[6] From act IV, scene iv, of Cyril Tourneur's *The Revenger's Tragedy* (1607). [Eds.]

dinner, and, it may be, fall asleep over them both. What is the price-current of an honest man and patriot to-day? They hesitate, and they regret, and sometimes they petition; but they do nothing in earnest and with effect. They will wait, well disposed, for others to remedy the evil, that they may no longer have it to regret. At most, they give only a cheap vote, and a feeble countenance and Godspeed, to the right, as it goes by them. There are nine hundred and ninety-nine patrons of virtue to one virtuous man. But it is easier to deal with the real possessor of a thing than with the temporary guardian of it.

All voting is a sort of gaming, like checkers or backgammon, with a   12 slight moral tinge to it, a playing with right and wrong, with moral questions; and betting naturally accompanies it. The character of the voters is not staked. I cast my vote, perchance, as I think right; but I am not vitally concerned that that right should prevail. I am willing to leave it to the majority. Its obligation, therefore, never exceeds that of expediency. Even voting *for the right* is *doing* nothing for it. It is only expressing to men feebly your desire that it should prevail. A wise man will not leave the right to the mercy of chance, nor wish it to prevail through the power of the majority. There is but little virtue in the action of masses of men. When the majority shall at length vote for the abolition of slavery, it will be because they are indifferent to slavery, or because there is but little slavery left to be abolished by their vote. *They* will then be the only slaves. Only *his* vote can hasten the abolition of slavery who asserts his own freedom by his vote.

I hear of a convention to be held at Baltimore, or elsewhere, for the   13 selection of a candidate for the Presidency, made up chiefly of editors, and men who are politicians by profession; but I think, what is it to any independent, intelligent, and respectable man what decision they may come to? Shall we not have the advantage of his wisdom and honesty, nevertheless? Can we not count upon some independent votes? Are there not many individuals in the country who do not attend conventions? But no: I find that the respectable man, so called, has immediately drifted from his position, and despairs of his country, when his country has more reason to despair of him. He forthwith adopts one of the candidates thus selected as the only *available* one, thus proving that he is himself *available* for any purposes of the demagogue. His vote is of no more worth than that of any unprincipled foreigner or hireling native, who may have been bought. O for a man who is a *man*, and, as my neighbor says, has a bone in his back which you cannot pass your hand through! Our statistics are at fault: the population has been returned too large. How many *men* are there to a square thousand miles in this country? Hardly one. Does not America offer any inducement for men to settle here? The American has dwindled into an Odd Fellow,—one who may be known by the development of his organ of gregariousness, and a manifest lack of intellect and cheerful self-reliance; whose first and chief concern, on coming into the world, is to see that Almshouses[7] are in good repair; and, before yet he has lawfully donned the virile garb, to collect a fund for the support of the widows and orphans that may be; who, in short, ventures to live only by the aid of the Mutual Insurance company, which has promised to bury him decently.

It is not a man's duty, as a matter of course, to devote himself to 14 the eradication of any, even the most enormous wrong; he may still properly have other concerns to engage him; but it is his duty, at least, to wash his hands of it, and, if he gives it no thought longer, not to give it practically his support. If I devote myself to other pursuits and contemplations, I must first see, at least, that I do not pursue them sitting upon another man's shoulders. I must get off him first, that he may pursue his contemplations too. See what gross inconsistency is tolerated. I have heard some of my townsmen say, "I should like to have them order me out to help put down an insurrection of the slaves, or to march to Mexico—see if I would go;" and yet these very men have each, directly by their allegiance, and so indirectly, at least, by their money, furnished a substitute. The soldier is applauded who refuses to serve in an unjust war by those who do not refuse to sustain the unjust government which makes the war; is applauded by those whose own act and authority he disregards and sets at naught; as if the state were penitent to that degree that it hired one to scourge it while it sinned, but not to that degree that it left off sinning for a moment. Thus, under the name of Order and Civil Government, we are all made at last to pay homage to and support our own meanness. After the first blush of sin comes its indifference; and from immoral it becomes, as it were, *un*moral, and not quite unnecessary to that life which we have made.

The broadest and most prevalent error requires the most disinter- 15 ested virtue to sustain it. The slight reproach to which the virtue of patriotism is commonly liable, the noble are most likely to incur. Those who, while they disapprove of the character and measures of a government, yield to it their allegiance and support are undoubtedly its most conscientious supporters, and so frequently the most serious obstacles to reform. Some are petitioning the state to dissolve the Union, to disregard the requisitions of the President. Why do they not dissolve it themselves,—the union between themselves and the state,—and refuse to pay their quota into its treasury? Do not they stand in the same relation to the state that the state does to the Union? And have not the same reasons prevented the state from resisting the Union which have prevented them from resisting the state?

How can a man be satisfied to entertain an opinion merely, and 16 enjoy *it*? Is there any enjoyment in it, if his opinion is that he is aggrieved? If you are cheated out of a single dollar by your neighbor,

---

[7] Poorhouses; county homes that provided for the needy. [Eds.]

you do not rest satisfied with knowing that you are cheated, or with saying that you are cheated, or even with petitioning him to pay you your due; but you take effectual steps at once to obtain the full amount, and see that you are never cheated again. Action from principle, the perception and the performance of right, changes things and relations; it is essentially revolutionary, and does not consist wholly with anything which was. It not only divides states and churches, it divides families; ay, it divides the *individual*, separating the diabolical in him from the divine.

Unjust laws exist: shall we be content to obey them, or shall we 17 endeavor to amend them, and obey them until we have succeeded, or shall we transgress them at once? Men generally, under such a government as this, think that they ought to wait until they have persuaded the majority to alter them. They think that, if they should resist, the remedy would be worse than the evil. But it is the fault of the government itself that the remedy *is* worse than the evil. *It* makes it worse. Why is it not more apt to anticipate and provide for reform? Why does it not cherish its wise minority? Why does it cry and resist before it is hurt? Why does it not encourage its citizens to be on the alert to point out its faults, and *do* better than it would have them? Why does it always crucify Christ, and excommunicate Copernicus and Luther, and pronounce Washington and Franklin rebels?

One would think, that a deliberate and practical denial of its author- 18 ity was the only offense never contemplated by government; else, why has it not assigned its definite, its suitable and proportionate penalty? If a man who has no property refuses but once to earn nine shillings for the state, he is put in prison for a period unlimited by any law that I know, and determined only by the discretion of those who placed him there; but if he should steal ninety times nine shillings from the state, he is soon permitted to go at large again.

If the injustice is part of the necessary friction of the machine of gov- 19 ernment, let it go, let it go: perchance it will wear smooth,—certainly the machine will wear out. If the injustice has a spring, or a pulley, or a rope, or a crank, exclusively for itself, then perhaps you may consider whether the remedy will not be worse than the evil; but if it is of such a nature that it requires you to be the agent of injustice to another, then, I say, break the law. Let your life be a counter friction to stop the machine. What I have to do is to see, at any rate, that I do not lend myself to the wrong which I condemn.

As for adopting the ways which the state has provided for remedy- 20 ing the evil, I know not of such ways. They take too much time, and a man's life will be gone. I have other affairs to attend to. I came into this world, not chiefly to make this a good place to live in, but to live in it, be it good or bad. A man has not everything to do, but something; and because he cannot do *everything*, it is not necessary that he should do *something* wrong. It is not my business to be petitioning the Governor or the Legislature any more than it is theirs to petition me; and if they should not hear my petition, what should I do then? But in this case the state has provided no way: its very Constitution is the evil. This may seem to be harsh and stubborn and unconciliatory; but it is to treat with the utmost kindness and consideration the only spirit that can appreciate or deserve it. So is all change for the better, like birth and death, which convulse the body.

I do not hesitate to say, that those who call themselves Abolitionists should at once effectually withdraw their support, both in person and property, from the government of Massachusetts, and not wait till they constitute a majority of one, before they suffer the right to prevail through them. I think that it is enough if they have God on their side, without waiting for that other one. Moreover, any man more right than his neighbors constitutes a majority of one already. 21

I meet this American government, or its representative, the state government, directly, and face to face, once a year—no more—in the person of its tax-gatherer; this is the only mode in which a man situated as I am necessarily meets it; and it then says distinctly, Recognize me; and the simplest, the most effectual, and, in the present posture of affairs, the indispensablest mode of treating with it on this head, of expressing your little satisfaction with and love for it, is to deny it then. My civil neighbor, the tax-gatherer, is the very man I have to deal with,—for it is, after all, with men and not with parchment that I quarrel,—and he has voluntarily chosen to be an agent of the government. How shall he ever know well what he is and does as an officer of the government, or as a man, until he is obliged to consider whether he shall treat me, his neighbor, for whom he has respect, as a neighbor and well-disposed man, or as a maniac and disturber of the peace, and see if he can get over this obstruction to his neighborliness without a ruder and more impetuous thought or speech corresponding with his action. I know this well, that if one thousand; if one hundred, if ten men whom I could name;—if ten *honest* men only,— say if *one* HONEST man, in this State of Massachusetts, *ceasing to hold slaves,* were actually to withdraw from this copartnership, and be locked up in the county jail therefor, it would be the abolition of slavery in America. For it matters not how small the beginning may seem to be: what is once well done is done forever. But we love better to talk about it: that we say is our mission. Reform keeps many scores of newspapers in its service, but not one man. If my esteemed neighbor, the State's ambassador, who will devote his days to the settlement of the question of human rights in the Council Chamber, instead of being threatened with the prisons of Carolina, were to sit down the prisoner of Massachusetts, that State which is so anxious to foist the sin of slavery upon her sister,—though at present she can discover only an act of inhospitality to be the ground of a 22 quarrel with her,—the Legislature would not wholly waive the subject the following winter.

Under a government which imprisons any unjustly, the true place 23 for a just man is also a prison. The proper place to-day, the only place which Massachusetts has provided for her freer and less desponding spirits, is in her prisons, to be put out and locked out of the State by her own act, as they have already put themselves out by their principles. It is there that the fugitive slave, and the Mexican prisoner on parole, and the Indian come to plead the wrongs of his race should find them; on that separate, but more free and honorable ground, where the State places those who are not *with* her, but *against* her,—the only house in a slave State in which a free man can abide with honor. If any think that their influence would be lost there, and their voices no longer afflict the ear of the State, that they would not be as an enemy within its walls, they do not know by how much truth is stronger than error, nor how much more eloquently and effectively he can combat injustice who has experienced a little in his own person. Cast your whole vote, not a strip of paper merely, but your whole influence. A minority is powerless while it conforms to the majority; it is not even a minority then; but it is irresistible when it clogs by its whole weight. If the alternative is to keep all just men in prison, or give up war and slavery, the State will not hesitate which to choose. If a thousand men were not to pay their tax-bills this year, that would not be a violent and bloody measure, as it would be to pay them, and enable the State to commit violence and shed innocent blood. This is, in fact, the definition of a peaceable revolution, if any such is possible. If the tax-gatherer, or any other public officer, asks me, as one has done, "But what shall I do?" my answer is, "If you really wish to do anything, resign your office." When the subject has refused allegiance, and the officer has resigned his office, then the revolution is accomplished. But even suppose blood should flow. Is there not a sort of blood shed when the conscience is wounded? Through this wound a man's real manhood and immortality flow out, and he bleeds to an everlasting death. I see this blood flowing now.

I have contemplated the imprisonment of the offender, rather than 24 the seizure of his goods,—though both will serve the same purpose,—because they who assert the purest right, and consequently are most dangerous to a corrupt State, commonly have not spent much time in accumulating property. To such the State renders comparatively small service, and a slight tax is wont to appear exorbitant, particularly if they are obliged to earn it by special labor with their hands. If there were one who lived wholly without the use of money, the State itself would hesitate to demand it of him. But the rich man—not to make any invidious comparison—is always sold to the institution which makes him rich. Absolutely speaking, the more money, the less virtue; for money comes

strongest. What force has a multitude? They only can force me who obey a higher law than I. They force me to become like themselves. I do not hear of *men* being *forced* to live this way or that by masses of men. What sort of life were that to live? When I meet a government which says to me, "Your money or your life," why should I be in haste to give it my money? It may be in a great strait, and not know what to do: I cannot help that. It must help itself; do as I do. It is not worth the while to snivel about it. I am not responsible for the successful working of the machinery of society. I am not the son of the engineer. I perceive that, when an acorn and a chestnut fall side by side, the one does not remain inert to make way for the other, but both obey their own laws, and spring and grow and flourish as best they can, till one, perchance, overshadows and destroys the other. If a plant cannot live according to its nature, it dies; and so a man.

The night in prison was novel and interesting enough. The prison- 29 ers in their shirt-sleeves were enjoying a chat and the evening air in the doorway, when I entered. But the jailer said, "Come, boys, it is time to lock up;" and so they dispersed, and I heard the sound of their steps returning into the hollow apartments. My room-mate was introduced to me by the jailer as "a first-rate fellow and a clever man." When the door was locked, he showed me where to hang my hat, and how he managed matters there. The rooms were whitewashed once a month; and this one, at least, was the whitest, most simply furnished, and probably the neatest apartment in the town. He naturally wanted to know where I came from, and what brought me there; and, when I had told him, I asked him in my turn how he came there, presuming him to be an honest man, of course; and, as the world goes, I believe he was. "Why," said he, "they accuse me of burning a barn; but I never did it." As near as I could discover, he had probably gone to bed in a barn when drunk, and smoked his pipe there; and so a barn was burnt. He had the reputation of being a clever man, had been there some three months waiting for his trial to come on, and would have to wait as much longer; but he was quite domesticated and contented, since he got his board for nothing, and thought that he was well treated.

He occupied one window, and I the other; and I saw that if one 30 stayed there long, his principal business would be to look out the window. I had soon read all tracts that were left there, and examined where former prisoners had broken out, and where a grate had been sawed off, and heard the history of the various occupants of that room; for I found that even here there was a history and a gossip which never circulated beyond the walls of the jail. Probably this is the only house in the town where verses are composed, which are afterward printed in a circular form, but not published. I was shown quite a long list of verses which were composed by some young men who had been detected in an attempt to escape, who avenged themselves by signing them.

I pumped my fellow-prisoner as dry as I could, for fear I should 31 never see him again; but at length he showed me which was my bed, and left me to blow out the lamp.

It was like traveling into a far country, such as I had never expected 32 to behold, to lie there for one night. It seemed to me that I never had heard the town-clock strike before, nor the evening sounds of the village; for we slept with the windows open, which were inside the grating. It was to see my native village in the light of the Middle Ages, and our Concord was turned into a Rhine stream, and visions of knights and castles passed before me. They were the voices of old burghers that I heard in the streets. I was an involuntary spectator and auditor of whatever was done and said in the kitchen of the adjacent village-inn,—a wholly new and rare experience to me. It was a closer view of my native town. I was fairly inside of it. I never had seen its institutions before. This is one of its peculiar institutions; for it is a shire town.[8] I began to comprehend what its inhabitants were about.

In the morning, our breakfasts were put through the hole in the 33 door, in small oblong-square tin pans, made to fit, and holding a pint of chocolate, with brown bread, and an iron spoon. When they called for the vessels again, I was green enough to return what bread I had left; but my comrade seized it, and said that I should lay that up for lunch or dinner. Soon after he was let out to work at haying in a neighboring field, whither he went every day, and would not be back till noon; so he bade me good-day, saying that he doubted if he should see me again.

When I came out of prison,—for some one interfered, and paid that 34 tax,—I did not perceive that great changes had taken place on the common, such as he observed who went in a youth and emerged a tottering and gray-headed man; and yet a change had to my eyes come over the scene,—the town, and State, and country,—greater than any that mere time could effect. I saw yet more distinctly the State in which I lived. I saw to what extent the people among whom I lived could be trusted as good neighbors and friends; that their friendship was for summer weather only; that they did not greatly propose to do right; that they were a distinct race from me by their prejudices and superstitions, as the Chinamen and Malays are; that in their sacrifices to humanity they ran no risks, not even to their property; that after all they were not so noble but they treated the thief as he had treated them, and hoped, by a certain outward observance and a few prayers, and by walking in a particular straight though useless path from time to time, to save their souls. This may be to judge my neighbors harshly; for I believe that many of them are not aware that they have such an institution as the jail in their village.

---

[8] County seat. [Eds.]

It was formerly the custom in our village; when a poor debtor came 35 out of jail, for his acquaintances to salute him, looking through their fingers, which were crossed to represent the grating of a jail window, "How do ye do?" My neighbors did not thus salute me, but first looked at me, and then at one another, as if I had returned from a long journey. I was put into jail as I was going to the shoemaker's to get a shoe which was mended. When I was let out the next morning, I proceeded to finish my errand, and, having put on my mended shoe, joined a huckleberry party, who were impatient to put themselves under my conduct; and in half an hour,—for the horse was soon tackled,—was in the midst of a huckleberry field, on one of our highest hills, two miles off, and then the State was nowhere to be seen.

This is the whole history of "My Prisons."   36

I have never declined paying the highway tax, because I am as 37 desirous of being a good neighbor as I am of being a bad subject; and as for supporting schools, I am doing my part to educate my fellow-countrymen now. It is for no particular item in the tax-bill that I refuse to pay it. I simply wish to refuse allegiance to the State, to withdraw and stand aloof from it effectually. I do not care to trace the course of my dollar, if I could, till it buys a man or a musket to shoot one with,—the dollar is innocent,—but I am concerned to trace the effects of my allegiance. In fact, I quietly declare war with the State, after my fashion, though I will still make what use and get what advantage of her I can, as is usual in such cases.

If others pay the tax which is demanded of me, from a sympathy 38 with the State, they do but what they have already done in their own case, or rather they abet injustice to a greater extent than the State requires. If they pay the tax from a mistaken interest in the individual taxed, to save his property, or prevent his going to jail, it is because they have not considered wisely how far they let their private feelings interfere with the public good.

This, then, is my position at present. But one cannot be too much on 39 his guard in such a case, lest his action be biased by obstinacy or an undue regard for the opinions of men. Let him see that he does only what belongs to himself and to the hour.

I think sometimes, Why, this people mean well, they are only igno- 40 rant; they would do better if they knew how: why give your neighbors this pain to treat you as they are not inclined to? But I think again, This is no reason why I should do as they do, or permit others to suffer much greater pain of a different kind. Again, I sometimes say to myself, When many millions of men, without heat, without ill will, without personal feeling of any kind, demand of you a few shillings only, without the possibility, such is their constitution, of retracting or altering their present demand, and without the possibility, on your side, of appeal to any other millions, why expose yourself to this overwhelming brute force? You do not resist cold and hunger, the winds and the waves, thus obstinately; you quietly submit to a thousand similar necessities. You do not put your head into the fire. But just in proportion as I regard this as not wholly a brute force, but partly a human force, and consider that I have relations to those millions as to so many millions of men, and not of mere brute or inanimate things, I see that appeal is possible, first and instantaneously, from them to the Maker of them, and, secondly, from them to themselves. But if I put my head deliberately into the fire, there is no appeal to fire or to the Maker of fire, and I have only myself to blame. If I could convince myself that I have any right to be satisfied with men as they are, and to treat them accordingly, and not accordingly, in some respects, to my requisitions and expectations of what they and I ought to be, then, like a good Mussulman[9] and fatalist, I should endeavor to be satisfied with things as they are, and say it is the will of God. And, above all, there is this difference between resisting this and a purely brute or natural force that I can resist this with some effect; but I cannot expect, like Orpheus,[10] to change the nature of the rocks and trees and beasts.

I do not wish to quarrel with any man or nation. I do not wish to 41 split hairs, to make the fine distinctions, or set myself up as better than my neighbors. I seek rather, I may say, even an excuse for conforming to the laws of the land. I am but too ready to conform to them. Indeed, I have reason to suspect myself on this head; and each year, as the tax-gatherer comes round, I find myself disposed to review the acts and position of the general and State governments, and the spirit of the people, to discover a pretext for conformity.

> "We must affect our country as our parents,
> And if at any time we alienate
> Our love or industry from doing it honor,
> We must respect effects and teach the soul
> Matter of conscience and religion,
> And not desire of rule or benefit."[11]

I believe that the State will soon be able to take all my work of this 42 sort out of my hands, and then I shall be no better a patriot than my fellow-countrymen. Seen from a lower point of view, the Constitution, with all its faults, is very good; the law and the courts are very respectable; even this State and this American government are, in many respects, very admirable, and rare things, to be thankful for, such as a

---

[9] Muslim. [Eds.]

[10] Legendary Greek poet and musician who played the lyre so beautifully that wild beasts were transfixed by his music and rocks and trees moved. [Eds.]

[11] From *The Battle of Alcazar* (1594), a play by George Peele (1558?–1597?). [Eds.]

great many have described them; but seen from a point of view a little higher, they are what I have described them; seen from a higher still, and the highest, who shall say what they are, or that they are worth looking at or thinking of at all?

However, the government does not concern me much, and I shall 43 bestow the fewest possible thoughts on it. It is not many moments that I live under a government, even in this world. If a man is thought-free, fancy-free, imagination-free, that which *is not* never for a long time appearing *to be* to him, unwise rulers or reformers cannot fatally interrupt him.

I know that most men think differently from myself; but those 44 whose lives are by profession devoted to the study of these or kindred subjects content me as little as any. Statesmen and legislators, standing so completely within the institution, never distinctly and nakedly behold it. They speak of moving society, but have no resting-place without it. They may be men of a certain experience and discrimination, and have no doubt invented ingenious and even useful systems, for which we sincerely thank them; but all their wit and usefulness lie within certain not very wide limits. They are wont to forget that the world is not governed by policy and expediency. Webster[12] never goes behind government, and so cannot speak with authority about it. His words are wisdom to those legislators who contemplate no essential reform in the existing government; but for thinkers, and those who legislate for all time, he never once glances at the subject. I know of those whose serene and wise speculations on this theme would soon reveal the limits of his mind's range and hospitality. Yet, compared with the cheap professions of most reformers, and the still cheaper wisdom and eloquence of politicians in general, his are almost the only sensible and valuable words, and we thank Heaven for him. Comparatively, he is always strong, original, and, above all, practical. Still, his quality is not wisdom, but prudence. The lawyer's truth is not Truth, but consistency or a consistent expediency. Truth is always in harmony with herself, and is not concerned chiefly to reveal the justice that may consist with wrong-doing. He well deserves to be called, as he has been called, the Defender of the Constitution. There are really no blows to be given to him but defensive ones. He is not a leader, but a follower. His leaders are the men of '87.[13] "I have never made an effort," he says, "and never propose to make an effort; I have never countenanced an effort, and never mean to countenance an effort, to disturb the arrangement as originally made, by which the various States came into the Union." Still thinking of the sanction which the Constitution gives to slavery, he says, "Because it was a part of the original compact,—let it stand." Notwithstanding his

---

[12] Daniel Webster (1782–1852), legendary American orator, lawyer, and statesman. [Eds.]
[13] The 1787 framers of the Constitution. [Eds.]

special acuteness and ability, he is unable to take a fact out of its merely political relations, and behold it as it lies absolutely to be disposed of by the intellect,—what, for instance, it behooves a man to do here in America to-day with regard to slavery,—but ventures, or is driven, to make some such desperate answer as the following, while professing to speak absolutely, and as a private man,—from which what new and singular code of social duties might be inferred? "The manner," says he, "in which the governments of those States where slavery exists are to regulate it is for their own consideration, under their responsibility to their constituents, to the general laws of propriety, humanity, and justice, and to God. Associations formed elsewhere, springing from a feeling of humanity, or any other cause, have nothing whatever to do with it. They have never received any encouragement from me, and they never will."

They who know of no purer sources of truth, who have traced up 45 its stream no higher, stand, and wisely stand, by the Bible and the Constitution, and drink at it there with reverence and humility; but they who behold where it comes trickling into this lake or that pool, gird up their loins once more, and continue their pilgrimage toward its fountain-head.

No man with a genius for legislation has appeared in America. 46 They are rare in the history of the world. There are orators, politicians, and eloquent men, by the thousand; but the speaker has not yet opened his mouth to speak who is capable of settling the much-vexed questions of the day. We love eloquence for its own sake, and not for any truth which it may utter, or any heroism it may inspire. Our legislators have not yet learned the comparative value of free-trade and of freedom, of union, and of rectitude, to a nation. They have no genius or talent for comparatively humble questions of taxation and finance, commerce and manufacturers and agriculture. If we were left solely to the wordy wit of legislators in Congress for our guidance, uncorrected by the seasonable experience and the effectual complaints of the people, America would not long retain her rank among the nations. For eighteen hundred years, though perchance I have no right to say it, the New Testament has been written; yet where is the legislator who has wisdom and practical talent enough to avail himself of the light which it sheds on the science of legislation?

The authority of government, even such as I am willing to submit 47 to,—for I will cheerfully obey those who know and can do better than I, and in many things even those who neither know nor can do so well,— is still an impure one: to be strictly just, it must have the sanction and consent of the governed. It can have no pure right over my person and property but what I concede to it. The progress from an absolute to a limited monarchy, from a limited monarchy to a democracy, is a progress toward a true respect for the individual. Even the Chinese philosopher was wise enough to regard the individual as the basis of the empire. Is a democracy, such as we know it, the last improvement possible in government? Is it not possible to take a further step towards recognizing and organizing the rights of man? There will never be a really free and enlightened State until the State comes to recognize the individual as a higher and independent power, from which all its own power and authority are derived, and treats him accordingly. I please myself with imagining a State at last which can afford to be just to all men, and to treat the individual with respect as a neighbor; which even would not think it inconsistent with its own repose if a few were to live aloof from it, not meddling with it, nor embraced by it, who fulfilled all the duties of neighbors and fellow-men. A State which bore this kind of fruit, and suffered it to drop off as fast as it ripened, would prepare the way for a still more perfect and glorious State, which also I have imagined, but not yet anywhere seen.

Responding to Reading

1. What moral or political choice does each of the following statements by Thoreau imply?
   - "'That government is best which governs least'" (1).
   - "All men recognize the right of revolution" (8).
   - "All voting is a sort of gaming, like checkers or backgammon" (12).
   - "Under a government which imprisons any unjustly, the true place for a just man is also a prison" (23).
   - "I did not see why the schoolmaster should be taxed to support the priest, and not the priest the schoolmaster" (26).
2. Do you believe civil disobedience is ever necessary? If so, under what circumstances?
3. Do you see any advantages in obeying a law, however unjust, rather than disobeying it? Explain.

LETTER FROM BIRMINGHAM JAIL

Martin Luther King, Jr.

One of the greatest civil rights leaders and orators of this century (see also p. 457), Martin Luther King, Jr. (1929–1968), was also a Baptist minister and winner of the 1964 Nobel Peace Prize. He was born in Atlanta, Georgia, and earned degrees from four institutions. Influenced by Thoreau and Gandhi, King altered the spirit of African-American protest in the United States by advocating nonviolent civil disobedience to achieve racial equality. King's books include Letter from Birmingham Jail *(1963) and* Where Do We Go from Here: Chaos or Community? *(1967). King was assassinated on April 4, 1968. The following letter, written in 1963, is his eloquent and impassioned response to a public statement by eight fellow clergymen in Birmingham, Alabama, who appealed to the citizenry of the city to "observe the principles of law and order and common sense" rather than join in the principled protests that King was leading.*

MY DEAR FELLOW CLERGYMEN:[1]   1

While confined here in the Birmingham city jail, I came across your recent statement calling my present activities "unwise and untimely." Seldom do I pause to answer criticism of my work and ideas. If I sought to answer all the criticisms that cross my desk, my secretaries would have little time for anything other than such correspondence in the course of the day, and I would have no time for constructive work. But since I feel that you are men of genuine good will and that your criticisms are sincerely set forth, I want to try to answer your statement in what I hope will be patient and reasonable terms.

I think I should indicate that I am here in Birmingham, since you   2
have been influenced by the view which argues against "outsiders coming in." I have the honor of serving as president of the Southern Christian Leadership Conference, an organization operating in every southern state, with headquarters in Atlanta, Georgia. We have some eighty-five affiliated organizations across the South, and one of them is the Alabama Christian Movement for Human Rights. Frequently we share staff, educational, and financial resources with our affiliates. Several months ago the affiliate here in Birmingham asked us to be on call to engage in a nonviolent direct-action program if such were deemed necessary. We readily consented, and when the hour came we lived up to our promise. So I, along with several members of my staff, am here because I was invited here. I am here because I have organizational ties here.

But more basically, I am in Birmingham because injustice is here.   3
Just as the prophets of the eighth century B.C. left their villages and carried their "thus saith the Lord" far beyond the boundaries of their home towns, and just as the Apostle Paul left his village of Tarsus and carried the gospel of Jesus Christ to the far corners of the Greco-Roman world, so am I compelled to carry the gospel of freedom beyond my own home town. Like Paul, I must constantly respond to the Macedonian call for aid.

Moreover, I am cognizant of the interrelatedness of all communities   4
and states. I cannot sit idly by in Atlanta and not be concerned about

---

[1] This response to a published statement by eight fellow clergymen from Alabama (Bishop C. C. J. Carpenter, Bishop Joseph A. Durick, Rabbi Milton L. Grafman, Bishop Paul Hardin, Bishop Holan B. Harmon, the Reverend George M. Murray, the Reverend Edward V. Ramage and the Reverend Earl Stallings) was composed under somewhat constricting circumstances. Begun on the margins of the newspaper in which the statement appeared while I was in jail, the letter was continued on scraps of writing paper supplied by a friendly Negro trusty, and concluded on a pad my attorneys were eventually permitted to leave me. Although the text remains in substance unaltered, I have indulged in the author's prerogative of polishing it for publication.

what happens in Birmingham. Injustice anywhere is a threat to justice everywhere. We are caught in an inescapable network of mutuality, tied in a single garment of destiny. Whatever affects one directly, affects all indirectly. Never again can we afford to live with the narrow, provincial "outside agitator" idea. Anyone who lives inside the United States can never be considered an outsider anywhere within its bounds.

You deplore the demonstrations taking place in Birmingham. But 5 your statement, I am sorry to say, fails to express a similar concern for the conditions that brought about the demonstrations. I am sure that none of you would want to rest content with the superficial kind of social analysis that deals merely with effects and does not grapple with underlying causes. It is unfortunate that demonstrations are taking place in Birmingham, but it is even more unfortunate that the city's white power structure left the Negro community with no alternative.

In any nonviolent campaign there are four basic steps: collec- 6 tion of the facts to determine whether injustices exist; negotiation; self-purification; and direct action. We have gone through all these steps in Birmingham. There can be no gainsaying the fact that racial injustice engulfs this community. Birmingham is probably the most thoroughly segregated city in the United States. Its ugly record of brutality is widely known. Negroes have experienced grossly unjust treatment in the courts. There have been more unsolved bombings of Negro homes and churches in Birmingham than in any other city in the nation. These are the hard, brutal facts of the case. On the basis of these conditions, Negro leaders sought to negotiate with the city fathers. But the latter consistently refused to engage in good-faith negotiation.

Then, last September, came the opportunity to talk with leaders of 7 Birmingham's economic community. In the course of the negotiations, certain promises were made by the merchants—for example, to remove the stores' humiliating racial signs. On the basis of these promises, the Reverend Fred Shuttlesworth and the leaders of the Alabama Christian Movement for Human Rights agreed to a moratorium on all demonstrations. As the weeks and months went by, we realized that we were the victims of a broken promise. A few signs, briefly removed, returned; the others remained.

As in so many past experiences, our hopes had been blasted, and 8 the shadow of deep disappointment settled upon us. We had no alternative except to prepare for direct action, whereby we would present our very bodies as a means of laying our case before the conscience of the local and the national community. Mindful of the difficulties involved, we decided to undertake a process of self-purification. We began a series of workshops on nonviolence, and we repeatedly asked ourselves: "Are you able to accept blows without retaliating?" "Are you able to endure the ordeal of jail?" We decided to schedule our direct-action program for the Easter season, realizing that except for

Christmas, this is the main shopping period of the year. Knowing that a strong economic-withdrawal program would be the by-product of direct action, we felt that this would be the best time to bring pressure to bear on the merchants for the needed change.

Then it occurred to us that Birmingham's mayoral election was 9 coming up in March, and we speedily decided to postpone action until after election day. When we discovered that the Commissioner of Public Safety, Eugene "Bull" Connor,[2] had piled up enough votes to be in the run-off, we decided again to postpone action until the day after the run-off so that the demonstrations could not be used to cloud the issues. Like many others, we wanted to see Mr. Connor defeated, and to this end we endured postponement after postponement. Having aided in this community need, we felt that our direct-action program could be delayed no longer.

You may well ask, "Why direct action? Why sit-ins, marches, and so 10 forth? Isn't negotiation a better path?" You are quite right in calling for negotiation. Indeed, this is the very purpose of direct action. Nonviolent direct action seeks to create such a crisis and foster such a tension that a community which has constantly refused to negotiate is forced to confront the issue. It seeks so to dramatize the issue that it can no longer be ignored. My citing the creation of tension as part of the work of the non-violent-resister may sound rather shocking. But I must confess that I am not afraid of the word "tension." I have earnestly opposed violent tension, but there is a type of constructive, nonviolent tension which is necessary for growth. Just as Socrates felt that it was necessary to create a tension in the mind so that individuals could rise from the bondage of myths and half-truths to the unfettered realm of creative analysis and objective appraisal, so must we see the need for nonviolent gadflies to create the kind of tension in society that will help men rise from the dark depths of prejudice and racism to the majestic heights of understanding and brotherhood.

The purpose of our direct-action program is to create a situation so 11 crisis-packed that it will inevitably open the door to negotiation. I therefore concur with you in your call for negotiation. Too long has our beloved Southland been bogged down in a tragic effort to live in monologue rather than dialogue.

One of the basic points in your statement is that the action that I and 12 my associates have taken in Birmingham is untimely. Some have asked: "Why didn't you give the new city administration time to act?" The only answer that I can give to this query is that the new Birmingham administration must be prodded about as much as the outgoing one, before it will act. We are sadly mistaken if we feel that the election of

---

[2] An ardent segregationist, Connor ordered police officers to use police dogs and fire hoses to break up civil rights demonstrations. (Conner lost his bid for mayor.) [Eds.]

Albert Boutwell as mayor will bring the millennium to Birmingham. While Mr. Boutwell is a much more gentle person than Mr. Connor, they are both segregationists, dedicated to maintenance of the status quo. I have hoped that Mr. Boutwell will be reasonable enough to see the futility of massive resistance to desegregation. But he will not see this without pressure from devotees of civil rights. My friends, I must say to you that we have not made a single gain in civil rights without determined legal and nonviolent pressure. Lamentably, it is an historical fact that privileged groups seldom give up their privileges voluntarily. Individuals may see the moral light and voluntarily give up their unjust posture; but, as Reinhold Niebuhr[3] has reminded us, groups tend to be more immoral than individuals.

We know through painful experience that freedom is never voluntarily given by the oppressor; it must be demanded by the oppressed. Frankly, I have yet to engage in a direct-action campaign that was "well timed" in the view of those who have not suffered unduly from the disease of segregation. For years now I have heard the word "Wait!" It rings in the ear of every Negro with piercing familiarity. This "Wait" has almost always meant "Never." We must come to see, with one of our distinguished jurists, that "justice too long delayed is justice denied."[4]   13

We have waited for more than 340 years for our constitutional and God-given rights. The nations of Asia and Africa are moving with jetlike speed toward gaining political independence, but we still creep at horse-and-buggy pace toward gaining a cup of coffee at a lunch counter. Perhaps it is easy for those who have never felt the stinging darts of segregation to say, "Wait." But when you have seen vicious mobs lynch your mothers and fathers at will and drown your sisters and brothers at whim; when you have seen hate-filled policemen curse, kick, and even kill your black brothers and sisters; when you see the vast majority of your twenty million Negro brothers smothering in an airtight cage of poverty in the midst of an affluent society; when you suddenly find your tongue twisted and your speech stammering as you seek to explain to your six-year-old daughter why she can't go to the public amusement park that has just been advertised on television, and see tears welling up in her eyes when she is told that Funtown is closed to colored children, and see ominous clouds of inferiority beginning to form in her little mental sky, and see her beginning to distort her personality by developing an unconscious bitterness toward white people; when you have to concoct an answer for a five-year-old son who is asking, "Daddy, why do white people treat colored people so mean?"; when you take a cross-country drive and find it necessary to sleep night after night in the uncomfortable corners of your   14

---

[3] American religious and social thinker (1892–1971). [Eds.]
[4] Attributed to British statesman William Ewart Gladstone (1809–1898), a stalwart of the Liberal Party who also said, "You cannot fight the future. Time is on our side." [Eds.]

automobile because no motel will accept you; when you are humiliated day in and day out by nagging signs reading "white" and "colored"; when your first name becomes "nigger," your middle name becomes "boy" (however old you are) and your last name becomes "John," and your wife and mother are never given the respected title "Mrs."; when you are harried by day and haunted by night by the fact that you are a Negro, living constantly at tiptoe stance, never quite knowing what to expect next, and are plagued with inner fears and outer resentments; when you are forever fighting a degenerating sense of "nobodiness"— then you will understand why we find it difficult to wait. There comes a time when the cup of endurance runs over, and men are no longer willing to be plunged into the abyss of despair. I hope, sirs, you can understand our legitimate and unavoidable impatience.

You express a great deal of anxiety over our willingness to break   15 laws. This is certainly a legitimate concern. Since we so diligently urge people to obey the Supreme Court's decision of 1954 outlawing segregation in the public schools, at first glance it may seem rather paradoxical for us consciously to break laws. One may well ask: "How can you advocate breaking some laws and obeying others?" The answer lies in the fact that there are two types of laws: just and unjust. I would be the first to advocate obeying just laws. One has not only a legal but a moral responsibility to obey just laws. Conversely, one has a moral responsibility to disobey unjust laws. I would agree with St. Augustine[5] that "an unjust law is no law at all."

Now, what is the difference between the two? How does one deter-   16 mine whether a law is just or unjust? A just law is a man-made code that squares with the moral law or the law of God. An unjust law is a code this is out of harmony with the moral law. To put it in the terms of St. Thomas Aquinas:[6] An unjust law is a human law that is not rooted in eternal law and natural law. Any law that uplifts human personality is just. Any law that degrades human personality is unjust. All segregation statutes are unjust because segregation distorts the soul and damages the personality. It gives the segregator a false sense of superiority and the segregated a false sense of inferiority. Segregation, to use the terminology of the Jewish philosopher Martin Buber,[7] substitutes an "I-it" relationship for an "I-thou" relationship and ends up relegating persons to the status of things. Hence segregation is not only politically, economically, and sociologically unsound, it is morally wrong and sinful. Paul Tillich[8] has said that sin is separation. Is not segregation an existential expression of man's tragic separation, his awful estrangement, his terrible sinfulness? Thus it

---

5 Italian-born missionary and theologian (?–c.604) [Eds.]
6 Italian philosopher and theologian (1225–1274). [Eds.]
7 Austrian existentialist philosopher and Judaic scholar (1878–1965). [Eds.]
8 American philosopher and theologian (1886–1965). [Eds.]

is that I can urge men to obey the 1954 decision of the Supreme Court, for it is morally right; and I can urge them to disobey segregation ordinances, for they are morally wrong.

Let us consider a more concrete example of just and unjust laws. An 17 unjust law is a code that a numerical or power majority group compels a minority group to obey but does not make binding on itself. This is *difference* made legal. By the same token, a just law is a code that a majority compels a minority to follow and that it is willing to follow itself. This is *sameness* made legal.

Let me give another explanation. A law is unjust if it is inflicted on 18 a minority that, as a result of being denied the right to vote, had no part in enacting or devising the law. Who can say that the legislature of Alabama which set up that state's segregation laws was democratically elected? Throughout Alabama all sorts of devious methods are used to prevent Negroes from becoming registered voters, and there are some counties in which, even though Negroes constitute a majority of the population, not a single Negro is registered. Can any law enacted under such circumstances be considered democratically structured?

Sometimes a law is just on its face and unjust in its application. For 19 instance, I have been arrested on a charge of parading without a permit. Now, there is nothing wrong in having an ordinance which requires a permit for a parade. But such an ordinance becomes unjust when it is used to maintain segregation and to deny citizens the First-Amendment privilege of peaceful assembly and protest.

I hope you are able to see the distinction I am trying to point out. In 20 no sense do I advocate evading or defying the law, as would the rabid segregationist. That would lead to anarchy. One who breaks an unjust law must do so openly, lovingly, and with a willingness to accept the penalty. I submit that an individual who breaks a law that conscience tells him is unjust, and who willingly accepts the penalty of imprisonment in order to arouse the conscience of the community over its injustice, is in reality expressing the highest respect for law.

Of course, there is nothing new about this kind of civil disobedi- 21 ence. It was evidenced sublimely in the refusal of Shadrach, Meshach, and Abednego to obey the laws of Nebuchadnezzar, on the ground that a higher moral law was at stake.[9] It was practiced superbly by the early Christians, who were willing to face hungry lions and the excruciating pain of chopping blocks rather than submit to certain unjust laws of the Roman Empire. To a degree, academic freedom is a reality today

---

[9] In the book of Daniel, Nebuchadnezzar commanded the people to worship a golden statue or be thrown into a furnace of blazing fire. When Shadrach, Meshach, and Abednego refused to worship any god but their own, they were bound and thrown into a blazing furnace, but the fire had no effect on them. Their escape led Nebuchadnezzar to make a decree forbidding blasphemy against their god. [Eds.]

because Socrates practiced civil disobedience.[10] In our own nation, the Boston Tea Party represented a massive act of civil disobedience.

We should never forget that everything Adolf Hitler did in Germany 22 was "legal" and everything the Hungarian freedom fighters[11] did in Hungary was "illegal." It was "illegal" to aid and comfort a Jew in Hitler's Germany. Even so, I am sure that, had I lived in Germany at the time, I would have aided and comforted my Jewish brothers. If today I lived in a Communist country where certain principles dear to the Christian faith are suppressed, I would openly advocate disobeying that country's anti-religious laws.

I must make two honest confessions to you, my Christian and 23 Jewish brothers. First, I must confess that over the past few years I have been gravely disappointed with the white moderate. I have almost reached the regrettable conclusion that the Negro's great stumbling block in his stride toward freedom is not the White Citizen's Counciler or the Ku Klux Klanner, but the white moderate, who is more devoted to "order" than to justice; who prefers a negative peace which is the absence of tension to a positive peace which is the presence of justice; who constantly says, "I agree with you in the goal you seek, but I cannot agree with your methods of direct action"; who paternalistically believes he can set the timetable for another man's freedom; who lives by a mythical concept of time and who constantly advises the Negro to wait for a "more convenient season." Shallow understanding from people of good will is more frustrating than absolute misunderstanding from people of ill will. Lukewarm acceptance is much more bewildering than outright rejection.

I had hoped that the white moderate would understand that law 24 and order exist for the purpose of establishing justice and that when they fail in this purpose they become the dangerously structured dams that block the flow of social progress. I had hoped that the white moderate would understand that the present tension in the South is a necessary phase of the transition from an obnoxious negative peace, in which the Negro passively accepted his unjust plight, to a substantive and positive peace, in which all men will respect the dignity and worth of human personality. Actually, we who engage in nonviolent direct action are not the creators of tension. We merely bring to the surface the hidden tension that is already alive. We bring it out in the open, where it can be seen and dealt with. Like a boil that can never be cured so long as it is covered up but must be opened with all its ugliness to the natural medicines of air and light, injustice must be exposed, with all the

---

[10]The ancient Greek philosopher Socrates was tried by the Athenians for corrupting their youth through his use of questions to teach. When he refused to change his methods of teaching, he was condemned to death. [Eds.]

[11]The Hungarian anti-Communist uprising of 1956 was quickly crushed by the army of the USSR. [Eds.]

tension its exposure creates, to the light of human conscience and the air of national opinion, before it can be cured.

In your statement you assert that our actions, even though peaceful, 25 must be condemned because they precipitate violence. But is this a logical assertion? Isn't this like condemning a robbed man because his possession of money precipitated the evil act of robbery? Isn't this like condemning Socrates because his unswerving commitment to truth and his philosophical inquiries precipitated the act by the misguided populace in which they made him drink hemlock? Isn't this like condemning Jesus because his unique God-consciousness and never-ceasing devotion to God's will precipitated the evil act of crucifixion? We must come to see that, as the federal courts have consistently affirmed, it is wrong to urge an individual to cease his efforts to gain his basic constitutional rights because the quest may precipitate violence. Society must protect the robbed and punish the robber.

I had also hoped that the white moderate would reject the myth 26 concerning time in relation to the struggle for freedom. I have just received a letter from a white brother in Texas. He writes: "All Christians know that the colored people will receive equal rights eventually, but it is possible that you are in too great a religious hurry. It has taken Christianity almost two thousand years to accomplish what it has. The teachings of Christ take time to come to earth." Such an attitude stems from a tragic misconception of time, from the strangely irrational notion that there is something in the very flow of time that will inevitably cure all ills. Actually, time itself is neutral; it can be used either destructively or constructively. More and more I feel that the people of ill will have used time much more effectively than have the people of good will. We will have to repent in this generation not merely for the hateful words and actions of the bad people, but for the appalling silence of the good people. Human progress never rolls in on wheels of inevitability; it comes through the tireless efforts of men willing to be co-workers with God, and without this hard work, time itself becomes an ally of the forces of social stagnation. We must use time creatively, in the knowledge that the time is always ripe to do right. Now is the time to make real the promise of democracy and transform our pending national elegy into a creative psalm of brotherhood. Now is the time to lift our national policy from the quicksand of racial injustice to the solid rock of human dignity.

You speak of our activity in Birmingham as extreme. At first I was 27 rather disappointed that fellow clergymen would see my nonviolent efforts as those of an extremist. I began thinking about the fact that I stand in the middle of two opposing forces in the Negro community. One is a force of complacency, made up in part of Negroes who, as a result of long years of oppression, are so drained of self-respect and a sense of "somebodiness" that they have adjusted to segregation; and in part of a few middle-class Negroes who, because of a degree of academic and economic security and because in some ways they profit by segregation, have become insensitive to the problems of the masses. The other force is one of bitterness and hatred, and it comes perilously close to advocating violence. It is expressed in the various black nationalist groups that are springing up across the nation, the largest and best-known being Elijah Muhammad's Muslim movement. Nourished by the Negro's frustration over the continued existence of racial discrimination, this movement is made up of people who have lost faith in America, who have absolutely repudiated Christianity, and who have concluded that the white man is an incorrigible "devil."

I have tried to stand between these two forces, saying that we need 28 emulate neither the "do-nothingism" of the complacent nor the hatred and despair of the black nationalist. For there is the more excellent way of love and nonviolent protest. I am grateful to God that, through the influence of the Negro church, the way of nonviolence became an integral part of our struggle.

If this philosophy had not emerged, by now many streets of the 29 South would, I am convinced, be flowing with blood. And I am further convinced that if our white brothers dismiss as "rabblerousers" and "outside agitators" those of us who employ nonviolent direct action, and if they refuse to support our nonviolent efforts, millions of Negroes will, out of frustration and despair, seek solace and security in black-nationalist ideologies—a development that would inevitably lead to a frightening racial nightmare.

Oppressed people cannot remain oppressed forever. The yearning 30 for freedom eventually manifests itself, and that is what has happened to the American Negro. Something within has reminded him of his birthright of freedom, and something without has reminded him that it can be gained. Consciously or unconsciously, he has been caught up by the *Zeitgeist*,[12] and with his black brothers of Africa and his brown and yellow brothers of Asia, South America, and the Caribbean, the United States Negro is moving with a sense of great urgency toward the promised land of racial justice. If one recognizes this vital urge that has engulfed the Negro community, one should readily understand why public demonstrations are taking place. The Negro has many pent-up resentments and latent frustrations, and he must release them. So let him march; let him make prayer pilgrimages to the city hall; let him go on freedom rides—and try to understand why he must do so. If his repressed emotions are not released in nonviolent ways, they will seek expression through violence; this is not a threat but a fact of history. So I have not said to my people, "Get rid of your discontent." Rather, I have tried to say that this normal and healthy discontent can be channeled

---

[12] The spirit of the times. [Eds.]

into the creative outlet of nonviolent direct action. And now this approach is being termed extremist.

But though I was initially disappointed at being categorized as an 31 extremist, as I continued to think about the matter I gradually gained a measure of satisfaction from the label. Was not Jesus an extremist for love: "Love your enemies, bless them that curse you, do good to them that hate you, and pray for them which despitefully use you, and persecute you." Was not Amos an extremist for justice: "Let justice roll down like waters and righteousness like an ever-flowing stream." Was not Paul an extremist for the Christian gospel: "I bear in my body the marks of the Lord Jesus." Was not Martin Luther an extremist: "Here I stand; I cannot do otherwise, so help me God." And John Bunyan: "I will stay in jail to the end of my days before I make a butchery of my conscience." And Abraham Lincoln: "This nation cannot survive half slave and half free." And Thomas Jefferson: "We hold these truths to be self-evident, that all men are created equal. . . ." So the question is not whether we will be extremists, but what kind of extremists we will be. Will we be extremists for hate or for love? Will we be extremists for the preservation of injustice or for the extension of justice? In that dramatic scene on Calvary's hill three men were crucified. We must never forget that all three were crucified for the same thing—the crime of extremism. Two were extremists for immorality, and thus fell below their environment. The other, Jesus Christ, was an extremist for love, truth, and goodness, and thereby rose above his environment. Perhaps the South, the nation, and the world are in dire need of creative extremists.

I had hoped that the white moderate would see this need. Perhaps I 32 was too optimistic; perhaps I expected too much. I suppose I should have realized that few members of the oppressor race can understand the deep groans and passionate yearnings of the oppressed race, and still fewer have the vision to see that injustice must be rooted out by strong, persistent, and determined action. I am thankful, however, that some of our white brothers in the South have grasped the meaning of this social revolution and committed themselves to it. They are still all too few in quantity, but they are big in quality. Some—such as Ralph McGill, Lillian Smith, Harry Golden, James McBridge Dabbs, Ann Braden, and Sarah Patton Boyle—have written about our struggle in eloquent and prophetic terms. Others have marched with us down nameless streets of the South. They have languished in filthy, roach-infested jails, suffering the abuse and brutality of policemen who view them as "dirty nigger-lovers." Unlike so many of their moderate brothers and sisters, they have recognized the urgency of the moment and sensed the need for powerful "action" antidotes to combat the disease of segregation.

Let me take note of my other major disappointment. I have been so 33 greatly disappointed with the white church and its leadership. Of course, there are some notable exceptions. I am not unmindful of the fact that each of you has taken some significant stands on this issue. I commend you, Reverend Stallings, for your Christian stand on this past Sunday, in welcoming Negroes to your worship service on a nonsegregated basis. I commend the Catholic leaders of this state for integrating Spring Hill College several years ago.

But despite these notable exceptions, I must honestly reiterate that I 34 have been disappointed with the church. I do not say this as one of those negative critics who can always find something wrong with the church. I say this as a minister of the gospel, who loves the church; who was nurtured in its bosom; who has been sustained by its spiritual blessings and who will remain true to it as long as the cord of life shall lengthen.

When I was suddenly catapulted into the leadership of the bus 35 protest in Montgomery, Alabama, a few years ago, I felt we would be supported by the white church. I felt that the white ministers, priests, and rabbis of the South would be among our strongest allies. Instead, some have been outright opponents, refusing to understand the freedom movement and misrepresenting its leaders; all too many others have been more cautious than courageous and have remained silent behind the anesthetizing security of stained glass windows.

In spite of my shattered dreams, I came to Birmingham with the 36 hope that the white religious leadership of this community would see the justice of our cause and, with deep moral concern, would serve as the channel through which our just grievances could reach the power structure. I had hoped that each of you would understand. But again I have been disappointed.

I have heard numerous southern religious leaders admonish their 37 worshipers to comply with a desegregation decision because it is the law, but I have longed to hear white ministers declare: "Follow this decree because integration is morally right and because the Negro is your brother." In the midst of blatant injustices inflicted upon the Negro, I have watched white churchmen stand on the sideline and mouth pious irrelevancies and sanctimonious trivialities. In the midst of a mighty struggle to rid our nation of racial and economic injustice, I have heard many ministers say: "Those are social issues, with which the gospel has no real concern." And I have watched many churches commit themselves to a completely otherworldly religion which makes a strange, un-Biblical distinction between body and soul, between the sacred and the secular.

I have traveled the length and breadth of Alabama, Mississippi, and 38 all the other southern states. On sweltering summer days and crisp autumn mornings I have looked at the South's beautiful churches with their lofty spires pointing heavenward. I have beheld the impressive outlines of her massive religious-education buildings. Over and over I have found myself asking: "What kind of people worship here? Who is their God? Where were their voices when the lips of Governor Barnett[13] dripped with words of interposition and nullification? Where were they when Governor Wallace[14] gave a clarion call for defiance and hatred? Where were their voices of support when bruised and weary Negro men and women decided to rise from the dark dungeons of complacency to the bright hills of creative protest?"

Yes, these questions are still in my mind. In deep disappointment I have wept over the laxity of the church. But be assured that my tears have been tears of love. There can be no deep disappointment where there is not deep love. Yes, I love the church. How could I do otherwise? I am in the rather unique position of being the son, the grandson, and the great-grandson of preachers. Yes, I see the church as the body of Christ. But, oh! How we have blemished and scarred that body through social neglect and through fear of being nonconformists. ₃₉

There was a time when the church was very powerful—in the time when the early Christians rejoiced at being deemed worthy to suffer for what they believed. In those days the church was not merely a thermometer that recorded the ideas and principles of popular opinion; it was a thermostat that transformed the mores of society. Whenever the early Christians entered a town, the people in power became disturbed and immediately sought to convict the Christians for being "disturbers of the peace" and "outside agitators." But the Christians pressed on, in the conviction that they were "a colony of heaven," called to obey God rather than man. Small in number, they were big in commitment. They were too God-intoxicated to be "astronomically intimidated." By their effort and example they brought an end to such ancient evils as infanticide and gladiatorial contests. ₄₀

Things are different now. So often the contemporary church is a weak, ineffectual voice with an uncertain sound. So often it is an archdefender to the status quo. Far from being disturbed by the presence of the church, the power structure of the average community is consoled by the church's silent—and often even vocal—sanction of things as they are. ₄₁

But the judgment of God is upon the church as never before. If today's church does not recapture the sacrificial spirit of the early church, it will lose its authenticity, forfeit the loyalty of millions, and be dismissed as an irrelevant social club with no meaning for the twentieth century. Every day I meet young people whose disappointment with the church has turned into outright disgust. ₄₂

---

[13] Ross Barnett, segregationist governor of Mississippi, best known for his resistance to the integration of the University of Mississippi in 1962. [Eds.]

[14] George Wallace, segregationist governor of Alabama, best known for standing in the doorway of a University of Alabama building to block the entrance of two black students who were trying to register. [Eds.]

Perhaps I have once again been too optimistic. Is organized religion 43 too inextricably bound to the status quo to save our nation and the world? Perhaps I must turn my faith to the inner spiritual church, the church within the church, as the true *ekklesia*[15] and the hope of the world. But again I am thankful to God that some noble souls from the ranks of organized religion have broken loose from the paralyzing chains of conformity and joined us as active partners in the struggle for freedom. They have left their secure congregations and walked the streets of Albany, Georgia, with us. They have gone down the highways of the South on tortuous rides for freedom. Yes, they have gone to jail with us. Some have been dismissed from their churches, have lost the support of their bishops and fellow ministers. But they have acted in the faith that right defeated is stronger than evil triumphant. Their witness has been the spiritual salt that has preserved the true meaning of the gospel in these troubled times. They have carved a tunnel of hope through the dark mountain of disappointment.

I hope the church as a whole will meet the challenge of this decisive 44 hour. But even if the church does not come to the aid of justice, I have no despair about the future. I have no fear about the outcome of our struggle in Birmingham, even if our motives are at present misunderstood. We will reach the goal of freedom in Birmingham and all over the nation, because the goal of America is freedom. Abused and scorned though we may be, our destiny is tied up with America's destiny. Before the pilgrims landed at Plymouth, we were here. Before the pen of Jefferson etched the majestic words of the Declaration of Independence across the pages of history, we were here. For more than two centuries our forebears labored in this country without wages; they made cotton king; they built the homes of their masters while suffering gross injustice and shameful humiliation—and yet out of a bottomless vitality they continued to thrive and develop. If the inexpressible cruelties of slavery could not stop us, the opposition we now face will surely fail. We will win our freedom because the sacred heritage of our nation and the eternal will of God are embodied in our echoing demands.

Before closing I feel impelled to mention one other point in your 45 statement that has troubled me profoundly. You warmly commended the Birmingham police force for keeping "order" and "preventing violence." I doubt that you would have so warmly commended the police force if you had seen its dogs sinking their teeth into unarmed, nonviolent Negroes. I doubt that you would so quickly commend the policemen if you were to observe their ugly and inhumane treatment of Negroes here in the city jail; if you were to watch them push and curse old Negro women and young Negro girls; if you were to see them slap and kick old Negro men and young boys; if you were to observe them,

---

[15] The Greek word for the early Christian church. [Eds.]

as they did on two occasions, refuse to give us food because we wanted to sing our grace together. I cannot join you in your praise of the Birmingham police department.

It is true that the police have exercised a degree of discipline in han- 46 dling the demonstrators. In this sense they have conducted themselves rather "nonviolently" in public. But for what purpose? To preserve the evil system of segregation. Over the past few years I have consistently preached that nonviolence demands that the means we use must be as pure as the ends we seek. I have tried to make clear that it is wrong to use immoral means to attain moral ends. But now I must affirm that it is just as wrong, or perhaps even more so, to use moral means to preserve immoral ends. Perhaps Mr. Connor and his policemen have been rather nonviolent in public, as was Chief Pritchett in Albany, Georgia, but they have used the moral means of nonviolence to maintain the immoral end of racial injustice. As T. S. Eliot[16] has said, "The last temptation is the greatest treason: To do the right deed for the wrong reason."

I wish you had commended the Negro sit-inners and demonstra- 47 tors of Birmingham for their sublime courage, their willingness to suffer, and their amazing discipline in the midst of great provocation. One day the South will recognize its real heroes. They will be the James Merediths,[17] with the noble sense of purpose that enables them to face jeering and hostile mobs, and with the agonizing loneliness that characterizes the life of the pioneer. They will be old, oppressed, battered Negro women, symbolized in a seventy-two-year-old woman in Montgomery, Alabama, who rose up with a sense of dignity and with her people decided not to ride segregated buses, and who responded with ungrammatical profundity to one who inquired about her weariness: "My feets is tired, but my soul is at rest." They will be the young high school and college students, the young ministers of the gospel and a host of their elders, courageously and nonviolently sitting in at lunch counters and willingly going to jail for conscience' sake. One day the South will know that when these disinherited children of God sat down at lunch counters, they were in reality standing up for what is best in the American dream and for the most sacred values in our Judaeo-Christian heritage, thereby bringing our nation back to those great wells of democracy which were dug deep by the founding fathers in their formulation of the Constitution and the Declaration of Independence.

Never before have I written so long a letter. I'm afraid it is much too 48 long to take your precious time. I can assure you that it would have been much shorter if I had been writing from a comfortable desk, but

---

[16] American-born British poet (1888–1965), winner of the 1948 Nobel Prize for literature. [Eds.]

[17] First African-American to enroll at the University of Mississippi, after federal troops were brought in to control demonstrators protesting his enrollment. [Eds.]

what else can one do when he is alone in a narrow jail cell, other than write long letters, think long thoughts, and pray long prayers?

If I have said anything in this letter that overstates the truth and indicates an unreasonable impatience, I beg you to forgive me. If I have said anything that understates the truth and indicates my having a patience that allows me to settle for anything less than brotherhood, I beg God to forgive me. 49

I hope this letter finds you strong in the faith. I also hope that cir- 50 cumstances will soon make it possible for me to meet each of you, not as an integrationist or a civil-rights leader but as a fellow clergyman and a Christian brother. Let us all hope that the dark clouds of racial prejudice will soon pass away and the deep fog of misunderstanding will be lifted from our fear-drenched communities, and in some not too distant tomorrow the radiant stars of love and brotherhood will shine over our great nation with all their scintillating beauty.

Yours for the cause of Peace and Brotherhood,   51
MARTIN LUTHER KING, JR.

Responding to Reading

1. What decision do the clergy members King addresses believe he should rethink? Do you believe King would have been justified in arguing that he had no other alternative than to protest? Would you accept this argument?

2. In paragraph 30, King says, "Oppressed people cannot remain oppressed forever." Do you think world events of the last few years confirm or contradict this statement? Explain.

3. Throughout this letter, King uses elaborate diction and a variety of rhetorical devices: he addresses his audience directly; makes frequent use of balance and parallelism, understatement, and metaphor; and makes many historical and religious allusions. What effect do you think King intended these rhetorical devices to have on the letter's original audience of clergymembers? Does King's elaborate style enhance his argument, or does it just get in the way? Explain.

LIFEBOAT ETHICS: THE CASE
AGAINST "AID" THAT HARMS

Garrett Hardin

Biologist Garrett Hardin (1915–) writes on moral and ethical issues in his field. His books include Filters against Folly: How to Survive Despite Economists, Ecologists, and the Merely Eloquent *(1985),*

Living within Limits: How Global Population Growth Threatens Widespread Social Disorder (1992), and The Ostrich Factor: Our Population Myopia *(1999). He often takes unpopular positions on subjects such as ecology and the scarcity of resources, and he is a fierce advocate of population limits. He has said, "Population is not a global problem. It is produced in each bedroom, a very local activity. So population control needs to be local." In this essay, which originally appeared in 1974 in* Psychology Today, *Hardin uses the metaphor of the wealthy nations of the world as lifeboats to illustrate the rights of both the needy and the rich in the problem of distributing the world's food. (Note that some of the world conditions on which Hardin bases his arguments have changed in the years since his essay was written.)*

Environmentalists use the metaphor of the earth as a "spaceship" in   1 trying to persuade countries, industries and people to stop wasting and polluting our natural resources. Since we all share life on this planet, they argue, no single person or institution has the right to destroy, waste, or use more than a fair share of its resources.

But does everyone on earth have an equal right to an equal share of   2 its resources? The spaceship metaphor can be dangerous when used by misguided idealists to justify suicidal policies for sharing our resources through uncontrolled immigration and foreign aid. In their enthusiastic but unrealistic generosity, they confuse the ethics of a spaceship with those of a lifeboat.

A true spaceship would have to be under the control of a captain,   3 since no ship could possibly survive if its course were determined by committee. Spaceship Earth certainly has no captain; the United Nations is merely a toothless tiger, with little power to enforce any policy upon its bickering members.

If we divide the world crudely into rich nations and poor nations,   4 two thirds of them are desperately poor, and only one third comparatively rich, with the United States the wealthiest of all. Metaphorically each rich nation can be seen as a lifeboat full of comparatively rich people. In the ocean outside each lifeboat swim the poor of the world, who would like to get in, or at least to share some of the wealth. What should the lifeboat passengers do?

First, we must recognize the limited capacity of any lifeboat. For   5 example, a nation's land has a limited capacity to support a population and as the (current energy crisis) has shown us, in some ways we have already exceeded the carrying capacity of our land.

So here we sit, say 50 people in our lifeboat. To be generous let us   6 assume it has room for 10 more, making a total capacity of 60. Suppose the 50 of us in the lifeboat see 100 others swimming in the water outside, begging for admission to our boat or for handouts. We have several options: we may be tempted to try to live by the Christian ideal of being "our brother's keeper," or by the Marxist ideal of "to each according to his needs." Since the needs of all in the water are the same, and since they can all be seen as "our brothers," we could take them all into our boat, making a total of 150 in a boat designed for 60. The boat swamps, everyone drowns. Complete justice, complete catastrophe.

Since the boat has an unused excess capacity of 10 more passen- 7 gers, we could admit just 10 more to it. But which 10 do we let in? How do we choose? Do we pick the best 10, the neediest 10, "first come, first served"? And what do we say to the 90 we exclude? If we do let an extra 10 into our lifeboat, we will have lost our "safety factor," an engineering principle of critical importance. For example, if we don't leave room for excess capacity as a safety factor in our country's agriculture, a new plant disease or a bad change in the weather could have disastrous consequences.

Suppose we decide to preserve our small safety factor and admit no 8 more to the lifeboat. Our survival is then possible although we shall have to be constantly on guard against boarding parties.

While this last solution clearly offers the only means of our survival, 9 it is morally abhorrent to many people. Some say they feel guilty about their good luck. My reply is simple: "Get out and yield your place to others." This may solve the problem of the guilt-ridden person's conscience, but it does not change the ethics of the lifeboat. The needy person to whom the guilt-ridden person yields his place will not himself feel guilty about his good luck. If he did, he would not climb aboard. The net result of conscience-stricken people giving up their unjustly held seats is the elimination of that sort of conscience from the lifeboat.

This is the basic metaphor within which we must work out our 10 solutions. Let us now enrich the image, step by step, with substantive additions from the real world, a world that must solve real and pressing problems of overpopulation and hunger.

The harsh ethics of the lifeboat become even harsher when we con- 11 sider the reproductive differences between the rich nations and the poor nations. The people inside the lifeboats are doubling in numbers every 87 years: those swimming around outside are doubling on the average, every 35 years, more than twice as fast as the rich. And since the world's resources are dwindling, the difference in prosperity between the rich and the poor can only increase.

As of 1973, the U.S. had a population of 210 million people, who 12 were increasing by 0.8 percent per year. Outside our lifeboat, let us imagine another 210 million people (say the combined populations of Colombia, Ecuador, Venezuela, Morocco, Pakistan, Thailand and the Philippines), who are increasing at a rate of 3.3 percent per year. Put differently, the doubling time for this aggregate population is 21 years, compared to 87 years for the U.S.

Now suppose the U.S. agreed to pool its resources with those seven 13 countries, with everyone receiving an equal share. Initially the ratio of

Americans to non-Americans in this model would be one-to-one but consider what the ratio would be after 87 years, by which time the Americans would have doubled to a population of 420 million. By then, doubling every 21 years, the other group would have swollen to 354 billion. Each American would have to share the available resources with more than eight people.

But, one could argue, this discussion assumes that current population 14 trends will continue, and they may not. Quite so. Most likely the rate of population increase will decline much faster in the U.S. than it will in the other countries, and there does not seem to be much we can do about it. In sharing with "each according to his needs," we must recognize that needs are determined by population size, which is determined by the rate of reproduction, which at present is regarded as a sovereign right of every nation, poor or not. This being so, the philanthropic load created by the sharing ethic of the spaceship can only increase.

The fundamental error of spaceship ethics, and the sharing it 15 requires, is that it leads to what I call "the tragedy of the commons." Under a system of private property, the men who own property recognize their responsibility to care for it, for if they don't they will eventually suffer. A farmer, for instance, will allow no more cattle in a pasture than its carrying capacity justifies. If he overloads it, erosion sets in, weeds take over, and he loses the use of the pasture.

If a pasture becomes a commons open to all, the right of each to use 16 it may not be matched by a corresponding responsibility to protect it. Asking everyone to use it with discretion will hardly do, for the considerate herdsman who refrains from overloading the commons suffers more than a selfish one who says his needs are greater. If everyone would restrain himself all would be well; but it takes only one less than everyone to ruin a system of voluntary restraint. In a crowded world of less than perfect human beings, mutual ruin is inevitable if there are no controls. This is the tragedy of the commons.

One of the major tasks of education today should be the creation of 17 such an acute awareness of the dangers of the commons that people will recognize its many varieties. For example, the air and water have become polluted because they are treated as commons. Further growth in the population or per-capita conversion of natural resources into pollutants will only make the problem worse. The same holds true for the fish of the oceans. Fishing fleets have nearly disappeared in many parts of the world; technological improvements in the art of fishing are hastening the day of complete ruin. Only the replacement of the system of the commons with a responsible system of control will save the land, air, water and oceanic fisheries.

In recent years there has been a push to create a new commons 18 called a World Food Bank, an international depository of food reserves to which nations would contribute according to their abilities and from which they would draw according to their needs. This humanitarian proposal has received support from many liberal international groups, and from such prominent citizens as Margaret Mead, U.N. Secretary General Kurt Waldheim, and Senators Edward Kennedy and George McGovern.

A world food bank appeals powerfully to our humanitarian 19 impulses. But before we rush ahead with such a plan, let us recognize where the greatest political push comes from, lest we be disillusioned later. Our experience with the "Food for Peace program," or Public Law 480, gives us the answer. This program moved billions of dollars worth of U.S. surplus grain to food-short, population-long countries during the past two decades. But when P.L. 480 first became law, a headline in the business magazine *Forbes* revealed the real power behind it: "Feeding the World's Hungry Millions: How It Will Mean Billions for U.S. Business."

And indeed it did. In the years 1960 to 1970, U.S. taxpayers spent a 20 total of $7.9 billion on the Food for Peace program. Between 1948 and 1970, they also paid an additional $50 billion for other economic-aid programs, some of which went for food and food-producing machinery and technology. Though all U.S. taxpayers were forced to contribute to the cost of P.L. 480, certain special interest groups gained handsomely under the program. Farmers did not have to contribute the grain; the Government, or rather the taxpayers, bought it from them at full market prices. The increased demand raised prices of farm products generally. The manufacturers of farm machinery, fertilizers and pesticides benefited by the farmers' extra efforts to grow more food. Grain elevators profited from storing the surplus until it could be shipped. Railroads made money hauling it to ports, and shipping lines profited from carrying it overseas. The implementation of P.L. 480 required the creation of a vast Government bureaucracy, which then acquired its own vested interest in continuing the program regardless of its merits.

Those who proposed and defended the Food for Peace program in 21 public rarely mentioned its importance to any of these special interests. The public emphasis was always on its humanitarian effects. The combination of silent selfish interests and highly vocal humanitarian apologists made a powerful and successful lobby for extracting money from taxpayers. We can expect the same lobby to push now for the creation of a World Food Bank.

However great the potential benefit to selfish interests, it should not 22 be a decisive argument against a truly humanitarian program. We must ask if such a program would actually do more good than harm, not only momentarily but also in the long run. Those who propose the food bank usually refer to a current "emergency" or "crisis" in terms of world food supply. But what is an emergency? Although they may be infrequent and sudden, everyone knows that emergencies will occur from time to time. A well-run family, company, organization or country prepares for the likelihood of accidents and emergencies. It expects them, it budgets for them, it saves for them.

What happens if some organizations or countries budget for acci- 23 dents and others do not? If each country is solely responsible for its own well-being, poorly managed ones will suffer. But they can learn from experience. They may mend their ways, and learn to budget for infrequent but certain emergencies. For example, the weather varies from year to year, and periodic crop failures are certain. A wise and competent government saves out of the production of the good years in anticipation of bad years to come. Joseph taught this policy to Pharoah in Egypt more than 2,000 years ago. Yet the great majority of the governments in the world today do not follow such a policy. They lack either the wisdom or the competence, or both. Should those nations that do manage to put something aside be forced to come to the rescue each time an emergency occurs among the poor nations?

"But it isn't their fault!" Some kind-hearted liberals argue, "How 24 can we blame the poor people who are caught in an emergency? Why must they suffer for the sins of their governments?" The concept of blame is simply not relevant here. The real question is, what are the operational consequences of establishing a world food bank? If it is open to every country every time a need develops, slovenly rulers will not be motivated to take Joseph's advice. Someone will always come to their aid. Some countries will deposit food in the world food bank, and others will withdraw it. There will be almost no overlap. As a result of such solutions to food shortage emergencies, the poor countries will not learn to mend their ways, and will suffer progressively greater emergencies as their populations grow.

On the average, poor countries undergo a 2.5 percent increase in 25 population each year; rich countries, about 0.8 percent. Only rich countries have anything in the way of food reserves set aside, and even they do not have as much as they should. Poor countries have none. If poor countries received no food from the outside, the rate of their population growth would be periodically checked by crop failures and famines. But if they can always draw on a world food bank in time of need, their population can continue to grow unchecked, and so will their "need" for aid. In the short run, a world food bank may diminish that need, but in the long run it actually increases the need without limit.

Without some system of worldwide food sharing, the proportion of 26 people in the rich and poor nations might eventually stabilize. The overpopulated poor countries would decrease in numbers, while the rich countries that had room for more people would increase. But with a well-meaning system of sharing, such as a world food bank, the growth differential between the rich and the poor countries will not only persist, it will increase. Because of the higher rate of population growth in the poor countries of the world, 88 percent of today's children are born poor, and only 12 percent rich. Year by year the ratio becomes worse, as the fast-reproducing poor outnumber the slow-reproducing rich.

A world food bank is thus a commons in disguise. People will have 27 more motivation to draw from it than to add to any common store. The less provident and less able will multiply at the expense of the abler and more provident, bringing eventual ruin upon all who share in the commons. Besides, any system of "sharing" that amounts to foreign aid from the rich nations to the poor nations will carry the taint of charity, which will contribute little to the world peace so devoutly desired by those who support the idea of a world food bank.

As past U.S. foreign-aid programs have amply and depressingly 28 demonstrated, international charity frequently inspires mistrust and antagonism rather than gratitude on the part of the recipient nation.

The modern approach to foreign aid stresses the export of technol- 29 ogy and advice, rather than money and food. As an ancient Chinese proverb goes: "Give a man a fish and he will eat for a day; teach him how to fish and he will eat for the rest of his days." Acting on this advice, the Rockefeller and Ford Foundations have financed a number of programs for improving agriculture in the hungry nations. Known as the "Green Revolution," these programs have led to the development of "miracle rice" and "miracle wheat," new strains that offer bigger harvests and greater resistance to crop damage. Norman Borlaug, the Nobel Prize winning agronomist who, supported by the Rockefeller Foundation, developed "miracle wheat," is one of the most prominent advocates of a world food bank.

Whether or not the Green Revolution can increase food production 30 as much as its champions claim is a debatable but possibly irrelevant point. Those who support this well-intended humanitarian effort should first consider some of the fundamentals of human ecology. Ironically, one man who did was the late Alan Gregg, a vice president of the Rockefeller Foundation. Two decades ago he expressed strong doubts about the wisdom of such attempts to increase food production. He likened the growth and spread of humanity over the surface of the earth to the spread of cancer in the human body, remarking that "cancerous growths demand food, but, as far as I know, they have never been cured by getting it."

Every human born constitutes a draft on all aspects of the environ- 31 ment: food, air, water, forests, beaches, wildlife, scenery and solitude. Food can, perhaps, be significantly increased to meet a growing demand. But what about clean beaches, unspoiled forests, and solitude? If we satisfy a growing population's need for food, we necessarily decrease its per capita supply of the other resources needed by men.

India, for example, now has a population of 600 million, which 32 increases by 15 million each year. This population already puts a huge load on a relatively impoverished environment. The country's forests are now only a small fraction of what they were three centuries ago, and floods and erosion continually destroy the insufficient farmland that remains. Every one of the 15 million new lives added to India's population puts an additional burden on the environment, and increases the economic and social costs of crowding. However humanitarian our intent, every Indian life saved through medical or nutritional assistance from abroad diminishes the quality of life for those who remain, and for subsequent generations. If rich countries make it possible, through foreign aid, for 600 million Indians to swell to 1.2 billion in a mere 28 years, as their current growth rate threatens, will future generations of Indians thank us for hastening the destruction of their environment? Will our good intentions be sufficient excuse for the consequences of our actions?

My final example of a commons in action is one for which the pub- 33 lic has the least desire for rational discussion—immigration. Anyone who publicly questions the wisdom of current U.S. immigration policy is promptly charged with bigotry, prejudice, ethnocentrism, chauvinism, isolationism or selfishness. Rather than encounter such accusations, one would rather talk about other matters, leaving immigration policy to wallow in the crosscurrents of special interests that take no account of the good of the whole, or the interests of posterity.

Perhaps we still feel guilty about things we said in the past. Two 34 generations ago the popular press frequently referred to Dagos, Wops, Polacks, Chinks and Krauts, in articles about how America was being "overrun" by foreigners of supposedly inferior genetic stock. But because the implied inferiority of foreigners was used then as justification for keeping them out, people now assume that restrictive policies could only be based on such misguided notions. There are other grounds.

Just consider the numbers involved. Our Government acknowl- 35 edges a net inflow of 400,000 immigrants a year. While we have no hard data on the extent of illegal entries, educated guesses put the figure at about 600,000 a year. Since the natural increase (excess of births over deaths) of the resident population now runs about 1.7 million per year, the yearly gain from immigration amounts to at least 19 percent of the total annual increase, and may be as much as 37 percent if we include the estimate for illegal immigrants. Considering the growing use of birth-control devices, the potential effect of educational campaigns by such organizations as Planned Parenthood Federation of America and Zero Population Growth, and the influence of inflation and the housing shortage, the fertility rate of American women may decline so much that immigration could account for all the yearly increase in population. Should we not at least ask if that is what we want?

For the sake of those who worry about whether the "quality" of the 36 average immigrant compares favorably with the quality of the average resident, let us assume that immigrants and nativeborn citizens are of exactly equal quality, however one defines that term. We will focus here only on quantity; and since our conclusions will depend on nothing else, all charges of bigotry and chauvinism become irrelevant.

World food banks *move food to the people*, hastening the exhaustion of 37 the environment of the poor countries. Unrestricted immigration, on the other hand, *moves people to the food*, thus speeding up the destruction of the environment of the rich countries. We can easily understand why poor people should want to make this latter transfer, but why should rich hosts encourage it?

As is the case of foreign-aid programs, immigration receives sup- 38 port from selfish interests and humanitarian impulses. The primary selfish interest in unimpeded immigration is the desire of employers for cheap labor, particularly in industries and trades that offer degrading work. In the past, one wave of foreigners after another was brought into the U.S. to work at wretched jobs for wretched wages. In recent years the Cubans, Puerto Ricans and Mexicans have had this dubious honor. The interests of the employers of cheap labor mesh well with the guilty silence of the country's liberal intelligentsia. White Anglo-Saxon Protestants are particularly reluctant to call for a closing of the doors to immigration for fear of being called bigots.

But not all countries have such reluctant leadership. Most educated 39 Hawaiians, for example, are keenly aware of the limits of their environment, particularly in terms of population growth. There is only so much room on the islands, and the islanders know it. To Hawaiians, immigrants from the other 49 states present as great a threat as those from other nations. At a recent meeting of Hawaiian government officials in Honolulu, I had the ironic delight of hearing a speaker, who like most of his audience was of Japanese ancestry, ask how the country might practically and constitutionally close its door to further immigration. One member of the audience countered: "How can we shut the doors now? We have many friends and relatives in Japan that we'd like to bring here some day so that they can enjoy Hawaii too." The Japanese-American speaker smiled sympathetically and answered: "Yes, but we have children now, and someday we'll have grandchildren too. We can bring more people here from Japan only by giving away some of the land that we hope to pass on to our grandchildren some day. What right do we have to do that?"

At this point, I can hear U.S. liberals asking: "How can you justify 40 slamming the door once you're inside? You say that immigrants should be kept out. But aren't we all immigrants, or the descendants of immi-grants? If we insist on staying, must we not admit all others?" Our crav-ing for intellectual order leads us to seek and prefer symmetrical rules and morals: a single rule for me and everybody else; the same rule yes-terday, today and tomorrow. Justice, we feel, should not change with time and place.

We Americans of non-Indian ancestry can look upon ourselves as   41
the descendants of thieves who are guilty morally, if not legally, of stealing this land from its Indian owners. Should we then give back the land to the now living American descendants of those Indians? However morally or logically sound this proposal may be, I, for one, am unwilling to live by it and I know no one else who is. Besides, the logical consequence would be absurd. Suppose that, intoxicated with a sense of pure justice, we should decide to turn our land over to the Indians. Since all our other wealth has also been derived from the land, wouldn't we be morally obliged to give that back to the Indians too?

Clearly, the concept of pure justice produces an infinite regression   42
to absurdity. Centuries ago, wise men invented statutes of limitations to justify the rejection of such pure justice, in the interest of preventing continual disorder. The law zealously defends property rights. Drawing a line after an arbitrary time has elapsed may be unjust, but the alterna-tives are worse.

We are all the descendants of thieves, and the world's resources are   43
inequitably distributed. But we must begin the journey to tomorrow from the point where we are today. We cannot remake the past. We can-not safely divide the wealth equitably among all peoples so long as peo-ple reproduce at different rates. To do so would guarantee that our grandchildren, and everyone else's grandchildren, would have only a ruined world to inhabit.

To be generous with one's own possessions is quite different from   44
being generous with those of posterity. We should call this point to the attention of those who, from a commendable love of justice and equality, would institute a system of the commons, either in the form of a world food bank, or of unrestricted immigration. We must convince them if we wish to save at least some parts of the world from environmental ruin.

Responding to Reading

1. Hardin presents his problem as one that has no comfortable solution. One alternative, welcoming all who wish to come into the lifeboat, is "complete justice, complete catastrophe" (6); the other, retaining the crucial "safety factor," is both "the only means of our survival" and "morally abhorrent to many people" (8–9). Does Hardin see these two alternatives as ethically and practically unacceptable? Do you? Is it really an either/or situation, or are there some solutions he ignores?

2. Does Hardin's use of the lifeboat metaphor clarify his arguments and present the problem he describes in vivid terms? Or do you find it simplistic, distracting, or irrelevant?

3. In paragraph 2, Hardin asks, "But does everyone on earth have an equal right to an equal share of its resources?" That is, are some people more—or less—deserving than others? How would you answer this question?

DOG LAB

Claire McCarthy

A pediatrician at an inner-city clinic in Boston, Claire McCarthy graduated from Harvard Medical School and worked as a resident at Boston's Children's Hospital. During her medical training, she kept extensive journals to "help her understand the dramatic changes she was witnessing herself and the overwhelming events she was participating in at the hospital each day." These provided the basis of her book Learning How the Heart Beats: The Making of a Pediatrician *(1995), which physician and writer Richard Selzer (see p. 532) has called a "moving personal rendition of the anguish and the joy of one doctor's becoming." McCarthy's latest book is* Everyone's Children: A Pediatrician's Story of an Inner-City Practice *(1998). In the following chapter from* Learning How the Heart Beats, *McCarthy recalls a controversial lab lesson in which students studied the cardiovascular system of a sedated living dog, a lesson culminating in the cutting open of the dog's chest and the dog's ultimate death.*

When I finished college and started medical school, the learning changed fundamentally. Whereas in college I had been learning mostly for learning's sake, learning in order to know something, in medical school I was learning in order to *do* something, do the thing I wanted to do with my life. It was exhilarating and at the same time a little scary. My study now carried responsibility.

The most important course in the first year besides Anatomy was Physiology, the study of the functions and processes of the human body. It was the most fascinating subject I had ever studied. I found the intricacies of the way the body works endlessly intriguing and ingenious: the way the nervous system is designed to differentiate a sharp touch from a soft one; the way muscles move and work together to throw a ball; the wisdom of the kidneys, which filter the blood and let pass out only waste products and extra fluid, keeping everything else carefully within. It was magical to me that each organ and system worked so beautifully and in perfect concert with the rest of the body.

very important that we do the right thing, but the right thing seemed variable and unclear.

I was quiet during these discussions. I didn't want to kill a dog, but 14 I certainly wanted to take advantage of every learning opportunity offered me. And despite the fact that the course instructor had said our grades wouldn't be affected if we didn't attend the lab, I wasn't sure I believed him, and I didn't want to take any chances. Even if he didn't incorporate the lab report into our grades, I was worried that there would be some reference to it in the final exam, some sneaky way that he would bring it up. Doing well had become so important that I was afraid to trust anyone; doing well had become more important than anything.

I found myself waiting to see what other people would decide. I 15 was ashamed not to be taking a stand, but I was stuck in a way I'd never been before. I didn't like the idea of doing the lab; it felt wrong. Yet for some reason I was embarrassed that I felt that way, and the lab seemed so important. The more I thought about it, the more confused I became.

Although initially the students had appeared divided more or less 16 evenly between the camps, as the lab day drew nearer the majority chose to participate. The discussions didn't stop, but they were fewer and quieter. The issue seemed to become more private.

I was assigned to the second lab day. My indecision was becoming 17 a decision since I hadn't crossed my name off the list. I can still change my mind, I told myself. I'm not on a team yet, nobody's counting on me to show up. One of my classmates asked me to join his group. I hedged.

The day before group lists had to be handed in, the course instruc- 18 tor made an announcement. It was brief and almost offhand: he said that if any of us wished to help anesthetize the dogs for the lab, we were welcome to do so. He told us where to go and when to be there for each lab day. I wrote the information down.

Somehow, this was what I needed. I made my decision. I would do 19 the lab, but I would go help anesthetize the dogs first.

Helping with the anesthesia, I thought, would be taking full respon- 20 sibility for what I was doing, something that was very important to me. I was going to *face* what I was doing, see the dogs awake with their tails wagging instead of meeting them asleep and sort of pretending they weren't real. I also thought it might make me feel better to know that the dogs were treated well as they were anesthetized and to be there, help- ing to do it gently. Maybe in part I thought of it as my penance.

The day of the first lab came. Around five o'clock I went down to 21 the Friday afternoon "happy hour" in the dormitory living room to talk to the students as they came back. They came back singly or in pairs, quiet, looking dazed. They threw down their coats and backpacks and made their way to the beer and soda without talking to anyone. Some, once they had a cup in their hands, seemed to relax and join in conversations; others took their cups and sat alone on the couches. They all looked tired, worn out.

"Well?" I asked several of them. "What was it like?"   22

Most shrugged and said little. A few said that it was interesting and   23
that they'd learned a lot, but they said it without any enthusiasm. Every
one of them said it was hard. I thought I heard someone say that their
dog had turned out to be pregnant. Nobody seemed happy.

The morning of my lab was gray and dreary. I overslept, which I   24
hardly ever do. I got dressed quickly and went across the street to the
back entrance of the lab building. It was quiet and still and a little dark.
The streets were empty except for an occasional cab. I found the open
door and went in.

There was only one other student waiting there, a blond-haired   25
woman named Elise. I didn't know her well. We had friends in common, but we'd never really talked. She was sweet and soft-spoken; she
wore old jeans and plaid flannel shirts and hung out with the activist
crowd. She had always intimidated me. I felt as though I weren't political enough when I was around her. I was actually a little surprised that
she was doing the lab at all, as many of her friends had chosen not to.

We greeted each other awkwardly, nodding hello and taking our   26
places leaning against the wall. Within a few minutes one of the teaching assistants came in, said good morning, pulled out some keys, and
let us into a room down the hall. Two more teaching assistants followed
shortly.

The teaching assistants let the dogs out of cages, and they ran   27
around the room. They were small dogs; I think they were beagles. They
seemed happy to be out of their cages, and one of them, white with
brown spots, came over to me with his tail wagging. I leaned over to pet
him, and he licked my hand, looking up at me eagerly. I stood up again
quickly.

The teaching assistant who had let us in, a short man with tousled   28
brown hair and thick glasses, explained that the dogs were to be given
intramuscular injections of a sedative that would put them to sleep.
During the lab they would be given additional doses intravenously as
well as other medications to stop them from feeling pain. We could
help, he said, by holding the dogs while they got their injections. Elise
and I nodded.

So we held the dogs, and they got their injections. After a few   29
minutes they started to stumble, and we helped them to the floor. I
remember that Elise petted one of the dogs as he fell asleep and that she
cried. I didn't cry, but I wanted to.

When we were finished, I went back to my room. I sat at my desk,   30
drank my coffee, and read over the lab instructions again. I kept thinking

about the dogs running around, about the little white one with the brown spots, and I felt sick. I stared at the instructions without really reading them, looking at my watch every couple of minutes. At five minutes before eight I picked up the papers, put them in my backpack with my books, and left.

The lab was held in a big open room with white walls and lots of windows. The dogs were laid out on separate tables lined up across the room; they were on their backs, tied down. They were all asleep, but some of them moved slightly, and it chilled me. 31

We walked in slowly and solemnly, putting our coats and back-packs on the rack along the wall and going over to our assigned tables. I started to look for the dog who had licked my hand, but I stopped myself. I didn't want to know where he was. 32

Our dog was brown and black, with soft floppy ears. His eyes were shut. He looked familiar. We took our places, two on each side of the table, laid out our lab manuals, and began. 33

The lab took all day. We cut through the dog's skin to find an artery and vein, into which we placed catheters. We injected different drugs and chemicals and watched what happened to the dog's heart rate and blood pressure, carefully recording the results. At the end of the day, when we were done with the experiments, we cut open the dog's chest. We cut through his sternum and pulled open his rib cage. His heart and lungs lay in front of us. The heart was a fist-size muscle that squeezed itself as it beat, pushing blood out. The lungs were white and solid and glistening under the pleura that covered them. The instructor pointed out different blood vessels, like the aorta and the superior vena cava. He showed us the stellate ganglion, which really did look like a star. I think we used the electrical paddles of a defibrillator and shocked the dog's heart into ventricular fibrillation, watching it shiver like Jell-O in front of us. I think that's how we killed them—or maybe it was with a lethal dose of one of the drugs. I'm not sure. It's something I guess I don't want to remember. 34

Dan was the anesthesiologist, the person assigned to making sure that the dog stayed asleep throughout the entire procedure. Every once in a while Dan would get caught up in the experiment and the dog would start to stir. I would nudge Dan, and he would quickly give more medication. The dog never actually woke up, but every time he moved even the slightest bit, every time I had to think about him being a real dog who was never going to wag his tail or lick anyone's hand again because of us, I got so upset that I couldn't concentrate. In fact, I had trouble concentrating on the lab in general. I kept staring at the dog. 35

As soon as we were finished, or maybe a couple of minutes before, I left. I grabbed my coat and backpack and ran down the stairs out into the dusk of the late afternoon. It was drizzling, and the medical school looked brown and gray. I walked quickly toward the street. 36

I was disappointed in the lab and disappointed in myself for doing 37
it. I knew now that doing the lab was wrong. Maybe not wrong for
everyone—it was clearly a complicated and individual choice—but
wrong for me. The knowledge I had gained wasn't worth the life of a
dog to me. I felt very sad.

The drizzle was becoming rain. I slowed down; even though it was 38
cold, the rain felt good. A couple of people walking past me put up their
umbrellas. I let the rain fall on me. I wanted to get wet.

From the moment you enter the field of medicine as a medical stu- 39
dent, you have an awareness that you have entered something bigger
and more important than you are. Doctors are different from other people, we are told implicitly, if not explicitly. Medicine is a way of life, with
its own values and guidelines for daily living. They aren't bad values;
they include things like the importance of hard work, the pursuit of
knowledge, and the preservation of life—at least human life. There's
room for individuality and variation, but that's something I realized
later, much later. When I started medical school I felt that not only did I
have to learn information and skills, I had to become a certain kind of
person, too. It was very important to me to learn to do the thing that a
doctor would do in a given situation. Since the course instructor, who
represented Harvard Medical School to me, had recommended that we
do the lab, I figured that a doctor would do it. That wasn't the only reason I went ahead with the lab, but it was a big reason.

The rain started to come down harder and felt less pleasant. I 40
walked more quickly, across Longwood Avenue into Vanderbilt Hall.
I could hear familiar voices coming from the living room, but I didn't
feel like talking to anyone. I ducked into the stairwell.

I got to my room, locked the door behind me, took off my coat, and 40
lay down on my bed. The rain beat against my window. It was the time
I usually went running, but the thought of going back out in the rain
didn't appeal to me at all. I was suddenly very tired.

As I lay there I thought about the course instructor's discussion of 42
the spectrum of morality and drawing lines. Maybe it's not a matter of
deciding which animals I feel comfortable killing, I thought. Maybe it's
about drawing different kinds of lines: drawing the lines to define how
much of myself I will allow to change. I was proud of being a true student, even if it did mean becoming a little like an automaton. But I still
needed to be the person I was before; I needed to be able to make some
decisions without worrying about what a doctor would do.

I got up off the bed, opened a can of soup, and put it in a pan on the 43
hot plate to warm. I got some bread and cheese out of the refrigerator,
sat down at my desk, and opened my Biochemistry text.

Suddenly I stopped. I closed the text, reached over, and turned on 44
the television, which sat on a little plastic table near the desk. There
would be time to study later. I was going to watch television, read a

newspaper, and call some friends I hadn't called since starting medical school. It was time to make some changes, some changes back.

Responding to Reading

1. Summarize the two main schools of thought about whether or not to participate in "dog lab." Do the students really have a choice? Explain.
2. Why did McCarthy decide to help anesthesize the dogs? Does her decision make sense to you?
3. Did McCarthy believe that the knowledge she gained was worth the sacrifice of the dog? Do you agree with her? Do you think her experience in "dog lab" changed her? Do you think it made her a better doctor? Explain.

DEATH AND JUSTICE: HOW CAPITAL PUNISHMENT AFFIRMS LIFE

Edward I. Koch

Ed Koch (1924–   ) was born in The Bronx, New York, and attended the City College of New York and New York University Law School. After practicing law privately, he served for eight years in the U.S. House of Representatives and later for two years on the New York City Council. He was elected mayor of New York City in 1978 and served for three terms. Since his 1988 defeat in a race for a fourth term, the colorful Koch has been a political commentator, lecturer, syndicated columnist, and presiding judge on television's The People's Court. *His books include such memoirs and opinion pieces as* Mayor *(1984) and* Citizen Koch *(1992) and a series of mysteries, most recently* Murder on 34th Street *(1997). The following opinion piece was published in 1985.*

Last December a man named Robert Lee Willie, who had been convicted of raping and murdering an 18-year-old woman, was executed in the Louisiana state prison. In a statement issued several minutes before his death, Mr. Willie said: "Killing people is wrong. . . . It makes no difference whether it's citizens, countries, or governments. Killing is wrong." Two weeks later in South Carolina, an admitted killer named Joseph Carl Shaw was put to death for murdering two teenagers. In an appeal to the governor for clemency, Mr. Shaw wrote: "Killing is wrong when I did it. Killing is wrong when you do it. I hope you have the courage and moral strength to stop the killing."

It is a curiosity of modern life that we find ourselves being lectured on morality by cold-blooded killers. Mr. Willie previously had been convicted of aggravated rape, aggravated kidnapping, and the murders of a Louisiana deputy and a man from Missouri. Mr. Shaw committed another murder a week before the two for which he was executed, and admitted mutilating the body of the 14-year-old girl he killed. I can't help wondering what prompted these murderers to speak out against killing as they entered the death-house door. Did their newfound reverence for life stem from the realization that they were about to lose their own?

Life is indeed precious, and I believe the death penalty helps to 3 affirm this fact. Had the death penalty been a real possibility in the minds of these murderers, they might well have stayed their hand. They might have shown moral awareness before their victims died, and not after. Consider the tragic death of Rosa Velez, who happened to be home when a man named Luis Vera burglarized her apartment in Brooklyn. "Yeah, I shot her," Vera admitted. "She knew me, and I knew I wouldn't go to the chair."   — establish authority

During my 22 years in public service, I have heard the pros and 4 cons of capital punishment expressed with special intensity. As a district leader, councilman, congressman, and mayor, I have represented constituencies generally thought of as liberal. Because I support the death penalty for heinous crimes of murder, I have sometimes been the subject of emotional and outraged attacks by voters who find my position reprehensible or worse. I have listened to their ideas. I have weighed their objections carefully. I still support the death penalty. The reasons I maintain my position can be best understood by examining the arguments most frequently heard in opposition.

1. *The death penalty is "barbaric."* Sometimes opponents of capital punishment horrify with tales of lingering death on the gallows, of 5 faulty electric chairs, or of agony in the gas chamber. Partly in response to such protests, several states such as North Carolina and Texas switched to execution by lethal injection. The condemned person is put to death painlessly, without ropes, voltage, bullets, or gas. Did this answer the objections of death penalty opponents? Of course not. On July 22, 1984, *The New York Times* published an editorial that sarcastically attacked the new "hygienic" method of death by injection, and stated that "execution can never be made humane through science." So it's not the method that really troubles opponents. It's the death itself they consider barbaric.

Admittedly, capital punishment is not a pleasant topic. However, 6 one does not have to like the death penalty in order to support it any more than one must like radical surgery, radiation, or chemotherapy in order to find necessary these attempts at curing cancer. Ultimately we may learn how to cure cancer with a simple pill. Unfortunately, that day has not yet arrived. Today we are faced with the choice of letting the cancer spread or trying to cure it with the methods available, methods that one day will almost certainly be considered barbaric. But to give up and do nothing would be far more barbaric and would certainly delay the discovery of an eventual cure. The analogy between cancer and murder is imperfect, because murder is not the "disease" we are trying to cure. The disease is injustice. We may not like the death penalty, but it must be available to punish crimes of cold-blooded murder, cases in which any other form of punishment would be inadequate and, therefore, unjust. If we create a society in which injustice is not tolerated, incidents of murder—the most flagrant form of injustice—will diminish.

2. *No other major democracy uses the death penalty.* No other major 7 democracy—in fact, few other countries of any description—are plagued by a murder rate such as that in the United States. Fewer and fewer Americans can remember the days when unlocked doors were the norm and murder was a rare and terrible offense. In America the murder rate climbed 122 percent between 1963 and 1980. During that same period, the murder rate in New York City increased by almost 400 percent, and the statistics are even worse in many other cities. A study at M.I.T. showed that based on 1970 homicide rates a person who lived in a large American city ran a greater risk of being murdered than an American soldier in World War II ran of being killed in combat. It is not surprising that the laws of each country differ according to differing conditions and traditions. If other countries had our murder problem, the cry for capital punishment would be just as loud as it is here. And I daresay that any other major democracy where 75 percent of the people supported the death penalty would soon enact it into law.

3. *An innocent person might lie executed by mistake.* Consider the work 8 of Hugo Adam Bedau, one of the most implacable foes of capital punishment in this country. According to Mr. Bedau, it is "false sentimentality to argue that the death penalty should be abolished because of the abstract possibility that an innocent person might be executed." He cites a study of the 7,000 executions in this country from 1893 to 1971, and concludes that the record fails to show that such cases occur. The main point, however, is this. If government functioned only when the possibility of error didn't exist, government wouldn't function at all. Human life deserves special protection, and one of the best ways to guarantee that protection is to assure that convicted murderers do not kill again. Only the death penalty can accomplish this end. In a recent case in New Jersey, a man named Richard Biegenwald was freed from prison after serving 18 years for murder; since his release he has been convicted of committing four murders. A prisoner named Lemuel Smith, who while serving four life sentences for murder (plus two life sentences for kidnapping and robbery) in New York's Green Haven Prison, lured a woman corrections officer into the chaplain's office and strangled her. He then mutilated and dismembered her body. An additional life sentence for Smith is meaningless. Because New York has no death penalty statute, Smith has effectively been given a license to kill.

But the problem of multiple murder is not confined to the nation's 9
penitentiaries. In 1981, 91 police officers were killed in the line of duty
in this country. Seven percent of those arrested in the cases that have
been solved had a previous arrest for murder. In New York City in 1976
and 1977, 85 persons arrested for homicide had a previous arrest for
murder. Six of these individuals had two previous arrests for murder
and one had four previous murder arrests. During those two years the
New York police were arresting for murder persons with a previous
arrest for murder on the average of one every 8.5 days. This is not surprising when we learn that in 1975, for example, the median time served
in Massachusetts for homicide was less than two-and-a-half years. In
1976 a study sponsored by the Twentieth Century Fund found that the
average time served in the United States for first-degree murder is ten
years. The median time served may be considerably lower.

4. *Capital punishment cheapens the value of human life.* On the con- 10
trary, it can be easily demonstrated that the death penalty strengthens
the value of human life. If the penalty for rape were lowered, clearly it
would signal a lessened regard for the victims' suffering, humiliation,
and personal integrity. It would cheapen their horrible experience, and
expose them to an increased danger of recurrence. When we lower
the penalty for murder, it signals a lessened regard for the value of the
victim's life. Some critics of capital punishment, such as columnist
Jimmy Breslin, have suggested that a life sentence is actually a harsher
penalty for murder than death. This is sophistic nonsense. A few killers
may decide not to appeal a death sentence, but the overwhelming
majority make every effort to stay alive. It is by exacting the highest
penalty for the taking of human life that we affirm the highest value of
human life.

5. *The death penalty is applied in a discriminatory manner.* This factor no 11
longer seems to be the problem it once was. The appeals process for a condemned prisoner is lengthy and painstaking. Every effort is made to see
that the verdict and sentence were fairly arrived at. However, assertions
of discrimination are not an argument for ending the death penalty but
for extending it. It is not justice to exclude everyone from the penalty of
the law if a few are found to be so favored. Justice requires that the law
be applied equally to all.

6. *Thou Shalt Not Kill.* The Bible is our greatest source of moral inspi- 12
ration. Opponents of the death penalty frequently cite the sixth of the
Ten Commandments in an attempt to prove that capital punishment is
divinely proscribed. In the original Hebrew, however, the Sixth Commandment reads, "Thou Shalt Not Commit Murder," and the Torah
specifies capital punishment for a variety of offenses. The biblical viewpoint has been upheld by philosophers throughout history. The greatest thinkers of the 19th century—Kant, Locke, Hobbes, Rousseau,

Montesquieu, and Mill—agreed that natural law properly authorizes the sovereign to take life in order to vindicate justice. Only Jeremy Bentham was ambivalent. Washington, Jefferson, and Franklin endorsed it. Abraham Lincoln authorized executions for deserters in wartime. Alexis de Tocqueville, who expressed profound respect for American institutions, believed that the death penalty was indispensable to the support of social order. The United States Constitution, widely admired as one of the seminal achievements in the history of humanity, condemns cruel and inhuman punishment, but does not condemn capital punishment.

7. *The death penalty is state-sanctioned murder.* This is the defense with 13 which Messrs. Willie and Shaw hoped to soften the resolve of those who sentenced them to death. By saying in effect, "You're no better than I am," the murderer seeks to bring his accusers down to his own level. It is also a popular argument among opponents of capital punishment, but a transparently false one. Simply put, the state has rights that the private individual does not. In a democracy, those rights are given to the state by the electorate. The execution of a lawfully condemned killer is no more an act of murder than is legal imprisonment an act of kidnapping. If an individual forces a neighbor to pay him money under threat of punishment, it's called extortion. If the state does it, it's called taxation. Rights and responsibilities surrendered by the individual are what give the state its power to govern. This contract is the foundation of civilization itself.

—— Everyone wants his or her rights, and will defend them jealously. 14 Not everyone, however, wants responsibilities, especially the painful responsibilities that come with law enforcement. Twenty-one years ago a woman named Kitty Genovese was assaulted and murdered on a street in New York. Dozens of neighbors heard her cries for help but did nothing to assist her. They didn't even call the police. In such a climate the criminal understandably grows bolder. In the presence of moral cowardice, he lectures us on our supposed failings and tries to equate his crimes with our quest for justice.

The death of anyone—even a convicted killer diminishes us all. But 15 we are diminished even more by a justice system that fails to function. It is an illusion to let ourselves believe that doing away with capital punishment removes the murderer's deed from our conscience. The rights of society are paramount. When we protect guilty lives, we give up innocent lives in exchange. When opponents of capital punishment say to the state: "I will not let you kill in my name," they are also saying to murderers: "You can kill in your *own* name as long as I have an excuse for not getting involved."

It is hard to imagine anything worse than being murdered while 16 neighbors do nothing. But something worse exists. When those same neighbors shrink back from justly punishing the murderer, the victim dies twice.

Responding to Reading

1. How, according to Koch, does capital punishment affirm the fact that life is precious? Do you accept his logic? Can you argue that just the opposite is true?

2. In paragraphs 5 through 14, Koch systematically examines seven popular arguments in opposition to the death penalty. Does he successfully refute each of these arguments? Can you think of any he does not address? Do changes that have occurred since this essay was written—for example, the availability of DNA testing or the decline in the murder rate in many U.S. cities—weaken (or strengthen) any of his arguments? Explain.

3. What is your reaction to the tone and content of each of these statements?

   - "And I daresay that any other major democracy where 75 percent of the people supported the death penalty would soon enact it into law" (7).

   - "If government functioned only when the possibility of error didn't exist, government wouldn't function at all" (8).

   - "Simply put, the state has rights that the private individual does not" (13).

THE NEED FOR A MORATORIUM ON EXECUTIONS

Russell Feingold

Born in Janesville, Wisconsin, Russell Feingold (1953–   ) graduated from the University of Wisconsin, attended Oxford University as a Rhodes Scholar, and received his law degree from Harvard University. In 1983, he was elected to the Wisconsin State Senate, where he served for ten years, and he is currently in his second term as a U.S. senator. A Democrat and a long-time opponent of the death penalty, Feingold sponsored a Senate bill to abolish the federal death penalty in 1999, and in April 2000, he cosponsored the National Death Penalty Moratorium Act. As of this writing, neither piece of legislation has come up for a vote by the full Senate. In the following speech, delivered before the Senate in June 2000, Feingold argues in favor of the National Death Penalty Moratorium Act.

Mr. President[1], the Federal Government has not executed a person 1 in the name of the people of the United States of America since 1963. For 37 years, we as a people have not taken that fateful, irreversible, step. I

---

[1]Here, Feignold addresses Al Gore, then-vice president of the United States, in his role as president of the senate. [Eds.]

rise today because all that is apparently about to change. Since January, 1
I have come to the Senate floor several times to urge my colleagues to
support a moratorium on executions and a review of the administration
of capital punishment. Mr. President, the need for that moratorium has
now become more urgent.

During the Senate recess just ended, a Federal judge in Texas set 2
a date for the execution of Juan Raul Garza. In only two months, on
August 5, he could become the first prisoner that the Federal Government has put to death since 1963. In the early hours of a Saturday morning, when most Americans will be sleeping, Federal authorities will
strap Mr. Garza to a gurney at a new Federal facility in Terre Haute,
Indiana. They will put the needle in his vein. And they will deliver an
injection that will kill him.

Mr. President, I rise today to invite my colleagues to consider the 3
wisdom of this action. More and more Americans, including prosecutors, police, and those fighting on the front lines of the battle against
crime, are rethinking the fairness, the efficacy, and the freedom from
error of the death penalty. Senator Leahy, a former federal prosecutor,
has introduced the Innocence Protection Act, of which I am proud to be
a cosponsor. Congressman Delahunt and Congressman LaHood have
introduced the same bill in the House. Congressman Delahunt, also a
former prosecutor, is concerned that our current system of administering the death penalty is far from just. He has said: "If you spent 20 years
in the criminal Justice system, you would be very concerned about what
goes on."

In my own home state of Wisconsin, at least eleven active and for- 4
mer state and federal prosecutors have said that executions do not deter
crime and could result in executing the innocent. Michael McCann, the
well-respected District Attorney of Milwaukee County, has said that
prosecution is a human enterprise, bound to have mistakes. Mr. President, police—the people on the front lines of the battle against crime—
are coming out against the death penalty. They are finding that it is
bad for law enforcement. Recently, when police chiefs were asked about
the death penalty, they said that it was counterproductive. Capital cases
are incredibly resource-intensive. They do not yield a reduction in crime
proportional to other, more moderate law-enforcement activities. A former police chief of Madison, Wisconsin, for example, has said that he
fears that the death penalty would make police officers' jobs more dangerous, not less so. He expressed concern that a suspect's incentive to
surrender peacefully is diminished when the government has plans to
execute.

Mr. President, ours is a system of justice founded on fairness and 5
due process. The Framers of our democracy had a healthy distrust for
the power of the state when arrayed against the individual. Many of the
lawyers in the early United States of America had on their shelf a copy

of William Blackstone's Commentaries on the Laws of England, where it is written: "For the law holds, that it is better that ten guilty persons escape, than that one innocent suffer." And Benjamin Franklin wrote, "That it is better 100 guilty Persons should escape than that one innocent Person should suffer. . . ." Our Constitution and Bill of Rights reflect this concern for the protection of the individual against the might of the state. The fourth amendment protects: "The right of the people to be secure in their persons, houses, papers, and effects, against unreasonable searches and seizures. . . ." The fifth amendment protects against being "deprived of life, liberty, or property, without due process of law. . . ." The sixth amendment guarantees that "the accused shall enjoy the right . . . to have the assistance of counsel for his defense." And the eighth amendment prohibits "cruel and unusual punishments."

Mr. President, as you well know, our system of government is 6 deeply grounded in the defense of the individual against the power of the government. Our Nation has a proud tradition of safeguarding the rights of its citizens. But more and more, we are finding that when a person's very life is at stake, our system of justice is failing to live up to the standards that the American people demand and expect. More and more, Americans are finding reason to believe that we have a justice system that can, and does, make mistakes. Americans' sense of justice demands that if new evidence becomes available that could shed light on the guilt or innocence of a defendant, then the defendant should be given the opportunity to present it.

Unfortunately, apparently, the people of New York and Illinois are 7 the only ones who understand this. They have enacted laws allowing convicted offenders access to the biological evidence used at trial and modern DNA testing. If you are on death row in a state other than Illinois or New York, you might be able to show a court evidence of your guilt or innocence based on new DNA tests. But Mr. President, your ability to do so rests on whether you're lucky enough to get a prosecutor to agree to the test or convince a court that it should be done. Or, as we have seen very recently, your ability to show your innocence may rest with the decision of the governor. And that raises the risk of a political decision, not necessarily one that is based solely on fairness or justice.

Mr. President, I am not surprised that both Texas Governor George 8 Bush and Virginia Governor James Gilmore are no longer confident that every prisoner on death row in their states is guilty and has had full access to the courts. Allowing death row inmates the benefit of a modern DNA test is the fair and just thing to do. But scores of other death row inmates, in Texas, in Virginia, and around the country, may also have evidence exonerating them. They may have DNA evidence. Or they may have other exonerating evidence. We must ensure that all inmates with meritorious claims of innocence have their day in court.

In the basic experimental design, two people come to a psychology 4 laboratory to take part in a study of memory and learning. One of them is designated as a "teacher" and the other a "learner." The experimenter explains that the study is concerned with the effects of punishment on learning. The learner is conducted into a room, seated in a kind of miniature electric chair; his arms are strapped to prevent excessive movement, and an electrode is attached to his wrist. He is told that he will be read lists of simple word pairs, and that he will then be tested on his ability to remember the second word of a pair when he hears the first one again. Whenever he makes an error, he will receive electric shocks of increasing intensity.

The real focus of the experiment is the teacher. After watching the 5 learner being strapped into place, he is seated before an impressive shock generator. The instrument panel consists of thirty lever switches set in a horizontal line. Each switch is clearly labeled with a voltage designation ranging from 15 to 450 volts. The following designations are clearly indicated for groups of four switches, going from left to right: Slight Shock, Moderate Shock, Strong Shock, Very Strong Shock, Intense Shock, Extreme Intensity Shock, Danger: Severe Shock. (Two switches after this last designation are simply marked XXX.)

When a switch is depressed, a pilot light corresponding to each 6 switch is illuminated in bright red; an electric buzzing is heard; a blue light, labeled "voltage energizer," flashes; the dial on the voltage meter swings to the right; and various relay clicks sound off.

The upper left-hand corner of the generator is labeled SHOCK GEN- 7 ERATOR, TYPE ZLB, DYSON INSTRUMENT COMPANY, WALTHAM, MASS. OUTPUT 15 VOLTS–450 VOLTS.

Each subject is given a sample 45-volt shock from the generator 8 before his run as teacher, and the jolt strengthens his belief in the authenticity of the machine.

The teacher is a genuinely naïve subject who has come to the labo- 9 ratory for the experiment. The learner, or victim, is actually an actor who receives no shock at all. The point of the experiment is to see how far a person will proceed in a concrete and measurable situation in which he is ordered to inflict increasing pain on a protesting victim.

Conflict arises when the man receiving the shock begins to show 10 that he is experiencing discomfort. At 75 volts, he grunts; at 120 volts, he complains loudly; at 150, he demands to be released from the experiment. As the voltage increases, his protests become more vehement and emotional. At 285 volts, his response can be described only as an agonized scream. Soon thereafter, he makes no sound at all.

For the teacher, the situation quickly becomes one of gripping 11 tension. It is not a game for him; conflict is intense and obvious. The manifest suffering of the learner presses him to quit; but each time he hesitates to administer a shock, the experimenter orders him to continue. To extricate himself from this plight, the subject must make a clear break with authority.[3]

The subject, Gretchen Brandt,[4] is an attractive thirty-one-year-old medical technician who works at the Yale Medical School. She had emigrated from Germany five years before.   12

On several occasions when the learner complains, she turns to the experimenter coolly and inquires, "Shall I continue"? She promptly returns to her task when the experimenter asks her to do so. At the administration of 210 volts, she turns to the experimenter, remarking firmly, "Well, I'm sorry, I don't think we should continue."   13

EXPERIMENTER: The experiment requires that you go on until he has learned all the word pairs correctly.
BRANDT: He has a heart condition, I'm sorry. He told you that before.
EXPERIMENTER: The shocks may be painful but they are not dangerous.
BRANDT: Well, I'm sorry, I think when shocks continue like this, they are dangerous. You ask him if he wants to get out. It's his free will.
EXPERIMENTER: It is absolutely essential that we continue . . .
BRANDT: I'd like you to ask him. We came here of our free will. If he wants to continue I'll go ahead. He told you he had a heart condition. I'm sorry. I don't want to be responsible for anything happening to him. I wouldn't like it for me either.
EXPERIMENTER: You have no other choice.
BRANDT: I think we are here on our own free will. I don't want to be responsible if anything happens to him. Please understand that.

She refuses to go further and the experiment is terminated.   14

The woman is firm and resolute throughout. She indicates in the interview that she was in no way tense or nervous, and this corresponds to her controlled appearance during the experiment. She feels that the last shock she administered to the learner was extremely painful and reiterates that she "did not want to be responsible for any harm to him."   15

The woman's straightforward, courteous behavior in the experiment, lack of tension, and total control of her own action seem to make   16

---

[3] The ethical problems of carrying out an experiment of this sort are too complex to be dealt with here, but they receive extended treatment in the book from which this article is adapted. [The book is *Obedience to Authority* (New York: Harper & Row, 1974)—Eds.]

[4] Names of subjects described in this piece have been changed.

disobedience a simple and rational deed. Her behavior is the very embodiment of what I envisioned would be true for almost all subjects.

Before the experiments, I sought predictions about the outcome 17 from various kinds of people—psychiatrists, college sophomores, middle-class adults, graduate students and faculty in the behavioral sciences. With remarkable similarity, they predicted that virtually all subjects would refuse to obey the experimenter. The psychiatrists specifically predicted that most subjects would not go beyond 150 volts, when the victim makes his first explicit demand to be freed. They expected that only 4 percent would reach 300 volts, and that only a pathological fringe of about one in a thousand would administer the highest shock on the board.

These predictions were unequivocally wrong. Of the forty subjects 18 in the first experiment, twenty-five obeyed the orders of the experimenter to the end, punishing the victim until they reached the most potent shock available on the generator. After 450 volts were administered three times, the experimenter called a halt to the sessions. Many obedient subjects then heaved sighs of relief, mopped their brows, rubbed their fingers over their eyes, or nervously fumbled cigarettes. Others displayed only minimal signs of tension from beginning to end.

When the very first experiments were carried out, Yale undergrad- 19 uates were used as subjects, and about 60 percent of them were fully obedient. A colleague of mine immediately dismissed these findings as having no relevance to "ordinary" people, asserting that Yale undergraduates are a highly aggressive, competitive bunch who step on each other's necks on the slightest provocation. He assured me that when "ordinary" people were tested, the results would be quite different. As we moved from the pilot studies to the regular experimental series, people drawn from every stratum of New Haven life came to be employed in the experiment: professionals, white-collar workers, unemployed persons, and industrial workers. *The experimental outcome was the same as we had observed among the students.*

Moreover, when the experiments were repeated in Princeton, Munich, 20 Rome, South Africa, and Australia, the level of obedience was invariably somewhat *higher* than found in the investigation reported in this article. Thus one scientist in Munich found 85 percent of his subjects obedient.

Fred Prozi's reactions, if more dramatic than most, illuminate the 21 conflicts experienced by others in less visible form. About fifty years old and unemployed at the time of the experiment, he has a good-natured, if slightly dissolute, appearance, and he strikes people as a rather ordinary fellow. He begins the session calmly but becomes tense as it proceeds. After delivering the 180-volt shock, he pivots around in his chair and, shaking his head, addresses the experimenter in agitated tones:

PROZI: I can't stand it. I'm not going to kill that man in there. You hear him hollering?

EXPERIMENTER: As I told you before, the shocks may be painful, but . . .

PROZI: But he's hollering. He can't stand it. What's going to happen to him?

EXPERIMENTER (his voice is patient, matter-of-fact): The experiment requires that you continue, Teacher.

PROZI: Aaah, but, unh, I'm not going to get that man sick in there—know what I mean?

EXPERIMENTER: Whether the learner likes it or not, we must go on, through all the word pairs.

PROZI: I refuse to take the responsibility. He's in there hollering!

EXPERIMENTER: It's absolutely essential that you continue, Prozi.

PROZI (indicating the unused questions): There's too many left here, I mean, Jeez, if he gets them wrong, there's too many of them left. I mean, who's going to take the responsibility if anything happens to that gentleman?

EXPERIMENTER: I'm responsible for anything that happens to him. Continue, please.

PROZI: All right. (Consults list of words.) The next one's "Slow—walk, truck, dance, music." Answer, please. (A buzzing sound indicates the learner has signaled his answer.) Wrong. A hundred and ninety-five volts. "Dance." (Zzumph!)

learner (yelling): Let me out of here! My heart's bothering me! (Teacher looks at experimenter.)

EXPERIMENTER: Continue, please.

LEARNER (screaming): Let me out of here! You have no right to keep me here! Let me out of here, my heart's bothering me, let me out!

PROZI (shakes head, pats the table nervously): You see, he's hollering. Hear that? Gee, I don't know.

EXPERIMENTER: The experiment requires . . .

PROZI (interrupting): I know it does, sir, but I mean—hunh! He don't know what he's getting in for. He's up to 195 volts! (Experiment continues, through 210 volts, 225 volts, 240 volts, 255 volts, 270 volts, at which point Prozi, with evident relief, runs out of word-pair questions.)

EXPERIMENTER: You'll have to go back to the beginning of that page and go through them again until he's learned them all correctly.

PROZI: Aw, no. I'm not going to kill that man. You mean I've got to keep going up with the scale? No sir. He's hollering in there. I'm not going to give him 450 volts.

Cannot control his laughter at this point no matter what he does.   27
Clenching fist, pushing it onto table.   28

In an interview after the session, Mr. Braverman summarizes the   29
experiment with impressive fluency and intelligence. He feels the experiment may have been designed also to "test the effects on the teacher of
being in an essentially sadistic role, as well as the reactions of a student
to a learning situation that was authoritative and punitive." When asked
how painful the last few shocks administered to the learner were, he
indicates that the most extreme category on the scale is not adequate (it
read EXTREMELY PAINFUL) and places his mark at the edge of the scale with
an arrow carrying it beyond the scale.

It is almost impossible to convey the greatly relaxed, sedate quality   30
of his conversation in the interview. In the most relaxed terms, he
speaks about his severe inner tension.

> EXPERIMENTER: At what point were you most tense or nervous?
> MR. BRAVERMAN: Well, when he first began to cry out in pain,
> and I realized this was hurting him. This got worse when he
> just blocked and refused to answer. There was I. I'm a nice
> person, I think, hurting somebody, and caught up in what
> seemed a mad situation . . . and in the interest of science, one
> goes through with it.

When the interviewer pursues the general question of tension, Mr.   31
Braverman spontaneously mentions his laughter.

"My reactions were awfully peculiar. I don't know if you were   32
watching me, but my reactions were giggly, and trying to stifle laughter.
This isn't the way I usually am. This was a sheer reaction to a totally
impossible situation. And my reaction was to the situation of having to
hurt somebody. And being totally helpless and caught up in a set of circumstances where I just couldn't deviate and I couldn't try to help. This
is what got me."

Mr. Braverman, like all subjects, was told the actual nature and pur-   33
pose of the experiment, and a year later he affirmed in a questionnaire
that he had learned something of personal importance: "What appalled
me was that I could possess this capacity for obedience and compliance
to a central idea, i.e., the value of a memory experiment, even after it
became clear that continued adherence to this value was at the expense of
violation of another value, i.e., don't hurt someone who is helpless and not
hurting you. As my wife said, 'You can call yourself Eichmann.[5] I hope I
deal more effectively with any future conflicts of values encounter."

---

[5] Nazi officer, executed in 1962, who engineered the mass extermination of Jews. Many concentration
camp officials defended themselves afterward by saying they were "just following orders." [Eds.]

One theoretical interpretation of this behavior holds that all people 34 harbor deeply aggressive instincts continually pressing for expression, and that the experiment provides institutional justification for the release of these impulses. According to this view, if a person is placed in a situation in which he has complete power over another individual, whom he may punish as much as he likes, all that is sadistic and bestial in man comes to the fore. The impulse to shock the victim is seen to flow from the potent aggressive tendencies, which are part of the motivational life of the individual, and the experiment, because it provides social legitimacy, simply opens the door to their expression.

It becomes vital, therefore, to compare the subject's performance 35 when he is under orders and when he is allowed to choose the shock level.

The procedure was identical to our standard experiment, except that 36 the teacher was told that he was free to select any shock level on any of the trials. (The experimenter took pains to point out that the teacher could use the highest levels on the generator, the lowest, any in between, or any combination of levels.) Each subject proceeded for thirty critical trials. The learner's protests were coordinated to standard shock levels, his first grunt coming at 75 volts, his first vehement protest at 150 volts.

The average shock used during the thirty critical trials was less than 37 60 volts—lower than the point at which the victim showed the first signs of discomfort. Three of the forty subjects did not go beyond the very lowest level on the board, twenty-eight went no higher than 75 volts, and thirty-eight did not go beyond the first loud protest at 150 volts. Two subjects provided the exception, administering up to 325 and 450 volts, but the overall result was that the great majority of people delivered very low, usually painless, shocks when the choice was explicitly up to them.

This condition of the experiment undermines another commonly 38 offered explanation of the subjects' behavior—that those who shocked the victim at the most severe levels came only from the sadistic fringe of society. If one considers that almost two-thirds of the participants fall into the category of "obedient" subjects, and that they represented ordinary people drawn from working, managerial, and professional classes, the argument becomes very shaky. Indeed, it is highly reminiscent of the issue that arose in connection with Hannah Arendt's 1963 book, *Eichmann in Jerusalem.* Arendt contended that the prosecution's effort to depict Eichmann as a sadistic monster was fundamentally wrong, that he came closer to being an uninspired bureaucrat who simply sat at his desk and did his job. For asserting her views, Arendt became the object of considerable scorn, even calumny. Somehow, it was felt that the monstrous deeds carried out by Eichmann required a brutal, twisted personality, evil incarnate. After witnessing hundreds of ordinary persons submit to the authority in our own experiments, I must conclude that Arendt's conception of the banality of evil comes closer to the truth than one might dare imagine. The ordinary person who shocked the victim did so out of a sense of obligation—an impression of his duties as a subject—and not from any peculiarly aggressive tendencies.

This is, perhaps, the most fundamental lesson of our study: ordinary 39 people, simply doing their jobs, and without any particular hostility on their part, can become agents in a terrible destructive process. Moreover, even when the destructive effects of their work become patently clear, and they are asked to carry out actions incompatible with fundamental standards of morality, relatively few people have the resources needed to resist authority.

Many of the people were in some sense against what they did to the 40 learner, and many protested even while they obeyed. Some were totally convinced of the wrongness of their actions but could not bring themselves to make an open break with authority. They often derived satisfaction from their thoughts and felt that—within themselves, at least—they had been on the side of the angels. They tried to reduce strain by obeying the experimenter but "only slightly" encouraging the learner, touching the generator switches gingerly. When interviewed, such a subject would stress that he had "asserted my humanity" by administering the briefest shock possible. Handling the conflict in this manner was easier than defiance.

The situation is constructed so that there is no way the subject can 41 stop shocking the learner without violating the experimenter's definitions of his own competence. The subject fears that he will appear arrogant, untoward, and rude if he breaks off. Although these inhibiting emotions appear small in scope alongside the violence being done to the learner, they suffuse the mind and feelings of the subject, who is miserable at the prospect of having to repudiate the authority to his face. (When the experiment was altered so that the experimenter gave his instructions by telephone instead of in person, only a third as many people were fully obedient through 450 volts.) It is a curious thing that a measure of compassion on the part of the subject—an unwillingness to "hurt" the experimenter's feelings—is part of those binding forces inhibiting his disobedience. The withdrawal of such deference may be as painful to the subject as to the authority he defies.

The subjects do not derive satisfaction from inflicting pain, but they 42 often like the feeling they get from pleasing the experimenter. They are proud of doing a good job, obeying the experimenter under difficult circumstances. While the subjects administered only mild shocks on their own initiative, one experimental variation showed that, under orders, 30 percent of them were willing to deliver 450 volts even when they had to forcibly push the learner's hand down on the electrode.

Bruno Batta is a thirty-seven-year-old welder who took part in the 43 variation requiring the use of force. He was born in New Haven, his parents in Italy. He has a rough-hewn face that conveys a conspicuous lack of alertness. He has some difficulty in mastering the experimental procedure and needs to be corrected by the experimenter several times. He shows appreciation for the help and willingness to do what is required. After the 150-volt level, Batta has to force the learner's hand down on the shock plate, since the learner himself refuses to touch it.

When the learner first complains, Mr. Batta pays no attention to 44 him. His face remains impassive, as if to dissociate himself from the learner's disruptive behavior. When the experimenter instructs him to force the learner's hand down, he adopts a rigid, mechanical procedure. He tests the generator switch. When it fails to function he immediately forces the learner's hand onto the shock plate. All the while he maintains the same rigid mask. The learner, seated alongside him, begs him to stop, but with robotic impassivity he continues the procedure.

What is extraordinary is his apparent total indifference to the learner; 45 he hardly takes cognizance of him as a human being. Meanwhile, he relates to the experimenter in a submissive and courteous fashion.

At the 330-volt level, the learner refuses not only to touch the shock 46 plate but also to provide any answers. Annoyed, Batta turns to him, and chastises him: "You better answer and get it over with. We can't stay here all night." These are the only words he directs to the learner in the course of an hour. Never again does he speak to him. The scene is brutal and depressing, his hard, impassive face showing total indifference as he subdues the screaming learner and gives him shocks. He seems to derive no pleasure from the act itself, only quiet satisfaction at doing his job properly.

When he administers 450 volts, he turns to the experimenter and 47 asks, "Where do we go from here, Professor?" His tone is deferential and expresses his willingness to be a cooperative subject, in contrast to the learner's obstinacy.

At the end of the session he tells the experimenter how honored he 48 has been to help him, and in a moment of contrition, remarks, "Sir, sorry it couldn't have been a full experiment."

He has done his honest best. It is only the deficient behavior of the 49 learner that has denied the experimenter full satisfaction.

The essence of obedience is that a person comes to view himself as 50 the instrument for carrying out another person's wishes, and he therefore no longer regards himself as responsible for his actions. Once this critical shift of viewpoint has occurred, all of the essential features of obedience follow. The most far-reaching consequence is that the person feels responsible to the authority directing him but feels no responsibility *for* the content of the actions that the authority prescribes. Morality does not disappear—it acquires a radically different focus: the subordinate person feels shame or pride depending on how adequately he has performed the actions called for by authority.

Language provides numerous terms to pinpoint this type of moral- 51 ity: *loyalty, duty, discipline* all are terms heavily saturated with moral meaning and refer to the degree to which a person fulfills his obligations to authority. They refer not to the "goodness" of the person per se but to the adequacy with which a subordinate fulfills his socially defined role. The most frequent defense of the individual who has performed a heinous act under command of authority is that he has simply done his duty. In asserting this defense, the individual is not introducing an alibi concocted for the moment but is reporting honestly on the psychological attitude induced by submission to authority.

For a person to feel responsible for his actions, he must sense that ⁵² the behavior has flowed from "the self." In the situation we have studied, subjects have precisely the opposite view of their actions—namely, they see them as originating in the motives of some other person. Subjects in the experiment frequently said, "If it were up to me, I would not have administered shocks to the learner."

Once authority has been isolated as the cause of the subject's behav- ⁵³ ior, it is legitimate to inquire into the necessary elements of authority and how it must be perceived in order to gain his compliance. We conducted some investigations into the kinds of changes that would cause the experimenter to lose his power and to be disobeyed by the subject. Some of the variations revealed that:

> *The experimenter's physical presence has a marked impact on his* ⁵⁴ *authority.* As cited earlier, obedience dropped off sharply when orders were given by telephone. The experimenter could often induce a disobedient subject to go on by returning to the laboratory.

> *Conflicting authority severely paralyzes action.* When two exper- ⁵⁵ imenters of equal status, both seated at the command desk, gave incompatible orders, no shocks were delivered past the point of their disagreement.

> *The rebellious action of others severely undermines authority.* In ⁵⁶ one variation, three teachers (two actors and a real subject) administered a test and shocks. When the two actors disobeyed the experimenter and refused to go beyond a certain shock level, thirty-six of forty subjects joined their disobedient peers and refused as well.

Although the experimenter's authority was fragile in some ⁵⁷ respects, it is also true that he had almost none of the tools used in ordinary command structures. For example, the experimenter did not threaten the subjects with punishment—such as loss of income, community ostracism, or jail—for failure to obey. Neither could he offer incentives. Indeed, we should expect the experimenter's authority to be much less than that of someone like a general, since the experimenter has no power to enforce his imperatives, and since participation in a psychological experiment scarcely evokes the sense of urgency and dedication found in warfare. Despite these limitations, he still managed to command a dismaying degree of obedience.

I will cite one final variation of the experiment that depicts a 58 dilemma that is more common in everyday life. The subject was not ordered to pull the lever that shocked the victim, but merely to perform a subsidiary task (administering the word-pair test) while another person administered the shock. In this situation, thirty-seven of forty adults continued to the highest level of the shock generator. Predictably, they excused their behavior by saying that the responsibility belonged to the man who actually pulled the switch. This may illustrate a dangerously typical arrangement in a complex society: it is easy to ignore responsibility when one is only an intermediate link in a chain of action.

The problem of obedience is not wholly psychological. The form 59 and shape of society and the way it is developing have much to do with it. There was a time, perhaps, when people were able to give a fully human response to any situation because they were fully absorbed in it as human beings. But as soon as there was a division of labor things changed. Beyond a certain point, the breaking up of society into people carrying out narrow and very special jobs takes away from the human quality of work and life. A person does not get to see the whole situation but only a small part of it, and is thus unable to act without some kind of overall direction. He yields to authority but in doing so is alienated from his own actions.

Even Eichmann was sickened when he toured the concentration 60 camps, but he had only to sit at a desk and shuffle papers. At the same time the man in the camp who actually dropped Cyclon-b into the gas chambers was able to justify *his* behavior on the ground that he was only following orders from above. Thus there is a fragmentation of the total human act; no one is confronted with the consequences of his decision to carry out the evil act. The person who assumes responsibility has evaporated. Perhaps this is the most common characteristic of socially organized evil in modern society.

Responding to Reading

1. What is the "dilemma inherent in submission to authority" (2)? How do Milgram's experiments illustrate this dilemma? Why do you suppose virtually no one predicted that the subjects would continue to obey the orders of the experimenter?

2. Do you see the subjects as ordinary people—cooperative, obedient, and eager to please—or as weak individuals, too timid to defy authority? Explain.

3. In paragraph 51, Milgram says, "The most frequent defense of the individual who has performed a heinous act under command of authority is that he has simply done his duty." In your opinion, can such a defense ever excuse a "heinous act"? If so, under what circumstances?

THE RULES OF THE GAME

Carl Sagan

An astronomer, biologist, physicist, and popular science writer, Carl Sagan (1934–1996) was born in New York City and educated at the University of Chicago. A professor at Cornell, he lectured widely at other universities on subjects ranging from the birth of the cosmos to the threat of the nuclear arms race. His many books, which did much to educate average readers about a variety of scientific matters, include The Cosmic Connection *(1973);* The Dragons of Eden *(1977), winner of the Pulitzer Prize;* Cosmos *(1980), which provided the basis for a widely watched PBS television series that Sagan cowrote and narrated;* A Path Where No Man Thought: Nuclear Winter and the End of the Arms Race *(1989); and* Pale Blue Dot *(1994). He was also instrumental in developing NASA's Mariner, Viking, and Voyager interplanetary missions. The winner of many awards for his academic work, his television documentary, and his humanitarian achievements, Sagan, according to one critic, "sends out an exuberant message: science is not only vital for humanity's future well-being, but it is rousing good fun as well." His posthumously published* Billions and Billions: Thoughts on Life and Death at the Brink of the Millennium *(1997) was written as Sagan was undergoing ultimately unsuccessful treatment for cancer. In the following essay from that book, he explores the various moral codes people may choose to live by.*

Everything morally right derives from one of four sources: it concerns either full perception or intelligent development of what is true; or the preservation of organized society, where every man is rendered his due and all obligations are faithfully discharged; or the greatness and strength of a noble, invincible spirit; or order and moderation in everything said and done, whereby is temperance and self-control.

—Cicero, *De Officiis*, I, 5 (45–44 b.c.)

I remember the end of a long ago perfect day in 1939—a day that power- 1
fully influenced my thinking, a day when my parents introduced me to the wonders of the New York World's Fair. It was late, well past my bedtime. Safely perched on my father's shoulders, holding onto his ears, my mother reassuringly at my side, I turned to see the great Trylon and Perisphere, the architectural icons of the Fair, illuminated in shimmering blue pastels. We were abandoning the future, the "World of Tomorrow, "for the BMT subway train. As we paused to rearrange our possessions, my father got to talking with a small, tired man carrying a tray around his neck. He was selling pencils. My father reached into the crumpled brown paper bag that held the remains of our lunches, withdrew an apple, and handed it to the pencil man. I let out a loud wail. I disliked apples then, and had refused this one both at lunch and at dinner. But I had, nevertheless, a proprietary interest in it. It was my apple, and

my father had just given it away to a funny-looking stranger—who, to com-
pound my anguish, was now glaring unsympathetically in my direction.

Although my father was a person of nearly limitless patience and tender- 2
ness, I could see he was disappointed in me. He swept me up and hugged me
tight to him.

"He's a poor stiff, out of work," he said to me, too quietly for the man to 3
hear. "He hasn't eaten all day. We have enough. We can give him an apple."

I reconsidered, stifled my sobs, took another wistful glance at the World of 4
Tomorrow, and gratefully fell asleep in his arms.

Moral codes that seek to regulate human behavior have been with 5
us not only since the dawn of civilization but also among our precivi-
lized, and highly social, hunter-gatherer ancestors. And even earlier.
Different societies have different codes. Many cultures say one thing
and do another. In a few fortunate societies, an inspired lawgiver lays
down a set of rules to live by (and more often than not claims to have
been instructed by a god—without which few would follow the pre-
scriptions). For example, the codes of Ashoka (India), Hammurabi
(Babylon), Lycurgus (Sparta), and Solon (Athens), which once held
sway over mighty civilizations, are today largely defunct. Perhaps they
misjudged human nature and asked too much of us. Perhaps experience
from one epoch or culture is not wholly applicable to another.

Surprisingly, there are today efforts—tentative but emerging—to 6
approach the matter scientifically; i.e., experimentally.

In our everyday lives as in the momentous relations of nations, we 7
must decide: What does it mean to do the right thing? Should we help
a needy stranger? How do we deal with an enemy? Should we ever take
advantage of someone who treats us kindly? If hurt by a friend, or
helped by an enemy, should we reciprocate in kind; or does the totality
of past behavior outweigh any recent departures from the norm?

Examples: Your sister-in-law ignores your snub and invites you over 8
for Christmas dinner; should you accept? Shattering a four-year-long
worldwide voluntary moratorium, China resumes nuclear weapons testing; should we? How much should we give to charity? Serbian soldiers
systematically rape Bosnian women; should Bosnian soldiers systematically rape Serbian women? After centuries of oppression, the Nationalist
Party leader F. W. de Klerk[1] makes overtures to the African National
Congress; should Nelson Mandela and the ANC have reciprocated? A
coworker makes you look bad in front of the boss; should you try to get
even? Should we cheat on our income tax returns? If we can get away
with it? If an oil company supports a symphony orchestra or sponsors a
refined TV drama, ought we to ignore its pollution of the environment?

---

[1] Of South Africa. [Eds.]

Should we be kind to aged relatives, even if they drive us nuts? Should you cheat at cards? Or on a larger scale? Should we kill killers?

In making such decisions, we're concerned not only with doing right 9 but also with what works—what makes us and the rest of society happier and more secure. There's a tension between what we call ethical and what we call pragmatic. If, even in the long run, ethical behavior were self-defeating, eventually we would not call it ethical, but foolish. (We might even claim to respect it in principle, but ignore it in practice.) Bearing in mind the variety and complexity of human behavior, are there any simple rules—whether we call them ethical or pragmatic—that actually work?

How do we decide what to do? Our responses are partly deter- 10 mined by our perceived self-interest. We reciprocate in kind or act contrary because we hope it will accomplish what we want. Nations assemble or blow up nuclear weapons so other countries won't trifle with them. We return good for evil because we know that we can thereby sometimes touch people's sense of justice, or shame them into being nice. But sometimes we're not motivated selfishly. Some people seem just naturally kind. We may accept aggravation from aged parents or from children, because we love them and want them to be happy, even if it's at some cost to us. Sometimes we're tough with our children and cause them a little unhappiness, because we want to mold their characters and believe that the long-term results will bring them more happiness than the short- term pain.

Cases are different. Peoples and nations are different. Knowing how 11 to negotiate this labyrinth is part of wisdom. But bearing in mind the variety and complexity of human behavior, are there some simple rules, whether we call them ethical or pragmatic, that actually work? Or maybe we should avoid trying to think it through and just do what feels right. But even then how do we *determine* what "feels right"?

The most admired standard of behavior, in the West at least, is the 12 Golden Rule, attributed to Jesus of Nazareth. Everyone knows its formulation in the first-century Gospel of St. Matthew: **Do unto others as you would have them do unto you.** Almost no one follows it. When the Chinese philosopher Kung-Tzi (known as Confucius in the West) was asked in the fifth century B.C. his opinion of the Golden Rule (by then already well-known), of repaying evil with kindness, he replied, "Then with what will you repay kindness?" Shall the poor woman who envies her neighbor's wealth give what little she has to the rich? Shall the masochist inflict pain on his neighbor? The Golden Rule takes no account of human differences. Are we really capable, after our cheek has been slapped, of turning the other cheek so it too can be slapped? With a heartless adversary, isn't this just a guarantee of more suffering?

The Silver Rule is different: **Do not do unto others what you would** 13 **not have them do unto you.** It also can be found worldwide, including, a generation before Jesus, in the writings of Rabbi Hillel. The most inspiring twentieth-century exemplars of the Silver Rule were Mohandas Gandhi and Martin Luther King, Jr. They counseled oppressed peoples not to repay violence with violence, but not to be compliant and obedient either. Nonviolent civil disobedience was what they advocated—putting your body on the line, showing, by your willingness to be punished in defying an unjust law, the justice of your cause. They aimed at melting the hearts of their oppressors (and those who had not yet made up their minds).

King paid tribute to Gandhi as the first person in history to convert 14 the Golden or Silver Rules into an effective instrument of social change. And Gandhi made it clear where his approach came from: "I learnt the lesson on nonviolence from my wife, when I tried to bend her to my will. Her determined resistance to my will on the one hand, and her quiet submission to the suffering my stupidity involved on the other, ultimately made me ashamed of myself and cured me of my stupidity in thinking that I was born to rule over her."

Nonviolent civil disobedience has worked notable political change 15 in this century—in prying India loose from British rule and stimulating the end of classic colonialism worldwide, and in providing some civil rights for African-Americans—although the threat of violence by others, however disavowed by Gandhi and King, may have also helped. The African National Congress (ANC) grew up in the Gandhian tradition. But by the 1950s it was clear that nonviolent noncooperation was making no progress whatever with the ruling white Nationalist Party. So in 1961 Nelson Mandela and his colleagues formed the military wing of the ANC, the *Umkhonto we Sizwe*, the Spear of the Nation, on the quite un-Gandhian grounds that the only thing whites understand is force.

Even Gandhi had trouble reconciling the rule of nonviolence with 16 the necessities of defense against those with less lofty rules of conduct: "I have not the qualifications for teaching my philosophy of life. I have barely qualifications for practicing the philosophy I believe. I am but a poor struggling soul yearning to be . . . wholly truthful and wholly nonviolent in thought, word and deed, but ever failing to reach the ideal."

"Repay kindness with kindness," said Confucius, "but evil with jus- 17 tice." This might be called the Brass or Brazen Rule: **Do unto others as they do unto you.** It's the *lex talionis*, "an eye for an eye, and a tooth for a tooth," *plus* "one good turn deserves another." In actual human (and chimpanzee) behavior it's a familiar standard. "If the enemy inclines toward peace, do thou also incline toward peace," President Bill Clinton quoted from the Qur'an[2] at the Israeli-Palestinian peace accords. Without having to appeal to anyone's better nature, we institute a kind of operant

---

[2] The Koran, or sacred book of Islam. [Eds.]

conditioning,[3] rewarding them when they're nice to us and punishing them when they're not. We're not pushovers but we're not unforgiving either. It sounds promising. Or is it true that "two wrongs don't make a right"?

Of baser coinage is the Iron Rule: **Do unto others as you like, before they do it unto you.** It is sometimes formulated as "He who has the gold makes the rules," underscoring not just its departure from, but its contempt for the Golden Rule. This is the secret maxim of many, if they can get away with it, and often the unspoken precept of the powerful.   18

Finally, I should mention two other rules, found throughout the living world. They explain a great deal: One is **Suck up to those above you, and abuse those below.** This is the motto of bullies and the norm in many nonhuman primate societies. It's really the Golden Rule for superiors, the Iron Rule for inferiors. Since there is no known alloy of gold and iron, we'll call it the Tin Rule for its flexibility. The other common rule is **Give precedence in all things to close relatives, and do as you like to others.** This Nepotism Rule is known to evolutionary biologists as "kin selection."   19

Despite its apparent practicality, there's a fatal flaw in the Brazen Rule: unending vendetta. It hardly matters who starts the violence. Violence begets violence, and each side has reason to hate the other. "There is no way to peace," A. J. Muste said. "Peace *is* the way." But peace is hard and violence is easy. Even if almost everyone is for ending the vendetta, a single act of retribution can stir it up again: A dead relative's sobbing widow and grieving children are before us. Old men and women recall atrocities from their childhoods. The reasonable part of us tries to keep the peace, but the passionate part of us cries out for vengeance. Extremists in the two warring factions can count on one another. They are allied against the rest of us, contemptuous of appeals to understanding and loving-kindness. A few hotheads can force-march a legion of more prudent and rational people to brutality and war.   20

Many in the West have been so mesmerized by the appalling accords with Adolf Hitler in Munich in 1938 that they are unable to distinguish cooperation and appeasement. Rather than having to judge each gesture and approach on its own merits, we merely decide that the opponent is thoroughly evil, that all his concessions are offered in bad faith, and that force is the only thing he understands. Perhaps for Hitler this was the right judgment. But in general it is not the right judgment, as much as I wish that the invasion of the Rhineland had been forcibly opposed. It consolidates hostility on both sides and makes conflict much more likely. In a world with nuclear weapons, uncompromising hostility carries special and very dire dangers.   21

---

[3] A process of behavioral modification. [Eds.]

Breaking out of a long series of reprisals is, I claim, very hard. There 22
are ethnic groups who have weakened themselves to the point of extinction because they had no machinery to escape from this cycle, the Kaingáng of the Brazilian highlands, for example. The warring nationalities in the former Yugoslavia, in Rwanda, and elsewhere may provide further examples. The Brazen Rule seems too unforgiving. The Iron Rule promotes the advantage of a ruthless and powerful few against the interests of everybody else. The Golden and Silver Rules seem too complacent. They systematically fail to punish cruelty and exploitation. They hope to coax people from evil to good by showing that kindness is possible. But there are sociopaths who do not much care about the feelings of others, and it is hard to imagine a Hitler or a Stalin being shamed into redemption by good example. Is there a rule between the Golden and the Silver on the one hand and the Brazen, Iron, and Tin on the other which works better than any of them alone?

With so many different rules, how can you tell which to use, which 23
will work? More than one rule may be operating even in the same person or nation. Are we doomed just to guess about this, or to rely on intuition, or just to parrot what we've been taught? Let's try to put aside, just for the moment, whatever rules we've been taught, and those we feel passionately—perhaps from a deeply rooted sense of justice—*must* be right.

Suppose we seek not to confirm or deny what we've been taught, 24
but to find out what really works. Is there a way to *test* competing codes of ethics? Granting that the real world may be much more complicated than any simulation, can we explore the matter scientifically?

We're used to playing games in which somebody wins and some- 25
body loses. Every point made by our opponent puts us that much further behind. "Win-lose" games seem natural, and many people are hard-pressed to think of a game that isn't win-lose. In win-lose games, the losses just balance the wins. That's why they're called "zero-sum" games. There's no ambiguity about your opponent's intentions: Within the rules of the game, he will do anything he can to defeat you.

Many children are aghast the first time they really come face to face 26
with the "lose" side of win-lose games. On the verge of bankruptcy in Monopoly, they plead for special dispensation (forgoing rents, for example), and when this is not forthcoming may, in tears, denounce the game as heartless and unfeeling—which of course it is. (I've seen the board overturned, hotels and "Chance" cards and metal icons spilled onto the floor in spitting anger and humiliation—and not only by children.) Within the rules of Monopoly, there's no way for players to cooperate so that all benefit. That's not how the game is designed. The same is true for boxing, football, hockey, basketball, baseball, lacrosse, tennis, racquetball, chess, all Olympic events, yacht and car racing, pinochle, potsie, and partisan politics. In none of these games is there an opportunity to

practice the Golden or Silver Rules, or even the Brazen. There is room only for the Rules of Iron and Tin. If we revere the Golden Rule, why is it so rare in the games we teach our children?

After a million years of intermittently warring tribes we readily 27 enough think in zero-sum mode, and treat every interaction as a contest or conflict. Nuclear war, though (and many conventional wars), economic depression, and assaults on the global environment are all "lose-lose" propositions. Such vital human concerns as love, friendship, parenthood, music, art, and the pursuit of knowledge are "win-win" propositions. Our vision is dangerously narrow if all we know is win-lose.

The scientific field that deals with such matters is called game theory, 28 used in military tactics and strategy, trade policy, corporate competition, limiting environmental pollution, and plans for nuclear war. The paradigmatic game is the Prisoner's Dilemma. It is very much non-zero-sum. Win-win, win-lose, and lose-lose outcomes are all possible. "Sacred" books carry few useful insights into strategy here. It is a wholly pragmatic game.

Imagine that you and a friend are arrested for committing a serious 29 crime. For the purpose of the game, it doesn't matter whether either, neither, or both of you did it. What matters is that the police say they think you did. Before the two of you have any chance to compare stories or plan strategy, you are taken to separate interrogation cells. There, oblivious of your Miranda rights ("You have the right to remain silent . . ."), they try to make you confess. They tell you, as police sometimes do, that your friend has confessed and implicated you. (Some friend!) The police might be telling the truth. Or they might be lying. You're permitted only to plead innocent or guilty. If you're willing to say anything, what's your best tack to minimize punishment?

Here are the possible outcomes: 30

If you deny committing the crime and (unknown to you) your 31 friend also denies it, the case might be hard to prove. In the plea bargain, both your sentences will be very light.

If you confess and your friend does likewise, then the effort the 32 State had to expend to solve the crime was small. In exchange you both may be given a fairly light sentence, although not as light as if you both had asserted your innocence.

But if you plead innocent and your friend confesses, the state will 33 ask for the maximum sentence for you and minimal punishment (maybe none) for your friend. Uh-oh. You're very vulnerable to a kind of double cross, what game theorists call "defection." So's he.

So if you and your friend "cooperate" with one another—both 34 pleading innocent (or both pleading guilty)—you both escape the worst. Should you play it safe and guarantee a middle range of punishment by confessing? Then, if your friend pleads innocent while you plead guilty, well, too bad for him, and you might get off scot-free.

When you think it through, you realize that whatever your friend 35
does you're better off defecting than cooperating. Maddeningly, the same
holds true for your friend. But if you both defect, you're both worse off
than if you had both cooperated. This is the Prisoner's Dilemma.

Now consider a repeated Prisoner's Dilemma, in which the two play- 36
ers go through a sequence of such games. At the end of each they figure
out from their punishment how the other must have pled. They gain
experience about each other's strategy (and character). Will they learn to
cooperate game after game, both always denying that they committed
any crime? Even if the reward for finking on the other is large?

You might try cooperating or defecting, depending on how the 37
previous game or games have gone. If you cooperate overmuch, the other
player may exploit your good nature. If you defect overmuch, your friend
is likely to defect often, and this is bad for both of you. You know your
defection pattern is data being fed to the other player. What is the right
mix of cooperation and defection? How to behave then becomes, like any
other question in Nature, a subject to be investigated experimentally.

This matter has been explored in a continuing round-robin com- 38
puter tournament by the University of Michigan sociologist Robert
Axelrod in his remarkable book *The Evolution of Cooperation*. Various
codes of behavior confront one another and at the end we see who wins
(who gets the lightest cumulative prison term). The simplest strategy
might be to cooperate all the time, no matter how much advantage is
taken of you, or never to cooperate, no matter what benefits might
accrue from cooperation. These are the Golden Rule and the Iron Rule.
They always lose, the one from a superfluity of kindness, the other from
an overabundance of ruthlessness. Strategies slow to punish defection
lose—in part because they send a signal that noncooperation can win.
The Golden Rule is not only an unsuccessful strategy; it is also dangerous for other players, who may succeed in the short term only to be
mowed down by exploiters in the long term.

Should you defect at first, but if your opponent cooperates even 39
once, cooperate in all future games? Should you cooperate at first, but if
your opponent defects even once, defect in all future games? These
strategies also lose. Unlike sports, you cannot rely on your opponent to
be always out to get you.

The most effective strategy in many such tournaments is called 40
"Tit-for-Tat." It's very simple: You start out cooperating, and in each subsequent round simply do what your opponent did last time. You punish
defections, but once your partner cooperates, you're willing to let
bygones be bygones. At first, it seems to garner only mediocre success.
But as time goes on the other strategies defeat themselves, from too much
kindness or cruelty, and this middle way pulls ahead. Except for always
being nice on the first move, Tit-for-Tat is identical to the Brazen Rule. It
promptly (in the very next game) rewards cooperation and punishes

to throw away the happiness of thousands for the chance of the happiness of one: that would be to let guilt within the walls indeed.

The terms are strict and absolute; there may not even be a kind 11 word spoken to the child.

Often the young people go home in tears, or in a tearless rage, when 12 they have seen the child and faced this terrible paradox. They may brood over it for weeks or years. But as time goes on they begin to realize that even if the child could be released, it would not get much good of its freedom: a little vague pleasure of warmth and food, no doubt, but little more. It is too degraded and imbecile to know any real joy. It has been afraid too long ever to be free of fear. Its habits are too uncouth for it to respond to humane treatment. Indeed, after so long it would probably be wretched without walls about it to protect it, and darkness for its eyes, and its own excrement to sit in. Their tears at the bitter injustice dry when they begin to perceive the terrible justice of reality, and to accept it. Yet it is their tears and anger, the trying of their generosity and the acceptance of their helplessness, which are perhaps the true source of the splendor of their lives. Theirs is no vapid, irresponsible happiness. They know that they, like the child, are not free. They know compassion. It is the existence of the child, and their knowledge of its existence, that makes possible the nobility of their architecture, the poignancy of their music, the profundity of their science. It is because of the child that they are so gentle with children. They know that if the wretched one were not there snivelling in the dark, the other one, the flute-player, could make no joyful music as the young riders line up in their beauty for the race in the sunlight of the first morning of summer.

Now do you believe in them? Are they not more credible? But there 13 is one more thing to tell, and this is quite incredible.

At times one of the adolescent girls or boys who go to see the child 14 does not go home to weep or rage, does not, in fact, go home at all. Sometimes also a man or woman much older falls silent for a day or two, and then leaves home. These people go out into the street, and walk down the street alone. They keep walking, and walk straight out of the city of Omelas, through the beautiful gates. They keep walking across the farmlands of Omelas. Each one goes alone, youth or girl, man or woman. Night falls; the traveler must pass down village streets, between the houses with yellow-lit windows, and on out into the darkness of the fields. Each alone, they go west or north, towards the mountains. They go on. They leave Omelas, they walk ahead into the darkness, and they do not come back. The place the they go towards is a place even less imaginable to most of us than the city of happiness. I cannot describe it at all. It is possible that it does not exist. But they seem to know where they are going. the ones who walk away from Omelas.

Responding to Reading

1. Why do you think Le Guin's narrator keeps asking readers whether or not they "believe," whether they accept what she is saying as the truth? *Do* you "believe"? What do you find most unbelievable? What do you find most believable?

2. Are the ones who walk away from Omelas any less morally responsible for the child's welfare than those who keep the child imprisoned? Or do you believe there is a difference between actively doing something "wrong" and passively allowing it to happen?

3. Why does the logic of the story require that the child be present? Why must the child suffer? Might it be argued that our society has its own equivalent of the child locked in the closet and that we are guilty of failing to act to save this child?

the American public appears to be as badly informed about the real nature of science as it ever was. Such undiluted ignorance, coupled with the strong anti-intellectual tradition in the U.S., provides congenial climate for creationism to leap once more to the fore, along with school prayer, sex education, Proposition 13, and the other favorite issues of the populist, conservative movement. Much of the success of recent creationist efforts lies in a prior failure to educate our children about science—how it is done, by whom, and how its results are to be interpreted.

Today's creationists usually cry for "equal time" rather than for 3 actually substituting the Genesis version of the origin of things for the explanation preferred by modern science. (The recent trial in California is an anachronism in this respect because the plaintiff simply affirmed that his rights of religious freedom were abrogated by teaching him that man "descended from apes"). At the heart of the creationists' contemporary political argument is an appeal to the time-honored American sense of fair play. "Look," they say, "evolution is only a theory. Scientists cannot agree on all details either of the exact course of evolutionary history, or how evolution actually takes place." True enough. Creationists then declare that many scientists have grave doubts that evolution actually has occurred—a charge echoed by Ronald Reagan during the campaign, and definitely false. They argue that since evolution is only a theory, why not, in the spirit of fair play, give equal time to equally plausible explanations of the origin of the cosmos, of life on earth, and of mankind? Why not indeed?

The creationist argument equates a biological, evolutionary system 4 with a non-scientific system of explaining life's exuberant diversity. Both systems are presented as authoritarian, and here lies the real tragedy of American science education: the public is depressingly willing to see merit in the "fair play, equal time" argument precisely because it views science almost wholly in this authoritarian vein. The public is bombarded with a constant stream of oracular pronouncements of new discoveries, new truths, and medical and technological innovations, but the American education system gives most people no effective choice but to ignore, accept on faith, or reject out of hand each new scientific finding. Scientists themselves promote an Olympian status for their profession; it's small wonder that the public has a tough time deciding which set of authoritarian pronouncements to heed. So why not present them all and let each person choose his or her own set of beliefs?

Of course, there has to be some willingness to accept the expertise 5 of specialists. Although most of us "believe" the earth is spherical, how many of us can design and perform an experiment to show that it must be so? But to stress the authoritarianism of science is to miss its essence. Science is the enterprise of comparing alternative ideas about what the cosmos is, how it works, and how it came to be. Some ideas are better than others, and the criterion for judging which are better is simply the relative power of different ideas to fit our observations. The goal is greater understanding of the natural universe. The method consists of constantly challenging received ideas, modifying them, or, best of all, replacing them with better ones.

So science is ideas, and the ideas are acknowledged to be merely 6 approximations to the truth. Nothing could be further from authoritarianism—dogmatic assertions of what is true. Scientists deal with ideas that appear to be the best (the closest to the truth) given what they think they know about the universe at any given moment. If scientists frequently act as if their ideas *are* the truth, they are simply showing their humanity. But the human quest for a rational coming-to-grips with the cosmos recognizes imperfection in observation and thought, and incorporates the frailty into its method. Creationists disdain this quest, preferring the wholly authoritarian, allegedly "revealed" truth of divine creation as an understanding of our beginnings. At the same time they present disagreement among scientists as an expression of scientific failure in the realm of evolutionary biology.

To the charge that "evolution is *only* a theory," we say "all science is 7 theory." Theories are ideas, or complex sets of ideas, which explain some aspect of the natural world. Competing theories sometimes coexist until one drives the other out, or until both are discarded in favor of yet another theory. But it is true that one major theory usually holds sway at any one time. All biologists, including biochemists, molecular geneticists, physiologists, behaviorists, and anatomists, see a pattern of similarity interlocking the spectrum of millions of species, from bacteria to timber wolves. Darwin finally convinced the world that this pattern of similarity is neatly explained by "descent with modification." If we imagine a genealogical system where an ancestor produces one or more descendants, we get a pattern of progressive similarity. The whole array of ancestors and descendants will share some feature inherited from the first ancestor; as each novelty appears, it is shared only with later descendants. All forms of life have the nucleic acid RNA. One major branch of life, the vertebrates, all share backbones. All mammals have three inner ear bones, hair, and mammary glands. All dogs share features not found in other carnivores, such as cats. In other words, dogs share similarities among themselves in addition to having general mammalian features, plus general vertebrate features, as well as anatomical and biochemical similarities shared with the rest of life.

How do we test the basic notion that life has evolved? The notion of 8 evolution, like any scientific idea, should generate predictions about the natural world, which we can discover to be true or false. The grand prediction of evolution is that there should be one basic scheme of similarities interlocking all of life. This is what we have consistently found for over 100 years, as thousands of biologists daily compared different organisms. Medical experimentation depends upon the interrelatedness of life. We test drugs on rhesus monkeys and study the effects of caffeine on rats because we cannot experiment on ourselves. The physiological systems of monkeys are more similar to our own than to rats. Medical scientists know this and rely on this prediction to interpret the significance of their results in terms of human medicine. Very simply, were life not all interrelated, none of this would be possible. There would be chaos, not order, in the natural world. There is no competing, rational biological explanation for this order in nature, and there hasn't been for a long while.

Creationists, of course, have an alternative explanation for this 9 order permeating life's diversity. It is simply the way the supernatural creator chose to pattern life. But any possible pattern could be there, including chaos—an absence of any similarity among the "kinds" of organisms on earth—and creationism would hold that it is just what the creator made. There is nothing about this view of life that smacks of prediction. It tells us nothing about what to expect if we begin to study organisms in detail. In short, there is nothing in this notion that allows us to go to nature to test it, to verify or reject it.

And there is the key difference. Creationism (and it comes in many 10 guises, most of which do not stem from the Judeo-Christian tradition) is a belief system involving the supernatural. Testing an idea with our own experiences in the natural universe is simply out of bounds. The mystical revelation behind creationism is the opposite of science, which seeks rational understanding of the cosmos. Science thrives on alternative explanations, which must be equally subject to observational and experimental testing. No form of creationism even remotely qualifies for inclusion in a science curriculum.

Creationists have introduced equal-time bills in over 10 state legisla- 11 tures, and recently met with success when Governor White of Arkansas signed such a bill into law on March 19 (reportedly without reading it). Creationists also have lobbied extensively at local school boards. The impact has been enormous. Just as the latest creationist bill is defeated in committee, and some of their more able spokesmen look silly on national TV, one hears of a local school district in the Philadelphia environs where some of the teachers have adopted the "equal time" or "dual model" approach to discussing "origins" in the biology curriculum on their own initiative. Each creationist "defeat" amounts to a Pyrrhic victory for their opponents. Increasingly, teachers are left to their own discretion, and whether out of personal conviction, a desire to be "fair," or fear of parental reprisal, they are teaching creationism along with evolution in their biology classes. It is simply the path of least resistance.

Acceptance of equal time for two alternative authoritarian explana- 12 tions is a startling blow to the fabric of science education. The fundamental notion a student should get from high school science is that people can confront the universe and learn about it directly. Just one major inroad against this basic aspect of science threatens all of science education. Chemistry, physics, and geology—all of which spurn biblical revelation in favor of direct experience, as all science must—are jeopardized every bit as much as biology. That some creationists have explicitly attacked areas of geology, chemistry, and physics (in arguments over the age of the earth, for example) underscores the more general threat they pose to all science. We must remove science education from its role as authoritarian truthgiver. This view distorts the real nature of science and gives creationists their most potent argument.

The creationists' equal-time appeal maintains that evolution itself 13 amounts to a religious belief (allied with a secular humanism) and should not be included in a science curriculum. But if it is included, goes the argument, it must appear along with other religious notions. Both are authoritarian belief systems, and neither is science, according to this creationist ploy.

The more common creationist approach these days avoids such 14 sophistry and maintains that both creationism and evolution belong in the realm of science. But apart from some attempts to document the remains of Noah's Ark on the flanks of Mt. Ararat, creationists have been singularly unsuccessful in posing testable theories about the origin, diversity, and distribution of plants and animals. No such contributions have appeared to date either in creationism's voluminous literature or, more to the point, in the professional biological literature. "Science creationism" consists almost exclusively of a multipronged attack on evolutionary biology and historical geology. No evidence, for example, is presented in favor of the notion that the earth is only 20,000 years old, but many arguments attempt to poke holes in geochemists' and astronomers' reckoning of old Mother Earth's age at about 4.6 billion years. Analysis of the age of formation of rocks is based ultimately on the theories of radioactive decay in nuclear physics. (A body of rock is dated, often by several different means, in several different laboratories. The results consistently agree. And rocks shown to be roughly the same age on independent criteria (usually involving fossils) invariably check out to be roughly the same age when dated radiometrically. The system, although not without its flaws, works.) The supposed vast age of any particular rock can be shown to be false, but not by quoting Scripture.

All of the prodigious works of "scientific creationism" are of this 15 nature. All can be refuted. However, before school boards or parent groups, creationists are fond of "debating" scientists by bombarding the typically ill-prepared biologist or geologist with a plethora of allegations, ranging from the second law of thermodynamics (said to falsity evolution outright) to the supposed absence of fossils intermediate between "major kinds." No scientist is equally at home in all realms of physics, chemistry, geology, and biology in this day of advanced specialization. Not all the proper retorts spring readily to mind. Retorts

history; rather they are "extreme antisemites" whose aim is "to confuse the matter by making it appear as if they are engaged in genuine scholarly effort when, of course, they are not." The following chapter from Denying the Holocaust *focuses specifically on Lipstadt's argument that by accepting advertisements in which Holocaust deniers outline their claims, college newspapers can inadvertently add legitimacy to those claims.*

This is not a public stagecoach that has to take everyone who buys a ticket.

—Benjamin Franklin

In the early 1990s American college campuses became loci of inten- 1 sive activity by a small group of Holocaust deniers. Relying on creative tactics and assisted by a fuzzy kind of reasoning often evident in academic circles, the deniers achieved millions of dollars of free publicity and significantly furthered their cause. Their strategy was profoundly simple. Bradley Smith, a Californian who has been involved in a variety of Holocaust denial activities since the early 1980s, attempted to place a full-page ad claiming that the Holocaust was a hoax in college newspapers throughout the United States. The ad was published by papers at some of the more prestigious institutions of higher learning in the United States.

Entitled "The Holocaust Story: How Much Is False? The Case for 2 Open Debate," the ad provoked a fierce debate on many of the campuses approached by Smith. His strategy was quite straightforward: He generally called a paper's advertising department to ascertain the charge for publication of a full-page ad and then submitted camera-ready copy and a certified check in the proper amount. On occasion he inquired in advance whether a paper would be willing to run this particular ad. Even when he was rejected, the attempt to place the ad won him significant media attention. Campus newspapers began to use his name in headlines without identifying him, assuming readers would know who he was. Articles, letters, and op-ed pieces defended Holocaust denial's right to make its "views" known. But not all the results were necessarily what Smith would have wanted. On some campuses there was a backlash against him and Holocaust denial. Courses on the Holocaust that had languished on the back burner for an extended period materialized in the next semester's offerings. Campus administrators admitted that the ad constituted the final push necessary to move these courses from the planning stage to the schedule books. Professors from a wide variety of disciplines included discussion of the Holocaust in their courses. Movies, speakers, photographic exhibits and other presentations relating to the Holocaust were brought to campus. Students participated in rallies, teach-ins, and protests.

This response prompted some observers to argue that the contro- 3 versy had a positive impact. Students had become increasingly aware not only of the Holocaust but of the contemporary attempt to subvert history and spread antisemitism. While this may be a relatively accurate analysis of the immediate outcome of Smith's endeavor, there is another more sobering and pessimistic aspect to the matter. Analysis of the students', faculty's, and administration's responses reveals both a susceptibility to the worst form of historical revisionism and a failure to fully understand the implications of Holocaust denial, even among those who vigorously condemned it. . . .

The ad Smith began to circulate in the spring of 1991 contained the 4 deniers' familiar litany of claims. It declared the gas chambers a fraud, photographs doctored, eyewitness reports "ludicrously unreliable," the Nuremberg trials a sham, and camp internees well fed until Allied bombings destroyed the German infrastructure in the most "barbarous form of warfare in Europe since the Mongol invasions," preventing food from being delivered and causing the inmates to starve. According to Smith the notion of a Nazi attempt to destroy the Jews was the product of Allied efforts to produce "anti-German hate propaganda." Today that same propaganda was used by powerful forces to "scape-goat old enemies," "seek vengeance rather than reconciliation," and pursue a "not-so-secret political agenda."

He repeated the familiar protest that his sole objective was to 5 uncover the truth through an open debate on the Holocaust—debate that had been suppressed by a powerful but secret group on campus as part of their larger political agenda. "Let's ask these people—what makes such behavior a social good? Who benefits?"

The ad contended that denial was forcing "mainline Holocaust his- 6 torians" to admit the "more blatant examples" of Holocaust falsehoods. It was the deniers who had forced them to revise the "orthodox" Holocaust story. They had had to admit that the number of Jews killed at Auschwitz was far smaller than originally claimed, and had been made to confess that the Nazis did not use Jewish cadavers for the production of soap. It is correct that in recent years newly revealed documentation has allowed scholars to assess more precisely the number of Jews thought to have been murdered at Auschwitz.[1] It is also accurate that scholars have long written that despite wartime rumors to the contrary,

---

[1] The memorial stone at Auschwitz lists the number of victims of the camp as 4 million. Research now indicates that the number of people who died in the Auschwitz/Birkenau gas chambers was between 1.5 and 2 million, of whom 85 to 90 percent were Jews.

the Nazis apparently did not use Jewish cadavers for soap. There has been a wide array of other "revelations" by Holocaust historians, all part of the attempt to uncover the full details of one of the most horrifying acts of human destruction. Smith suggested to his readers that scholars and others who work in this field, all of whom vigorously repudiate Holocaust denial, have been compelled to admit the truth of deniers' claims: "We are told that it is 'anti-Jewish' to question orthodox assertions about German criminality. Yet we find that it is Jews themselves like Mayer, Bauer, Hier, Hilberg, Lipstadt and others who beginning [sic] to challenge the establishment Holocaust story." This notion—that deniers have exposed the truth and mainline historians are scrambling to admit it—remains a linchpin of the deniers' strategy. It has two objectives: to make it appear that Jewish scholars are responding to the pressure of the deniers' findings and to create the impression that Holocaust deniers' "questions" are themselves part of a continuum of respectable scholarship. If establishment scholars, particularly those who are Jews, can question previously accepted truths, why is it wrong when Bradley Smith does the same?

Though much of the ad consisted of familiar rhetoric, Smith added a new twist that had a particular resonance on American college campuses. Since the 1980s the concept of "political correctness" has been a source of academic conflict. Conservative political groups have accused the "liberal establishment" of labeling certain topics politically incorrect and therefore ineligible for inclusion in the curriculum. Smith framed his well-worn denial arguments within this rhetoric, arguing that Holocaust revisionism could not be addressed on campus because "America's thought police" had declared it out of bounds. "The politically correct line on the Holocaust story is, simply, it happened. You don't debate 'it.'" Unlike all other topics students were free to explore, the Holocaust story was off limits. The consequences, he charged, were antithetical to everything for which the university stood. "Ideology replaces free inquiry, intimidation represses open debate, and . . . the ideals of the university itself are exchanged for intellectual taboos." While most students who had to decide whether the ad should be published did not overtly succumb to CODOH's use of the political correctness argument, many proved prone to it, sometimes less than consciously—a susceptibility evident in their justifications for running the ad. Among the first universities to accept the ad were Northwestern, the University of Michigan, Duke, Cornell, Ohio State, and Washington University.[2]

---

[2] The papers discussed in this chapter function as private newspapers. The courts have broadly defined their editorial discretion to accept or reject ads. In situations of "state action," where a state university administration controls the newspaper's content, the courts may prohibit content-based rejection of the ads. Discretion of Student Editors to Accept or Reject Holocaust Revisionist Advertisements (ADL Legal Affairs Dept., Feb. 1992).

At the University of Michigan the saga of the ad had a strange twist. 8
Smith mailed camera-ready copy directly to the *Michigan Daily*.
According to the paper's business manager, the ad "slipped through
without being read." When it appeared the business staff was appalled
to learn what they had allowed to happen. On the following day they
placed a six-column ad in the paper apologizing for running Smith's ad
and acknowledging that its publication had been a mistake. They
declared it a "sorrowful learning experience for the staff." The manager
told the *Detroit Free Press*, "We make mistakes like any organization."

The story might well have ended here—an example of faulty mon- 9
itoring by a segment of the staff of the *Michigan Daily*—but the issue
became more complicated when, despite the fact that those responsible
for running the ad acknowledged doing so as a mistake, the editorial
board attempted to transform a blunder into a matter of principle. They
recast a snafu as an expression of freedom of speech. On the same day
that the advertising staff published its apology, the front page carried an
editorial explaining that, though the editors found the ad "offensive and
inaccurate," they could not condone the censorship of "unpopular
views from our pages merely because they are offensive or because we
disagree with them." Editor in chief Andrew Gottesman acknowledged
that had the decision been in his hands, he would have printed the ad.
He argued that rejecting it constituted censorship, which the editorial
board found unacceptable.

The following day a campus rally attacked both Holocaust denial 10
and the paper's editorial policies. Stung by student and faculty con-
demnations and afraid that its editorial was being interpreted as an
endorsement of CODOH, the editorial board devoted the next issue's
lead editorial to the topic. Condemning Holocaust denial as "absurd"
and "founded on historical fiction and anti-Jewish bigotry," they dismissed it as irrational, illogical, and ahistorical propaganda. The editors
accurately assessed the ad as lacking intellectual merit. Nonetheless,
they continued to support its publication. Their powerful condemnation of Holocaust denial in general and Smith's ad in particular
appeared under a banner quoting Supreme Court Justice Hugo Black's
opinion on free speech: "My view is, without deviation, without exception, without any ifs, buts, or whereases, that freedom of speech means
that you shall not do something to people either for the views they have
or the views they express or the words they speak or write."

The strange set of circumstances at Michigan—snatching a consti- 11
tutional principle from the jaws of a mistake—was further complicated
by the entry of the university's president, James Duderstadt, into the
debate. In a letter to the *Daily* he declared the ad the work of "a warped
crank" and proclaimed that denying the Holocaust was to "deny our
human potential for evil and to invite its resurgence." But he, too,
defended the paper's decision, which was more of a nondecision, to run

the ad. The president asserted that the *Daily* had a long history of editorial freedom that had to be protected even when "we disagree either with particular opinions, decisions, or actions." Most disturbing was Duderstadt's elevation of Smith's prejudices to the level of opinions.

There was no doubt about the message the editors and the presi- 12 dent were trying to convey: As absurd, illogical, and bigoted as the ad may be, First Amendment guarantees were paramount. The dictates of the American Constitution compelled the *Daily* to publish. None of those involved seemed to have considered precisely what the First Amendment said: "Congress shall make no law . . . abridging the freedom of speech or of the press." Those who argued that free speech guarantees acceptance of the ad ignored the fact that the First Amendment prevents *government* from interfering in any fashion with an individual's or group's right to publish the most outlandish argument. The *New York Times* made this point in an editorial when it adamantly repudiated the notion that this was a First Amendment question: "Government may not censor Mr. Smith and his fellow 'Holocaust revisionists,' no matter how intellectually barren their claims."

To call rejection of the ad censorship was to ignore the fact that, 13 unlike the government, whose actions are limited by the First Amendment, these papers do not have a monopoly of force. If the government denies someone the right to publish, they have no other option to publish in this country. But if a paper rejects someone's column, ad, or letter, there are always other publications. The First Amendment does not guarantee access to a private publication. It is designed to serve as a shield to protect individuals and institutions from government interference in their affairs. It is not a sword by which every person who makes an outlandish statement or notorious claim can invoke a Constitutional right to be published.[3] Nor did the *Michigan Daily* seem to notice how Justice Black, whom they quoted, framed it: "you shall not do something to people. . . ." No one was advocating "doing" anything to Smith.

One of the most ardent advocates of the free-speech argument was 14 the *Duke Chronicle*. In an editorial column the editor in chief, Ann Heimberger, justified the paper's decision by acknowledging that while the paper knew it could reject the ad, it "chose" to accept it as an expression of the paper's desire to "support the advertiser's rights." The editorial board believed that it was not the paper's responsibility to protect "readers from disturbing ideas," but to "disseminate them."

---

[3] In 1931, in *Near v. Minnesota*, the Supreme Court struck down a state attempt to gag a paper's freedom to publish "malicious, scandalous or defamatory" material. Fred W. Friendly, *Minnesota Rag* (New York, 1981).

Echoing his Michigan colleague, Duke University president Keith 15
Brodie repeated the free-speech defense in a statement that, though it
contained a strong refutation of the ad, was more vigorous in its support of the *Chronicle's* publication of the ad. To have "suppressed" the
ad, he argued, would have violated the university's commitment to free
speech and contradicted its "long tradition of supporting First
Amendment rights."

When the *Cornell Daily Sun* ran the ad, the editors justified the deci- 16
sion in an editorial statement warning that "page twenty will shock
most readers" but proclaimed that it was not the paper's role to
"unjustly censor advertisers' viewpoints." Echoing their colleagues on
many of the other campuses that printed the ad, the editors declared
that they decided to print it because the "First Amendment right to
free expression must be extended to those with unpopular or offensive ideas." Neeraj Khemlani, the editor in chief of the *Daily Sun*, said
his role was not to "protect" readers. Cornell president Frank H. T.
Rhodes joined his colleagues at Duke and Michigan in defending the
paper's decision.

The University of Montana's paper, the *Montana Kaimin*, also used 17
the First Amendment to defend its publication of the ad. The editor contended that it was not the paper's place to "decide for the campus community what they should see." The University of Georgia's paper, the
Red and Black, expressed the hope that publishing the ad would affirm
America's unique commitment to "allowing every opinion to be heard,
no matter how objectionable, how outright offensive, how clearly
wrong that opinion may be." After the ad appeared the paper's editor
defended the decision by describing it as "a business decision," arguing
that "if the business department is set up to take ads, they darn well better take ads." Given the juxtaposition of these two explanations, there
was, as Mark Silk, an editorial writer for the *Atlanta Constitution*,
pointed out, something dubious about "this high-minded claim."

After an extensive debate Washington University's *Student Life* 18
decided to run the ad. When the ad appeared in the paper, Sam Moyn,
the opinion editor, was responsible for conveying to the university community the reasoning behind the staff's "controversial action." The editors, he wrote, conceived of this as a free-speech issue: "The abridgment
of Mr. Smith's rights endangers our own." The *St. Louis Post Dispatch*
defended the students' actions. Declaring the ad "offensive, provocative
and wrong," it praised the student newspaper's courage to print it and
stated that its actions strengthened the cause of freedom of speech. The
University of Arizona also depicted its actions as protecting the First
Amendment. The editor in chief, Beth Silver, proclaimed that the mission of student newspapers is "to uphold the First Amendment and run
things that are obviously going to be controversial and take the heat for

it." This attitude—we have to do what is right irrespective of the costs— was voiced by a number of papers. Ironically, it echoed a theme frequently voiced by the deniers themselves: We will tell the truth, the consequences notwithstanding.

At Ohio State University the decision-making process was com- 19 plex. The *Lantern's* advertising policy is in the hands of a publications committee comprising faculty, students, editorial board members, and the paper's business manager. University policy requires committee approval before acceptance of an ad designating a religious group. The committee voiced five to four to reject CODOH's submission. But the story did not end there. Enjoined by the committee's decision from running the ad, the *Lantern's* editor, Samantha G. Haney, used her editorial powers to run it as an op-ed piece, explaining that the paper had an "obligation" to do so. This decision gave Smith added legitimacy and saved him the $1,134 it would have cost to place a full-page ad in the paper.

A lengthy editorial explaining the *Lantern's* decision condemned 20 Bradley Smith and his cohorts as "racists, pure and simple" and the ad as "little more than a commercial for hatred." Nonetheless the newspaper had to publish it because it could not only "run things that were harmless to everyone." Haney and her staff rejected the suggestion that they turn to the Ohio State History Department to "pick apart" the ad fact by fact. That, they explained, might suggest that the ad had some "relevancy" and some "substance," which they were convinced it did not. Given that one of the rationales the *Lantern* offered for publishing the article was that "truth will always outshine any lie," its refusal to ask professional historians to elucidate how the ad convoluted historical fact seemed self-defeating. It seemed to reflect an understandable reluctance to accord denial legitimacy. There is no better example of the fragility of reason than the conclusion by these editorial boards that it was their obligation to run an ad or an op-ed column that, according to their *own* evaluation, was totally lacking in relevance or substance.

In contrast to the position adopted by James Duderstadt at the 21 University of Michigan, Ohio State's president, Gordon Gee, attacked the decision to give Smith space in the newspaper, declaring the deniers' arguments "pernicious" and "cleverly disguised" propaganda that enhanced prejudice and distorted history.

When this issue was being debated at Ohio State, a CBS reporter 22 came to that campus to film a segment on Holocaust denial for a network show on hatred and extremism in the United States. Alerted in advance to the pending controversy, the cameras were conveniently present when the editor received a call from Smith congratulating her for running the ad and standing up for the principles of free speech and free press. When Haney hung up, the television reporter, who was standing nearby, asked how she felt. She turned and somewhat plaintively observed that she thought she had been had.

Not all the papers subscribed to the First Amendment argument; 23 indeed, some explicitly rejected it. The University of Tennessee's *Daily Beacon* dismissed the idea that not running the ad harmed the deniers' interests: It was not "censorship or even damaging." Pennsylvania State University's *Daily Collegian*, which had been one of the first to receive an ad from Smith, denied that the issue was one of free speech. After seeing student leaders and numerous individuals on campus inundated with material by deniers, the paper reasoned that those behind the ad had sufficient funds to propagate their conspiracy theory of Jewish control without being granted space in the paper.

In an eloquent editorial the *Harvard Crimson* repudiated Smith's 24 claim to a free-speech right to publish his ad. To give CODOH a forum so that it could "promulgate malicious falsehoods" under the guise of open debate constituted an "abdication" of the paper's editorial responsibility. The University of Chicago *Maroon* agreed that while the deniers "may express their views," it had "no obligation at any time to print their offensive hatred."

The argument that not publishing the ad constituted censorship 25 was not only a misinterpretation of the First Amendment but disingenuous. The editorial boards that reached this decision ignored the fact that they all had policies that prevented them from running racist, sexist, prejudicial, or religiously offensive ads. (Some of the papers in question even refuse cigarette ads.) How could they square their "principled" stand for absolute freedom of speech with policies that prevented them from publishing a range of ads and articles? Why was Bradley Smith entitled to constitutional protection while an ad for an X-rated movie, *Playboy*, the KKK, or Marlboros was not? Recognizing this inconsistency, some of the boards tried to reconcile these two seemingly contradictory positions by adopting a stance that drew them even further into the deniers' trap. They argued that Holocaust denial was not antisemitic and therefore not offensive. The *Cornell Daily Sun* editorial board determined that the "ad does not directly contain racist statements about Jewish people." Valerie Nicolette, the *Sun's* managing editor, told the *Chronicle of Higher Education* that the editors had evaluated the ad based on their standards of "obscenity and racism" and decided that it passed. When a group of Jewish students at Duke met with the editorial board of the *Duke Chronicle* to protest the running of the ad, they were told that the paper's policy was not to run any ad that was "racist or contained ethnic slurs" but that this ad did not fall into that category.

Andrew Gottesman, who vigorously argued that he could not con- 26 done "censorship" of Smith's advertisement and whose *Michigan Daily* published its ringing denunciation of Holocaust denial under Justice Hugo Black's interpretation of the First Amendment, admitted that there were ads he would not run in the paper. This ad, however, did not deserve to be "banned from the marketplace of ideas, like others might be." Among those he would ban were a Ku Klux Klan announcement of lynching or a beer ad with a woman holding a beer bottle between her breasts. For Gottesman keeping such sexist and racist ads out of the paper would not constitute censorship; keeping Smith's out would. When Washington University's *Student Life* published the ad, an editorial explained that it did so in the interest of preventing "freedom of ideas from disappearing from its newspapers." Yet the same paper includes the following policy statement on its advertising rate card: "*Student Life* reserves the right to edit or reject any advertisement which does not comply with the policies or judgment of the newspaper."

The claim that the rejection of the ad constituted censorship also 27 revealed the failure of editorial staffs and, in certain cases, university presidents to think carefully about what their papers did regularly: pick and choose between subjects they covered and those they did not, columns they ran and those they rejected, and ads that met their standards and those that did not. The *Daily Tar Heel*, the paper of the University of North Carolina, proclaimed that as soon as an editor "takes the first dangerous step and decides that an ad should not run because of its content, that editor begins the plunge down a slippery slope toward the abolition of free speech." What the *Tar Heel* failed to note was that newspapers continuously make such choices. As Tom Teepen, the editor of the *Atlanta Constitution's* editorial page, observed, "Running a newspaper is mainly about making decisions, not about ducking them." In fact the *Duke Chronicle*, whose editor had wondered how newspapers founded on the principles of free speech and free press could "deny those rights to anyone," had earlier rejected an insert for *Playboy* and an ad attacking a fraternity.

While some papers justified their decision by arguing that the ad 28 was not antisemitic and others leaned on the censorship argument, an even more disconcerting rationale was offered by many papers. They argued that however ugly or repellent Smith's "ideas," they had a certain intellectual legitimacy. Consequently it was the papers' responsibility to present these views to readers for their consideration. Those editors who made this argument fell prey to denial's attempt to present itself as part of the normal range of historical interpretation. That they had been deceived was evident in the way they described the contents of the ad. The editor in chief of the *Cornell Daily Sun* described the ad as containing "offensive *ideas*." The *Sun* argued that it was not the paper's role to "unjustly censor advertisers' *viewpoints*," however "unpopular or offensive." In a similar vein the *University of Washington Daily* defended giving Smith op-ed space because the paper must constitute a "forum for diverse *opinions* and *ideas*." Ironically, six weeks earlier, when it rejected the ad, it had described Smith's assertions as "so obviously false as to be unworthy of serious debate." The paper insisted that the op-ed column it eventually published was different because it was Smith's "opinion" and did not contain the "blatant falsehoods" of the ad. In the column Smith asserted that for more than twelve years he has been unable to find "one bit of hard evidence" to prove that there was a plan to "exterminate" the Jews, and that the gas-chamber "stories" were "allegations" unsupported by "documentation or physical evidence."

The *Michigan Daily* engaged in the same reasoning. It would not 29 censor "unpopular *views*" simply because readers might disagree with them. In a show of consistency, two weeks after Smith's ad appeared, the *Daily* supported the decision by Prodigy, the computer bulletin board, to allow subscribers to post Holocaust denial material. Prodigy, they contended, was similar to a newspaper, and like a newspaper it must be a *"forum for ideas."* In another suggestion that Smith's views were worthy of debate, the editor in chief of the *Montana Kaimin* argued that "this man's *opinions*, no matter how ridiculous they may be, need to be heard out there." According to the editor in chief of Washington University's *Student Life*, the board voted to run the ad because "we didn't feel comfortable censoring offensive *ideas*."

The *Ohio State Lantern's* explanation of why it let Smith have his 30 "public say" despite the fact that it condemned Smith and CODOH as "racist, pure and simple," was more disturbing than the decision itself. The *Lantern* argued that it was "repulsive to think that the quality, or total lack thereof, of any idea or opinion has any bearing on whether it should be heard." It is breathtaking that students at a major university could declare repulsive the making of a decision based on the "quality" of ideas. One assumes that their entire education is geared toward the exploration of ideas with a certain lasting quality. This kind of reasoning essentially contravenes all that an institution of higher learning is supposed to profess.

The editors of Washington University's *Student Life* demonstrated a 31 similar disturbing inconsistency. They dismissed Smith's claim to be engaged in a quest for the truth, describing him as someone who "cloaks hate in the garb of intellectual detachment." They believed that Smith was posing as a "truth seeker crushed by a conspiratorial society." Given their evaluation of Smith, his tactics, and the way conspiracy theorists have captured the imagination of much of American society, what followed was particularly disconcerting. Notwithstanding all their misgivings, the editors decided that they must give "Mr. Smith the benefit of the doubt if we mean to preserve our own rights." In an assertion typical of the confused reasoning that student papers nationwide displayed on this issue, the *Student Life* editors acknowledged that they could have suppressed Smith's views "if we attributed motives to him that contradict his statements. But we cannot in good conscience tell Mr. Smith that we 'know' him and his true intentions." Was not the fact that he was denying a historical fact about whose existence there is no debate among any reputable scholars indicative of something significant? The editorial board had concluded that "if we refused Mr. Smith's advertisement, we could censor anyone based on ulterior motives that we perceive them to harbor." At what point would the board feel it was appropriate to make a decision based on the objective merits of the information contained in the ad?

In this instance what the paper considered to be ulterior motives is 32 what scholars call coming to a conclusion based on a wide variety of facts, including historical data. In giving Smith the "benefit of the doubt," the editors fell prey to the notion that this was a rational debate. They ignored the fact that the ad contained claims that completely contravened a massive body of fact. They transformed what the *Harvard Crimson* described as "vicious propaganda" into iconoclasm.

The most controversial interpretation about precisely what this ad 33 represented was expressed by the *Duke Chronicle*. In a column justifying the paper's decision to run the ad, Ann Heimberger contended that "Revisionists are . . . reinterpreting history, a practice that occurs constantly, especially on a college campus." In a private meeting with Jewish student leaders on the Duke campus, the editors reiterated this argument. The students were told that the ad was neither racist nor antisemitic but was part of an ongoing "scholarly debate." The Duke editorial board viewed the advertisement more as "a political argument than as an ethnic attack." In editorials, articles, and interviews, those at the helm of the *Duke Chronicle* repeatedly referred to Holocaust denial as "radical, unpopular *views*," and "disturbing *ideas*" and argued that the ad was not a "slur" but an "*opinion*." By doing so they not only clung to their First Amendment defense, they gave the ad historical and intellectual legitimacy. . . .

There were, of course, those college newspapers that had no problem 34 evaluating the ad's intellectual value. The *Harvard Crimson* repudiated the idea that the ad was a "controversial argument based on questionable facts." In one of the most unequivocal evaluations of the ad, the *Crimson* declared it "vicious propaganda based on utter bullshit that has been discredited time and time again." More than "moronic and false," it was an attempt to "propagate hatred against Jews." The editorial board of the University of Pennsylvania's *Daily Pennsylvanian* argued that "running an ad with factual errors that fostered hate" was not in the best interests of the paper.

The *MIT Tech* simply decided that it would not accept an ad that it 35 knew "did not tell the truth." For the *Brown Daily Herald* the ad was "a pack of vicious, antisemitic lies" parading as "history and scholarship."

The *Daily Nexus*, the publication of the University of California at Santa Barbara, refused the ad because of its "blatant distortions of truth and its offensive nature." The paper described receiving the ad itself and the more than one thousand dollars to print it as "chilling." The *Dartmouth Review*, no stranger to controversy, also rejected the ad. It acknowledged that by so doing it was denying "someone a forum through which to speak to the paper's readership" but explained that it had a "bond of trust" with the public, which expected it to abide by "standards of accuracy and decency." Accepting an ad "motivated by hatred and informed by total disregard to the truth" would be to violate that trust. The *Chicago Maroon* saw no reason why it should run an ad whose "only objective is to offend and incite hatred." The *Yale Daily News* "simply" let Smith know that it found the ad "offensive."

Some of the papers that ran the ad did so on the basis of what may 36 be called the light-of-day defense, a corollary of the free-speech argument: In the light of day truth always prevails over lies. Neeraj Khemlani of the *Cornell Sun* believed that by running the ad he had done the Jewish people a favor—reminding them that there were a "lot of people out to get [them]," which was something they needed to know. This attitude is reminiscent of the concept of "saving" the Jews (or women, African Americans, or any other potentially vulnerable group) despite themselves. Michael Gaviser, business manager of the *Daily Pennsylvanian*, decided to run the ad because of his belief that Smith was a "dangerous neo-Nazi" of whom the public had to be aware. (His decision was reversed by the editorial board.)

This assault on the ivory tower of academe illustrated how 37 Holocaust denial can permeate that segment of the population that should be most immune to it. It was naive to believe that the "light of day" can dispel lies, especially when they play on familiar stereotypes. Victims of racism, sexism, antisemitism, and a host of other prejudices know of light's limited ability to discredit falsehood. Light is barely an antidote when people are unable, as was often the case in this investigation, to differentiate between reasoned arguments and blatant falsehoods. Most sobering was the failure of many of these student leaders and opinion makers to recognize Holocaust denial for what it was. This was particularly evident among those who argued that the ad contained ideas, however odious, worthy of discussion. This failure suggests that correctly cast and properly camouflaged, Holocaust denial has a good chance of finding a foothold among coming generations.

This chapter ends where it began. Given the fact that even the 38 papers that printed the ad dismissed Smith's claims in the most derogatory of terms—absurd, irrational, racist, and a commercial for hatred— one might argue that the entire affair had a positive outcome. Rarely did the ad appear without an editorial or article castigating Holocaust denial. Students were alerted to a clear and present danger that can easily take root in their midst. Courses on the Holocaust increased in number. One could argue that all this is proof that CODOH's attempt to make Holocaust denial credible backfired.

My assessment is far more pessimistic. It is probably the one issue 39 about which I find myself in agreement with Bradley Smith. Many students read both the ad and the editorials condemning it. Some, including those who read neither but knew of the issue, may have walked away from the controversy convinced that there are two sides to this debate: the "revisionists" and the "establishment historians." They may know that there is tremendous controversy about the former. They may not be convinced that the two sides are of equal validity. They may even know that the deniers keep questionable company. But nonetheless they assume there *is* an "other side." That is the most frightening aspect of this entire matter.

Responding to Reading

1. Do you believe the college newspapers Lipstadt discusses had a responsibility to publish the ad that called the Holocaust a hoax, or do you believe they had the right (or even the responsibility) *not* to publish it? Explain your position. Do you see any possibility of compromise—for example, publishing the ad along with a detailed opposing viewpoint?
2. Holocaust scholar Raul Hilberg has criticized Lipstadt for writing her book, arguing that it gives the Holocaust deniers valuable publicity. Do you think this criticism of Lipstadt is valid? How would Lawrence Krauss (p. 754) respond to this objection?
3. Regardless of the legal definition of *free speech*, do you believe that all viewpoints should be allowed to reach an audience? Or do you think some ideas are so inaccurate, so morally repugnant, or so dangerous that they do not deserve to be heard? What specific views, if any, do you believe should *not* be aired?

REVISING OUR PREJUDICES: THE HOLOCAUST AND FREEDOM OF SPEECH

Francois Tremblay

Francois Tremblay was born in Quebec, Canada, in 1978 and is a student at the University of Quebec at Montreal. He is, in his words, an "active rationalist," and he sponsors The Liberator: A Controversial E-zine for Free Thinkers *at <http://liberator.net/>. The following was posted there on May 19, 2000.*

The social disease that we call "Political Correctness" infects all areas 1
of life, even history. Now, history is not an exact science, that much is true.
But some people have vested interests in history, for various reasons: ideological support, political support, moral support, and others. And there
is no other issue that polarizes opinion and interest more than the subject
of the World War II holocaust, mostly directed against the Jews.

It is therefore not a surprise that the Irving trial, which began in 2
January, attracted a lot of press attention. So did the verdict pronounced
on April 11th. It was an important trial on many points of view: on freedom of speech, on the Holocaust, on political motivations. David Irving,
who is without doubt the most celebrated revisionist historian in the
world, had sued for libel a writer named Deborah Lipstadt, who wrote
a book called *Denying the Holocaust—The Growing Assault on Truth and
Memory*. Lipstadt maintained that Irving, who is otherwise a great historian, has distorted evidence and maintained double standards in his
examination of the Holocaust question in order to support his neo-Nazi
political aspirations.

The judge found that almost without exception all of the evidence on 3
which this position was based was correct, and that therefore Irving's
claim was false. In fact, it is very surprising, by reading the detailed verdict, how Irving distorted clear evidence and blew out of proportion
small facts or even lies. How could such an acclaimed historian, who did
ground-breaking work on World War II (as the judge himself acknowledged in numerous occasions), also be such an inveterate liar when faced
with the facts of the Nazis and their involvement in the mass murder of
Jews? Of course one might say that opportunism was an important factor. Being involved in neo-Nazi politics made the Holocaust an easy target for Irving; after all, he is mostly a World War II historian.

The trial was interesting, as I said, for many reasons. One of these 4
is that it sums up very clearly the evidence for and against the notion of
the Holocaust, and the Nazis' involvement in it, in calm and impartial
terms. This is not a coincidence, since a trial is not usually the place for
passions to run high. Therefore it serves this very important purpose.

The main point of contention put forward by revisionists is the all- 5
eged non-existence of the gas chambers, at Auschwitz and other camps.
The Leuchter report, the main document used to refute the Holocaust,
was admitted even by Irving to contain gross scientific mistakes, mistakes
which made it completely unuseful as a study of the gassing question.
Apart from the lack of internal documentation of the number of victims,
all the evidence points to the existence of the Holocaust as described by
historical authorities. This lack can also be explained, although with more
difficulty (for more information on the codes used by the Nazis, consult
Eichmann's testimony to the Israeli police made before his trial).

This trial has also hopefully shed some light on the terrible libel laws 6
in the UK. In Britain, any person accused of libel must make the proof that

his propositions are true to their most important extent. Not only need there not be any proof of actual harm, but the burden is on the accused, not the accuser. That is a blow to freedom of speech, there is no doubt about it. What's worse is that British anti-libel laws were even more stringent during the eighties, and were toned down by the Defamation Act of 1996.

Surely such a set-up discourages free expression in a great way, 7 especially for newspapers. Personally I am against any libel law, as a consequence of free speech. Saying something bad against someone does not hurt this person directly or his property; it is left to each individual to assess the evidence presented and make his own conclusion. Assuming that people are so simple as to believe everything they read is silly, even if nobody ever lost money underestimating public stupidity (except, I suppose, John Travolta and his flop *Battlefield Earth*, but that's a story for another time).

It is not really my argument here to show that the Holocaust did 8 happen, since it seems to me that this question has been resolved without doubt, to the satisfaction of any rational standard of evidence. I have no doubt that all revisionists are sorely misguided or lying. I am not saying this to be politically correct—heavens forbid—it is simply my educated opinion.

I am a lot more disgusted at censorship than I am at revisionism. 9 Holocaust Revisionism is a false and politically motivated position on a terrible incident. Censorship, done by the supposedly "good guys," is far more revolting. At least revisionism does not suppress anyone, and it attempts to use facts (although in a rather shallow way) to make a point. Censorship in no form whatsoever attempts to maintain the merest facade of righteousness; it is an unqualified and undisguised attack on each and every one of us.

There is no doubt that the Holocaust was a most evil event from all 10 points of view. However, I do not subscribe to the theory that discussing the validity of the evidence for such events is a lack of respect for anyone. Mainstream historians themselves have disputed, for example, the estimate of four million victims at Auschwitz, and have established it as being a gross misrepresentation. The real figure turns more realistically around a million victims. Such a "revision" does not make the impact of these individual deaths and the means used any less horrifying. Saying that one million people died instead of four is not a lack of respect to the children or grandchildren of the victims. Even if such was true, nobody has the right to not be offended. Whenever such a "revision" offends anyone or not is irrelevant.

Not only that, but historians, with good reasons, repeat that the 11 Holocaust is a historical fact. If that is so, there shouldn't be any fear about revisionism. Historians should be the first people to encourage rational examination. Of course there is an extent to which such discussion proves to be unfruitful, like we observe with biology and creationism. In fact both beliefs are similar in some ways: they are motivated by particular ideologies and supported by pseudo-scientific inquiry. Creationism is much too popular to be banned, however. I don't know any biologist who seeks to purge creationist thought from society: it is with a renewed delight that they jump on the latest nonsense from our Christian friends.

Because of the persecution made towards revisionists, it is tempting 12 to take their side. Irving himself, according to the LA Times, has been denied entry in Canada, Italy, Germany and Austria because of his activities—and Holocaust denial laws. In most of Europe, "alternate views on the Holocaust" are forbidden by law. As Irving says, "[t]hey regard me as dangerous, and the word 'dangerous' puzzles me. I don't go around punching people in the face. . . . 'Dangerous' can only mean dangerous to their interests, either in the long term or the short term." One is tempted to extrapolate on these interests. What do they have to hide? During the trial, Irving's books (*Hitler's War* and *Goebbels*) have been shown conclusively to be tapestries of lies and deceptions. It should be as easy as shooting fish in a barrel to refute Irving, and even write books on the subject to expose his deceptions. What is so important that people must be fined, jailed or expelled? Not wanting to hurt anyone's feelings? It wouldn't be the first time that governments enforce sensitivity with violence. It's not only immensely stupid, but ironically self-defeating, much like Christian rock.

Why the vested interests on both sides of the fence about this piece 13 of history? Like all fields of inquiry, history is supposed to be impartial. True, many revisonsists are associated with neo-Nazi movements, but it is perfectly normal for quacks in all disciplines to associate with people who will want to hear what they have to say. Hatred and violence is hardly the way to convert *anyone* to your views: it only makes martyrs and creates disillusionment. Nazi Germany learned that lesson too late, and we still haven't learned it.

Hating the Hateful

Martyrs, the revisionists have in spades. Countless students or 14 teachers have been expelled for their views, and countless people have been harassed, attacked or banned from countries for propagating the word of revisionism. The most prominent Internet revisionist, Ernst Zündel, has been the target of three assassination attempts. Fred Leuchter, who wrote the infamous "Leuchter Report" denying the existence of gas chambers, was arrested, jailed and ruined financially in Germany for giving an anti-Holocaust lecture. And so on.

There is no point to this charade. Instead of letting them recite their 15
litany of false statements and complaints, we create martyrs. This strategy
has never worked before and it will not work any more now—let alone
having a strategy altogether. The question of the Holocaust, as
of most other false popular ideas, does not require a "strategy." It is
mostly a partly good sense, partly scientific question. For example, some
revisionists say Auschwitz was not used as a death camp since it had a
swimming pool. This kind of stupidity is just the result of a lack of good
sense. Another argument often used is that delousing chambers have a
much higher residual concentration of Zyklon-B than the gas chambers,
and that therefore the chambers were not used to gas people. This is a scientific question, which is easy to understand if you consult any basic textbook on the subject: the concentration necessary to kill human beings is
much smaller than the concentration necessary to kill microscopic organisms. I think that an uninformed reader, stumbling upon the Leuchter
Report or some other revisionist literature, could easily believe that the
Holocaust is a myth. That's the problem of being uninformed, you see.
From a pragmatic viewpoint, it would be much more effective to inform
a large segment of these people rather than imprison their most vocal representatives.

As I said, by censoring the revisionists, we are unwittingly imitat- 16
ing the kind of people that we want to suppress. Censorship is not
unique to Nazi-like societies, but is certainly one of their characteristics.
Hitler had all the "bad art" and "non-German art" exposed to ridicule
and relegated to dusty attics. Now we are exposing all the "bad ideas"
and "non- acceptable ideas" to litigation. There is a double standard,
though; we certainly don't persecute creationists or astrologers for their
opinions, false or destructive as they may be. Perhaps this is because
most delusions are seen as harmless.

I also note that we often rationalize this behaviour by classifying 17
revisionism as "hate speech" (it is officially qualified as such in Canada). I suppose that is a convenient way of pushing embarrassing issues
away: "they're just hateful people." The mere notion of "hate speech" is
ridiculous. How does it go? If you insult someone because you hate
him, it's not so bad, but if you insult someone because you hate his race,
it's an outrage? To me, an insult is an insult, any way it is presented. I
have no more qualms about getting insulted because of my race or
nationality any more than being insulted because of my opinions. I suspect that is a more rational attitude than the Mother Superior-ing that
we see flourish today, although I'll leave the more thorough appraisal as
an exercise for the readers.

The notion of hate is also subjective, in the manner that we use it. 18
To Christians, an atheist web site may be hate speech. To a homeopath,
a web site on chemistry may be hate speech. Politicians can get away

with defining hate into existence since they follow the general consensus of what is "politically correct." We see once again that democracy produces very dangerous effects—hate laws are little more than organized mob lynchings.

Not only should there not be any laws to regulate speech, but governments should be ideologically neutral, except for politics, of course. The notion of a "Holocaust-denial law" is as ridiculous as creationism in schools, or a law saying that the long established value called Pi is equal to 3. It's just not the government's job to determine what is true and what is not. Politicians are there to administrate nations, not to determine scientific truths. 19

I have gone a long way from Irving, but I think it is a point that deserves to be made. The Irving trial gave the occasion to the media to once more appraise the two sides of the debate. And that's what a free society is all about. 20

Responding to Reading

1. Tremblay clearly states that he is convinced that, contrary to assertions by revisionist historian David Irving, "the Holocaust did happen" (8), yet he adds, "I am a lot more disgusted at censorship than I am at revisionism" (9). How does he explain his position? How would Deborah Lipstadt (p. 763) respond to this explanation? Why does Tremblay object to the characterization of revisionism as "hate speech"?

2. In paragraph 11, Tremblay likens the revisionist historians who question accepted views of the Holocaust to creationists, whose ideas he brands "nonsense." Why does he make this analogy? How does it help to support his position on censorship?

3. According to Tremblay, it is the fact that so many people are "uninformed" that makes them believe nonsensical ideas; he feels we should educate such people "rather than imprison their most vocal representatives" (15). Would Niles Eldredge (p. 757) agree?

───────────── **WIDENING THE FOCUS** ─────────────

- Kevin J.H. Dettmar, "Grasping the Dark Images of Rock" (p. 290)
- Wendy Kaminer, "Testifying: Television" (p. 307)
- Jack Kevorkian, "A Case of Assisted Suicide" (p. 587)

Responding to the Image

1. This is a photograph of a rally of the Aryan Nation, a neo-Nazi organization, that took place in Coeur d'Alene, Idaho, in 1999. As you can see, the rally and the subsequent march through town drew a number of anti-Nazi protesters. How would you respond to a public rally on your campus espousing ideas that you found deeply offensive?

2. Originally a benevolent symbol, the swastika has become indelibly associated with the evils of Nazism and anti-Semitism. Why do you think it has continued to be such a potent image?

--------- WRITING ---------

Making Choices

1. What moral and ethical rules govern your behavior? Considering the rules Carl Sagan discusses in "The Rules of the Game" as well as the ethical guidelines set forth by several other writers in this chapter, define and explain your own personal moral code.

2. The question of whether or not to act to end another's suffering—possibly at one's own expense—is explored, implicitly or explicitly, in both "The Deer at Providencia" by Annie Dillard, "Shooting an Elephant" by George Orwell, and "The Ones Who Walk Away from Omelas" by Ursula Le Guin. What are your own feelings about this issue? You may also consider ideas explored in the essays by Lawrence J. Schneiderman, Jack Kevorkian, or Stephen L. Carter in Chapter 8.

3. Henry David Thoreau says, "Unjust laws exist: shall we be content to obey them, or shall we endeavor to amend them, and obey them until we have succeeded, or shall we transgress them at once?" (17). Choose a law or practice that you consider unjust, and write an essay in which you tell why you believe it should be disobeyed. Use ideas from Thoreau's essay to support your points.

4. Is all life equally valuable? Explain your position on this issue, considering the ideas raised by Garrett Hardin and those raised by Anna Mae Halgrim Seaver in Chapter 8.

5. Stanley Milgram believes that his study illustrates Hannah Arendt's controversial theory, showing that "ordinary people, simply doing their jobs, and without any particular hostility on their part, can become agents in a terrible destructive process" (39). Cite examples from your own experience to support his conclusion.

6. Martin Luther King, Jr., Milgram, and Thoreau all consider the difficulties of resisting majority rule, standing up to authority, and protesting against established rules and laws. Did you ever submit to authority even though you thought you should not have? Write an essay in which you describe your experience. What were the consequences of your act? (Or, describe a time when you stood up to authority. What motivated you? Was your resistance successful? Would you do the same thing again?) Be sure you draw a conclusion from your experience, and state this conclusion as your thesis.

7. What do you believe we gain and lose by using animals in scientific research? Do you believe this practice should be continued? If so, with which animals? Under what circumstances? If not, why not?

What alternative do you propose? Reread Claire McCarthy's "Dog Lab" and Annie Dillard's "The Deer at Providencia" before you begin your essay.

8. Which of the two roads identified in Robert Frost's "The Road Not Taken" have you chosen? In what sense has that choice "made all the difference"?

9. How free should speech on your campus be? After reading Deborah Lipstadt's "Denying the Holocaust" and Francois Tremblay's "Revising Our Prejudices," write an editorial for your school newspaper in which you discuss the kinds of statements that should be censored, and explain why. If you believe no ideas should be censored, support that position.

10. Read all the essays in the Focus section of this chapter. Then, write an essay in which you answer the question "Are all ideas created equal?" taking a stand on whether or not "nonsense—ideas widely denounced by eminent scientists and historians"—should be given a public forum. (You may want to discuss the role of the Internet in providing this forum.)

11. **For Internet research:** The controversy over teaching evolution and creationism in public schools has a long history in the United States. You can learn more about this controversy at sites sponsored by the National Center for Science Education (<http://www. NatCenSciEd.org/> the People for the American Way (<http:// www.pfaw.org/issues/education/creationism. shtml>), and the law school at the University of Missouri at Kansas City (<http//www. law.umkc.edu/faculty/projects/FTrials/conlaw/evolution.htm>). Using information you access on these sites, the readings by Krauss and Eldredge in this chapter, and other sources you may find, write an essay in which you explore some of this history and examine reasons why the controversy remains so potent.

Credits

BARBARA TUCHMAN, "The Black Death," from A DISTANT MIRROR: THE CALAM-
ATOUS FOURTEENTH CENTURY by Barbara Tuchman. © 1978.

KATE TUTTLE, "Television and African Americans," from *Africana.com*.

ALICE WALKER, "Beauty: When The Other Dancer is the Self" from *In Search of Our
Mothers' Gardens*. Copyright © 1967 by Alice Walker. Reprinted with the permission of Harcourt Brace and Company.

E. B. WHITE, "Once More to the Lake" from *Essays of E. B. White*. Copyright 1941 by
E. B. White. Reprinted with the permission of HarperCollins Publishers, Inc.

BARBARA DAFOE WHITEHEAD, "The Girls of Gen-X." Reprinted with permission from
The American Enterprise.

MARIE WINN, "Television: The Plug-in Drug"" from *The Plug-In Drug*. Copyright ©
1967, 1985 by Marie Winn Miller. Reprinted with the permission of Viking
Penguin, a division of Penguin Putnam Inc.

RICHARD WRIGHT, "The Library Card" from *Black Boy*. Copyright 1937, 1942, 1944,
1945 by Richard Wright, renewed © 1973 by Ellen Wright. Reprinted with the
permission of HarperCollins Publishers, Inc.

MALCOLM X, "A Homemade Education" from *The Autobiography of Malcolm X* by
Malcolm X with the assistance of Alex Haley. Copyright © 1964 by Alex
Haley and Malcolm X. Copyright © 1965 by Alex Haley and Malcolm X,
copyright © 1965 by Alex Haley and Betty Shabazz. Reprinted with the permission of Random House, Inc.

WILLIAM ZINSSER, "College Pressures" from *Blair & Ketchum's Country Journal* 6, no.
4 (April 1979). Copyright © 1979 by William K. Zinsser. Reprinted with the
permission of the author and Carol Brissie.

Photo Credits

Chapter 01 page 79 Novastock/PhotoEdit

Chapter 02 page 162 © The New Yorker Collection 1999 Robert Weber from
cartoonbank.com. All Rights Reserved; page 163 © The New Yorker
Collection 1992 Mike Twohy from cartoonbank.com. All Rights Reserved.

Chapter 03 page 253 Danny Johnston, AP/Wide World Photo

Chapter 04 page 333 Peter Byron, Photo Researchers, Inc.

Chapter 05 page 388 Shirley Zeiberg, Pearson Education/PH College

Chapter 06 page 461 Lennox McLendon, AP/Wide World Photos

Chapter 07 page 518 Terry Vine, Stone

Chapter 08 page 597 Steve Fenn/ABC News/HO, AP/Wide World Photos

Chapter 09 page 647 Linda Remsburg/The Mining Journal, AP/Wide World Photos

Chapter 10 page 782 Alan Steiner/Coeur d'Alene Press, AP/Wide World Photos

Index of Authors and Titles

"Age of Optimism, An," 469
"American Dreamer," 406
Amselle, Jorge
   "¡Inglés Sí!," 249
Angelou, Maya
   "Graduation," 102
"ARIA," 232

"Barbie Doll," 338
"Bards of the Internet: If E-Mail
      Represents the Renaissance of
      Prose, Why Is So Much of It
      Awful?," 495
Barry, Lynda
   "The Sanctuary of School," 99
"Beauty: When the Other Dancer Is
      the Self," 42
"Black Death, The," 522
Borosage, Robert L.
   "Misplaced Priorities: A Focus on
      Guns," 577
Boyle, T. Coraghessan
   "Top of the Food Chain," 632
Brady, Judy
   "Why I Want a Wife," 348
Brown, Leslie S.P.
   "Who Cares About the
      Renaissance?," 140

Carson, Rachel
   "The Obligation to Endure," 614
Carter, Stephen L.
   "Rush to Lethal Judgment," 592
Carver, Raymond
   "My Father's Life," 49
"Case of Assisted Suicide, A," 587
"Celebrity Journalism, the Public,
      and Princess Diana," 271
Christensen, Sally Thane
   "Is a Tree Worth a Life?," 629
"Civil Disobedience," 664
Cofer, Judith Ortiz
   "The Myth of the Latin Woman:

I Just Met a Girl Named
      Maria," 412
"College Pressures," 127
"Computers," 473
"Creationism Isn't Science," 757

"Death and Justice: How Capital
      Punishment Affirms Life," 714
"Declaration of Independence, The,"
      449
"Deer at Providencia, The," 654
"Denying the Holocaust," 763
Dettmar, Kevin J. H.
   "Grasping the Dark Images of
      Rock," 290
Dillard, Annie
   "The Deer at Providencia," 654
"Dog Lab," 707
"Do Not Go Gentle into That Good
      Night," 569
Douglass, Frederick
   "Learning to Read and Write," 167
Dunn, Ashley
   "Two Views of Technology's
      Promise," 465

Edmundson, Mark
   "On the Uses of a Liberal
      Education: Lite Entertainment
      for Bored College Students,"
      145
Eighner, Lars
   "On Dumpster Diving," 421
Ehrenreich, Barbara
   "The Myth of Man as Hunter,"
      643
Eldredge, Niles
   "Creationism Isn't Science," 757
Elmer-Dewitt, Phillip
   "Bards of the Internet: If E-Mail
      Represents the Renaissance of
      Prose, Why Is So Much of It
      Awful?," 495

"End of Serendipity, The," 478
"Equal Time for Nonsense," 754
"Ethics," 652
"Ethics of Euthanasia, The," 581

Faludi, Susan
"The Future of Men," 385
Feingold, Russell
"The Need for a Moratorium on
Executions," 719
Forster, E. M.
"My Wood," 611
"Four-Letter Words Can Hurt You,"
181
Frost, Robert
"The Road Not Taken," 651
"Future of Men, The," 385

Gates, Henry Louis, Jr.
"One Internet, Two Nations,"
499
"Girls of Gen X, The," 372
"Giving Saturday Morning Some
Slack," 266
"Global Village Finally Arrives, The,"
303
Goodall, Jane
"A Plea for the Chimps," 559
Gordon, Suzanne
"What Nurses Stand For," 543
Gore, Al
"The Wasteland," 603
"Government and the Internet:
Haves and Have-nots," 514
"Graduation," 102
"Grasping the Dark Images of Rock,"
290
Grisham, John
"Unnatural Killers," 318
"Growing Up Game," 637
Gup, Ted
"The End of Serendipity," 478
Gutmann, Stephanie
"Sex and the Soldier," 357

Hardin, Garrett
"Lifeboat Ethics: The Case against
"Aid" That Harms," 697

Hayakawa, S. I.
"Reports, Inferences,
Judgements," 197
Hayden, Robert
"Those Winter Sundays," 11
Henry, William A., III
"In Defense of Elitism," 134
Hochschild, Arlie
"The Second Shift," 351
Hoffman, Alice
"The Perfect Family," 57
"Hollow Claims about Fantasy
Violence," 326
Holt, John
"School Is Bad for Children," 83
"Homemade Education, A," 173
"How It Feels to Be Colored Me,"
432
"Human Cost of an Illiterate Society,
The," 189
Hurston, Zora Neale
"How It Feels to Be Colored Me,"
432
Huxley, Aldous
"Propaganda under a
Dictatorship," 214

"If John Dewey Were Alive Today,
He'd Be a Webhead," 482
"I Have a Dream," 457
"Imelda," 532
"Inaugural Address," 453
"In Defense of Elitism," 134
"Informing Ourselves to Death,"
486
"¡Inglés Sí!," 249
"Is a Tree Worth a Life?," 629
Iyer, Pico
"The Global Village Finally
Arrives," 303

Jefferson, Thomas
"The Declaration of
Independence," 449
"Just Walk On By," 417

Kaminer, Wendy
"Testifying: Television," 307

Kennedy, John F.
  "Inaugural Address," 453
Kevorkian, Jack
  "A Case of Assisted Suicide," 587
King, Martin Luther, Jr.
  "I Have a Dream," 457
  "Letter from Birmingham Jail,"
    682
King, Robert D.
  "Should English Be the Law?," 238
Kingsolver, Barbara
  "Stone Soup," 60
Kingston, Maxine Hong
  "No Name Woman," 25
Koch, Edward I.
  "Death and Justice: How Capital
    Punishment Affirms Life," 714
Kozol, Jonathan
  "The Human Cost of an Illiterate
    Society," 189
  "Savage Inequalities," 112
Krauss, Lawrence
  "Equal Time for Nonsense," 754
Kübler-Ross, Elisabeth
  "On the Fear of Death," 570
Kuriloff, Peshe
  "If John Dewey Were Alive Today,
    He'd Be a Webhead," 482

Lawrence, Barbara
  "Four-Letter Words Can Hurt
    You," 181
Lawrence, Charles R., III
  "The Telltale Heart: Apology,
    Reparation, and Redress," 436
Lazarus, Emma
  "The New Colossus," 452
"Learning to Read and Write," 167
Le Guin, Ursula K.
  "The Ones Who Walk Away from
    Omelas," 747
Leo, John
  "When Life Imitates Video," 329
"Letter from Birmingham Jail," 682
"Letter to President Pierce, 1855," 601
"Library Card, The," 398
"Lifeboat Ethics: The Case against
    "Aid" That Harms," 697

Lipstadt, Deborah
  "Denying the Holocaust," 763

Malcolm X
  "A Homemade Education," 173
"Marked Women," 366
Matsuda, Mari
  "The Telltale Heart: Apology,
    Reparation, and Redress," 436
McCarthy, Claire
  "Dog Lab," 707
McGrath, Charles
  "Giving Saturday Morning Some
    Slack," 266
"Men We Carry in Our Minds, The,"
    345
Milgram, Stanley
  "The Perils of Obedience," 725
"Misplaced Priorities: A Focus on
    Guns," 577
Momaday, N. Scott
  "The Way to Rainy Mountain," 36
"Mother Tongue," 184
Mukherjee, Bharati
  "American Dreamer," 406
Murphy, Cullen
  "Recycling: No Panacea," 620
"My Father's Life," 49
"Myth of Man as Hunter, The," 643
"Myth of the Cave, The," 89
"Myth of the Latin Woman: I Just Met
    a Girl Named Maria, The," 412
"My Wood," 611
"My World Now," 566

"Need for a Moratorium on
    Executions, The," 719
Negroppante, Nicholas
  "An Age of Optimism," 469
"New Colossus, The," 452
Nilsen, Alleen Pace
  "Sexism in English: Embodiment
    and Language," 203
"No Name Woman," 25

"Obligation to Endure, The," 614
Olds, Sharon
  "Rite of Passage," 339

"Once More to the Lake," 20
"On Dumpster Diving," 421
"One Internet, Two Nations," 499
"One Last Time," 12
"Ones Who Walk Away from
    Omelas, The," 747
"On the Fear of Death," 570
"On the Uses of a Liberal Education:
    Lite Entertainment for Bored
    College Students," 145
Orwell, George
    "Politics and the English
        Language," 220
    "Shooting an Elephant," 658
"Our Animal Rites," 640

Pastan, Linda
    "Ethics," 652
"Perfect Family, The," 57
"Perils of Obedience, The," 725
Peterson, Brenda
    "Growing Up Game," 637
Piercy, Marge
    "Barbie Doll," 338
Plato
    "The Myth of the Cave," 89
"Plea for the Chimps, A," 559
"Politics and the English Language,"
    220
Postman, Neil
    "Informing Ourselves to Death,"
        486
"Pregnant with Possibility," 475
"Professions for Women," 340
"Propaganda under a Dictatorship,"
    214
Purdy, Jedediah
    "Shades of Green," 625

Quindlen, Anna
    "Our Animal Rites," 640

Rathje, William
    "Recycling: No Panacea," 620
Rawlins, Gregory J.E.
    "Pregnant with Possibility," 475
"Reading the River," 96
"Recycling: No Panacea," 620

"Reports, Inferences,
    Judgements," 197
"Reversing Our Prejudices: The
    Holocaust and Freedom of
    Speech," 77
Rhodes, Richard
    "Hollow Claims about Fantasy
        Violence," 326
"Rite of Passage," 339
"Road Not Taken, The," 651
Rodriguez, Richard
    "ARIA," 232
"Rules of the Game, The," 738
"Rush to Lethal Judgment," 592

Sagan, Carl
    "The Rules of the Game," 738
Saltzman, Joe
    "Celebrity Journalism, the Public,
        and Princess Diana," 271
"Sanctuary of School, The," 99
Sanders, Scott Russell
    "The Men We Carry in Our
        Minds," 345
Sanger, Margaret
    "The Turbid Ebb and Flow of
        Misery," 553
"Savage Inequalities," 112
Schneiderman, Lawrence J.
    "The Ethics of Euthanasia," 581
"School Is Bad for Children," 83
Seattle, Chief
    "Letter to President Pierce, 1855,"
        601
    "We May Be Brothers," 392
Seaver, Anna Mae Halgrim
    "My World Now," 566
"Second Shift, The," 351
Selzer, Richard
    "Imelda," 532
"Sex, Lies, and Advertising," 274
"Sex and the Soldier," 357
"Sexism in English: Embodiment and
    Language," 203
"Shades of Green," 625
Shatzman, Aaron M.
    "When Learning Hurts," 142
"Shooting an Elephant," 658

"Should English Be the Law?,"
238

Smiley, Jane
"There They Go, Bad-Mouthing
Divorce Again," 76

Sommers, Christina Hoff
"The War against Boys," 380

Soto, Gary
"One Last Time," 12

Span, Paula
"Women and Computers: Is There
Equity in Cyberspace?," 502

Stafford, William
"Traveling through the Dark," 645

Staples, Brent
"Just Walk On By," 417
"Why Colleges Shower Their
Students with A's," 125

Steinem, Gloria
"Sex, Lies, and Advertising,"
274

"Stone Soup," 60

Symonds, Matthew
"Government and the Internet:
Haves and Have-nots," 514

Tan, Amy
"Mother Tongue," 184

Tannen, Deborah
"Marked Women," 366

"Television: The Plug-In Drug," 257

"Television and African Americans,"
297

"Telltale Heart: Apology, Reparation,
and Redress, The," 436

"Testifying: Television," 307

"There They Go, Bad-Mouthing
Divorce Again," 76

Thomas, Dylan
"Do Not Go Gentle into That
Good Night," 569

Thomas, Lewis
"Computers," 473

Thoreau, Henry David
"Civil Disobedience," 664

"Those Winter Sundays," 11

Tocqueville, Alexis de
"Why the Americans Are So

Restless in the Midst of Their
Prosperity," 395

"Top of the Food Chain," 632

"Traveling through the Dark," 645

Tremblay, Francois
"Reversing Our Prejudices: The
Holocaust and Freedom of
Speech," 77

Tuchman, Barbara
"The Black Death," 522

"Turbid Ebb and Flow of Misery,
The," 553

Tuttle, Kate
"Television and African
Americans," 297

Twain, Mark
"Reading the River," 96

"Two Views of Technology's
Promise," 465

"Unexpected Legacy of Divorce,
The," 67

"Unnatural Killers," 318

Walker, Alice
"Beauty: When the Other Dancer
Is the Self," 42

Wallerstein, Judith
"The Unexpected Legacy of
Divorce," 67

"War against Boys, The," 380

"Wasteland, The," 603

"Way to Rainy Mountain, The," 36

"We May Be Brothers," 392

"What Nurses Stand For," 543

"When I Heard the Learn'd
Astronomer," 98

"When Learning Hurts," 142

"When Life Imitates Video," 329

White, E. B.
"Once More to the Lake," 20

Whitehead, Barbara Dafoe
"The Girls of Gen X," 372

Whitman, Walt
"When I Heard the Learn'd
Astronomer," 98

"Who Cares About the
Renaissance?," 140

"Why Colleges Shower Their
    Students with A's," 125
"Why I Want a Wife," 348
"Why the Americans Are So Restless
    in the Midst of Their
    Prosperity," 395
Winn, Marie
    "Television: The Plug-In Drug,"
    257
"Women and Computers: Is There
    Equity in Cyberspace?," 502
Woolf, Virginia
    "Professions for Women," 340
Wright, Richard
    "The Library Card," 398

Zinsser, William
    "College Pressures," 127